"Phillips sets a bountiful table, filled with a wealth of delicious dishes, engaging personal narratives, characters, and abundant knowledge of China and its culinary treasures."

—MELISSA CALDWELL, editor of *Gastronomica*

ALL UNDER HEAVEN

All Under Heaven

Recipes from the 35 Cuisines of China

Written & illustrated by
CAROLYN PHILLIPS

Foreword by
KEN HOM

MCSWEENEY'S
SAN FRANCISCO

TEN SPEED PRESS
Berkeley

McSWEENEY'S
www.mcsweeneys.net

TEN SPEED PRESS
Berkeley

Published in the United States by Ten Speed Press, an imprint of the Crown Publishing Group, a division of Penguin Random House LLC, New York, in association with McSweeney's.
www.crownpublishing.com
www.tenspeed.com
www.mcsweeneys.net

Ten Speed Press and the Ten Speed Press colophon are registered trademarks of Penguin Random House LLC.

McSweeney's and colophon are registered trademarks of McSweeney's, an independent publisher.

Portions of this work previously appeared, sometimes in slightly different form, in *Lucky Peach* and the *San Francisco Chronicle*, and on The Huffington Post, Food52, and Zester Daily.

Library of Congress Cataloging-in-Publication Data
Phillips, Carolyn J., author.
All under heaven : recipes from the 35 cuisines of China / written and illustrated by Carolyn Phillips ; introduction by Ken Hom.—First edition.
     pages cm
 Includes bibliographical references and index.
 1. Cooking, Chinese. I. Title.
TX724.5.C5P486 2016
641.5951—dc23
                          2015029244

Hardcover ISBN: 978-1-60774-982-0
eBook ISBN: 978-1-60774-983-7

Printed in China

Design by Dan McKinley
Cover Design by Ashley Lima

10 9 8 7 6 5 4 3 2 1

First Edition

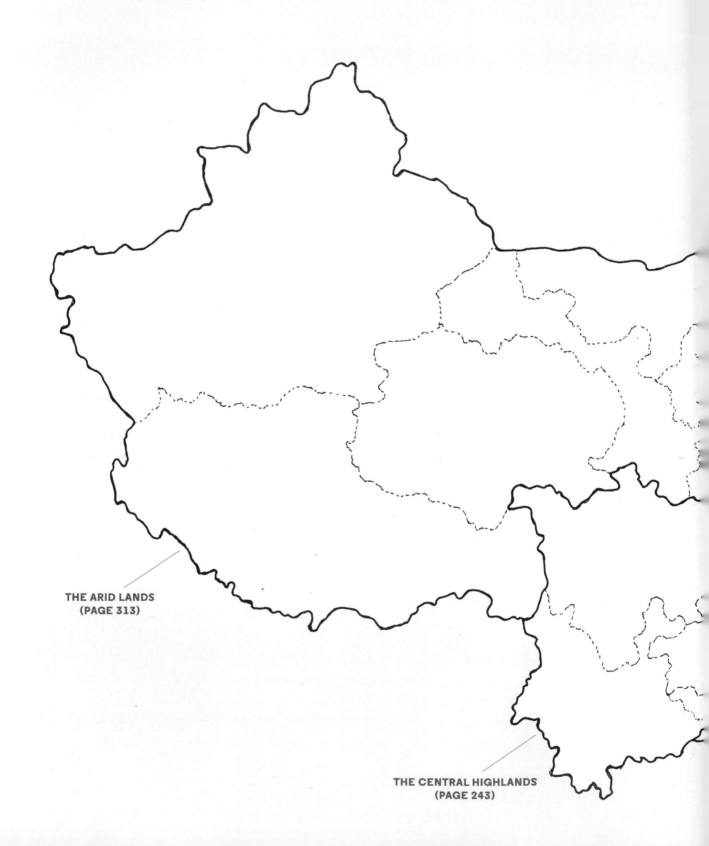

THE ARID LANDS
(PAGE 313)

THE CENTRAL HIGHLANDS
(PAGE 243)

THE NORTH AND
MANCHURIAN NORTHEAST
(PAGE 1)

This book is dedicated with humble thanks to the people of Taiwan, Mainland China, and the Chinese diaspora, to their inventive ancestors, and to the endless generations of inspired cooks who together created the best food in the world.

THE YANGTZE RIVER &
ITS ENVIRONS
(PAGE 69)

THE COASTAL SOUTHEAST
(PAGE 153)

FOREWORD

Fifty-six years ago, when I first worked in my uncle Paul's restaurant in Chicago's Chinatown, I remember that we had two large refrigerators in the kitchen. The first one was for the non-Chinese diners: it was filled with chop suey; the then very popular patties of egg foo yung, ready to be reheated and sauced; and battered pieces of pork for the sweet-and-sour plates. The second refrigerator was filled with fresh scallops and sea conch, dim sum dumplings, birds' nests bound for soup, and braised pigeons. The gulf between those fridges could not have been wider. Our non-Chinese diners had only a vague idea of what Chinese food was truly about.

Since then, the West's idea of Chinese cuisine has changed dramatically. No doubt this transformation has come about for many reasons, the first and foremost being China's rise from a poor, underdeveloped country racked by turmoil, revolution, and self-inflicted wounds to one of the leading economic powers in the world. The renaissance of one of Earth's oldest civilizations has captured the global imagination. China's growth, culturally and economically, has had an enormous impact on all our lives—including on the way we eat.

For four decades, I have taught Chinese cooking to both interested amateurs and professional chefs, and over the years I've witnessed how Chinese cookery has evolved outside of China. When I began teaching, in the early 1970s, Chinese food in the United States and in Great Britain was mediocre. Trade embargos restricted the flow of authentic Chinese ingredients and foodstuffs, and many of the Chinese immigrants who came to the West were not actual chefs. The result was cheap fare adapted to the milieus the immigrants lived in. In the States, chop suey, an invented perversion of stir-fried leftovers, became a standard item on Chinese menus; in Britain, Chinese takeaway shops often served curry and chips. As China opened up, though, the quality of Chinese cooking improved immensely. New floods of immigrants brought with them a sense of authentic Chinese cuisine.

Funnily enough, a similar sea change occurred in China itself. I remember how disappointed I was, thirty years ago, by the food I ate in China. It was cooked without passion, care, or love, and served with surly service on top. Good and varied ingredients were hard to come by, and many of the best chefs had already left the country. Fortunately, home cooking still thrived, despite the state's attempt at promoting communal kitchens. And in the wake of the economic reforms of the late 1970s, farmers were allowed to grow what they wanted. Within a few years, foreigners began opening restaurants to take advantage of the economic boom, and five-star hotels popped up to meet the demands of travelers from all over the world. Those restaurants and hotels rehired the Chinese chefs who had been lost to Hong Kong and Singapore, and the result was a reemergence of Chinese cuisine. The ever-growing middle class was soon demanding better cooking; enterprising restaurateurs and food companies rose up to respond to their appetites. Chefs and home cooks alike revisited old recipes and started inventing new ones. Today, Chinese food has never been better.

I have always welcomed any book that expands the horizons of our knowledge of Chinese food; now comes one of the best I have seen in ages. *All Under Heaven* is not just a mere cookbook—in fact, it may be the most comprehensive work to date on an incredibly complex subject. Carolyn Phillips's monumental exploration of Chinese cuisine documents classic recipes in exacting detail, but it is also infused with her personal observations and insight, as well as with illuminating bits of historical information. Her meticulous research has helped fill gaps in my own understanding of how certain recipes developed. There are simple, widely known recipes for the novice cook here, such as Guangdong-Style Steamed Fish, but also lesser known and more challenging preparations, such as Beijing-Style Smoked Chicken. I cannot praise Carolyn's work enough; I am sure that, in the coming years, *All Under Heaven* will come to be considered a classic, as well as an invaluable reference for any serious cook's kitchen. ●

—*Ken Hom*

Widely regarded as one the world's greatest authorities on Chinese cooking, Ken Hom, OBE, is an award-winning celebrity chef, television host, and best-selling author of thirty-six books that have been published in more than sixteen languages.

AUTHOR'S NOTE

China's cuisines have always proved too tantalizing for me to ignore. When I arrived in Taipei as a young student in the mid-1970s, though, I didn't have an inkling of what was in store for my palate—nothing I ate was anything like the so-called Chinese food I had eaten in the States. As I started to roam around the city, fragrant aromas lured me into little restaurants that plied me with specialties from all over China. Taipei was still a quiet place then, but by wandering its labyrinth of alleys and side streets, I discovered not just the home-style dishes and street snacks of the local Taiwanese and Hakka people, but also delicacies imported by Mainlanders from Shandong in the north down to Guangdong in the south, and from Shanghai in the east out into China's Muslim west.

What had happened was this: in the wake of China's communist revolution in 1949, millions of Nationalist sympathizers from all across the country retreated to Taiwan. This huge influx made the island into a

A WORD ABOUT THE INGREDIENTS

Good news to all of you who are new to cooking China's cuisines: many of these recipes do not need exotic ingredients. And for those of you eager to build these dishes from the ground up, instructions are provided in the Basic Recipes section toward the back of the book.

Some of the more obscure ingredients mentioned may not yet be widely available in your area, but I have faith that since these are the things the Chinese people love to eat, sooner or later they will be showing up on grocery shelves. So, keep searching— it's worth the effort.

Do note that the soy sauce called for in this book should be Chinese, rather than Japanese, as their salt contents and flavors are very different. Other condiments, like sweet wheat paste, have simply been mistranslated for way too long (see page 490), and so I've done my best to clarify and define these ingredients, as well as provide their Chinese names for ease of shopping. Check out the Glossary on page 475 and the Tips below many recipes for more detailed information on just about everything mentioned in *All Under Heaven*.

As you stock up your Chinese pantry, don't forget to visit Latino, Korean, Southeast Asian, Indian, and other markets. Throughout the book I give suggestions for where to find things, but you never know where certain ingredients will pop up, so keep your eyes open. The main thing to look for is freshness and quality. Store your dried treasures in jars in a cool place; if they stay in their bags, they may get buggy, and you want anything that may already be infested to remain very much contained.

Meats and poultry taste best when they are raised with care, so try to find organic or natural meats, as well as free-range birds and eggs. Vegetables and fruits should be very

fresh, unsprayed whenever possible, and in season. Rice, flour, and other dry ingredients can, of course, be purchased in East Asian markets, but they are often available in bulk bins at health food stores, too—fast turnover is key here.

Some recipes here note potential substitutions. For example, rock sugar might be listed first, followed by regular sugar. This means that rock sugar is my first choice, and I often make an effort to explain the reasons why this makes a difference in the recipe's Tips.

Do note that few of these recipes are set in stone. You should feel free to make your own substitutions (like ground turkey for ground pork), adjust the sweet-savory ratio to fit your palate, garnish the foods in whatever way makes you happy, and swap out or even omit certain ingredients (like Chinese medicinal herbs) if they are just not available in your area. That being said, pastry and candy are the main exceptions here, as they require a delicate balancing of chemical reactions and textures. Adjust the amount of sugar in such a recipe only in small increments, and do not expect good results when you substitute whole wheat flour for white Chinese flour (see page 386).

Shopping should be a lot of fun; one of my greatest pleasures is visiting Chinese markets and Chinatowns whenever I get the chance, though online stores are beginning to make a huge range of resources available only a click away. There are whole new worlds of flavor in store for you, and the offerings are only going to get better.

About the serving sizes: These are for multicourse meals served in the Chinese manner; see page 493 for some suggestions. If you're planning on having, say, a Western-style meal with only one main dish plus a side and a starch, you should increase the amounts accordingly.

microcosm of China's cuisines. By the time I arrived, there was no better place to be eating Chinese food.

After eight wonderful years there, I moved back to California with my husband, J. H. Huang. I still wanted to eat the many Chinese dishes we loved, but no American restaurants were offering them. I soon started buying every Chinese-language cookbook I could lay my hands on and bugging our Chinese friends for their secrets. This was my introduction to the deeper layers of Chinese home cooking. My late father-in-law and others taught me the recipes they had learned from their families, and through them I gained a new appreciation of the country's rich culinary traditions. As the years passed and my husband and I continued to travel back and forth across the Pacific, my fascination turned into an all-consuming obsession. I worked during the day as a professional Mandarin interpreter, and I spent my nights studying the patchwork of cuisines that was slowly being revealed to me.

There are eight traditional Chinese "great cuisines": the foods of Shandong, Jiangsu, Zhejiang, Fujian, Guangdong, Anhui, Hunan, and Sichuan. But that roster was far too humble, in my view; it left out more of China's foods than it included. The "great cuisines" concept was not developed until the Qing dynasty (1644-1911), and even now many people argue about what it comprises. Anhui, in particular, gets short shrift; it used to be incredibly wealthy, due to the salt trade, but it's since become an economic backwater, and now few people can even name an Anhui dish.

I wanted to gain a broader understanding of China's major cuisines and to better understand how they related to one another. By my count, the country boasts *at least* five major gastronomic regions and thirty-five unique cuisines. (I define a "cuisine" as a food tradition with its own distinctive dishes, ingredients, and cooking styles.) In my studies, I noted how regional flavors and ingredients repeated themselves, how certain recipes reemerged in neighboring provinces with little twists, and how China's history and minority peoples colored the foods in each place. I became entranced by things like the enormous impact Hui Muslims have had on the entire North and West; how imported ingredients seeped through harbors where foreigners docked their ships; and how, in spite of everything, the foods I was learning about still remained unequivocally Chinese.

So, who eats what in China, and how do I draw the lines? My biggest discovery was this: YOU EAT WHAT YOU SPEAK. With this realization, much became clear. The people of Hainan, for example, speak the Chaozhou dialect, and so it makes sense that their foods look and taste like those of Chaozhou, albeit with a tropical twist.

There are other factors, of course: overlay an ethnolinguistic map with maps of China's climate and topography, and new delineations become clear. Each of the five regions explored in this book is shaped by its climate and geography, which give the foods within them a kind of commonality. You can, in other words, use ingredients from one cuisine to make something from a culinary neighbor without encountering too much trouble. This snapped the last pieces into place, and my five culinary regions,[1] and their respective cuisines, quickly became distinct:

- The ageless North and Manchurian Northeast—Shandong, Beijing, Tianjin, Hebei, and the Northeast

- The elegant Yangtze River environs—Huai Yang, Jiangsu, Shanghai, Zhejiang, Northern Fujian, Anhui, Henan, Hubei, and Jiangxi

- The savory Coastal Southeast—the Hakka, Chaozhou, Southern Fujian, Taiwan, Taiwan's Military Families, Hainan, Guangdong and Southern Guangxi, Pearl River Delta, Macau, and Hong Kong

- The spicy Central Highlands—Sichuan, Hunan, Yunnan, Guizhou, and Northern Guangxi

- The arid Northwest—Shaanxi, Shanxi, Gansu, the Great Northwest, Inner Mongolia, and Tibet

Of course, *All Under Heaven* is by no means encyclopedic; as far as China's foods are concerned, what lies between these covers is little more than the tip of the iceberg. Rather, this book is meant to be a subjective compilation of my personal favorites from each part of the country. The reason for this is simple: China's culinary traditions are so vast, ancient, and varied that each one of the thirty-five cuisines touched upon here deserves a book of its own. But I hope that I've provided a place for you to start, and a glimpse beneath the surface.

Eating my way through so much of what China has to offer has been the adventure of a lifetime. Named after what the Chinese people called their country in ancient times—Tiānxià 天下, or "All Under Heaven"—this book is my attempt to provide a framework for China's many food traditions and the forces that shaped them, and to offer curious readers a guide to the world's greatest unknown culinary treasure trove.

Thank you for allowing me to share my delicious obsession with you. Now, let's eat. ●

---

1. Please note that the borders of these regions are only approximate, for ingredients and cooking styles rarely obey the hard lines on a map.

THE NORTH & MANCHURIAN NORTHEAST

SHANDONG · BEIJING · TIANJIN · HEBEI · THE NORTHEAST

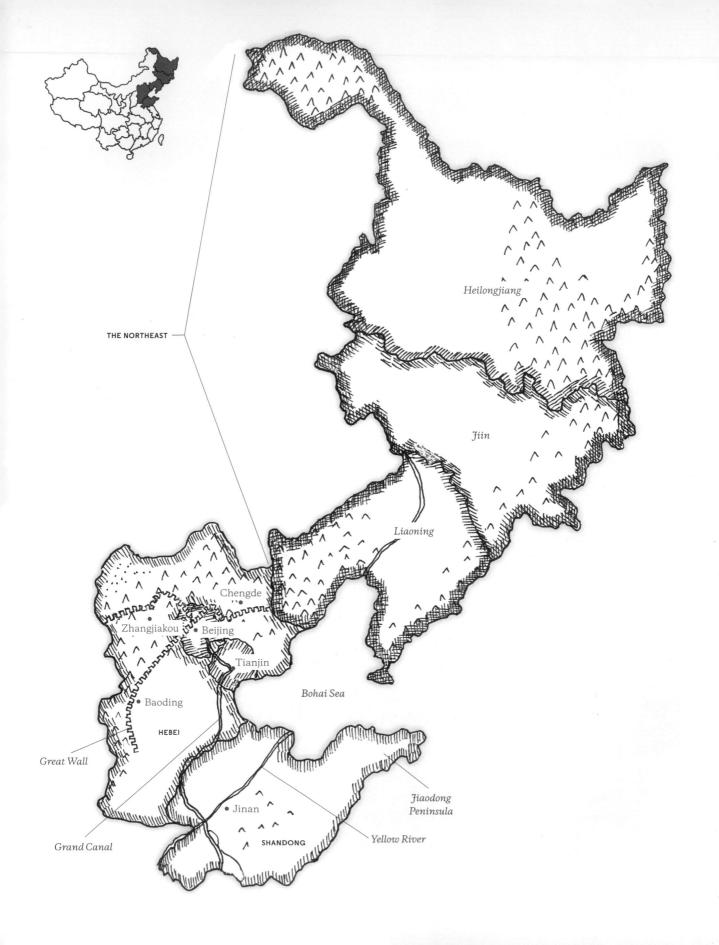

THE NORTHEAST

Heilongjiang

Jiin

Liaoning

Chengde

Zhangjiakou • Beijing

Tianjin

Baoding

Bohai Sea

HEBEI

Great Wall

Jinan

Jiaodong
Peninsula

Grand Canal

SHANDONG

Yellow River

PREVIOUS SPREAD:
The color black and the *xuanwu*,
an intertwined tortoise and serpent,
symbolize the North.

"Chinese people love to eat, and perhaps, comparatively speaking, the people of Beijing love to eat more than anyone else."

中國人饞，也許北京人比較起來更饞。

—LIANG SHIH-CHIU, AUTHOR, TRANSLATOR,
AND BEIJING NATIVE (1903–87)

A welcoming attitude toward the ingredients and ideas of other lands and peoples has lent incredible depth and variety to China's foods. This is especially true in the country's northern region, which is home to the cuisines of Shandong, Beijing, Tianjin, Hebei, and the Northeast. Nowhere else on Mainland China does Han Chinese[1] cooking combine with Muslim, Mongolian, Manchurian, and even Russian food traditions as well as it does in these five areas.

This is due, in no small part, to the region's geography. The terrain here is less hilly than it is in other ancestral Han borderlands. As a result, despite the presence of the Great Wall, this territory was more susceptible to foreign intrusions. Some of these invading groups set down roots in northern China, becoming part of the local culture and bringing with

---

1. One of five humans is Han Chinese, making the Han the largest ethnic group in the world. Their name comes from the Han dynasty that unified China under one ruler; they now constitute over 90 percent of China's population. The country also includes many other ethnicities that have been assimilated to varying degrees, and all can be referred to simply as "Chinese," just as all citizens of the United States are called "Americans."

them an unequivocal preference for lamb, beef, and bread. Additionally, the Silk Road passed through this region, and its presence greatly influenced the area's local foods. Middle Eastern traders traveling along its multiple routes introduced Mediterranean spices and foodstuffs. Everything from carrots, dates, and peaches to black pepper, grapes, and cucumbers was shuttled along these ancient highways, usually en route to Beijing and the even more ancient capital that is now Xi'an.

But after all is said and done, with the notable exception of the Manchurian Northeast, this region's cooking styles have always remained firmly grounded in the food traditions of the Han. Pork, green onion, garlic, and ginger are all featured prominently in this group of recipes. To fully understand this region's cuisine, we must turn first to Shandong, where a dominant food culture has thrived since the beginning of recorded history.

SHANDONG

This coastal province lies at the mouth of the Yellow River, and its fertile alluvial fields nurtured the ancient communities here. Northern cooking has been so heavily influenced by this province's rich and savory local dishes that the entire region's cuisine is often referred to as the "Shandong School." The extent to which Shandong has shaped the region's diet is evident in the popularity of Daokou Poached Chicken (page 110). This moist and flavorful dish has traveled as far inland as Anhui and Henan, establishing itself as a local specialty in those provinces. With its deep aromas of soy sauce, caramelized sugar, rice wine, green onions, and fresh ginger, Daokou Poached Chicken epitomizes the rich cuisines of the North.

Shandong has three very influential culinary branches. The first is composed of dishes designed by the descendants of Confucius,[2] whose refined and subtle sensibilities can be tasted in dishes like Yellow-Braised Duck (page 31). The other two branches are defined by location: one follows the long coastal area of the Jiaodong Peninsula, while the other is centered in the capital of Jinan, on the Yellow River. The Jiaodong Peninsula is home to a wealth of creative seafood dishes, such as Sweet-and-Sour Carp (page 22), while Jinan's foods often feature an abundance of fresh garlic, as evidenced in the recipe for Cold Garlic Chicken (page 13). Garlic, in general, plays a major role in this region's cuisine. One elderly Shandongnese friend demonstrated this for me when he popped a whole raw clove into his mouth and said, "We eat these like peanuts."

BEIJING

As a center of culture and political power, Beijing has historically attracted chefs and ingredients from every corner of the country. Some of its ancient imperial dishes are still enjoyed today, such as Consort's Chicken Wings (page 12) made with red wine. Other fare was imported from the surrounding countryside, like Corn Thimbles (page 58). Street foods here tend to be the province of China's Hui Muslims. This ethnic group congregated in Beijing and its port city of Tianjin and introduced juicy Chinese Hamburgers (page 52), as well as the inspiration for famous palace dishes like Tasimi (page 35). Cuisines from the South also played a big role in shaping this city's foods. Chief among them was the Tan family cuisine, which was first introduced to the city by an official from Guangdong. These recipes gradually evolved into such renowned dishes as

---

2. Confucius is called Kong Fuzi (Master Kong) in China; his Western name is a Latinized version of his Chinese one.

Peking duck and shark fin soup (my mock version is on page 16).

Much of Beijing's culinary excellence, however, can be traced back to Confucius's descendants in Shandong. These officials took the family's refined cooking styles to the Forbidden City, including the recipes for dishes such as Abalone Shreds with Mung Bean Sprouts (page 24) and Jade and Pearls (page 28).

TIANJIN

Eighty miles southeast of Beijing lies Tianjin harbor. The cuisines of these two cities have much in common, but Tianjin's influences are more traditionally Han Chinese than Muslim. In this great seaport, pork often takes the place of lamb or beef in pasta- or bread-wrapped street foods, as evidenced in the recipes for Ignored by the Dog Filled Buns (page 48) and Potstickers (page 50).

Tianjin also has a more southern flair than Beijing, thanks to the influences that have wafted up the Grand Canal[3] from the Yangtze River Delta. This man-made watercourse connects the North with the culinary epicenters of the South. As a result, eaters of Tianjin dishes will note Zhejiang's propensity for sweetness and vinegar, Jiangsu's insistence on the finest and freshest ingredients, and Shanghai's adoption of Western flavors like catsup. All of these influences are present in such dishes as Braised Prawns (page 25), whose deceptively nondescript name belies its remarkable flavors and complex origins.

HEBEI

Beijing and Tianjin used to lie within the confines of Hebei Province, but now they are independent metropolises. The remainder of Hebei Province curls around them on the North China Plain. Fertilized by the flood-prone Yellow River's annual gift of silt, this rich farmland has allowed Beijing to grow into one of the world's greatest cities. Farther north, these alluvial lands gradually transition into the steppes and

deserts of Mongolia and northwestern China. As mentioned previously, this flat terrain made Hebei and other northern provinces more susceptible to invasion than other, hillier borderlands. Culinary traditions here are, as a result, deeply shaded by contributions from Mongols, Manchurians, and many others who sidestepped the Great Wall.

These influences have given Hebei three unique culinary spheres. The first is Zhangjiakou, which lies west of Beijing and was once an important caravan stop in the tea trade; mutton and baked flatbreads called *gezhabing* are popular here. South of that is Baoding, which sidles up against the more arid province of Shanxi. This region is known for its simple fare, such as braised donkey meat and toasted biscuits. Finally, along the northern edge of the province, refined court dishes define the culinary landscape. The Manchurian Qing dynasty's imperial family had its summer residence in the rolling hills near Chengde, and their impact can still be noted in dishes like Golden Pouches (page 34).

THE NORTHEAST

Just northeast of Chengde and past the Great Wall is the expansive territory often referred to as "Manchuria" by Westerners. Today, most Chinese refer to this area as the Northeast, not Manchuria, a name that is often negatively associated with Japanese imperialism. The region consists of a group of three closely related

---

3. The Grand Canal is the largest artificial waterway in the world. Work on the canal began in 486 BCE, but it was not expanded into a vital link between the Yangtze and the North until almost eleven hundred years later, when China's southern cities began to emerge as economic centers.

provinces: Liaoning, Jilin, and Heilongjiang. With Siberia wrapping around its top and the icy Russian port of Vladivostok to the east, the region has designed its foods to be nourishing and warming.

Dishes in the Northeast can be divided into two camps: the products of local cooks and the imported flavors of the Shandongnese who immigrated here a little more than a century ago. In addition, Slavic influences can be tasted throughout the region, in everything from crudités to the local oxtail dish Russian Soup (page 19). Soured cabbage here is traditionally made at home, providing families with healthy greens in the midst of the long, relentless winters. The Chinese have been making sauerkraut since at least the fifth century BCE,[4] so it is quite possible that it was introduced to Europe by Genghis Khan's hordes. Called "soured vegetable" in Chinese, it is often used throughout the region in clear soups like Lamb Hotpot (page 20).

My late mother-in-law immediately comes to mind whenever I think about North China. Born and raised in Tianjin, Chou Yueh-ming was the child of a warlord, and she grew up living like a princess. That all ended with the breakout of China's civil war in 1927 and the subsequent assassination of her father.

Nationalist forces would battle Communist forces for the next ten years, until the combatants temporarily ceased hostilities in order to defend against a Japanese invasion. It was around this time, with the Japanese on the brink of attacking Tianjin, that my husband's grandmother dressed her teenage daughter up as a boy and snuck her onto a ship bound for Vietnam. From there she walked all the way up to the Nationalist redoubt in Kunming, in south-central China, where she entered the local university and later met and married my husband's father.

She never lived in Tianjin again, but the foods of North China gave her joy as few other things could. I soon learned that cooking North China specialties did quite a bit to soften her opinion of me, the foreign bride of her eldest son. Visiting us in our lousy studio apartment in Long Beach, she would nibble on things like Corn Thimbles (page 58) and muse about her childhood: how her mother's insistence that she have unbound feet had allowed her to escape Tianjin before it fell to the Japanese, for example. Sometimes, in the middle of one of these stories, she would pause

and a shadow would pass across her face. You had the sense that she was seeing a world and a people that no longer existed.

Such is the power of food and memory. ●

---

4. *The Rites of Zhou* (*Zhōulǐ* 周禮), written during the Spring and Autumn Period (772–476 BCE), refers to it as *jū* 菹, and the *Shuowen* dictionary defines it as "sour vegetable."

THE RECIPES

V = VEGETARIAN OR VEGAN OPTION

Liángbàn dòugān báicàixin 涼拌豆乾白菜心

Napa Cabbage with Pressed Bean Curd

BEIJING · SERVES 4 TO 6

1 small head (under 1 pound) light green napa cabbage
1 teaspoon sea salt
2 squares pressed bean curd
2 tablespoons toasted sesame seeds (page 413)
    or finely chopped toasted peanuts (page 411)
3 tablespoons toasted sesame oil
1 teaspoon sugar, or to taste
1 to 2 teaspoons pale rice vinegar, or to taste
1 jalapeño pepper, seeded and thinly sliced, optional
¼ cup coarsely chopped cilantro
1 green onion, trimmed and thinly sliced

Despite being located in the northern latitudes, Beijing is insanely hot and humid in the summer; the nearby deserts of Mongolia also push warm sirocco-like winds into the city. As a result, Beijing residents have developed some pretty wonderful dishes designed for the heat.

Besides being refreshing, Napa Cabbage with Pressed Bean Curd has the added advantage of requiring no cooking whatsoever. The cabbage is lightly salted and then tossed with the rest of the ingredients to make a salad that one could describe as a Chinese-style coleslaw.

But the dish is distinctly Chinese. Instead of using mayonnaise, for example, it is seasoned with a light, palate-cleansing vinaigrette. And rather than carrots, it features slender slivers of pressed bean curd, toasted sesame seeds, chopped cilantro, green onions, sesame oil, and a touch of rice vinegar. Just like coleslaw, though, this dish is a perfect accompaniment to barbecue, fried chicken, or roast meats.

1. If possible, start this recipe at least 4 hours before serving, but do not add the cilantro and green onions until the last minute. (They'll turn soggy if added earlier.) Rinse the cabbage, shake it dry, and cut it in half. Cut out and discard the core and then chop the cabbage into ½-inch pieces. Place the cabbage in a colander and toss with the salt; let the cabbage drain while you prepare the rest of the ingredients.

2. Rinse the bean curd and slice each piece horizontally into 4 thin slices. Then cut these slices in half before cutting them crosswise into tiny matchsticks. Place the bean curd in a medium work bowl and add the sesame seeds (or peanuts), oil, sugar, vinegar, and optional jalapeño pepper.

3. Squeeze out the excess liquid in the cabbage by pressing it between your hands. Drop the squeezed cabbage into the work bowl without rinsing it. Combine the cabbage with the other ingredients, taste, adjust the seasoning, and chill covered for a few hours. Just before serving, toss in the cilantro and green onion.

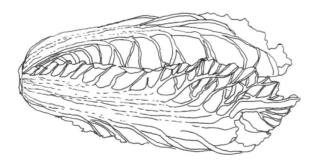

Shāo máodòu 燒茅豆

Soybean Pods

THE NORTHEAST · SERVES 4 TO 6

Lots of people think that cooked whole soybean pods are a Japanese invention, but they are also enjoyed in many parts of China. Soybeans have been there forever, and cooking them this way is easy, nutritious, cheap, and delicious.

Rather than simply simmering their soybeans in salted water, cooks in China's great Northeast toss in whole Sichuan peppercorns and five-spice powder to add extra flavor. They often also clip off both ends of the pods before their hot bath, so that all of those spices can saturate the little jade beans.

Good hot, better warm, and best cold, soybean pods are a great way to inaugurate a summer evening's festivities.

1 pound frozen soybeans (*edamame*) in their
    pods (see Tips)
2 teaspoons whole Sichuan peppercorns
1½ teaspoons five-spice powder (page 441
    or store-bought)
1½ teaspoons sea salt
3 cups water

1. Defrost the soybeans by soaking them in lukewarm water, or defrost the bag overnight in the refrigerator. Drain the soybeans and use a pair of kitchen shears to trim off both ends of the pods.

2. Place the soybeans in a 2-quart saucepan with the Sichuan peppercorns, five-spice powder, salt, and water. Add more water as necessary to cover the soybeans. Bring the water to a boil over high heat, then reduce the heat to maintain a gentle simmer. Cook the soybeans for about 15 minutes. Test one of the beans; it should have lost its beany taste and be slightly soft. Drain the beans in a colander, shaking them so that the excess water is removed and the peppercorns slither to the bottom of the colander.

3. Remove the soybeans to a covered container, discarding most of the peppercorns in the process. Cover the container and chill. Eat like any other soybean pods: tease the beans from the pod with your teeth and discard the pod.

You can almost never buy fresh soybeans, so frozen is the way to go. If you are a stickler for freshness, plant them yourself. They're an easy crop and they grow fast.

Packages for these pods will usually display their Chinese name as *máodòu* 毛豆, which has the same pronunciation as 茅豆. The first one means "fuzzy beans," while the second means "thatch beans."

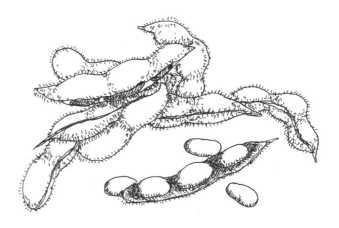

Bōcài huāshēng 菠菜花生

Spinach and Peanuts

BEIJING · SERVES 4 TO 6

When summer gets under way, one way to make food more appealing is to offer a spread of what the Chinese call *kāiwèicài* 開胃菜 or "stomach opener dishes." Many of these dishes involve cold salads or chilled veggies, and they can be very refreshing in hot weather. As with all things Chinese, though, the secret is in the balance, the timing, and the brilliant contrasts between flavor and texture.

Spinach and Peanuts can be served chilled or slightly warm. If you are making it ahead of time, wait until the last minute to toss in the dressing and peanuts so that the spinach remains emerald green and the peanuts stay crunchy.

1 bunch (about 12 ounces) spinach,
    as tender as possible
3 or more tablespoons sauce from sweet pickled garlic
    cloves (page 433), or 1 clove garlic, finely minced,
    1 tablespoon dark soy sauce, 1 tablespoon black
    vinegar, and 1 tablespoon sugar
2 to 3 tablespoons toasted sesame oil
¼ cup fried peanuts (page 411)

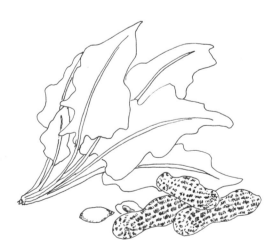

1. Clean the spinach (see Tips) and remove any tough stems. To blanch the spinach, bring about 2 inches of water to a boil in a large (2-quart) covered saucepan, add the spinach, cover the pot again, and then quickly toss the spinach with a pair of tongs as soon as the water boils again. Once all of the leaves have wilted but are still bright green and barely cooked, drain the spinach in a colander. Spray cold water over the spinach to stop it from cooking further (this will preserve its color). Gently squeeze the spinach dry and chill it if you are not serving it immediately.

2. If you are making the sauce from scratch, mix the garlic, soy sauce, vinegar, and sugar together and let the flavors develop for a few minutes.

3. To make the dressing, combine the sesame oil with either the sauce from the sweet pickled garlic cloves or the sauce you just made. Taste and adjust the seasoning.

4. Just before serving, toss the spinach with the sauce and the fried peanuts. Serve cold.

The best way to wash spinach is to use the trick I learned from Marian Morash's *Victory Garden Cookbook*: wash the spinach in a tub of warm water, which is easier on your hands and makes swishing the leaves around a whole lot more pleasant. Rinse and swish the spinach, changing the water after each rinsing until there is absolutely no sand left in the bottom of the tub. Then shake the leaves dry (you don't need to get them totally dry for this dish because they are going to be blanched).

Chinese dishes rarely call for spinach to be stemmed. If you have a tough bunch of spinach, though, this is a great time to learn how to remove the stems: grab the leaves with one hand while pulling up on the stems like a zipper with the other. This is a skill that will come in handy often. You can toss the leftover stems into your soup, or you could chop them finely, blanch or stir-fry them, and season as desired.

Jīsī lāpí 雞絲拉皮

Manchurian Chicken Salad

THE NORTHEAST · SERVES 6 TO 8

This is a popular appetizer in the northern provinces, with many places claiming to have invented it. But from what I've been able to determine, Manchurian Chicken Salad is a native of the Northeast.

This recipe makes twice the amount of dressing you'll need for an appetizer, but I am firm in recommending that you make this extra amount because it is a fabulous salad dressing.

BEAN SHEETS
3 dried mung bean sheets
Boiling water, as needed
1 tablespoon toasted sesame oil

CHICKEN AND CUCUMBERS
12 to 16 ounces cooked, boneless chicken
2 Persian or other small, seedless cucumbers

DRESSING
1 inch fresh ginger, peeled
1 green onion, green part only
½ cup toasted sesame paste (page 413)
½ cup toasted sesame oil
1 tablespoon black vinegar
3 tablespoons sugar
¼ cup regular soy sauce
3 tablespoons prepared mustard (Dijon is great here)
¼ cup water

GARNISH
2 tablespoons toasted sesame seeds (page 413)
1 small bunch cilantro, optional

1. Place the dried mung bean sheets in a large work bowl and pour the boiling water over them to cover. The sheets will begin to soften in a few minutes, so if any areas are sticking above the water, use tongs to jab them down. Allow the sheets to soak and rehydrate for about 30 minutes while you prepare the rest of the meal, or follow package directions.

2. Shred or cut the chicken into thin strips. You can remove the skin if you like, but I enjoy the added texture and flavor that skin can bring. Trim the ends off of the cucumbers, smack them open (see page 449), and cut them into 2-inch lengths. Cover the chicken and cucumbers and chill them until it's time to serve the dish.

3. Finely grate the ginger and chop the green onion into small pieces. Melt the sesame paste and sesame oil together in a small frying pan, using a silicone spatula to scrape the bottom. Add the vinegar, sugar, soy sauce, and mustard, then mix together. Taste and adjust as necessary. Stir in the ginger and onions, then loosen up the dressing with the water; you should end up with a sauce that has the consistency of heavy cream. Pour it into a wide bowl to cool.

4. Drain the mung bean sheets and pour cold water over them. You must do this carefully; they will have turned completely clear at this point and will be rather fragile. You probably won't have to cut the sheets, since they tend to fall apart into bite-sized pieces all by themselves. Gently toss them with the sesame oil to keep them from sticking together. You can make the recipe ahead of time up to this point and chill everything.

5. Just before serving, layer the mung bean sheets on your serving platter, then the cucumbers and chicken, and pour half of the dressing over the top. Garnish with sesame seeds and cilantro and serve with the extra dressing on the side.

Guìfēi jīchì 貴妃雞翅

Consort's Chicken Wings

BEIJING · SERVES 4

Although it has been present in China's food traditions for centuries, red wine never became popular as a beverage, perhaps because rice wine and white liquors better complement the fermented flavors of things like soy sauce and sweet wheat paste (see page 462). In any case, it plays a central role in this dish, which first appeared in the eighth century CE, when along with fresh lychees (page 146), these chicken wings were one of Consort Yang Guifei's favorite things to eat. I often serve them next to a pile of Spinach and Peanuts (page 10), which complements the flavors and colors of the chicken nicely.

CHICKEN

8 chicken wings

3 tablespoons regular soy sauce

2 cups peanut or vegetable oil (used oil is
    all right if it smells fresh)

SAUCE

1 leek, split and cleaned (see page 450),
    or 5 green onions, trimmed

5 slices fresh ginger

7 tablespoons regular soy sauce

6 tablespoons Shaoxing rice wine

1½ cups water

2 tablespoons rock sugar or other sugar

¾ cup good red table wine

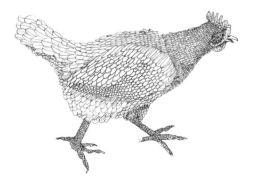

1. Pull off and discard any feathers, loose fat, or skin on the wings. Cut each wing into three sections, but use the tips for something else. Place the wings in a work bowl and toss them with the soy sauce to coat.

2. Heat the oil over medium-high heat in a wok until a chopstick inserted in the oil immediately bubbles all over. Drain the wings and discard the soy sauce. Fry the chicken wings in batches of all drumettes and all middle sections so that they fry evenly, about 15 minutes each. When each piece is golden brown, remove to a colander and place this in the sink. Rinse the oil off the wings under running water to make the final flavors as light as possible.

3. Drain off all but 1 tablespoon of the oil from the wok. Set the wok over high heat and toss in the leek or green onions with the ginger. Stir-fry them quickly until browned and then add the soy sauce, rice wine, water, and rock sugar. When the mixture comes to a boil, add the browned chicken wings. Bring the sauce to a boil again and then lower to a simmer. Cook the wings uncovered for about 1 hour, until the sauce is reduced and the wings are very tender. Remove the ginger and the leeks (or green onions); save them for a snack, as they are very tasty but not particularly good looking.

4. Add the red wine to the chicken and bring the sauce to a boil once more. Simmer the sauce for 15 to 20 minutes so that the chicken can absorb the wine flavors; the sauce should again be reduced and thick. Taste and adjust the flavors. Serve the wings hot, cold, or warm.

Use good soy sauce and wines. Because very few ingredients are involved here, all the flavors play a prominent role.

The sauce can be used afterward to cook bean curd, carrots, or potatoes. It will jell up once it gets cold because of the chicken skin, so remove the chicken pieces before you refrigerate it.

Shāndōng shāojī 山東燒雞

Cold Garlic Chicken

SHANDONG · SERVES 6 TO 8

The first time I sampled this dish was when a friendly Shandongnese restaurateur served it to my husband and me as his house specialty. To make the dish, the chef said he fried, steamed, and chilled a whole chicken. Then he chopped it up, set it on a bed of sliced cucumber, and doused it in a garlicky vinaigrette. After experimenting with the dish myself, I realized that I prefer to make it with boneless dark meat only. Its moist, springy texture works as a wonderful foil against the deeply seasoned sauce and the crisp cucumbers.

CHICKEN

6 chicken thighs, or 8 to 10 drumsticks, with the skin on
¼ cup regular soy sauce
Vegetable or peanut oil, as needed
2 teaspoons ground toasted Sichuan
    peppercorns (page 441)
1 finger fresh ginger, thinly sliced (about ¼ cup)
3 green onions, trimmed and cut into 2-inch lengths

GARNISH

5 or 6 Persian or other small, seedless cucumbers
2 tablespoons regular soy sauce
2 tablespoons black vinegar
1 tablespoon finely chopped garlic
1 tablespoon toasted sesame oil
2 tablespoons reserved liquid from the steamed chicken
Chopped cilantro, optional

1. Place the chicken pieces in a plastic bag with the soy sauce and marinate them for 1 hour, squishing the bag every now and then to make sure that every surface is nicely tanned. Drain off and discard the soy sauce and pat the pieces dry. Heat 1 inch of oil in a large, flat frying pan over medium-high heat and then place the chicken in the pan in a single layer. Do this in two or three batches, if necessary. Fry the chicken for about 20 minutes until it is golden brown all over, adjusting the temperature as necessary to ensure an even heat that browns the skin without blackening the juices. Remove the chicken to a heatproof plate that will fit into your steamer (see page 49), draining off as much oil as possible.

2. Scatter the ground Sichuan peppercorns, ginger, and green onions over the fried chicken, making sure that all of the pieces are well dusted. I adore the piney flavor that toasted Sichuan peppercorns give this dish, and often use extra, but you should follow your palate. Steam the chicken for about 1 hour, adding more water as needed, until the juices run clear when the thickest part is pierced with a knife. Remove from the heat, let the chicken come to room temperature, discard the seasonings, and remove the bones. Reserve 2 table-spoons of the chicken juices. Shred the chicken into thick strips, keeping as much skin on the meat as possible and plucking out any veins, bones, gristle, or tendons that you run across. Chill the shredded chicken in a covered container for up to 3 days.

3. About 1 hour before you want to serve this dish, trim the cucumbers, smack them open (see page 449), cut them into 2-inch lengths, and arrange them on a serving plate. Mix together the soy sauce, vinegar, garlic, sesame oil, and reserved chicken juices in a measuring cup or small bowl. Arrange the chicken on top of the cucumbers and then pour the sauce over everything so that the cucumbers and chicken have a chance to get flavored up. Garnish with chopped cilantro, if you like.

Lǔ niújiàn, niújīn, niúzá 滷牛腱、牛筋、牛雜

Braised Beef Shank, Tendons, and Variety Meats

BEIJING · SERVES 8 TO 12

Muslim-influenced dishes in Beijing are without a doubt some of my favorite in the region. Much of this has to do with the creative ways in which every bit of an animal is used. In the West, we tend to toss out the less meaty parts of the animal, but that is not the case in China. Chinese cooks use these parts because they are frugal, but also because they appreciate the intriguing textures that the heart, stomach, and shin have to offer.

These variety meats are the kinds of things that most Beijing-style Muslim restaurants offer as a matter of course. If they are small, family-run places, they will display them right in the front window, the same way Cantonese delis hang ducks and pigs near the sidewalk. The flavors in braises such as this one are rich and savory, as they are based on a spice-infused marinade colored by soy sauce and slightly sweetened with rock sugar.

For dinner at these Muslim-style eateries, my husband and I would usually have a plate of cool braised liver, tendons, and heart to start off. This might be followed by eggs, bean curd, and thick seaweed cooked in the braising liquid that was used for the meats. If it was breakfast, we might order tender braised shank served in Shaobing (page 56), a truly great way to start the day.

MAIN INGREDIENTS

2 pounds (more or less) boneless beef shank,
    or 1 pound beef shank plus 1 beef heart (see Tips)
2 beef tendons, about 1¼ to 1½ pounds
1 pound honeycomb tripe
½ cup thinly sliced fresh ginger
4 green onions
6 tablespoons regular soy sauce
4 star anise
½ stick cinnamon
1 tablespoon fennel seeds
1 tablespoon whole Sichuan peppercorns
½ cup (more or less) rock sugar or brown slab sugar
2 dried Thai chilies, optional
1 piece aged tangerine peel, optional
1 cup mild rice wine, optional

VARIATIONS (WITH RECIPES AT RIGHT)

1 pound beef liver or other variety meats
12 (medium or large) eggs, at room
    temperature (see Tips)
1 pound pressed bean curd
    or very firm bean curd
½ long strip dried kombu seaweed
    (or 1 cup any other variety), soaked
    in cool water overnight

TO SERVE

Thinly sliced green onions
Toasted sesame oil and thinly sliced green onions,
    for garnish if serving bean curd and/or seaweed

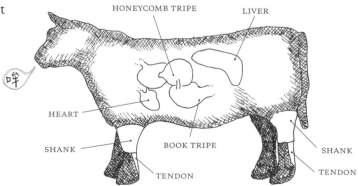

1. Rinse the shank and place in the pot of a pressure cooker with the cleaned heart (see page 459). (If you don't have a pressure cooker, see Tips following the Russian Soup recipe on page 19.) Rinse the tendons and add them to the pot. Carefully wash out every crevice of the tripe before prepping it (see Tips) and tossing it in with the other meats. Cover the meats with water, bring the water to a boil over high heat, lower the heat, simmer the meats for about 10 minutes, and then dump out the water.

2. Rinse the scum off of the meats and the pot. Return the meats to the pot and add all of the remaining ingredients, as well as enough water to cover the meats (or right below the maximum level for the pot). Cover the pressure cooker, bring it to a boil over high heat, lower it to medium, and cook the meat on high pressure for 1 hour. Release the steam and open the pressure cooker.

3. Carefully remove the shank (and heart, if used) to a bowl. Cover the pot again and cook over high pressure for another 30 minutes, until the tendons and tripe are absolutely tender. Fish the tendons and tripe out and add them to the shank. Bring the liquid to a boil, lower the heat to medium-high, and boil the liquid down until it is flavorful and you have about 1 cup left (about 30 minutes). Pour this reduced liquid through a sieve held over the meat and let it come to room temperature. Cover and refrigerate overnight. (If you are cooking beef liver, too, remember that it requires much less cooking than the other meats, so blanch it and then simmer it in the reduced liquid until it is done to your liking. Refrigerate it overnight in that sauce with the rest of the meats.)

4. All of these meats can be served hot, cold, or at room temperature. They are easiest to slice, however, when they are cold, and you can either serve them immediately, cover them and let them come to room temperature, or steam them before serving. Garnish with thinly sliced green onions.

BRAISED EGGS

To prepare hard-boiled eggs, see the Tips. Peel the eggs once they have cooled down. Place them in the reduced liquid from Step 3, covering them as needed with water, soy sauce, sugar, spices, and so on, so that the sauce is not too diluted. Cook them without the lid on (see Tips) for an hour or two, turn off the heat, cover the eggs, and let them sit overnight. Simmer them uncovered the next day for an hour or two, then let them rest. They will be best 2 or 3 days after they are first made, as this gives them time to absorb the sauce.

BRAISED BEAN CURD AND SEAWEED

If you want to simmer some pressed bean curd or seaweed here, make sure that you will not be cooking anything else in your sauce, as both bean curd and seaweed are dominating flavors. Place either the bean curd or seaweed in a pan, cover them with the sauce from Step 3, and simmer them for about 1 hour. The bean curd will need to sit in the sauce for a day or two before it is flavorful. Cook the bean curd without the lid on unless you like a honeycomb effect (lots of elongated bubbles). The seaweed needs to simmer in the sauce only until tender. Serve both chilled with a sprinkle of sesame oil and some green onions.

Variety meats can be found at good butcher shops; if they're not in stock, the butcher can probably order them. Tripe is often thought to have a strong smell, but nowadays this variety meat is cleaned so well and even bleached that this is rarely the case. For advice on tendons, see page 120.

Whenever you make hard-boiled eggs for recipes like this, look for two things: the smallest ones possible, and eggs that are not too fresh. Smaller ones absorb the sauce's flavors faster, and older ones are easier to peel. When cooking them, keep the lid off; otherwise, pressure will build up in the pan and the egg whites will have a honeycomb texture. Gently stirring the eggs as the water comes to a boil will keep the yolks centered in the still-soft whites; once the water begins to boil, the whites will have set and you can stop stirring. Never boil the eggs at full blast, though, as this will make the whites tough. A gentle simmer is enough. They will also be cooked in the sauce, so there's no need to overdo it. For more information, see page 461.

Huángmèn sùyúchì 黃燜素魚翅

Mock Shark Fin Soup

BEIJING · SERVES 6 TO 8

Traditionally consumed by an exclusive and wealthy minority, shark fin soup has become increasingly popular as China's citizenry has grown more affluent. Shark populations have plummeted as a result of this heightened demand. In addition to being destructive, the practice is also highly wasteful. Just like the tusks of elephants, only one part of the shark has any real value: its fins. As a result, after a captured shark has been harvested for its fins, the rest of its body is often dumped back into the ocean like a piece of garbage.

This all prompts the question, what is it about shark fin soup that is so appealing to the Chinese palate? The answer is simple: its gelatinous quality. Many of China's most prized ingredients—sea cucumbers, tendons, swallows' nests, and jellyfish, to name a few—are savored because of their texture, rather than their flavor. In and of themselves

they have little or no taste, but what they do have is a gentle chewiness that is loved by the Chinese almost as much as Americans adore crunchy things.

Shark fin soup originated in Guangdong, where dried seafood has played an important role in the cuisine for centuries. Then, in the latter half of the 19th century, imperial official and poet Tan Zongjun took shark fin soup to Beijing, along with many other dishes, which are now collectively known as Tan family cuisine (see page 4).

Fortunately, vegetarian shark fin is a remarkable substitute, so we can still dine well without endangering sharks. This new version of the soup, which I've developed from the blueprint created by Tan's favorite chef, Cao Jincheng, provides the same delicate, traditional flavors, but punctuates them with ersatz shark fin instead of the real thing. Here, as in Cao's original creation, everything but the stock ends up flying almost below your sensory radar. The green onions, dried scallops, and ginger hover in the background, and the small piece of Chinese ham lends just a faint smoky saltiness.

4 small (¾-inch) dried scallops (about ½ ounce)

½ ounce Chinese-style ham or prosciutto, about 2 × ¾ × ¾ inch

5 pounds chicken backs or other meaty bones

1 duck, breast meat and legs removed (see Tips); reserve 1 leg

4 quarts water

2 inches fresh ginger, thinly sliced (about ¼ cup)

4 green onions, trimmed

1 chicken breast

1 package (16 ounces) frozen vegetarian shark fin

1 tablespoon sugar

½ cup Shaoxing rice wine

1. Place the dried scallops in a heatproof bowl and cover them with warm tap water. As soon as they have plumped up, use a paring knife to trim off any tough fibers or debris. Rinse the ham and trim off the skin. Cut one-fourth of the ham against the grain into paper-thin slices and then mince the slices evenly; this will be used as garnish. Chop the rest of the ham into about 6 pieces for the stock.

2. Remove any organs or big pieces of fat on the chicken backs and duck carcass and trim as needed. Place the poultry in a stockpot and cover with cool tap water. Bring the water to a boil and simmer for about 1 minute to remove any impurities, then dump the contents into a colander set in the sink. Rinse the chicken and duck under cool water, washing off any scum. Return the chicken and duck to the rinsed-out stockpot, cover with the water, and add the scallops, ham chunks, ginger, and green onions. Bring to a full boil, lower the heat to a gentle simmer, and cook uncovered for about 3 hours to get every bit of flavor from the ingredients. At this point, the liquid should be reduced to about 8 cups and the bones should be completely broken down.

3. While the stock is cooking, prepare the poached meat garnishes by placing the chicken breast and duck leg in a small saucepan and covering them with at least 2 inches of water. Bring the water to a boil, then dump it out and rinse off the chicken and duck.

4. Rinse the pan, return the chicken and duck to it, add the chicken breast, and add water to cover. Bring to a boil again, cover, turn off the heat, and let the chicken and duck poach undisturbed for about 15 minutes. Check the meat by piercing with a chopstick; the juices should run clear. Pour the cooking liquid into the stockpot. When the chicken and duck pieces are cool enough to handle, remove and discard the skin and bones and shred the meat into long strips. Place the minced ham in a heatproof bowl and steam for about 5 minutes; discard any juices. Taste the ham, and if it is too salty, rinse with boiling water. Drain it in a small, fine sieve and taste again; repeat as necessary.

5. Pour the stock through a large, fine sieve placed over a 2-quart casserole with a lid, preferably a sandpot. Use a heavy spoon to press all the juices from the solids before discarding them. You should have a nice bit of yellow fat floating on the top, which is quite delicious, but it may be skimmed off, if you prefer.

6. Defrost the vegetarian shark fin by placing the package in a large bowl and covering it with hot water, adding more hot water as necessary. When it has completely defrosted, pour the contents into a sieve (don't use a colander, as the holes are too big) and rinse under cool tap water. Drain well. Add the drained vegetarian shark fin to the stock in the casserole or sandpot and bring it to a boil, along with the sugar and rice wine. Lower the heat to a simmer and cook uncovered for 20 to 30 minutes, until it absorbs the flavors and plumps up a bit.

7. Gently stir in the shredded chicken and duck to heat through. Sprinkle the minced ham on top and serve at once, either in a tureen or in delicate soup bowls. This soup is best when eaten immediately while the vegetarian shark fin is still firm and the flavors are perfectly balanced.

The duck breast and leg should be used for something else; see the index for suggestions.

Some recipes suggest using cellophane noodles—also called mung bean noodles or *fensi*—in place of the mock shark fin, but these noodles soften too quickly and turn gluey.

Clear Beef Soup with Chinese Herbs and Radishes

BEIJING · SERVES AT LEAST 6

This soup will turn into a crystalline broth that jells into a solid mass when chilled. This is due to the beef shanks and tendons, which transfer their elasticity to the soup as it cooks. The resulting broth has an amazing body and depth. All it needs are some Chinese radishes, which offer a gentle crispness and a suggestion of sweetness. I sometimes like to toss in tripe (see Tips, page 15) and a couple more of those tendons, so that I can serve them as a separate appetizer.

SOUP

2 pounds boneless beef shank, plus 1 split shank bone, if possible
2 beef tendons (1¼ to 1½ pounds)
1 pound honeycomb or book tripe, rinsed, optional
1 large leek, split and cleaned (see page 450)
½ cup thinly sliced fresh ginger
½ cup mild rice wine
2 bay leaves
1 teaspoon sea salt
3 pieces dried licorice root
1 star anise
½ stick cinnamon
1 tablespoon whole Sichuan peppercorns
1 tablespoon whole black peppercorns
1 piece Dahurian angelica root, optional
5 slices lovage root, optional
2 smallish Chinese radishes (about 1 pound)

GARNISH

Chopped cilantro

1. Start this recipe at least a day before you wish to serve it. Place the meats in a large stockpot and cover with water. Bring the water to a boil over high heat, lower the heat, and simmer the meats for about 10 minutes, then dump out the water. Rinse the scum off the meats and the pot, then return the meats to the pot.

2. Add the leek, ginger, rice wine, bay leaves, and salt to the stockpot. Toss in the herbs and spices after either tying them in a piece of coarse cheesecloth or placing them in a large mesh ball. Add enough water to cover the meats. Bring the water to a boil, then lower it to a gentle simmer, cooking the soup uncovered and adding more boiling water as needed to keep the meats submerged.

3. When the optional tripe is very tender (check after 2 hours), remove it from the stock. The tendons and shank should gently cook for 3 to 5 hours to become tender. Remove them from the stock as they become ready, let the meats come to room temperature, cover, and chill; serve these either on top of a noodle soup or as an appetizer (see Tip), but their role in this recipe is now over.

4. Strain out the solids and let the stock come to room temperature before covering and refrigerating it. If you like, you can remove most of the fat after it has congealed on top.

5. Peel the radishes. Be sure to get rid of any fibrous webbing below the skin. Cut them into thin slices and then into matchsticks. Bring the stock to a boil in a large pan or wok and then add the radishes. Bring to a boil again and then lower to a gentle simmer. Cook the radishes only until they are tender, 10 to 15 minutes. Taste and adjust the seasoning. Serve with some chopped cilantro on top.

To serve chilled meats as an appetizer, slice them very thinly and toss with a seasoned oil (see pages 434 and 435), as well as some julienned green onions or chopped cilantro, and either salt or soy sauce to taste.

Luósòng tāng 羅宋湯

Russian Soup

THE NORTHEAST · SERVES 6 AS A MAIN DISH

This is the Chinese version of borscht, Russia's quintessential soup. Even the name in Chinese tells you that: *luosong* means (and sounds like) "Russian." But here those earthy, Slavic flavors of carrot, tomato, and parsley have been tempered and emboldened by ginger, rice wine, soy sauce, and (yes) catsup.

My secret for the perfect oxtail soup is a pressure cooker. Now, if you don't use one because you have been terrified by your mom's story about the exploding chicken incident of 1959, you are in for some good news, because today's high-quality pressure cookers are safe, easy, and effective.

BEEF AND BROTH

3 tablespoons peanut or vegetable oil

2 inches fresh ginger, thinly sliced (about ¼ cup)

1 oxtail (2 to 2½ pounds), cut into chunks by the butcher

1 large onion, cut into 1-inch chunks

6 cloves garlic, lightly smashed

2 bay leaves

6 cups water

¼ cup mild rice wine

¼ cup regular soy sauce

½ cup catsup

VEGETABLES

3 small Yukon Gold or other potatoes

3 carrots, peeled

1 can (28 ounces) whole tomatoes (see Tips)

GARNISH

Handfuls of parsley or cilantro, chopped

1. Ideally, start this recipe a day before you plan to serve it—although you can also prep and cook this within 90 minutes. Heat the pot of a pressure cooker over high heat and then add the oil. Toss in the ginger and fry it for a few seconds. Add the oxtail and let it sear on both sides before removing it along with the ginger. Leave the oil in the pan. Add the onion and garlic, tossing them around in the hot oil until the onion is lightly browned. Return the oxtail and ginger to the pan along with the bay leaves, water, rice wine, soy sauce, and catsup. Cover the pressure cooker and cook the oxtail on high pressure for 55 minutes. Remove from the heat and let the pressure drop naturally for around 10 minutes before opening the lid.

2. While the oxtail is cooking away, cut each potato into eighths (I leave them unpeeled). Roll-cut the carrots into pieces about 1 inch long (see page 449). Place the potatoes and carrots in a medium saucepan. Drain the juices from the tomatoes into the saucepan. Slice each tomato into pieces about ¾ inch thick and add them to the saucepan. Pour just enough water into the saucepan to cover the root vegetables and bring the pan to a boil. Reduce the heat and simmer the vegetables until they are cooked to your taste, 15 to 20 minutes.

3. Add the vegetables to the soup, taste, and adjust the seasoning. If you have time, let the soup come to room temperature, cover, and refrigerate overnight. Remove most of the fat before heating up the soup. Ladle the soup into individual soup bowls or serve it in a terrine. Garnish with lots of chopped parsley or cilantro and serve with bread or rice.

If you don't have a pressure cooker, use a Dutch oven and proceed as directed in Step 1, browning the meat and onions, adding the other ingredients, and then simmering the meat until it is tender, which should take about 3 hours.

This is a cold-weather soup, so when you make it, good tomatoes may not be available. That's why I recommend canned ones.

Shuàn yángròu 涮羊肉

Lamb Hotpot

THE NORTHEAST · SERVES 4 TO 6 AS A MAIN DISH

Hotpots are a favorite winter dish in China's northern half. From Shaanxi to Manchuria, each community renders this dish in its own, idiosyncratic way. The hotpot is thought to have gotten its start in either the Northeast or Mongolia—accounts differ. One story even attributes its invention to Kublai Khan. I like the hotpot because it is a very sensible way for a bunch of people to get warm and eat well with a minimum amount of fuss. In fact, this is more of an assembly than an actual recipe.

Of all the different takes on the hotpot out there, this recipe is my favorite. Part of the reason lies in the delicious contrast between the rich lamb, the soured cabbage, and the meaty, frozen bean curd. By putting a block of firm bean curd in the freezer, you end up with a honeycombed, chewy sponge that sucks up all the dipping sauces perfectly.

But it is those dipping sauces that are my ultimate reason for choosing this hotpot over all others. My husband and I used to order it all the time in downtown Taipei at the Shanxi Restaurant (like I said, this is popular all over), where long rows of different condiments and sauces would be lined up. We'd mix together our own favorite concoctions and nibble on some of the sweet pickled garlic cloves (page 433) placed on our table. Then we'd start dunking the paper-thin pieces of lamb into the boiling broth, plucking them out as soon as they turned from pink to gray, and giving them a quick bath in our sauce before eating them.

You don't have to have a fancy copper Mongolian hotpot to make the perfect winter dinner, but it doesn't hurt. Mongolian hotpots have a funnel that allows the fumes from the fuel to waft away while the soup bubbles around it in a moat. The cheaper traditional Chinese hotpots have little hearth-like inserts in the bottom where liquid fuel can be burned, and Japanese shabu-shabu pots can be operated using electricity (you can also place some of them on induction cooktops),

so the equipment possibilities are broad enough to fit any budget. I've even used an ancient electric wok at times that works just fine.

A note on the Chinese name for this recipe, which is sometimes translated as "rinsed lamb" or something equally gruesome: *shuan* actually means to swish something around in a liquid—for example, the hot broth.

MEAT AND VEGETABLES

1 pound boneless lamb with fat, very thinly sliced
    (see Tips)
1 head pickled napa cabbage
1 bunch spinach, any tough stems discarded
    and cleaned (see page 10)
4 blocks (14 ounces each) firm bean curd,
    frozen solid and then defrosted
2 bundles cellophane noodles,
    soaked in cool water until soft

DIPPING CONDIMENTS (ALL OR SOME—AMOUNTS CAN BE ADJUSTED—SET OUT IN SMALL BOWLS)

2 cubes red fermented bean curd "cheese" (page 420)
3 tablespoons salted garlic chive flowers
2 tablespoons fish sauce
6 tablespoons toasted sesame paste (page 413)
¼ cup red chili oil (page 435)
¼ cup regular soy sauce
¼ cup black vinegar
¼ cup sugar
¼ cup toasted sesame oil
2 cloves garlic, finely chopped
2 green onions, trimmed and finely chopped
1 small bunch cilantro, finely chopped

Sweet pickled garlic cloves (as many as you like; page 433)
Fried peanuts (as many as you like; page 411)
Shaobing (about 2 per diner; page 56), hot

HOTPOT

¼ cup mild rice wine
4 cups boiling unsalted chicken stock (page 380),
    or as needed
Freshly ground black pepper

1. If your meat has not been cut for you by your butcher, freeze it until it is fairly firm, then cut it against the grain into razor-thin slices; the length and width do not matter as long as the slices are small enough to stick in your mouth without effort when cooked. Roll the slices up, arrange them on a serving platter, cover with plastic wrap, and freeze.

2. Rinse the napa cabbage, cut off and discard any tough pieces, and slice it against the grain into ½-inch pieces. Try to keep the original shape of the cabbage as you arrange it on a serving platter. Use a salad spinner to remove all the excess water from the spinach and pile it up in a large serving bowl. Gently squeeze the water out of the bean curd as if it were a sponge, then cut it into rectangles; arrange on a serving platter. Drain the cellophane noodles, cut them in half with kitchen shears, and arrange them in a serving bowl.

3. Give each of your guests a pair of chopsticks and a Chinese soupspoon. Lay out the little bowls and dishes with the dipping condiments; put little spoons in there, as well, so that diners can pick and choose among the selections, adjusting the seasonings to fit their own tastes. While they are busy doing that, place the meat, vegetables, bean curd, and cellophane noodles on the table around the hotpot and remove the plastic wrap. Lay out bowls of the sweet pickled garlic and peanuts, and heat up the *shaobing*.

4. Light the fuel (or plug in the heating element) for your hotpot. Add the rice wine to the stock, pour enough of the stock into the hotpot so that the liquid fills it no more than halfway, grind in some pepper, and toss in a few thicker pieces of the soured cabbage. Bring out the hot *shaobing* and cover them with a napkin to keep them warm. When the stock comes to a full boil again (and not before), have all of the guests pick up pieces of meat and swish them around in the hot stock to cook them thoroughly before dipping them in their sauces. After a few rounds of the meat, add the frozen bean curd and some of the vegetables to the stock. Top off the hotpot with more boiling stock as needed. When all of the meat is finished, add the rest of the vegetables and the cellophane noodles to the stock. This big bowl of soup signals the end of the hotpot meal.

Sourcing good meat is a demanding task, as the quality varies from store to store. You can try asking your butcher to prepare the meat for you—get a couple of pounds to make it worth his or her while—by freezing it and then cutting it on the deli slicer. It will usually roll up naturally into curls that way, which keeps the slices from sticking to one another.

Chinese and Korean grocery stores often have lamb, beef, and pork already cut and ready for hotpots, usually packed by their own butcher shop and stored in the freezer.

Tángcù lǐyú 糖醋鯉魚

Sweet-and-Sour Carp

SHANDONG · SERVES 4 TO 6

This carp recipe is one of Shandong's most famous dishes. It has many variations, including squirrel fish (*sōngshǔ lǐyú* 松鼠鯉魚), which was one of my first loves after I arrived in Taipei.

At northern banquets, this is always served as a whole fish because it is just so beautiful that way. For more casual dining, feel free to use fillets of any good firm-fleshed, mild-flavored fish. This is definitely not a difficult dish to master, although it looks spectacular when made with a whole fish. Basically, the fish is deeply scored through the skin, coated with cornstarch, and deep-fried. It is then quickly doused with the sauce. As with most traditional Chinese sweet-and-sour dishes, the sauce is merely a backdrop for the lightly coated ingredients and in no way resembles the overwhelming, sugary sweet-and-sour sauces that are so often served at American Chinese restaurants.

FISH

1 whole or filleted fish (1½ pounds or so),
    such as carp or bass
1 teaspoon sea salt
Peanut or vegetable oil for frying
Cornstarch, as needed

SAUCE

2 green onions, trimmed and finely chopped
2 tablespoons peeled and finely chopped fresh ginger
3 cloves garlic, finely chopped
¼ cup black vinegar
3 tablespoons rock sugar
2 tablespoons regular soy sauce
¼ cup unsalted chicken stock (page 380)
1 tablespoon cornstarch mixed with
    3 tablespoons water

GARNISH

Finely shredded baby white ginger and/or
    tender green onions

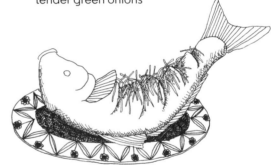

SHANDONG'S CUISINE IS MORE OR LESS divided along a north-south axis because the terrain is just so accommodating to this sort of thing. Although most of this province is a flat adjunct to the North China Plain that spreads all the way from Beijing south to Anhui and Hubei, the central area is a high dividing line covered with mist-shrouded mountains. On the east coast is a long hilly arm called the Jiaodong Peninsula that juts out into the sea toward Korea. Because western Shandong is located within what was even in imperial times considered easy traveling distance to Beijing, traditional

dishes here tend to be more refined and at times even glorious pieces of art, such as this Sweet-and-Sour Carp.

Shandong remains a place that shimmers with the glow of the nation's earliest history and culture. This is only natural, as Shandong was the land of Confucius over two thousand years ago. And, contrary to popular belief, the Great Sage was not concerned solely with thinking great thoughts. He also had much to say about food, as when he pointed out that "the way you cut your meat reflects the way you live," and when he mused that he could be

happy with nothing but coarse rice to eat, water to drink, and his bent arm for a pillow.

Appropriately enough, it was just after the age of Confucius that Shandong's cuisine was introduced to the palace kitchens as *guānfǔ cài* 官府菜 ("food from officials' residences"), the lavish dishes that are closely intertwined with the culinary traditions of Confucius's descendants (see page 4). An utterly refined way of cooking that could rival France's haute cuisine, these dishes are what graced the banquets of noblemen, powerful officials, and eventually even the emperors in Beijing.

1. Pat the fish dry inside and out with a paper towel, then prep the fish using the "peony blossom" technique (see below). Sprinkle the inside and outside of the fish with the salt, including the slashes, and let it marinate while you prepare the rest of the ingredients.

2. Heat a wok over medium heat until it starts to smoke, and then add about 3 inches of oil. While the oil is heating up, arrange the sauce ingredients near the stove. Have a Chinese spider or slotted spoon, some chopsticks, and a wok spatula ready, and prepare a serving platter.

3. Hold the fish up by the tail over a wide plate so that the slashes flap open. Coat the entire exterior of the fish—including the slashes—with cornstarch. Lightly shake the fish so that the excess cornstarch drops onto the plate. Sprinkle a pinch of the cornstarch into the oil, and if it immediately bubbles up and disappears, lower the fish gently, by the tail, into the oil. This will give the slashes the opportunity to open up wide. Adjust the heat as necessary to have a merry bubbling all around the fish, but not so hot that the exterior browns faster than the flesh can cook. Ladle the hot oil all over the fish, including the head. Rather than lifting the fish up to move it around, wait until it has browned in one section before gently shaking the wok to loosen the fish and nudge it to where you want it. When one side is a golden brown, use your spatula and chopsticks to gingerly turn the fish over; keep the tail raw for as long as possible to prevent it from breaking. (The tail can be browned right at the end.) When the second side is completely golden brown, use your spider and spatula to lift it carefully out of the hot oil and onto the waiting serving platter. If, in spite of your best efforts, the fish breaks apart at some point, simply rearrange it as well as you can on the platter and hide any gaps with the garnish.

4. Remove all but 2 tablespoons of the oil from the wok. Set it over medium-high heat and add the green onions, ginger, and garlic. Stir them around for about 10 seconds to release their fragrance, then add the vinegar, sugar, soy sauce, and stock. Bring the sauce to a boil, adjust the seasoning, and quickly stir in the cornstarch mixture. As soon as it bubbles, pour the sauce evenly over the fish and garnish as desired before rushing it to the table.

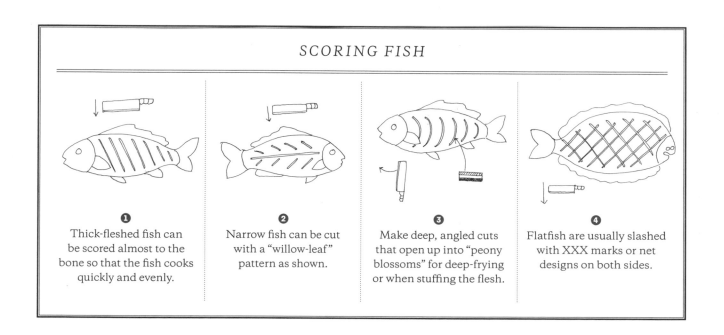

SCORING FISH

❶ Thick-fleshed fish can be scored almost to the bone so that the fish cooks quickly and evenly.

❷ Narrow fish can be cut with a "willow-leaf" pattern as shown.

❸ Make deep, angled cuts that open up into "peony blossoms" for deep-frying or when stuffing the flesh.

❹ Flatfish are usually slashed with XXX marks or net designs on both sides.

Bàosī yínyá 鲍丝银芽

Abalone Shreds with Mung Bean Sprouts

SHANDONG AND BEIJING · SERVES 4

This beautiful dish is very subtly flavored, making it an understated classic worthy of a palace meal. To begin with, the bean sprouts have both their heads and tails nipped off so that only the pure white stalks remain. These are then stir-fried with only a suggestion of green onion and ginger. The abalone is cut to complement the sprouts and quickly simmered in a gentle mixture of stock and rice wine to cut the fishiness a bit. Easy and elegant, this dish suggests strong influences from the Confucian family style of cooking.

7 to 8 ounces fresh, frozen, or canned abalone (see Tips)
12 ounces very fresh mung bean sprouts
1 cup salted or unsalted chicken stock (page 380)
2 tablespoons Shaoxing rice wine
½ teaspoon sea salt, or to taste (for unsalted stock)
1 teaspoon cornstarch mixed with 1 tablespoon water
2 tablespoons peanut or vegetable oil
2 green onions, white parts only, trimmed and finely minced
1 tablespoon peeled and finely minced fresh ginger

1. If you are using fresh or thawed frozen abalone, trim off the foot and any tough parts. If you are using canned abalone, simply rinse it off, pat it dry, and then trim off any discolored areas. Cut the abalone across the grain into thin slices, then cut them crosswise into matchsticks that are about the same width and length as the white stalks of the bean sprouts.

2. Next, prep the bean sprouts by using your fingernails to pinch off the heads and the whiskery tails (see Tips). Don't skip this step—it's an essential part of this dish's preparation. If you aren't using the trimmed sprouts right away, place them in a bowl and cover with ice water; they will keep well this way for a day or two if refrigerated.

3. Pour the stock and rice wine into a small saucepan and bring to a boil over high heat. Add the salt and abalone, bring to a boil, and then lower the heat to a simmer. Gently cook the abalone for about 15 minutes, until it is tender and the stock has reduced to an almost syrupy texture. Pour in the cornstarch mixture and gently stir the abalone over low heat until the sauce thickens. Remove the saucepan from the heat but keep it warm.

4. Drain the sprouts in a colander and shake off all the water. Pat them lightly with a tea towel to get rid of as much water as possible (see Tips). Set a wok over high heat until it starts to smoke and then pour in the oil. Add the green onions and ginger to the oil and stir them around quickly to release their fragrance. Add the bean sprouts and stir-fry them quickly until they just lose their rawness, then toss in 2 or 3 tablespoons of the abalone's sauce. Taste and adjust the seasoning. Scoop the bean sprouts out onto a serving plate, then pour the abalone and sauce over the center of the sprouts. Serve immediately.

Farm-raised abalone is the best choice here, according to the Monterey Bay Aquarium's Seafood Watch. Because canned abalone often tastes of the can, place the julienned abalone in a sieve or colander, set this in the sink, and douse it liberally with boiling water. Try a piece, and if it tastes fresh, proceed to the next step. If not, blanch it once more.

Another alternative is the large sea snail called "king top shell" that is sold in cans. Very tender and tasty, it mimics abalone admirably.

Because all the ingredients are white here, this dish looks fantastic if plated on something of a deep, contrasting color. No garnishes are needed in that case. Otherwise, tuck some cilantro into the side of the bean sprouts to add a touch of color.

When you nip off the heads and tails of the sprouts (see page 450), they turn into a completely different vegetable: much better mannered, much prettier, and also much more pleasant on the tongue.

Since you don't want the bean sprouts to boil instead of stir-fry, make sure they are as dry as possible. This will give them a much crunchier texture.

Gānshāo dàmíngxiā 乾燒大明蝦

Braised Prawns

TIANJIN · SERVES 4 TO 6

This was the favorite dish of Popo, my late mother-in-law. She left Tianjin just before the city fell to a large-scale Japanese invasion in 1937, so the foods of her childhood were one of the few ways she could connect with her old home. Whenever she visited us in Taipei, we would rush her over to the only restaurant in town that specialized in those dishes, a new place called Tiānjīn wèi 天津味, or "Tianjin Flavors."

We would order this dish right off the bat. Although the restaurant listed them as "dry-cooked big prawns," Popo always referred to them as "braised shrimp" (*áo xiā* 熬蝦), and there would be a purr in her voice and a gleam in her eyes whenever she said those two words. A couple plates of freshly made fried flatbreads (page 54) would arrive about the same time as the prawns, so that we could dip the flatbread in the sauce. We would happily eat our way through every offering on the table, with Popo polishing off more prawns than anyone.

This dish shows better than any map ever could how close Tianjin is to Shanghai. Catsup, because it provides color and a subtle layer of sweet-and-sour to any sauce, is one of those foreign ingredients that was adopted by chefs at the mouth of the Yangtze. And because Tianjin was just a short journey up the Grand Canal from there, the things that folks in Shanghai adopted soon found their way into Tianjin's kitchens, as well.

Prawns are one of Tianjin's best-loved ingredients, and here they receive that special treatment that always made my mother-in-law so very happy.

PRAWNS

2 pounds large fresh prawns or shrimp with the shell on (see Tips)
2 tablespoons ginger juice (page 481)
2 tablespoons Shaoxing rice wine
½ cup peanut or vegetable oil

SAUCE

2 green onions, trimmed and finely chopped
2 tablespoons peeled and finely chopped fresh ginger
3 tablespoons fermented rice (page 415 or store-bought)
3 tablespoons catsup
¼ cup Shaoxing rice wine
3 tablespoons boiling water

1. Rinse the prawns and pat them dry. Prep them according to the directions for shell-on shrimp or prawns on page 457.

2. Place the prepped prawns in a medium work bowl and toss them with the ginger juice and rice wine. Let them sit in this marinade—tossing them every once in a while when you think of it—while you prepare the rest of the ingredients.

3. Heat a wok over high heat until it starts to smoke, and then add the oil. As soon as the oil begins to shimmer, add half of the prawns to the hot oil and stir them around quickly. The second that the prawns turn an even pink and the shells begin to pull back from the incisions, use a Chinese spider or slotted spoon to remove them to a clean medium work bowl. Repeat with the second half of the prawns.

4. Drain off all but 2 tablespoons of the oil to make the sauce. Still over high heat, add the green onions and ginger and stir them quickly around in the hot oil to release their fragrance. Add the remaining sauce ingredients and bring them to a boil. Add the prawns to the sauce and toss them around over high heat until they are completely coated. Plate the prawns and sauce. Serve immediately.

Get fresh prawns if at all possible; both the flavor and the texture will be much better. When all else fails, frozen ones are okay, but defrost and drain them thoroughly.

Chopped steamed crab is good here, too. To be honest, an old shoe would probably taste wonderful in this sauce.

Jingshì xūnjī 京式薰雞

Beijing-Style Smoked Chicken

BEIJING · SERVES 4 TO 6

Smoked meats are popular throughout many parts of China. The smoking process is generally used to season these meats, not to cook them; as in this recipe, the meats are usually cooked first and then dunked in a smoker for a few minutes to add flavor.

The length of this recipe makes it look like a whole lot of effort, but the actual hands-on work doesn't add up to more than a few minutes—the rest is just a matter of waiting around. Moreover, this dish is often prepared using small (usually homemade) smokers rather than in smokehouses, so anyone can join in the fun.

One thing to keep in mind is that there should be enough fuel in the smoker for it to quickly add a nice color and aroma to the bird. Smoking for too long burns the sugar, which will make the smoke taste sour.

CHICKEN

1 whole roasting chicken (5 to 6 pounds) or large whole
  fryer with giblets
¼ cup white liquor or Shaoxing rice wine
2 tablespoons toasted Sichuan peppercorn salt (page 440)
Spray oil

FUEL AND SHEEN

½ cup raw rice of any kind
½ cup dry tea leaves of any kind
½ cup sugar of any kind
A couple of tablespoons of aromatics (aged tangerine
  peel, star anise, stick cinnamon, and the like; see Tips)
Toasted sesame oil

1. Place the chicken in a large work bowl, rub half of the liquor inside the cavity, and then massage half of the peppercorn salt in there, as well. Rub the outside of the chicken and the giblets with the rest of the liquor and peppercorn salt and marinate for an hour or so.

2. Spray a large, high-rimmed, heatproof platter with oil. Lay the chicken on the plate and tuck the giblets into the chicken's cavity. Pour any marinade in the bowl over the chicken. Place the chicken in a steamer (see page 49) and steam over high heat for about an hour, until the chicken is about 80 percent done, adding more water as needed. To check for doneness, pierce the thigh with a chopstick; it should go in easily but release pink juice. Remove the chicken (and the giblets from the cavity) and let it cool to room temperature. Then place the chicken in a breezy area so the skin dries completely, as this will allow the smoke to adhere to the surface.

3. Prepare your smoker (see the diagram to the right, and use the rice, tea, sugar, and aromatics as your fuel). Position the chicken in the center of the smoker. Place the smoker on a rear burner—where the suction from the overhead fan is usually better—and turn the heat under it on high. Wait until the smoke grows thick, then cover the smoker; if you are using an old wok, wrap the foil lining around the edge of the lid, leaving only a small opening for the smoke to escape.

4. Smoke the chicken for about 10 minutes (the time may need to be adjusted slightly depending upon the size of the chicken and how hot your stove is). Turn off the heat and let the chicken sit in the slowly cooling smoke for another 10 minutes. The chicken is done when the skin is a dark mahogany color.

5. Cool the chicken and then lightly rub some sesame oil on the skin to give it some sheen. Use a cleaver to cut the cold or cool chicken into whatever size pieces you want (see page 460). If the chicken is still pink inside, or if you want to serve it hot, wrap it in foil and bake at 350°F for about 15 minutes, until heated through.

I have a small electric fan that I put on the counter whenever something needs to be quickly dried—like this chicken, for example. I position the chicken on a trivet or on a wire rack over a plate, and then I turn the bird over when one side is dry.

Vary the flavors by using different aromatics and wines. Save your stale raw rice and tea leaves for the smoker, since they end up being just fuel.

HOMEMADE SMOKER SETUP

❶
To make your own smoker, find an old wok and cover that you won't use anymore for stove-top cooking (the high heat will destroy the wok's finish). If you don't have these, find them at a used-goods store or a garage sale.

❷
Line the inside of the wok and cover with heavy-duty foil.

❸
Make a small nest out of another piece of heavy-duty foil to hold the fuel and place this at the bottom of the wok.

❹
Fill the nest with the fuel and place a round wire cake rack on top. Spray the rack with oil.

❺
Cover the wok and set it over high heat. When white smoke emerges from under the lid in a steady stream, open the lid.

❻
Arrange the food you want to smoke on the rack.

❼
Cover the wok and fold the foil up and over the lid to seal in the smoke, leaving only one small opening for the smoke to escape. Direct the smoke toward the back so that it is easily sucked up by your overhead fan.

❽
After you are done smoking, turn off the heat and let the wok cool down slowly.

❾
Remove the food from the smoker. Clean the rack and discard the fuel nest. The foil in the lid and wok can be used a couple of times more until they wear out or tear.

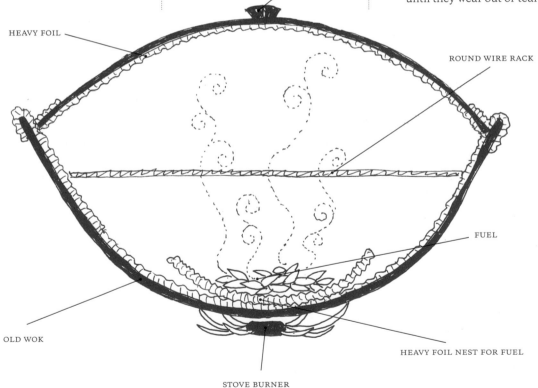

LID

HEAVY FOIL

ROUND WIRE RACK

FUEL

OLD WOK

HEAVY FOIL NEST FOR FUEL

STOVE BURNER

Liu jipú 溜雞脯

Jade and Pearls

BEIJING · SERVES 4 TO 6

The literal Chinese translation of this dish—"poached chicken breasts with starch"—does little to communicate its complexity and beauty. With its elegance and understated flavors, this dish is a prime example of Confucian-family cooking.

Instead of simply chopping up the white meat into small pieces and braising them with fresh peas, the chicken in this dish is forced through the holes of a slotted spoon into warm oil, where it is briefly poached. Egg whites and stock elevate the texture of the meat, and tiny fresh peas provide a sweetness that contrasts well with the buttery sauce. Serve this in small heated bowls with little soupspoons.

STOCK AND PEAS

2 cups unsalted chicken stock (page 380)

3 thin slices fresh ginger

2 green onions, trimmed

2 tablespoons Shaoxing rice wine

½ teaspoon sea salt

1 cup baby peas, fresh or frozen

CHICKEN

8 ounces skinless, boneless chicken breast, chilled

2 tablespoons unsalted chicken stock (page 380), chilled

1 tablespoon Shaoxing rice wine, chilled

5 large egg whites, chilled and lightly beaten

½ teaspoon sea salt

THE REST

2 cups rendered chicken fat or peanut
    or vegetable oil

1 teaspoon cornstarch mixed with 2 tablespoons water

LOCATED AT THE EDGE OF THE GOBI DESERT, on a historic trade route that connected North China with the princes of Venice and the traders of Samarkand, ancient Beijing sat at the crossroads of history. As the centuries passed, it became a city of assorted cuisines pulsating with the aromas of faraway cultures and exotic spices.

In Chinese, the name Běijīng 北京 says it all: the northern capital. It is this close relationship between imperial power and interesting geography that has shaped the city's cuisine. Well, that and the fact that the ambitious officials and their talented

chefs flocked to the powerful center of the greatest empire Asia has ever known, bringing with them rare ingredients and the finest the world had to offer.

Beijing's foods do not belong solely to the rich and famous, though, for wedged as it is up close to the Great Wall, both the city and its cuisine have benefited from the myriad neighboring influences that have trickled in over the years, as well. Hui Muslim (page 4) dishes, for example, came to form the bedrock for local foods and street snacks, providing a steady hum of Central Asian spices, rich aromas of beef

and lamb suggesting culinary homelands somewhere along the ancient Silk Roads, and a love for breads and pasta so contagious that all of northern and western China long ago caught this fever.

Now, in the alleys of Beijing, pork can be found sidling up to many formerly halal dishes, with soy sauce emphasizing the deep savoriness of the meats and putting a decidedly Chinese spin on Muslim flavors. And local wheaten foods like *jiaozi* and *baozi* have become happy marriages of flavors from both edges of the Asian continent.

1. Place the stock in a wide pan and add the ginger and green onions. Bring the stock to a full boil and then lower it to a gentle simmer. Let the stock become slowly seasoned while you work on the rest of the ingredients. After it has reduced to about half, strain out the solids and add the rice wine and salt.

2. Pick over the peas, removing any less-than-perfect ones or pea shells. If they are frozen, rinse them in cool tap water to defrost them completely and then drain. Set the peas aside. Prepare small serving bowls and keep them hot in a pan of water or in a heated oven. Have small saucers ready for them to sit on, as well.

3. Pat the breast meat dry with a paper towel. Use the towel to grasp one end of the breast as you scrape away any silver skin, tendons, and fat. You should be left with nothing but pure white meat. Use a Chinese knife to cut the meat into a very small dice before mincing it. Use the back of two Chinese knives or cleavers (see page 458) to then beat the chicken into a very light and fine pulp. (You could, of course, use already ground breast meat or do this in a processor, but it will not be as light and fluffy.) Use your blade to scrape up all of the meat and place it in a medium work bowl. Use chopsticks or a silicone spatula to beat in the stock, rice wine, egg whites, and salt in one direction (see page 458), as this will further lighten the loose mixture.

4. To shape and poach the chicken "pearls," first pour the fat or oil into a wide frying pan or wok. Place the oil over medium heat until it barely begins to shimmer, as you want the chicken to slowly poach rather than fry. Have two slotted spoons ready (see Tips for information on using the correct type of spoon), as well as a ladle, the bowl of chicken forcemeat, and a clean plate. Hold one slotted spoon about 4 inches above the oil, then ladle about ¼ cup of the forcemeat into the slotted spoon. Slowly rotate the spoon over the oil so that little balls of the forcemeat drop into the warm oil, using the back of the ladle to nudge the forcemeat through. Put the wet slotted spoon and ladle down. Gently swirl the pearls of chicken around in the oil, adjusting the heat as necessary so that they just begin to bubble and turn white. Once all of the little pearls have become pale, use the dry slotted spoon to scoop them onto the waiting plate. Repeat with the rest of the forcemeat until all of the chicken is cooked.

5. Bring the pan of stock to a boil and add the peas. When they are just barely done, gently slide in the little balls of chicken. Mix these together by swirling the pan—do not use a spatula, as it might break them apart. Taste and adjust the seasoning, adding more rice wine or salt as needed. Keep swirling the pan as you add the cornstarch slurry, and as soon as the sauce has thickened, divide the dish among the waiting bowls. Serve immediately.

The slotted spoon must have round holes about ⅛ inch in diameter. Chinese round slotted spoons traditionally have holes like this and can be found in most Chinese supermarkets and kitchenware stores. A good alternative would be the kind of slotted spoon that is used in molecular gastronomy to scoop out spherification "caviar" from a calcium bath.

Frozen peas work well here, as long as they are baby peas and of excellent quality. Do remember that frozen peas have already been blanched, so they need to be cooked for only a second or two.

The heated china of your serving bowls will keep the fat from congealing. Place the bowls on small saucers along with little spoons.

Qīngzhēng rénshēn jī 清蒸人參雞

Ginseng Steamed Chicken

THE NORTHEAST · SERVES 4 TO 6

This is a warming, subtle dish that highlights many northern Manchurian flavors, such as native ginseng and dried mushrooms. There is a reason why dried mushrooms and a dried bamboo shoot are called for here instead of fresh ones: they have a nice fermented edge that lends the dish a wintry feel.

Ginseng has almost magical properties in Chinese folklore (see page 42). It is considered an exceptional tonic in Chinese medicine, known for restoring health, alleviating emotional and physical stress, and balancing cholesterol levels. Because ginseng—sort of like mandrake root—resembles a human body with arms and legs, it is often thought of as having human-like consciousness, or what the Chinese refer to as *língxìng* 靈性.

4-inch piece dried ginseng (or 5-inch piece fresh ginseng, if available)
Boiling water, as needed
1 large dried bamboo shoot
6 dried black mushrooms
1 whole fryer chicken (3 to 4 pounds)
1 teaspoon sea salt
¼ cup mild rice wine
3 green onions, trimmed
2 tablespoons peeled and thinly sliced fresh ginger
1-inch cube Hunan-style cured pork (see charcuterie, page 478), cut into thin julienne

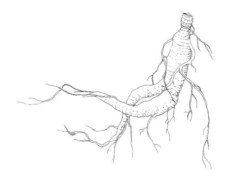

1. Start this dish at least 6 hours before serving; it is even better the next day. Rinse the dried ginseng and place it in a small work bowl. Cover it with boiling water and let it soak until plumped up a bit, about 4 hours. Set up a steamer (see page 49), place the bowl and the soaking water in the steamer, and steam the ginseng over high heat for about 30 minutes, by which time it should have softened up. Remove the ginseng from the hot liquid (reserve that water), and when it is cool enough to handle, slice it into small, thin pieces. (Fresh ginseng does not need to be soaked, so just steam it in a pool of water until tender.)

2. While the ginseng is soaking, rinse the bamboo shoot and mushrooms, place them in a medium work bowl, and cover them with boiling water. Allow them to soak until they are plump. Drain them, reserving the liquid. Shred the bamboo shoot with your hands into thin strips and cut off any tough parts. Cut the bamboo shreds into 1-inch pieces. Remove the stems from the mushrooms and cut the caps into quarters.

3. Pat the chicken dry with paper towels, tucking under the wing tips (see page 461). Rub the inside and outside of the chicken with the salt and rice wine and place it in a shallow, heatproof bowl. Scatter the ginseng, bamboo shoot, mushrooms, green onions, ginger, and ham in and around the chicken. Pour the bamboo and mushroom soaking waters into the bowl.

4. Place the bowl with the chicken in a steamer (see page 49) and steam for about 1 hour, adding more water as needed, until clear juices run when the thigh is pierced to the bone. Remove the bowl with the chicken from the steamer and transfer the chicken to a shallow serving bowl. Discard the flabby green onions, then pour the rest of the solids and juices into a wok, bring to a boil, skim off any scum, and adjust the seasoning. Pour this over the chicken and serve.

Huángmèn yākuài 黄焖鸭块

Yellow-Braised Duck

SHANDONG · SERVES 4 TO 6

Peking duck is the most popular way to prepare duck in northern China for the simple reason that it is a glorious way to show off its different flavors and textures. First the skin is served, then the meat, and finally a rich broth made from the bones. When my husband and I lived in Taipei, we would often be served additional duck courses, such as a buttery custard made with duck yolks, or perhaps braised duck feet as an appetizer.

As famous as Peking duck might be, restricting one's familiarity with northern-style duck to one preparation would be a real pity. Other local ways of serving duck might not look as spectacular, but they are just as flavorful, like this deliciously easy one from Shandong.

DUCK

3 whole duck legs, or ½ duck (about 1½ pounds)

2 green onions, trimmed

4 slices fresh ginger

2 teaspoons whole Sichuan peppercorns

6 tablespoons Shaoxing rice wine

VEGETABLES

Good handful of snow pea pods

1 medium carrot

1 winter bamboo shoot, fresh or frozen and defrosted (page 122)

6 wood ear fungus, fresh or dried and plumped up

SAUCE

1 tablespoon peanut or vegetable oil

1 green onion, trimmed and chopped

1 tablespoon peeled and finely minced fresh ginger

1 tablespoon regular soy sauce

1 teaspoon rock sugar

2 teaspoons cornstarch mixed with 2 tablespoons water

1. Start this at least 3 hours and up to a day ahead of when you plan to serve it to give the duck time to be cooked and chilled. Use a very sharp knife or fork to prick the duck skin all over; this will help release the fat and lessen skin shrinkage. Place the duck in a medium saucepan, add the green onions, ginger, and peppercorns, pour the rice wine over everything, and then add just enough water to barely cover the duck. Bring the water to a full boil, lower it to a gentle simmer, and cook the duck this way for about 15 minutes. Remove the duck from the pan, let it cool down until it is room temperature, and then chill. Strain the juices and discard the solids.

2. Chop the duck into neat pieces ½ to ¾ inch wide, doing your best to keep the skin attached to the meat, and arrange the duck into its original shape. Use your knife to scoop these pieces up—still keeping their shape intact—and place them in a shallow bowl. About 30 minutes before serving, pour the strained juices over the duck and steam it (see page 49) for 15 minutes over boiling water.

3. While the duck is steaming, pull the strings off of the snow pea pods, peel the carrot and slice it on the diagonal into thin shavings, cut the bamboo shoot into thin slices, and tear the wood ears into pieces about the size of a quarter. Bring a few cups of water to a boil in a wok and blanch each vegetable separately until just barely done. Scatter the vegetables on the bottom of a serving platter.

4. To make the sauce, set a cleaned wok over high heat and then add the oil. When the oil begins to barely smoke, add the green onion and ginger. Stir these around for about a minute, then add the soy sauce and sugar. Gently slide the duck and the juices into the wok and bring the sauce to a boil. As soon as the sauce has reduced and thickened slightly, drizzle the cornstarch around the edge of the duck and shake the wok to mix it in while doing your best not to mess up the duck slices. Taste and adjust the seasoning. Once the sauce is glossy and thick, slide it and the duck over the waiting vegetables. Serve immediately.

Rock Sugar Pork Shank

SHANDONG · SERVES 4 TO 6

Like all good braised pork shank dishes in China, this recipe is a study in reductions. Popular in Shandong and in Beijing, its origin story is a great one.

A young man from Shandong named Liu Fengxiang arrived in the capital and found himself at a small shop in the Xidan district run by a man from Shanxi. The shop sold pig parts braised in the northern manner, and Liu was hired to help out. However, business was never any good, so the man from Shanxi left, leaving Liu to run the place by himself.

Later on, Liu was purchasing some supplies at the market when he happened to see an old store sign in an antiques shop. On the sign were three characters—*tiān fú hào* 天福號, or "the shop blessed by Heaven"—written in the powerful calligraphic style of Yan Zhenqing. Liu bought it for his own place and changed the name of his shop to Tianfuhao. Passersby recognized the stunning calligraphy, and business began to improve for Liu.

As with any other shop of this kind where food has to be both made and sold by a skeleton crew, the pork was cooked at night so that there would be something to sell the next day. One night, Liu's son was tending the stove, and he fell asleep while the pork shanks were bubbling. When he woke up, the meat was just on the verge of falling apart, so his father salvaged the pork as best he could and readied it for the day's customers.

It so happened that a high-ranking official in the corrections ministry passed by and bought one of those overcooked shanks to dine on that night. He found it extremely tender, and he returned for more the next day, praising their pork to the skies.

Then one evening, just as they were about to close, that same official rushed in and told Liu that he had to make the best shank of his life. He was going to present it to the Dowager Empress Cixi the next day. Elated and terrified, Liu made a number of shanks, tweaking each one as he went so that he would have a variety to choose from in the morning.

Palace eunuchs appeared before noon, and Liu presented them with the dowager empress's carefully prepared lunch. The dowager empress enjoyed her meal so much, she requested that Liu deliver several shanks directly to the Forbidden City. Eventually, Liu began supplying meats to the palace on a daily basis.

Nowadays, it is difficult to find anyone who slowly steams these shanks the traditional way in a slightly sweet sauce. It is that slow steaming that changes the texture of the pork and allows it to gradually absorb the layers of spice and caramel and wine. Steaming also helps the skin render almost all of its fat while still preserving its shape, turning it into a trembling, custardy layer that is not in the least greasy.

PORK

1 pork shank (about 3 pounds with bone in and skin on, see Tips)
Boiling water, as needed
1 tablespoon honey
½ to 1 cup peanut or vegetable oil for frying
1 tablespoon fennel seeds
1 stick cinnamon
1 tablespoon whole Sichuan peppercorns
2 inches fresh ginger, smashed with the side of a cleaver
2 green onions, trimmed and lightly smashed
2 tablespoons regular soy sauce
¼ cup Shaoxing rice wine
2 tablespoons rock sugar
2 teaspoons cornstarch mixed with in 2 tablespoons water

GARNISH

2 to 3 green onions, trimmed and cut into thin julienne

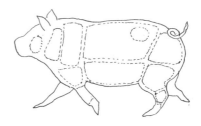

1. Start this at least 2 and preferably 3 or more days before serving. Pat the pork shank dry but leave the skin on, as this will be intensely delicious by the end of the recipe. Use tweezers to remove any hairs (see page 459); a chef's kitchen torch is useful for burning off anything that is stubborn. There are two ways to proceed with the bone: you can either leave it on the shank and remove in Step 3, or you can use a thin boning knife to remove the bone from the raw meat (see page 459). Place the shank in a medium saucepan and cover it with boiling water. Return the water to a boil over high heat and then lower it to a simmer; cook the shank for about 10 minutes, dump out the water and scum, and rinse the shank thoroughly. Rinse out the saucepan well and place the shank back in there.

2. Cover the pork with enough boiling water so that it is submerged by at least an inch. Bring to a boil over high heat and then reduce to a simmer. Slowly cook the shank uncovered for about 1½ hours, adding more boiling water as necessary, at which point the pork should be tender and there should be a layer of fat on top of the liquid.

3. Turn off the heat and carefully remove the pork from the liquid; set it aside on a plate to cool down until it is easy to handle. At that point, if the bone is still in the meat, twist it until it comes loose and then pull it out; discard the bone. Defat the braising liquid and then pour it through a sieve to remove all of the solids. (The shank can be made ahead of time up to this point; the meat and sauce should be refrigerated separately.)

4. Wipe the shank dry with a clean paper towel. Warm the honey until it is runny and then smear it all over the skin (but not over the meaty end). Warm the oil over medium heat in a tall pan with as small a base as possible (one that is about an inch wider than the shank is perfect—the oil will explode all over the place if you are not careful). When the oil is hot enough to form bubbles on a chopstick, use long metal tongs to place the shank skin-side down into the oil, then immediately cover the pan with a spatter screen. Carefully turn the shank over in the oil as it browns, adjusting the heat as necessary. When the skin is the color of maple syrup, remove the pan from the heat. After the spattering dies down, use tongs to remove the shank to a heatproof bowl that is large enough to hold both the shank and a cup or so of liquid.

5. Prepare a steamer (see page 49) that is deep and wide enough to comfortably hold the bowl with the pork shank. Tie the fennel seeds, cinnamon, and Sichuan peppercorns in a cheesecloth bag or put them in a mesh ball, then add them to the pork shank along with the ginger, smashed green onions, soy sauce, and rice wine. Place the sugar and a few tablespoons water in a stainless steel pan and heat over high heat, swishing the mixture gently as needed until it caramelizes (see page 446), then add this to the liquid. Pour a cup or so of the strained braising liquid over the pork, reserving the rest for something else. Steam the pork for about 2 hours over medium heat, adding more water to the steamer as needed. Taste and adjust the seasoning, adding extra rock sugar, soy sauce, or wine if you wish. Turn the pork over and let it steam for another 2 hours, then turn off the heat and let the pork cool down in the sauce. Cover the bowl and refrigerate overnight or up to a couple of days.

6. Steam the pork for about another 2 hours before serving. Remove the shank to a serving bowl. Pour the sauce into a small saucepan and adjust the seasoning a final time. Bring the sauce to a boil, lower the heat to medium, and stir in the cornstarch slurry. Cook the sauce while stirring constantly until it is thick and glossy. Pour this over the shank and garnish with the julienned green onions. I like to serve the hot pork with a small, sharp knife on the side so that guests can admire it whole before someone slices it into wedges.

The skin should cover the entire shank, and the fat should be an even layer.

Cooking the pork without any salt at the beginning is key to keeping the meat tender.

Hébāo lǐjí 荷包里脊

Golden Pouches

HEBEI · SERVES 4 TO 6

Although the Manchurian people ruled all of China from 1644 to 1911, their dishes had little effect on Han cuisine. In fact, the influence went in the opposite direction, with the ingredients and cooking styles of Shandong and Beijing altering the Northeast's foods in many ways. This dish is one example of court cuisine from the early Qing that shows Han influences. Called Golden Pouches, these tiny omelet skins are filled with simply seasoned chopped pork loin and then sautéed until the rectangular packets are crispy on the outside and juicy on the inside. Crunchy cilantro sprigs and nutty sesame oil round out these delicious eggy puffs.

I have tweaked the traditional dish a bit, using a slightly more fatty cut of pork. I also slipped in a touch of the northern region's sweet wheat paste and ginger to provide more depth and contrast.

OMELET WRAPPERS

3 large eggs
Pinch of sea salt
Peanut or vegetable oil as needed

PORK

4 ounces good boneless pork (15 percent fat),
    such as from the shoulder or neck
1 green onion, trimmed
2 tablespoons peeled and finely chopped fresh ginger
1 tablespoon sweet wheat paste
1 teaspoon soy sauce
2 tablespoons Shaoxing rice wine
Peanut or vegetable oil for frying

GARNISH

½ cup cilantro sprigs, tough stems removed
1 tablespoon toasted sesame oil

1. First make the omelet wrappers: lightly beat the eggs and salt together. Place a wok over medium-high heat and swirl in around a teaspoon of the oil to coat the bottom. Pour in a teaspoon of the egg mixture and rapidly swirl the wok around to form a very thin omelet. As soon as the top sets (which is very quickly), use a wok spatula to remove it to a plate without flipping it over first. Repeat with the rest of the oil and eggs to make about 24 wrappers.

2. Chop the pork by hand until it is a fine mince. Finely chop the green onion and add it to the pork along with the ginger, sweet wheat paste, soy sauce, and rice wine. Mix this well and divide the pork into 24 balls (or however many wrappers you have). Working on 1 packet at a time, place a meatball in the center of a wrapper and fold the sides of the wrapper over the meat. Gently flatten the packet and straighten up the sides with the palms of your hands to form an even rectangle. Make this look nice, as it was designed for the emperor. Repeat with the rest of the wrappers and meat until done. (This dish can be prepared ahead of time up to this point and refrigerated on a baking sheet.)

3. Just before serving, place a wok over medium heat. Film the bottom with oil and place some of the packets in the pan, being careful they do not touch. Fry them gently on one side until they are golden and then flip them over. When both sides are fried and the pork is cooked through, remove the packets to a serving platter and keep them warm. Repeat with the rest of the packets until all are cooked.

4. Arrange the cilantro around the edge of the platter and sprinkle the packets with the sesame oil. Serve immediately. To eat, place a sprig or two of cilantro on each packet, so that you have contrast in every bite.

Tāsìmì 它似蜜

Tasimi

BEIJING · SERVES 4 TO 6

There are a couple of possible explanations for the name of this dish. The most common one is as follows: The Dowager Empress Cixi was presented with this new preparation for lamb, and she was so impressed that she asked the chef what it was called. Flummoxed at this unusual attention, the chef could not find the words to answer. The dowager empress mused over the dish and commented, "It's like honey" (*tā sì mì* 它似蜜).

Nearly every story about the origin of a Beijing dish winds up in the dowager empress's lap for some reason. I'm not quite sure why, but there you have it. This lamb does have a touch of sweetness, but it's not overt. Rather, this dish offers a comforting combination of sweet, savory, spicy, tart, and creamy notes that perfectly complement the tender lamb.

1 pound lamb loin or other tender cut
4 teaspoons ginger juice (page 481)
4 teaspoons cornstarch
2 teaspoons regular soy sauce
4 teaspoons Shaoxing rice wine
1 tablespoon black vinegar
5 tablespoons (or so) toasted sesame oil
1 tablespoon sugar
2 tablespoons sweet wheat paste

1. Cut the lamb into thin slices across the grain, and then place the slices in a medium work bowl. Stir in the ginger juice, cornstarch, soy sauce, rice wine, and vinegar. Cover the bowl and marinate the lamb for at least 20 minutes and up to 3 hours.

2. Place a wok over high heat, and when it starts to smoke, add the sesame oil. Swirl the oil around to coat the lower half and add the lamb, as well as any marinade. Break up any big clumps and then lightly brown the meat. When all of the lamb is just barely done, add the sugar and sweet wheat paste, toss the meat well, and serve.

BEIJING IS PROTECTED BY THE GREAT WALL, WHICH IS KNOWN IN CHINESE BY THE MORE MODEST name of the Long City Walls (Chángchéng 长城). It is not a single ribbon stretching across the north, but rather a series of large barricades erected in vulnerable areas.

To be honest, though, these fortifications never really worked as well as hoped. Some of China's former enemies—namely the Mongols, Jurchens, and Manchurians—eventually managed not only to invade their giant southern neighbor but also to ensconce emperors of their own on the Dragon Throne.

That being said, this is after all China, and unlike boring places that boast of sterile things like racial purity or closed-loop bloodlines, China did as she always has and assimilated these foreign bodies. The people blended in varying degrees into the Chinese mainstream, while their foods were inevitably embraced and transformed, sparking local cuisines with delicious layers of exotic influences.

Kāiyáng báicài 開洋白菜

Napa Cabbage with Dried Shrimp

SHANDONG AND TAIWAN'S MILITARY FAMILIES ·
SERVES 4 TO 6

2 tablespoons dried shrimp
Boiling water, as needed
1 head napa cabbage (about 2 pounds)
6 tablespoons peanut or vegetable oil
4 green onions, trimmed and finely chopped
4 teaspoons peeled and finely minced fresh ginger
1 tablespoon regular soy sauce
1 tablespoon pale rice vinegar

Most evenings when my husband and I got off of work in Taipei, I would be way too tired to cook. Fortunately for us, the little mom-and-pop restaurants that dotted the city offered an amazing variety of foods from all over China. One of our favorites was a little place that served up northern-style dishes. *Jiaozi* (page 44) were always on the menu because the chef was from Shandong. But for dinner we usually wanted something more substantial, so we would order one of the set meals. These were called *kèfàn* 客飯, and this way we could pick and choose two or three entrées from a short list of cheap favorites. They would be served with small bowls of the house soup, as well as some white rice. At the time, this would cost only about four dollars, which made eating out even more pleasurable.

This simple dish was a permanent fixture there, and it is one that we returned to again and again. It is little more than shredded napa cabbage flavored with chopped dried shrimp and aromatics. I know, this does not sound at all exciting, but the seasoning is marvelous, and it turns a boring pile of cabbage into a delightful dish.

1. Place the shrimp in a small heatproof bowl and cover them with boiling water. Let them soak until the water has cooled off. Drain the shrimp, reserving the water, then clean the shrimp individually, removing any sandy veins or foreign matter. Chop them finely.

2. Rinse the cabbage, shake it dry, and cut it lengthwise in half. Discard the core and finely shred the white bottom half of the leaves across the grain (see page 449), and then shred the greener leaves. Keep these two piles separate.

3. Set a wok over high heat and add the oil when the wok begins to smoke. Toss in the chopped shrimp, green onions, and ginger. Fry these for about a minute, until they are just beginning to brown, then add the white parts of the cabbage leaves to the wok. Stir-fry the cabbage over high heat until it starts to brown on the edges, then scoot everything up the side of the wok. Add the greener parts of the leaves and toss these over high heat until they begin to wilt. Finally, mix everything together and pour the soy sauce and vinegar over the vegetables. Toss until the seasoning is well distributed. Taste and adjust the seasoning. Serve hot.

Qīngchǎo sùantái 清炒蒜薹

Stir-Fried Garlic Stems

SHANDONG · SERVES 4 TO 6

This is one of my favorite vegetables, but it is available for only a few weeks every year. The long, thin, emerald flower stems that emerge from garlic bulbs at the first sign of warm weather are called scapes, and they embody all of the warm flavors you'd expect from garlic, but with a subtler, more vegetal taste.

The Chinese simply call them "garlic stems" and love them dearly. A doctor friend from Nanjing lives nearby, and at least half of his backyard is dedicated to rows of garlic bulbs. He plants them in the cold days of autumn so that he can have as many garlic stems as he desires when the end of spring arrives.

1 bunch fresh garlic stems (about 1½ pounds)
3 tablespoons peanut or vegetable oil
1 teaspoon sea salt
2 tablespoons Shaoxing rice wine

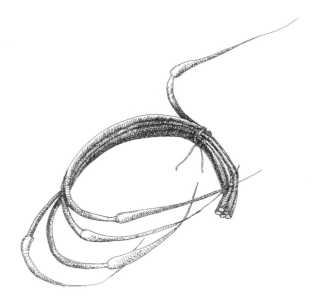

1. Rinse the garlic stems and trim off the flower heads. Cut them into 1-inch or so lengths as directed in Tips, using a paring knife.

2. Heat a wok over high heat until it smokes, then pour in the oil. Add the salt and swirl it around for a few seconds, then toss in the garlic stems. Stir-fry them until they turn jade green, then pour the rice wine over everything. Toss them again a few times. Taste and adjust the seasoning. Serve hot.

Note that the flower is not eaten here, just the tender stem. If you've ever looked at an onion or other allium blossom, you'll know why: it's a spiky little ball—all long pins with the flowers at the very end.

Select garlic stems that are green all over—even the blossom sheaths should be green rather than yellow. If they are anything other than green, that means their short season has passed and the stems will be tough. To be sure they are in season, use the time-honored fingernail test: if your nail goes easily into the bottom half of the stems, they are still tender enough to eat.

Once you get your stems home, wrap them in plastic and refrigerate immediately to stop any more of the blossoming action. Then, within a few days, rinse the stems and trim off the flower heads about ½ inch down, where the stems start to turn dark green. Discard the heads.

Use a paring knife to cut each stem, one at a time. If you want to turn them into inch-long pieces, as here, start at the top and lop off the lengths one at a time. As soon as you start to encounter resistance, that means the skin of the stem is becoming tough and you should discard it.

If, on the other hand, you have uniformly tough scapes, you should think about dicing them finely. When you do this, only dice a few at a time so that you don't cut into deadwood, as dicing can only do so much. No matter what, if you are at all concerned about the tenderness of your stems, cut them shorter so that they will become more tender.

Wrap the stems in plastic wrap and store them in the fridge. If they look a bit dry, you can plunk them into a jar of water first—they are flowers, after all.

Dìsānxiān 地三鲜

Three Fruits of the Earth

THE NORTHEAST · SERVES 4 TO 6

Heilongjiang, the northernmost province in the Northeast, does not have a huge repertoire of famous recipes, but this one should definitely put it on the map. Simple and inspired, it takes three foreign imports—eggplants from the Middle East and potatoes and sweet peppers from the Americas—and transforms them into a local favorite.

It might seem rather Provençal in style on the surface, but a closer look shows that this is not the case at all: the inclusion of ginger sets this dish firmly in the realm of Chinese cooking. Pair this recipe with simply seasoned barbecued or braised meats for a true taste of the Northeast.

2 Chinese or 3 Japanese eggplants
1 fist-sized Yukon Gold potato or similar variety
1 cup peanut or vegetable oil for frying
1 large sweet red pepper
1 tablespoon finely minced garlic
1 tablespoon peeled and finely minced fresh ginger
1 green onion, trimmed and finely chopped
½ teaspoon sea salt
½ cup boiling water

1. Trim off the caps of the eggplants and roll-cut them into pieces around 1 inch in length and ½ inch thick (see page 449.) Cut the potato lengthwise into quarters and then cut it into pieces of approximately the same size and shape as the eggplant. (You should end up with about 2 cups of each vegetable.)

2. Heat the oil in a wok over high heat and fry the eggplant first, tossing it occasionally, until the pieces are nicely browned. Use a slotted spoon to remove the eggplant to a serving plate. Reheat the oil and add the potatoes, frying them until golden all over and cooked through. Remove them from the oil and add them to the eggplant.

3. Cut the pepper in half and remove the stem end and seeds. Slice the flesh into wide strips and then diagonally into diamonds about the same size as the eggplant. Drain off all but a tablespoon of oil from the wok and heat the oil over high heat. Add the peppers, garlic, ginger, green onion, and salt and quickly stir-fry them for a few seconds to release their fragrance. Add the cooked eggplant and potatoes and the boiling water. Bring everything to a boil and quickly simmer the vegetables together for a few minutes. Taste and adjust the seasoning. Serve hot.

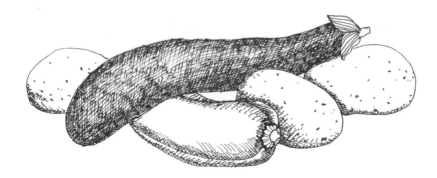

Qīngjiāo chǎo tǔdòusī 青椒炒土豆絲

Stir-Fried Potato and Green Chili Threads

BEIJING · SERVES 4 TO 6

1 pound potatoes (preferably Yukon Gold), peeled or
　unpeeled, cut into thin (⅛-inch) matchsticks
3 tablespoons peanut or vegetable oil, plus more as needed
1 teaspoon sea salt
2 tablespoons peeled and finely chopped fresh ginger
½ cup finely chopped green onions
2 to 3 green jalapeño peppers, seeded and sliced into
　long, thin strips

Just about every self-respecting northern Chinese restaurant in the United States has this dish on the menu. If you have never had lightly cooked potatoes that retain their natural crunchiness, you are in for a treat. The secret lies in selecting the right tubers: my go-to variety is Yukon Gold, which keep their shape as they cook and also retain their snappy character.

This dish is very versatile. You can use as many chilies as you like. If you have little kids or are just heat averse, cook the chilies with the potatoes to reduce their vibrancy to a muted hum. Otherwise, add them toward the end so that they barely warm through and retain their spark. You can also add things like finely chopped garlic, dried instead of fresh chilies, or a splash of vinegar toward the end of the cooking—it all depends on your preferences.

By the way, northern and northeastern Chinese refer to potatoes as *tudou* (earth beans), while in many southern areas they are known as *mǎlíngshǔ* 馬鈴薯, literally "horse bell tubers," because they have the same round shape and size as the bells that used to be hung from harnesses (see the illustration below). And there are other names as well: in Shandong, the potato is called an "earth egg," in Anhui it's referred to as "Western sweet potato," and in southern Fujian and Chaozhou it's called "Dutch tuber."

1. The potatoes can remain unpeeled, if you like. Don't cut them too finely because they will mush up. Place the potato matchsticks in a medium work bowl and cover with cool water while you prepare the rest of the ingredients. Just before cooking them, drain the potatoes well, dump them out onto a tea towel, and pat them as dry as you possibly can. This way they will fry rather than steaming into a fat clump.

2. Heat a wok over high heat until it starts to smoke, then add the oil and salt. Swirl the oil around to lightly dissolve the salt, then toss in the ginger and green onions. Quickly fry them for about 30 seconds to release their aromas and then add the potatoes. (If you like your chilies milder, add them at this point so that they cook more.) Toss the potatoes once in a while so that they lightly brown. (Add the chilies at this point if you want more of a kick.) Taste and adjust the seasoning. Serve hot.

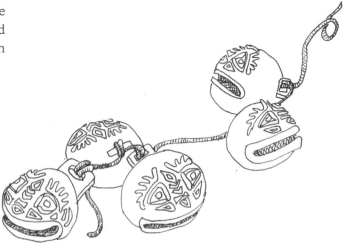

Cōngshāo qiumǔěr 蔥燒秋木耳

Wood Ears Braised with Green Onions

THE NORTHEAST · SERVES 4 TO 6

Mushrooms of every stripe grow in the forests of the Northeast. Often they are treated with minimal seasonings to allow the character of each particular mushroom to emerge. Wood ears—a direct translation of their Chinese name—are a fairly bland fungus that smells mildly fishy when fresh and grows mainly on alder trees. Its allure, then, is more about its delightful gelatinous texture than its flavor. Collected mainly in the fall, wood ears are used in China for medicinal purposes, often to lower cholesterol.

Fresh wood ears are best if you can find them, and cultivated varieties are becoming more common in markets, at least near where I live in the San Francisco Bay Area. But dried ones are good, too. They can easily be rehydrated by pouring boiling water over them. Like dried black mushrooms, these plumped-up wood ears will not be as tender as fresh ones, and their flavor will be a bit more subdued.

1 medium leek or 4 green onions
4 cups (or so) lightly packed fresh wood ear fungus
    or 1 cup dried wood ear fungus, plumped up
2 tablespoons peanut or vegetable oil
6 tablespoons mild rice wine
2 tablespoons oyster sauce
4 teaspoons regular soy sauce, or to taste
2 teaspoons sugar

1. Trim the dark green leaves off the leek, cut it in half through the root, and then wash between the leaves very carefully to remove all of the grit (see page 450). Pat the leek dry. Cut the leek on the diagonal into thin shreds. (If using green onions, simply cut both the white and green parts into 2-inch lengths.) Carefully rinse the fresh or rehydrated wood ears and either shake or pat them dry; trim off any hard bits and tear the large ears into quarter-sized pieces.

2. Heat a wok over high heat until it starts to smoke, then add the oil. Swirl it around and add all of the leek shreds or green onion. Quickly stir-fry them until they barely begin to brown, then toss in the wood ears. Stir-fry these together until the wood ears are almost cooked through. Fresh ones will start to pop when this happens.

3. Add the rice wine, oyster sauce, soy sauce, and sugar to the wood ears and toss them thoroughly. Taste and adjust the seasoning. Serve hot.

Store raw wood ears like any other mushroom: without rinsing and in a paper bag, which will absorb any extra moisture and keep down both fungal invasions and rot.

Dry ones keep pretty much forever if stored in a sealed container in a dark cupboard.

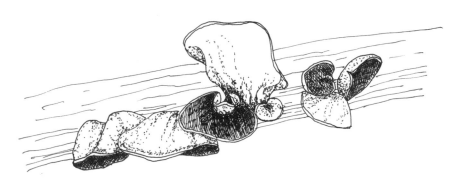

Guōtā dòufǔ 鍋塌豆腐

Panfried Bean Curd

SHANDONG · SERVES 4 TO 6

This cooking method, called *guota* ("to collapse in a wok"), is native to Shandong. It involves layering ingredients like fish, meat, vegetables, and bean curd into small, egg-covered packets before frying and braising them. The packets puff up as they are fried and then crumple down during the short braise. This charming idea stood little chance of remaining a local secret. Although it was most likely created in the capital city of Jinan during the Ming dynasty, it gradually made its way to Shanghai, Tianjin, and Beijing, where it appeared on the Qianlong emperor's table in the mid-Qing dynasty. A recipe that has been around as long as this one naturally has many variations. I have had this served to me in Muslim-style restaurants as a sort of omelet filled with slices of bean curd, for example.

To my mind, though, nothing can beat this version, which tastes like the great seaports of Shanghai or Tianjin, thanks to the dried shrimp roe.

BEAN CURD

1 block (14 to 16 ounces) firm bean curd

½ teaspoon sea salt

1 cup (or so) peanut or vegetable oil

3 tablespoons all-purpose or Chinese flour (page 386)

2 large egg yolks lightly beaten with 2 teaspoons water

SAUCE

2 tablespoons peanut or vegetable oil

2 teaspoons dried shrimp roe

2 green onions, trimmed

1 tablespoon peeled and finely minced fresh ginger

2 tablespoons Shaoxing rice wine

½ cup salted or unsalted chicken stock (page 380)

Sea salt to taste

4 leaves romaine or other crispy lettuce

1. Cut the bean curd in half lengthwise and then cut it crosswise into 8 even slices, which will give you a total of 16 pieces. Lay these flat on a dry tea towel and sprinkle them with the salt. Give the bean curd about 30 minutes (and up to 2 hours in a cool kitchen) to release most of its moisture. Pat the tops of the slices dry before you proceed.

2. Pour enough oil into a wide frying pan to completely cover the bottom at a depth of about ¼ inch. Place the pan over medium heat. While the oil is slowly heating up, pat the flour on all sides of the bean curd slices and then dip them completely in the egg yolks before gently laying them in the hot oil so that they do not touch (you will probably have to do this in two batches). The oil should immediately bubble up around the slices, and the egg batter should puff up without browning too quickly. When the slices are golden brown on the bottom, flip them over gently and let them brown on the other side. Remove to a rimmed plate.

3. Pour all of the oil out of the pan, wipe it clean, and add the oil for the sauce. Over medium heat, sprinkle in the shrimp roe and move it around in the oil until it starts to bubble and darken. Add the green onions and ginger. Stir these together for a few seconds to release their fragrance, then pour in the rice wine and stock and add the salt. As soon as the sauce boils, arrange the fried bean curd slices in the sauce, preferably in a single layer. Turn the slices over once.

4. Clean and wipe the platter. Slice the lettuce in a thin chiffonade (very fine pieces) and place these on the platter. As soon as the sauce has been almost completely absorbed, arrange the bean curd slices attractively on top of the lettuce. Scrape any sauce or aromatics left in the pan onto the slices.

If shrimp roe is not available in your area, you can either omit it and add a bit more salt to the dish as desired, or else toss in some soaked and dried shrimp or scallops that have been finely chopped.

Zhájiàng miàn 炸醬麵

Zhajiang Noodles

THE NORTHEAST AND TAIWAN'S MILITARY
FAMILIES · SERVES 2 OR 3 AS A MAIN DISH

Popular throughout most of northeast China, this dish has been compared to pasta Bolognese: a rich meat sauce balanced on top of chewy strands of dough. But that's where the similarities end. *Zhajiang mian* means "deep-fried sauce noodles," which has always confused me, because the sauce for this dish is panfried. It wasn't until very recently that I came upon an explanation. You see, most folks think of this dish as being from Beijing, but after some research, I learned that it probably originated in the Northeast, where it is also known as *zájiàng miàn* 雜醬麵, or "mixed sauce noodles." *Zha* and *za* sound very much alike, and my personal theory is that these two were mixed up at some point.

The idea for adding eggplant came from the wonderful Chinese writer Liang Shih-chiu (who is quoted at the beginning of this chapter). In an essay called "Noodles" (*Miàntiáo* 麵條), he wrote,

"Our family once was taught by a lofty personage to add cubed eggplant when the sauce was almost done . . . and the secret lay in doing one's best to make the sauce on the noodles not too salty."

I've enjoyed endless variations on this dish, but this recipe is the best I have ever tasted. However, as with great simple foods elsewhere, perfection demands a couple of very important requirements.

First, the pasta should be handmade and fresh. No dried noodles here, please. In fact, you should use pulled noodles (page 354) if at all possible—although rolled noodles are also good (see page 388). Second, make the pasta flat and wide, if you can, because you'll need really big noodles to temper the powerfully seasoned sauce. Third, don't drown the noodles with sauce. You want a good balance of sauce to pasta so that your tongue is initially hit with the salty, meaty taste of the *zhajiang*, and then soothed by the sweet noodles. The cucumber garnish is cleansing and slightly tannic, which provides even more contrast. Some people like to sprinkle green onions on top, and I am not opposed to a few slices per bite, but don't overdo it.

IN THE NORTHEAST, LOCAL SPECIALTIES LIKE WILD GAME, MUSHROOMS, FERNS, GINSENG, wood ears, golden pheasants, and daylily buds are used to great effect in such dishes as Wood Ears Braised with Green Onions (page 40) and Ginseng Steamed Chicken (page 30).

Ginseng is the true prize for local foragers. In the past, larger households in the Northeast often hired workers to harvest wild ginseng during the summer. Called *wābàngchuí* 挖棒槌—or "dig, club, hammer"—they carried dried provisions along with strips of red cloth, a ball of red thread, and a cudgel for protection. The red cloth was torn into strips to mark their path in the deep mountain forests. When a clump of ginseng was located, they would first encircle it with sticks in order to "restrain" it; a piece of red thread was then tied onto a stalk. As mentioned earlier (page 30), ginseng often seems to have arms and legs, and so it probably appeared capable of escape unless magically confined.

NOODLES AND EGGPLANT

1 pound fresh, wide wheat noodles
    (see headnote for suggestions)
8 cups boiling water
2 small eggplants
2 to 4 tablespoons peanut or vegetable oil

SAUCE

1 tablespoon peanut or vegetable oil
8 ounces ground pork (15 percent fat)
½ medium yellow onion, cut into ½-inch dice
2 tablespoons peeled and minced fresh ginger
3 cloves garlic, finely minced
2 tablespoons mild rice wine
6 to 8 tablespoons toasted sesame oil
3 tablespoons sweet wheat paste
1 tablespoon regular soy sauce
2 teaspoons sugar
¼ cup hot water

GARNISH

1 Persian or other small seedless cucumber,
    trimmed and julienned
1 green onion, trimmed and julienned, optional

1. Prepare your own noodles or buy fresh ones that are wide and have a nice texture, like pappardelle. Shake the noodles out onto a tea towel and loosen the strands. Cover them with the towel to keep them from drying out. Have the water in a pot on the stove with the lid on to keep it hot.

2. Clean and trim the eggplants and then cut them into ½-inch cubes without peeling. They can be deep-fried or roasted in the oven. To fry them, heat the oil in a wok over medium-high heat and fry the eggplants until they are browned all over; to bake, toss the eggplants in some oil and bake at 350°F for about 15 minutes, turning them over now and then until they are completely browned. Remove the eggplants to a work bowl.

3. To prepare the sauce, heat the 1 tablespoon oil in a wok over medium-high heat and add the pork, onion, ginger, and garlic. Lower the heat to medium and cook, stirring occasionally, until the onions are translucent. Raise the heat to medium-high again and fry the mixture until it has some browned edges.

4. Pour in the rice wine and stir it around quickly to stop the caramelization. Scoop the mixture up one side of the wok. Raise the heat to high, pour the sesame oil into the wok, and add the sweet wheat paste. Stir the paste in the oil to break it up into a smooth layer and to fry out any raw flavors. Add the soy sauce and sugar. Mix the meat mixture into the sauce and toss this around over the heat. Pour in the hot water and stir the sauce to incorporate the water. Lower the heat to a simmer and cook gently for 10 to 15 minutes. Add the eggplant, taste and adjust the seasoning, and then cook the sauce for another 3 minutes.

5. Just before serving, cook the noodles until done, making sure to keep them nice and chewy. Use a Chinese spider or slotted spoon to remove them to noodle bowls, but don't pour out the noodle water. Ladle the sauce on top of each mound of noodles and garnish with the cucumbers and the optional green onions. Serve a bowl of the hot noodle water on the side to each person as a soup. Your diners should toss the noodles with the sauce and garnish before eating.

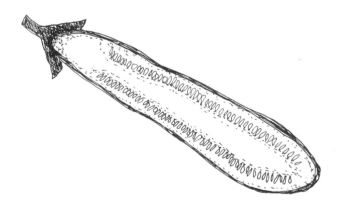

Dǎlǔ miàn 打滷麵

Dalu Noodle Soup

ALL OVER NORTHERN CHINA AND TAIWAN'S MILITARY
FAMILIES · SERVES 4

Shandong lays claim to this noodle soup, as do Shanxi
and Hebei, but regardless of how it is prepared, it is
almost always a can't-lose proposition. Known as 打滷麵,
which means "make stew noodles," or *dàlǔ miàn* 大滷麵,
"big stew noodles," this dish features a mixture of finely
shredded vegetables and meats served in a thick broth
with slithery noodles. This recipe is my husband's
favorite take on it.

VEGETABLES AND MEAT

1 cup fresh wood ear fungus, or ¼ cup dried, plumped up

1 carrot or ½ cup dried daylily flowers

½ large winter bamboo shoot, fresh or frozen and
    defrosted

2 green onions, trimmed

4 black mushrooms, fresh or dried and plumped up

2 cups shredded napa cabbage

1 tablespoon peanut or vegetable oil

4 ounces boneless pork, cut into fine julienne

2 tablespoons rinsed and finely chopped Sichuan
    pickled tuber

STOCK AND SEASONING

4 cups pork or chicken stock (page 381 or 380),
    preferably unsalted

2 teaspoons regular soy sauce (if stock is unsalted)

1 teaspoon sugar

Freshly ground black pepper to taste

1 tablespoon cornstarch mixed with 3 tablespoons water

2 large eggs, lightly beaten

1 tablespoon toasted sesame oil

1 tablespoon black vinegar

NOODLES

1 pound fresh wheat noodles (page 387)

1. As you prep the vegetables, keep them in separate
piles. Trim off any hard bits and then cut the wood
ears into fine shreds. Peel the carrot and cut it into
fine julienne (or, if using daylily flowers, soak them
in boiling water until soft and then remove the hard
base). Finely shred the bamboo shoot. Slice the white
parts of the green onions into 1-inch pieces and chop
the other sections into thin circles to use as a garnish.
Remove the stems from the mushrooms and cut the
caps into julienne. Rinse the cabbage and shake it dry.

2. Set a wok over high heat until it smokes and then add
the oil. Swirl it around in the wok and add the 1-inch
pieces of green onion; stir-fry these for about 30 seconds to release their fragrance, then add the pork,
pickled Sichuan tuber, wood ears, carrot or daylily
flowers, bamboo shoot, mushroom shreds, and cabbage. Toss these over high heat for about 5 minutes,
or until the volume is reduced by half.

3. Add the stock, soy sauce, sugar, and pepper to the
vegetables and bring to a boil. Let simmer for 5 to
10 minutes and then stir in the cornstarch slurry until
the stock thickens. Drizzle the beaten eggs in a spiral
on top so that they cook quickly and evenly, and then
gently stir them in. Immediately remove the wok from
the heat.

4. Bring a large pot of water to a boil and cook the
noodles until they are al dente. Drain the noodles
and distribute them among however many bowls you
are using. Divide the soup among the bowls, sprinkle
each bowl with the green onion garnish, and dribble
some sesame oil and vinegar over the top. Serve hot.
Have your diners lightly toss the soup and noodles
before digging in.

Zhēngjiǎo, shuǐjiǎo 蒸餃、水餃

Steamed and Boiled Jiaozi

ALL OVER NORTHERN CHINA AND TAIWAN'S MILITARY
FAMILIES · MAKES 36 AND SERVES 3 TO 4

There are many different types of Chinese dough, but this recipe discusses the two most basic forms: hot dough and cold dough. Hot dough (literally "scalded dough" or *tàngmiàn* 燙麵) is usually made with just white flour and boiling water. This direct, moist heat removes the rawness from the flour and turns it into supple dough, without a hint of dryness. Cold dough (*léngshuǐmiàn* 冷水麵), on the other hand, is more resilient. Even when rolled out very thinly, it will not break while being stirred in a pot of boiling water. For this reason, hot dough is used for steamed *jiaozi*, and cold dough is used for boiled *jiaozi*.

Just about anything you like can be used to stuff *jiaozi*. Check out the pork filling in the recipe for Potstickers (page 50) or any of the *baozi* fillings (pages 48, 132, and 300) for additional ideas. Meats, poultry, and seafood should be chopped very finely or ground; vegetables can be slightly larger to provide contrasting texture. Fat of some sort is almost always included to give the *jiaozi* good flavor.

Both of these *jiaozi* (often called "dumplings" in English; see page 365) are common throughout the year, but boiled *jiaozi* are particularly popular at northern Chinese celebrations for the Lunar New Year. Rolling, filling, wrapping, and eating them is a communal affair—a time for laughter, gossip, and the sharing of news.

ROLLING OUT AND FILLING STEAMED *JIAOZI*
1 recipe plain hot-water dough (page 386)
1 recipe any kind of filling (see the headnote and the
    recipes on page 47)
Extra flour as needed

1. For directions on how to shape and wrap *jiaozi*, follow the diagram on page 46.

2. Place the filled *jiaozi* in an oiled or lined steamer (see page 49). Steam them for about 15 minutes, until done. Serve hot.

ROLLING OUT AND FILLING BOILED *JIAOZI*
1 recipe plain cold-water dough (page 387)
1 recipe any kind of filling (see the headnote and the
    recipes on page 47)
Extra flour as needed

1. For directions on how to shape and wrap *jiaozi*, follow the diagram on page 46.

2. Bring a large pot of water to a boil over high heat. Add about a dozen *jiaozi* to the boiling water and bring it back to a full boil while stirring gently with a wooden spoon. Pour about a cup of cool water into the pot and bring the water back to a boil. Repeat this one more time, at which point the *jiaozi* should be floating. Remove them to a serving platter with a slotted spoon. Cook the remainder in the same way. Serve each batch immediately as it is cooked.

JIAOZI

There are two ways to roll out and separate the dough into Ping-Pong ball–sized pieces.

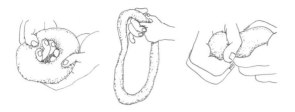

❶

A The old-fashioned way is to shape the dough into a ball and then work a hole into the center to form a big doughnut. Pull the doughnut into a long hoop that is about an inch in diameter. Snap open the hoop to make a rope, and then break off inch-long pieces of dough.

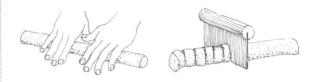

❶

B The second way is to simply roll the dough out into a long rope about an inch in diameter. Use a pastry scraper to cut the rope into inch-long pieces.

Now that you have your individual pieces of dough, proceed with the following steps.

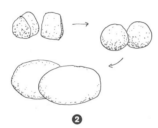

❷

Dust the inch-long pieces with flour, roll each piece into a ball, and then flatten it into a round disk. Roll out each piece into a wrapper about 2 inches in diameter, turning the disk with one hand while wielding your rolling pin with the other. Lightly dust the wrappers and cover them with a tea towel. Fill immediately and keep them covered, or freeze them for later.

❸

To fill the *jiaozi*, place a wrapper on the palm of your nondominant hand and use the other hand to place the filling in the center.

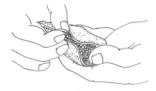

❹

Fold the wrapper over the filling, matching up the edges as they meet, to form a half-moon shape. Press down on the edges to seal. This forms a basic *jiaozi* perfect for boiling.

❺

If you are planning to steam the *jiaozi*, consider these shapes, too: wavy edged, V-shaped folds, hat shaped, and with a braided edge.

SHRIMP AND PORK FILLING

Xiānxiā zhūròu xiàn 鮮蝦豬肉餡

Enough for about 36 *jiaozi*

1 pound shrimp, fresh or frozen and defrosted
2 pounds ground pork (30 percent fat)
½ cup peeled and finely chopped fresh ginger
6 tablespoons regular soy sauce
¼ cup mild rice wine
2 teaspoons sugar
Freshly ground black pepper to taste
8 large leaves napa cabbage
2 teaspoons sea salt
8 green onions, trimmed and finely chopped

1. Peel and devein the shrimp (see page 457). Coarsely chop them (¼-inch pieces), place in a work bowl, add the pork, ginger, soy sauce, rice wine, sugar, and black pepper, and mix well.

2. Finely chop the cabbage and toss it with the salt. Wait about half an hour, then squeeze it dry in your fists. Toss the pork and shrimp with the cabbage and onions. Adjust the seasoning (see Tips). Fill the *jiaozi* as shown to the left.

Uncooked *jiaozi* freeze beautifully, so try to make more than you think you will need. Freeze the extra uncooked *jiaozi* on a cloth-covered baking sheet; make sure that they do not touch one another or they will stick together. As soon as they are very hard, remove them to a resealable plastic freezer bag and return to the freezer. Boil or steam the *jiaozi* without defrosting them first.

Any leftover cooked *jiaozi* can be lightly fried in a few tablespoons of oil over medium-high heat until golden all over. They are just about as delicious as the freshly cooked ones.

One of the best places to roll out dough is the underside of a pull-out chopping board. Put a damp cloth on your counter to keep the board from moving around and place the board on top of that. Then, when you are through making the wrappers, be sure you turn the board right side up before you put it away in order to protect its smooth surface.

Before filling the *jiaozi*, fry a small amount of the filling—no additional oil should be necessary—and taste. Adjust the seasoning as needed.

GOURD AND EGG FILLING

Mùxī hùguā xiàn 木樨瓠瓜餡 or *Mùxū hùguā xiàn* 木須瓠瓜餡

Enough for about 36 *jiaozi*

3½ to 4 pounds edible bottle gourds (or pumpkin or chayote)
1½ teaspoons sea salt
¼ cup peanut or vegetable oil
8 large eggs, lightly beaten
½ cup peeled and finely chopped fresh ginger
3 tablespoons regular soy sauce
3 tablespoons mild rice wine
1 tablespoon sugar
Freshly ground black pepper to taste
4 teaspoons toasted sesame oil
8 fresh or dried and plumped up black mushrooms, stemmed and finely chopped
½ cup green onion oil (page 434) or additional peanut or vegetable oil
4 green onions, trimmed and finely chopped

1. Up to a day before filling the *jiaozi*, peel and trim the gourds, remove any seeds, grate coarsely, and place in a colander in the sink. Toss the shredded gourd with the salt. Wait for about an hour and then squeeze the gourd dry in your fists. You should have 5 to 6 cups, packed. Place the shredded gourd in a large work bowl.

2. Warm the oil in a wok over medium-low heat, add the eggs, and scramble until curds have formed but the eggs are not dried out. Add them to the work bowl and gently break the eggs apart into small clumps.

3. Toss in the ginger, soy sauce, rice wine, sugar, pepper, sesame oil, mushrooms, and green onion oil. Place the filling in a covered container and refrigerate.

4. Up to an hour before filling the *jiaozi*, toss the gourd mixture with the green onions. Adjust the seasoning (see Tips). Fill the *jiaozi* as shown to the left.

Gǒubùlǐ bāozi 狗不理包子

Ignored by the Dog Filled Buns

TIANJIN · MAKES 16 *BAOZI*

This is without a doubt the most famous dish of Tianjin. Part of it has to do with history, and part of it has to do with that odd name: Ignored by the Dog. It all started with a guy named Gao Guiyou who was born near Tianjin and whose family called him by a very common and affectionate nickname in northern China: Doggy, or Gǒuzi 狗子. He worked at a steamed foods shop on the Grand Canal, where his skills soon became renowned. At the tender age of seventeen, he opened up his own shop called Déjùhào 德聚號, where he sold street snacks like steamed pork buns. He was so busy banging out these *baozi* that he never had time to talk to his customers, who soon started saying that "the doggy sells *baozi* but ignores people." Soon, the real name of this *baozi* shop was forgotten and customers referred to it as the place where they were ignored by the dog.

This recipe is just a simple combination of pork and steamed dough. The pork has water slowly added to it, and this water plumps up the meat and then turns into a savory broth as the buns steam.

FILLING

1 pound ground pork (15 percent fat)
2 ounces finely chopped pork fat
2 tablespoons regular soy sauce
¾ cup cool water
1 tablespoon toasted sesame oil
½ teaspoon sea salt
2 green onions, trimmed and finely chopped
3 tablespoons peeled and finely chopped fresh ginger

WRAPPERS

1 recipe fast steamed bread dough (page 400, prepared up through Step 4)
Spray oil

1. First, make the filling: on a chopping board, use a heavy knife to chop the pork and fat together until they make a very fine paste (see page 458). After about 5 minutes of dedicated attention, the meat and fat should be uniformly combined and very light. Use your knife to scoop the meat into a medium work bowl.

2. Use one hand as a paddle and hold the bowl with your other hand. Mix in the soy sauce with your hand, then add the water in about 5 increments, stirring rapidly in one direction with your hand so that the meat becomes lighter and lighter (see page 458). When the water from one addition has been completely absorbed, add a bit more. After all of the water has been beaten in, mix in the sesame oil, salt, green onions, and ginger. Smooth down the top of the meat mixture, cover the bowl with plastic wrap, and chill the mixture for at least 3 hours.

3. Roll the fast steamed bread dough out into a rope 16 inches long before cutting it into even 1-inch pieces. Form these pieces into 3½-inch balls and cover them with either a damp tea towel or plastic wrap. Cut out 16 (2-inch) squares of parchment or wax paper. Spray these with some oil.

4. See pages 406 to 407 for directions on how to form and fill the *baozi*.

5. To steam the *baozi*, bring the water under your steamer (see the diagram to the right) to a full boil, place the *baozi* in the steamer baskets so that they are about an inch apart, set the baskets on the steamer, and cover the top basket. Steam the *baozi* over high heat for about 7 minutes, then turn off the heat and let the steam settle down before opening up the baskets—this will help keep the *baozi* from deflating. Serve hot.

That small bump in the center of the dough circle makes the wrapper more even, since the dough is bunched up at the top.

Ignored by the Dog Filled Buns traditionally have exactly eighteen folds on top. It's a nice touch to aim for but not absolutely necessary.

STEAMER SETUP

❶

Place bamboo or steel steamer baskets over a wide pan or wok that you will no longer use for stir-frying. Fill the bottom of the pan with water to just below the baskets and drop a few pennies into the water. Once the water is boiling, if you can't hear the pennies rattling about in the pan, it means you are almost out of water.

❷

For larger items like a whole fish or chicken, I use a steel wok with a glass cover, although any wide and deep pan can be used. Place a trivet in the wok or pan, fill with water to just below the trivet, and add a couple of pennies as in Step 1.

❸

Make sure that the cover fits tightly and that you have enough headroom for the steam to circulate freely. A glass cover is nice because you can easily see what is going on.

❹

I use a wide pair of wire tongs that I got from a Chinese kitchen supply store to remove hot plates from a steamer. Canning jar lifters will work well, too, if they are wide enough.

Guōtiē 鍋貼

Potstickers

TIANJIN · MAKES 24 POTSTICKERS AND SERVES ABOUT 4

Potstickers have become commonplace at Asian restaurants in the United States, but what most of these establishments call "potstickers" are previously frozen pork *jiaozi* (page 45) with boring fillings and leaden skins. They are pale shadows compared to what can be found in places like Tianjin. These potstickers are delicious in part because the ethereally light wrappers are handmade but also because the filling is so juicy and flavorful. Once you've eaten handmade *guotie*, you will fall in love, too. They are perfect for breakfast with a hot bowl of Congee (page 226), as an afternoon snack, or as part of a dim sum feast. They can even be made ahead of time up to the last step, which means they are great for entertaining.

WRAPPERS

1 recipe plain hot-water dough (page 386)

FILLING

1 pound ground pork (30 percent fat recommended)
1 teaspoon mushroom powder or sea salt
½ teaspoon sugar
1 teaspoon regular soy sauce
2 tablespoons Shaoxing rice wine
2 tablespoons chopped cilantro
1 green onion, trimmed and finely chopped
2 tablespoons peeled and minced fresh ginger

¾ cup peanut or vegetable oil

1. Prepare the wrappers according to the instructions on page 46 up through Step 2.

2. On a clean cutting board, use a heavy cleaver to chop the pork until it is fine and a bit sticky. Place the meat in a medium work bowl and add the rest of the filling ingredients. Use your hand to stir them around in one direction to fully incorporate them, then pick the meat up and slam it back into the bowl around 10 times to make it bouncy and resilient. Divide the filling into 24 pieces and roll each piece into a cigar shape.

3. Fill the potstickers (see the diagram to the right). The potstickers can be made ahead of time up to this point and either covered with plastic wrap and refrigerated or frozen as you would freeze uncooked *jiaozi* (see tips, page 47).

4. Fry the potstickers just before serving: heat a flat-bottomed frying pan (preferably nonstick) over medium heat until the edges of the pan are very hot. Follow the directions at right to cook and serve the potstickers.

SHAPING, FILLING, AND COOKING POTSTICKERS

 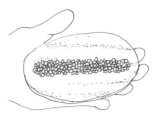 

❶

Shape your rested dough into a rope 24 inches long and then cut the rope into twenty-four 1-inch pieces. Roll each piece out into a circle 5 inches in diameter as directed in Step 2 of the diagram on page 46. The wrapper should be smooth, elastic, and even. Lightly dust it with some flour and cover it with a towel. Repeat with the rest of the dough until you have 24 wrappers.

❷

To wrap the potstickers, hold a wrapper flat in one hand and center one of the meat cigars in the wrapper with your other hand.

❸

Pinch the edges together, leaving a ¾-inch opening at both ends. Lightly crimp the edges in a wavy pattern, if you like. Cover the filled potsticker with a tea towel and repeat with the rest of the wrappers and filling until all are done.

❹

Pour some oil (about 1½ tablespoons per potsticker) into a hot, flat frying pan over medium heat. Arrange as many potstickers in the pan as will fit without squeezing—though they should touch one another.

❺

Pour water (again, about 1½ tablespoons per potsticker) into the pan and immediately cover it with a tight-fitting lid. Fry-steam the potstickers for about 5 minutes, until you can hear by the popping oil that the water has been absorbed. Remove the lid and continue to fry the potstickers until their bottoms are a golden, crispy brown.

❻

Loosen them with a thin spatula and turn them out onto a serving plate with the brown bottoms on top.

Xiànbǐng 餡餅

Chinese Hamburgers

BEIJING · MAKES 16 AND SERVES 8

My future husband introduced me to these juicy little burgers that northerners call *xianbing* when he took me to a Muslim eatery near downtown Taipei. It was yet another one of those nondescript little holes-in-the-wall where amazing food sails out of the kitchen with little more than a shrug and a smile. Or so it seemed. Along with the hamburgers we had a rich broth filled with all sorts of vegetables and meats and pasta. It was heaven.

I was so impressed with the meal that I immediately invited my American buddy Mike over to have the same lunch. The problem was that I couldn't remember what anything was called, and my Chinese was still so lousy that I was unable to figure out from the menu on the wall what it was we had eaten. So I winged it. The guy at the counter gave me a strange look and headed into the back.

Now, I had regaled Mike with how great these burgers were, so he was grinning from ear to ear with anticipation, a particularly hungry glow in his eyes. Imagine his surprise, then, when the cook himself emerged from the kitchen and set down a plate of plain, dry, unadorned flour biscuits, along with a big bowl of the water in which *jiaozi* (page 45) had been boiled.

Fortunately for me, Mike had already had a similar experience at another restaurant when he ordered what the menu clearly described as "field chicken"

(*tiánjī* 田雞) and was startled to find that this was a euphemism for the whole cooked frog staring back at him. In spite of his gracious good humor, I knew that, from then on, I'd have to start writing the names of foods down to save myself further embarrassment.

But back to those burgers. Calling them "hamburgers" is really a disservice, but no English word provides a better translation. What they are is much more exciting: ground beef with an equal amount of chopped garlic chives and a bunch of seasonings, all wrapped in a thin piece of dough that is sautéed on both sides until the outside is crispy.

FILLING

1 pound ground chuck
1 teaspoon sea salt
5 tablespoons cool water
2 tablespoons regular soy sauce
1 clove garlic, finely minced
1 tablespoon peeled and finely minced fresh ginger
1 tablespoon mild rice wine
1 tablespoon peanut or vegetable oil
1 small bunch (about 1 inch across) garlic chives, trimmed and finely chopped
½ cup chopped onion

WRAPPERS

2½ cups Chinese flour (page 386)
½ cup boiling water

Peanut or vegetable oil for frying

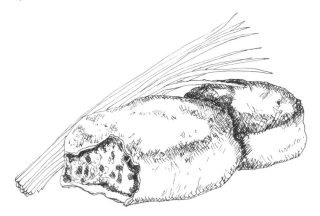

1. At least 4 hours before serving, make the meat filling. Place the meat on a chopping board and use a heavy knife to finely chop it back and forth in different directions. Scoop the meat up into a medium work bowl, sprinkle the salt on top, and use one hand to hold the bowl as you use your other hand to stir around the meat in one direction (see page 458). When the meat feels light and airy, add the water a tablespoon at a time, beating it in until it is fully incorporated. Continue to use your hand to beat in the soy sauce, garlic, ginger, rice wine, and oil. Smooth down the top of the meat, place the chives and onions on top (don't mix them in yet; see Tips), cover the bowl, and refrigerate it for at least 3 hours.

2. For directions on making and filling the wrappers, see the diagram on pages 406 to 407, steps 1 through 10, plus 12 and 13.

3. Place a seasoned cast-iron or nonstick frying pan over medium heat, film the bottom of the pan with some oil, and reduce the heat to medium-low. Loosely arrange some of the pastries in the hot pan with their pleated sides down and about 1 inch between them. Slowly cook them until they are a crisp golden brown on the bottom. Carefully turn them over with a spatula, cover, and cook this side as well until crispy and golden, about 10 minutes in total. Repeat with the rest of the pastries until done, and either eat them as they are cooked (best!) or keep them on a baking sheet in a 275°F oven for up to 30 minutes until you wish to serve them.

The big secrets to successfully making *xianbing* were discovered through trial and error. The problem is that the juices have to be carefully sealed inside the dough, but the wrappers can be neither too thick (tough) nor too thin (fragile). To give yourself the best shot, I recommend that you roll the dough out into 5½-inch-wide circles. This will give you just enough wrapper to perfectly cover the filling, but it will still be thick enough that it won't tear while the burgers are being fried.

Forming a point on the top of the *xianbing* and then nipping it off was also a major discovery. This technique seals in the juices and fat and also removes the extra dough that would otherwise form a tough pillow at the bottom of the hamburgers.

Cook the pastries uncovered at a relatively low temperature. This gives the meat time to steam cook while the exterior slowly fries to a crisp.

Fry the pleated side to a dark golden brown and then flip it over only once, because those pleats sometimes leak when they harden. Also, be very careful when you touch the sides of the *xianbing*: they are unfried and soft, and can pierce easily.

To eat the *xianbing*, cradle one in a Chinese soupspoon and use chopsticks with your other hand. If the pastry is very hot, take a little nip out of one edge and pour the juices into your spoon; sip this while you wait for the *xianbing* to cool down.

THE APPRECIATION OF DIFFERENT TEXTURES sets the foods of China apart from all others. Among Chinese dining cognoscenti, exciting consistency is considered on par with aroma and flavor as the most important qualities in a dish. Achieving correct mouthfeel and textural balance depends upon a number of factors that are discussed throughout this book.

Take pork skin and fat: When you make Rock Sugar Pork Shank (page 32), a piece of skin-on pork is coated with honey before being fried to a crispy brown, which caramelizes the sugar and toughens up the skin enough so that it remains in one piece during a long braise. During the actual cooking process, though, the fat under the skin and between the tender meaty strata is rendered, leaving behind only pillowy layers that will end up melting on the tongue, a texture called "slippery," *huá*.

At the same time, the skin will release its collagen into the sauce, which leaves a slight stickiness, *nián*, on the lips. What remains of the skin is so soft that it falls apart at the slightest touch and yet is full of flavor—its texture, though, is completely different from that of the fat and the meat, and so it supplies the final textural fillip of softness (*ruǎn*), providing you with tactile heaven in one mouthful.

Cōngyóubǐng, zhuābǐng 蔥油餅、抓餅

Fried Scallion and Flaky Flatbreads

ALL OVER NORTHERN CHINA · EACH RECIPE
MAKES 6 (8-INCH) BREADS AND SERVES 4 TO 6

Fried scallion flatbreads have become a staple at many Chinese restaurants on the American side of the Pacific. But the problem is that few places make their own breads anymore, relying instead on commercially made products that are frozen and then cooked whenever an order comes in. I find this strange, because fried scallion flatbreads (their Chinese name, *congyoubing*, literally means "green onion and oil flatbreads") are so easy to make and so delicious.

Flaky flatbreads—what the Chinese call "grabbed flatbreads" (*zhuabing*)—are crispier and in some ways more enticing. They are also a bit more difficult to make, but not by much. Instead of being cut into wedges like the fried scallion flatbreads, these are served whole as fluffed-up mounds, a whorl of crispy strands on the outside encircling a moist, tender center, very much like an Indian *paratha*.

My husband and I ate plain scallion flatbreads for years in Taipei before *zhuabing* took the city by storm. Soon everyone was making and selling them, but the best were at my late mother-in-law's favorite haunt, Tianjin Flavors (see page 25).

DOUGH

2½ cups Chinese flour (page 386), plus more as needed
1 cup boiling water
Peanut or vegetable oil, as needed

PASTE AND SEASONINGS

½ cup Chinese flour (page 386)
1 teaspoon sea salt
½ to 1 teaspoon ground toasted Sichuan peppercorns
   (page 441), optional
¼ cup melted lard or white shortening
2 tablespoons peanut or vegetable oil
4 green onions, trimmed and very finely chopped
   (about ⅔ cup)
Peanut or vegetable oil for frying

1. To make the dough, place the flour in a medium work bowl. Use chopsticks to stir in the boiling water until large flakes have formed. Turn the dough out onto a lightly floured board and knead it gently, adding a little extra flour as needed, until the dough is as soft as an earlobe. Rinse out the bowl, wipe it dry, and pour in a little oil. Toss the ball of dough around in the oil and then cover the bowl with either plastic wrap or a damp towel. Let the dough rest for 20 to 30 minutes.

2. While the dough is resting, make a thin paste by mixing together in a small bowl the flour, salt, optional Sichuan peppercorns, lard (or shortening), and oil. Set the green onions next to the paste.

3. For directions on shaping, frying, and serving both types of flatbread, see the diagram to the right.

❶

Divide the dough into 6 equal portions and roll each portion into a smooth ball. Working on 1 piece at a time, and keeping the other portions covered so that they do not dry out, use a Chinese rolling pin to roll the ball out into a strip about 12 inches long, then pull gently on both ends to create a strip 18 inches long. Smear one-sixth of the paste on top of the strip and sprinkle one-sixth of the onions all the way down the strip.

❷

Roll up the strip from one of the long sides to form a rope, and then pull this rope gently to form a strand 24 inches long. Repeat with the rest of the dough and paste until you have 6 strands.

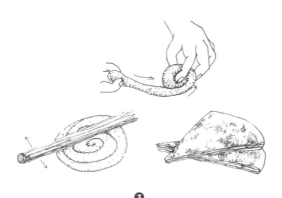

❸

A *To make Fried Scallion Flatbreads,* coil the strand until you have a flat circle, then roll this circle out into an 8-inch disk. Repeat with the rest of the strands until you have 6 disks. (The uncooked breads can be frozen on plastic wrap-lined baking sheets at this point and then stored in a resealable plastic bag.) Heat a flat frying pan over medium-high heat and then film the bottom with oil. As soon as the oil is hot, place a bread in the pan. Cover the pan and fry until the bottom is golden and the bread is puffy. Turn the bread over, cover again, and fry until the second side is also golden. Remove to a plate lined with paper towels and keep the bread warm in a 250°F oven for up to 20 minutes. Cut each flatbread into 6 or so wedges.

❸

B *To make Flaky Flatbreads,* first use a sharp knife to make 7 or 8 slashes down the length of each strand. Then lightly coil the strands (don't mash them together) to form flat circles, and roll these circles out into 8-inch disks. (The uncooked breads can be frozen on plastic wrap-lined baking sheets at this point and then stored in a resealable plastic bag.) Fry the breads as directed in Step 3a. To serve the breads, do something different: while the breads are still very hot, place them, one at a time, on a paper towel and—while handling the flatbread through the towel—scrunch the edges toward the center, to make the breads light and fluffy. Serve without slicing.

Shāobǐng 燒餅

Shaobing

NORTHERN CHINA AND BEYOND · MAKES 16

These flaky biscuits are a favorite breakfast in northern China. They usually cradle fried crullers called *yóutiáo* 油條 or are packed with razor-thin slices of braised beef shank (page 14). Either way, they make for a perfect first meal of the day.

Shaobing were traditionally baked in tandoor-like ovens, but nowadays regular ovens are usually substituted. I've met the old and new halfway by baking these on a pizza stone in a hot oven. The unglazed tile simulates the super-hot surface of the tandoor, which makes the breads puff up quickly and adds a nice crispy edge.

Different places put their own spin on these biscuits. However, I always enjoyed *shaobing* for breakfast in Taipei with nothing more than sesame seeds on top, so that's the recipe I've provided below.

DOUGH

1 recipe northern-style puff pastry (page 390)

FILLING

½ cup Chinese flour (page 386)

6 tablespoons toasted sesame oil

½ teaspoon salt

½ to 1 teaspoon ground toasted Sichuan peppercorns (page 441), optional

TOPPING

2 tablespoons sugar

2 tablespoons water

½ cup raw sesame seeds, unhulled or white

Toasted sesame oil, peanut oil, or vegetable oil for rolling out the dough

CHINESE CULINARY THEORY HAS A GALAXY of descriptive words for flavors, but the basic roster comes down to the sourness (*suān* 酸) of vinegar and pickles, the sweetness (*tián* 甜) of sugar and fruits, the bitterness (*kǔ* 苦) of mustard greens and green tea, the heat (*là* 辣) of chili peppers and ginger, the saltiness (*xián* 鹹) of soy sauce and fermented black beans, the fragrance (*xiāng* 香) of rice wine and fresh green onions, the funkiness (*chòu* 臭)

of fish sauce and dried shrimp, and the *xianwei* (*xiān* 鮮) of black mushrooms and beef. Sometimes two other flavors—the delicious moldiness (*méi* 霉) of things like bean curd "cheese" and the fermented flavors (*zāo* 糟) of red wine lees—are also included; if it were up to me, I would also add another: the smokiness (*xūn* 薰) of, well, smoked foods. So, what is *xianwei*? Basically, it means something on the order of "meaty" or "deliciously savory," and the

Japanese word *umami* is often used to describe it.

Other sensations that can't be considered flavors exist in our foods, as well. Temperature is one; texture (see page 53), considered particularly important in Chinese cuisine, is another. China also prizes that strange sensation called "numbing" (*má* 麻). Almost always caused by the oils in Sichuan peppercorns, this is a tingling feeling on the lips and tongue.

---

1. Make the puff pastry as directed and defrost, if necessary. Cover the dough with a clean tea towel or plastic wrap and keep it in a cool place. Prepare a smooth surface (see Tips, page 47) to roll out the dough and have a Chinese rolling pin, pastry scraper, pastry brush, and baking sheet lined with plastic wrap ready. Place a pizza stone or a large unglazed tile on a rack in the bottom third of your oven and heat it to 400°F.

2. To make the filling, place the flour in a dry wok (see Tips) and stir over medium-high heat until it changes from white to a pale tan. Empty the cooked flour into a small work bowl and stir in the sesame oil, salt, and optional ground Sichuan peppercorns. Divide the filling into 16 pieces.

3. Prepare the topping by boiling together the sugar and water (a microwave works well for this), stirring until the sugar dissolves and allowing it to cool to room temperature in a small work bowl; pour the sesame seeds onto a rimmed plate.

4. Now make the *shaobing*: work on filling each piece of dough one by one, keeping the others covered at all times and being sure to either cover the finished uncooked pastries or immediately bake them, as you don't want to let the dough dry out (see Tips). Clean your flat work surface and rub it generously with either sesame oil or plain oil. Place a piece of dough in front of you with the cut edges at 12 and 6 o'clock. Roll the piece out to a rough square about 5 inches all around, then place one portion of the filling in the center. Enclose the filling completely by folding each edge over the filling: left, right, top, and bottom. Turn the packet over and press down lightly on it, then use your dough scraper to pick it up.

5. Hold the packet between the palms of both hands and mold it gently to seal the folds. Brush the smooth side of the dough with the glaze and then press this side down firmly onto the sesame seeds. Place the dough seed-side down on your oiled work surface and roll it out into a rectangle with lightly rounded ends about 5½ × 3 inches. The uncooked *shaobing* can be prepared up to this point and frozen (see Tips).

6. To cook the *shaobing*, lay as many as you want to bake, seed-side down, on the hot pizza stone and bake for 8 to 15 minutes (depending upon your oven). Flip the pastries over after they have puffed up and are nicely browned on the bottom. When both sides are a golden brown, remove and eat immediately or let cool. Leftover baked pastries can be reheated in an oven or toaster oven; never use a microwave, as it will usually give you a very tough and flabby pastry.

Whenever flour is used in the filling of Chinese pastry, it is almost always dry-fried first to remove its raw taste.

One of the keys to successfully making Chinese puff pastry is ensuring that the uncooked dough never dries out through over-exposure to the air. It is equally important not to use too much flour as you roll out and shape the pastries. Either of these errors will give you dry dough, and the pastries will end up cracked, broken, or tough. Dry dough also prevents the pastries from puffing up because cracks form and allow steam to escape.

If you want to freeze all or some of these pastries, do so before you bake them. Lay the uncooked pastries on a plastic wrap–lined baking sheet, freeze them until solid, and pack them in resealable plastic bags. They will only need a few extra minutes of baking, and they can be baked without defrosting.

To open up a *shaobing*, use kitchen shears to cut up one of the long edges and through both short edges. This will give you a book-shaped wrapper.

Wōwotóu'er 窩窩頭兒

Corn Thimbles

TIANJIN · MAKES ABOUT 12 AND SERVES 3 OR 4

1 cup finely ground cornmeal
2 tablespoons all-purpose flour
½ teaspoon baking powder
2 teaspoons sugar
½ teaspoon sea salt
6 tablespoons water, plus more as needed

After marrying in Yunnan's capital of Kunming and then traveling around the country with her air force pilot husband and children, my mother-in-law settled in Taiwan in 1949 before finally making the United States her home. She wasn't able to find the food she loved in any of those places, though, until I hit upon this and other Tianjin recipes.

When we were first getting to know each other, I was unaware of this, and I asked her about what she used to eat. She was not a terribly good cook, but she loved to dine almost as much as I do, and she began reminiscing about the foods of northern China. She was able to paint me a picture of a world of food that no longer existed for her.

One of the things she missed the most were the little corn thimbles known as *wowotou'er*. There is no direct translation for this word, but many little snacks and pastries in the North are called *wowo*. Corn, of course, came from the New World, so *wowotou'er* were probably first made from millet flour. Millet has a nice stickiness to it, which you will be familiar with if you have ever made Millet Porridge (to the right). Cornmeal, on the other hand, can be a little difficult to shape into something like these thimbles. To up the stickiness factor, I've added a bit of flour. I've also added some sugar to heighten the corn flavor and a touch of baking powder and salt to lighten the dough.

When I first made these for my mother-in-law, she demolished them with glee. Later on, I made thimbles for her out of other things, such as chestnut flour, and she enjoyed them with equal relish. This dish always reminds me of her.

1. Set aside an hour or so the first time you make these. This will give you enough time to practice and redo them a couple of times. Set up a steamer (see page 49), and line a steamer basket with either a square of damp muslin or a sheet of steamer paper. Turn the steamer on with the covered basket on top so that the inside of the steamer gets hot and moist. Steam the basket and liner this way for at least 10 minutes while you prepare the corn thimbles.

2. Mix the cornmeal and flour with the baking powder, sugar, and salt. Add the 6 tablespoons water and mix it into the dry ingredients. Squeeze a piece of dough in your fist; if it forms a cigar shape easily without crumbling, it's ready to go. If not, dribble in just enough water as needed (see Tips). Note that you probably will need to add a bit more water later on as the cornmeal starts to absorb it, so keep some water nearby.

3. Put a walnut-sized piece of dough in one hand and shape it into a ball. Insert the forefinger of your other hand into the ball to form a thimble shape. Smooth the outside into a cone or dome, whichever you prefer. Sit the thimble right-side up on your work surface; if it crumbles or looks less than steady, pop it back into the dough and try again. Repeat until you have formed a dozen or so *wowotou'er*.

4. Place the corn thimbles on the hot muslin or steamer paper. Cover and steam for 30 to 40 minutes, until the cornmeal cooks completely through. Remove the *wowotou'er* from the steamer. You can serve them immediately or freeze them for later (see Tips). Serve with something hot and soupy.

The water content of cornmeal and flour can vary, so it's difficult to give a precise amount of water here. Add only as much water as you need at first, and then sprinkle in more as you go along to keep the dough moist and supple. If you happen to add too much water, just add a bit more cornmeal.

Steamer liner paper is great to have on hand. It's very cheap and you don't have to bother with washing steamer liners. Plus, it's relatively nonstick. Get a package in the housewares section of a Chinese market.

To prepare the *wowotou'er* for freezing, put the cooled thimbles on a small sheet in a single layer, freeze them until solid, and then store them in a resealable plastic bag. To reheat the frozen thimbles, place them with or without defrosting in a lined steamer and steam until heated through.

Xiǎomǐ zhōu 小米粥

Millet Porridge

BEIJING · MAKES ABOUT 4 CUPS AND SERVES 2

Zhou sounds so lovely in Chinese, but English translations like "porridge," "mush," and "gruel" don't sound nearly as appealing, bringing to mind Oliver Twist rather than a bowl of something hot, comforting, and delicious.

Zhou can be made from a variety of different grains. In Beijing, millet—or "little rice" (*xiaomi*)—is the grain of choice, although sorghum (see page 65) does have its faithful adherents. Millet's tiny yellow balls are popular not only because of their low cost but also for their gentle, milky flavor and their slightly rough texture, which is quite different from rice.

Zhou is generally served in large soup bowls, since it is meant to be the main starchy component of the meal, what the Chinese call *zhǔshí* 主食. So, while this recipe makes about 4 cups, it is designed to serve two people. Depending upon the time of day (breakfast, afternoon snack, or a late-night meal), you can accompany it with simple side dishes of hard-boiled brined eggs (page 422), white or red fermented bean curd "cheese" (page 420 or 421), and/or fried peanuts (page 411).

4 cups water
½ cup millet, preferably organic and fresh

1. Bring the water to a boil in a saucepan over high heat. Stir in the millet.

2. Lower the heat to medium and stir the millet occasionally until it "blooms," meaning that the grains have popped. This should take about 30 minutes. Serve hot in winter and lukewarm in summer.

Millet is available at most Chinese markets that don't cater exclusively to a southern Chinese clientele, but I prefer to buy mine in bulk at health food stores, where it is generally very fresh and often organic.

Lǘ dǎgǔn 驢打滾

Rolling Donkeys

BEIJING · MAKES ABOUT 12

These tea sweets are originally from Beijing, where they were a palace favorite during the times of the emperors. They are called "Rolling Donkeys" because they are the same color as the fine particles that coat Beijing during dust storms. The traditional recipe calls for a red bean paste filling and a dusting of ground toasted soybeans, but my husband once suggested that I use finely chopped peanuts as a substitute, and that's worked out terrifically.

This dish doesn't keep and turns hard within a day, so make it the morning that you want to serve it and store it covered at room temperature until it's time to eat.

1½ cups sticky rice flour
1½ cups water
1 cup sweetened red bean paste
2 tablespoons toasted sesame oil
½ teaspoon sea salt
1½ cups skinned, toasted peanuts (page 411)
    or toasted soybean flour (page 410)

1. Mix the rice flour and water together to form a dough. Knead the dough until smooth, adding just a bit more water if needed. Form the dough into a smooth ball. Wrap the ball in a piece of cheesecloth and steam it for about 40 minutes, adding more water to the steamer (see page 49) as necessary. At the end of the steaming time, remove the dough from the steamer and let it cool down until you can work with it without burning your fingers, but don't let it get cold.

2. While the dough is steaming, gently fry the bean paste and sesame oil together until the bean paste absorbs the oil. Sprinkle on the salt, mix well, and remove the bean paste to a plate to cool off completely. Grind the peanuts until they are a fine powder but don't let them turn into peanut butter; the best way to do this is in small batches so that the peanuts don't heat up. Pulse the peanuts in a small processor or blender until they are chopped very finely, remove to a bowl, and then process the rest in small increments until done. (Or, use the soybean flour.)

3. Spread about a cup of the ground peanuts (or soybeans) on a smooth, clean work surface, like the underside of a cutting board. Place the warm dough on top of the peanuts and use wet hands to pat it out into a square. Shape the dough into a 12 × 8-inch rectangle, scooting the peanuts under the dough as you adjust it so that the dough doesn't stick to the board.

4. Use a silicone spatula to smooth the bean paste over the dough, leaving a 1-inch strip on one of the 12-inch edges, which will eventually be the outside of the roll. Starting from the other 12-inch edge, roll up the dough over the bean paste so that it looks like a jelly roll, using a pastry scraper as needed to encourage the dough to turn over. Gently pinch the long edge into the roll. Use a thin, sharp knife to take a thin slice off of both of the rolled-up ends to even things up, then cut the roll into 12 pieces. Dust the pieces with the remaining ground peanuts and serve with hot tea. You can eat these with little bamboo skewers or small forks, or you can pick them up with your hands.

Kāikǒuxiào 開口笑

Laughing Doughnut Holes

BEIJING · MAKES ABOUT 20

The recipe for Laughing Doughnut Holes, or *kaikouxiao* ("open mouth laughs"), has been in our family for decades. Traditionally made around the Lunar New Year as a treat for the young, these doughnut holes are a nostalgic comfort food for many Chinese. However, they are very easy to toss together, and there is no reason why they need to be made only during the spring festivities.

I suggest you use dark brown sugar instead of granulated. They're both delicious here, but for some reason the dark sugar makes these doughnuts especially light and crunchy.

These are best eaten as soon as they are fried, so plan to make them just before you serve them. They can, of course, sit around for a short while and still be quite tasty. Serve them with hot tea and coffee, or with milk for the kids.

1 cup Chinese flour (page 386)

1 teaspoon baking powder

1 tablespoon solid fat (unsalted butter, lard, or white shortening), at room temperature

1 tablespoon water

1 large egg, at room temperature

¼ cup sugar (dark brown or granulated)

½ teaspoon sea salt

¼ cup (or so) raw sesame seeds, black or white

2 to 3 cups peanut or vegetable oil

1. Mix the flour and baking powder together in a small work bowl. Use a mixer to beat the fat, water, egg, sugar, and salt together to form a thin batter. Slowly mix in the flour and baking powder to form a soft dough.

2. Place the sesame seeds in a medium bowl. Use one hand to scoop out the dough, and wet the other one to shape the dough into balls. Spoon a piece of dough about the size of a walnut (see Tips) and drop it into the sesame seeds. Use your dry hand to roll the dough around in the seeds until it is completely coated, then lightly roll between your palms to form a small ball. Repeat with the rest of the dough until you have 20 or so small balls coated with sesame, rinsing your hands as necessary.

3. Prepare a plate next to the stove and cover it with a paper towel. Heat the oil in a small saucepan (see Tips) over medium heat until a wooden chopstick inserted in the oil bubbles all over. Gently slide some of the balls into the hot oil. They will expand to twice their original size as they fry, so don't crowd the pan.

4. Lightly shake the pan so that the balls roll over on their own; if any need help, just nudge them with the chopstick. When the balls are browned all over and have split, remove them with a slotted spoon and place them on the paper towel. Repeat with the rest of the balls until done. Serve immediately, if possible. Keep any uneaten doughnuts in a resealable plastic bag.

You don't need to be too exacting when scooping out the dough balls. As long as they all are about the size of a walnut, they will cook evenly.

Adjust the heat as necessary. The oil has to be hot enough to fry the dough quickly. If it is too cold, the dough will soak up the oil. On the other hand, if the oil is too hot, the dough will burn before the insides have cooked. So, test the oil with your chopstick and then monitor the heat as you fry the doughnuts.

Get the sesame-coated balls as close to the oil as you safely can before sliding them in. This will cut down on splashing.

Bási píngguǒ 拔絲蘋果

Toffee Apples

SHANDONG · SERVES 8 TO 12

During my first years in Taipei, this was my favorite dessert. The chef would dip chunks of apple in batter, deep-fry them, and then toss them in hot caramel. While a waitress rushed all of this to the table, another server would present a large tureen filled with ice water and ice cubes. We would use our chopsticks to pick up a piece of fried apple, which was dripping with threads of hot caramel, and quickly dunk it in the ice water so that the caramel hardened. The result was a molten apple interior that contrasted with an icy candy exterior, the fried batter functioning as a sort of pie-crust intermediary. If there was one moment when I fell in love with North China's foods, it was when I had my first bite of this.

As I learned more about this dish, I discovered that all sorts of things were given the toffee treatment: bananas, pineapple, orange sweet potatoes, lotus seeds, and Chinese yams, among others. It seemed that each northern region had its own favorite, and I was more than happy to eat my way through them all.

This recipe is not at all difficult to master. It just requires that the cook have everything prepped and ready to go before guests sit down to dinner. After the last dish has been served, the cook can serve some hot tea and disappear into the kitchen to fry the apples and make the caramel.

APPLES

1 pound sweet apples (see Tips)
1 tablespoon fresh lemon juice

BATTER

¼ cup cornstarch
¼ cup Chinese flour (page 386)
¼ teaspoon sea salt
¼ teaspoon double-acting baking powder
1 large egg
¼ cup ice water
1 teaspoon vanilla or black walnut extract, optional

Peanut or vegetable oil for frying
¼ cup Chinese flour (page 386)
Bowl of ice water with some ice cubes

CARAMEL AND FINISHING TOUCHES

1 tablespoon peanut or vegetable oil
6 tablespoons turbinado or raw sugar
2 tablespoons water
1 tablespoon fresh lemon juice
Finely grated zest of 1 lemon
2 teaspoons toasted sesame seeds (page 413)

1. Peel and core the apples, cut each one into 8 wedges, and then cut each wedge in half crosswise to make 16 fat pieces per apple. Place the apple chunks in a bowl of cool water with the lemon juice so that they don't turn brown. (This can be done up to a couple of hours ahead of time; cover and refrigerate if your kitchen is warm.)

2. To make the batter, mix together the cornstarch, flour, salt, and baking powder in a medium work bowl. Just before you are ready to fry the apples, whisk together the egg, ice water, and optional extract in a small bowl and then stir this mixture into the dry ingredients to form a slightly lumpy batter (see Tips).

3. To fry the apples, heat about 3 inches of oil in a wok over medium-high. Heat your oven to 275°F and have a baking sheet lined with parchment paper ready. While the oil is heating up, drain the apples, pat them dry in a towel, and toss them with the ¼ cup flour. Coat a large handful of the dusty apples with the batter. Slide them one by one into the hot oil. Cook these in batches so that they do not stick to one another or cool the oil down too fast, adjusting the heat as necessary. Fry them until they are crispy golden brown. As they turn brown, remove them with a Chinese spider or slotted spoon to the parchment paper and keep them warm in the oven. Repeat with the rest of the apples until all are fried; stash them in the oven if you are not serving them right away. Lightly oil a serving platter and place the bowl of ice water in the center of the dining table.

4. It is easiest to see how done the caramel is if it is made in a light-colored pan rather than a dark wok, so pour the oil into a large stainless-steel frying pan. Reduce the heat under the pan to medium before adding the sugar, water, and lemon juice. Cover the pan for a few minutes so that the steam washes down any sugar crystals. This will prevent the caramel from seizing up. Remove the cover and stir the liquid occasionally with a silicone spatula until the sugar syrup thickens and starts to change color. Stir constantly to keep the sugar from burning as it turns a golden brown. Remove the pan from the heat, quickly mix in the lemon zest and sesame seeds, and then toss in the hot fried apples, coating them as completely as possible. Empty the caramel-coated apples onto the platter and rush them to the table. Have your guests pluck pieces of the apple, dunk them in the ice water, and enjoy.

Get a good-flavored apple, like Fuji or Pacific Rose. You can substitute 1 pound bananas or other fruits. Treat them like the apples, but cut softer fruits into larger pieces so they do not cook through and soften too quickly.

Be sure not to mix the batter ahead of time or the double-acting baking powder will lose its power.

Separate any clumps of caramelized apples as you work your way through the plate.

The Chinese name for this translates to "pulled thread apples." When you pull the hot apples out of the pile with your chopsticks, you should try to make the caramel threads as long and as thin as possible before dipping the apples in the ice water.

TIANJIN WOULD NOT EXIST AS MUCH MORE than a simple seaport if it weren't for China's capital being around 70 miles away. Not only that, but Tianjin has a direct channel to northern and southern flavors thanks to its position on the Grand Canal that starts in Beijing and flows through Shandong and Jiangsu to its terminus on the Yangtze River.

And so, while Shandong has exerted a certain degree of influence on Tianjin's cuisine, her banquet dishes reflect the foods of Jiangsu and Zhejiang. Tianjin is so similar in many ways to Jiangsu's culinary epicenter of Yangzhou that it actually used to be referred to as "little Yangzhou." However, the uniqueness of this port city's foods lies in its seafood—spectacular prawns and crabs here vie with saltwater fish to be the stars of the local banquets.

The cuisine we now know of as Tianjin's started to take shape in the mid-eighteenth century and reached its pinnacle around a hundred years later when foreigners settled there after the Opium Wars. Tianjin then turned into a place where lavish living became the standard, an elegance that is still reflected in its banquet dishes and its appreciation for stellar ingredients.

Dòujiāng 豆漿

Soymilk

NORTHERN CHINA AND BEYOND ·
MAKES 6 TO 8 CUPS

The most popular soymilk in Taipei was made in the suburb of Yonghe, but my favorite place was a little shop in the tiny port of Danshui. The guy who worked there was from Ningbo, and he sold delicious, icy glasses of fresh soymilk. It was the perfect refreshment after a long, hot hike over the mountains from our old home in Beitou.

There is a big difference between commercial and homemade soymilk. When you pour out a hot bowl of freshly made soymilk, it will be thicker and richer than you might be used to, sort of like half-and-half rather than 2 percent milk. You can dissolve rock sugar into the soymilk for a sweet angle, or you can go the savory route, adding a sprinkle of chili oil, pork fluff, cilantro, and finely sliced crullers (my favorite). Either way, hot soymilk is best enjoyed at breakfast.

The secrets to great soymilk are few. First, the dried beans have to be fresh, preferably not GMO (genetically modified), and organic. Second, the beans must be soaked overnight so that they completely plump up. Third, soymilk should be slowly simmered for a couple of hours to eliminate any suggestion of rawness and concentrate the aromas.

Please note that this is a slight pain in the neck to make if you do not have a soymilk machine, which automatically soaks, grinds, and cooks the milk for you. If you love soymilk, think about getting one and then pouring the ready-made milk into a saucepan, where it can be concentrated to your liking.

8 ounces tan soybeans plus 8 ounces black soybeans
(or 1 pound of one or the other; see Tips)

FOR SWEET SOYMILK
Rock sugar (preferred) or granulated sugar

FOR SAVORY SOYMILK
Red chili oil (page 435), pork fluff, chopped cilantro
and/or green onions, soy sauce, thinly sliced fried
Chinese crullers as desired

1. Pick over the beans and soak them overnight in cool tap water to cover by a couple of inches; they will double in size as they soak. The next morning, drain the beans in a colander and rinse lightly.

2. If you don't have a soymilk machine, prepare a large, tall stockpot (see Tips) and a blender, as well as a large bowl and a long silicone spatula. To strain the soymilk, I've come to depend on a pair of large chinois (a conical sieve also known as a China cap; I use a coarse one on top of a fine-mesh one), although a pair of large sieves perched over the stockpot will work well, too (see Tips). Grind the beans in your blender, using a ratio of approximately 2 parts beans to 3 parts water. When the beans have been thoroughly pulverized, pour the mush into your paired-up sieves and let the soymilk drain into the stockpot. When the ground soybeans are as dry as a bowl of oatmeal, dump them into the large bowl. Clean out the fine sieve, and then repeat until all the soymilk has been strained.

3. There is still a lot of soymilk left in the beans, so stir about 4 cups water into the ground beans and strain the milk one more time. Remove the sieves and bring the soymilk to a boil over medium heat, stirring often to keep the proteins from burning on the bottom (see Tips). As it is coming to a boil for the first time, the top will start to be covered with foam. *Don't leave the pot when this happens* because, at this point, the soymilk might suddenly rise up and spill over the sides. To avoid that, stir the milk constantly as it comes to a boil and adjust the heat.

4. Reduce the heat to low and slowly simmer the soymilk until it is reduced by a third or a half, or to whatever consistency you prefer. Sweeten it with sugar to taste or pour the unsweetened hot soymilk into individual soup bowls and let diners garnish their bowls with the condiments. Leftover soymilk should be cooled to room temperature, poured into covered containers, and refrigerated as soon as possible. Use it within 3 days, as it can coagulate or turn sour.

I like to make soymilk out of a mixture of regular tan soybeans and black ones, so that I end up with a milky, caramel-colored drink.

A tall stockpot is perfect here because the soymilk will foam up as it starts to boil, and the extra headroom will help prevent it from bubbling over.

You may season the soymilk with nuts or seeds. I especially like to add a couple of tablespoons of toasted sesame seeds (page 413) to the soybeans when I am grinding them in the blender.

Using a pair of sieves (one coarse and one fine) speeds the draining process because most of the ground soybeans will be trapped in the coarse sieve, while the smaller particles will be filtered by the fine mesh. If just one sieve is used, it tends to get clogged up quickly and frustration mounts, especially if you are doing this in the early morning with your first cup of coffee.

Sometimes the heat will be too high or the pot's bottom too thin, in which case the soymilk might start to burn. If you notice this happening, immediately remove the pot from the heat and pour the soymilk into another pot. Then lower the heat a bit and continue to simmer the soymilk.

If you are using an automatic soymilk machine, you should, of course, follow the manufacturer's instructions.

HEBEI DID NOT EXIST PRIOR TO 1928, AS IN Ming and Qing times it was a huge district called Zhílì 直隸, meaning that it was "directly governed" by the central government, sort of like Washington, D.C. This area has been continually occupied by the Chinese and their evolutionary ancestors; Peking Man roamed these lands hundreds of thousands of years ago.

The cuisine of Hebei generally flies under the radar of even the most discerning Chinese gastronome. This is understandable, for while by all rights this province should be the star of the North (after all, Beijing and Tianjin are its famous

progeny), once these two were lopped off and made independent municipalities, Hebei was left with only a handful of small cities, and its territory forms a strange loop around Beijing and Tianjin with a tiny dot in the middle to make, I suppose, geography lessons more interesting.

Sorghum is grown here and for all intents and purposes is a grain eaten mainly by the very poor, as the red variety is especially dry and tough compared to more luxurious things like wheat and rice. But sorghum has a wild side that blossoms when it is brewed into the white lightning called *gāoliáng* 高粱 (see page 492), which

incidentally is also the Chinese name for sorghum itself.

Millet used to be one of the cornerstones of the North's many impoverished areas, but the introduction of maize from the Americas (see page 350) gave the local people considerable relief from this rather bland cereal and soon took millet's place in many grain-based creations. These tiny yellow seeds still speak of home and childhood to many people, though, which is part of what makes a bowl of Millet Porridge (page 59) so comforting.

Guìhuā suānméi tāng 桂花酸梅湯

Chilled Sour Plum Infusion

BEIJING · MAKES 4 CUPS

I drank my first glass of Chilled Sour Plum Infusion, or *suanmei tang*, on a ridiculously hot afternoon in Taipei—the kind of early fall day that the Chinese call *qiū lǎohǔ* 秋老虎, or "autumn tiger." It was so hot out that even the cicadas were too tired to trill, and for some stupid reason I was walking down the street, finding it increasingly difficult to breathe and keep my eyes open at the same time.

Passing by a sweets shop, I noticed someone downing a big glass of reddish liquid, beads of condensation gathering on his glass.

I swung the door open and was greeted by a blast of cold air. With my red face and soggy clothes, I must have appeared to be in obvious distress, because as soon as I stepped inside, a wide-eyed shop girl said, "Help yourself" and pointed to a refrigerated case on the other side of the shop, which was full of icy homemade foods and drinks.

Sticking my head as far into the refrigerator as physically possible, I asked, "What's this?" and held up a sealed plastic glass of whatever the other person had been enjoying. "*Suanmei tang*," said the shop girl, adding, "It's our own secret recipe." I whacked a straw through the plastic lid and began to drink. It was icy cold and full of complex aromas: scents of fruit and flower and an underlying woody taste. Sweet and salty and sour at the same time, it was unlike anything I had ever tasted.

I drank a second glass a bit more slowly, lingering over the diverse flavors. There was definitely licorice root, and obviously sour plums were involved. But I couldn't tease out the rest of the ingredients. *Why does there always have to be a secret recipe?* I thought.

That same day I wandered down a few storefronts to an herbalist's shop and asked the guy in charge if I could get the makings for *suanmei tang*. "Of course!" he said. Then he carefully weighed out each ingredient and wrapped up the herbs. He even told me how much sugar and water to use. Not much of a secret after all, I'm afraid.

Almost any good Chinese supermarket will have the fixings for this traditional Beijing-style drink, and will even have it prepared as a concentrate in a bottle. But your best bet is always an herbalist shop, where the ingredients will be freshest. The plums, hawthorn fruits, licorice root, and osmanthus blossoms will all be available there, but you can usually only find the osmanthus blossom syrup in busy Chinese supermarkets that cater to a non-southern clientele.

The following recipe makes a concentrate that is easy to store in the refrigerator for a few days during the hot summer months.

3 or 4 sour dried black plums

Small handful of sliced dried hawthorn fruits

Small handful of sliced dried licorice root

Small handful of dried jamaica flowers, optional

4 cups water

2 walnut-sized pieces of rock sugar, or to taste,
 or agave syrup to taste

Salt to taste, optional

2 tablespoons osmanthus blossom syrup, or 2 tablespoons
 dried osmanthus blossoms plus ¼ teaspoon sea salt

1. Place the plums, hawthorn fruits, licorice root, and optional jamaica flowers in a sieve and rinse them well under running water. Shake them dry and place them in a 2-quart saucepan. Pour the 4 cups water over the dry ingredients and let them soak for at least an hour to plump them up.

2. Bring the pot to a full boil, then lower the heat to a gentle simmer for about 1 hour. Add the rock sugar and optional salt and simmer the infusion until the sugar melts; taste and add more sugar if you want. Add either the osmanthus syrup or the osmanthus blossoms and salt to the hot liquid so that the flavors can steep together, and then let the infusion come to room temperature.

3. Chill the concentrate overnight to allow the flavors to develop. Strain and add enough ice water to make 4 cups, or to taste. Serve icy cold without any ice.

Once you get the basics down, feel free to improvise. Some people like aged tangerine peel in here as well (get that at a Chinese herbalist's, too). But if you do add it, take the jamaica flowers out.

If you have a garden and you live in a temperate climate, consider growing some Chinese plants like *Osmanthus fragrans* (sweet olive) and Chinese dates. I've found that there are many Chinese plants that can be grown here in California, for example. Check with your local garden center, university, or agricultural extension program. I can't recommend highly enough the scent of osmanthus in full bloom. The Chinese regard it as one of the most refined floral aromas.

There's a reason for not adding ice: as with iced coffee, you do not want to dilute the drink. Chill the infusion and serve it in small glasses if the weather is hot. Keep the rest of it ready in a thermos or a covered pitcher.

A Western but lovely twist is to use chilled carbonated water to top off the glasses at the end.

Use rock sugar rather than granulated sugar. Regular sugar turns sour in the mouth, while rock sugar stays sweet.

THE CHINESE PRINCIPLE OF *HUŎHÒU* 火候 ("fire and time") is central to creating great food, for it means that a good cook knows how to apply the exact amount of heat for the precise amount of time in order to achieve the desired result.

The first half of this principle requires that a cook be familiar with how heat expresses itself. And so, as your senses become more attuned to the many signals sent their way, you will notice them more acutely. Some are sounds, like the pinging of water in a pan as it dries up, the rapid spatter of frying oil that needs to be tended to, or the change in tempo as a steamer hits its stride. Others are aromas, as caramelization signals itself with the smell of sugars in foods creeping from golden toward burned, while an empty steamer gives off whiffs of calcified minerals.

If you want, you can determine the exact temperature of water just as the ancients taught. This sounds like magic, but it actually is quite simple: water boiling at sea level looks different at each stage of its progress toward boiling. The following chart was adapted from the classic *Records on Tea*, but can of course be applied to any type of food preparation:

Shrimp eyes (xiāyǎn 蝦眼): Very tiny bubbles form at the bottom of the pan at 158°F to 176°F

Crab eyes (xièyǎn 蟹眼): Bubbles grow slightly larger and gentle wisps of steam rise at 176°F to 185°F

Fish eyes (yúyǎn 魚眼): Bubbles grow larger still and start to float to the top at 185°F to 194°F

Rope of pearls (liánzhū 連珠): Bubbles turn into wide streams that break the surface at 194°F to 203°F

Raging torrents and thundering waves (shēngpō gǔlàng 勝波鼓浪): A full rolling boil at 203°F to 212°F

THE YANGTZE RIVER & ITS ENVIRONS

HUAI YANG · JIANGSU · SHANGHAI · ZHEJIANG · NORTHERN FUJIAN
ANHUI · HENAN · HUBEI · JIANGXI

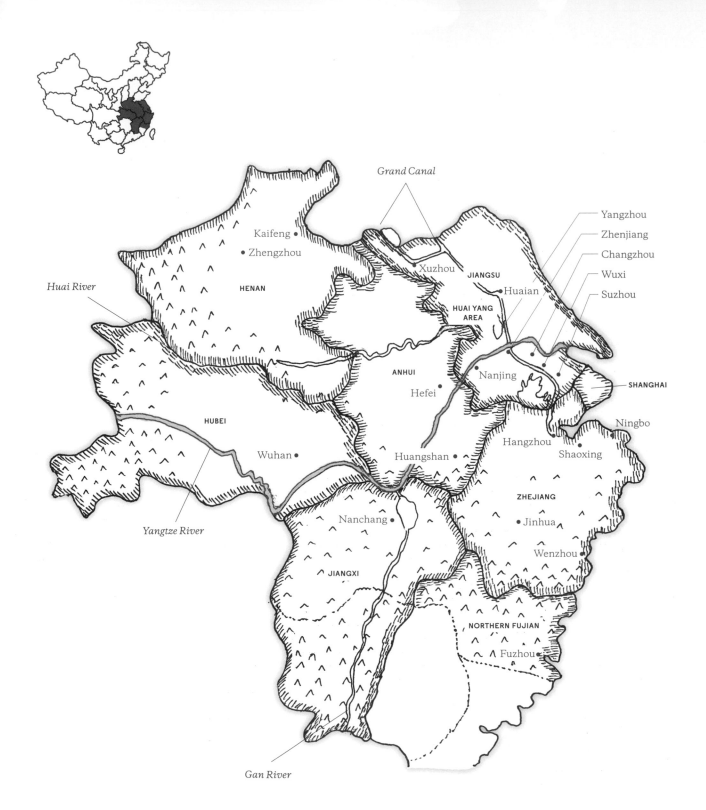

Grand Canal

Yangzhou
Zhenjiang
Changzhou
Wuxi
Suzhou

Huai River

Kaifeng
Zhengzhou

HENAN

Xuzhou

JIANGSU

Huaian

HUAI YANG
AREA

ANHUI

Hefei

Nanjing

SHANGHAI

Wuhan

HUBEI

Huangshan

Hangzhou

Shaoxing

Ningbo

Yangtze River

ZHEJIANG

Jinhua

Nanchang

Wenzhou

JIANGXI

NORTHERN FUJIAN

Fuzhou

Gan River

"Above is Heaven, and below is Suzhou and Hangzhou."

上有天堂，下有蘇杭。

—(SONG) FAN CHENGDA, *ANNALS OF THE WU REGION* (1192)

If China's food culture were to have an epicenter, it would no doubt be located somewhere near the lower reaches of the Yangtze River. Half of China's Eight Great Cuisines are found here, and China's gourmet elite have long held the region in high regard.[1] The Yangtze is also the traditional dividing line between North and South, which means that inspiration from all over the country can be found here, from the most ancient cooking techniques of Henan and Shandong to the cutting-edge dishes of cosmopolitan Shanghai.

The Yangtze[2] begins in Sichuan's massive mountain ranges, then gathers strength as it travels across the breadth of China before joining the Pacific at Shanghai. The Chinese call it the "Long River" because it stretches across so much of the country. It is deep enough for seagoing

---

1. During the Ming and Qing dynasties, Chinese food scholars divided their culinary traditions into four broad categories: Shandong, Suzhou (Jiangsu), Guangdong, and Sichuan. These were expanded and redefined in the late nineteenth century, creating the Eight Great Cuisines we know today. Jiangsu, Zhejiang, Anhui, and Fujian are the Great Cuisines found in the lower Yangtze region. The other Great Cuisines are Shandong, Guangdong, Hunan, and Sichuan. All eight cuisines highlight Han Chinese tastes and aesthetics—minority cuisines have traditionally not been included.

2. The Yangtze's name evolved out of a mistake. Foreign travelers to Zhejiang and Jiangsu named the river after a harbor there, Yangzijin. After a while, even the Chinese called the lower reaches of the river—from Nanjing down to Shanghai—Yángzi Jiāng 揚子江, or the "Yangtze River." Nowadays, however, the Chinese call the entire river Cháng Jiāng 長江 (Long River).

vessels to sail a thousand miles upriver, and, as a result, communities along the Yangtze have long been able to trade and interact. This is reflected in the shared interests of their cuisines: freshwater fish and crustaceans, tender bamboo shoots, mild vinegars, and rice wines. The Yangtze sensibility is particularly notable in dishes such as Fried Fish in a Sea Moss Batter (page 102), Freshwater Eels with Yellow Chives (page 109), and West Lake Piquant Fish (page 101).

Pork and poultry are central to all of the Yangtze area's cuisines, too. They are usually cooked until tender and juicy and infused with flavor via marinades, dry rubs, smoke, and braises. The region's favorite seasonings are fresh ginger, salt, and green onions, as well as soy sauce, vinegar, and the local Shaoxing rice wine. Vegetable dishes are unaffected and fresh, and pickles brighten up everything from meats to starches. The emphasis here is almost always on pure, natural flavors or simple, elegant combinations.

More than any other part of China, the Yangtze region is also home to many diverse vegetarian cuisines, called *sùcài* 素菜 or *zhāishí* 齋食, which are designed for followers of Mahayana Buddhism. Popular vegetarian dishes include Four Happiness Gluten and Vegetables (page 124) and Vegetarian Goose (page 82). Some cooks even go so far as to follow vegan precepts, which require that no animal products of any kind be consumed. Other adherents of Chinese Buddhism forbid the consumption of strong-smelling produce, such as chives,

onions, chilies, and garlic. This is based on the teachings of the Surangama Sutra, as well as the belief that aromatics such as these incite powerful, destructive emotions and attract the attention of evil spirits.

The most sophisticated of all the region's cuisines, though, grew out of the idyllic landscape in northern Jiangsu. We'll begin our tour of the foods of the lower Yangtze there, with a look at Huai Yang cuisine.

HUAI YANG

Named after the Huai and Yangtze Rivers that sandwich the area, the lush and verdant lands of the Huai Yang are auspiciously located near the Grand Canal, which flows between Beijing to the north and Hangzhou to the south. Much of the cuisine in the area is centered in the city of Yangzhou, which was a major trading center for salt until the nineteenth century. As a result, the city was home to many salt brokers, and they helped turn it into a lavish place to live and to eat as early as a thousand years ago.

Similar in many ways to the foods of the province of Jiangsu that surrounds it, Huai Yang cuisine emphasizes the flavors of Shaoxing wine and black mushrooms. Pork, freshwater fish, bean curd, vegetables, and the little steamed pork buns called Xiaolongbao (page 132) all reach sublime heights here. Yangzhou-Style Lion Heads (page 96), Crystalline Jellied Pork (page 90), and Molded Ham, Chicken, and Bean Curd Shreds (page 126) are also local favorites.

JIANGSU

Situated for the most part on the Yangtze plains, this province is so webbed with canals that the Chinese often refer to it as "the land of water." Its most important city is Suzhou, which is often called the Venice of the East. Suzhou is known for its food as well as its waterways, and deeply seasoned dishes like Suzhou "Smoked" Fish (page 85) and Vegetarian Dongpo Pork (page 79) encapsulate many of its refined aesthetics. Just to the west of Suzhou is Wuxi, a city that is split in half by Lake Tai. Long a hub for business and commerce, Wuxi's culinary highlights include many dishes with a sweet edge, such as Wuxi Spareribs (page 119). And finally, there is Nanjing, which was founded around the time of Christ and reached its apex during the Tang dynasty. Even then, the city was recognized as an exceptional culinary nerve center. Take, for example, this assessment of Nanjing banquets from scholar-official Tao Gu in the mid-900s:

> The pickled mustard greens [are so shiny they] could reflect one's face, the wonton broth [so clear it] could be used to wet an inkstone, and the crêpes [so thin that] words could be read [through them]; each grain of rice is distinct yet soft and chewy, the pasta tensile enough to act as a belt, the vinegar delicious enough to drink as wine, and the fried pastries so crisp they could startle a person five kilometers away.

Today the city has over 8 million residents, and it is still considered an excellent place to go out eating. Good examples of the local repertoire are Nanjing Saltwater Duck (page 113) and Drunken Eggs with Molten Centers (page 84).

SHANGHAI

Problems arise whenever anyone tries to define the tastes and textures of Shanghainese food. Lying at the confluence of so many cuisines—at the mouth of the Yangtze, next to the Pacific, near the Grand Canal, and within a stone's throw of all sorts of railways and highways—the dishes here seem to be the children of a thousand mothers. But, in fact, Shanghainese cuisine was developed upon a strong foundation of Jiangsu and Zhejiang culinary principles, along with direct influences from the Huangshan (Yellow Mountain) area in Anhui Province.

The Shanghainese refer to their way of cooking as "our gang's food." The cuisine is highly seasonal and prominently features saltwater and freshwater fish. The best local dishes are often seasoned with toasted green onions, which lend a deep savoriness to many recipes. Examples of these include Fried Green Onion Noodles (page 134) and Slow-Braised Bok Choy (page 125), as well as Cold Braised Little Fish with Green Onions (page 86), in which small saltwater fish no longer than four inches are cooked in a slightly

vinegary sauce so slowly that their bones dissolve. Western influences can be found in this international port, too, with catsup added to certain sauces, as in Bombs over Tokyo (page 106).

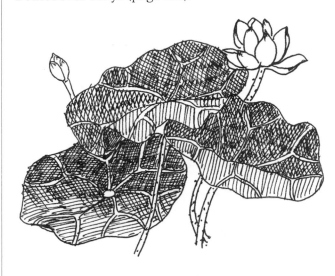

ZHEJIANG

This beautiful land is often referred to in Chinese as "Heaven on Earth," and such a description could easily be applied to its food culture. The Grand Canal ends here, in the former national capital of Hangzhou. As a result, Hangzhou has always been an important culinary nexus. A handful of other major food cities in Zhejiang possess their own bodies of recipes, including the seaside town of Ningbo, the more inland city of Shaoxing (most famous for its sherry-like rice wines), and the rather isolated coastal town of Wenzhou at the mouth of the Ou River.

Many of Zhejiang's most breathtaking dishes, like Stir-Fried Shrimp with Longjing Tea (page 104), are paeans to seafood. But Zhejiang also has a number of popular freshwater fish dishes, such as Sister-in-Law Song's Fish Chowder (page 93). Pork and poultry are treated with almost reverential care here and are usually cooked until perfectly tender, as in Braised Tendons with Dried Shrimp Roe (page 120).

NORTHERN FUJIAN

Fujian cuisine is considered one of the Eight Great Cuisines of China, but the foods of Southern Fujian are so different from those of the north that they are considered here as part of Region 3, the Coastal Southeast (see page 153). Known for its seafood and delicious fresh fruit, the cuisine of the northern coast—from the edge of Zhejiang all the way down past Fuzhou—tends to be very light and slightly sweet, and so it rightly belongs here, alongside its Yangtze River brethren.

One seasoning in particular is emblematic of Northern Fujian cuisine: red wine lees (page 418). This beautiful creation becomes the basis for rich, aromatic sauces for pork, poultry, and seafood, as well as red fermented bean curd "cheese" (page 420). It is particularly notable in the crunchy fritters known as Drunken Scarlet Eels (page 108). Other common seasonings in Northern Fujian foods are black vinegar, Shaoxing rice wine, and fish sauce.

A unique and important ingredient in Northern Fujian are the paper-like sheets called "swallow's skin" (*yànpí* 燕皮). Made from a paste of pounded pork shanks rather than flour—but still tasting more like pasta than anything else—these wonton wrappers resemble large wafers. Another notable ingredient here is sticky rice, which—in addition to being the main ingredient of the local rice wine—finds its way into all sorts of culinary creations, both sweet and savory, including Lotus Leaf Eight Treasure Rice (page 142).

Anhui, Henan, Hubei, and Jiangxi are grouped together at the end of this discussion because their cooking styles can be viewed as a viable sub-branch of this region. Located far from the ocean, these four landlocked provinces feature many delicious ways of preparing freshwater fish, as well as red meats, poultry, and bean curd. The influence of the spicy Central Highlands (page 243) can be tasted in the local tinglings of chili peppers, which increase in both heat and quantity as one heads south- and westward. But northern flavors show up here, too—particularly in the local noodles and the occasional lamb dish.

ANHUI

Anhui cuisine is probably the least well known of the Eight Great Cuisines. Connected to the North China Plain in its upper regions, this province is located right next to Henan, where China's civilization first took hold. Like Yangzhou, Anhui became involved in the incredibly lucrative salt trade, and this made it a hotbed for fine dining. One of the products of this era is a remarkable dish known as Wuwei Smoked Duck (page 112).

Food in Anhui tends to feature a lot of powerful, ripe flavors, as well as fermented and cured ingredients. Dry-cured hams are often used to season the local dishes, as in Chestnut Bean Curd (page 128). Some food connoisseurs here claim that the culinary classics farther downstream in Jiangsu and Zhejiang owe much to Anhui, including Yangzhou-Style Lion Heads (page 96) and Crab Shell Pastries (page 130).

HENAN

This ancient land is known as "the mother of the Eight Great Cuisines." Over the millennia, a cuisine developed here that is a celebration of northern and southern aesthetics. Although the top part of Henan is located far enough above the Yangtze to share North China's deep-rooted preference for pasta and bread, dishes in southern Henan tend to feature the rice and fresh fish of its river valleys.

The condiments and flavorings that are most often used in Henan—ginger, garlic, Sichuan peppercorns, sesame paste, aged vinegar, and green onions—are similar to those used along the Yangtze River. As in the rest of the region, freshwater fish are the stars of the local cuisine, along with pork, poultry, and bean curd. In the upper areas that are part of the North China Plain, lamb becomes the meat of choice, as evidenced in the recipe for Huaidian Smoked Lamb (page 121).

HUBEI

Called "the land of a thousand lakes," much of this humid, subtropical area is fertilized by the Yangtze. The capital city of Wuhan has existed longer than Xi'an and Beijing, and the wealthy have lived here in comfort for centuries, cultivating a refined cuisine. Freshwater fish from the rivers that flow past this city are featured in almost every full meal; in fact, this one ingredient dominates all discussion of the local cuisine. Seasonings tend to be gentle and highlight the sweet flavors of the local catch.

Apart from its fish, Hubei is well known for its Pearl Meatballs (page 116). The recipe for this dish features a mixture of sticky rice, fish, and pork, thereby satisfying two of the local stipulations for a proper meal: "If there's no soup, there is no meal; if there is no fish, there is no meal; if there are no meatballs, there is no meal." But if one ingredient encapsulates the flavors of Hubei, it is the lotus root. Enshrined in such local dishes as hearty Lotus Root and Pork Rib Soup (page 92), this beautifully patterned vegetable adds a wonderful crispness to many recipes here.

JIANGXI

Just to the east of Hubei is Jiangxi. This province is edged by the wide Yangtze and so, like many other cuisines in this area, rice and freshwater fish play a huge role in the local recipes. Also contributing to this area's cuisine are the thriving Hakka neighborhoods in the southern mountain ranges (their foods are discussed as part of the Coastal Southeast, page 153), and the communities farther east in the Central Highlands region (page 243) that favor spicier dishes.

Meats—particularly pork and poultry—are cured here in much the same way that they are in Hunan. These Hunan-inspired foods tend to be more heavily seasoned and fiery than those of Jiangxi's northerly neighbors. Another striking characteristic of Jiangxi's cuisine is its long-term love affair with bean curd (see Lively Bean Curd, page 127). In general, though, surrounded as it is by so many culinary powerhouses, the local foods here suggest a variety of influences. Historically, Jiangxi's cuisine has been described as "the head of Wu [Jiangsu] and the tail of Chu [Hunan], with ingredients from Guangdong as prepared in Fujian." The result is a very heady mix, as can be tasted in Three-Cup Chicken (page 204).

The director at Taipei's National Museum of History was the man responsible for teaching me how to properly appreciate the classic dishes of the lower Yangtze River Valley. Dr. Ho Hao-tien was a true gourmand, and over the five wonderful years when I worked with him at the museum, I tagged along whenever he took a foreign guest out to eat, which, fortunately, happened quite a lot. Dr. Ho was a native of Zhejiang, and so we often dined on the foods of both his homeland and neighboring Jiangsu, with regular detours into the cuisines of Hunan, Sichuan, and Beijing.

I had a cozy arrangement with the museum: I did not have to stay at the office all day as long as I got my work done on time. Back then, few foreigners remained in Taiwan after their initial year or two of language studies, so there were many interesting jobs

to be had. As a result, I would bang out my translations at the museum as fast as I could and then pick up work at other cultural institutions, such as the National Central Library next door. The director there, Prof. Wang Chen-ku, was also serious about eating, and both he and my immediate boss (and, later, good friend), Teresa Wang Chang, would often take me along for stellar business meals, too. With them, I got to eat completely different kinds of dishes, as they were respectively from Hebei and Anhui. The connection quickly became clear: the more work I had, the more I got to dine out.

By my fourth year there, I must have had ten different positions at the same time, which, in my mind, meant lots of delicious meals at a wide range of restaurants. I never had any problem balancing the different jobs until Dr. Ho invited the great Cambridge scholar Joseph Needham to the museum for a special banquet. When I entered the room, I found every one of my bosses staring up at me. Dr. Ho introduced me with my Chinese name by saying, "This is our interpreter, Fei Kailing." And then one after the other, each director laughed and said, "She's our interpreter, as well." I prayed that the floor would crack open between my feet and swallow me up, but no such luck. After wagging their fingers at me for what seemed a very long time, we got down to the serious business of toasting one another repeatedly and eating an exquisite meal put together by some of the best chefs on the island. My sins were absolved, at least for the moment. ●

THE RECIPES

V = VEGETARIAN OR VEGAN OPTION

Cōngyóu báiluóbōsī 蔥油白蘿蔔絲

Raw Radish Threads with Green Onion Oil

JIANGSU • SERVES 4 TO 6

This dish caught my eye when I was rearranging my cookbook shelves. It was the first recipe in a 1970s paperback by Huang Shaomo (writing under the pseudonym Yunlinyisou) called *How to Make the Famous Dishes of China* (*Zhōngguó míngcài cāozuòfǎ* 中國名菜操作法). I had never heard of the dish before, but it looked oddly intriguing, and I thought it was interesting that Mr. Huang had chosen it as the first recipe in his book. After making it myself, I learned why: it's brilliant.

This appetizer or side dish conveys the essence of the home-style cooking of Jiangsu Province, in which humble ingredients are treated simply, allowing their elemental flavors to shine. The dish is little more than shredded raw radish topped with green onions and hot oil. The original recipe calls for the football-shaped Chinese or Korean radish, but you can instead use Chinese icicle radishes or even colored Asian radishes.

1 white Chinese or Korean radish (2 pounds or so)
2 teaspoons sea salt
3 green onions, trimmed
¼ cup peanut or vegetable oil

1. Peel the radish and trim off the root end. If you are grating it by hand, leave on the stem end to act as a handle; otherwise, discard it.

2. Grate the radish either by hand or with a food processor. I personally prefer the long threads that are made with a Chinese grater, but not using one certainly isn't a deal breaker. Place the grated radish in a colander set in the sink or on a large plate. Toss the radish threads with the salt and let the moisture from the radish drip out over an hour or two.

3. Gently squeeze clumps of the radish threads between your hands to remove the remaining water and place the squeezed radish in a medium work bowl. Refrigerate the threads for at least an hour or two, so they are well chilled.

4. Slice the green onions as thinly as you can and place in a heatproof bowl. Heat the oil in a small saucepan or wok until it just barely starts to smoke and immediately pour it over the green onions. Use chopsticks to move the onions around in the hot oil so that they cook evenly, and then let the onions and oil come to room temperature.

5. Up to an hour before serving, thoroughly toss the radish threads with the onions and oil; taste and adjust the seasoning, if necessary.

Sù Dōngpō 素東坡

Vegetarian Dongpo Pork

JIANGSU · SERVES 4 TO 6

Part of the fun of the best Chinese meals is the element of surprise, of humor, of twisted expectations. For example, I often serve this dish, which looks like a huge hunk of pig flesh, to the vegetarians or vegans at my table, and wait for their horrified reaction. You can drag this out for a bit, depending on your mood, before telling them that what they have in front of them is actually a piece of winter melon, not pork belly.

The genius of this dish—which is a play on the name of the famous poet and gastronome Su Dongpo (page 114)—lies in the ability of winter melon to take on some of the attributes of pork. The rind that lies under the skin, for example, comes to resemble crispy, rich pork skin. And the melon flesh, too, when braised in a wine-and-spice-infused sauce, looks like meat and takes on a gentle suggestion of pork's buttery and savory flavors.

Winter melon is in season during the late summer, but it is available most of the year in areas with large Chinese populations. Because it can grow to a breathtaking size, it is often sold in chunks. You will want only one chunk, unless you are planning to feed and fool an army.

1-pound piece winter melon, as flat and as square
    as possible
½ cup peanut or vegetable oil
1 finger fresh ginger, thinly sliced (about ¼ cup)
2 green onions, trimmed and cut into 2-inch lengths
½ cup Shaoxing rice wine
¼ cup regular soy sauce
1 to 2 tablespoons rock sugar
2 star anise
½ stick cinnamon
¼ cup water

1. Scrape off any seeds and fibers in the winter melon, trim the edges so that they are even and white, and cut off the rind with a heavy knife—just trim off the green skin, and don't go too deeply into the flesh, as you want that slightly hard area under the green part to serve as your "pork rind." Then score that peeled area diagonally in a crosshatch pattern in lines about ½ inch apart and ½ inch deep. Wipe the squash dry with a paper towel so that it doesn't splatter when you fry it.

2. Heat the oil in a wok over medium-high heat until it starts to shimmer. A wooden chopstick inserted into the oil should immediately be covered with bubbles. Fry just the skin side of the melon until it is an even brown. Remove the melon to a small plate and drain out all but ¼ cup of the oil in the wok.

3. Heat the oil again over medium-high heat and stir-fry the ginger and green onions, then toss in the rest of the ingredients. Bring the mixture to a boil and add the winter melon to the wok, this time skin-side up. Reduce the heat to low and slowly simmer the winter melon for about an hour, turning it gently only two times while it is cooking. At this point you should be able to insert a wooden chopstick into the center very easily; cook for another 15 minutes so that your melon becomes deliciously soft, loses its squash flavor, and soaks up the sauce. Taste and adjust the seasoning.

4. You may serve the dish immediately by using 2 spatulas to carefully transfer the very tender melon to a plate. Strain the sauce, and if it is not yet syrupy, boil it over high heat until it's thick and glossy. Pour it around the melon and serve.

5. If you want to make this dish ahead of time, let both the winter melon and the strained sauce come to room temperature, place them in a container, and store covered in the refrigerator; steam (see page 49) the melon for about 10 minutes, until it is completely heated through, before serving.

Cōngkào fāyádòu 蔥燴發芽豆

Sprouted Fava Beans

SHANGHAI • SERVES 6 TO 8

Sprouted fava beans are quite popular in traditional Shanghai-style restaurants, where they usually accompany other light appetizers and tea or beer. These small dishes are meant to stimulate the palate and relax diners while the main meal is being prepared. Although rarely seen this side of the Pacific, Shanghai's silky sprouted favas are remarkably flavorful and the perfect way to begin a meal.

2 cups unpeeled dried fava beans (see Tips)
8 green onions, trimmed
½ cup peanut or vegetable oil
5 thin slices fresh ginger
2 tablespoons Shaoxing rice wine
1 cup water
2 tablespoons fish sauce (or to taste; see Tips for alternatives)
Toasted sesame oil, optional

1. Start this recipe about 5 days before you plan to serve it. Rinse the beans in a colander, place them in a medium work bowl, and cover them with at least 2 inches of cool tap water. Soak the beans for 24 hours to fully plump them up.

2. Drain the beans, dump them back in the bowl, and cover the bowl with a kitchen towel. Place the bowl in a slightly warm place like the kitchen counter, rinsing and draining the beans every 12 hours. Keep the beans covered and moistened this way until the vast majority of them have grown rootlets ¼ to ½ inch long, a process that will take 2 to 4 days. The beans can be prepared ahead of time up to this point and refrigerated in a resealable plastic bag for around 5 days.

3. Cut the green onions into ¼-inch lengths; you should have about 2 cups. Warm the oil in a saucepan, Chinese sandpot, or wok over medium heat until it starts to shimmer, then add the green onions. Stir the onions around and add the ginger. Lower the heat to medium-low and gently cook the green onions and ginger until they are browned, which will add a nice nuttiness to the sauce. Remove and reserve about half of the oil and green onions as garnish.

4. Add the sprouted beans, rice wine, water, and fish sauce to the pot, bring everything to a boil over high heat, and then cover the pot tightly and lower the heat to medium-low. Simmer the beans for 25 to 30 minutes, checking now and then to stir them and to ensure that the liquid has not been boiled off. Add some water if the beans are getting too dry.

5. When the beans are perfectly done, some of them will have split their casings and the meat of the beans will be soft. If there is still liquid left, quickly boil it down until the oil starts to bubble and spit. Pour both the beans and their sauce into a medium work bowl to cool them to room temperature. Add the reserved oil and onions and toss. Taste and adjust the seasoning. Refrigerate the beans overnight.

6. Serve the beans slightly chilled or at room temperature and sprinkle a bit of sesame oil on top, if you wish. The beans are traditionally picked up one by one with chopsticks, with the diner using his or her teeth to ease the bean out of its inedible casing. Discard the skin by plucking it from your lips with your chopsticks and you will look very proper.

The best place to find good-quality unpeeled dried fava beans is in a Middle Eastern market with a fast turnover.

I have added a touch of fish sauce here (and in some other recipes, for that matter), which is not traditional, but it supplies a wonderful layer of *xianwei* (savoriness and depth) that I love. Chicken stock (page 380) or mushroom stock (page 381) plus salt to taste is a suitable alternative.

Sōnghuā pídàn dòufǔ 松花皮蛋豆腐

Bean Curd with Pine Flower Preserved Eggs

HUBEI AND JIANGXI · SERVES 4 TO 6

2 or 3 preserved eggs

1 block (14 ounces or so) soft bean curd (see Tips)

2 tablespoons Sichuan pickled tuber

1 green onion, green parts only

2 tablespoons coarsely chopped cilantro

½ teaspoon sea salt

1 teaspoon sugar

1 teaspoon pale rice vinegar

1 teaspoon black vinegar

¼ cup toasted sesame oil

This is a classic East China hot-weather dish—another incredibly simple yet dazzling combination from the Yangtze River area. The one place my husband and I could always count on to do this dish right was a wonderful mid-priced restaurant in downtown Taipei, Fùxīngyuán 復興園. We became such regular customers there that, as soon as we walked in the door, the cook would prepare this dish just the way I liked it—with an extra egg—and it would be set on our table only seconds after we'd been poured hot tea.

Generally referred to as simply *pidan doufu*, or bean curd with preserved eggs, this dish relies on the quality of the ingredients, the perfect ratio of bean curd to egg, and the proper execution of the tangy sauce that tops it. The bean curd must be the soft, custardy type, and the preserved eggs should be of the pine flower (*songhua*) variety, meaning that crystalline patterns have formed under the shells (see page 480).

Preserved eggs get a bad rap because of their appearance and the touristy names associated with them: "thousand-year-old egg" or "century egg" or even "millennium egg." The fact is, they're not at all old, and they should be enjoyed while they are relatively fresh because they will dry out if left out for too long. When opened, the whites will have turned a clear, dark amber, and the yolks will be runny and grayish green but taste remarkably buttery.

1. Peel the eggs, rinse them gently to remove any tiny bits of shell, and slice them into thin wedges.

2. Bring a small saucepan half full of water to a boil and slip in the block of soft bean curd; bring the water to a boil again and then discard the water and carefully rinse the hot bean curd under cool tap water. Drain well and place on a cutting board. Cut the bean curd lengthwise in half and then cut it crosswise into thin pieces (⅛ to ¼ inch wide). Use your knife to gently lift up the fragile slices and fan them out on a rimmed serving plate. Arrange the sliced eggs on top.

3. Rinse the pickled tuber and chop it very finely. Thinly slice the onion greens. Scatter the pickled tuber, green onion, and cilantro over the top of the eggs. Boil the salt, sugar, vinegars, and sesame oil in a wok over high heat until they bubble furiously; taste this mixture and adjust as necessary, then drizzle it over the greens to wilt them. Serve slightly warm.

You can use either "soft" or "extra-soft" bean curd here. But keep in mind that although the extra-soft kind will taste very good, it might look messier, as it tends to fall apart easily.

The bean curd is quickly blanched in this recipe to gently firm it up (so that it's easier to slice) and to remove any scent of the packaging.

Different areas of China make their own versions of this classic. In Taiwan, for example, the egg is often served whole over a square of tender bean curd. Pork fluff or shaved dried bonito (showing the old Japanese influence here) are then placed on top, often with a healthy drizzle of soy paste instead of the vinegar and hot oil.

Wǔbǎo sù'é 五寶素鵝

Vegetarian Goose

SHANGHAI • MAKES 2 GOOSE "BREASTS" AND
SERVES 6 TO 8

Vegetarian dishes in China are often named after ani-mals or cuts of meat. Some dishes, like this one, are only loosely related to the meat they reference. Others are startlingly similar in appearance to their name-sakes, such as Vegetarian Dongpo Pork (page 79).

Many of China's meatless creations rely on meat substitutes, like vegetarian chicken and ham, which are usually made out of balled-up soy skins (see page 489) that have been braised in a marinade. Most of these dishes are pretty tasty. But nowhere are they more exalted than along the Yangtze River, which has long been home to a large Buddhist population. The meatless dishes pioneered by the Buddhists there have become incredibly popular, even among carnivores. One of the most famous dishes is this one, Vegetarian Goose. You can vary the ingredients as you wish, but try to keep a nice balance of colors and textures, which might mean substituting something like wood ear fungus for the black mushrooms.

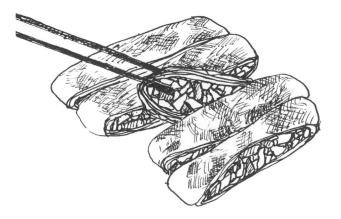

FILLING

3 black mushrooms, fresh or dried and plumped up
3 soy batons, soaked in hot water until soft,
    or 2 extra soy skins, shredded
¼ cup dried daylily flowers, soaked in boiling water until soft
½ cup julienned winter bamboo shoots, defrosted if frozen
    and peeled and blanched if fresh (see Tip, page 122)
1 medium carrot, peeled and julienned
2 tablespoons peanut or vegetable oil
1 tablespoon Sichuan pickled tuber, rinsed and julienned

SAUCE

¾ cup filtered mushroom soaking liquid
    or unsalted mushroom stock (page 381)
2 tablespoons regular soy sauce
2 tablespoons sugar
1 tablespoon toasted sesame oil

2 large soy skins (circles about 24 inches in diameter)
1 teaspoon cornstarch mixed with 2 teaspoons water
Peanut or vegetable oil for frying

1. Cut the stems off of the mushrooms, then slice the caps into thin julienne and place in a medium work bowl. Trim off and discard any tough pieces on the soy batons, then shred or cut the soft parts (or the extra soy skins) into thin julienne before tossing them in with the mushrooms. Drain the daylily flowers, pick out and discard any tough pieces, hand-shred the largest blossoms, and add them to the bowl along with the bamboo shoots and carrot.

2. To prepare the sauce, combine all of the ingredi-ents in a measuring cup and stir to dissolve the sugar.

3. To finish the filling, place a wok over high heat until it smokes a bit, then pour in the oil. Swirl the oil around and add the Sichuan tuber. Stir-fry quickly, tossing in all the vegetables. Pour in half the sauce and continue to stir-fry the vegetables until the sauce has been absorbed; taste and adjust the seasoning. Scrape the filling out into a medium work bowl, hollowing out the center to allow the steam to escape, and let the filling cool down until it is easy to handle, about 20 minutes.

4. For directions on filling and shaping the packets, follow the directions in the diagram below, using the soy skins and cornstarch paste.

5. To steam the packets, place them, seam-side down, directly in an oiled steamer (see page 49) without a plate (which would collect water). Steam them over medium heat for about 10 minutes, then remove them and let them cool to room temperature. The dish can be prepared ahead of time up to this point and refrigerated for up to 3 days.

6. Just before serving, warm a frying pan over medium heat until a flick of water immediately turns to steam, then film the bottom with oil. When the oil is hot, lay the packets, seam-side down, in the pan. Fry both sides, turning once, until golden brown and crispy. Cut into inch-wide slices and serve warm. No dipping sauce is needed.

VEGETARIAN GOOSE PACKETS

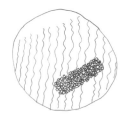

❶ Lay one of the soy skins on a flat surface and keep the other one completely covered in a plastic bag (they dry out and crack very quickly). Use a pastry brush to spread half of the sauce over the surface of the soy skin, except for the very top edge. Pile half of the filling in the center of the bottom half of the circle to make a firm rectangle approximately 8 × 4 inches.

❷ Fold the left and right sides over the filling and press down gently before folding the bottom edge up and over the filling.

❸ Continue to roll the packet up until you have a piece about 8 × 4 inches. Seal the edge with the cornstarch paste.

❹ Flatten the packet slightly with the palms of your hands, cover it carefully to keep it from drying out, and repeat this step with the other soy skin and the rest of the filling.

Tángxīn huādiāo zuìdàn 糖心花雕醉蛋

Drunken Eggs with Molten Centers

JIANGSU • MAKES 6 EGGS

In many boiled egg recipes, the whites get over-cooked and you end up with something that seems like a facsimile of a Ping-Pong ball. If you try to cook the eggs less, they tend to look soggy and runny and anything but appetizing. Fortunately, the folks in the Jiangsu capital of Nanjing have found the solution to this problem.

In this recipe, the whites are cooked for a mere thirty seconds, made to sit in the hot water for another three minutes, and then quickly cooled down. This gives the whites the texture of a tender custard, while the yolks balance that fine line between raw and cooked. Add to that a good dousing of Shaoxing rice wine and an infusion of dried salted plums, ginger, lemon zest, and whole peppercorns and you have a remarkably complex and textured dish.

6 large eggs, about a week old and at room temperature

1 cup water, plus more as needed

7 dried salted plums

1 inch fresh ginger, smashed with the side of a cleaver

1 tablespoon sea salt

1 teaspoon whole white or black peppercorns

Zest from ½ lemon, in wide strips

1 cup Shaoxing rice wine, plus more as needed

1. Start this recipe more than a day before you plan to serve it. Use a sharp tack or pin to poke a hole in the round end of the egg—just barely break through the shell without puncturing the inside of the egg (see page 461).

2. Put the eggs in a small saucepan and cover with cool tap water by about 1 inch. Place the pan uncovered on the stove and bring to a boil as you stir, which

will help center the yolks. *As soon as the water comes to a full boil, where big bubbles are bursting over the surface, start counting down 30 seconds.* At the end of 30 seconds, remove the pan from the heat, cover, and wait for exactly 3 minutes. Then immediately drain the eggs and cover them with cool tap water. Change the water a few times until it remains cool. Drain the eggs and lightly crack them all over with the back of a spoon, but don't remove the shell.

3. Rinse the saucepan, add the water, dried salted plums, ginger, salt, peppercorns, and lemon zest, and bring to a boil. Lower the heat to a bare simmer and cook the marinade for about 5 minutes. Let cool to room temperature and then add the rice wine.

4. Place the eggs in a tall, narrow container—this allows them to soak in as little marinade as possible. Pour the marinade over the eggs, cover, and refrigerate for a few hours. Add more rice wine if needed for the marinade to completely cover the eggs. When the eggs are cold, shell and return them to the marinade for 24 to 36 hours. If you are not eating them within 36 hours, remove the eggs from the marinade so they don't get too salty.

5. Serve the eggs as a simple appetizer by slicing them in half and serving on any light and refreshing vegetable, like microgreens or radish shoots or finely shredded leeks. Or serve them as a summer breakfast on hot toast, with noodles or Congee (page 226), or as a midnight snack.

You can play around with the flavorings, but be sure and to not use anything oily; the eggs should come across as clean and greaseless.

Traditionally this dish is made with fresh duck eggs, but because they are relatively difficult to find in the States, I've substituted large hen eggs. Feel free to use whatever type of eggs you like. However, do know that you'll have to experiment a bit in order to get the texture the way you want it, since the size of the egg will greatly affect the cooking time. The only thing I'd add is that your eggs should be organic and free range: the better quality egg you use, the better the result.

Sūshì xūnyú 蘇式薰魚

Suzhou "Smoked" Fish

JIANGSU • SERVES 4 TO 6

As you may have noticed, this section includes more appetizer recipes than any other in this book. That is because people from the lower reaches of the Yangtze—especially the literati and well-to-do—revel in leisurely dining. The "little dishes" here are meant to be lingered over, complemented by a cup of warm rice wine, hot green tea, or even the occasional beer (see page 87).

In Suzhou, the relaxed enjoyment of good food is a way of life. This appetizer, which is prepared in advance and served cold, is one of Suzhou's most famous fish dishes. It's not actually smoked, though it looks like it has spent some time in a smoker, which likely explains its name.

FISH AND MARINADE

1 whole mild-flavored, firm-fleshed fish,
    like pomfret or carp (1½ to 2 pounds)
3 green onions, trimmed
Walnut-sized piece of fresh ginger
2 star anise
¼ cup regular soy sauce
3 tablespoons Shaoxing rice wine
Peanut or vegetable oil for frying

SAUCE

2 green onions, trimmed
3 tablespoons Shaoxing rice wine
¼ cup regular soy sauce
½ cup water
6 tablespoons sugar
1 tablespoon five-spice powder (page 441 or store-bought)
1 tablespoon toasted sesame oil

1. Start this dish a day ahead of time. Clean and scale the fish. Gut it, cut off the head, fins, and tail, and rinse the fish carefully before patting it dry with a paper towel. Slice the fish crosswise into 1-inch-wide strips, cutting it on a sharp diagonal. Place the fish slices in a medium work bowl.

2. Smash the green onions and ginger with a wide knife and add them to the fish along with the star anise, soy sauce, and rice wine. Toss the fish with these ingredients and let it marinate in a cool place for at least 30 minutes and up to a couple of hours. Pour off and discard the marinade, then lightly pat the fish dry with a paper towel.

3. Pour about 1 inch of the oil into a wok and place it over medium heat. When hot, add about half of the slices to the wok, being careful not to crowd them. Gently shake the wok to keep the fish from sticking. Don't turn the slices over often, as they will break up once they are cooked. Instead, wait until one side is golden brown before gently flipping them over. Fry the other side until golden and remove the cooked fish to a clean plate. Repeat with the rest of the fish.

4. Skim any fried bits off of the oil and then set it over high heat until a wooden chopstick inserted into it immediately begins to bubble furiously and the oil shimmers. Add a few of the fish slices to the wok (be careful of any spattering) and carefully fry them until both sides are dark brown and crispy. Remove the slices and repeat with small batches of the rest of the fish.

5. Combine all the sauce ingredients in a medium saucepan, bring to a boil, and then simmer for 5 minutes. Remove from the heat and add the fried fish. Gently toss the fish in the sauce, let it come to room temperature, and then cover and refrigerate it. Whenever you think of it, turn the fish over so that every side is permeated with the sauce.

6. To serve, remove the fish from the marinade and pick off any ginger or onions clinging to it. Place the best-looking pieces on top and serve as is or topped with some finely shredded green onion.

Cōngkào xiǎoyú 蔥燽小魚

Cold Braised Little Fish with Green Onions

SHANGHAI AND ZHEJIANG · SERVES 4 TO 6

The reigning doyenne of Chinese cookbooks, Florence Lin, once reminisced to me about her mother making this dish for the family when she was still a child in Ningbo. Her mother didn't cook the dish often, she said, but once in a while she would make a big batch of these little fishes. The family would then leisurely eat them over the course of a week.

The traditional Shanghainese recipe for this dish calls for small crucian carp, which are close to impossible to find in the States. I have therefore come to rely, instead, on small croakers and drum fish. The vinegar slowly dissolves the bones of these fish, leaving delicate morsels to enjoy with a hot cup of rice wine. This is Yangtze cooking at its very best.

FISH

1 pound fresh or frozen small (4 inches or less) croakers or drum fish, with or without the heads but preferably not gutted (see Tips)

3 tablespoons Shaoxing rice wine

3 tablespoons regular soy sauce

3 tablespoons black vinegar

¾ cup peanut or vegetable oil (tea oil, discussed on page 437, is also good here)

SAUCE

¼ cup peeled and julienned ginger

2 bunches (about 12) green onions, trimmed and cut into 2-inch lengths

¼ cup Shaoxing rice wine

3 tablespoons regular soy sauce

2 tablespoons black vinegar

1 tablespoon rock sugar

3 cups boiling water

1 teaspoon toasted sesame oil

1. Make this dish a day before serving. Pat the fish dry with paper towels, leaving them whole and ungutted if you find roe inside them (see Tips). Place them in a large work bowl and toss them with the rice wine, soy sauce, and vinegar. Press the fish down lightly into the marinade so that they all get a chance to soak up the flavors. Let them marinate for at least 30 minutes and up to 1 hour at room temperature, gently tossing them whenever you think of it. This not only makes the flavors cleaner by removing excess water and extra fishiness, but it also colors the skin when the soy sauce caramelizes during the frying in the next step.

2. Have a medium-sized work bowl ready next to the stove. Place a flat, nonreactive (see Tips), heavy-bottomed frying pan over medium-high heat until it is very hot and then add the oil. When the oil starts to shimmer, drain the marinade off of the fish and discard. Remove the pan from the heat so that you don't get burned and gently but quickly lay about half of the fish, one at a time, in the hot oil—putting in only as many as will fit in a loose single layer on the bottom. Return the pan to the heat and fry the fish quickly on both sides until browned, using a spatter screen to protect yourself. When they are golden but not cooked through, gently lift them out of the pan and lay them in the bowl. Repeat with the rest of the fish.

3. When all of the fish have been browned, fry the ginger and green onions in the pan in the remaining oil until they are nicely browned, too. Don't skimp on the browning, as this is what gives the dish its distinctive flavor. Slide the fish on top of the ginger and green onions and add the remaining rice wine, soy sauce, vinegar, sugar, and water. Wait until the water has been added to the pan before trying to rearrange the fish, as they will then be happy to swim about in the sauce; shake the pan gently to evenly distribute them. Bring the pan to a full boil, and then lower the heat so that you have only the barest simmer. Cook the fish uncovered very slowly for about 3 hours, until the liquid has been reduced to a syrupy sauce. Gently swirl the pan now and then to make sure the fish are not sticking, but do not flip them over or fool around with them—they will break apart easily. Sprinkle on the sesame oil.

4. When the fish have come to room temperature, carefully slide them into a rimmed dish, arrange the cooked green onions and ginger on top, pour the sauce over everything, cover with plastic wrap, and refrigerate the fish overnight. Remove the fish from the refrigerator about an hour before serving so that the harsh chill dissipates. Since the vinegar will often dissolve the calcium in the bones, you might be able to eat the entire fish, but of course encourage caution in children and other people who might not fully understand this concept.

Try different varieties of fish to see what pleases you best. If you live near the ocean, check out the local catches for tasty varieties.

If your fish have small scales, you can probably skip scaling them, as their scales will dissolve in the vinegar.

Some East Asian markets have small fish in their frozen section, which can be quite good. Try to use sustainable varieties; the Monterey Bay Aquarium has a great website called Seafood Watch that is very helpful in this regard.

If you happen to luck onto fish that are filled with roe, do not gut them or open them up in any way, as the eggs will pour out into the frying oil and be ruined. Instead, after cooking, eat as the Chinese do: suck out the roe as a special treat and then eat around the guts, which often will become virtually nonexistent after frying. This is much more pleasurable than it sounds.

Use a nonreactive pan here—stainless steel is good—because the vinegar is an acid that will corrode things like iron, giving the food a metallic taste.

ONE OF THE PERENNIAL DRAWS OF AN OLD-school Shanghainese restaurant is the lavish, delicatessen-style army of cold dishes always arrayed near its front counter. Many of this region's appetizers would feel right at home in such a glass case: Drunken Chicken (page 89), Suzhou "Smoked" Fish (page 85), Sprouted Fava Beans (page 80), and Four Happiness Gluten and Vegetables (page 124) are good examples.

Called *péntóucài* 盆頭菜 (basins of food) in the local dialect, these are the kinds of dishes that chefs whip up as soon as they get to work. Even before

refrigeration was common, appetizers like these were savory enough to sit out for a day and still be perfect for the most discerning diners.

Many of this region's entrées are braised or slow cooked, meaning that much of a restaurant's menu can be prepared days ahead of time; the chefs need only to heat dishes up when an order comes in. Braised meat dishes in particular taste better if they are allowed to sit around for a while, and so the combination of *pentoucai* with slow-cooked meats makes this region's cuisine very chef-friendly.

A number of this region's appetizers also work wonderfully as the basic components for a simple lunch: hot steamed rice or noodle soup can be topped with whatever is handy, like the "smoked" fish or braised gluten. Many of my favorite restaurants in Taipei even had the rice ready to go in the form of Crusty Vegetable Rice (page 131). If we happened to drop by with a bunch of people for a more lavish meal, all the chef had to do was flash-fry some pea shoots and toss together a hot soup. Need I point out that this template makes fancy dinners at home a breeze, too?

Gānshāo yúxiàba 乾燒魚下巴

Soy-Braised Fish Collar

SHANGHAI · SERVES 4

In the West, fish heads are predestined for the cat or the garbage can. With a big fish head, though—and I'm talking about something that is at least a pound in size—there's a lot of acreage you can work with. The head and collar of a fish have the most interesting musculature of the entire body. They are also full of nooks and crannies, and this dynamic texture captures whatever seasoning you use in interesting ways.

In this dish, a family favorite that I devised a long time ago after tasting it during a luxurious banquet, the area just behind the fish head—called the "collar" in English and the "chin" in Chinese—is braised until it caramelizes. The sauce is dark and sticky and features green onion, ginger, and rice wine.

4 halves (about 2 pounds) very fresh collar from a
    wild-caught amberjack (aka hamachi)
    or other firm-fleshed yet mild large sea fish
6 tablespoons peanut or vegetable oil
5 tablespoons thinly sliced fresh ginger
2 cups cut-up green onions, in 1-inch lengths
6 tablespoons regular soy sauce
4 tablespoons (or so) crushed rock sugar or brown slab sugar
½ cup Shaoxing rice wine, divided in half

1. Rinse the collars carefully under cool running water, making sure that all viscera and gills have been removed. Thoroughly scrape off all scales under running water. Carefully go over the skin a couple of times with a paring knife to ensure that it is scale free, since the skin is delicious and those tiny scales will ruin everything. Pat the collars very dry with a paper towel so they will fry in the oil rather than steam.

2. Heat the oil in a large, flat-bottomed frying pan over medium-high heat until a small piece of ginger immediately sizzles when added. Place the ginger and the collars skin-side down in the hot oil. Sear the collars on one side without moving them so that a light crust is formed (page 454). Shake the pan and flip the collars over. Add the green onions and shake the pan so that they shimmy down under the fish. When the second side of the fish is golden, too, add the soy sauce, sugar, and half of the rice wine. Reduce the heat to low, cover the pan, and let the fish slowly cook for about 10 minutes. Uncover the pan, raise the heat to medium-high, and when the sauce has been reduced to a heavy syrup, gently turn the fish over and add the other half of the rice wine. Cook uncovered until the sauce has once again been reduced to the consistency of honey; you will be able to smell caramel as the sauce reaches its perfect state of gooeyness. The fish may be prepared ahead of time up to this point and gently reheated under the broiler in the final step.

3. Remove from the heat and place the fish skin-side up on a lightly oiled broiler pan. Scrape all of the sauce and ginger and onions onto the fish. Broil the fish a few inches from the coils until the edges have caramelized and the sauce is very sticky.

Asian markets often have a wonderful array of fish, including varieties and cuts that Western markets might not offer.

If you decide to plunge in and prepare a fish head, just substitute one whole fish head for the four collar halves. Split (or have your fishmonger split) the head down the middle and remove the gills. Rinse the head, scale the skin carefully, pat it dry, and proceed as with the collar.

Rock sugar (as well as other solid sugars like Chinese brown slab) is the secret to obtaining the luxurious mouthfeel of many Chinese sauces; it melts into a silky layer that does not leave a sour aftertaste, which white sugar tends to do.

Zuìjī 醉雞

Drunken Chicken

JIANGSU · SERVES 4 TO 6

My museum boss in Taipei was from East China, and he knew everything about that area's food. We would often spend long business lunches working our way through most of what a given chef had to offer. Almost every banquet he took me to started out with something that was "drunken," which meant that it had been soaked in Shaoxing rice wine. My favorite was always this chicken recipe.

It is not hard to understand why: juicy poached chicken is lightly seasoned with salt and spices, and then rice wine is added to its rich broth. The chicken rests in this heady sauce, absorbing all the flavors. A sparkling aspic adds an alcoholic punch to the dish, so that the first taste on the tongue is like a chilled glass of sherry. Bright red wolfberries lend a touch of sweetness and color to this magnificently simple recipe.

2 boneless chicken breasts
Boiling water and ice water, as needed
½ cup Shaoxing rice wine
1 cup unsalted chicken stock (page 380); if not naturally
    jelled from skin, add ½ envelope (1¼ teaspoons)
    powdered gelatin
1 tablespoon ginger juice (page 481)
¼ piece brown slab sugar or small piece
    (about 2 teaspoons) rock sugar
Mushroom powder or sea salt to taste
2 tablespoons wolfberries

1. Early on the day you wish to serve this, pat the chicken dry and trim off any excess fat. Place the meat in a small saucepan and cover it with boiling water. Poach gently over medium-low heat for 20 minutes and then remove the chicken. Save the stock for something else and plunge the meat into a bowl of ice water while you prepare the rest of the ingredients.

2. While the meat is cooking and cooling, pour the rice wine and stock into a medium saucepan. Add the ginger juice and sugar, as well as mushroom powder or salt to taste. Bring the stock to a boil, add the wolfberries, and simmer gently for about 2 minutes. Cool to room temperature.

3. Place the cooked meat in a lidded container, pour in the cooled stock, cover, and refrigerate for at least 4 hours and up to 1 day. Do not prepare more than 1 day before serving or the texture of the meat will turn powdery.

4. To serve, remove the chicken from the marinade and slice into ½-inch-wide pieces, keeping as much of the aspic attached to the meat as possible. Arrange attractively on a plate, sprinkle the chicken with the plumped-up wolfberries, and garnish as desired.

Shuǐjīng yáoròu 水晶肴肉

Crystalline Jellied Pork

HUAI YANG · SERVES 8 TO 10

It is said that on a hot summer day three centuries ago, the owner of a pub on Jiuhai Jie (the aptly named "Ocean of Wine Street") in the city of Zhenjiang brought four pork shanks back to his shop in order to cure them. Instead of salt, however, he grabbed the saltpeter his father-in-law used to make firecrackers and rubbed it into the meat. The saltpeter cured the pork beautifully and the result was an instant classic.

Nowadays, this dish is still sometimes called "saltpeter pork" (*xiāoròu* 硝肉), although pink curing salt (page 486) is more commonly used. When done right, the dish is composed of flecks of rosy pork bound in a flavorful aspic. The spices, herbs, and wine are perfectly balanced, and the pork is juicy. Little saucers of Zhenjiang's finest black vinegar and peaked mounds of finely shredded ginger traditionally accompany this appetizer. A cup of warm Shaoxing rice wine is all that is needed to complete the picture.

My love for this dish is what inspired me to truly delve into the study of Chinese cooking. Over the years, I have spent a whole lot of time trying to re-create this wonder as it first appeared to me, and I think I've come pretty close. It takes a bit of time and effort, but everything can be done leisurely over a number of days. I encourage you to try it: this one is a showstopper.

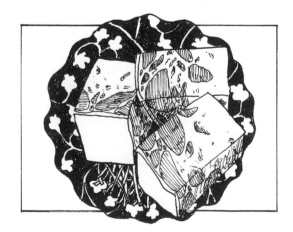

PORK AND RUB

1 excellent-quality front pork leg shank with skin on; bone out, if possible

1 tablespoon Shaoxing rice wine

⅛ teaspoon pink salt

1 tablespoon coarse sea salt

STOCK

2 star anise

2 teaspoons whole Sichuan peppercorns

6 slices fresh ginger

3 green onions, trimmed

Boiling water, as needed

1 tablespoon coarse sea salt

Pinch of alum

½ cup Shaoxing rice wine

JELLY

2¼ cups pork stock from Step 3, divided into ¾ cup and 1½ cups

6 tablespoons Shaoxing rice wine

1 tablespoon ginger juice (page 481)

3 envelopes (¼ ounce each) powdered gelatin

Pinch of alum

1 teaspoon sugar

Lard, melted and cooled, if making ahead

DIPPING SAUCE (PER PERSON)

1 tablespoon finely shredded fresh ginger (young white ginger is best)

2 tablespoons black vinegar

1. Start this recipe at least 5 days before serving. Pat the shank dry with a paper towel and place it on a clean working surface. If the bone is still in the shank, slice down the thinnest side of the shank, which would be its front; use a boning knife to cut the meat and tendons carefully away from the bone (see page 459), and use the bone for something else.

2. Remove any hairs with heavy-duty tweezers or needle-nose pliers (see page 459). Do your best to get rid of them by holding the skin up against the light to locate any finer hairs. (This might take some time, so get yourself comfortable and do as good a job as you can. You will be able to go over the skin once more when it is cooked.) Place the boned shank skin-side up on a cutting board, and use a sharp paring knife to stab the skin side repeatedly until you have little holes all over, about 1 inch apart. Place the rice wine in a small bowl and add both the pink salt and the sea salt. Rub this mixture all over the meat and skin, especially in the holes, before placing the pork in a resealable plastic bag. Refrigerate the pork for 3 days, turning the bag over occasionally and massaging the meat and skin from outside the bag. The pork will turn a nice rosy color when it is ready.

3. Place the meat and skin in a colander and carefully rinse off the entire cure, rubbing the pork lightly as you clean it. Transfer the pork to a work bowl, cover with cool tap water, and let it soak for about an hour to get rid of most of the pink salt. Bring a wide pot of water to a boil and blanch the pork for 3 to 5 minutes. While the pork is blanching, place the star anise, peppercorns, ginger, and green onions in a cheesecloth bag or mesh ball. Empty out the water and clean the pot. Set a small trivet in the bottom of the pot to keep the pork from sticking to the bottom or burning, and arrange the pork on the trivet with the meat side facing up. Add the cheesecloth sachet to the pot. Cover the pork with boiling water and add the salt, alum, and rice wine. Bring to a boil, again uncovered, and then lower the heat to a gentle simmer. Cook the pork uncovered for 30 minutes and then turn the meat over so the skin side is on top. (If there are still hairs sticking out of the skin, remove them with tweezers at this point.) Continue to cook the meat uncovered for another 3 hours, adding more boiling water as necessary, until the skin is as soft and relaxed as a piece of wet silk. Remove the meat and skin to a work bowl and let them cool down until easy to handle but not yet cold. Discard the sachet of spices. While the meat and skin are cooling off, pour the stock through a fine-mesh sieve into a large measuring cup or work bowl. Cool the stock to room temperature and skim off the fat.

4. Use a small loaf pan (about 4-cup capacity) to hold the jellied pork. First, take the skin and lay it fat-side up on a cutting board. Cut off and discard all of the fat, veins, and mushy parts so that you have only a thin, beige layer left. Trim the soft pork skin as necessary to make it fit into the bottom of the pan, with the fat side of the skin facing up. Rip the pork meat into fine shreds, discarding any fat or sinews. Scatter the pork evenly over the top of the skin.

5. To make the jelly, measure out ¾ cup of the cooled stock and add both the rice wine and ginger juice. Sprinkle the powdered gelatin on top and let it soften while you heat up the remaining 1½ cups stock in a small saucepan. Add the alum and sugar to the hot stock, bring it to a boil, then remove from the heat and use a silicone spatula to stir in the softened gelatin mixture. Stir until the gelatin dissolves completely. Taste and adjust the seasoning, then pour the stock over the shredded pork. Use your spatula to gently poke the pork and fluff it up a bit in the stock so that shards of pork are suspended in the jelly. Let the jelly come to room temperature before covering the pan with plastic wrap and refrigerating it overnight. Any extra stock can be frozen and used the next time you make this aspic, or you can use it as any other pork stock. If you will not be serving the pork for 3 days, pour a thin layer of melted lard on top of the solid jelly to keep it from molding.

6. Just before serving, scrape off and discard any fat that has collected on the surface. Unmold the pan by rinsing the bottom and sides with hot tap water until the aspic comes loose but is not yet melting. Invert a plate on top of the pan and invert the pan onto the plate. Then cut the jellied pork from the top into pieces about 1 inch square on top and 2 inches thick, so that each piece has a bit of the skin at one end. Arrange the rectangles on a serving plate—these can be stacked, if you wish, or arrayed in a sunburst pattern. Serve this very cold and on a chilled plate. Place big pinches of the ginger on small sauce dishes, drizzle the vinegar around the ginger so that it stays white, and serve. Dip each piece of the jellied pork into the vinegar and arrange a few strands of the ginger on top before eating.

Lián'ǒu páigǔ tāng 蓮藕排骨湯

Lotus Root and Pork Rib Soup

HUBEI · SERVES 4 TO 6

Hubei is so speckled with still bodies of water that it is sometimes called "The Land of Fish and Rice." And the name is apt, for fishing is a major part of Hubei culture and fish is featured at almost every meal. But another important resource is harvested in those ponds, as well: lotuses.

Pink lotus blossoms cover the lakes and ponds of Hubei in high summer. Their leaves are gathered around this time and used as scented wrappers for pork and chicken (page 286) or desserts (page 142). Also harvested are the heavy green pods filled with ivory seeds that can be found after the flowers have faded. These seeds are soft and delicate when fresh and starchy when dried. The greatest harvest of all, though, happens after the leaves have died and cold winds send the plants into hibernation. This is when the long, white rhizomes are dug up.

Harvesting these rhizomes is backbreaking work. The roots are hidden under layers of thick, cold, gray mud, and workers have to gently feel around with their feet for the roots, then pull them out without breaking them. The most prized rhizomes are the fat, long, juicy specimens that are almost meaty. They are delicious in this hearty soup, which is best served in late autumn or early winter, the peak of the lotus root season.

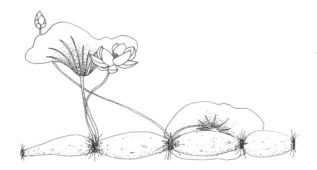

½ side of pork ribs or a pork neck (about 1¼ pounds)
Peanut or vegetable oil
2 inches fresh ginger
3 to 4 green onions, trimmed
Boiling water, as needed
¼ cup Shaoxing rice wine
Sea salt to taste
Freshly ground black pepper
2 lotus roots
1 green onion, trimmed and finely chopped
Handful of cilantro, coarsely chopped

1. Start this recipe at least a day before you want to serve it. Whack the meat into smallish pieces to expose the marrow. Pour ½ inch or so of oil in a frying pan and place it over medium-high heat, and then brown the meat on all sides before removing it to a stockpot.

2. Brown the ginger in the pan and add it to the pork. Add the whole green onions and cover the ribs with the boiling water. Pour in the rice wine before bringing everything to a full boil. Lower the heat to a gentle simmer. Cook uncovered for about an hour, until the meat is very tender. Keep the soup in a cool place overnight.

3. The next day, skim off the fat and discard along with the limp cooked onions and ginger. Bring the soup to a boil; add the salt and pepper to taste and adjust the seasoning as desired.

4. Peel and clean the lotus roots (see page 451) and roll cut them (see page 449) into pieces about 1 inch wide. If you notice any mud at all inside the roots, wash it off carefully. Add the lotus roots to the soup and bring it to a boil again before lowering the heat to a simmer. Cook the lotus roots until tender, about 30 minutes. Portion out the soup into large individual bowls, sprinkle them with the chopped green onions and cilantro, and serve hot.

Sòngsǎo yúgēng 宋嫂魚羹

Sister-in-Law Song's Fish Chowder

ZHEJIANG · SERVES 4

Light and delicious, this fish chowder is a classic recipe from old Hangzhou, the capital of Zhejiang Province. The dish has a lot of history behind it, with the earliest written reference to it appearing some eight hundred years ago. At first glance it seems like a complicated recipe, but it is actually quite easy to put together.

First and foremost, you must have a good freshwater fish. Its fresh sweetness is key in terms of bringing out the qualities of the other ingredients. You will also find crunchy bamboo shoots in here, which provide just the right textural component, while mushrooms and ham add their own savory flavors to the mix. The beauty of this chowder is breathtaking when it's prepared correctly.

12 ounces firm white freshwater fish, like carp;
    mild sea fish like bass can also be used
1 tablespoon ginger juice (page 481)
½ teaspoon sea salt
5 large black mushrooms, fresh or dried and plumped up
A little over 1-inch cube Chinese-style ham or Hunan-style
    cured pork (see charcuterie, page 478)
½ winter bamboo shoot, defrosted if frozen and peeled
    and blanched if fresh (see Tip, page 122)
1 tablespoon fresh peanut or vegetable oil
1 tablespoon peeled and finely shredded fresh ginger
3 cups boiling unsalted chicken stock (page 380),
    or 3 cups boiling water plus 2 teaspoons fish sauce
2 large egg whites, lightly beaten
1 tablespoon black vinegar, or to taste
1 tablespoon cornstarch or water chestnut flour
    mixed with 3 tablespoons water
Chopped cilantro for garnish

1. Rinse the fish, pat it dry, and remove any skin or bones. Place the fish in a single layer on a heatproof rimmed dish, sprinkle it with the ginger juice and salt, and steam it (see page 49) for 10 to 15 minutes, until it flakes easily. Discard the juices and let the fish cool down while you prepare the rest of the ingredients, and then flake it into small petals while plucking out any bones you find.

2. Remove the stems from the mushrooms. Cut the caps horizontally into 3 layers (or 2 if the caps are thin), then cut these layers into matchsticks. Trim any skin or tendons off of the ham and cut it against the grain into thin slices and then crosswise into matchsticks. Do the same with the bamboo shoot. You should end up with about ¼ cup each of the julienned ham and bamboo shoot. Keep the ham separate from the mushrooms and bamboo shoot.

3. Add the oil and ginger to a medium-sized sandpot or casserole and place it over medium-high heat. Once the ginger releases its fragrance, add the mushrooms and bamboo shoot. Stir these around in the hot oil, and when they start to go limp, pour in the hot stock. Bring the stock to a boil over high heat and then reduce it to medium. Let the stock and the vegetables cook together for a couple of minutes before adding the ham and flaked fish.

4. After about a minute, remove the sandpot from the heat. Lightly beat the egg whites again and then pour them through a sieve in a fine thread all over the soup. Do not mix the chowder at this point; instead, give the whites a chance to set and form delicate flowers all over the surface.

5. Return the sandpot to the heat and bring the soup to a boil before lowering the heat to a simmer. Blend in the vinegar and the cornstarch mixture, stir the chowder gently until it thickens, adjust the seasoning with salt if needed, and then garnish with the cilantro. Serve immediately.

Shāguō yútóu 砂鍋魚頭

Fish Head Sandpot

JIANGSU • SERVES 4

Winter in Taipei was wonderful because it meant that I could hunker down to great, warming meals after work—either with the museum director and coworkers or alone with my husband. If it was a museum meal, it was invariably one of those delicious extravaganzas that went on until the restaurant closed. But when left to our own devices, my husband and I usually gravitated to simpler places that specialized in home-style Mainland dishes. Many of the chefs at these restaurants had fled to the island in 1949, and their dishes spoke of lands they had left behind on the other side of the Taiwan Strait.

Taipei in the late 1970s and early 1980s was filled with many such refugees, mostly middle-aged men. As a result, there was an extraordinary diversity of Mainland cuisines available to eaters in the city. You could go out and try food from some far-flung highland village, and just down the block you could eat at a restaurant that specialized in the cuisine of an eastern metropolis. It seemed that every place, from the tiniest holes-in-the-wall to the greatest dining palaces, offered Fish Head Sandpot during the winter, and all were good, but I especially loved the versions that were served at the little Yangtze home-style restaurants.

At its best, this soup does not taste fishy at all but, rather, is fragrant with mushrooms, pork, and vegetables. Carp heads have a nice ratio of meat to bones and offer an interesting range of consistencies in every bite. The final addition of silky mung bean sheets that soak up all the flavors really makes this recipe, in my opinion. This is another one of those classic dishes that seem unremarkable at first glance but will make you understand the Chinese obsession with texture and balanced flavors.

FISH HEAD AND MARINADE

½ large big-head carp head (a little over 1 pound), scaled, cleaned, and whacked into about 6 pieces by the fishmonger
¼ cup regular soy sauce
2 tablespoons Shaoxing rice wine

MAIN SEASONINGS

6 tablespoons peanut or vegetable oil
8 thin slices fresh ginger
4 green onions, trimmed and cut into 2-inch lengths
4 ounces pork belly, with skin removed, thinly sliced against the grain
1 winter bamboo shoot, defrosted if frozen and peeled and blanched if fresh (see Tip, page 122), cut into ½-inch-thick slices
10 black mushrooms, fresh or dried and plumped up, stemmed and caps torn in half
1 dried Thai chili
2½ cups unsalted chicken stock (page 380)
¼ cup Shaoxing rice wine
1 tablespoon regular soy sauce
½ teaspoon rock sugar

EXTRA TOUCHES

Sea salt, as needed
2 dried mung bean sheets
Boiling water, as needed
1 block (14 ounces or so) soft bean curd
1½ pounds (more or less) pale napa cabbage
1½ cups unsalted chicken stock (page 380)

1. This dish can be enjoyed the same day that you cook it but is much better the second day. Rinse the fish head under cool tap water in a colander and pat dry with a paper towel. Place the pieces in a medium work bowl and toss with the soy sauce and rice wine; let the fish head marinate while you prepare the rest of the ingredients. Have a wok ready, as well as an 8-cup covered sandpot or casserole.

2. Place your wok over high heat and then add the oil. Toss in the ginger and green onions and stir-fry them until they are browned. Place the ginger and green onions on the bottom of the sandpot. Add the pork belly to the wok and stir-fry that over high heat until it too is browned all over, then add it to the sandpot. Stir-fry the bamboo shoot and mushrooms over high heat until they are lightly browned before tossing them into the sandpot, as well.

3. If oil has collected in the bottom of the sandpot, pour it back into the wok and then turn the heat down to medium-high before starting to brown the fish heads; you will need to do this in two batches. Fry the head pieces skin-side first; when they have browned, shake the wok to loosen them (see Tips) before turning the pieces over and frying the other side. Add the browned pieces to the sandpot and repeat with the rest of the fish head pieces until done.

4. Add the chili to the sandpot along with the stock, rice wine, soy sauce, and rock sugar. Bring to a boil and let simmer for about half an hour. If you are serving this the next day, remove the sandpot from the heat and let the soup come to room temperature before covering and refrigerating; slowly warm it on the stove before proceeding to Step 5. If you are serving this the same day, simmer the soup for another half hour before removing it from the heat and going directly to the next step.

5. Bring a large pot of water to a boil and add the salt while you prepare the dried mung bean sheets, bean curd, and cabbage. Place the dried mung bean sheets in a medium work bowl and cover with boiling water, or follow package directions. Drain them as soon as they have softened and separated into smaller pieces, then add these to the sandpot. Cut the bean curd in half and then crosswise another 5 or 6 times to give you 10 or 12 pieces. Prepare the cabbage by cutting it in half and removing the core. Cut the leaves into 1-inch squares. Simmer the bean curd in the salted water for about 10 minutes to remove the excess liquid and firm it up. Use a Chinese spider or slotted spoon to carefully lift out the slices and place them in the sandpot. Blanch the cabbage until it becomes slightly translucent; drain it in a colander set in the sink and then add it to the sandpot along with the stock. Shake the sandpot gently to stir, bring the soup to a boil, taste and adjust the seasoning, and serve hot.

Be *very* careful of two bones in a carp's head: each is shaped like an S and is as sharp as a needle at both ends. They can be deadly if caught in the throat, as well as farther down the digestive system. For this reason, serve carp heads only to adults and only to people who will eat carefully. The flavors here are very much worth the price of admission.

Shaking a wok to loosen browned ingredients serves two purposes. First, the meat will only release itself willingly when it is fully caramelized (see page 454). As a result, shaking the wok—instead of turning the meat with a spatula—allows you to clearly determine when it is ready. Second, if you avoid using a spatula, the caramelized sugars will stay attached to the meat and not become glued to the spatula or wok. (If the caramelized ingredient refuses to shake loose freely, you may nudge it with your spatula.)

If you cannot locate mung bean sheets, consider making your own mung bean jelly (page 250). The jelly can be cut into very thin slices, which can then be added to the sandpot at the end of the recipe so they heat through without having a chance to break apart.

Yángzhōu qīngtāng shīzitóu 揚州清湯獅子頭

Yangzhou-Style Lion Heads

HUAI YANG • SERVES 4

Lion heads are familiar to those who love Shanghainese food. Most places that serve them offer only red-cooked lion heads, in which the meatballs are braised with soy sauce. That version is tasty, but I particularly like the Yangzhou recipe presented here because it allows for more delicate and nuanced flavors.

Yangzhou-Style Lion Heads differ from the Shanghainese versions in several ways. One major departure is the way in which the meatballs are prepared. Instead of a couple of meatballs piled into a sandpot or casserole with extra stuff like cabbage, these lion heads are double-boiled all alone in individual cups.

Then there is the way the pork is cooked: half of it is hand-chopped to create an airy texture and then extra pork fat is added—lots of fat, probably more than makes you comfortable. But don't be alarmed, for most of it will melt into the soup and then be skimmed out before the dish is served.

There are a few other tweaks. A handful of chopped shrimp is tossed in, as well as bits of crunchy water chestnuts, which add a nice texture. There's also lots of ginger juice added (instead of chopped ginger), a heavy dose of Shaoxing rice wine, and some good chicken stock.

MEATBALLS

1 pound ground pork (15 percent fat), divided in half
6 ounces pork fat
8 large shelled shrimp (8 ounces), fresh or frozen and defrosted
6 water chestnuts, fresh or frozen and defrosted, or 2 ounces jicama
2 green onions, white parts only, trimmed
2 tablespoons ginger juice (page 481)
¼ cup Shaoxing rice wine
1 teaspoon mushroom powder or sea salt
1 teaspoon sugar
1½ tablespoons cornstarch
1 tablespoon old-fashioned rolled oats, finely chopped

STOCK

3 cups unsalted chicken stock (page 380)
1 teaspoon sea salt, or to taste
3 tablespoons Shaoxing rice wine
1 tablespoon ginger juice
Extra chicken stock, optional

1. Prepare 4 (1-cup) covered jars (see Tips) and a wide covered pot that easily holds the jars. Place half of the ground pork in a deep work bowl and the other portion on a chopping board. Finely chop this second half for about 5 minutes, as this will help bind the meatballs together. Scrape the meat up with your knife and add it to the other pork.

2. Chop the fat into pieces somewhere between the size of a soybean and a kernel of corn. Add them to the pork. Clean the shrimp (see page 457), chop the meat very finely, and then add it to the bowl. Trim the water chestnuts and chop them into pieces just a little larger than grains of rice before tossing them into the bowl. Finely mince the white parts of the green onions and add them to the pork, along with the ginger juice, rice wine, mushroom powder or salt, sugar, cornstarch, and oats. Hold the rim of the bowl with one hand while you rapidly mix the pork together with your other hand. Keep beating the mixture until it is light and fluffy (see page 458).

3. Divide the pork into 4 equal portions and roll these into balls. Slap 1 ball at a time from one hand to the other, sort of like a baseball pitcher warming up. This really helps to make the lion heads springy. Then roll each one back into a demure ball and drop these into the waiting jars.

4. Mix the stock with salt to taste plus the rice wine and ginger juice. Taste and adjust the flavors as needed. Pour equal amounts of the stock into each jar; it should cover the meatballs but still be about an inch from the top. Cover the jars with both lids (or the foil as noted in the Tips), place them in the pot, fill the pot with hot water until it is halfway up the sides of the jars, and place it over high heat. Cover the pot, and as soon as the water boils, reduce the heat to a good simmer and set the timer for 2 hours, adding more boiling water as necessary to maintain the level. The lion heads can be prepared ahead of time up to this point.

5. Remove the jars from the pot. Carefully pour out all the hot stock from each jar into a heatproof 4-cup measuring cup. Repeat this a couple of times because the meatballs will ooze out more juices as they sit. If you are serving them immediately, use a turkey baster to draw up the stock from the bottom of the cup, leaving the wide band of melted lard on top, and then discard the fat. If you are doing this ahead of time, you can just let the stock cool and then remove the hard layer of fat. Taste the stock and adjust the seasoning as needed. Bring the defatted stock to a full boil and pour it back into the jars. If you find the stock too fishy or salty for your palate, use the optional fresh chicken stock instead and season to taste. Serve the lion heads very hot in their jars, with saucers underneath.

Yangzhou-Style Lion Heads are traditionally cooked and served in little covered clay jars that have two lids. The jars are placed in the bottom of a large pot, with water coming halfway up the sides of the jars. Two lids are placed on the jars to prevent any water from entering them, and the individual containers keep any violent heat or movement from breaking down the meatballs, while giving the cooking stock the chance to absorb the meat's juices and vice versa.

If you don't have these kinds of jars, use jelly jars and cover them tightly with foil. You can also tie string around the jars so that the foil stays put.

You can serve the lion heads in the jars if the jars are attractive. Otherwise, serve the meatballs and their soup in bowls. No matter the final serving container, place a small saucer under each serving dish to keep from burning your hands or those of your diners. Eat the lion heads with chopsticks and spoon up the soup.

Shāo sùhuángquè 燒素黃雀

Braised Vegetarian Finches

JIANGSU · SERVES 4 TO 6

There was a great Buddhist restaurant in downtown Taipei about a block from the Taiwan Provincial Museum. My husband and I would often go there, and we'd always order the same thing: Braised Vegetarian Finches. These are parcels of vegetables and bean curd wrapped in soy sheets, fried, and then braised in a delicate sauce. Vegetarian finches get their name from the little "wings" that the wrappers form when they're tied into knots. They are best served with some steamed bread (pages 398 and 400) or lots of rice to soak up all the tasty sauce.

Chinese Buddhists who follow the strictest rules for their vegan cuisine never use alcohol, onions, chives, chili peppers, garlic, or anything else that could be considered addictive and draw attention away from the pure nature of the food that is being prepared (see page 72). I don't think that I could ever go that route, but in the spirit of authenticity, I've listed all of the "addictive" seasonings and the eggs as optional.

Salted water for blanching

4 black mushrooms, fresh or dried and plumped up

4 heads baby bok choy (about 3 inches in length)

1 carrot, peeled and cut into small dice

1 tablespoon peanut or vegetable oil,
     optional if using the eggs

3 large eggs, beaten, optional

1 block (14 ounces or so) firm bean curd

¼ cup shelled green soybeans (*edamame*),
     rinsed in warm water and drained

1 green onion, trimmed and thinly sliced, optional

3 tablespoons light soy sauce, divided into
     1 tablespoon and 2 tablespoons

1 teaspoon toasted sesame oil

2½ teaspoons sugar, divided into ½ teaspoon
     and 2 teaspoons

8 soy skins (circles about 24 inches in diameter),
     fresh or dried

¼ cup peanut oil, or as needed

1½ cups (or more) unsalted mushroom stock
     (page 381), filtered mushroom soaking liquid,
     or water

1 tablespoon Shaoxing rice wine, optional

5 thin slices fresh ginger, optional

Toasted sesame oil

Shredded green onion or chopped cilantro
     for garnish, optional

I DON'T ALWAYS PEEL MY FRESH MATURE ginger . . . that's my deep, dark secret. It all depends on a variety of factors: If the ginger is super-juicy and the peel is relatively young, few people will notice if the skin is hanging around. The only exception is when it is very finely julienned for a dipping sauce. Second, if it either sliced or smashed in order to season a braise or soup, skip the peeling, for these chunks will be removed later on; ginger that is getting juiced should never get peeled, either—that would be a waste of time.

To peel ginger, first lop off all those little protuberances that poke out along the edges of a nice, juicy hunk of the rhizome. The pieces smaller than ½ inch can be saved for a stew or discarded. Second, use a short paring knife to scrape down from the base toward the tip so that you go with the grain of the ginger. Third, slice off a thin piece from the length of ginger so that it will rest safely against your cutting board.

To julienne ginger, lay the ginger flat against the cutting board, with the knife in your dominant hand and your nondominant hand curled up on the ginger; the knuckles on this nondominant hand are doing some important work here, as they will guide your blade and also determine how thick the pieces are. Cut straight down gently and evenly while pushing the knife a bit, which allows the blade to glide through the ginger.

Finally, once you have a stack of ginger slices, stack them flat against the cutting board in piles of 3 or 4, and then start slicing them into thin threads.

1. Bring a medium-sized pot of salted water to a boil. Meanwhile, stem the mushrooms, cut the caps into a small dice, and toss them into a large bowl. Split the baby bok choy into quarters lengthwise, rinse them carefully to remove any grit, shake dry, and cut into small dice. Toss the bok choy into the boiling water and let it blanch for no more than 20 seconds, until it turns a brilliant green. Scoop it out of the pot and run some cold water on it to stop the cooking. Drain, then squeeze any excess water out before adding the bok choy to the mushrooms. Toss the diced carrots into the boiling water and let them blanch for about a minute, then rinse under cold water, drain, and add these to the mushrooms, too.

2. If you are adding eggs to the mix, heat the peanut or vegetable oil in a wok until it starts to shimmer, then add the eggs and stir-fry them until they are cooked through. Cut them up into small pieces with your spatula and add them to the mushrooms. Remove any hard edges from the block of bean curd and mash it up into a fine paste before adding it to the mushrooms along with the soybeans. Add the optional chopped green onion, 1 tablespoon soy sauce, sesame oil, and ½ teaspoon sugar to the bowl and toss the ingredients well to mix.

3. If you are using dried soy skins, remove them one at a time, rinse them under warm water, gently shake dry, and cut in half. If you are using fresh skins, just remove 1 sheet at a time and cut it in half. Keep all the other skins well covered so that they don't dry and crack. To roll up the "finches," see the diagram below. This will make 16 knots.

4. Heat the ¼ cup oil in a wok until it shimmers, then add the knots a few at a time so that they don't crowd one another. Fry them on every side until they are golden and remove to a plate as they are done. Repeat with the rest of the knots until all have been fried, adding more oil as necessary.

5. Drain the oil out of the wok and lightly wipe it with a paper towel. Pour the stock, optional rice wine, remaining 2 tablespoons soy sauce, optional ginger, and remaining 2 teaspoons sugar into the wok and bring to a boil. Add the fried knots, toss them gently, cover, and let cook for about 2 minutes, gently turning them over about halfway through so that they all get bathed in the sauce, adding more stock as needed. When most of the sauce has been absorbed, sprinkle on a bit of sesame oil, remove them to a serving platter, and dust with the optional green onion or cilantro. Serve hot or slightly warm.

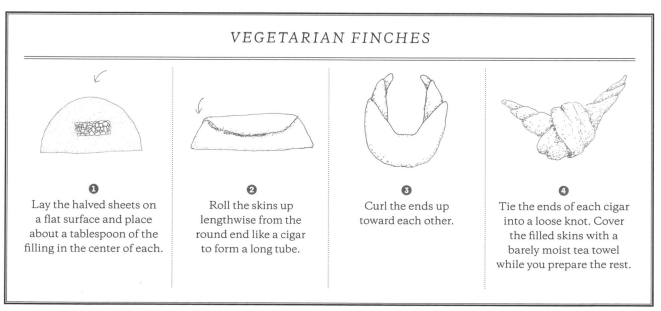

VEGETARIAN FINCHES

❶ Lay the halved sheets on a flat surface and place about a tablespoon of the filling in the center of each.

❷ Roll the skins up lengthwise from the round end like a cigar to form a long tube.

❸ Curl the ends up toward each other.

❹ Tie the ends of each cigar into a loose knot. Cover the filled skins with a barely moist tea towel while you prepare the rest.

Qīngzhēng xiānyú 清蒸鲜鱼

Steamed Fish Jiangsu Style

JIANGSU • SERVES 4

This gentle dish goes by the unassuming Chinese name of "plain steamed fresh fish," but it is in fact quite beautiful and delicately seasoned with Chinese ham, black mushrooms, thin slices of ginger, and spoonfuls of Shaoxing rice wine: a simple set of ingredients that yields a subtle, deeply satisfying dish.

In addition to these Yangtze staples, I've added fresh bamboo shoots for a bit of crunch. Also, if you happen to have a piece of caul fat lying around the freezer, this is a good dish to use it on. You can do as my father-in-law liked to do and wrap it around the fish instead of adding plain oil, and the fat will melt into the fish and sauce, taking this savory meal up a notch.

1 (1-pound) mild-flavored fresh fish, such as grass carp, yellow croaker, bass, mullet, or hake

1 teaspoon sea salt

1 large or 2 small black mushrooms, fresh or dried and plumped up

½ winter bamboo shoot, defrosted if frozen and peeled and blanched if fresh (see Tip, page 122), optional

8 thin slices Chinese-style ham or Hunan-style cured pork (see charcuterie, page 478), about 1 × 2 inches

1 inch fresh ginger, thinly sliced

2 green onions, trimmed and shredded

3 tablespoons Shaoxing rice wine

2 tablespoons peanut or vegetable oil

Freshly ground black pepper

1. Clean and scale the fish, pat dry with a paper towel, and either fillet both sides or butterfly it by splitting it down the belly and flattening the whole fish. Cut 4 deep diagonal slashes into each fillet or side of the fish (see page 23). Sprinkle the salt on all sides of the fish and rub it gently into the flesh.

2. Stem the mushrooms and slice on the diagonal into 8 long, wide pieces. If you're using the fresh bamboo shoot, peel and slice it thinly; if using the frozen shoot, just thinly slice it. Boil the slices in salted water to cover until tender (about 10 minutes for fresh and 2 minutes for frozen), then drain and rinse well.

3. Make a little sandwich of a slice of mushroom, optional bamboo shoot, and ham and stuff it into a slash in the fish. Repeat with the rest of the mushroom, bamboo shoot, and ham until the slashes on both sides of the fish are filled. Lay the fillets or whole fish on a heatproof plate that easily fits into your steamer (see page 49). Sprinkle any leftover bamboo shoot pieces on top, as well as the ginger, green onions, rice wine, and oil, and dust the fish with a few grinds of black pepper.

4. Bring the water in your steamer to a full boil and place the platter with the fish in the steamer. Steam the fish until done, which will be 10 to 20 minutes, depending upon the fish and how hot your steamer is. As soon as the fish is ready (see page 101, Step 2), serve it immediately.

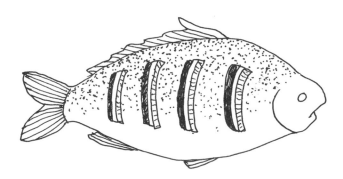

Xīhú cùyú 西湖醋魚

West Lake Piquant Fish

ZHEJIANG · SERVES 4 TO 6

Big nights out for my husband and I as a couple in Taipei during the early 1980s usually consisted of hitting up the bookstores on Chongqing South Road and then heading over to one of our favorite restaurants whenever we got a craving for this dish. A good touch of sugar balances out the sourness, but this is not a sweet sauce; as the Chinese name tells you right up front, this is "West Lake vinegar fish."

The sweet-and-sour element is very gentle here, and there is no batter to overwhelm you. That being said, there is also nothing to hide any flaws in the fish, so get the best you can. Carp is the fish of choice in China when it comes to dishes like this one, but we do have some pretty good freshwater fish in the United States. I'd recommend trout, which ends up being a perfect foil for the sauce and the shredded ginger garnish.

FISH

1 to 1½ pounds very fresh trout or similar freshwater fish, either whole or fillets with skin still attached
Boiling water, as needed
¼ cup thinly sliced fresh ginger
1 teaspoon sea salt

SAUCE

2 cups unsalted chicken stock (page 380)
½ cup green onion oil (page 434)
½ cup peanut or vegetable oil
¼ cup black vinegar
6 tablespoons (or so) rock sugar
1 teaspoon sea salt
½ cup peeled and finely julienned fresh ginger (or preferably young ginger), divided in half
2 teaspoons cornstarch mixed with 2 tablespoons Shaoxing rice wine

1 pound fresh whole egg dough noodles (page 389 or store-bought)

1. Scale the fish carefully, rinse gently under cool tap water, and pat dry with paper towels. Remove any dark film in the stomach cavity, and if the sides are thicker than ¼ inch, make tiny gashes wherever they are thickest (see page 23) to help the fish cook evenly. A whole fish should be butterflied.

2. Fill a wide pan or wok with boiling water to about 3 inches deep; add the ginger slices and salt and bring to a full boil again. Turn off the heat and lay the fish, skin-side up, in the hot water. Cover the pan and let the fish sit for about 8 minutes for thin (¼ inch thick) and 10 minutes for thicker fish. Pierce the thickest piece with a chopstick; if it goes through very easily, use a Chinese spider or slotted spoon to very carefully lift the fish out of the water and onto a rimmed platter. Discard the water.

3. While the fish is poaching, bring a large pot of water to a boil so you can cook the noodles in Step 4. Then prepare the sauce: bring the chicken stock to a boil over medium-high heat and add the green onion oil, peanut oil, vinegar, sugar, salt, and half the julienned ginger. When this comes to a boil again, stir in the cornstarch slurry and keep stirring until the sauce thickens. Taste, adjust the seasoning, and keep the sauce warm.

4. Boil the noodles until they are barely cooked; this should take only a minute or two. Taste one as soon as the noodles float, and if they are done, drain them in a colander set in the sink.

5. To serve, pour off and discard any water that has collected around the fish. Arrange the fish in an attractive pattern and pour about half of the sauce all over it. Sprinkle most of the remaining julienned ginger on top. Put the cooked noodles in a deep bowl and toss with the rest of the sauce, then sprinkle a bit of ginger on top as decoration. Serve immediately.

Táitiáo sūyú 苔條酥魚

Fried Fish in a Sea Moss Batter

ZHEJIANG • SERVES 4

Sea moss is an aquatic plant, and it's a lot like seaweed in the sense that it is green and tastes of the ocean. But it looks quite different, growing in long, hairlike strands instead of wide leaves. These strands are hacked off in hanks, left to dry, and then used as seasoning for a variety of different things. I have even used them to season shortbread cookies, of all things (page 145).

In this recipe, the sea moss adds a wonderful accent to the batter, but the success of the dish, as usual, hinges on the quality of the fish. In Hangzhou, the capital of Zhejiang Province, grass carp is generally the fish of choice. Native to Asia and widely cultivated in China, the carp is considered an invasive species in the United States, having been dumped into many American waterways in the late 1970s in a misguided attempt to control aquatic weeds. In any case, it's a great option, but if you cannot get your hands on one, any other mild, delicate fish will do the trick. I'd recommend yellow croaker, bass, mullet, or hake.

FISH

1 whole mild-flavored fish (1¼ to 1½ pounds)
     or 1 pound fillets
2 green onions, trimmed and coarsely chopped
1 tablespoon Shaoxing rice wine
Juice and zest of ½ lemon
1 tablespoon ginger juice (page 481)
¼ teaspoon sea salt
Freshly ground black pepper

BATTER

1 large hank of sea moss (about 2 ounces)
Peanut or vegetable oil for frying
6 tablespoons pastry flour
2 tablespoons cornstarch, plus more for dusting
¼ teaspoon sea salt
½ teaspoon baking powder
¼ cup peanut or vegetable oil
¼ cup ice water, plus more as needed
¼ cup Shaoxing rice wine, chilled

DIP

Dry-fried salt and pepper (page 440)

MOSSES AND SEAWEEDS OF EVERY VARIETY season the foods of China, adding color, texture, and nutrition to dishes from all corners of the land.

One of the most famous is the dark green, almost blackish flossy moss called *fǎcài* 髮菜, or "hair vegetable." Rather neutral in flavor, it is commonly added to dishes because its Chinese name sounds like *fācái* 發財, or "getting rich," which lends the suggestion of prosperity to a gathering. Often described as being some sort of seaweed—and it certainly looks as if it would be at home in the ocean—it is actually a type of terrestrial plant that grows mainly in the wild desert lands around the

Gobi and the Qinghai plateau. Because of over-harvesting, many sophisticated Chinese diners have begun refusing to eat it until it has become sustainable once again.

Sea moss (see the recipe above and on page 145), on the other hand, grows rampantly in long strands in tidal areas and serves as a tasty seasoning for many Chinese dishes, especially in the coastal Yangtze River area. It is becoming more common in Chinese markets that are geared toward people from eastern China and is usually found in plastic bags near the seaweed.

Seaweed in Chinese cooking can generally be divided into laver and kelp.

Laver seaweed (*zǐcài* 紫菜, or "purple vegetable") is, like sea moss, a variety of algae that clings to rocks. Usually sold under its Japanese name, nori, laver is dried in thin sheets. Kelp (*hǎidài* 海帶, or "sea ribbon") grows in large forests, with its roots clinging to the ocean floor, and is usually sold under its Japanese name, kombu.

A final variety of seaweed is called "sea vegetable," or *hǎicài* 海菜. It tends to be sold as colorful assortments of delicate seaweeds, much like spring mix greens. They are usually fresh but packed with salt, and so only need a quick soak in cool water before they are ready to be eaten raw with a light dressing of some sort.

1. Scale and rinse the fish, then pat it dry. If you are using a whole fish, cut off the fins. Then use a sharp knife to remove the fillets from both sides of the fish; run your hands down the inner side of the fillets and use tweezers to remove any small bones. Press down on the head of the fish to flatten it completely and reserve the skeleton, if you wish (see Step 4), and then place it in a medium work bowl. No matter whether you are using a whole fish or just fillets, cut the fillets into inch-wide pieces and make shallow, vertical slashes every ¾ inch to help the fish cook evenly, and then place the fish in the work bowl. Put the green onions, rice wine, lemon zest and juice, ginger juice, salt, and pepper in a small food processor or blender and whirl them together to pulverize the solids. Gently toss the fish with this marinade and let it sit in a cool spot for 20 to 30 minutes.

2. Rinse the sea moss and wring it with your hands, squeezing it as dry as you can using a paper towel. Separate the sea moss out into smaller hanks; the best way to do this is to place it in a paper bag before you fiddle with it, so that the shards don't fly all over the place. Pour the oil to a depth of 3 inches into a wok, warm it over medium heat until it starts to shimmer, and then fry the sea moss; poke it around with chopsticks to keep it from burning or browning too quickly. When it is crispy and has turned a deep olive, put it back in that paper bag, which will absorb most of the oil. Keep the oil in the wok for frying the fish.

3. Place the cooled fried sea moss in a food processor and pulse until pulverized. Add the flour, cornstarch, salt, and baking powder and pulse these together to combine them well. Mix together the oil, ice water, and chilled rice wine. With the processor running, pour in the oil mixture into the flour mixture to form a light batter, adding more ice water if needed to make a pancakelike batter.

4. Set the oil over medium-high heat until it starts to shimmer. If you'd like to use the fish skeleton for presentation, lightly dust the head and tail with cornstarch and then lower the skeleton, head first, into the hot oil. Fry it on both sides until it is lightly browned, including the tail. Lay the skeleton on a long oval platter.

5. Next, toss the fillets with a bit of cornstarch and then use your chopsticks to dip each slice of fish in the batter before quickly transferring it to the hot oil. Fry as many pieces as fit loosely into the wok so that they do not stick. When both sides are a light gold, remove them to the serving plate and set them back in place on the skeleton, if desired, or simply arrange them like Lincoln Logs on a serving plate. When all of the fish has been fried, serve it immediately with the dry-fried salt and pepper as a dip.

Lóngjǐng xiārén 龍井蝦仁

Stir-Fried Shrimp with Longjing Tea

ZHEJIANG · SERVES 4

Few restaurants serve this Hangzhou specialty with any success. The oil must be absolutely fresh, as any off flavors will be immediately noticeable. The seasoning of the shrimp should taste aromatic and slightly leafy, with the gentle tannins of the tea leaves acting as a counterbalance to the natural sweetness of the crustaceans. Good-quality green tea leaves are the main seasoning, so add more of the brewed leaves to the shrimp if they are not fully flavored.

You will notice that only a tiny bit of salt and a small dash of rice wine are needed; be sure not to add more, or the delicate nuances of the dish will be thrown off. When done right, the shrimp will be crunchy, juicy, pink, and dotted with green bits of tea.

2 tablespoons Longjing (dragon well) green tea leaves

½ cup boiling water left to cool for a couple of minutes

1 pound medium (31/40) shelled shrimp, fresh or frozen and defrosted

1 large egg white, lightly beaten

½ teaspoon sea salt

1 teaspoon cornstarch

6 tablespoons peanut or vegetable oil, plus more if needed

2 teaspoons Shaoxing rice wine

1. Place the tea leaves in a sieve and pour some hot water over them to rinse off any dust. Then put them in a cup or bowl and pour the boiled water over them. Allow the leaves to steep while you prepare the rest of the ingredients. Just before you start to fry the shrimp, drain the tea into another cup and reserve 2 or more tablespoons of the plumped-up leaves. Use the rest of the leaves for a nice cup of tea after dinner (for directions on how to brew green tea, see The Perfect Pot of Chinese Tea, page 150).

2. Clean the shrimp (see page 457). Rinse them thoroughly, shake dry in a colander, and place in a medium work bowl. Toss them with the egg white, salt, and cornstarch and allow them to marinate for 10 to 30 minutes. Drain well and discard the marinade.

3. Have a serving platter next to the stove. Heat a wok over high heat until the iron starts to smoke a bit and then pour in the oil and swirl it around. Add the drained shrimp to the hot oil and stir-fry them very quickly until they are only half done, which means that they are just beginning to turn opaque. Remove the shrimp from the wok to the platter, but drain all of the oil back into the wok.

4. Toss the tea leaves into the hot oil, stir-fry them for about 20 seconds to release their fragrance, and then add the shrimp, brewed tea, and rice wine. Toss these together quickly until the shrimp are cooked through and pink but still juicy. Immediately transfer them to the platter and serve hot.

Jiāoyán sūxiā 椒鹽酥蝦

Crunchy Salt-and-Pepper Shrimp

JIANGSU • SERVES 4

Many places in China have their own versions of this classic. In Sichuan, for example, cooks add lots of fresh chilies and garlic. But this recipe from Jiangsu really appeals to me because it allows the sweetness of the shrimp to shine through. Also, the shells in this version are perfectly done: crisp and flavorful, they are as tasty as potato chips.

To be honest, I usually don't care for what passes for salt-and-pepper shrimp in most restaurants. Even if the shrimp are of good quality—which is never guaranteed even if they are alive when you purchase them—the shells aren't crunchy enough, the meat is overcooked, there's too much salt, or the oil is not fresh. If it seems like I'm picky when it comes to this dish, it's only because when it is done well, it is sublime. This one may take a couple of practice runs to get down, but once you master it, Crunchy Salt-and-Pepper Shrimp will be an all-time favorite.

8 ounces medium shrimp (31/40 count, or smaller
    if you like), fresh or frozen and defrosted, with shells
    and tails on and preferably with their heads
1 tablespoon Shaoxing rice wine
2 tablespoons cornstarch
2 to 3 cups frying oil, preferably rice bran oil (used oil is
    all right if it smells fresh)
½ teaspoon sea salt
½ teaspoon freshly ground black pepper
1 green onion, trimmed and finely chopped
1 clove garlic, finely chopped

1. First prep the shrimp (see page 457). Shrimp with or without their heads should be allowed to keep their shells, tails, and feet.

2. Place the shrimp in a colander and rinse them under cool running water. Have a medium work bowl ready as you use a paper towel to dry them off, pressing down slightly to squeeze out any extra water. Place the dried-off shrimp in the bowl. Toss them with the rice wine and then the cornstarch. Let them marinate while you prepare the rest of the ingredients. Have everything prepared before you start frying the shrimp, as it proceeds very quickly.

3. Have a wok ready, as well as wooden chopsticks, a Chinese spider or slotted spoon, a serving dish lined with parchment paper, and a bowl for the used oil. Pour the oil into the wok and place it on high heat. When a chopstick inserted into the hot oil is immediately covered with bubbles, add about half of the shrimp, sliding them individually by their tails into the oil so that you don't get splashed. Lower the heat to medium and fry the shrimp quickly until they are a golden brown all over. Remove them with a slotted spoon and chopsticks to the serving dish. Repeat with the other half of the shrimp, adjusting the heat as necessary.

4. When the shrimp are fried and crispy, pour out all of the oil into the waiting bowl, leaving only a film of oil inside the wok. Heat the wok over high, add the salt, pepper, green onion, and garlic, and quickly toss these together for a few seconds to take the raw edge off of the aromatics. Add all of the shrimp, toss them quickly just to coat them with the seasoning, and then serve immediately. The whole shrimp can be eaten; the legs in particular are nice and brittle.

Hōngzhà Dōngjīng 轟炸東京

Bombs over Tokyo

SHANGHAI · SERVES 8

When it comes to food, we pay plenty of attention to taste, scent, and appearance, but rarely do we focus on sound. This dish from Shanghai has a wonderful aural quality: once the boiling sauce hits the freshly fried rice crusts, the whole thing crackles with noise.

This dish is known by many names, from the confident "best dish in the world" (*tiānxià dìyī cài* 天下第一菜) to the pedestrian "rice crust shrimp" (*guōbā xiārén* 鍋粑蝦仁). In English, it is commonly referred to as "sizzling rice shrimp" or "rice crust shrimp." In China, though, it has often gone by a name that came about in the 1930s and 1940s during the Second Sino-Japanese War: Bombs over Tokyo.

But names have a way of adapting as history moves on, and by the time I arrived in Taiwan in the 1970s, the name of the dish had been changed to Bombs over Moscow, for Japan had come to be seen as less of an enemy and more of an important trading partner. In any case, through all the name changes, the dish remains the same: a loud and excellent table-pleaser.

RICE CRUSTS

1½ cups short-grain white rice
Small amount of vegetable oil

SHRIMP

8 ounces small (41/50 count or smaller) shelled shrimp, fresh or frozen and defrosted
1 teaspoon sea salt
1 large egg white, lightly beaten
1 tablespoon cornstarch

SAUCE

4 ounces boneless chicken breast
2 cups unsalted chicken stock (page 380)
Sea salt to taste
2 tablespoons Shaoxing rice wine
2 tablespoons sugar
6 tablespoons catsup
2 teaspoons toasted sesame oil
2 teaspoons pale rice vinegar
¼ cup chopped black mushrooms, fresh or dried and plumped up
2 tablespoons cornstarch mixed with ¼ cup unsalted chicken stock

FINAL TOUCHES

4 cups peanut or vegetable oil
¼ cup cooked baby peas or green soybeans (*edamame*), fresh or frozen

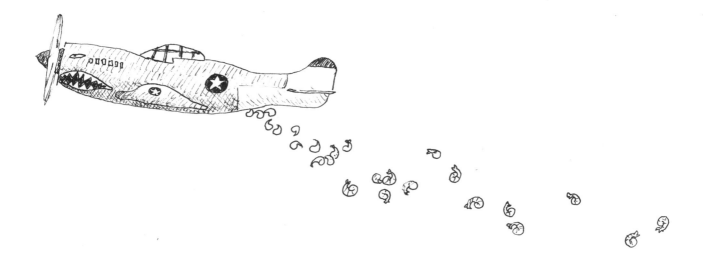

1. Start this recipe at least a day before you wish to serve it. First make the rice crusts, which will need time to thoroughly dry out before you can deep-fry them. Cook the rice according to the directions on page 382 or on the package, using either a rice cooker or a saucepan. Lightly oil a large, flat-bottomed frying pan and heat the oven to 175°F.

2. When the rice has cooled enough to handle easily, spread a layer of rice about ½ inch thick over the bottom of the pan. You may need to do this in two or three batches. Don't smash the rice down, but use wet hands and a wet silicone spatula to gently flatten it. Cook the rice over medium heat, shaking the pan occasionally to keep the rice from sticking. Do this until the bottom of the rice starts to crackle and turns light golden brown in patches. Flip the rice over (it's okay if it breaks) and cook the other side. Transfer the cooked rice to a large baking sheet and place it in the oven.

3. Dry-fry the rest of the rice in the same way, then dry out the rice crusts in the oven for a few hours until they are completely hard and crisp. Break the crusts into pieces that are about 2 inches square. You can make these ahead of time; just let them cool off before storing them in a plastic bag in the refrigerator, where they will stay fresh for a long time.

4. Clean the shrimp (see page 457). Pat the shrimp dry with a paper towel, place them in a bowl, and toss them with the salt and egg white. Sprinkle the cornstarch over the shrimp and toss them again to coat well.

5. Remove any skin and cartilage from the chicken breast and cut the meat into inch-wide strips. Heat the stock in a large saucepan, adding salt to taste. Add the chicken to the stock, turn the heat down to a gentle simmer, and poach the chicken until it is done. Remove the chicken from the stock, cool it slightly, and shred into fine pieces. Bring the stock to a boil again and stir in the rice wine, sugar, catsup, sesame oil, vinegar, and mushrooms, as well as the shredded chicken; taste and adjust the seasoning as needed. You can prepare the dish ahead of time up to this point.

6. About 10 minutes before you wish to serve this dish, put the rice crusts within reach by the stove, the sauce in a saucepan, and 2 large serving bowls and a Chinese spider or slotted spoon next to the stove.

7. Start by placing the oil in a wok over medium-high heat. As soon as the oil starts to shimmer, go back to the stock: bring it to a gentle simmer, stir in the cornstarch slurry until the sauce is thick and glossy, add the shrimp to the stock one at a time so that they don't stick together, and finally toss in the peas or soybeans.

8. While the shrimp are poaching in the stock, the oil should have arrived at the right temperature. To test it, drop a few grains of the rice crust into the hot oil; they should immediately puff up and rise to the surface without burning. If the oil is too hot, add a bit more oil; if it's too cool, increase the heat. Add the rice crust squares and any large crumbs to the hot oil and stir them constantly. As soon as they puff up, use a Chinese spider to remove the rice crusts to a large rimmed serving bowl. You may need to do this in two or three batches, but make haste, as the rice needs to be hot in order to explode when it's covered with the sauce.

9. Immediately pour the hot shrimp sauce into another large bowl and bring both the sauce and rice crusts to the table in separate dishes. Place the bowl with the rice crusts on the dining table and quickly pour the shrimp sauce over the rice crusts while they are still hot; you and your guests will be rewarded with a loud crackling noise. Serve the rice crusts and the sauce in small soup bowls and eat them right away while the rice is still crisp.

Zuìzāo hǎimán 醉糟海鳗

Drunken Scarlet Eels

NORTHERN FUJIAN · SERVES 4 TO 6

I was first introduced to Northern Fujian's exciting cuisine by my husband's beloved graduate school mentor, Wang Men-ou. A native of Fuzhou, Professor Wang once took us out for a meal at his favorite place. Everything there was delicious, but my favorite dish was Drunken Scarlet Eels.

In this recipe, the eel is coated in a batter flavored with red wine lees. It's also seasoned with two other subtle elements: five-spice powder and curry powder. Because Fuzhou, the capital of Fujian, was one of the five treaty ports (see page 162) opened up to the West following the First Opium War in the nineteenth century, things like curry gained something of a foothold there, as well as in Hong Kong and Macau (see Portuguese Chicken, page 195).

FISH AND MARINADE

6 (or so) ounces fillet of fresh conger eel, monkfish, or mullet

1 tablespoon red wine lees (page 418)

1½ tablespoons wine from red wine lees or other rice wine

2½ teaspoons sugar

¼ teaspoon five-spice powder (page 441 or store-bought)

¼ teaspoon curry powder

BATTER

5½ tablespoons pastry flour

¼ cup cornstarch

1 teaspoon baking soda

1 teaspoon sea salt

2 tablespoons red wine lees (page 418)

About 7 tablespoons ice water

1½ teaspoons peanut or vegetable oil

1½ teaspoons toasted sesame oil

1 large egg white

Peanut or vegetable oil for frying

Extra pastry flour for breading the fish

Dry-fried salt and pepper (page 440)

1. This is best started early on the day you wish to eat it. Clean the fish and trim off any dark meat or skin. As you work with the fish, run your fingers gently up and down the flesh and use tweezers to pull out any errant bones. Cut the fish diagonally against the grain into wide, ¼-inch-thick slices. Mix the marinade's red wine lees and the rice wine in a small work bowl and use a spoon to mash up any lumps in the lees. Mix in the rest of the marinade ingredients, add the fish, and toss thoroughly with the marinade. Cover and refrigerate for 6 to 8 hours to marinate the fish.

2. In a medium work bowl, mix together the flour, cornstarch, baking soda, and salt. Mash in the batter's red wine lees and add the ice water and both oils before stirring this into the dry ingredients. Refrigerate the batter for 10 to 15 minutes to give the flour time to absorb some of the liquid; add more ice water if it is thicker than pancake batter. Keep the batter chilled. Just before you fry the fish, beat the egg white until it forms soft peaks and then fold it into the batter.

3. About 15 minutes before serving, pour oil into a wok to a depth of about 2 inches for deep-frying. Set the oil over medium-high heat while you prepare the fish in the next step, but remove it from the heat if it starts to get too hot. Have a small baking sheet lined with parchment paper next to the stove and heat an oven or toaster oven to 300°F.

4. Pour about ½ cup of the extra flour into a small work bowl. Working on a slice or two at a time, coat the fish lightly with the flour and then dip each piece thoroughly into the batter before sliding it into the hot oil. Working in batches, fry the fish evenly on both sides until it starts to brown and then remove to the paper-lined baking sheet; adjust the heat as necessary to make the batter explode in the hot oil but not burn. Keep the fish hot in the oven while you fry the rest. When all of the fish has been fried, serve immediately with the dry-fried salt and pepper as a dip.

Jǐuhuáng chǎo shànhú 韭黃炒鱔糊

Freshwater Eels with Yellow Chives

JIANGSU AND ANHUI • SERVES 4

This dish features two ingredients that have yet to take hold outside of China: yellow chives and freshwater eels. Both are subtly flavored and refined, which makes them a perfect match. The true beauty of this dish, though, lies in the tangle of contrasting textures and colors: crisp golden leaves against tender tan fish. The sauce is appropriately understated, providing a backdrop of light, savory notes.

The one ingredient folks usually get wrong in this recipe is the yellow chives. They must be the thick, meaty kind, not leafy and wispy. Fat yellow chives will stay springy and full of juice and thus provide a satisfying crunch.

EELS AND CHIVES

1 package (8 ounces) frozen small freshwater eels (see Tips)
1 bunch of fresh, bouncy, thick yellow chives
    (9 or 10 ounces)
¼ cup peanut or vegetable oil
8 thin slices fresh ginger
2 green onions, trimmed, smacked with
    the side of a cleaver, and cut into 2-inch lengths
2 tablespoons Shaoxing rice wine
¼ cup boiling water
2 tablespoons light soy sauce
1 tablespoon sugar
Freshly ground black pepper
1 teaspoon cornstarch mixed with 1 tablespoon water

TOPPING

1 clove garlic, finely minced
1 green onion, green part only, trimmed and
    finely julienned
2 tablespoons finely shredded young ginger
¼ cup chopped cilantro, optional
3 tablespoons toasted sesame oil

1. Defrost the eels, place them in a colander, and rinse them well with cool tap water. Pick over the eels carefully and discard any bits of skin or guts. Pat them lightly dry with a paper towel and cut them crosswise in half. They will shrink as they cook, so don't make them too small.

2. Pick over the yellow chives and remove any stringy leaves, dirt, and so forth; you should be left with only chubby, springy leaves. Trim off the tough parts on the root ends, rinse the chives, shake them dry, and then cut them into pieces about 1½ inches long.

3. Place a wok over high heat and add the oil. Fry the ginger and green onions, then discard them after they have turned a deep brown and scented the oil. Stir-fry the eels in the oil for a minute or so, then toss in the rice wine. After about a minute, pour in the boiling water and soy sauce and sprinkle in the sugar and pepper. Bring the sauce to a high boil and toss the eels as they cook. When the liquid has boiled down to about half the original amount, stir in the cornstarch slurry. As soon as the sauce has thickened, toss in the yellow chives and cook them quickly, only until they have lost their raw edge. Taste and adjust the seasoning, then scoop the eels and chives out onto a serving plate.

4. Rinse out and dry the wok, then return it to high heat. While it is heating up, sprinkle the raw garlic, green onions, young ginger, and optional cilantro over the top of the eels and chives. As soon as the wok is very hot, pour the sesame oil into the wok. When it starts to smoke, drizzle it over the garnishes on the dish to quickly cook them and release their fragrance. Serve immediately and toss the dish at the table.

The name for these eels may be translated into English in several different ways. What you need to look for on the package is the word "wild," as well as the Chinese characters for freshwater eels (*shanhu* 鱔糊). Keep them frozen unless you are cooking them that day.

Dàokǒu shāojī 道口燒雞

Daokou Poached Chicken

HENAN · SERVES 6 TO 8

This is Henan's most famous dish, and my husband and I used to eat it all the time in Taipei. The best place to order it was at a little restaurant on a sleepy, narrow street called Yongkang, near the downtown area. The place was run by a gentleman from Henan, who worked the stoves in the back while his wife and children served the food.

Yongkang Street was the first area I became familiar with in Taipei. The Chinese family I boarded with lived only two blocks to the north, and my language school was also nearby. I can barely recognize the place anymore: all of the humble little stores—including that Daokou chicken restaurant—were torn down and replaced by fancier ones as the area transformed into one of Taipei's hippest neighborhoods. I often think of their delicious chicken, though, and this recipe is the closest I've come to re-creating it.

POACHING BROTH

4 cups unsalted chicken stock (page 380) or water

½ cup Shaoxing rice wine

¼ cup fish sauce (if no stock is used), or salt to taste

¼ cup light soy sauce

1 tablespoon rock sugar

1 piece aged tangerine peel or large handful of homemade dried orange peel

1 tablespoon whole sand ginger

1 tablespoon whole black peppercorns

1 tablespoon whole Sichuan peppercorns

1 tablespoon fennel seeds

4 star anise

½ dried arhat fruit, or increase sugar to taste

½ stick cinnamon

1 teaspoon whole cloves

3 black cardamom pods

CHICKEN

1 whole chicken (3 to 4 pounds), trimmed

½ cup maltose or honey

4 cups toasted sesame oil or rice bran oil, or other vegetable oil mixed with some toasted sesame oil

ANCIENT HISTORY PERMEATES THE CULTURE and the foods of Henan, resulting in a cuisine that celebrates northern and southern tastes, reflects the four seasons, and is flavored with a sure hand.

Much of China's civilization and its first cooking methods grew up in this timeless province. As Henan is the mother of China's cuisines, it should come as no surprise that it was also where one of China's first recorded banquets took place, in about 537 BCE.

Henan is the home of the predecessor of Chinese culinary professionals, Yi Yin. This early Shang dynasty philosopher is credited with setting down some of the initial rules that guided the growth of China's many cuisines over the ensuing millennia, such as the need for a chef to understand the nature of the ingredients being used and how to turn even off-putting flavors into delicious food through the mastery of cooking skills.

Food remained a big deal in Henan for thousands of years, and so, for example, while the West was locked down in the terrors of the Dark Ages, the largest metropolis in the world—Kaifeng—offered over one hundred famous eating places.

Situated in northeastern Henan on the Yellow River, this former capital truly was an international city. It even became home to a small Jewish community that still exists. Kaifeng was located on a branch route of the Silk Road, and the ancestors of these Jews may have traveled on it from Persia or India. They had a synagogue and other traditional buildings, such as a ritual bath and kosher butcher. However, unlike China's vast population of Hui Muslims, they never had much of an impact on Henan's cuisine—perhaps because there were so few of them.

1. Toss all of the poaching broth ingredients together in a large, narrow pasta pot, then fill it two-thirds full with water; it should be just wide enough to hold the chicken. Bring the ingredients to a boil and then allow them to simmer while you prepare the chicken.

2. Pat the chicken all over with a paper towel to ensure that the skin is dry and tacky, since the maltose will glide off of any wet areas. Fold the wings underneath themselves so that they lie flat against the body, and tie the legs together along with the tail so that you have a nice, tight, football-shaped chicken (see page 461); this will help keep any pieces from burning and allow all of the chicken to brown evenly.

3. Melt the maltose or honey until it is runny, place the chicken on a clean plate, and then use a pastry brush to completely coat the chicken with the syrup. If the maltose starts to harden, just reheat it as needed.

4. Heat the oil in a wok until a chopstick inserted in the oil immediately bubbles all over. Do not drop any moisture into the oil after this point, as it will explode and possibly burn you. Adjust the heat to maintain a steady bubbling that does not burn the chicken. Gently lower the chicken into the oil and carefully turn it over and around in the hot oil so that all of the surfaces are a deep, mahogany brown. I like to use 2 bamboo tongs to do this, as they can be shoved into the top and bottom cavities, prop up the chicken as it browns on a wobbly side, and even flip it up on its end. Try not to use metal spatulas, which will tear the skin. If the skin does happen to tear in places anyway, or if it sticks to the wok, don't worry, as the chicken will be chopped up before serving and no one will be the wiser.

5. When the chicken is completely browned, lower it into the poaching broth and add boiling water, if needed, to cover the chicken. Bring the broth to a boil and then reduce the heat to the lowest setting, which should give you a very, very slow simmer. Cover the pot and allow the chicken to gently poach for about 2 hours, then turn off the heat and let the chicken rest in the covered pot until the broth is warm, at least another 2 hours. Use a Chinese spider or a wide strainer to help you carefully lift the chicken out of the broth and onto a plate—use extreme care, as it will fall apart easily. Drain any liquids back into the pot, let the chicken come to room temperature, and then chill it for at least 4 hours or overnight. Chop into pieces (see page 460) and serve at room temperature or slightly warm.

The frying oil may be strained, refrigerated, and used again. The poaching liquid can be strained and frozen.

I have modified the original recipe a bit by adding fish sauce to give extra depth to the flavors. The traditional way of making Daokou chicken also calls for thirteen Chinese herbs, some of which are quite difficult to locate in the United States. The ones listed here are generally easy to find in areas with large Chinese populations, but just leave out whatever you cannot find—the chicken will still be great.

Wúwéi xūnyā 無為薰鴨

Wuwei Smoked Duck

ANHUI • SERVES 6 TO 8

This duck dish from Wuwei County in Anhui has been around for at least 250 years. It's commonly a star in Anhui cookbooks—as rare as these might be—and with good reason: the vinegar in the sauce cuts the richness of the crispy duck skin beautifully, and the meat is tender and smoky.

Most smoked foods in this book use smoke as a final step to either cook or season the ingredients. In this dish, however, and in Sichuan's Camphor Tea Duck (page 284), the bird is smoked in the middle of the process, halfway between a quick brining and a slow braise. What you end up with is a dish with considerable depth and nuance.

DUCK

1 whole duck, fresh or frozen and fully thawed
4 teaspoons sea salt
⅛ teaspoon pink salt
Spray oil
Handful of applewood smoking chips

BRAISING LIQUID

2 teaspoons fennel seeds
4 star anise
1 stick cinnamon
2 teaspoons whole Sichuan peppercorns
½ cup regular soy sauce
¼ cup black vinegar
2 tablespoons rock sugar
8 green onions, trimmed
12 slices fresh ginger
4 cups boiling water

GARNISH

Toasted sesame oil, as needed
Cilantro sprigs

1. Pat the duck dry, inside and out. Remove any extra fat around the cavity. Combine the sea salt and pink salt and rub the inside and outside of the duck thoroughly. Chill the bird for about 2 hours.

2. Bring about 8 cups water to a boil; a tall pasta pot is perfect. Rinse the duck thoroughly. If the duck does not have a head and feet, tie the legs together at the bottom joint and slip a loop of butcher's twine around the body under the wings (see page 461). Place a large work bowl next to the stove. Pick up the bird by its legs and dunk it a few times, way down into the boiling water, as this will tighten the skin around the duck and close the pores. Put the duck in the bowl and then pick it up from the neck, or with the twine under its wings, and repeat the dunking process. Remove the duck to the bowl and use a clean towel to lightly rub the duck's skin to remove any loose surface matter, leaving a white, shiny skin that will absorb the smoke.

3. Lightly spray the inside of your smoker (see page 27) with oil to keep the duck from sticking. Heat the wood chips in your smoker; when you have a fine haze winding up toward the stove fan, which should be on full blast, place the duck in the smoker and return the cover. Smoke the duck for about 5 minutes per side, then remove it to the work bowl.

4. Clean your pot and put a trivet in the bottom of it. Pack the dry spices into a mesh ball or cheesecloth bag and toss this into the pot along with the rest of the ingredients for the braising liquid. Bring the pot to a full boil and simmer for about 10 minutes; taste and adjust the seasoning. Add the duck, bring the pot to a full boil once again, and then lower the heat to a simmer. Slowly cook the bird for about 45 minutes. Remove the duck to a platter and let it cool before cutting it into 1-inch-wide pieces (see page 460). It can be steamed if you wish to serve it hot, but the bird is much easier to cut up when it is cold. Drizzle sesame oil over the duck; it is good warm, hot, or at room temperature. Serve with some cilantro tucked all around.

Nánjīng yánshuǐ yā 南京鹽水鴨

Nanjing Saltwater Duck

JIANGSU • SERVES 6

Summer months in many parts of China are brutal, and on some days it can be very difficult to work up enthusiasm for food there. But man (and woman) cannot survive on ice cream and beer alone, and so the denizens of Jiangsu have come up with some pretty great summer foods. This simple yet delicious duck dish is one such example.

In this recipe, the duck is salted overnight, cooked in nothing more than water, salt, and aromatics, and then chilled. It's that easy. As far as what cut of duck to get, I'd recommend duck legs. They are a heck of a lot cheaper than buying an entire bird, they slice up easily once cold, and they are almost all meat. You will need a heavy cleaver to whack up the legs, however, so if you don't have one, get duck breasts instead. They are just as tasty, and they can easily be boned and sliced once cooked.

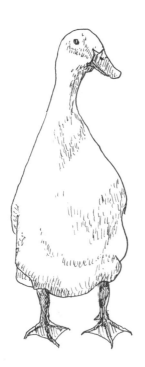

DUCK AND SALT RUB

4 whole duck legs (thighs attached) with skin on
2 tablespoons coarse sea salt
2 teaspoons five-spice powder (page 441 or store-bought)
2 teaspoons ground toasted Sichuan peppercorns (page 441)

BRAISING LIQUID

2 green onions, trimmed
1 star anise
5 slices fresh ginger
2 teaspoons sea salt

1. Start this 2 days before you wish to serve it. Pat the duck dry and pluck off any pinfeathers you find, as well as the thin yellow skin. Place the legs in a plastic container. Sprinkle them with the salt and spices, rubbing the seasonings thoroughly into every part of the legs. Cover the container and chill for about 24 hours.

2. The next day, rinse the duck legs in plenty of cool tap water, being sure to get rid of all the salt and spices. Place the legs in a small saucepan and add the rest of the ingredients, as well as water to barely cover. Bring the water to a full boil, then lower the heat to a simmer. Poach the legs for 30 minutes and then remove the pan from the heat. Let the legs cool in the liquid. Remove the cooled legs to a resealable plastic bag and refrigerate overnight. Just before serving, use a very sharp heavy cleaver to whack the legs into ½-inch-wide slices. Serve cold or just slightly chilled.

Nanjing Saltwater Duck also makes a delicious appetizer or bar snack that will serve around 12.

Dōngpō ròu 東坡肉

Dongpo Pork

JIANGSU • SERVES 4

Few restaurants in the States, at present, serve this sublime dish from Jiangsu. In fact, few Jiangsu dishes are popular outside of China, even though most Chinese epicures revere the province's cuisine. Dongpo Pork happens to be one of the region's most famous dishes, and it's said to have been the brainchild of one of China's greatest poets, Su Dongpo.

To make the dish well, you must have excellent ingredients, a liberal touch with the wine bottle, and the willingness to wait for the pork to cook slowly. The finished product is buttery but not greasy, and it has a fine sweetness to it that is slightly offset by the sharpness of the green onion and ginger. The tender meat and the light, almost gelatinous skin make this another one of those sublimely textured dishes that the Chinese excel at creating.

PORK

4 pieces thick, long dried grass or butcher's twine
Boiling water, as needed
1 pound pork belly (see Tips) with the skin on

SAUCE

3 walnut-sized pieces of rock sugar
3 tablespoons peanut or vegetable oil
4 cups Shaoxing rice wine
4 cups water
5 green onions, trimmed but left whole
1 thumb-sized piece of fresh ginger, thinly sliced
4 star anise
½ stick cinnamon
3 tablespoons regular soy sauce

RICE WINES ARE AS MUCH A PART OF CHINA'S food culture as tea, especially in the Yangtze River area. Jiangsu and Zhejiang in particular enjoy a historic reputation for the exceptional quality of their wines. In fact, this region is a bit like the Loire Valley in France when it comes to discussions of a wine-based food culture, as countless dishes have been designed to complement wine and also incorporate it as a main component in the seasoning.

Rice wines are almost always served very warm in small porcelain or pottery pitchers. They are poured out into tiny wine cups that tend to be a bit wider than teacups. Good rice wine is sipped to allow for the proper appreciation of its aroma as it travels from the tongue on down to the throat. It is invariably accompanied by savory bar snacks that allow for relaxed lingering and slow imbibing.

The Yangtze's rice wines tend to be amber colored, and so they are collectively referred to as "yellow wine" (*huángjiǔ* 黃酒). Shaoxing rice wine (*Shàoxīng jiǔ* 紹興酒), which is often specified as an ingredient in this book, is named after the town in Zhejiang where it is produced. *Huādiāo* 花雕 literally means "carved" and is a Shaoxing varietal, while mild rice wine, or "cooking wine" (*liàojiǔ* 料酒), is of lesser quality than the wines destined for drinking and usually has a bit of salt added to deter its direct consumption. A good example of the latter is Taiwanese *mijiu* (see page 171).

Like their Western counterparts, the best Chinese rice wines can range in sweetness from dry or brut (*gān* 乾) to syrupy elixirs (*nóngtián* 濃甜) that pair well with dessert. The colors likewise can be anywhere from clear to a deep brown. All are nondistilled and made mainly from rice, of course, and they rely on the same mold used in fermented rice (page 415).

1. Start this recipe at least a day ahead of time, and up to 3 or 4 days earlier if you have that much leeway—the flavor only improves over a couple of days. If you're using strands of grass to tie up the pork, soak them in a large bowl of boiling water to soften them; if you're using twine, have it handy on the counter along with a pair of kitchen shears.

2. Make sure the pork is well chilled as it slices much easier when it's very cold. Pull out any hairs you find (see page 459) and trim the edges so that the pork becomes an even rectangle. Save those scraps for something else, or throw them in the pot later on for the cook's treat. Cut the pork into 4 equal portions. Tie each piece up with a length of grass or twine so it looks like a Christmas present minus the fancy bow (see the illustration below).

3. Bring a pot of water to a boil and toss in the pork. Blanch it for 5 or 10 minutes to remove all the impurities. Dump out the water, then rinse off the pork and pat it dry.

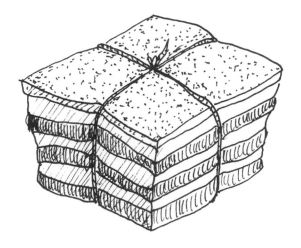

4. Place the sugar and oil in a large, light-colored saucepan (stainless steel is good) over medium heat and gently stir until the sugar melts and caramelizes (see page 33, Step 5). You can whack at any large pieces now and then to help them break down as it heats up. Once it's caramelized to a nice golden brown, add all of the rice wine, water, green onions, ginger, star anise, and cinnamon. Bring the sauce to a boil and add the pork, skin-side up. Simmer over medium heat for an hour, add the soy sauce, cover the pot, and continue to cook over the lowest heat for about 2 hours, stirring occasionally. Don't add more water unless it's truly necessary. Taste the sauce and make any adjustments at this point. If you add extra sugar, wine, or soy sauce, bring the sauce to a boil again so that the raw flavors of these ingredients are mellowed. The sauce will be thick and the pork very tender by now, so turn off the heat and let the pork continue to soak up the juices for another couple of hours.

5. Once this time is up, place the pork in a small sandpot or casserole dish and strain the juices over it. Discard the solids. Cover and chill the pork at least overnight and for up to a few days. A little more than a half an hour before you want to serve it, scrape off the congealed fat and reserve it for stir-fries, as it is delicious. Steam the covered sandpot for about 30 minutes and serve this dish hot right out of the container. As you serve your guests, snip open the packages so that the pork can be enjoyed without struggle.

The best pork belly has many thin, alternating layers of meat and fat (for information on selecting pork belly, see page 485).

Don't use a really salty soy sauce, which is usually called "dark soy sauce" and looks kind of like molasses (see page 489).

Zhēnzhūwán 珍珠丸

Pearl Meatballs

HUBEI • SERVES ABOUT 6 TO 8

This beautiful dish incorporates all of the classic tastes of Hubei: sticky rice, pork, fresh fish, and sweet water chestnuts. The recipe comes from Xiantao, a city in central Hubei, on the delta where the Han and Yangtze Rivers meet. In olden days this town was known for three dishes: rice crumb pork (see the Sichuanese version on page 286), the pale meatballs known as *zhēngbáiwán* 蒸白丸 (literally "steamed white balls"), and these Pearl Meatballs.

If my memory serves, a variation on this dish might have been the first real Chinese dish I ever prepared as a kid (Chun King canned chow mein notwithstanding). I seem to remember a recipe for this coming out of one of my mother's hausfrau magazines, perhaps *Woman's Day* or *Good Housekeeping*. It looked a lot like the porcupine meatballs that were making the rounds of the suburbs in those days, minus the tomato sauce of course, and it was a tantalizing glimpse of what food from China could taste like (although it was made that day with canned water chestnuts, supermarket pork, and whatever passed for rice then—Uncle Ben's, perhaps). Fast-forward a decade and there I am in Taipei eating real pearl meatballs and realizing that they could be something infinitely more delicious.

MEATBALLS

2 cups long-grain sticky rice, rinsed and soaked
    at least 2 hours
Spray oil
8 ounces chilled fatback (or firm belly fat
    or other solid, unrendered pork fat)
4 water chestnuts, fresh or frozen and defrosted,
    peeled and coarsely chopped
8 ounces chilled ground pork (15 percent fat)
6 ounces chilled, boned, skinned flatfish of any kind,
    coarsely chopped
1 tablespoon peeled and finely chopped fresh ginger
2 large eggs
1 teaspoon sea salt
Lots of freshly ground black pepper, or to taste
2 green onions, trimmed and coarsely chopped
1 tablespoon Shaoxing rice wine
3 tablespoons cornstarch

DIPPING SAUCE

¼ cup any kind of chili paste
    (page 437 or 438 recommended)
Soy sauce and black vinegar to taste

THE YANGTZE AND ITS TRIBUTARIES HAVE fertilized temperate Hubei for thousands of years, with eons of silt layers nurturing her rich agricultural lands. Such abundance led to dishes renowned as early as 2,500 years ago, back when Hubei was known as the great kingdom of Chu. Even earlier than that, this was a land where rhinoceros and other proud beasts roamed around a great freshwater lake romantically called the Cloud Dream Marsh.

Hubei's capital city of Wuhan has been around a very long time, too—longer than even Xi'an and Beijing—and it is connected via the Yangtze to so many other interior cities that (geographically speaking, at least) it is considered a Chinese version of Vienna. As a result, the wealthy have lived here in comfort for centuries and developed a cuisine fueled by very hefty wallets. Unlike the cooking traditions of China's great seaports, the cuisine of this inland city was only very marginally affected by its status as a foreign concession following the Opium Wars (see page 162), when the Hankou part of Wuhan was administered by the British, French, Russians, Germans, and Japanese.

Just to the east of Hubei is Jiangxi, a province that also has more than a few toes dipped into the Yangtze River and is dominated by a huge river valley edging China's largest freshwater body, Lake Poyang. While the Yangtze flows from west to east, Jiangxi's Gan River courses from south to north. Meandering almost directly through the middle of the province, the Gan is what allowed Jiangxi to flourish, for rugged terrain cut off easy land travel to the east, south, and west.

Many of the mountains surrounding Jiangxi are so virtually uninhabitable by man that, as late as a few decades ago, they were some of the last places where the South China tiger was sighted. Many other animals roam the mist-shrouded peaks and valleys and occasionally find themselves on the local dinner tables.

1. Drain the rice in a sieve set in the sink while you prepare the rest of the ingredients. Have a basket steamer set up (see page 49)—metal works best here for cleanup—and spray the inside of the steamer with oil.

2. Cut the pork fat into very small cubes and place half of it in a small work bowl with the water chestnuts. Place the other half in a food processor along with the ground pork, fish, and ginger. Process the meat mixture for a couple of minutes, scraping it down as needed, until you have an even, fine paste. Add the eggs, salt, pepper, green onions, rice wine, and cornstarch and process again until they are fully incorporated and the filling is light and fluffy. This can also be done by hand using the method described on page 458. Empty the filling into the bowl with the water chestnuts and fat, then mix these together by hand.

3. Put the rice in a wide, shallow bowl and place it on your work space next to the meatball mixture. Use a metal spoon to scoop a generous tablespoon of the meat and shape it roughly into a ball before dropping it into the rice. Repeat this a couple of times until the top of the rice is about half covered with meatballs. Then pick up a meatball and turn it over in the rice; place it in your cupped hand and roll it around to shape the ball. Pat on more rice if there are bald spots and place the finished meatball in a steamer basket. Repeat with the rest of the meatballs until done, setting them about an inch apart so that they do not stick to one another. This will probably take 3 or 4 baskets to finish. If you have extra rice after finishing the meatballs—and you most definitely will—use it to make some Congee (page 226), or toss it in some soup for a quick lunch. Steam the meatballs over high heat for 10 to 15 minutes, until done.

4. To make the dipping sauce, mix the chili sauce with soy sauce and vinegar to taste. Serve the meatballs hot with the dipping sauce. They can be served right out of the steamer baskets, if you like. The best way to do this is to steam all of the meatballs ahead of time, cool them on a baking sheet (they can be refrigerated for a day or two, as well), and then place the cold meatballs in the steaming baskets so that they barely touch. Steam them again until hot.

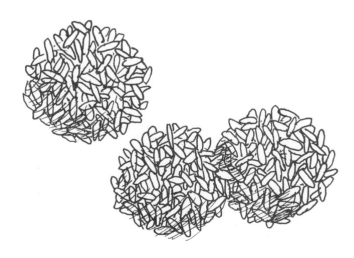

Méicài kòuròu 梅菜扣肉

Shaoxing-Style Pork Belly

ZHEJIANG · SERVES 4 TO 6

Getting this one dish right took me decades, but in the end it was worth it. When done right—like here—a perfect balance is struck between sweet and savory, meat and vegetable, fresh and preserved, tender and chewy. A specialty of Zhejiang, this pork belly is seasoned by dark, flaky Shaoxing-style *meicai*, a preserved mustard green whose name literally means "plum vegetable." This always struck me as strange until I one day realized that the original name was *méicài* 霉菜, or "molded vegetable," since the mustard is ripened much like soy sauce, another specialty of the region.

PORK

1 pound pork belly, with the skin on

1 tablespoon dark soy sauce

¼ cup frying oil

VEGETABLES AND THE REST

6 ounces Shaoxing-style preserved mustard greens
    (do not use Hakka-style *meicai*; see page 485)

¼ cup Shaoxing rice wine

¼ cup thinly sliced fresh ginger

3 green onions, trimmed but left whole

Piece of rock sugar (about the size of a large cherry),
    or more as needed

1½ teaspoons white liquor

1. Trim the pork and pluck out any hairs on the skin (see page 459). Place the pork skin-side down into the soy sauce to marinate while you prepare the rest of the ingredients. Pat the pork dry just before frying. Have a wok ready, as well as the oil and a pot of cool tap water.

2. Place the *meicai* in a sieve and rinse it with very warm tap water. As soon as it has softened up a bit, squeeze it dry. Work apart the clumps and use kitchen shears to chop any largish pieces. Place the *meicai* in a medium heatproof bowl and toss it with the rice wine.

3. Set the wok over medium-high heat, add the oil, and fry *only the skin* of the pork. Cover the wok with a spatter screen, and when the skin is a nice brown, transfer the pork to the cool water. As soon as it can be handled easily, slice the pork crosswise into pieces about ¼ inch thick.

4. Arrange the pork slices over the *meicai* and then sprinkle on the ginger slices. Lay the whole green onions on top, and finally add the rock sugar.

5. Set the bowl inside a steamer (see page 49) and cover the bowl with a saucer. Steam the pork for around 2 hours, remove it from the steamer, and let it come to room temperature. Remove the green onions and reserve the ginger slices. Drain the sauce out into a measuring cup and refrigerate it until the fat hardens and can be easily removed.

6. Line the inside of a heatproof 6-cup bowl with the pork slices by first placing 1 or 2 of the prettiest slices at the very bottom and then covering the sides by overlapping them in an attractive pattern. Mound the *meicai* in the middle and lightly pack it down. Drizzle in the white liquor and sauce, and arrange the ginger slices back on top.

7. Steam the bowl as in Step 5 for another 4 hours or so. Pour off the sauce into a measuring cup, invert a rimmed plate over the bowl, and flip the pork over onto the plate. Pour the sauce around the mound of pork and serve.

Wúxí páigǔ 無錫排骨

Wuxi Spareribs

JIANGSU • SERVES 4

My love affair with Wuxi Spareribs is a long and passionate one. It started when I worked at the museum in Taiwan. I would interpret when the director took foreign guests out to banquets, and whenever we ended up at one of Taipei's many fancy Jiangsu-style restaurants, I'd practically hold my breath, praying that Wuxi Spareribs would be served.

SPARERIBS

1 side of pork spareribs (2 to 2½ pounds)
    cut lengthwise in half
½ cup regular soy sauce
Peanut or vegetable oil for frying

SAUCE

6 green onions, trimmed, smashed with
    the side of a cleaver, and cut into 1-inch lengths
4 pieces fresh ginger (about 1 cup), smashed with
    the side of a cleaver
6 tablespoons Shaoxing rice wine
4 star anise
2 sticks cinnamon
3 to 4 cups boiling water, or as needed
¼ cup rock sugar, plus more if desired
1 teaspoon dark soy sauce
Toasted sesame oil, optional

1. Have your butcher cut the ribs in half so that you're left with 2 long strips of riblets, and then cut between the bones and through the cartilage. Toss the riblets in a large bowl with the soy sauce and marinate them for 20 to 30 minutes.

2. Warm about 2 inches of oil in a wok over medium-high heat until it shimmers. Lift about half of the ribs out of the marinade (reserve this soy sauce for later), shake off any excess, and cautiously add them to the hot oil; use a spatter screen or cover to protect yourself. Deep-fry the ribs until they're dark brown, then repeat with the second half.

3. Pour off all but a tablespoon or two of the oil. Stir-fry the onions and ginger for about a minute and then add the soy sauce used as a marinade, as well as the rice wine, star anise, cinnamon, and 3 cups boiling water. Bring the sauce to a boil, add the ribs, and top it off with a bit more water if necessary to cover. Bring the sauce to a boil again and then lower to a gentle simmer. Cook the ribs covered for about 1½ hours, until the meatiest areas can be easily pierced with a chopstick, and then add the sugar and dark soy sauce. Remove the cover and continue to braise the ribs until they are meltingly tender, about 20 to 30 minutes. Remove the ribs to a platter before boiling down the sauce. Taste the sauce and adjust the seasoning.

4. Strain the thick sauce to remove all the seasonings and then pour it over the ribs. You can sprinkle just a few drops of sesame oil into the sauce to provide a bit more gloss, if you like.

This recipe can be multiplied easily. I usually make at least twice this amount so that I can have spareribs ready in the freezer.

Xiāzǐ niújīn 蝦籽牛筋

Braised Tendons with Dried Shrimp Roe

ZHEJIANG · SERVES 4 TO 6

In the West, the adjectives usually used to describe tendons are not that inspiring: tough, stringy, and tasteless. But they can be tender and delicious and are extremely versatile. Beef tendons aren't at all greasy and can be used as blank canvasses for a variety of different flavors (see pages 14 and 18).

In addition to tendons, this recipe uses another unsung ingredient: dried shrimp roe. The roe has a remarkable rust-red color and an alluring aroma. If you've never tried shrimp roe before, you're in for something special. Tossed together with ginger, green onions, and fish sauce, this entrée is always a surprise favorite at the table.

TENDONS
2 beef tendons, 1¼ to 1½ pounds
Boiling water, as needed

SAUCE
½ cup peanut or vegetable oil
¼ cup dried shrimp roe
2 teaspoons peeled and finely shredded fresh ginger
2 green onions, trimmed, split, and cut into 1-inch sections
¼ cup Shaoxing rice wine
2 tablespoons regular soy sauce
1 teaspoon fish sauce
2 teaspoons sugar
1 cup boiling water

TO FINISH
2 green onions, green parts only
2 teaspoons toasted sesame oil

1. Rinse the tendons and place them in a pan wide enough to hold them flat. Cover them with boiling water by at least 1 inch (see Tips), bring the water to a boil again over high heat, and then cover and lower the heat to a slow simmer. Gently cook them until they relax and can be easily pierced with a chopstick, about 3 hours. The tendons can also be quickly prepared in a pressure cooker in water to cover for 1 hour or until tender. Discard the liquid, cool the tendons to room temperature, place in a resealable plastic bag, and refrigerate them. The tendons can be cooked to this point up to 3 days ahead of when you are going to serve them.

2. Cut the tendons in half lengthwise, then quarter them lengthwise into strips about ½ inch wide all around. Cut these strips into pieces about 1 inch long.

3. Pour the oil into a cool wok and add the roe. Give the roe a few minutes to absorb most of the oil, then raise the heat under the wok to medium. Slowly cook the roe until it looks liquid and bubbly, then add the tendons, ginger, and green onions. Cook for a few minutes to coat the tendons with the roe. Raise the heat to high and pour in the rice wine. As the wine cooks down, add the soy sauce, fish sauce, sugar, and boiling water. Bring the sauce to a boil and then lower the heat to medium. Cook the tendons, stirring occasionally to keep them from sticking, until almost all of the sauce has been absorbed. Taste and adjust the seasoning.

4. Just before serving, cut the leaves of the green onions into thin diagonal strips and add them to the hot tendons along with the sesame oil. Toss quickly and serve while the tendons are still hot.

The tendons will contract into tight balls as the water heats up, and before you know it, they will be as hard as rocks. They must be slowly simmered for about 3 hours (or cooked in a pressure cooker for about 1 hour) until they completely relax and return to their original size.

If you have extra cooked tendons, you can use them in recipes like Clear Beef Soup with Chinese Herbs and Radishes (page 18).

Huáidiàn xūn yángròu 槐店薰羊肉

Huaidian Smoked Lamb

HENAN · SERVES 4 TO 6

Huaidian, in eastern Henan, lies very close to Shangqiu, the capital of the Shang dynasty during the second millennium BCE. This dish has been around for at least a century; it's one of those recipes that doesn't look particularly intriguing at first glance. In fact, the last time I served this, my guests had a decidedly ho-hum look on their faces. That is, of course, until they took the first bite.

The lamb is brined for a few days, which turns the meat a rosy red and makes it moist and flavorful. The meat is then cooked with a handful of warm spices before being quickly smoked over wood chips. It might sound like a slow process, but there is very little actual work involved, and the results are unparalleled.

LAMB AND BRINE

1 pound lamb riblets or breast (or some other fatty
    but tasty cut of lamb, goat, or mutton that can be
    easily cut into smallish pieces)
4 cups water, divided in half
3 tablespoons sea salt

POACHING LIQUID

1 teaspoon whole black peppercorns
3 whole cloves
2 teaspoons whole Sichuan peppercorns
1 teaspoon fennel seeds
1 black cardamom pod, lightly crushed

SMOKING AND FINISHING

Large handful of wood chips (apple, oak,
    or another sweet variety)
Spray oil
2 teaspoons toasted sesame oil

1. Start this dish at least 2 days before you plan to serve it. Pat the lamb dry, and if the meat hasn't been cut into inch-wide strips between the bones, do it now. Bring half the water to a boil, add the salt, and stir to dissolve. Add the rest of the water to the brine and allow it to cool down completely. Place the lamb in the brine, toss it carefully so that each piece is coated and covered by the brine, cover, and refrigerate. Check the lamb after 24 hours; if it has turned a dark red, remove it from the brine and pat it dry. If not, brine it for another 12 to 24 hours, but not much longer than that, as the meat will become too salty.

2. Place the whole spices in a dry wok and stir over medium heat until they smell fragrant and start to pop. Pack the spices in a piece of cheesecloth or a mesh ball and place them in a large saucepan with the brined lamb. Cover the lamb with about 1 inch of water, bring to a boil, and then lower to a gentle simmer. Poach the lamb until it is very tender but not falling apart, about 30 minutes. Remove it from the liquid, drain it thoroughly, and let it cool until it is easy to handle. The dish can be prepared up to this point and refrigerated for a couple of days.

3. Prepare your smoker (see page 27) and place the wood chips at the bottom. Arrange the rack over the chips, spray it with oil, place the lamb on top of the grill with space between the pieces, cover, and then heat the smoker over high until white smoke begins to puff out of the top. After 3 minutes, turn off the heat, remove the smoker from the stove, and let the meat sit in the smoker for no more than another 5 minutes. Take the meat out of the smoker, rub it lightly with the sesame oil, and arrange on a serving platter. Serve warm or hot.

Yóumèn chūnsǔn 油燜春筍

Oil-Braised Spring Bamboo Shoots

ZHEJIANG • SERVES 4

This dish comes from the bamboo-laced mountains of Zhejiang. It goes by the Chinese name of "spring bamboo shoots braised in oil" and, unfortunately, cooks often take that name a bit too literally, bathing the bamboo in oil. To really do this dish right, the oil should be relatively light: it's there primarily to help the cooking process, but also to add a savory, creamy note to the stark cleanliness of the bamboo. The dish should not be seasoned with a heavy hand, either, because the delicacy of the stems' grassy flavor is easily overwhelmed.

You can serve this dish hot, cold, or at any point in between, so it's a great one to make ahead of time. I prefer to serve it when it is slightly warmer than room temperature. That way, the oil stays in the background of the dish and provides just the suggestion of richness.

14 to 16 ounces spring bamboo shoots, defrosted if
    frozen and peeled and blanched if fresh (see Tip)
1 cup water
2 tablespoons green onion oil (page 434),
    or fresh peanut or vegetable oil
1 teaspoon toasted sesame oil
2 tablespoons Shaoxing rice wine
2½ tablespoons regular soy sauce
1½ tablespoons sugar

1. Start this a day before you plan to serve it. Shred the bamboo shoots into thinnish strips by notching the stem end with a paring knife (go down about ½ inch or so if the stems are a bit hefty) and then pulling the bamboo shoot apart. Try to make all the strips more or less the same size—around ½ inch wide. I like to leave the strips long because I find them prettier that way (the interiors look like ladders), but cut them crosswise in half, if you wish.

2. Place the bamboo shoots, water, oils, rice wine, and soy sauce (but not the sugar) in a saucepan, cover, bring to a boil, and then lower the heat to a simmer. Cook the shoots covered for about 30 minutes, until they are completely tender at the thickest bases. Add the sugar, toss again, and cook over high heat uncovered until almost all of the sauce has evaporated. Cool, cover, refrigerate overnight, and serve the next day warm, cool, or hot.

Fresh bamboo shoots need to be blanched to remove their bitterness. To prepare fresh bamboo shoots, first peel them by slicing up the side with a very sharp blade, pressing down deeper as you reach the tip. Then, peel off the individual sheaths and trim off any tough bits. Next, place the peeled bamboo shoots in a saucepan, cover with water, and bring the water to a boil. Reduce the heat to a simmer and cook the shoots until the bases are tender, about 1 hour. If there are lots of different sizes of bamboo shoots in there, pluck out the little ones as they are done so they are not cooked to death. Rinse the shoots in cool tap water and drain in a colander. Frozen bamboo shoots have already been blanched, so all you need to do is defrost them thoroughly and rinse.

Jīnshā kǔguā 金沙苦瓜

Bitter Melons in Golden Sand

SHANGHAI · SERVES 4 TO 6

2 medium bitter melons
Boiling water, as needed
6 raw brined egg yolks (page 422 or store-bought)
2 cloves garlic
1 green onion, trimmed
¼ cup peanut or vegetable oil
2 to 3 teaspoons sugar
2 teaspoons sea salt

Golden sand is made by mashing up the yolks of brined eggs and then stir-frying them into a buttery sauce. It's used in a variety of dishes, and the last time my husband and I were in Shanghai, it was popular with many different chefs. Some of the things we had with golden sand were less than stellar—shellfish, for example, which I found too fatty and salty when combined with golden sand—but when it's used as a textural and flavorful contrast for a clean-tasting and simple main ingredient, the results can be inspired.

My favorite rendition matches up golden sand with bitter melons. The vegetables are cut into thin batons, blanched, cooled down, and then tossed in the sauce. This serves to leach out most of the bitterness and essentially cook the melon very rapidly, which preserves its exquisite color and crispness. The result is a beautiful trio of contrasts: the jade color of the vegetable against the amber, salted egg yolk; the crunchy melon and the creamy sauce; and the slightly bitter and yet slightly sweet flavors mingling with the salty and buttery aromas of the golden sand.

1. Wash and dry the bitter melons and trim off both ends, as well as any damaged areas. Split the melons lengthwise in half and scoop out both the seeds and any pith. Cut the melon halves crosswise into 2-inch or so lengths, then slice these pieces lengthwise into ¼-inch-thick strips.

2. Bring water to a boil in a medium saucepan and blanch the bitter melons for less than 1 minute, until they turn bright green and taste barely cooked. Rinse the bitter melons with cool tap water in a colander set in the sink and then shake them dry.

3. Use a fork to mash the egg yolks. Finely chop the garlic and green onion.

4. Place a wok over medium-high heat until hot and add the oil. As soon as the oil starts to shimmer, add the mashed egg yolks, garlic, and green onion and stir-fry them until the sauce foams up. Add the sugar and salt and then toss in the well-drained bitter melon, mixing it quickly to heat the pieces through. Taste and adjust the seasoning. Pour the melons onto a serving plate and scrape all of the sauce out of the wok on top of them. Serve while still very hot.

A general rule is, the lighter the green of the bitter melon, the less bitter it is.

This recipe calls for brined chicken eggs. If you are using duck or goose yolks, be sure to adjust the quantity accordingly. Also, because duck and goose eggs tend to have a gamy or fishy flavor, I'd recommend cutting each yolk in half, sprinkling them with a bit of white liquor or rice wine, and steaming them for about 5 minutes. Be sure to cool the yolks before mashing.

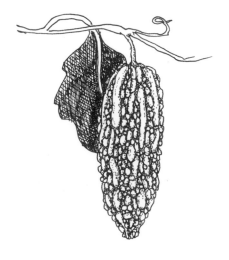

Sìxǐ kǎofū 四喜烤麩

Four Happiness Gluten and Vegetables

JIANGSU · SERVES 4 TO 6

The first Chinese funeral I attended in Taipei was followed by a banquet at a Buddhist-style restaurant. I had never eaten such good vegetarian food. It tasted like there was meat in most of the dishes, but upon closer inspection, the meat turned out to be clever substitutes made from either bean curd or wheat gluten.

Although wheat gluten has been given short shrift in Western fare, it's long been incorporated into Chinese cuisine; see page 482 for more information on gluten varieties.

Two secrets are key to success here: first, tear the gluten, rather than cut it into cubes. The ragged edges and various sizes will give texture and variety to something that is inarguably a very bland ingredient, and the bigger pieces will sponge up the rich sauce and make each bite intensely flavorful. Second, fry the gluten pieces until brown: the outsides will crisp up and become foils for the moist centers, giving them the mouthfeel that suggests meat.

4 ounces raised wheat gluten (page 403 or store-bought)
Peanut or vegetable oil for frying (used oil is all right if it smells fresh)
1 large wood ear fungus, fresh or dried and plumped up
1 large winter bamboo shoot, defrosted if frozen and peeled and blanched if fresh (see Tip, page 122)
24 dried daylily flowers, soaked in boiling water until pliable, or 1 carrot, peeled and thinly sliced
½ cup shelled green soybeans (*edamame*)
2 green onions, trimmed and cut into 1-inch lengths
4 slices fresh ginger
2 star anise
3 tablespoons dark soy sauce
1 tablespoon Shaoxing rice wine
Walnut-sized piece of rock sugar, or 1 tablespoon sugar
3 cups water
Soy sauce, sugar, and toasted sesame oil, as needed

1. Tear the gluten into pieces about 1 inch square or so; it's all right if you end up with crumbs and raggedy pieces, too, as these add complexity to the dish. Warm up about 2 inches of oil in a wok over medium-high heat until it begins to shimmer, add a small handful of the gluten, and fry it until it is golden all over. Remove the fried gluten to a plate, and then fry the rest of the gluten in batches of similarly sized pieces, so that the smaller bits don't stay in too long.

2. Drain the wood ear fungus and tear it into pieces about the same size as the shredded gluten. Slice the bamboo shoot into thin slices and cut these crosswise at an angle. Drain the daylily flowers, remove any tough parts, and tie them in pairs into knots. If the soybeans are frozen, rinse them in a colander under warm water to defrost them.

3. Drain all the oil out of the wok except for about 3 tablespoons and heat the oil over medium-high heat until it shimmers. Add the green onions and ginger and stir-fry them for a minute to release their fragrance. Add the wood ear pieces and bamboo shoot slices and stir-fry them for another minute. Toss in the star anise, soy sauce, rice wine, sugar, and water. Bring to a boil, add the fried gluten, and simmer for about half an hour;

all of the ingredients should be soft and flavorful by then. Add the daylily knots and green soybeans to the wok, stir gently, and cook uncovered for about 10 minutes. The sauce should be thick and glossy at this point. If not, use a slotted spoon to remove everything but the sauce from the wok. Simmer the sauce over medium-high heat and stir until it is reduced to the consistency of molasses. Return the gluten mixture to the wok and toss gently to coat. Taste and adjust the seasoning with more soy sauce, sugar, and sesame oil as needed.

4. Allow the dish to come to room temperature before serving. This can be made up to 3 days ahead of time and should be refrigerated if not eaten right away.

This kind of gluten spoils easily, so smell it carefully before you use it and discard it if there's a sour aroma. If it is not going to be used immediately, be sure to freeze it.

Try this as an appetizer, too.

Kàocài 燠菜

Slow-Braised Bok Choy

SHANGHAI · SERVES 4 TO 6

There is nothing more emblematic of Shanghai's cuisine than braised bok choy. It is widely loved in Jiangsu, and this particular preparation is a standby in any Shanghainese restaurant. The vegetables are gently cooked until they're completely tender, and the soy sauce, sugar, and oil are added in perfectly proportional amounts. This is home cooking at its finest.

1 pound (or so) bok choy, mustard cabbage, or other flavorful, slightly bitter vegetable
2 tablespoons green onion oil (page 434)
1 tablespoon regular soy sauce
1½ teaspoons sugar
½ cup unsalted chicken stock (page 380) or water
Extra green onion oil and its fried green onions for garnish

1. Prepare this the day before you wish to serve it. Trim the vegetable into small, bite-sized pieces, and discard any tough stems or cores; if using baby bok choy, you may leave them whole or cut them in half. Clean them well, rinse, and drain.

2. Place the vegetables in a saucepan with the rest of the ingredients. Bring the pan to a boil, cover tightly, and reduce the heat to a simmer. Cook the vegetables covered for about 5 minutes, then uncover and stir. Cover and cook for another 5 to 10 minutes or so, until the vegetables are very tender. Taste and adjust the seasoning; they should taste slightly overseasoned since they will be served cold or cool, which will dull the sweet and salty flavors. Let the vegetables come to room temperature, place them and the sauce in a covered container, and chill overnight.

3. Arrange the vegetables attractively in a serving dish. Drizzle the green onion oil over the top and sprinkle with the fried onions. Serve cold or at room temperature.

Jī huǒ zhǔ gānsī 雞火煮乾絲

Molded Ham, Chicken, and Bean Curd Shreds

HUAI YANG • SERVES 4

This classic Yangzhou recipe is an inspired layering of sweet and salty ham, rich stock, delicate chicken, and hearty mushrooms that transfer much of their flavors to a billowy pile of bean curd. Together they create an extraordinary example of Huai Yang sensibilities. I like to let this dish sit overnight and then steam it again before serving: this changes the texture of the bean curd, making it expand and fluff up in a wonderful way. I stumbled on this possibility when I was forced to prepare this recipe so that I could serve it the next day at a friend's house.

1 chicken breast
2 cups boiling water, plus more for the bean curd
2 tablespoons thinly sliced fresh ginger
2 green onions, trimmed
2 large black mushrooms, fresh or dried and plumped up
1-inch cube Chinese-style ham or Hunan-style cured pork
    (see charcuterie, page 478)
2 cups unsalted chicken stock (page 380)
2 tablespoons Shaoxing rice wine
1 block (14 ounces or so) firm bean curd
Sea salt to taste

1. The day before you plan to serve this, remove the skin and excess fat from the chicken and place it in a medium saucepan. Add the boiling water, ginger, and whole green onions. Bring the water to a boil again, lower the heat to a simmer, and slowly cook the chicken for about 10 minutes. Remove the pan from the heat, cover it, and let the chicken sit in the hot bath for about 15 minutes. Take the chicken out of the pan and let it cool down until it can be handled easily. Use your hands to shred the chicken into thin pieces and save the cooking liquid for something else.

2. While the chicken is cooking and cooling down, prepare the rest of the ingredients: trim the stems off of the mushrooms, cut the caps horizontally into thin slices, and then cut these into very thin (⅛-inch-wide) matchsticks. Trim any fat or skin off of the ham, cut it against the grain into thin slices, and then across once again into matchsticks the same size as the mushrooms. Place the chicken stock and rice wine in a medium saucepan. Add the mushrooms and cook for a few minutes until they are tender, pluck them out with a slotted spoon, and pile them up in the center of a heatproof 4-cup bowl. Add the julienned ham to the hot stock and cook for a couple of minutes until it is soft, then remove it with a slotted spoon and arrange it in a ring around the mushrooms. Finally, add the shredded chicken to the stock and bring it to a boil before removing the chicken with the slotted spoon and arranging it in a circle around the ham.

3. Cut the bean curd into very thin (⅛-inch-thick) slices and then across into very thin (⅛-inch-wide) matchsticks. Place the bean curd into a colander and pour boiling water over it to quickly blanch it and remove any beany aromas. Gently slide the bean curd into the hot stock and slowly simmer it for about 5 minutes before using a large slotted spoon to remove the matchsticks to the bowl with the mushrooms and so forth. Pile the bean curd in a thick layer on top of the mushrooms, ham, and chicken. Taste the stock and adjust the seasoning with salt and more rice wine, if needed, before pouring it over the bean curd. Let the bowl come to room temperature, cover, and chill overnight.

4. About 30 minutes before serving, cover the bowl lightly with foil so that no water enters the stock and steam it (see page 49) on high until heated through. Pour all the stock out into a measuring cup, taste, and adjust the seasoning a final time, if needed. Invert a rimmed plate over the bowl and then invert the bowl and plate together. Remove the bowl, pour the stock over the bean curd, and serve.

Huó dòufu 活豆腐

Lively Bean Curd

JIANGXI · SERVES 4

No one I know can really explain how this dish came to be called "Lively Bean Curd." It's a specialty of Jiujiang, a town in Jiangxi Province located right on the edge of the Yangtze.

I like this dish for its contrast in textures more than anything else. Soft bean curd holds center stage here, but squeaky bits of black wood ear and pale yellow daylily flowers serve as interesting counterpoints. The meat, green onion, and stock offer very nice flavors, but really this recipe is all about the dynamic textures at play.

20 (or so) dried daylily flowers
Boiling water, as needed
6 (or so) wood ear fungus, fresh or dried and plumped up
¼ cup julienned pork or chicken
4 teaspoons regular soy sauce
1 tablespoon Shaoxing rice wine
1 tablespoon cornstarch
1 green onion, trimmed
1 block (14 ounces or so) soft bean curd
2 tablespoons peanut or vegetable oil
2 cups unsalted stock of any kind (page 380 or 381)
1 teaspoon toasted sesame oil

1. First, soak the daylily flowers in boiling water while you prepare the rest of the ingredients. Later on, after they have gotten fat and look once more like blossoms, discard the water before picking off any hard parts at the stem end and then peeling them lengthwise into 3 or 4 strips. Cut or tear the wood ears into dime-sized pieces, discarding any tough bits.

2. Place the meat in a small work bowl and toss it with the soy sauce, rice wine, and cornstarch. Let the pork or chicken marinate while you get the final ingredients ready.

3. Cut the green onion into ½-inch lengths. Drain the water off of the bean curd and rinse it lightly under cool tap water. Cut the block of bean curd lengthwise in half and then crosswise into ¼-inch-thick squares.

4. Set a wok over high heat and add the oil. When the oil is hot, swirl it around in the wok and toss in the meat and all of the marinade. Stir-fry until the meat turns from pink to gray and even has a bit of browning on the edges. Add the green onion, toss, and then add the daylily flowers and wood ears. Continue to stir-fry these until the flowers just start to wilt, then pour in all of the stock. Bring the stock to a boil and slide in the sliced bean curd, fanning it out across the stock so that it heats evenly. When it comes to a boil again, lower the heat and simmer the ingredients for about 5 minutes to heat the bean curd through. Taste and adjust the seasoning, sprinkle in the sesame oil, and serve hot in a bowl or rimmed plate.

Lì dòufu 栗豆腐

Chestnut Bean Curd

ANHUI · SERVES 4

Occasionally in Chinese cooking, a simple ingredient will be treated in such a way that it takes on a completely different character. That is what happens in this dish. Silky soft bean curd abandons its custard-like texture and bland taste to become something much fluffier and more delicious. It is flavored with three different kinds of meat—chicken stock, pork, and ham—and paired with three beloved southern Anhui ingredients: that ham, as well as a winter bamboo shoot and chestnuts.

This is great cold-weather fare. You can make this dish particularly refined if you discard the pork belly and charcuterie after simmering them with the chicken stock—by that stage, most of their flavor will have been transferred to the sauce. However, frugal home cooks can rarely afford such luxury, and so, for family dinners, these two meats can be chopped finely and returned to the sandpot just before serving.

2 cups unsalted chicken stock (page 380)

About 2 tablespoons thinly sliced pork belly

About 2 tablespoons thinly sliced Chinese-style ham
     or Hunan-style cured pork (see charcuterie, page 478)

5 slices fresh ginger

1 block (14 ounces or so) soft bean curd

Boiling water, as needed

½ large winter bamboo shoot, defrosted if frozen and
     peeled and blanched if fresh (see Tip, page 122),
     about 1 cup cubed

4 ounces shelled chestnuts, fresh or frozen and defrosted

2 teaspoons regular soy sauce

1 teaspoon sugar

1 teaspoon cornstarch mixed with
     2 tablespoons Shaoxing rice wine

1 green onion, trimmed and finely chopped,
     for garnish

1. Simmer the chicken stock with the pork belly, ham, and ginger in a covered saucepan for about an hour. Strain out the solids and pour the stock into a small (4-cup) sandpot. If you like, chop the meats into fine pieces, but discard the ginger and any skin on the cured pork.

2. While the stock is simmering, place the bean curd in a small saucepan and cover with boiling water. Bring the water to a boil again over high heat and then lower the heat to a gentle simmer. Slowly cook the bean curd for about 5 minutes to rid it of excess water and firm it up a bit, then cut it into ¾-inch cubes. Peel and cut the bamboo shoot into ¾-inch cubes. Cut or break the chestnuts in half.

3. Add the bean curd, bamboo shoot, and chestnuts to the hot strained stock. Bring the stock to a boil over high heat before lowering it to a gentle simmer. Add the soy sauce and sugar. Simmer these for about half an hour, then taste and adjust the seasoning. You can prepare this dish in advance up to this point, let it come to room temperature, and then cover and refrigerate it for up to 3 days. Before serving, bring it to a boil once more, stir the cornstarch mixture into the sauce until it thickens, and then toss in the reserved chopped meats, if you like. Sprinkle the top with the green onion, cover the sandpot briefly to wilt the onion, and serve.

Frozen chestnuts that are already shelled and peeled can be found in most Chinese supermarkets.

Zhá ǒupiàn 炸藕片

Fried Lotus Chips

HUBEI • MAKES AS MANY AS YOU WANT

These are not only tasty—they are also absolutely beautiful. Plus, they possess the faint taste of lotus, making them even more delicious than potato chips, and are super simple to make. You can serve them like regular chips or pile them around roast chicken for a special treat.

A mandoline is extremely handy here for cutting the roots into wafer-thin slices. What I do is trim off the end of one root and leave the other end on as a handle; then, I just shave the root into as many slices as possible until I reach the untrimmed end. Of course, as with all sharp blades, use care when slicing things on a mandoline, as fingers can get cut in a flash.

One odd thing about lotus roots that you should be aware of is that they produce a hairlike juice that makes it look like you have very fine follicles among your slices, even after the slices have been fried. So, don't be alarmed if you see what looks like blond locks weaving in and out of the chips—they are totally harmless and melt on the tongue.

Lotus roots
Peanut or vegetable oil (used is all right if it smells fresh)
Sea salt, as needed

1. Peel the lotus roots with a potato peeler and remove any soft or brown spots. Rinse off any mud that might have worked its way into the roots (see page 451). Shave the roots into thin slices using a mandoline or a very sharp knife.

2. Place a plate covered with a paper towel next to the stove. Heat a few inches of oil in a wok over medium-high heat until a wooden chopstick inserted in the oil bubbles all over. Add a handful of the lotus root slices to the hot oil and stir them around with the chopsticks so that they don't stick to one another. Stir and fry them until they are a light golden brown all over. Use a slotted spoon to remove them from the oil and place them on the paper towel to drain. Sprinkle the hot chips with the salt to taste. Repeat with the rest of the lotus root slices until done.

3. Cool to room temperature and either serve immediately or store in a resealable plastic bag, preferably with a paper towel to absorb any moisture or extra oil.

MY FIRST LESSON IN BAMBOO SHOOTS CAME one day when I was shopping at my favorite vegetable stand in Shipai on the outskirts of Taipei. Mr. Cong always happily instructed me on the proper selection and preparation of his stellar wares. He told me, for example, that the age of a radish could be determined by the width of the bunch of leaves on its top (thinner topknots meant they were sweeter and more tender), and that bamboo shoots should never have green tips, as this means they had seen too much sun and so were converting their sugars into bitter-tasting growth.

One day a couple of years later, I was grocery shopping in another local farmers' market when I came across a tarp laid out covered with freshly harvested winter bamboo shoots. I told the farmer that if they were sweet, I'd like about four of them, and he grabbed the ones nearest to him and stuffed them into a bag. I refused the bag, saying that they would be bitter, to which he laughed, "If you know how to figure out which are the sweet ones, you can have them all for free!" Silently thanking Mr. Cong, I picked out a large bagful of ivory-tipped shoots and handed them to the man. Crestfallen, he remained as good as his word and said, "They're yours." But knowing how much work had gone into this harvest, I plucked out four, gave him his money, and had some sweet bamboo shoots for dinner, as well as a new friend at the market.

Xièkéhuáng 蟹殼黃

Crab Shell Pastries

ANHUI AND SHANGHAI · MAKES 48

As with so many wonderful foods in the Jiangsu area, Crab Shell Pastries had their beginnings in Anhui. The pastry of these stuffed biscuits tastes very much like Shaobing (page 56), and the juicy green filling is mildly oniony. They were brought to Shanghai by the wealthy merchants who visited from the remote but beautiful Huangshan region in southern Anhui. These pastries are still just as popular back in Huangshan, where they are almost a required dish at banquets.

I would always try to nab these fresh out of the oven at my favorite Shanghainese bakery in Taipei. When made right, they are hard to beat.

FILLING
2 cups ground pork (15 percent fat)
2 teaspoons sea salt
Lots of freshly ground black pepper
8 cups finely chopped green onions (5 or 6 bunches)

TOPPING
½ cup toasted sesame seeds (page 413)
¼ cup sugar dissolved in ¼ cup boiling water

1 recipe southern-style puff pastry (page 392)

1. Place the pork in a large work bowl and use chopsticks to mix in the salt, pepper, and green onions. Divide the filling into 48 pieces and roll these into balls.

2. Line 2 baking sheets with a nonstick baking mat or parchment paper. Place your oven racks in the center of your oven and heat the oven to 350°F. Pour the sesame seeds into a wide bowl and have the cooled sugar water ready, along with a pastry brush. Working on 1 pastry at a time, flatten the ball of puff pastry out into a disk about 3½ inches wide, then place a ball of filling in the center and close the pastry around it (Steps 6 to 9 plus 13 on pages 406 to 407). Roll the ball lightly and press it seam-side down on a lined baking sheet before covering it with plastic wrap. Repeat with the rest of the puff pastry and filling.

3. Use a pastry brush to swab some of the sugar water on top of each pastry before immediately flipping the pastry over into the bowl of sesame seeds. Press down lightly to make the seeds stick to the sugar water, turn the pastry over, and return it to the baking sheet. Place the pastries at least ½ inch apart, as they will rise a little bit.

4. Bake the pastries, rotating the sheets back to front halfway through the cooking time, for about 25 minutes, until the pastries are a golden brown and puffy. Remove the pastries to a cooling rack and repeat this step with the rest of the pastries until all have been baked. Cool and store in an airtight container in the refrigerator; heat them up briefly in a 350°F oven before serving.

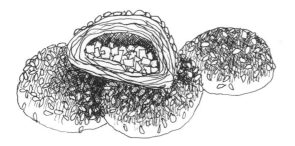

Càifàn 菜飯

Crusty Vegetable Rice

SHANGHAI · SERVES 2 AS A MAIN DISH,
4 AS A SIDE DISH

In addition to their *xiaolongbao* (page 132), Sōngjílóu 松吉樓, a restaurant run by old Jiangsu soldiers, made this dish incredibly well. I first learned about it when I watched a happy old Shanghainese gentleman order a bowl of *caifan* and tell the waiter to give him extra crust.

This is basically an eastern Chinese version of fried rice, but it is both much simpler and much more texturally interesting. The only important ingredients in here besides the rice are the vegetables and green onions. It is how the rice is cooked that turns this into a Shanghainese favorite: the rice is gently toasted on the bottom, then flipped and browned some more. This gives the dish a great crunch and also a delicate, toasty flavor.

1 pound (or so) small bok choy (see Tips)
2 green onions, trimmed
4 to 6 tablespoons oil or fat (see Tips), or more as needed
¼ cup thinly julienned Chinese-style ham or Hunan-style cured pork (see charcuterie, page 478), optional (see Tips)
½ to 1 teaspoon sea salt (less if you're using the ham)
4 cups cold cooked rice (short-grain white rice recommended)

1. Cut off the ends of the bok choy and separate the heads into leaves. Trim off any discolored bits and wash the vegetables carefully in a pan of water; rinse the leaves and make sure that no dirt is clinging to them. Shake them dry and coarsely chop the leaves into pieces no larger than ½ inch long. Cut the green onions into smallish pieces.

2. Heat ¼ cup oil or fat in a wok over high heat. Add the optional ham and the salt, swirl the wok to melt the salt, then add the chopped onions and bok choy. Stir-fry the veggies until the bok choy stems become translucent. Scoot them up the side of the wok, allowing the oil to drain back into the bottom. Add the cold rice to the wok and use a metal wok spatula to break up any clumps. Toss the rice in the hot oil, adding more oil as necessary to keep the rice from sticking. Use the spatula to lift up the rice from the bottom and shake it so that even the smaller clumps fall apart. When the rice is completely heated through, toss it with the cooked vegetables.

3. Next, make a crust form on the bottom of the rice by smoothing it into an even layer in the wok and turning the heat to medium-low; do not disturb the rice for about 5 minutes. When the rice makes a faint popping sound and smells like popcorn, lift up an edge to check. If it is golden brown, flip the rice over so that the crust is on the top. Allow the rice to form another crust on the bottom, adjusting the heat as necessary to brown the rice without burning it. When you have as much crunchy stuff as you like, toss the rice around to break up the crust and then serve it up while it is still very hot.

For the bok choy in this recipe, I recommend the variety called *wūtācài* 烏塌菜, or "black prostrate vegetable." It's called "black" because the leaves are a very dark green, and "prostrate" because the leaves grow out at a low angle to the ground, instead of straight up like most other bok choys.

You can boost the flavor a notch by adding ham and using some rendered fat for the oil.

Xiǎolóngbāo 小籠包

Xiaolongbao

HUAI YANG • MAKES 40

Xiaolongbao are tiny steamed buns filled with hot stock and ground meat. My favorite place to eat them in Taipei was Songjilou, the restaurant run by former soldiers from eastern China (see page 131). They cooked simple things from Jiangsu that were more like street food and snacks than regular meals. They were most renowned for their *xiaolongbao*, a Chinese name that simply means "little steamer basket buns." These filled parcels were designed to be dipped in black vinegar and draped with fresh ginger. You would eat them with a soupspoon, cradling them underneath so as not to waste a single drop of their juice.

I have played around considerably with the original recipe, in particular by adding the black vinegar and fresh ginger to the filling. It's much more pleasurable to eat them this way, I find, rather than having a harsh blast of vinegar on the tongue and threads of ginger slipping around.

Once you get the hang of cooking these, consider making extra jelly and freezing it. You can also make larger batches of these buns and freeze them just after they are wrapped.

CHICKEN STOCK JELLY

2 quarts unsalted chicken stock (page 380)

6 ounces (or so) pork skin

10 slices fresh ginger

3 green onions, trimmed and cut in half

MEAT FILLING

1 pound ground pork (15 percent fat), chilled

5 ounces unrendered pork fat (such as pork belly or fatback), partially frozen and then chopped very finely

1½ cups chicken stock jelly (above), crumbled but kept very cold

3 tablespoons peeled and finely minced fresh ginger

3 green onions, trimmed and finely minced

1 teaspoon sea salt

1 teaspoon regular soy sauce

1 teaspoon Shaoxing rice wine

1 teaspoon black vinegar

2 teaspoons sugar

2 teaspoons toasted sesame oil

DOUGH

1¼ cups all-purpose flour

5 tablespoons (more or less) boiling water

THE FIRST COMMONERS' COOKBOOK appeared in Zhejiang about 900 years ago. Called *Pǔjiāng Wúshì zhōngkuì lù* 浦江吳氏中饋錄 ("Homestyle Cooking by Wu of Pujiang"), it was written by a woman, and its recipes were very succinct but useful. For example, here are Ms. Wu's directions for making rice tamales: "Rinse sticky rice and stuff it with Chinese dates, chestnuts, dried persimmons, gingko nuts, and red beans, and then wrap with wild rice or bamboo leaves."

One of the most influential of China's cookbooks came out around 500 years later: *Suíyuán shídān* 隨園食單 ("The Sui Garden Gastronomy"). Written by the delightfully opinionated scholar Yuan Mei, his recipes for exquisite dishes from his home near Hangzhou are balanced with the grumblings of an amusingly cantankerous character, as in this anecdote:

A certain man in Xi'an was well known for his love of entertaining, but his food was really not all that good. One guest

finally asked him, "Are you and I on the best of terms?" The host said, "Of course!" His guest immediately knelt before him and pleaded, "If we are truly friends, then I have a request, and I will not get up again until you grant it." The host replied in surprise, "What is that request?" The guest answered, "From now on, whenever you invite people over, I beg you not to include me."

1. Make the chicken stock jelly by bringing all of its ingredients to a boil and then lowering the heat to a bare simmer. Cook the stock for about 2 hours, strain, discard the solids, and let the jelly cool to room temperature. Chill until solid. Reserve 1½ cups of the chicken stock jelly and freeze the rest for something else.

2. Mix the filling ingredients together by hand, using your hand as a paddle as you stir the filling *in one direction* until it is light and fluffy (see page 458). Keep the filling cold to prevent it from separating. When it is chilled and just before filling the *xiaolongbao*, divide the filling into 40 pieces and roll these into marbles; cover and keep them cold.

3. Prepare steamer baskets by lining them with steamer cloth or paper. You can also use large napa cabbage leaves, which must be steamed first to make them limp, but which make a great nonstick surface. Have your steamer ready (see page 49).

4. Now make the wrappers: place the flour in a small work bowl and stir in the boiling water to form a hot ball of dough that will quickly cool down. Knead the dough on a smooth surface, adding more flour if necessary to have a soft dough that feels like an earlobe when pressed. Cover the dough, let it rest for about 20 minutes, and then divide it into 40 pieces. Fill the *xiaolongbao* (see page 406 to 407) by rolling each ball of dough out into a circle that is about 3 inches in diameter. Place a marble of filling in the center, then pleat the edges around the filling—many tiny pleats are preferable, as they make the *xiaolongbao* more evenly shaped—until the filling is completely enclosed so that the juices will not leak out. Gently twist the top-knot to seal it securely. Place the filled *xiaolongbao* in your steamer baskets (but not over the heat yet) and cover. Repeat until all of the *xiaolongbao* have been filled. Only cook as many as you will serve immediately and freeze the rest (see Tips).

5. Steam fresh *xiaolongbao* for about 10 minutes and frozen ones for about 15 minutes. They can stay in the steamer for a short while longer without overcooking. Count on at least 10 *xiaolongbao* per person as the main course of a meal; as an appetizer, just a few will suffice.

To freeze the *xiaolongbao*, place them in a single layer on baking sheets lined with plastic wrap, freeze them solid, and then store them in resealable freezer bags.

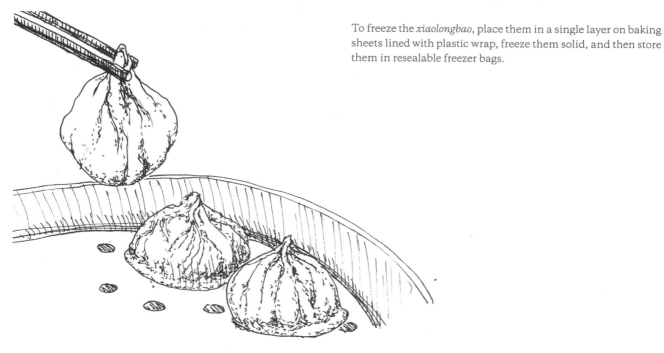

Cōngyóu bànmiàn 蔥油拌麵

Fried Green Onion Noodles

SHANGHAI · SERVES 4 TO 6

Don't let the simplicity of this recipe fool you; Fried Green Onion Noodles are seriously delicious. In the wake of my first attempt, my husband requested these noodles three days in a row. The fried onions and oil can be made ahead of time, and I recommend making extra because both are fantastic on just about anything savory: poached chicken, steamed fish, even fried eggs. This recipe can be scaled up easily, and it's great for parties.

FRIED ONIONS

12 green onions
1½ cups peanut or vegetable oil

SAUCE

¼ cup light soy sauce, plus more if needed
¾ cup unsalted chicken stock (page 380),
    plus more if needed
2 tablespoons small dried shrimp soaked for
    30 minutes in boiling water, optional

NOODLES

4 quarts water
2 tablespoons sea salt
12 ounces thin dried noodles of any kind

1. Clean and trim the green onions, pat them dry (this is important as you don't want them to spatter in the oil), and then slice them into either thin rounds or on an angle into long, thin ovals.

2. Line a plate with a paper towel and place it next to the stove along with a slotted spoon. Heat the oil in a wok over medium-high heat. When the oil just begins to shimmer, add a few pieces of the onion. What you want is for the onions to gently bubble, so adjust the

heat as needed and then add the rest of the onions. Stir the onions every minute or so and let them slowly cook, giving them a chance to release their fragrance and gradually dry out. Keep an eye on the onions, and as soon as they start to smell toasty and a few begin to brown, stir them almost constantly so they toast evenly.

3. Once almost all of them are brown, remove them from the oil with the slotted spoon and place them on the paper towel. Set the wok with the hot oil aside if you're going to continue the recipe immediately; otherwise, let the seasoned oil (which is the same as green onion oil, page 434) cool, then pour it into a clean glass jar and store in the refrigerator.

4. Pour the soy sauce and stock into a large work bowl and stir in about ¼ cup of the flavored oil. If you are using the dried shrimp, drain them, discard any sandy veins or foreign matter, and chop them into fine pieces.

5. Put the water in a large pot, add the salt, and bring to a boil. About 5 to 10 minutes before you want to serve this dish, stir the noodles into the water and gently swish them often so they don't stick together. As soon as the water starts to boil, lower the heat to a simmer and cook the noodles until they are barely done. Place a colander in the sink and drain the pasta into it, but don't rinse it, as the starch on the noodles will help to thicken the sauce and allow it to evenly coat each strand.

6. Put the cooked noodles into the work bowl with the sauce (and optional minced shrimp) and toss them well. You want the noodles slightly soupy since they'll absorb some of the sauce, so add more stock if needed. Taste and add a bit more soy sauce or green onion oil, if you want.

7. Divide the noodles and sauce among your serving bowls, garnish with all of the fried onions, and serve.

Pià'r chuān 片兒川

Hangzhou-Style Noodle Soup

ZHEJIANG · SERVES 4 TO 6 AS A MAIN DISH

This easy dish is from Hangzhou, a city along the Yangtze that is known for its fine culinary culture. The people there are selective even when it comes to a simple bowl of noodles, and this snack is a good example.

One interesting thing about this dish is its use of bamboo pith fungus (see page 263), a beautiful mushroom that grows in bamboo groves. These mushrooms are delicately fragrant and smell wonderful as they plump up in hot water, but they are mainly prized for their crunchy texture.

NOODLES

½ recipe plain cold-water dough (page 387),
    or 1 pound store-bought fresh pasta
1 teaspoon toasted sesame oil, divided in half

SOUP

12 ounces boneless pork or chicken
1 teaspoon sea salt
2 tablespoons cornstarch
2 tablespoons Shaoxing rice wine
1 ounce (about 20 whole) dried bamboo pith fungus
Boiling water, as needed
2 winter bamboo shoots, fresh or frozen and defrosted
2 cups salted Shanghainese greens
    (page 426 or store-bought)
½ cup peanut or vegetable oil
8 cups unsalted pork or chicken stock (page 381 or 380)
2 teaspoons regular soy sauce

1. Bring a large pot of water to a boil while you are working on the pasta, then reduce the heat to the lowest setting. Make the noodles according to the directions on page 388, cutting them to a width of ⅛ inch, or have the store-bought pasta ready.

2. Slice the meat (pork or chicken) about ¼ inch thick, place in a small work bowl, and toss with the salt, cornstarch, and rice wine; let the meat marinate while you ready the vegetables and cook the noodles. Place the bamboo pith fungus in a heatproof work bowl and cover with boiling water; when it's plumped up, pour off and toss the water. Cut off and discard the pinched bases as well as the frilly tops and then carefully rinse any foreign matter off of the main stalks. Chop the fungus into pieces about an inch long. If you are using fresh bamboo, peel it (see Tip, page 122), slice it thinly, simmer in boiling water until barely tender, drain, and rinse well. If using defrosted shoots, just thinly slice them. Place the salted greens in a sieve and rinse thoroughly under cool tap water; squeeze the greens dry and chop any large pieces.

3. Next, cook the noodles: have a large, clean work bowl next to the stove along with some chopsticks and a Chinese spider or slotted spoon. Shake the extra flour off of the pasta and then toss half of the pasta into the boiling water. Let the water come to a full boil again, stirring occasionally. Be sure not to let the water boil over. When the noodles are barely done—chewy, yet cooked—use your chopsticks and spider to remove them to the clean bowl. Toss them with half of the sesame oil to keep them from sticking. Repeat with the rest of the noodles and sesame oil.

4. Finally, cook the soup ingredients. Heat a wok over high heat until it barely starts to smoke, then pour in the oil. Swirl it around and then toss in the meat and any marinade. Stir-fry the meat, breaking apart any clumps, until it loses its pink color and just barely starts to brown; add the meat to the noodles. Pour out all but about 2 tablespoons of the oil and return the wok to high heat. Stir-fry the bamboo shoots and salted greens for about 20 seconds, then pour in the stock and the bamboo pith fungus. Bring the soup to a full boil and add the meat, noodles, and soy sauce. Taste and adjust the seasoning, bring the soup to a full boil again, and then divide among individual bowls. Serve very hot.

Chǎo nián'gāo (liǎngzhǒng) 炒年糕 (兩種)

Stir-Fried Rice Cakes Two Ways

ZHEJIANG • SERVES 2 AS A MAIN DISH

This recipe comes from Ningbo, a coastal city in Zhejiang Province. "Rice cakes" is one of those horrible translations that manages to supply all the wrong images, but there really is no equivalent in Western cuisine. *Nian'gao* like these are made of sticky rice that has been cooked, pounded into a paste, shaped, cooled, and then sliced. If you are fond of *mochi*, you will like *nian'gao*. The name actually means "year cakes" because various forms of these rice pastes are traditionally eaten in China during the Lunar New Year.

Nian'gao are fairly bland and offer only the natural sweetness of rice itself, but they match up well with other things. When stir-fried, as in this recipe, they will remain bouncy and chewy. My favorite preparation is the first recipe here, a vegan dish with wonderful textures: crisp bamboo shoots, green soybeans, and salted Shanghainese greens.

If you are more of a carnivore, though, the second recipe is for you. In that one, the robust flavors of the black mushrooms and pork get absorbed by the rice cakes. In other recipes, *nian'gao* might be thrown into a soup at the last minute in place of noodles. They're a wonderful starch and can be used in a variety of ways.

RICE CAKES WITH SALTED SHANGHAINESE GREENS, BAMBOO SHOOTS, AND GREEN SOYBEANS

Xuělǐhóng sǔnsī máodòu chǎo nián'gāo
雪裏紅筍絲毛豆炒年糕

3 tablespoons peanut or vegetable oil
4 green onions, trimmed and chopped
1 winter bamboo shoot, defrosted if frozen and peeled and blanched if fresh (see Tip, page 122), cut into julienne (about 1 cup)
1 cup shelled green soybeans (*edamame*), defrosted
About 1 cup (6 ounces) chopped salted Shanghainese greens (page 426 or store-bought), rinsed, squeezed dry, and any large pieces chopped
12 ounces (about 2¼ cups) sliced Ningbo-style rice cakes
2 tablespoons Shaoxing rice wine
1 cup boiling water

1. Place a wok over high heat and add the oil. Toss in the green onions and stir them around to release their fragrance. Before they start to brown, add the bamboo shoot and soybeans. Toss these in the hot oil for about 1 minute to heat them through, then add the salted greens. Toss these together for about 30 seconds and then add the rice cakes.

2. After you stir-fry the rice cakes for a minute or so, pour the rice wine and boiling water around the edge of the wok. Continue to toss the rice cakes until most of the liquid has been absorbed. Taste and adjust the seasoning, if necessary. Serve hot in bowls.

RICE CAKES WITH PORK AND VEGETABLES
Shànghǎi chǎo nián'gāo 上海炒年糕

4 ounces pork, julienned

2 teaspoons regular soy sauce

1 tablespoon Shaoxing rice wine

2 teaspoons cornstarch

5 black mushrooms, fresh or dried and plumped up

1 winter bamboo shoot, fresh or frozen and defrosted, peeled (see Tip, page 122)

1 small (12-ounce) napa cabbage

2 ounces Chinese-style ham or Hunan-style cured pork (see charcuterie, page 478)

1 green onion, trimmed

3 tablespoons peanut or vegetable oil

½ teaspoon sea salt

1 tablespoon peeled and julienned fresh ginger

12 ounces (about 2¼ cups) sliced Ningbo-style rice cakes

1 cup unsalted chicken stock (page 380) or strained mushroom soaking liquid

1 teaspoon toasted sesame oil

1. Place the pork in a small work bowl and mix it with the soy sauce, rice wine, and cornstarch. Let it marinate while you prepare the rest of the ingredients.

2. Stem the mushrooms and cut the caps into thin julienne. If using a fresh bamboo shoot, cut it into thin julienne, and place in a small saucepan. Cover with water and simmer until barely tender, then pour off the water and rinse well with cool water to stop the cooking. If using a defrosted bamboo shoot, simply cut the shoot into thin julienne. Cut the napa cabbage in half, discard the core, and cut it against the grain into fine strips. Shred the ham and the green onion into fine strips and keep them separate.

3. Place a wok over high heat and add the oil. Stir-fry the pork and marinade until the pork loses its pink color, then remove it and the crusty marinade from the wok to a clean work bowl, leaving the oil in the wok. Still over high heat, add the salt and then the ginger and green onions to the wok and finally the ham and mushrooms. Stir-fry these for a few seconds to release their fragrance before adding the bamboo shoots and cabbage. Stir-fry these until the cabbage starts to wilt and then add the rice cakes. Continue stir-frying, drizzling in the stock around the edge of the wok to keep the rice cakes from sticking. As soon as the rice cakes are tender, toss in the pork and sesame oil. Taste and adjust the seasoning before serving.

THE FOODS OF JIANGSU AND ZHEJIANG share so much in common that they almost seem to mirror each other. In fact, if you turn a map of the region on its side, the two provinces look like two halves of a large moth, its wide wings fanning out along the warm coast. If you squint your eyes just right, the pointy Shanghai Peninsula forms the head of this moth, which actually makes a kind of poetic sense, for China's biggest city has become a world-renowned gastronomic center in its own right, mainly because it is the downriver confluence of these two great cuisines.

As similar as Jiangsu and Zhejiang's foods may appear on the surface, there

are definite differences that reflect their geography: Jiangsu's coastline stretches up along the Yellow Sea toward the hearty northern schools, while Zhejiang's shoreline reaches down to warmer climes. The Yangtze has traditionally been the dividing line between saltiness on the north bank and sweetness on the south, and Zhejiang highlights this difference with a decided enthusiasm for rock sugar in its braises and sauces, as well as for its aromatic rice wines.

Country-style dry-cured hams season many of Zhejiang's dishes, too, lending gentle depth and savoriness to its cuisine. Great ham is produced in Jinhua, which

lies to the south of Hangzhou in the center of the province. Other great Chinese hams come from the cities of Xuanwei in Yunnan, Anfu in Jiangxi, and Rugao in Jiangsu.

The region is also known for another sort of charcuterie—"wind duck" (*fēngyā* 風鴨). The customary preparation involves slitting the animal open on the breast side so that the body is anchored with the spine all the way up through the head. A spiced dry rub seasons the bird, and then the body is propped open using split bamboo staves so that it ends up looking a bit like a kite. It is dried in the cool wind, hence "wind duck."

Jīnyín zǐcài yāoguǒ chǎofàn 金銀紫菜腰果炒飯

Gold and Silver Fried Rice

JIANGSU AND ZHEJIANG · SERVES 2 AS A MAIN DISH,
4 AS A SIDE DISH

The Yangtze region straddles the line between northern and southern China, and so both wheat and rice dishes are beloved here. This being eastern China, even fried rice is infused with a delicate sensibility, and Gold and Silver Fried Rice is an excellent example of the region's inspired approach to food.

Fried rice is generally eaten either as a snack or at home. It is never served as one of the main courses during a formal Chinese dinner; it would appear only as a final dish to fill up any understuffed bellies (see page 473). And so, when you are offered it (or any other starch) at the conclusion of such a banquet, do your best to refuse, claiming you are too full for another bite. This will give your host great pleasure, and you will be considered an excellent guest.

RICE
2 cups cooked long-grain white rice, chilled, or 1 cup
   jasmine or other long-grain white rice and 1½ cups
   water (or whatever your rice steamer calls for)

EVERYTHING ELSE
½ cup raw whole cashews (see Tips)
6 tablespoons peanut or vegetable oil,
   divided into ¼ cup and 2 tablespoons
½ teaspoon sea salt, plus a sprinkle
1½ cups or so chopped laver seaweed (see Tips)
2 or 3 large eggs, lightly beaten
1 teaspoon toasted sesame oil

1. If you do not have 2 cups cold cooked long-grain white rice, make some fresh. And if you do not have a rice steamer, you can easily cook it on the stove by following the directions on page 383. Scrape the rice out into a thin layer on a rimmed baking sheet and let it cool completely, tossing it lightly now and then to release the steam. Refrigerate it when it has cooled to room temperature. (The rice can be made ahead of time and either refrigerated or frozen. Defrost completely before proceeding.)

2. Lightly chop the cashews until they are the size of peas. Dry-fry them in a wok over medium heat until they start to brown on the edges and smell fantastic. Remove the nuts to a bowl.

3. Pour ¼ cup of the oil into the hot wok and swirl it around. Add the ½ teaspoon salt and all of the rice. Toss the rice over medium to medium-high heat until it starts to steam and turns golden in places. Add the laver seaweed and toss to make the seaweed start to break apart.

4. Make a well in the center of the rice, pour in the remaining 2 tablespoons oil, and then add the beaten eggs. Cook them in your oil well until they look curdled and are about half done. Add the nuts and toss everything together. Taste and adjust the seasoning with a sprinkle more salt. Drizzle the sesame oil over the top, give the rice a final toss, and serve.

Use pine nuts, or other nuts, if you prefer. Whatever nuts you use, they should be slightly soft so that they don't contrast with the texture of the rice too much.

Laver seaweed, or nori, is most easily found in Japanese or Korean grocery stores. The little individual packets are expensive, so buy the larger sheets, preferably freshly toasted. Chop the seaweed with kitchen shears.

A little sprinkle of sea salt at the end makes a world of difference in this dish. How much you add will depend on the saltiness of the seaweed, and your palate.

A NOTE ABOUT FRIED RICE

Fried rice is often mistaken for a culinary cliché. I love good fried rice, though, and make it for brunch or lunch when there's cold rice, a couple of eggs, and some tasty leftovers in the fridge. Many Chinese people look upon fried rice as mom's chef surprise, the dish that turns up just after the refrigerator has been cleaned.

Several Chinese areas have versions that are truly sophisticated, however. The best come from Guangdong and the Yangtze River Delta; two of my hands-down favorites are a Guangzhou-style fried rice with salted fish and chicken (page 222) and a vegetarian Shanghainese recipe that tastes like heaven (at left). To me, good fried rice is perfection in a bowl. It is so subtle and yet so satisfying that I can finish off a dish of it with pleasure even if nothing else is on the table, and yet so refined that it could also appear at the end of a banquet.

Here are my secrets for the best fried rice:

→ Use only long-grain white rice. Jasmine rice is perfect because it is not too starchy, which means it cooks up into fluffy, individual grains. Short-grain rice mushes up easily, and brown rice is too heavy.

→ Eat like the Chinese when you are dining with family and friends and use a big spoon instead of chopsticks. Just pile the rice into a bowl and dig in. If you are given a plate instead of a bowl for your rice, do as the Chinese do once again and ask for a fork. No one uses chopsticks for fried rice unless a bowl is involved.

→ Cook the rice ahead of time and let it cool completely, which means *at least* to room temperature. This helps separate the grains even further so that you end up with very light fried rice.

→ Fry the rice in a minimum of oil. This keeps the grains from getting soggy and heavy, and it also ensures that you taste the sweet flavor of the rice more than the flavor of the oil.

→ Always fully blend the other ingredients—both solids and seasonings—into the rice. Because the grains are fairly bland, use strong flavors, like salted fish and seaweed, that won't be washed out.

→ To get some toasty aromas into the rice, give it a chance to brown in the oil. This Shanghainese touch makes some of the mouthfuls a bit crunchy while others are soft.

→ Use whatever ingredients you want and consider making more than you immediately need. Fried rice can be reheated for a quick meal later in the week.

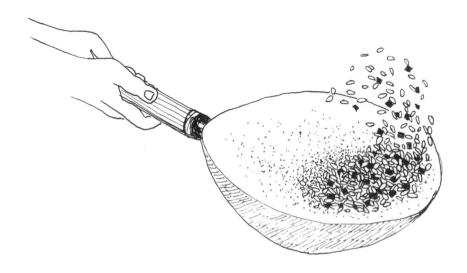

Xīn tài ruǎn 心太軟

Too Soft a Heart

SHANGHAI • MAKES 36

For a short while, my husband and I had a fun teahouse we'd go to in Taipei. As soon as we were seated, we would be served some hot towels and a couple of complimentary saucers filled with roasted peanuts and seasoned melon seeds. Then we would get down to the business of selecting our tea and the sweet and savory snacks that would accompany it. Too Soft a Heart was one of the confections available, and it has just the right balance of textures to go with a bracing pot of green tea.

This recipe is basically Chinese red dates stuffed with a *mochi*-like filling. The stuffed dates are fried, covered with a sauce made out of osmanthus blossoms, and steamed. They are best if eaten immediately, but they can be held for an hour or two. Do not refrigerate the dates once they've been cooked, as the rice dough will become hard and almost impossible to soften.

DATES

36 dried large Chinese red dates (see Tips),
    preferably pitted
Boiling water, as needed

FILLING

2 tablespoons wheat starch
1 tablespoon boiling water
¾ cup sticky rice flour
4 to 5 tablespoons cool water

SAUCE

3 walnut-sized pieces of rock sugar,
    or 4 tablespoons sugar or honey
1 cup water
1 tablespoon osmanthus blossom syrup, or grated
    zest and juice of ½ Meyer lemon, optional

Peanut or vegetable oil for frying (2 to 3 cups)

ONE OF OUR FAVORITE TAIPEI SPOTS WAS Astoria Cafe, a beat-up lounge downtown where we could while away an hour or two over fresh coffee and a plate of cookies. It was a simple coffee shop on a small street, across from a busy temple dedicated to the City God, or *chénghuángmiào* 城隍廟, the deity in charge of protecting Taipei. Food was offered in the many mom 'n 'pop eateries that surrounded it, the edges of the sidewalk were crammed with bicycles and motorbikes, and tarps were spread out everywhere and covered with things to buy. The neighborhood was, therefore, a very crowded, noisy, and fun place to meander.

The cafe, though, was a relatively quiet oasis for us, a place where local writers and artists liked to hang out, nibble on pastries made by the half-Russian owner, and argue endlessly over cups of fresh joe, which was still a relative rarity at that time.

It's been said that the First Lady then, Chiang Ching-kuo's Belarusian-born wife Faina (Chiang Fang-liang), had a standing weekly order at the place. Astoria was decidedly bohemian and hardly the kind of cafe where Madame Chiang could ever personally set foot, so the pastries were always delivered to the First Lady's residence. We went for the general weirdness of its habitués, though, such as a certain elderly poet and infamous roué who would invariably try to sneak one of his bare feet under the bottom of whatever young female admirer was sitting at his table. More than one person told us that he had all of his money stashed in a belt hidden under his robes.

More often than not, we would meet up with old friends, like the great folk art scholar Kuo Li-cheng. A Beijing native, she was an iconoclast of the first order. A short, sturdy, vital feminist, she had divorced her husband at a time when few women would have even considered such an action and the social shame it entailed. But Professor Kuo scoffed at this and all other nonsense, and this fearlessness extended into every aspect of her life. As she once quipped with a sideways glance at me, "I'm not scared of cops in the day nor of ghosts at night."

1. Soak the dates in boiling water to cover for about 10 minutes, until soft and pliable, and then drain. If you have pitted dates, use a pair of kitchen shears or a paring knife to cut a slit down the length of one side of each date to make sure no pit shards are hidden inside. If you are using dates that still have the pits in them, use a paring knife to cut one side of each date open lengthwise and remove the pit.

2. To make the filling, place the wheat starch in a small bowl, add the boiling water, and stir with a fork or chopsticks to make a paste. Add the rice flour and cool water to the paste and knead the mixture until a soft dough forms. Use only enough cool water to prevent the dough from sticking to your hands or the board. Place the dough back in the bowl and cover it with a piece of plastic wrap.

3. Put the rock sugar (or sugar or honey) and water in a small saucepan and bring to a boil. Lower the heat to a simmer and let the sauce gently bubble away until the sugar water has reduced to a thick syrup. Remove the sauce from the heat and add the optional osmanthus blossom syrup or the lemon juice and zest.

4. While the syrup is bubbling away, divide the dough into 36 pieces and roll each piece into a small marble. Stuff each date with a dough marble and gently close the date around the dough. Lay a sheet of parchment paper on a baking sheet and set it next to the stove along with a slotted spoon.

5. Pour about 2 inches of oil into a wok and place over medium heat. When a wooden chopstick dipped in the hot oil begins to bubble all over, add a handful of the dates, one at a time, being careful not to crowd them. Fry them until the rice dough puffs up: they don't need to brown; they just need to cook lightly all the way through. Remove the fried dates to the parchment paper to drain while you fry up the rest. These dates are at their absolute best when they are just out of the oil—they will still be slightly crispy—but you can prepare them an hour or so ahead of time up to this point and keep them in a relatively warm area.

6. Place all of the fried dates in a shallow, heatproof bowl. Pour the sauce over the dates and toss well. Serve them while they are still hot, or let them cool to room temperature.

Get the largest and softest dried dates you can find. Press them gently through their plastic bag to make sure of their texture. If possible, try to smell them through the plastic, too; fresh ones will smell sweet.

Some red dates at the store are not only pitted but also cooked in sugary water and then redried. They are meant to be snacks, but they work great in this recipe, as well. Just make sure that you adjust the sweetness accordingly.

Héyè bābǎofàn 荷葉八寶飯

Lotus Leaf Eight Treasure Rice

NORTHERN FUJIAN · SERVES 8 TO 10

What I've been told over the years is that Chinese dishes are often built around eight ingredients because eight is a lucky number. My own interpretation is that this is really just a good excuse to add lots of tasty things to a dish.

Eight treasure rice is one good example. It's found throughout much of China, and just about everyone has his or her own take on how it should be made. I've come to prefer a lighter confection, like the following version, which is an unabashedly personal riff off of a recipe from Northern Fujian.

In this recipe, the rice is tossed with black sugar, osmanthus blossom syrup, and browned butter. Eight treasure rice is usually filled with red bean paste, but I prefer to fill the rice with cooked pineapple, as its tartness provides a nice counterweight to the sweet rice. This is definitely not traditional, however, so I've included directions for the more common filling, as well. Either way works. The whole thing is wrapped in a lotus leaf, which lends the dessert a lovely summery feel.

RICE

1 pound round sticky rice
Cool water, as needed
3 tablespoons unsalted butter
¼ teaspoon sea salt
2 tablespoons dark brown sugar
2 tablespoons osmanthus blossom syrup or agave syrup

FILLING

½ ripe pineapple, peeled and cored
1½ tablespoons black or very dark brown sugar
Pinch of sea salt
¼ cup slivered or shredded unsweetened dried coconut

THE REST

1 dried lotus leaf, soaked in hot water until soft
Spray oil
8 lotus seeds, soaked in boiling water until soft and with their green sprouts removed (see page 289)
1 tablespoon raisins
1 tablespoon wolfberries
4 large dried Chinese red dates
6 dried pitted longans
1 tablespoon toasted sesame seeds (page 413)
2 tablespoons toasted pine nuts, almonds, walnuts, or some other tasty nut
3 fresh or frozen water chestnuts, peeled and sliced
Your choice of dried and candied fruits, toasted nuts, or the like

1. Rinse the rice in a strainer and then soak it in cool water for about 2 hours, until it passes the fingernail test (see page 480). Steam the rice in 2 steamer baskets lined with cloth (see page 417) for about 40 minutes, until it is tender but still nicely chewy. Brown the butter in a small saucepan or frying pan and then scrape it into a medium work bowl. Add the salt, sugar, and syrup to the butter. Add the cooked rice to the work bowl while the grains are still very hot so that the butter and sugar melt and form a nice goo that envelops the rice as it cools; taste and adjust the seasoning.

2. To make the filling, thinly slice the pineapple, place in a small saucepan, and add the sugar and salt. Bring the pineapple to a boil and then lower the heat to a simmer. While the pineapple is cooking, toast the coconut in a dry frying pan over medium heat, tossing it carefully so that it doesn't burn. When it is lightly toasted, remove the coconut to a small work bowl. As the pineapple cooks down, the sugars will start to caramelize and bubble, so use a silicone spatula to continually scrape the bottom of the pan to keep the sugar from burning. When the pineapple is cooked and the syrup is nice and thick, scrape the pineapple and syrup into the coconut.

3. Rinse the now-pliable lotus leaf well and pat it more or less dry. Select an 8-cup heatproof bowl and lay the leaf, green-side down, in the bowl: this will be the top of the dessert when you unmold it. Spray the stem side of the leaf with oil.

4. Now comes the fun part: decorating and filling the rice pudding. For directions on this, as well as serving the dessert, see the diagram below.

5. Place the bowl in the steamer and steam over medium heat for about 1 hour. Cool the dessert for 10 minutes or so, as this will help stabilize the rice. Bring the leaf-covered mound to the table and unveil it dramatically so your guests can enjoy the design before you all dig in.

If you want to make this the traditional way, use 5 tablespoons sugar in the rice instead of the brown sugar and syrup. Also melt 3 tablespoons lard and use it in place of the butter.

The most common filling is sweet red bean paste. To get rid of the metallic taste of the canned paste, set a wok over medium heat and add about 2 tablespoons toasted sesame oil. Stir in 1 cup sweetened red bean paste and ½ teaspoon sea salt. Fry the bean paste in the oil until the oil has been completely absorbed by the paste. Let cool before using. I also recommend that you reduce the sugar in the rice by half. You can also use the red bean paste on page 442, with or without the chestnuts.

The lotus leaf is optional. For plain eight treasure rice, coat the inside of an 8-cup heatproof bowl with lard or white shortening and then proceed to decorate and fill as directed.

MAKING & SERVING LOTUS LEAF EIGHT TREASURE RICE

❶
Squash the soaked and pliable lotus leaf into a large bowl with the stem side up, and the green side down, and the edges draped over the sides. Place your big red dates in the center and arrange everything else in concentric rings, around the dates, alternating colors as much as possible. Start adding the rice when you get about an inch up the sides of the bowl. Small spoonfuls at first are helpful because they will act like glue and keep things tidy.

❷
When the bowl is half full, smooth out a ½-inch depression in the rice (stay about ½ inch away from the edge so that the filling doesn't leak out) and layer in all of the filling. Add the rest of your decorations around the bowl, gluing them steady with more of the rice as needed, and then top off the bowl with the remaining rice. Fold the leaf edges over the rice and steam as directed.

❸
To serve, fold back the leaf away from the rice so it opens up like a flower. Invert a rimmed plate over the top of the bowl. Quickly flip the bowl over onto the plate, and remove first the bowl and then the leaf. Use a wide spoon to serve the rice in small bowls.

Júgēng tāngyuán 橘羹湯圓

Rice Pearl and Tangerine Petal Sweet Soup

JIANGXI · SERVES 4 TO 6

Sticky rice is popular all over China. It is especially prominent in dishes from the southern coastal zones, where it has turned into a staple of many local cuisines. Outside of these areas, though, it mainly appears as a flour that is mixed with cool water to form a paste, which is then either boiled, steamed, or fried; this is often referred to as *cíbā* 糍粑 in the southern regions (page 306) or "rice cakes" (page 136) in other places. It is even popular in North China, where it regularly appears in the local sweets, such as Rolling Donkeys (page 60). The paste is also used to make *tangyuan*, the rice-dough balls that are beloved in so many parts of China and are an integral part of both Winter Solstice and Lunar New Year celebrations. Large or small, stuffed or plain, sweet or savory, deep-fried or boiled, these chewy delights are invariably delicious.

But one of the most unusual recipes for sticky rice paste that I've come across is this one from Jiangxi Province. Virtually unknown outside Jiangxi, Rice Pearl and Tangerine Petal Soup is truly worthy of greater fame. The following recipe features canned mandarin segments, a slightly sweet broth, and plain little rice pearls. Because of the tangerines in the soup, which are a sign of good luck, this dish is often served for New Year. To make it even more festive, I've colored the rice flour with a touch of red food coloring.

RICE PEARLS

½ cup sticky rice flour

2 drops red food coloring, optional

¼ cup cool water

TANGERINES AND SOUP

2 cups water

1 can (11 ounces) mandarin orange segments, including the juice

2 to 3 tablespoons rock sugar or agave syrup

1. First make the rice pearls by placing the rice flour in a medium work bowl. Make a small well in the flour, stir the optional food coloring into the water, and mix this with the flour to form a soft dough. Place the dough on a smooth surface and knead it briefly. Roll the dough into a long rope about ½ inch thick, then break or cut the rope into about 36 pieces. Roll each piece into a small ball. These can be made ahead of time and frozen (see Tips).

2. Bring the water to a boil in a medium saucepan and then add the rice pearls in loose handfuls so that they do not stick together; stir after each addition to help separate the little balls. As soon as the water comes to a boil again and the pearls rise to the surface, add the can of mandarin orange segments and their juice and the sugar to the rice balls. Bring to a boil once again and add more sugar or agave syrup to taste. Serve immediately so the rice pearls do not soften.

There are many different brands of canned mandarin (tangerine) segments out there; get a high-quality one with light syrup.

The rice pearls can be made ahead of time and frozen on a baking sheet lined with plastic wrap. Try not to let them stick to one another and clump up. As soon as the rice pearls are hard, place them in a freezer bag and freeze them for up to a couple of months. If the balls look cracked or if the bag is full of ice crystals, discard them and make a new batch.

Táitiáo sū 苔條酥

Sea Moss Sandies

JIANGSU • MAKES 84 TO 96

One of my favorite local cookies when I lived in Taiwan was flavored with sea moss. I know that doesn't sound like the most tantalizing flavor in the world, but the sea moss brings with it a faint echo of the ocean and a salty edge that cuts the sweetness of what would otherwise be a plain, one-note cookie.

I experimented with these flavors a bit, and what I ended up with are buttery shortbread wafers with an unabashedly moss green hue. In addition to this gorgeous color, the saltiness and delectable aroma of the main ingredient remain highlighted here.

When you open your package of sea moss, it will look for all the world like you have a couple hanks of green hair. I've found that the best way to deal with this ingredient here is to toss the whole bunch into a food processor and pulse away until the sea moss is broken down into little shards. You can then proceed to make the rest of the cookie dough in the processor. It ends up taking no more than a few minutes to put together.

1 package (5 ounces) sea moss
2 cups Chinese flour (page 386)
½ cup powdered sugar, plus more for dusting, optional
1 cup (2 sticks) unsalted butter

1. Pull the sea moss apart into manageable strands, shake them to dislodge any sand, and place them in a food processor. Pulse the sea moss until coarsely chopped. Add the flour and powdered sugar and grind these dry ingredients together until the sea moss is reduced to a fine powder. Add the butter and pulse the mixture until a crumbly mass forms.

2. Divide the dough in half and place each piece on a sheet of plastic wrap. Form each half into a smooth log a little over 1 inch in diameter. Wrap the logs in the plastic wrap and either roll them up in silicone baking mats or slide them into empty paper towel tubes, which will help the logs keep their shape. If you have neither, roll the dough again on a flat board just before cutting it to make logs as round as possible. Freeze the dough for about 1 hour to make it easier to slice.

3. Heat the oven to 350°F. Cut the dough into ¼-inch-thick slices. Place them about 1 inch apart on baking sheets lined with nonstick baking mats or parchment paper.

4. Bake the cookies for 12 to 15 minutes, until the edges are golden; rotate the sheets back to front halfway through the baking time. The cookies will be fragile, so cool them on the baking sheets before removing them. If you wish, dust the cookies with a little powdered sugar before serving. The cookies taste best after they have cooled completely, as they are crispier and the sea moss flavor is more pronounced.

5. Store the cookies in an airtight container; freeze for longer storage.

Sea moss, or *taitiao* (moss strands), is becoming more and more common in Chinese groceries (see page 102), so look for it next time you're at an Asian grocery. It will probably be near the dried seaweed.

Shuǐjing lìzhi 水晶荔枝

Crystal Lychees

NORTHERN FUJIAN · SERVES 6 TO 8

During the Tang dynasty, imperial consort Yang Guifei was renowned for her appetite as much as she was for her beauty. She was a favorite of Emperor Xuanzong, and it is said that she loved lychees with such passion that a relay delivery system was instated by the emperor to quickly transport these fragile tropical fruits from southern China to the capital, Chang'an, in the north. Yang Guifei wanted them to be as fresh as possible, and if you've ever had a perfectly ripe lychee (or litchi), you'll understand why.

In Taiwan I was always more than willing to put up with the excruciatingly humid July weather just to eat fresh lychees. At their pinnacle of ripeness, they have a delectable sweet-and-sour taste that seems gently carbonated. Lychees are in season for only a very short time during the summer—about six weeks—so take advantage of their availability while you can.

2 pounds (more or less) fresh lychees,
    or 2 cans (20 ounces or so each) lychees
3¼ cups water, divided into ¼ cup and 3 cups
1 tablespoon powdered gelatin
3 tablespoons sugar, or to taste
¼ cup fresh lemon juice
Citrus or similar leaves for garnish, optional

1. Chill a 5- to 6-cup container in the freezer while you prepare the rest of the ingredients.

2. If you have fresh lychees, reserve about 6 of the prettiest ones unpeeled as a garnish. Rinse the rest of the fresh lychees, peel, and use a paring knife to remove the pits. Be sure to cut the fruit over a bowl so that you save any juices. If you're using canned lychees, drain the fruit and reserve the syrup. Measure the syrup and add enough water to make 4 cups liquid.

3. Pour ¼ cup of the water into a medium work bowl, sprinkle the gelatin on top, and let soften for 3 to 5 minutes. If using fresh lychees, bring the remaining 3 cups water to a boil in a saucepan. If using canned lychees, bring the syrup-water mixture to a boil in a saucepan. Remove the boiling liquid from the heat. Add the sugar to the gelatin mixture, then stir in the boiling water to dissolve the sugar and gelatin. Taste and add more sugar, if needed. Allow the liquid to come to room temperature and then add the lemon juice.

4. Arrange the lychees in the bottom of the chilled mold so that the cut sections face inside. This way you will have only smooth, rounded surfaces showing when you unmold the jelly. Pour a thin (½-inch) layer of the gelatin over the fruit and immediately refrigerate the mold for about 10 minutes, until the gelatin has solidified. Pour the rest of the gelatin into the mold, cover, and refrigerate for a few hours until the gelatin firms up.

5. Just before serving, briefly run warm tap water over the bottom of the mold to loosen it. Swiftly turn the mold over onto a plate and gently shake the mold again so the jelly plops down onto the serving plate. If it doesn't, run more warm water over the outside of the mold and try again. Garnish the jelly with the optional reserved lychees. Clean and dry some citrus leaves, if desired, and arrange them around the jelly. Serve immediately.

Jīnjú táng 金橘糖

Candied Kumquats

ANHUI · MAKES ABOUT 2 POUNDS

Candied kumquats are always one of the highlights of Chinese New Year. Good-quality ones are hard to find outside of China, but you can make them at home. Kumquats are given three hot baths to remove the bitterness from their skin and to tenderize them so that they will soak up the syrup later on.

The challenge with this recipe is keeping the fruits from bursting, because you want the finished candy to retain that lovely kumquat shape. The secret to this is pricking the fruit all over to allow steam to escape. The other key is not to boil them for more than a moment. Poaching and soaking the kumquats in hot syrup between boilings gives the skins time to toughen up again, which lends the candied skins their characteristic chewiness.

About 2 pounds kumquats
2 cups sugar, plus more for coating
2 cups cool water
Good pinch of sea salt
Good pinch of cream of tartar

1. This recipe will take a couple of days of leisurely preparation interspersed with long rests. Wash the kumquats carefully and discard any that don't look perfect. The ends of the stems can be left on the fruit if they are trimmed very short. Prick the kumquats all over (at least 10 times) with a pin or skewer. Place the kumquats in a 2-quart saucepan and cover with cool water. Bring the water to a boil, cover the pan, and remove it from the heat. Allow the water to cool down a bit (at least half an hour), pour off the water, cover the kumquats with fresh cool water, and bring the pot to a boil again. Boil and rest the kumquats 3 times. You can do this part ahead of time, if you wish, and refrigerate the cooked kumquats for a day or two.

2. In the same pan, combine the kumquats, sugar, water, salt, and cream of tartar. Bring the mixture to a full boil, then reduce the heat to very low so that there is almost no movement in the pan (the kumquats will be very tender at this point and can fall apart easily). Slowly cook the fruit for about an hour, until it looks translucent and dark. Remove from the heat, cover, and let the fruit sit overnight in the syrup.

3. The next day, bring the syrup and fruit to a boil, cover the pan, and turn off the heat. Let the kumquats and syrup return to room temperature. Do this 3 times until the kumquats look like balls of pure amber.

4. Thoroughly drain the kumquats (reserve the syrup for something else; see Tip) on a wire rack overnight. Place about 1 cup of sugar on a rimmed plate or tray and roll a few of the sticky kumquats at a time in the sugar until they are completely coated. Place the sugared kumquats in an airtight container with extra sugar around them and store in a cool, dark place.

The syrup can be used over pancakes or waffles, like a runny marmalade. It can also be used as a flavoring for sparkling water or as a delicious coating for baked ham. Use any broken kumquats for cooking (like in Lotus Leaf Eight Treasure Rice, page 142) and save the pretty ones for serving with tea.

Jiāngmǐ lián'ǒu 江米蓮藕

Sweet Stuffed Lotus Roots

JIANGSU • SERVES 6 TO 8

2 lotus roots (each about 6 inches long)
½ cup sticky rice or black sticky Thai rice (see Tip)
Boiling water, as needed
3½ ounces rock sugar (about the size of 2 large eggs)
½ cup osmanthus blossom syrup, or grated zest of
　　1 Meyer lemon plus a small handful of rock sugar
　　chips and ½ teaspoon sea salt

October is the best time of the year for lotus roots—or so I was told by a lotus farmer in Modesto, California, many years ago. He scoffed at the tubers that were for sale the rest of the year and told me they had been in storage for too long or weren't ripe enough. Surrounded as he was by ponds full of insanely beautiful lotus blossoms of every imaginable color, I figured he knew what he was talking about.

Lotus roots are actually long tubers that grow horizontally in the mud under the lotus plants; the real roots are the hairs that bristle out from between the white segments. Peeled and cut into slices, these tubers are lacy and perfectly patterned. You can cube them and then blanch and pickle the cubes (page 425), thinly slice them and deep-fry the slices to make chips (page 129), or use them as meaty chunks in Lotus Root and Pork Rib Soup (page 92).

This recipe is less sweet than most versions. I prefer to let the distinct aroma of the lotus root and rice shine through. If you would like it sweeter, add more rock sugar toward the end. As with all chilled desserts, keep in mind that the lotus root will taste less sweet when it is cold.

1. Using a potato peeler, peel the lotus roots and trim the joints at either end so that they lie flush with the root. Cut off about ¾ inch from one end, which will serve as a cap. Rinse out the insides with cool tap water, use a chopstick to scrape off any mud you see, and then drain the roots (see page 451).

2. Place the rice in a sieve and rinse under running water; shake dry. If using black Thai rice, grind it very coarsely in a mini food processor or mortar so that the grains are chopped more or less in half. For directions on how to stuff and cook the lotus roots, see the diagram at right.

3. Continue to cook the lotus roots for another hour, adding more water only if the sauce boils down too quickly. After the roots have been cooked for a total of 3 hours, remove them to a container to cool off. Add the osmanthus blossom syrup (or the lemon zest plus the extra sugar and the salt) to the pan and boil the sauce down rapidly until it is the consistency of maple syrup. Cool the sauce to room temperature and pour it over the lotus roots. Cover and refrigerate overnight or longer.

4. To serve, remove the caps and cut off the other ends. Cut the roots into slices about ½ inch thick. Arrange the slices, overlapping them, on a rimmed serving plate. Pour the sauce over the slices and serve with hot green tea.

Traditionally, round sticky rice fills the holes in the lotus root, but I prefer Thai black rice. It smells divine as it cooks and turns everything a beautiful shade of purple.

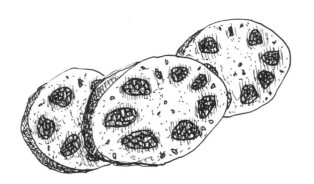

STUFFING & COOKING LOTUS ROOTS

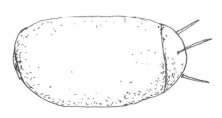

1

Use one hand as a funnel at the top of the lotus root and use the other to stuff the rice into the holes (a chopstick is useful for working the rice in).

2

Pat the outside to help shake the grains down, but don't pack the rice too tightly; it will need to expand as it cooks.

3

Use 3 toothpicks to pin the cap back onto the lotus root. Repeat this step with the other lotus root. (Discard any leftover rice, or use it for something else.)

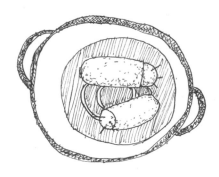

4

Place a small trivet in a pot that will easily hold the lotus roots in a single layer. One 7 to 8 inches in diameter should work great. Lay the stuffed lotus roots on the trivet and add boiling water to cover the roots by 1 inch. Bring the water to a boil again over high heat and then reduce the heat so that the water just simmers. Cook the lotus roots over gentle heat for 2 hours and then add the sugar.

Rúhé qīhǎo Zhōngguó chá 如何沏好中國茶

The Perfect Pot of Chinese Tea

EVERYWHERE IN CHINA

Tea made its way into China centuries ago, and it has long been the national drink of the Chinese people. Basically, there are three main kinds of tea leaves: green (unfermented), oolong (semi-fermented), and black (fermented). Green tea (*lùchá* 綠茶) has long needles with a fresh green color; oolong (*wūlóng* 烏龍) is dark olive and is curled from being rubbed before fermentation; and black tea (*hóngchá* 紅茶) tends to be wrinkled and inky. In addition, you can also find white tea (*báichá* 白茶), flower teas (*huāchá* 花茶, see page 311), and a large family of compressed black teas, which includes varieties like *pu'er* (*pǔer* 普洱) and the bowl-shaped *tuocha* (*tuóchá* 沱茶). And that's just the start of it.

The most important factors in tea preparation are water quality and temperature. Hard water tastes harsh, but if you use a water softener, the water will be salty. Use a good filter or spring water for the best results. When it comes to temperature, in general, the darker the tea leaves, the hotter the water should be. Green teas need to be brewed at temperatures between 140°F and 185°F in order to avoid dissolving their tannins. With oolong teas, strive for about 200°F, which can be achieved by bringing the kettle to a full boil and then letting it sit for a few minutes. Water must be at a full boil for black teas. Experience and personal tastes will outweigh any advice that can be given, however, since all of these teas have quirks that influence the end result. For example, the age of a tea and how the tea has been stored will determine the ideal water temperature and steeping time.

Get your loose-leaf tea from a reputable tea merchant, if possible, and see whether you can sample it before deciding. With the exception of compressed black teas (see Butter Tea, page 374), which are often aged for decades before reaching their peak potential, most teas are best when they are fresh. This is why you should not buy too much tea at one time, and keep what you do buy in an airtight container in a cool, dry, dark place.

THE COASTAL SOUTHEAST IS HOME TO some of China's finest teas. The best oolong tea, for example, comes from Southern Fujian and Taiwan. Even though the leaves are deep green, they produce a beautiful golden brew with a heady, floral scent. Nowhere is this tea appreciated more than in Chaozhou, home of the gentle art of the Chinese tea service. In Chaozhou, the tea service is called *gōngfu chá* 功夫茶, or "kung fu tea," but in places like Taiwan, it is more commonly referred to as "old people's tea," or *lǎorén chá* 老人茶.

Unlike the Japanese tea ceremony, which is more of a ritual, kung fu tea is a leisurely affair designed around the enjoyment of the fragrance, taste, and appearance of superior leaves. Friends gather at a low table and set out the necessary equipment on a wide tray: a small teapot, a pitcher for the brewed tea, a simmering pot of water, tiny eggshell cups, a bamboo spoon for the leaves, and a canister of either oolong or a compressed tea like *pu'er*. As the tea brews and the afternoon fades, they nibble on tea snacks like peanuts and toasted melon seeds—or even fancier offerings such as Too Soft a Heart (page 140) or Malay Sponge Cake (page 235)—until it is time to discuss where to gather for dinner.

In Guangdong, just about any sort of tea is enjoyed at dim sum teahouses. You will always be asked what kind of tea you prefer with your meal; green, oolong, jasmine, black, and *pu'er* teas are usually available, but the one I always ask for is a mixture of *pu'er* and chrysanthemum flowers called *júpǔ* 菊普. The bitterness and depth of this unique black tea cleanses the palate, while the blossoms lighten the beverage with a honeyed floral scent.

Hángzhōu júhuāchá 杭州菊花茶

Chrysanthemum Tea

ZHEJIANG • SERVES 4

Hangzhou is famous for its dried chrysanthemums, which are brewed as an herbal tea that smells of honey and is traditionally drunk as a steaming hot beverage in autumn. But the dried chrysanthemums are available all year-round, if you know where to look.

Lots of people slap the name "Hangzhou" on the package when they wrap up these little golden flowers, so look around for a quality Chinese dried-foods or herb shop that sells the real deal. The blossoms should be compressed into a little brick, and when you hold it up to your nose, it should smell intensely of fresh chrysanthemums. Keep the blossoms in a dark cupboard and use them up within a couple of months so that their flavor doesn't fade away.

1 handful (around 1 cup) dried chrysanthemum blossoms
Freshly boiled water
Rock sugar, honey, or agave syrup, optional

1. Place the blossoms in a saucepan or teapot. Cover them with freshly boiled water, swirl the flowers around to release any dust or flotsam, then dump out all the water. Immediately cover the blossoms with about 4 cups of slightly less hot water (bring the water to a full boil and then let it sit for a few minutes), cover, and let steep for about 5 minutes.

2. These blossoms are naturally honey flavored, but they certainly go well with whatever sweetener you like. Serve this tea hot or ice-cold. The flowers can be brewed one more time before their flavor is exhausted.

Hóngzǎo lù 紅棗露

Red Date Nectar

SHANGHAI • MAKES ABOUT 8 CUPS

Chinese red dates have an unfortunate English translation: "jujubes." I much prefer calling them red dates to avoid dredging up memories of movie theater candies that are not even remotely as delicious as these beautiful mahogany fruits.

8 ounces dried Chinese red dates
12 cups water, divided into 8 cups and 4 cups
Honey to taste

1. Rinse the dates and discard any imperfect ones. Slash each date in several places so that they fall apart easily as they cook. Place the dates in a large saucepan, add 8 cups of the water, and bring the water to a full boil. Lower the heat to a simmer, cover, and cook the dates slowly for an hour. Let the dates sit in the hot water until they are completely cooled down.

2. Strain the juice to remove the pulp, skins, and pits, and then press down lightly on the pulp. Return the solids to the saucepan, add the remaining 4 cups water, and simmer the dates covered for another 20 minutes or so to extract every last bit of flavor. Let the pan cool down, strain out the solids, and add this liquid to the first batch.

3. Taste the juice and add honey to taste, remembering that the nectar will taste less sweet when it is cold. Cover and chill the nectar for a couple of hours and serve it chilled.

THE COASTAL SOUTHEAST

THE HAKKA · CHAOZHOU · SOUTHERN FUJIAN · TAIWAN
TAIWAN'S MILITARY FAMILIES · HAINAN · GUANGDONG AND SOUTHERN GUANGXI
PEARL RIVER DELTA · MACAU · HONG KONG

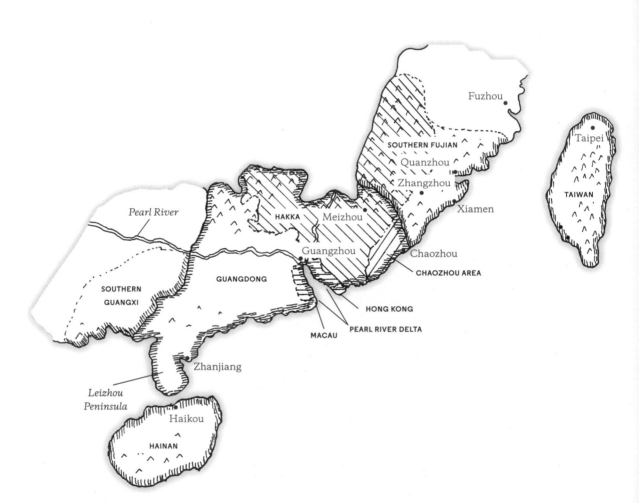

Pearl River

SOUTHERN FUJIAN

Fuzhou

Taipei

Quanzhou

Zhangzhou

TAIWAN

HAKKA   Meizhou

Xiamen

Guangzhou

Chaozhou

CHAOZHOU AREA

GUANGDONG

SOUTHERN
GUANGXI

HONG KONG

MACAU   PEARL RIVER DELTA

Zhanjiang

Leizhou
Peninsula

Haikou

HAINAN

PREVIOUS SPREAD:
The color red and a bird
symbolize the South.

"Almost all of the world's ingredients can be found in eastern Guangdong, but the rest of the world does not necessarily have all of eastern Guangdong's ingredients."

天下所有食貨，粵東幾盡有之，粵東所有之食貨，天下未必盡也。

—QU DAJUN, *NEW REPORTS ABOUT GUANGDONG* (1687)

Nestled along the southeastern coast of China lies a group of cuisines that share a deep love for poultry and pork, for both dried and fresh ingredients, for soups of any kind, and for the rich, savory flavors that only the region's fermented ingredients can provide. The coastal territories of this area—and they constitute the vast majority of the region—are well known for their delicious methods of preparing seafood. Meanwhile, further inland, in Southern Fujian and along the northeastern edge of Guangdong, cooking styles are still influenced by the ancient ingredients and techniques of the North China Plains.

The lower half of China's Coastal Southeast is home to what the West refers to as "Cantonese food," and which the Chinese call "the Guangdong School." Canton is actually the old name for the capital city of Guangzhou, which was derived from the Portuguese name for the city, Cantão. Its cuisine was shaped by the agricultural output of the enormous Pearl River, and it is known for its ethereal, delicate dishes. The food culture here has its heart in Guangzhou, and the dishes of this old city have gradually

155

trickled south and west. As a result, the Pearl River Delta, Southern Guangxi, Hong Kong, and Macau are now home to intriguing interpretations of Guangzhou's dishes.

In the northeastern half of Guangdong and in Southern Fujian, the cooking styles are vastly different. Here, among the rocky hills and rough coastlines along the South China Sea, a more down-home style of cooking is exhibited by three major cuisines: Hakka, Chaozhou, and Southern Fujian. These culinary traditions incorporate the indigenous cooking styles and fermented ingredients of the North China Plain, and they have served as a template for the foods on Taiwan and Hainan. Both of those islands have had many other culinary influences, as well, and over the past seventy years, Taiwan has become a second home to a kaleidoscope of cuisines, turning the island into a microcosm of everything China has to offer.

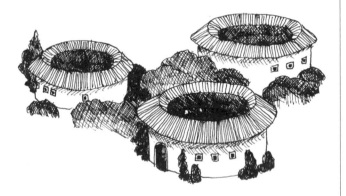

THE HAKKA

Almost two thousand years ago, wars and civil unrest on the North China Plain dislodged groups of Han Chinese and forced them into the south's less settled lands. These refugees were the ancestors of the people now known as the Hakka. Over the centuries, waves of people continued to flee south, and the Hakka developed communities in northeastern Guangdong's hill country and the surrounding areas. They also developed a cuisine that would become the backbone of southern China's heartiest foods.

Unlike most cuisines in China, Hakka food is defined by a group of people rather than a geographical region. The majority of the Hakka live in China's southeast quadrant, with the main concentration near Meizhou in northern Guangdong. Although no conclusive evidence exists proving exactly where the Hakka people originated, many scholars think they first migrated from the Yellow River in the north and arrived in Guangdong as early as the second century BCE. The fragile welcome they received was enshrined in the nickname locals gave them: Hakka, or "guest families."

The Hakka had to make do with whatever unclaimed territory they could find, and so frugality became a defining characteristic of their foods. Their dishes are simply seasoned with a variety of dried and fermented ingredients, which give recipes such as Pork Belly with Preserved Mustard Greens (page 207) and even a simple Salted Radish Omelet (page 179) their characteristically satisfying range of flavors and textures. With the exception of Hakka feast foods like Salt-Baked Chicken (page 200), expensive proteins are generally used as garnishes for starches and vegetables, as in Hakka Tamales (page 228). Echoes of their former homeland in the north can still be tasted in foods like Braised Stuffed Bean Curd (page 176), in which bean curd stands in for the wheat wrappers of Shandong-style *jiaozi* (page 45). Over time, the Hakka spread throughout the Coastal Southeast, and, as a result, some of their homey dishes can be found in the neighboring cuisines of Southern Fujian and Chaozhou.

CHAOZHOU

The river port of Chaozhou lies in eastern Guangdong, about halfway between the Hakka highlands and the Fujian coast. And so, while the greater Chaozhou area (also known as Teochew or Chiuchow) lies within the borders of Guangdong, its foods are most heavily influenced by the cuisines of the Hakka and Southern Fujian. In fact, these three cuisines are so closely related that they often claim one another's recipes as their own (this often happens with Sesame Oil Chicken Soup, page 171). The reason is simple: their adherents most likely have common ancestors. Although they arrived at different times, all three groups are believed to have descended from the Han Chinese who fled here from the North China Plain.

Chaozhou cuisine is most notable for the way seafood is prepared. Textural contrast is particularly essential here, as can be seen in Whole Dry-Fried Flounder (page 182), where the flatfish's frilly fins fry up like crispy potato chips. But flavor is important also, and two distinctive seasonings define most local foods: *shacha* (Chinese satay sauce) and fish sauce. *Shacha* is a complex mixture of dried ingredients: ground fish, scallops, shrimp, chilies, sesame seeds, and coconut, as well as fresh shallots. It adds a mysterious depth to Stir-Fried Rice Noodles and Satay Beef (page 220). Fish sauce, on the other hand, supplies a *xianwei* (see page 56) boost to buttery Chaozhou Shrimp Skewers (page 194).

SOUTHERN FUJIAN

Isolated from each other by forbidding mountains and a craggy coastline, the upper and lower expanses of Fujian Province developed independent cultures and dialects. Their foods are deliciously different, too: Northern Fujian's cuisine (see page 73) echoes the sweet, wine-infused flavors of its neighbor Zhejiang, while Southern Fujian's dishes resonate with the preserved and dried seasonings of Chaozhou and the Hakka. The cuisine in the south often contrasts strongly seasoned sauces or fillings against a gentle background of rice paste, rice noodles, or steamed rice, as can be tasted in Diced Braised Pork over Rice (page 208). Seafood makes its way into almost every meal. While it often appears as a straightforward panfried fish seasoned with a simple dash of salt, dishes such as Oyster Spring Rolls (page 168) offer more creative formulations. And every part of the pig is prized in Southern Fujian.

More than anything else, however, Southern Fujian's clear soups, thick chowders, and dipping sauces set its cuisine apart. These broths are usually based on pork or poultry and seasoned with ginger and medicinal herbs, as in Angelica Duck Soup (page 172). Many of its other soups are breathtakingly simple: for example, one night-market favorite involves giving fresh oysters a quick bath in boiling water and then seasoning this broth with slivered ginger and rice wine. And then there are Southern Fujian's delicious dipping sauces. Used in dishes like Blanched Squid with Garlicky Dipping Sauce (page 186) and those Oyster Spring Rolls, these sauces offer a bright contrast to the clean flavors of the meat or seafood they accompany.

TAIWAN

The majority of today's ethnic Taiwanese can trace their ancestry back to the cities of Quanzhou, Zhangzhou, and Xiamen in Southern Fujian (see page 225). All of these places happen to be located to the northeast of Chaozhou, which is one reason why the foods of Taiwan and Chaozhou share many flavors. Clear broths like herb-infused Sesame Oil Chicken Soup (page 171) are typical here, as well as rich, savory favorites such as Diced Braised Pork over Rice (page 208). Even the sweets seem related: the recipe for The Wife's Cookies of Chaozhou (page 232), for example, closely resembles the Taiwanese recipe for Sun Cookies (page 234). In addition to Southern Fujian and Chaozhou's influences, Taiwanese food is imbued with the flavors of the Japanese, who occupied the island from 1895 to 1945. This is clearly evidenced in dishes such as Cold Bamboo Shoots with Mayonnaise (page 162) and by the local penchant for sprinkling dried bonito (*katsuobushi*) shavings over Bean Curd with Pine Flower Preserved Eggs (page 81).

But Taiwan's traditional cuisines were reshuffled at the close of China's civil war in 1949, when countless Mainlanders followed Chiang Kai-shek, the leader of the Republic of China, into exile on the island.

Suddenly, for the first time ever, the cooking traditions of every region in China became available in one place. This is one of the reasons why many people in Taiwan now consider certain dishes that have incredibly distant origins, such as Yunnan's Cod with Crispy Bean Sauce (page 269), Shandong's Soymilk (page 64), Lanzhou Beef Noodle Soup (page 328), or Chaozhou's Whole Dry-Fried Flounder (page 182), as nothing less than Taiwanese specialties.

TAIWAN'S MILITARY FAMILIES

Juàncūncài 眷村菜, or "military family dishes," is a unique school of Taiwanese fusion cookery. These laid-back, home-style recipes often combine flavors from different regions throughout China. This cuisine emerged in Taiwan's military compounds, where officers and enlisted men lived with their families. These people came from different provinces, and the eateries they opened close by their homes mixed together cuisines from all over the country. The new dishes they created were highly savory and also economical. In Stir-Fried Grilled Breads (page 217), for example, an abundance of vegetables and starches stand in for the lack of meat, and satisfying pasta dishes such as Zhajiang Noodles (page 42) and Sesame Noodles (page 216) make for hearty and affordable meals all by themselves.

HAINAN

The foods of this subtropical isle located near the Gulf of Tonkin seem like a mix of the cuisines of Chaozhou, Southern Fujian, and Hawaii. Coconut and peanuts season the local Taro Rice (page 223), and the Lemon Cashews (page 163) taste a bit like the salted, preserved snacks that Hawaiians call "crack seed," which, by the way, were originally a Chaozhou treat. Sweets here are often made of sticky rice flour and steamed, as evidenced by the *mochi*-like creations called Ciba (page 306) that are also popular throughout the Coastal Southeast.

Since the island is almost directly connected to the Chinese mainland via the Leizhou Peninsula, some of Hainan's recipes have a distinct Cantonese cast. These are almost always the dishes with the lightest seasonings. One of Hainan's most famous foods, for example, is Hainan Chicken and Rice (page 198), which appears to be a local variation on Guangdong's White-Cut Chicken (page 196). As would be expected on a South China Sea island, seafood and tropical fruits are hugely important. Crab, in particular, is a famed local ingredient and finds its way onto most of Hainan's tables. When it comes to fruit, jackfruit is very popular and is often combined with things like chicken in simple stir-fries.

Guangdong and its related cuisines are grouped together here because all of them boast dishes with ethereal textures. Their delicate flavor spectrums also tend to be in stark contrast to the heartier cooking traditions of the Hakka, Southern Fujian, and Chaozhou. The following four stellar cuisines have all evolved in low wetlands and seaside metropolises within comfortable reach of Guangzhou. It is no wonder that Guangdong is the undisputed queen of southern China's cuisines.

GUANGDONG AND SOUTHERN GUANGXI

The Guangdong School invariably centers on the foods of the capital city. Straddling the network of rivers, channels, and streams that crisscross the Pearl River Delta, Guangzhou is home to fish dishes of every type, as well as to some of the country's best recipes for poultry and pork. To the west of Guangdong is the province of Guangxi. Because its lowermost flatlands used to be part of Guangdong, Southern Guangxi's dishes mirror those of its neighbor to the east, as in Wuzhou Paper-Wrapped Chicken (page 203), while Northern Guangxi (see page 248) and its tribal people are more aligned, taste-wise, with the spicy foods of the Central Highlands.

In Guangdong, simply treated fare like Guangdong-Style Steamed Fish (page 180) and White-Cut Chicken are paeans to the beauty of a single ingredient, while preserved ingredients provide powerful *xianwei* punches in dishes such as Steamed Minced Pork with Salted Fish (page 209). Guangzhou is known, too, for its dim sum, such as Cheong Fun (page 218). This ancient metropolis is also where many of China's finest roast meats first emerged, including Char Siu (page 206).

Rice is always found on the table in Guangzhou, and it often forms the foundation of a meal, as in Congee (page 226) and Crusty Rice with Charcuterie (page 221).

PEARL RIVER DELTA

Downriver from Guangzhou is a marshy land with an especially enchanting cuisine. A braided network of rivers and channels defines this region, which was home to the silk industry over five hundred years ago. Countless mulberry trees were planted to feed the silkworms, and the land beneath these trees was devoted to aquaculture. As a result, fish are a major staple of the region's cuisine (along with produce and, surprisingly, dairy cattle). The hub for all this abundance is Shunde, a town thought to be home to 80 to 90 percent of the Guangdong-style chefs in China.

Freshwater fish is so plentiful around here that it is sometimes substituted for other ingredients. For example, in Shunde Braised Fish Puffs (page 184), carp takes the place of bean curd in a startlingly delectable way. Another exciting dish from this cuisine is Shunde Raw Fish (page 164), in which paper-thin slices of uncooked grass carp are tossed in with fried garlic, dried laver seaweed, sesame seeds, toasty taro, and more. Few places in China adore fresh dairy as much as people do here, and cow's milk is used in inventive dishes such as Stir-Fried Milk with Crab (page 190) and Ginger Milk Pudding (page 230).

MACAU

Perched on the southern edge of the mouth of the Pearl River, Macau is composed of a tiny peninsula and two islands. For almost 450 years, until 1999, it was a Portuguese colony and, as a result, its foods demonstrate the most European influences of any Chinese cuisine. But the influences in Macau are not strictly Iberian. As one of the legacies of Portugal's colonial history, many international elements can be found in Macau. For example, you can taste the flavors of Goa, another former Portuguese colony on the west coast of India, in Portuguese Chicken (page 195), a creamy dish seasoned with curry and coconut milk. And the origins of African Chicken (page 202), a perennial local favorite in Macau, can possibly be traced back to Portugal's foray into Angola. More traditional Portuguese flavors can be tasted in recipes like Macanese Bacalau (page 166), a salt cod dish that is cooked with potatoes and black olives, as well as such Chinese touches as coconut cream and ginger.

HONG KONG

Hong Kong's dishes are the most well-known offspring of Guangzhou cuisine. The lingering culinary influence of Great Britain, which controlled this city on the northern edge of the Pearl River estuary until 1997, is one of the things that makes its foods so unique. Hong Kong Milk Tea (page 241) is a good example of Britain's influence. After the Chinese Civil War, many of the finest chefs from Guangzhou, the Pearl River Delta, and Chaozhou relocated here, and the presence of all these different cooking styles has fostered a culture of innovation and experimentation. Classic Hong Kong cuisine often emphasizes clear, fresh flavors, as in Savory Crab and Cellophane Noodles (page 192) and Typhoon Shelter Crab (page 188). Over the years, however, Hong Kong's tastes have moved toward clever reinterpretations of Guangzhou's specialties, such as Steamed Fish with Three Kinds of Olives (page 181).

My late father-in-law was the eldest son of a county governor. He was expected to marry the country girl his father had selected for him and inherit his father's prominent position in life. Despite this grooming and the relative luxury of his home in a Hakka village not too far from Meizhou, Huang Lung-chin left it all behind when he joined the fight against the Japanese invasion of his homeland in 1937. He became a decorated fighter pilot in the Nationalist Air Force, was severely wounded in one of his numerous dogfights, and was one of the few officers invited to Japan's official surrender in Nanjing in 1945.

In 1949, along with his young bride and their children, Huang Lung-chin left the Mainland for Taiwan, along with many other Nationalists. The Communists were closing in on Guangzhou, and my father-in-law and his family escaped on one of the last planes leaving the city. Chiang Kai-shek, the leader of the Nationalists, had promised that this exile would be temporary, and Huang Lung-chin assumed that he would return to his hometown one day. But the years passed, and the possibility of a return became more and more remote. He never saw his parents again.

When I finally met my father-in-law, he was a retired colonel with a shy smile. Gonggong, as I called him, had a tiny apartment in Los Angeles's Chinatown, where he cooked delicious Hakka- and Guangdong-style dishes. He reserved the most laborious ones for his Chinese New Year's Eve dinners, when all of the family would gather together. I was the only one who liked to help him in the kitchen, so I became his apprentice of sorts. He taught me how to cook fish perfectly, and through him, I fell in love with the savory dishes of his hometown.

It was at Gonggong's side that I first began to learn about Chinese cooking traditions. He was very generous with his knowledge, and he taught me the things his parents had once taught him. He turned out to be a fount of ancient culinary information. But perhaps more important, Gonggong taught me about self-reliance and perseverance: despite the historical and cultural hurdles he was forced to reckon with in his lifetime, Gonggong managed to fashion a life of his own design. He refused to be hemmed in by traditions or external forces that would have kept him bound to one place or one time or one way of living. Instead, he lived large and free, fearlessly pursuing his own path. He is, without doubt, my greatest inspiration. ●

THE RECIPES

V = VEGETARIAN OR VEGAN OPTION

Liángbàn zhúsǔn 涼拌竹筍

Cold Bamboo Shoots with Mayonnaise

TAIWAN · SERVES 4 TO 6

Taiwan spent fifty years under Japanese occupation, from 1895 to 1945, and the culinary influence has never left. The fresh seafood available on the island is part of the reason why the Japanese cuisine there is so wonderful, but I'm also fond of it because it has been inflected with Chinese flavors.

To make this local specialty, fat winter bamboo shoots are cooked until barely tender, chilled, and then drizzled with ribbons of Japanese mayo. Overall, it's a very simple dish, but make sure you check out the entry for winter bamboo shoots in the glossary (see page 476) for help in selecting the main ingredient.

1 pound winter bamboo shoots,
    fresh or frozen and defrosted
2 teaspoons sea salt
Curly lettuce leaves for garnish, optional
Kewpie brand mayonnaise, as needed

1. Start this recipe at least 4 hours—and up to 3 days—before serving. If using fresh bamboo shoots, peel them (see Tip, page 122). Trim off any less-than-perfect bits and cut the shoots into chunks about 1 inch all around; this uniform size will help them cook evenly.

2. Rinse the shoots and place them in a medium saucepan. Cover with water and add the salt. Bring the water to a full boil over high heat and then reduce the heat to maintain a gentle simmer. Cook the shoots until the thickest piece can be easily pierced with a paring knife, about 15 minutes for frozen shoots and about 30 minutes for fresh. Drain, rinse with cool tap water, and drain again in a colander. Allow them to cool to room temperature and then refrigerate for a couple of hours to chill them completely.

3. Just before serving, clean and dry the optional lettuce leaves and arrange them on a serving plate. Mound the chilled bamboo shoots on top of the lettuce and drizzle them with the mayo.

Another way to prepare your bamboo shoots is to cook them in salted, defatted chicken stock. If you like, you can season the stock with rice wine, ginger, and green onions. The bamboo shoots will be much more flavorful this way, and they won't need any garnish.

THERE IS A REASON WHY FOREIGN ingredients like catsup, Worcestershire sauce, curry, and mayonnaise have been adopted by many of China's cuisines, particularly along the long Pacific coast. It all has to do with treaty ports.

What happened was this: From 1760 to 1842, the only port open to foreign trade was Guangzhou (Canton), in Guangdong. China had many things Westerners and the Japanese wanted to buy, like tea, silk, and porcelain, but China itself needed so little that these foreigners had to pay for everything in silver. This cut seriously into the traders' profits. British merchants soon hit upon opium as the perfect item to sell to the Chinese, and this in turn became a serious social problem throughout China.

Before long, the Daoguang emperor (r. 1821–50) ordered his official Lin Zexu to burn all of the British opium held in Guangzhou, causing Guangzhou's foreign merchants to petition their own governments to in turn declare war on China. The resulting Opium Wars (1839–42) severely weakened the Qing government, Hong Kong was made a permanent British concession until 1997, and China was forced to capitulate to unequal treaties that turned eighty Chinese cities, including Shanghai, Nanjing, Tianjin, Ningbo, Fuzhou, and Guangzhou, into enclaves for occupiers from Great Britain, France, the United States, Russia, Japan, and other nations.

In the wake of these treaties, imported ingredients and culinary ideas brought exotic elements and new flavors to local dishes. Braised Prawns (page 25) were soon being tinged a brilliant scarlet by catsup, and a British confection was transformed into Malay Sponge Cake (page 235).

Níngméng yāoguǒ 檸檬腰果

Lemon Cashews

HAINAN · MAKES ABOUT 2 CUPS

One of Hainan's more interesting crops is the cashew, which grows in areas that are too dry for anything else. These nuts are actually seeds that grow on the bottom of a pear-shaped fruit, so each cashew must be individually harvested and shelled. In Hainan, they are sometimes deep-fried and then tossed with lemon, powdered hawthorn fruit (*shanzha*), and a light syrup. The resulting bar snack is wonderfully tart and salty.

1 large lemon

2½ tablespoons dried sliced hawthorn fruits

Freshly ground black pepper to taste (¼ to ½ teaspoon)

8 ounces raw cashews

Peanut or vegetable oil for deep-frying (used oil is all
    right if it smells fresh)

Spray oil

5 tablespoons sugar (2 tablespoons more if you want
    a sweeter coating)

2 tablespoons water

1 teaspoon sea salt

1. Scrub the lemon well, wipe dry, and zest it with a fine grater. Cut the lemon in half and squeeze out 3 tablespoons juice. Use a spice grinder to pulverize the hawthorn fruits, then shake them through a fine sieve to remove anything that isn't reduced to a powder, as the seeds can be extremely hard and have been known to crack teeth. Combine the hawthorn powder with the lemon zest and black pepper in a small bowl.

2. Place the cashews in a wok and barely cover them with cool oil. Turn on the heat to medium and slowly fry the nuts, stirring often, until they are golden brown. Adjust the heat as necessary to keep them bubbling nicely without burning. Don't walk away from the stove, as cashews brown very quickly. When the nuts are cooked through, empty the oil and nuts into a sieve set over a large, heatproof work bowl. Let the cashews drain while you prepare the syrup. Spray a large platter or rimmed baking sheet with oil.

3. Wipe out the wok and return it to the stove. Place the sugar, water, salt, and lemon juice in the wok and bring them to a boil over medium-high heat. Boil this mixture until it bubbles and becomes very thick, then add the fried cashews. Toss the nuts continuously in the syrup to coat them well; don't stop tossing until almost all of the syrup has been absorbed. At the last minute, add the lemon zest mixture. Toss again and turn the cashews out onto the platter to cool. Store in a tightly closed container, preferably in the refrigerator.

Shùndé yúshēng 順德魚生

Shunde Raw Fish

PEARL RIVER DELTA · SERVES 4 TO 6

Raw fish is usually known outside of China by its Japanese name, sashimi. But raw preparations are popular in China as well, where they've been enjoyed for at least two thousand years. They are particularly common in the Coastal Southeast, and my favorite rendition is this recipe, which comes from the Shunde area of the Pearl River Delta.

A visually stunning dish, this appetizer is usually reserved for a banquet. The fish slices are arranged in a single layer, often on a frozen platter or a large bed of ice. Unlike Japanese sashimi, the raw fish of Shunde are given a wide variety of complements: peanuts, sesame seeds, deep-fried taro, fried garlic, and other seasonings are served on the side for diners to use as garnishes. Here, though, I toss them all together, so that each bite has a delicious range of flavors and textures.

SEASONED GINGER

2 tablespoons finely shredded fresh young ginger or peeled and finely shredded fresh mature ginger

2 tablespoons sugar

2 tablespoons pale rice vinegar

1 tablespoon water

FRIED THINGS

2 cloves garlic, very thinly sliced

1 cup peanut or vegetable oil for frying, divided in half

½ bundle cellophane noodles

¼ cup peeled and julienned mature taro

FISH

8 to 10 ounces sashimi-grade Korean fluke or yellowtail fillet (see Tip)

DRY CONDIMENTS

2 tablespoons finely chopped toasted peanuts (page 411)

2 tablespoons toasted sesame seeds (page 413)

2 to 3 tablespoons finely shredded laver seaweed (nori)

MOIST CONDIMENTS

1 red jalapeño pepper, seeded and very thinly sliced

2 green onions, white parts only, trimmed and thinly julienned

¼ cup chopped cilantro, optional

¼ cup finely sliced lettuce (like romaine)

2 tablespoons finely chopped and rinsed Sichuan pickled tuber or Shanghai mustard pickles (page 427)

DRESSING

2 tablespoons strained seasoned vinegar (from Step 1)

1 tablespoon toasted sesame oil

1 to 2 tablespoons garlic oil from the fried garlic (from Step 2)

2 tablespoons fresh lemon juice, or to taste

½ teaspoon regular soy sauce, or to taste

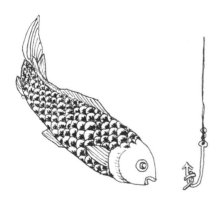

1. Chill a platter or individual salad plates for serving. Then make the seasoned ginger: place the ginger in a small work bowl. Mix together the sugar, vinegar, and water and microwave for about 30 seconds. Stir the liquid until the sugar dissolves and then pour it over the ginger. Marinate for at least 1 hour.

2. To make the fried garlic chips, first soak the garlic in cool water to cover for about 5 minutes and then rinse it until it feels slippery; this gets rid of the sticky juice that would otherwise make the garlic clump up. Drain the garlic well and pat the slices completely dry. Place a wok over medium heat, pour in half of the oil, and test how hot it is with a slice of garlic: if it floats and is immediately surrounded by bubbles, the oil is ready. Add all of the garlic and stir gently with chopsticks so that the slices float freely in the oil. Have a slotted spoon and plate lined with a paper towel ready. When the garlic turns a light golden brown, start paying close attention; as soon as it is a uniform golden brown, scoop it out with the spoon, shake off the oil, and spread the slices out on the paper towel. Immediately pour the garlic oil into a measuring cup and let it cool. To fry the cellophane noodles, heat the remaining oil in a wok over medium-high until it starts to shimmer. Break the cellophane noodles apart in a paper bag so that they don't shoot out all over your kitchen. Line a large work bowl with a paper towel and have a Chinese spider or slotted spoon ready. Drop one noodle into the oil, and if it immediately puffs up, the oil is ready; if it browns, lower the heat. Fry the noodles in small handfuls, removing them from the oil as soon as they are puffy and white. Finally, to fry the taro, sprinkle it into the hot oil and gently stir until the taro is lightly browned along the edges, then remove the taro and let it cool off on a paper towel.

3. Prepare the fish by removing the skin and any dark areas (unless you like the flavor of the dark meat, of course). Slice the fluke very thinly on the diagonal, which will give you nice, wide pieces. If you are using yellowtail, slice it on the diagonal into pieces about ⅛ inch thick. Arrange the fish slices on a plate, cover with plastic wrap, and refrigerate immediately.

4. Toss the fried garlic and the dry condiments together in a small work bowl. Toss the moist condiments together in a medium work bowl and keep them chilled.

5. Just before serving, drain the ginger and reserve the seasoned vinegar. Add the ginger, the dry condiments, and the raw fish to the moist condiments. Toss the mixture lightly together; your hands are the best utensils for this. To make the dressing, combine all of the ingredients in a small work bowl, adjusting the ingredients to taste. Drizzle the dressing into the fresh mixture and toss again as gently as possible. Taste and add whatever seasoning you think the dish needs, then serve it immediately on the chilled platter or chilled plates.

Excellent-quality farmed carp are not yet widely available here in the United States, but I have found two very good substitutes: farm-raised yellowtail (often sold under its Japanese name, *hamachi*) and the flatfish known as Korean fluke (or *hirame*). Yellowtail is very good in this dish: it is buttery and has a wonderful texture. However, if I'm being really meticulous, I would have to go with the fluke, which is a leaner fish and can be sliced much more thinly. You should be able to find both at Japanese-style fish shops.

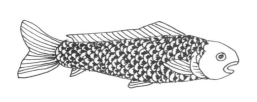

Zhá mǎjièxiu qíu 炸馬介休球

Macanese Bacalau

MACAU • SERVES 4 TO 6

Pretty much a riff on Portugal's ethereal *bacalau* (salt cod) croquettes, this dish is best made in the spring, when salt cod is freshest and most available in Italian and Portuguese delicatessens. Like many dishes from Macau, it displays a delicate balance of Chinese and Portuguese flavors. I've made a few slight alterations here, using coconut cream instead of whipping cream and tapenade instead of olives. I suggest serving this on a lightly dressed pile of spring greens.

CROQUETTES

8 ounces salt cod fillet
1 large (10 to 12 ounces) russet or other baking potato
2 tablespoons unsalted butter
2 green onions, trimmed and finely minced
2 large or 3 small cloves garlic, finely minced
2 teaspoons ginger juice (page 481)
2 teaspoons regular soy sauce
1 large egg, lightly beaten
Freshly ground black pepper
6 tablespoons tapenade, or pitted and chopped
    oil-cured black olives
½ cup finely chopped cilantro
½ cup chilled canned coconut cream
    (not coconut milk or sweetened cream of coconut),
    or chilled heavy cream

COATING

About 1 cup potato starch or cornstarch
2 large eggs, lightly beaten
2 cups dried bread crumbs (Japanese *panko*),
    or more as needed
Peanut or vegetable oil for frying

SALAD

¼ cup black vinegar
2 cloves garlic, finely minced
2 teaspoons Dijon mustard
½ teaspoon sea salt
6 tablespoons extra virgin olive oil
4 cups loosely packed baby greens (mizuna, arugula,
    spinach, and lettuce) or spring mix, chilled
Toasted sesame seeds (page 413) for garnish

1. Start this recipe at least 2 days before you wish to serve it. First, soak the salt cod in cool water to cover in the refrigerator, changing the water at least once a day. After 2 days, rinse the fish, pat it dry, and run your fingers over it carefully. Use tweezers to remove any errant bones, and pull off any silver skin you find. Flake the fish, tearing apart any tough sections; if a piece is too difficult to tear easily with your fingers, discard it. Coarsely chop the fish. You should have about 2 cups flaked fish.

2. Peel the potato and cut into quarters. Place in a saucepan, cover with water, and bring to a full boil. Reduce the heat to a simmer and cook until the potatoes are tender. Drain the potatoes and return them to the pan over low heat to cook off the excess moisture. After a few minutes, remove them from the stove, add the butter, and mash with a potato masher until smooth. (Do not use a food processor, as it will make the potatoes gummy.)

3. Scoop the mashed potatoes into a medium work bowl and add the flaked fish, green onions, garlic, ginger juice, soy sauce, egg, pepper, tapenade, and cilantro. Lightly mix everything together and then fold in the coconut or heavy cream. If you have the time, cover the mixture and chill it for an hour or two to make it easier to handle.

4. Next, prepare the coating, which consists of three layers. Place the potato starch in one work bowl, the eggs in another, and the bread crumbs in a third. Put 2 spoons each in the potato starch and the bread crumbs, plus a fork and a spoon in the eggs. (I like to use plastic spoons as they are thin and smooth.) Keep the utensils for each bowl separate so that they do not become heavily coated.

5. Now coat the croquettes: first, use the spoons from the potato starch bowl to scoop up about 2 tablespoons of the cod mixture. Form the cod into a rough ball and drop it into the starch. Toss the ball around to coat it, then shape it into a croquette (a long oval) between the palms of your hands. Lower this into the beaten eggs and gently roll it around to coat it completely. Lift it up with the fork so that most of the egg dribbles back into the bowl, then place the croquette in the bread crumbs. Use the 2 spoons in that bowl to gently roll the croquette around until it's covered completely. Shape it once again between the palms of your hands and then place it on a baking sheet. Repeat with the rest of the cod and coatings. The croquettes can either be refrigerated or frozen at this point, if you wish; they will not have to be defrosted before they are fried, but reduce the heat and extend the cooking time as needed to cook them through.

6. To fry the croquettes, set a large frying pan over medium heat until the edges are hot. Pour about ¼ inch oil into the pan. Sprinkle a couple of the bread crumbs in the oil; if they bubble immediately, the oil is ready. Reduce the heat to medium-low and gently slide in as many of the croquettes as you wish to fry, or as many as will fit without touching. While the croquettes are slowly frying, heat an oven to 250°F and line a clean baking sheet with some parchment paper or paper towels. Fry the croquettes until they are a deep golden brown—but not dark brown—on the bottom. Use a spatula to carefully turn each croquette over and fry the other side; each one will take about 5 minutes' total frying time. Remove them as they are done and place on the lined baking sheet. Keep them hot in the oven while you prepare the salad.

7. In a large bowl, mix together the vinegar, garlic, mustard, salt, and oil. Add the greens, toss well, and taste and adjust the seasoning. Distribute the salad among individual serving plates, piling it up in the center of each plate. Just before serving, arrange an equal number of the croquettes around the salads. Sprinkle with the sesame seeds. Serve immediately. The croquettes can be eaten with chopsticks or with a knife and fork.

Cuìpí héjuǎn 脆皮蚵卷

Oyster Spring Rolls

SOUTHERN FUJIAN AND TAIWAN • MAKES 12

This dish is a stunning appetizer and a wonderful accompaniment for cocktails or beer. Oyster Spring Rolls were probably invented in Quanzhou, in Southern Fujian, where so many of China's best oyster dishes originated. I like to serve them with little more than a simple dipping sauce of soy sauce, catsup, and garlic.

SAUCE

½ cup plus 1 tablespoon catsup

3 cloves garlic, very finely minced

3 tablespoons regular soy sauce

FILLING

10 ounces shucked oysters, preferably very small ones
    (½ inch or smaller)

4 ounces pork belly, with the skin removed, thinly sliced,
    and frozen until firm

4 ounces mung bean sprouts

4 green onions, trimmed

½ cup chopped cilantro

2 tablespoons Chinese flour (page 386)

½ teaspoon five-spice powder (page 441 or store-bought)

Freshly ground black pepper

2 tablespoons mild rice wine

1 tablespoon regular soy sauce

WRAPPERS

2 teaspoons Chinese flour (page 386)

1 tablespoon water

12 spring roll wrappers

Peanut or vegetable oil for frying

1. First, make the sauce by mixing the catsup with the garlic and soy sauce. Taste and adjust the seasoning, then let the sauce mellow at room temperature while you make the rest of the dish.

2. To make the filling, rinse the oysters, taking care to remove any shell bits. Place them in a small saucepan, add water to cover, and bring to a boil. Turn the heat down to a low simmer and cook the oysters for about 2 minutes; drain and discard the water. Allow the oysters to cool off while you prepare the rest of the ingredients. Coarsely chop the oysters if they are larger than ½ inch.

3. Chop the pork belly coarsely and place it in a mini food processor. Process the pork until it has been ground into tiny pieces. Rinse and shake the bean sprouts dry, then lightly break them up with your fingers into smallish pieces. Chop the green onions into ¼-inch pieces and place in a small work bowl. Place the cilantro and bean sprouts in a medium work bowl.

4. In a dry wok, stir-fry 2 tablespoons flour over medium heat until it starts to take on a golden tinge; this will remove any raw taste. Scrape the flour out into a small work bowl, rinse out the wok, and place the wok over medium-high heat. Add the pork without any additional oil and stir-fry until it is no longer pink, then toss in the green onions. Stir-fry these until they start to wilt, then add the five-spice powder, lots of black pepper, rice wine, soy sauce, and toasted flour. Toss everything together and then scrape it out into the work bowl with the cilantro and bean sprouts.

5. In a small bowl, make a paste out of the 2 teaspoons flour and 1 tablespoon water. Open your spring roll wrapper package and remove 12 wrappers; keep them covered with a tea towel at all times, as they will dry out and crack easily. (Any wrappers you won't be using should be placed in a resealable plastic bag and refrozen immediately.)

6. Wrap the spring rolls one at a time (for directions, see the diagram below). You can freeze the spring rolls at this point, in a single layer on some plastic wrap. When they are frozen solid, transfer them to a resealable freezer bag. They do not have to be defrosted before frying; simply lower the heat under the oil to medium-low to give them a bit more time to cook.

7. To fry the spring rolls, set a wok or frying pan over medium heat and pour in about ½ inch of oil. (If you have to cook these in batches, heat an oven or toaster oven to 275°F and have a small baking sheet lined with parchment paper or paper towels ready.) When the oil is hot, add as many spring rolls as will fit comfortably without touching. Fry them on one side until golden, then turn them over and fry the other side, 5 to 6 minutes total. Remove them to the paper towels, slice in half on the diagonal, and serve immediately with the dipping sauce.

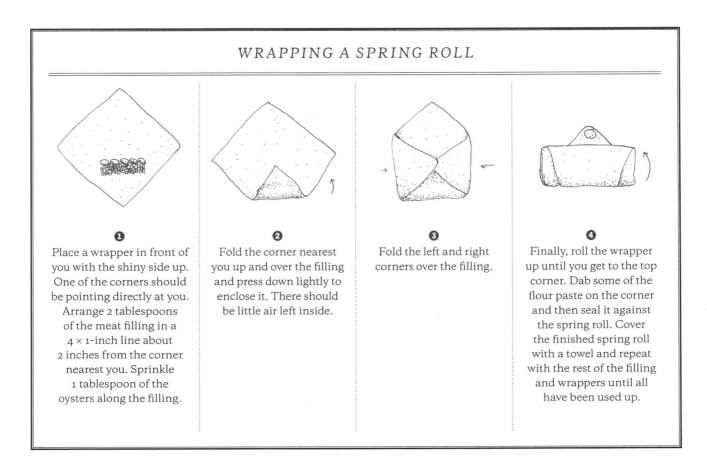

WRAPPING A SPRING ROLL

❶ Place a wrapper in front of you with the shiny side up. One of the corners should be pointing directly at you. Arrange 2 tablespoons of the meat filling in a 4 × 1-inch line about 2 inches from the corner nearest you. Sprinkle 1 tablespoon of the oysters along the filling.

❷ Fold the corner nearest you up and over the filling and press down lightly to enclose it. There should be little air left inside.

❸ Fold the left and right corners over the filling.

❹ Finally, roll the wrapper up until you get to the top corner. Dab some of the flour paste on the corner and then seal it against the spring roll. Cover the finished spring roll with a towel and repeat with the rest of the filling and wrappers until all have been used up.

Qīngdùn huāgū tāng 清燉花菇湯

Flower Mushroom Soup

GUANGDONG AND HONG KONG · SERVES 6 TO 8

12 (1-inch) dried flower mushrooms
8 cups water, divided into 2 cups and 6 cups
8 thin slices fresh ginger
2 green onions, trimmed
¼ cup mild rice wine
2 teaspoons sugar
2 tablespoons light soy sauce
1 tablespoon rendered chicken fat

The secret to this dish is procuring the right mushrooms. They're called "flower mushrooms" (*huagu*), and the best ones have traditionally come from Japan as high-grade shiitakes, though other places are beginning to produce them. The caps have natural furrows that look sort of like tortoise shells. Some places try to sell imitation versions, but if you look closely, you'll see that the real ones have little bumps and ridges, while the knockoffs have had their caps sliced with razors.

This is one of those rare cases in which dried ingredients outshine fresh ones. I recommend going to a Chinese herbalist for the mushrooms, if you have one in your area. Most times, if you are polite about it and ask permission, you will be allowed to poke and prod the dried mushrooms, which are usually sold loose. This allows you to check whether the flower mushrooms are genuine.

1. Start this recipe the night before you want to serve it by rinsing off the dried mushrooms in a colander and then placing them in a medium work bowl. Cover them with about 2 cups of the water and let them soak overnight. (You *can* cover them with boiling water if you're in a huge hurry, but neither the flavor nor the texture will be as good if you do so.)

2. The next day, cut the stems off the mushrooms using a pair of kitchen shears. Save the stems for your stockpot (see page 381) and reserve the soaking water for this soup. Place the trimmed mushrooms in a medium saucepan and carefully pour the soaking water through a fine-mesh sieve into the pan.

3. Add the remaining 6 cups water to the pan, as well as the ginger, whole green onions, rice wine, sugar, and soy sauce. Bring the water to a boil and then lower the heat to a gentle simmer. Cook the mushrooms for 30 to 45 minutes, until tender. Taste the stock and adjust the seasoning before removing the onions and adding the chicken fat. Serve very hot.

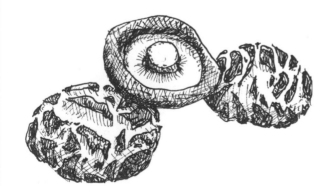

Máyóu jī tāng 麻油雞湯

Sesame Oil Chicken Soup

SOUTHERN FUJIAN, CHAOZHOU, AND TAIWAN •
MAKES 3 TO 4 QUARTS

This soup, whose smell reminds me of Taipei, is often given to nursing mothers as a part of *zuò yuèzi* 坐月子 (literally, "a month of sitting"). During this period, the new mom is supposed to relax and take care of herself and her new baby. She also gets to eat a lot of nourishing food courtesy of her own mother, mother-in-law, and aunts.

Believed to encourage blood flow and produce breast milk, this soup is one of the dishes most commonly served during a mother's confinement. The wood ear fungus is thought to combat high cholesterol, which many women suffer from after giving birth, and the ginger warms the blood, while the wolfberries act as an overall tonic. Traditional uses aside, I like to make this throughout the year, especially when anyone is feeling down or in need of a little extra TLC.

1 whole fryer chicken (3 to 4 pounds)
½ cup plus 2 tablespoons toasted sesame oil
1½ cups thinly sliced fresh ginger
7 cups mild rice wine (Taiwanese *mijiu* recommended)
2 to 3 cups wood ear fungus, fresh or dried and
    plumped up, trimmed and torn into pieces, optional
¼ cup wolfberries, optional
1 teaspoon regular soy sauce, optional
Dried rice noodles, optional

1. Pat the chicken dry and get rid of any extra fat or pinfeathers, and then use a cleaver to cut it into large pieces before whacking it across the bones into inch-wide chunks.

2. Place a wok over medium heat. When it is hot, add the oil and then the ginger. Stir the ginger occasionally as it fries so that it turns an even, golden brown. As it starts to brown a bit darker, scoot it up the sides of the wok, out of the oil, and then add all of the chicken. Turn the heat up a bit and brown the chicken on all sides, then mix the ginger back in.

3. When the chicken is nicely browned, add the rice wine, raise the heat to high, and bring the wine to a boil. Add the optional wood ears and wolfberries and then lower the heat to a gentle simmer and cook the chicken for about 30 minutes, until tender. Taste the soup and add the soy sauce only if necessary. (Be careful not to add too much—this dish might already be very savory, because cooking wines like Taiwanese *mijiu* contain salt.) If you wish to serve the soup over rice noodles, boil the noodles until barely tender and place them in the bottom of your soup bowls before ladling in the soup and chicken. Noodles or not, serve this very hot.

The black-skinned chickens called "silkies" in English and "black bone chickens" (*wūgǔ jī* 烏骨雞) in Chinese are considered especially nutritious and can often be found in the freezer case at Chinese groceries.

Taiwan-style rice wine is what gives this dish its distinctive flavor. The brand I use comes in a green glass bottle, has 1.5 percent salt, and says, in English, "Cooking michiu distilled spirit of rice, not for sale or use as a beverage."

Dānggui yā 當歸鴨

Angelica Duck Soup

SOUTHERN FUJIAN, CHAOZHOU, AND TAIWAN •
SERVES 4 TO 6

In China, food and medicine have long been seen as intimately related (see page 174), and some of the tastier Chinese medicinal herbs are also employed as seasonings. In certain cities, entire restaurants are devoted to nothing but restorative dishes that feature judicious pairings of meats, vegetables, and curative herbs.

Angelica Duck Soup, which is considered particularly good for the common cold and for any time a person feels weak and rundown, is often featured at such restaurants. It incorporates wolfberries, ginger, cinnamon, and other traditional Chinese herbs, like angelica and lovage root. The end result is a warming, wholesome, and healing meal.

1 whole duck (about 5 pounds)
6 thin slices fresh ginger
4 cups mild rice wine (Taiwanese *mijiu* recommended)
½ stick cinnamon
2 pieces Chinese angelica root
3 star anise
1 piece *shudi*, optional
2 slices lovage root
8 cups boiling water
1 teaspoon regular soy sauce, optional
¼ cup wolfberries
1 package (10½ ounces) dried rice vermicelli,
    more or less, depending upon how many
    people you want to serve

1. Chop (or have your butcher chop) the duck into 1-inch-wide pieces. Pat the pieces dry with a paper towel; remove any pinfeathers and viscera. Cut off and reserve the large lumps of fat around the neck and bottom of the bird. Melt the fat in a wok over medium heat until rendered; discard the solids.

2. Raise the heat to medium-high and add the ginger to the fat. Fry it until it turns a nice brown, then transfer it to a medium work bowl. Use the melted fat to fry the duck pieces in about 4 batches until brown, starting with the fattiest pieces so that the fat continues to render, and then transfer the browned duck to the bowl. Pour any fat in the bowl back into the wok but beware of the juices, which will spatter. Use a screen to protect yourself as necessary. Repeat with the rest of the duck until done and then pour out and reserve the fat.

3. Pour the rice wine into the wok and add all of the herbs and spices and the boiling water. Bring the water to a boil again and then lower the heat to a gentle simmer. Cover the wok and slowly simmer the flavor out of the herbs and into the broth for about 30 minutes.

4. Add the duck, fat (if you wish), and ginger to the broth. Bring the liquid to a boil again and then lower the heat to a simmer. Cover and simmer for about 1 hour. Taste the broth and add the soy sauce only if needed, then toss in the wolfberries, cover, and let the duck sit for another half hour to absorb the flavors. Taste and adjust the seasoning a final time. The duck can be prepared in advance up to this point, cooled, and refrigerated. Skim off the fat, if you wish.

5. To serve, heat the duck and broth to boiling, and at the same time bring a large pot of water to a boil and add the rice vermicelli. Bring the pot to a boil again, then lower to a simmer. When the vermicelli is barely done, drain it and divide it among large soup bowls. Ladle the duck, broth, and herbs over the noodles and serve.

Páigǔ gāncài tāng 排骨乾菜湯

Pork Rib and Dried Bok Choy Soup

GUANGDONG · SERVES 4 TO 6

Whenever you drop into an authentic Guangdong-style shop and order something like Crusty Rice with Charcuterie (page 221), this is most likely the soup that will be served on the side. Cheaper places will often skimp on the ingredients, but somehow the soup, which is customarily referred to as *lǎohuǒ tāng* 老火湯 (slow-cooked soup), is always flavorful. For this recipe, I like to soak the dried bok choy overnight and then chop it finely before adding it, which gives the vegetable a chance to break down a bit and become tender. After it is cooked, the bok choy ends up tasting slightly fermented and savory. I also add extra wine, which supplies the stock with a nice vibrancy, and throw in diced carrots, for their color as well as their sweetness.

2 bunches dried bok choy (about 3 ounces)

1 pound pork ribs, cut into 1-inch pieces by the butcher (see Tip)

1 leek, split and cleaned (see page 450)

¼ cup thinly sliced fresh ginger

1 cup mild rice wine, divided in half

1 carrot, peeled and finely diced

Freshly ground black pepper

Sea salt or mushroom powder to taste

1. Start this soup a day before you plan to serve it. Place the dried bok choy in a large pan or work bowl and cover with warm water. Let it soak overnight. The next day, drain off the water, rinse the boy choy gently, cut off the tough stem ends, and then chop into ½-inch pieces.

2. Separate the pork ribs, if necessary, and place them in a 4-quart saucepan. Cover with water and bring to a boil. Simmer the pork for about 5 minutes, dump out the water, and then rinse both the pork and the pan of any scum. Either chop the leek or split it in half lengthwise and tie it into 2 knots. Return the pork to the pan and add the ginger, leek, half of the rice wine, the bok choy, and water to cover. Bring the pan to a full boil and then lower the heat to a simmer. Cook the soup for at least 1 hour, until both the pork and the bok choy are very tender. Toss in the carrots and cook them for only a few minutes before pouring in the rest of the rice wine. Add pepper and either salt or mushroom powder to taste. Serve hot.

Another good cut for this soup is pork neck. Have the butcher chop it into bite-sized pieces.

Ròugǔ chá 肉骨茶

Meaty Bone Soup

CHAOZHOU AND SOUTHERN FUJIAN • SERVES 4

One of the most popular soups in Malaysia and Singapore is called *bak kut teh*, which means "meaty bone tea" in the Southern Fujian dialect. In Mandarin Chinese, the soup is called *rougu cha*. This aromatic and soothing dish was most likely brought to Southeast Asia by the Chaozhou travelers who eventually settled there. Like many soups from the Coastal Southeast (see pages 171 and 172), it is seasoned with Chinese medicinal herbs, and it's cheap and easy to make. Traditionally, the pork ribs are simply tossed into boiling water with the herbs and some garlic, but I have fooled around with the recipe to add extra depth and color.

The flavor of this soup is established by its herbs and spices—and there are quite a lot of them. The most common inclusions are Solomon's seal root (*yuzhu*), anise, angelica root, Chinese dates, licorice root, and star anise. But some cooks like to add wolfberries, aged tangerine peel, stick cinnamon, whole cloves, arhat fruit, and dried longans, among others. It all depends on how much underlying sweetness and fruitiness you're aiming for.

Luckily, you can find herb packets particularly designed for this soup in most well-stocked Chinese grocery stores. If you can't locate one of these packets, visit a Chinese herbalist and say that you need herbs and spices for *rougu cha*. You should be aware that this herbal broth will taste bitter and harsh at first. During the braising process, however, the broth will mellow as it encounters the flavors of the meat, sugar, wine, and soy sauce. Serve as is or over noodles along with a side of greens.

1 pound pork spareribs, cut in half lengthwise
        by the butcher (see Tips)
2 tablespoons regular soy sauce
1 package (2.1 ounces, more or less) *rougu cha* herbal mix
        (see Tips)
8 cups water
4 large dried black mushrooms, plumped up
Boiling water, as needed
¼ cup dried daylily flowers
3 tablespoons peanut or vegetable oil,
        divided into 2 tablespoons and 1 tablespoon
8 large cloves garlic, peeled and left whole
5 or 6 thin slices fresh ginger
½ cup mild rice wine
2 tablespoons rock sugar

THE CHINESE PRACTICE OF COOKING WITH therapeutic herbs belongs to the broader school of restorative, flavorful dishes called *yàoshàn* 藥膳, or "medicinal foods." On Chinese television and in printed media, many discussions of a recipe will include information on how that dish can be considered therapeutic, and on who should eat it and why.

Much of this is good common sense, of course: hot chicken soup is mom's penicillin just about everywhere in the world. But especially in the southeastern corner of China, healthy supplements often double as seasonings—wolfberries and ginger are good examples—while more powerful tonics like ginseng (see page 30) and angelica are added to curative soups such as Angelica Duck Soup (page 172) to heal the body in different ways.

Duck is used in that tonic because it is considered a "warming" ingredient, meaning that it raises the metabolism, just as "cooling" foods like watermelon and seaweed release the body's heat. When duck is combined with the antioxidants in wolfberries and the heat of ginger and cinnamon, the duck warms the body and invigorates the blood. Angelica Duck Soup has become an important home remedy for people who have caught a chill, as well as for women during their time of the month. But it is so tasty that the whole family can enjoy it, though children should probably be given only small portions.

1. Slice between the spareribs so that each bone is surrounded by meat. Place the riblets in a small work bowl, toss with the soy sauce, and let them sit in a cool area for an hour or so.

2. While the pork is marinating, rinse the whole dried herbs in a sieve, rinse off the little cloth sack that should have come in the herb packet, and then pack the sack with the herbs. (If there is no sack, use a mesh ball or wrap the herbs in cheesecloth.) If there is another sachet in the packet filled with the smaller herbs and spices, rinse this off as well. Place both sacks of herbs in a 3-quart saucepan, add the 8 cups water, cover, and bring to a boil. Reduce the heat to a gentle simmer and cook for 1 hour to make an herbal broth. Discard the herbs.

3. While the herbs are simmering, turn your attention to the dried ingredients. Drain the mushrooms and add their strained soaking liquid to the herbal broth. Remove the stems from the mushrooms and cut the caps in half. Place the daylily flowers in a small bowl and cover them with boiling water; after a few minutes, drain them and discard the water. Tie pairs of the blossoms into simple knots so that they don't fall apart. (These first three steps can be done ahead of time, if you like.)

I like the *rougu cha* herbal mixtures from Taiwan, but there are many different versions available. You can try them all and see which ones you prefer. Check the package to see how much meat is called for and adjust the recipe accordingly.

If you prefer chicken to pork, use a pound of chopped-up chicken legs instead and simmer for only 1 hour instead of 2 hours.

4. Place a wok over high heat. Add 2 tablespoons of the oil and swirl it around. Drain the ribs (you can add any leftover soy sauce to the soup in Step 5) and slide them into the hot wok. Adjust the temperature as needed to fry these up so that the marinade caramelizes and all sides of the ribs are browned. Remove the ribs from the wok and place them in a medium (8- to 10-cup) sandpot or casserole. Pour the remaining 1 tablespoon oil into the wok and fry the garlic and ginger over high heat until they are golden brown, then toss these into the pot along with the mushrooms and daylily blossoms.

5. Add the rice wine and rock sugar to the sandpot, then pour in just enough of the herbal broth to come up to the top of the ribs, but not so much that the broth bubbles out. Cover the sandpot and bring to a boil over medium heat, then reduce the heat to maintain a gentle simmer. Cook the ribs for 2 to 2½ hours, adding more of the herbal broth as needed to keep the ribs covered. (You will need most, if not all, of it; discard any extra.) Taste and adjust the seasoning before serving.

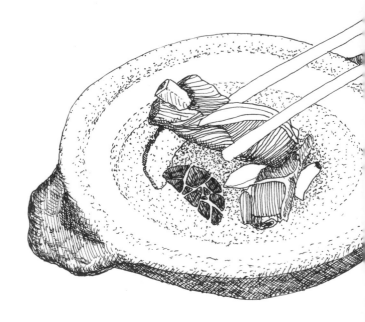

Niàng dòufǔ 釀豆腐

Braised Stuffed Bean Curd

HAKKA • SERVES 4

One of the truly classic dishes of the Hakka people, Braised Stuffed Bean Curd is also a family favorite; my late father-in-law would prepare it for the Chinese New Year. We would drive down to his little apartment in Los Angeles's Chinatown, where every imaginable surface would be covered with stuffed plastic bags from the local markets. After a hasty greeting, he would head back to work, happy in his element, working slowly but steadily on the New Year's feast.

For this dish, bean curd is cut into triangles and then stuffed with a meat filling. My father-in-law was particularly methodical when it came to the stuffing. He would deliberately scrape out the curd with one finger, taking five minutes with each tiny hole. One day, exhausted by this snail's pace, I banged out seven filled triangles in the same amount of time it took him to finish one, and then showed them to him in triumph. He looked over my triangles, nudged his glasses up the bridge of his nose in disgust, and then proceeded to redo all of them.

He used equal parts ground pork and fish paste in his filling. I am leery of the grayish stuff that passes for fish paste in most Chinese markets, so I add dried salted fish packed in oil instead. It has a wonderful saltiness, and its aroma blends nicely with the richness of the pork, the spiciness of the ginger, and the blandness of the bean curd.

SAUCE

2 cups unsalted chicken stock (page 380)

3 tablespoons mild rice wine

2 tablespoons thinly sliced fresh ginger

3 green onions, green parts only, cut into 1-inch pieces

1 to 2 tablespoons dark soy sauce (depending upon the saltiness of the fish)

STUFFING

1 tablespoon peeled and sliced fresh ginger

1 tablespoon old-fashioned rolled oats

4 ounces ground pork (15 percent fat)

1 piece (¾ to 1 ounce) salted fish packed in oil

3 green onions, white parts only, trimmed

BEAN CURD

1 block (14 ounces or so) regular bean curd

6 tablespoons cornstarch

Peanut or vegetable oil for frying (used oil is all right if it smells fresh)

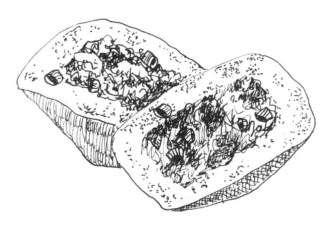

1. This dish is great the day it's made, but it's even better the next. First, make the sauce: put all of the ingredients into a medium sandpot or casserole and bring to a boil over high heat. Lower the heat to a constant but very low simmer, cover, and let the flavors mingle while you prepare the rest of the ingredients.

2. Place the ginger and rolled oats in a food processor and process until very finely chopped. Add the pork and pulse a few times. Pick over the fish carefully, removing all of the bones, which can catch in the throat, and any hard skin. Flake the fish a couple of times, running your fingers through it to find any last bones, and then add it to the processor. Toss in the green onions and pulse everything together until mixed; divide the filling into 8 pieces and roll these lightly into meatballs.

3. Pat the bean curd dry with a paper towel and cut it into quarters. Cut each square on the diagonal to form 8 triangles total. Use the small end of a melon baller (or a small spoon or a paring knife) to scoop out about one-third of the bean curd from the middle of the longest (diagonal) edge of each triangle, then sprinkle the inside of the scooped-out areas with cornstarch and pack a meatball firmly into each one. Dip the filled edge of each triangle into the cornstarch so that it covers the meat completely.

4. Heat a frying pan over medium heat and film the bottom with oil. When the oil starts to shimmer, place your triangles in the hot oil with the diagonal sides down. Fry those sides until golden brown. There is no need to fry the other sides, or even to drain the bean curd; when the filled side is fried, just gently deposit them in the sauce. Try to arrange the triangles so that the filled sides face up, as this will help to keep the meat from falling out. Bring the sauce to a boil and then lower it to a gentle simmer. Cover the sandpot and simmer for 25 to 30 minutes. Taste and adjust the seasoning, but keep in mind that the salted fish in the filling will provide a nice jolt of salt when you bite into the meatballs, so be careful not to overseason the sauce. Serve hot.

ANCIENT TRADITIONS CONTINUE TO GUIDE Hakka cuisine with a firm hand. This deeply conservative streak is grounded as much in economic necessity as it is in history. One study (*Kèjiā yǐnshí wénhuà* 客家飲食文化, by Wang Zengming) pointed out that the foods of the Hakka can be defined with four words: plain (*sù* 素), unrefined (*cū* 粗), wild (*yě* 野), and mixed (*zá* 雜).

The Hakka generally prepare meatless dishes (out of practicality rather than religious belief), and unpolished rice is eaten in place of more expensive white grains. Wild plants and animals are also incorporated into dishes, and when pigs are available, Hakka cooks are careful that every last morsel is turned into something good to eat.

Hakka food is also referred to as *Dōngjiāng cài* 東江菜 (East River cuisine), after the Dong River, which runs through the Meizhou area (see page 156) of Guangdong. Fujian, meanwhile, is home to a uniquely Hakkanese way of cooking rice: called "grass bag rice" (*cǎodài fàn* 草袋飯), the preparation consists of steaming soaked raw rice inside small woven grass pockets, which gives each grain a grassy aroma.

But rice is generally incorporated into traditional Hakka dishes as a paste or as rice noodles, as it is in Chaozhou and Southern Fujian. Rice-paste puddings called *guǒ* 粿, *mochi*-like *ciba* creations (page 306), *fāgāo* 發糕 cupcakes, chewy Hakka Tamales (page 228), and sticky *bǎn* 粄 patties are all traditional Hakka dishes, and have been so enthusiastically adopted by surrounding food cultures that they are often considered "traditional" dishes within the cuisines that borrowed them.

Xiānggū dàndòufu 香菇蛋豆腐

Fried Custard with Mushrooms

GUANGDONG · SERVES 4 TO 6

Custard is treated with special respect in Guangdong. Sweet or savory, steamed or baked, even the most basic custard dishes from this region are something to behold. This one is a personal favorite.

CUSTARD

8 large eggs

1¾ cups unsalted stock (page 380 or 381)

½ teaspoon sea salt

Spray oil

½ cup cornstarch

Peanut or vegetable oil for frying, as needed

BOK CHOY

2 tablespoons peanut or vegetable oil

1 teaspoon sea salt

1 pound baby bok choy, trimmed and cut into quarters

MUSHROOMS AND SAUCE

2 tablespoons peanut or vegetable oil

2 tablespoons peeled and julienned fresh ginger

3 green onions, trimmed and finely chopped

2 cloves garlic, finely chopped, optional

8 ounces mixed mushrooms, trimmed and cut into 1-inch (or so) pieces

¼ cup mild rice wine

2 tablespoons regular soy sauce

2 teaspoons rock sugar

½ cup unsalted stock

2 teaspoons cornstarch mixed with 2 tablespoons water

GARNISH

1 green onion, trimmed and chopped

1. First, lightly beat the eggs with the stock and salt. Spray an 8-inch square pan (or an 8-inch round one, depending upon the size of your steamer; see page 49) with oil. Pour the egg mixture through a sieve into the pan, as this will help to ensure an exceptionally smooth texture. Steam over medium-low heat for 15 to 20 minutes, until the custard is set. Remove the pan from the steamer, let it cool to room temperature, cover, refrigerate until chilled, and then cut the custard into 1-inch squares. Don't worry about any broken or strangely shaped pieces, as they can be fried first and placed in the bottom of the serving dish, where no one will notice.

2. About 20 minutes before serving, prepare the bok choy. Heat a wok over high heat until it starts to smoke and then swirl in the oil and salt. Add the bok choy and toss until the vegetables are just barely cooked and still crunchy. Remove them to a serving platter and shape them into a nest.

3. Toss the cubed custard in the cornstarch and shake off the excess. Heat a large, flat frying pan over medium-high heat. Add the oil to a depth of about ¼ inch. When a speck of cornstarch added to the oil immediately bubbles up and disappears, start with the less presentable pieces of custard and add just enough of them to the pan so that they are not crowded. Fry them on one side until golden, then turn them over. When they are completely browned, place them in the center of the bok choy nest. Repeat with the rest of the custard until done.

4. While the custard is frying, make the mushroom sauce: clean the wok and place it over high heat. Add the oil and then the ginger, green onions, and garlic and toss these together for about 10 seconds to release their fragrance. Throw in the mushrooms and toss until everything is coated with the oil. As the mushrooms start to brown, add the rice wine, soy sauce, sugar, and stock and adjust the seasoning. Swirl in the cornstarch slurry, pour the resulting mixture on top of the custard, and serve immediately with a sprinkle of green onions.

Jiǔcéngtǎ hōngdàn 九層塔烘蛋

Crispy Basil Omelet

HAKKA • SERVES 4

This omelet is a great everyday Hakka dish. Easy, cheap, and delicious, it's a good option if you're in a pinch, because all of the ingredients tend to be on hand. What makes this dish extraordinary is the quality that the basil takes on once it's fried: its peppery notes are toned down, and its texture becomes crispy. Try this omelet with Congee (page 226) for breakfast, or serve it alongside other dishes during lunch or dinner. Be sure to check out the salted radish and green onion variations, too.

1 bunch basil (any sort is great here)
1 cup peanut or vegetable oil
3 large eggs
Good pinch of sea salt, or to taste

1. Rinse the basil and pick the leaves off of the stems. Dry the leaves in a towel. Have ready a plate and a slotted spoon.

2. Pour the oil into a wok and heat over medium-high heat until a bamboo chopstick inserted in the hot oil immediately bubbles all over. Add a handful of the basil leaves to the hot oil and quickly stir them around until they quiet down. Immediately use the slotted spoon to scoop out the fried leaves; let them sit on the plate while you fry the rest of the basil in the same fashion.

3. Beat the eggs in a medium work bowl until they are frothy, then toss in the salt. Pour off all but a few tablespoons of the oil in the wok. (Reserve the poured-off oil as a nicely seasoned finishing oil, if you like.) Set the wok over high heat until the oil starts to shimmer. Reserve a few of the fried basil leaves as a garnish. Toss the rest into the raw eggs and then pour the egg mixture into the hot oil. Fry the omelet on the bottom, moving the eggs around with your chopsticks and turning the wok this way and that so that the eggs cook all over. Then lift the omelet a bit so that any raw egg can flow underneath and cook.

4. When the bottom of the omelet is golden brown, carefully flip it over and fry until the other side is brown. Remove to a plate, garnish with the reserved fried basil leaves, and serve immediately.

SALTED RADISH OMELET (*càipú dàn* 菜脯蛋)
One of the mainstays of any Hakka meal is an omelet made with salted radishes (*caipu*). This ocher ingredient can usually be found chopped and packed in plastic bags. To make this variation, use ⅓ cup chopped salted radishes in place of the basil and salt. Place the radish in a sieve and rinse it carefully under running water. Taste a piece and rinse it again if it is still very salty. Pat it dry and then fry it in oil before adding the beaten eggs; do not add extra salt.

GREEN ONION OMELET (*cōnghuā dàn* 蔥花蛋)
Follow the directions for a Crispy Basil Omelet, substituting 3 green onions for the basil. Trim the onions and slice them into thin rounds, then proceed as directed.

Guǎngdōng qīngzhēngyú 廣東清蒸魚

Guangdong-Style Steamed Fish

GUANGDONG · SERVES 4

Guangdong-style restaurants flourished in Taipei when I lived there, in large part because Taiwan boasted some of the freshest fish around. Freshness is and always has been key for recipes like this; with something so light and simple, nothing can be hidden. I always use my best soy sauce here, and I like to finish the dish with rice bran oil for its buttery flavor.

FISH

1 whole (about 1 pound) flatfish

1 teaspoon sea salt

½ cup peeled and finely shredded fresh ginger

1 large or 2 small green onions, trimmed

SAUCE

2 tablespoons regular soy sauce

1 tablespoon water

1 tablespoon mild rice wine

1½ teaspoons sugar

¼ cup vegetable oil (rice bran is best, though peanut and canola are good)

1. Clean the fish, removing the guts and gills, and then scale it; leave the head, tail, and fins attached. Use a sharp knife to cut 3 deep diagonal slashes on both sides of the fish (see page 23). Rub the salt into the cavity and the slashes, as well as on the outside. Place the fish on a platter that fits in your steamer. Set up your steamer equipment (see page 49).

2. Have the ginger ready and cut the green onions into fine julienne. Keep these in separate piles.

3. To make the sauce, stir together the soy sauce, water, rice wine, and sugar in a small work bowl until the sugar dissolves. Measure out the oil into a separate cup and have it next to the stove.

4. Pour water into the steamer, but don't let it reach the top of the trivet. Cover and bring to a full boil. Put a good pinch of the ginger inside of the fish's cavity and then sprinkle the rest along the top of the fish. Place the fish inside the steamer, cover, and steam on high. Start checking the fish at around 8 minutes, though it may take more than 12 minutes before it is perfectly done. Look inside of the slashes: when the bases are no longer pink, the fish is cooked. Make dead certain it's ready by plunging a chopstick through the thickest part; if it goes through it like it was piercing butter, remove the fish from the steamer. Drain off the salty liquid in the platter.

5. Sprinkle the green onions over the top of the fish. Pour the oil into a small saucepan set over high heat, and when it just starts to smoke, drizzle it down the length of the fish so it immediately cooks the green onions. Give the sauce a swirl and then pour it down the length of the fish, too. Serve immediately.

When you find a good fish, make sure the fishmonger leaves the head, tail, and fins on. They'll make the dish look nice, and there is a lot of fat located at the bottoms of the fins and in the head. The tail is always a joy to eat, too: it tends to have a firm, lively texture. Be sure to tell the fishmonger to leave any roe (that is, fresh caviar) he or she finds in the fish, too—it's delicious.

Try to buy a relatively small fish—a bit over a pound is ideal. You want it to steam quickly, and it must fit easily into your steamer. At home, I place the fish on a platter that barely fits inside a wide wok I have reserved just for steaming; a trivet holds the platter steady above the water, and a glass cover allows me to keep a close eye on the progress. Learning to calculate correctly when a fish is perfectly done takes a bit of practice and experience, but having a setup like this makes life a whole lot easier.

You don't have to use flatfish for this recipe, but it is a good fish to learn with, and the amount of sauce and so forth called for here is calibrated for this variety and size. Once you master flatfish, though, try orange roughy or rock cod or even sea bass.

Sānlǎn zhēngyú 三欖蒸魚

Steamed Fish with Three Kinds of Olives

HONG KONG • SERVES 4

Hong Kong has adopted many of Guangzhou's and Chaozhou's methods for cooking seafood and incorporated its own unique spins. Here, for example, a decidedly Western ingredient—extra virgin olive oil—joins the traditional seasonings of cured Chinese olives and olive vegetable. Together, this trio gives the fish a sublime aroma.

Because all three seasonings are oily and two contain salt, I like to use a relatively lean fish here. Flatfish are terrific; you can use either a whole fish or fillets. However, feel free to substitute something richer, like salmon, which also turns out quite tasty. I add a bit of lemon juice to lend a touch of tartness and balance out the mellow flavors.

Start this recipe at least an hour ahead of time so that you can prepare the preserved olives. The rest comes together in a flash.

PRESERVED OLIVES

4 ounces (or so) olive corners (see Tips)
2 tablespoons extra virgin olive oil
1 teaspoon sugar
½ teaspoon ground ginger

FISH

1 pound (or so) mild fish fillets, or 1 whole fish
    (about 1½ pounds) (see headnote)
½ teaspoon sea salt
6 preserved olives (from Step 1)
1 tablespoon olive vegetable, chopped (see Tips)
1 tablespoon finely shredded young ginger or
    peeled mature ginger
½ red jalapeño pepper, seeded and thinly sliced
¼ cup extra virgin olive oil
Juice of ½ lemon

1. This first step can be done far ahead of time, and you can even multiply the quantities if you like this seasoning as much as I do. Set up a steamer (see page 49). Place the olive corners, including any broken bits and pieces, in a sieve and rinse them well under tap water. Shake the olive corners dry and place them in a small heatproof bowl. Toss them with the olive oil, sugar, and ginger. Steam the olive corners for about 45 minutes, tossing them with a spoon every 15 minutes. Remove the olive corners from the steamer, cool, and refrigerate them in a covered jar until needed.

2. Prepare the fish about 30 minutes before you cook it. If you are using a whole fish, scale and gut it, remove the gills, and peel out any dark lining inside the cavity. Cut slashes through the thickest part of the fish's body so that it cooks evenly (see page 23). Rinse the whole fish or fish fillets and pat dry. Place the fish on a rimmed heatproof plate and rub the fish with the salt. Just before you proceed to the next step, discard any water that has accumulated on the plate. Bring the water in the steamer to a full boil.

3. Chop the preserved olives roughly, then place on top of the fish. Arrange the olive vegetable, ginger, and jalapeño along the top of the fish to create an attractive pattern of black, white, and red. Drizzle the olive oil evenly over the top. Place the fish in the steamer; steam the fillets for about 10 minutes or whole fish for about 15 minutes, until just cooked through. Squeeze the lemon juice over the fish and serve immediately.

Chinese olive corners (*lǎnjiǎo* 欖角) can usually be found in Guangdong-style markets and shops specializing in dried and preserved foods. They are available in plastic bags or in jars on the counter, where they are sold by the ounce.

Olive vegetable (*lǎncài* 欖菜) is typically stocked in the sauce aisle of Chinese grocery stores. Whole pits are often hiding inside, so be sure to chop the vegetable finely before using.

Gānjiān lónglì 乾煎龍利

Whole Dry-Fried Flounder

CHAOZHOU · SERVES 4 TO 6

It's taken me quite a while to figure out where this dish originated, but it most likely came from Chaozhou. Whole Dry-Fried Flounder is a direct translation of the most common Chinese name for this dish, *gan-jian longli*, although once in a while you find it referred to as *xiāngjiān lónglì* 香煎龍利 (fragrant fried flounder).

The emphasis here is on "whole" and "dry." It's important that the fish be whole, because when you fry it, the tiny bones in the fins turn into crunchy needles that are every bit as lovely as the meat. (The tail can be enjoyed, too, but the rest of the bones should be avoided.) The fish is "dry" because it's not coated with anything before it's fried; it's just wiped down and carefully placed into a pan over superhigh heat with lots of oil.

FISH

1 whole flounder or other flatfish (about 1 pound) (see Tips)

2 teaspoons sea salt

2 teaspoons mild rice wine

SAUCE

2 tablespoons peanut or vegetable oil

3 green onions, trimmed

3 tablespoons mild rice wine

3 tablespoons water or stock

2 teaspoons regular soy sauce, or to taste

½ teaspoon sugar

6 cups (or more) peanut or vegetable oil for frying (see Tips)

1. Clean the fish, removing the guts and gills, and then scale it. Leave the head, tail, and fins attached.

2. Pat the fish dry with a paper towel or two and lay it on a cutting board. Slash down the length of both sides of the body (see page 23).

3. Lay the fish on a platter and rub the salt into both sides. Sprinkle it with the rice wine and let it marinate for 10 to 20 minutes. At the end of this time, drain off all of the marinade and pat the fish very, very dry. Wipe out even the inside of the head and cavity so that there are no drops of water to explode in the hot oil. Lay the fish on a dry paper towel while you prepare everything else.

4. To make the sauce, in a small pan, heat the oil over high heat until it is sizzling, then add the green onions. Stir them quickly over high heat to release their fragrance, then add the rice wine, water or stock, soy sauce, and sugar. Bring the sauce to a boil, taste, and adjust the seasoning. Remove from the heat.

5. Pour at least 1½ inches of frying oil into a wok; you want enough hot oil to fry the fish rapidly and make it both crispy on the outside and succulent on the inside. Heat the oil over high heat until it starts to smoke. While you are waiting, have ready a serving platter, a pair of cooking chopsticks, a wok spatula, and either a spatter screen or a large lid.

6. While the oil is heating, turn off your phone and clear the kitchen of children and pets and anyone else who will get in your way.

7. Holding the fish by the tail in one hand and either the spatter screen or the lid in the other, slide the fish into the hot oil and immediately cover the wok with the screen or lid, as the water in the flesh will start to explode. This will die down fast, and if you can, keep your grip on the tail so that you can slide the fish around and give its entire body a chance to brown. Keep the tail raw as long as possible, as holding it will allow you to control the fish. If you have used enough hot oil, there is no need to flip the fish over; just lightly press down on it with your spatula and scoot it around so each part has a chance to be submerged. When the top of the fish looks done, slide the tail end in so it gets fried, too. This is a very thin part of the fish, so it will fry up fast.

8. Depending upon your fish, the heat of your stove, and the depth of the oil, the fish will be ready in 7 to 10 minutes. It should be golden brown all over, the fins and tail should be browned and crispy, and the meat should have pulled away from the bones where you slashed the flesh. Place your platter next to the wok. Use your chopsticks to steady the tail end as you lift up the fish with your spatula, drain off the oil, and place it carefully on your platter. If you feel uneasy about this, use two spatulas, or even ask someone to help. When you're done, turn off the heat and push the wok to the back of the stove, out of harm's way, to let the oil cool completely.

9. Bring the sauce to a quick boil and pour it over the fish. Serve immediately.

Do not use a fish that is much larger than a pound here, unless you have a restaurant-sized wok and stove. The ratio of fish to hot oil is important, and if the fish is too thick or too long, it won't cook quickly enough and will start to steam and crumble.

Be sure to use a large amount of oil here. This is crucial to rapidly achieving the correct balance of crisp edges and juicy meat. If you use too little oil, the fish will gently cook all the way down to the skeleton and dissolve into a sodden mess.

The oil can be reused, since flounder and other flatfish are very mild flavored. Strain the cooled oil and store it in the fridge. Throw it out whenever it starts to darken or has a strong aroma.

Salting the fish helps draw out more of its moisture, which is good, since water explodes in hot oil.

Once you master this dish, make it your own. Season it with other aromatics or even change the sauce. It's up to you.

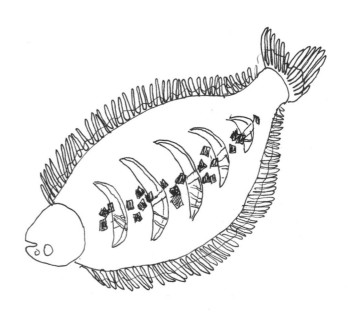

Shùndé huì yúfǔ 順德燴魚腐

Shunde Braised Fish Puffs

PEARL RIVER DELTA · SERVES 4 TO 6

In this dish, flaked fish is combined with beaten eggs and seasonings, then fried up into little golden spheres. This may not seem like much, but these fish puffs are easy, versatile, and remarkably delicious. They can be mostly made ahead of time, too, which allows the final braise to come together quickly. My father-in-law used to make fish paste dishes like this, and the aroma always reminds me of his tiny kitchenette and the great food that emerged from it.

Shunde's dishes tend to be designed for freshwater fish like carp or dace, since those are the most common species in the region's surrounding waterways and fishponds (see the drawing of just such a village at right). If those fish aren't available, use a mild saltwater fish. Any type of rockfish, flatfish, or even eel will work here, because the flesh is reduced to a pulp and its character disappears into the eggs. The fish mostly serves to create a nice consistency and add a gentle seasoning to the puffs.

FISH PUFFS

8 ounces white-fleshed fish fillets, skinned (see headnote)

¼ teaspoon sea salt

2 or 3 cloves garlic, finely minced

1 green onion, trimmed and finely minced

Freshly ground black pepper

2 teaspoons mild rice wine

5 teaspoons cornstarch

3 large eggs, separated

Peanut or vegetable oil for frying (used oil is all right if it smells fresh)

BRAISE

8 ounces black mushrooms, fresh or dried and plumped up

2 tablespoons peanut or vegetable oil

12 thin slices peeled fresh ginger

2 green onions, trimmed and cut into 1-inch lengths, whites and greens in separate piles

½ carrot, peeled and cut on the diagonal into thin slices

3 tablespoons mild rice wine

1 teaspoon oyster sauce

1 teaspoon sugar

1 cup unsalted chicken stock (page 380), or water

EVEN THOUGH THEY ARE ONLY AN HOUR away from each other, down-home Shunde looks completely different from gentrified Guangzhou—and its food tastes different, too. Situated within the Pearl River Delta, a marshy land that could best be compared to the bayous around New Orleans, the Shunde way with snake and alligator would give Cajun cooks a run for their money. The land is so webbed with rivers and creeks that it is said one encounters "water three steps out the door"; in some places, islets of human

civilization are connected to their fields by little footbridges.

The Pearl River Delta is also the traditional home of China's dairy cattle (see page 190), and so you would think that beef would be a star attraction. But it is rarely on the menu. Instead, chicken and an abundant array of fresh vegetables are cooked with the lightest of techniques. Local cooks also delight in the area's freshwater fish, which have traditionally been enjoyed raw (page 164).

Shunde-style raw fish is a very Chinese delight: paper-thin slices of the freshest grass carp are tossed with tiny shreds of fresh ginger, crunchy bits of some sort—usually deep-fried Indian olive kernels (see Tips, page 191), peanuts, or rice vermicelli—something sweet and crunchy like pears or fried taro or lotus root, a dash of sour courtesy of pickle bits, and the gentle seasoning of toasted sesame oil and salt. This is how it has long been done in Jun'an, the hometown of China's greatest martial arts star, Bruce Lee.

1. Rinse the fish and pat it dry. Remove any tiny bones or silver skin, then finely chop the fish into a paste, first using the blade side of your Chinese knife and then the back (see page 458). Scoop up the fish paste and place it in a medium work bowl, add the salt, and use chopsticks to stir it rapidly in one direction for a few seconds to dissolve the salt. Beat in the garlic, green onion, pepper, rice wine, and cornstarch until fluffy. Finally, stir in the egg yolks until everything is fully incorporated. In a separate bowl, beat the egg whites with a whisk until they form soft peaks. Fold the whites into the fish mixture with a silicone spatula until you have an even, cloudlike mass.

2. Set a clean plate and a Chinese spider or slotted spoon next to the stove. Place a wok over medium-high heat. When it's hot, add the oil to a depth of about 2 inches. Swirl the oil in the wok to coat the inside about halfway up and then lower the heat to medium. Use a clean spoon (plastic ones from the frozen-yogurt shop work well here) to scoop up a scant tablespoon of the fish mixture and use another spoon to scoot it into the oil as a ball. Gently fry the fish puff until it is golden on both sides. Add as many balls of the fish mixture as will fit very loosely in your wok, remembering that they will swell up as they cook; I cook about 8 balls at a time. Use chopsticks or the spider to remove the puffs to the waiting plate. Repeat with the rest of the mixture until it's all been fried. Set aside 12 of the puffs for this recipe and refrigerate the rest. The recipe can be done ahead of time up to this point.

3. Stem the mushrooms and cut or tear the cups into halves or quarters so that they are similar in size to the fish puffs.

4. Clean the wok and place it back over medium-high heat. When it is hot, add the 2 tablespoons oil. Swirl the oil in the wok to coat the inside about halfway up and then lower the heat to medium. Add the ginger, let it brown, and then raise the heat to high. Add the white parts of the green onions and toss them quickly in the scented oil before adding the mushrooms and carrot slices. Sear everything in the hot oil until the mushrooms are very lightly browned and then add the wine, oyster sauce, sugar, stock, and fish puffs. Bring the liquid to a full boil and reduce the heat to medium-high. Cover the wok and let the puffs braise for about 10 minutes, until most of the sauce has been absorbed. Uncover the wok and quickly reduce the sauce further over high heat until there is only a mere slick at the base of the wok. Taste and adjust the seasoning and then add the green parts of the onions. Toss everything together gently until the onions begin to wilt slightly. Serve hot in a wide bowl.

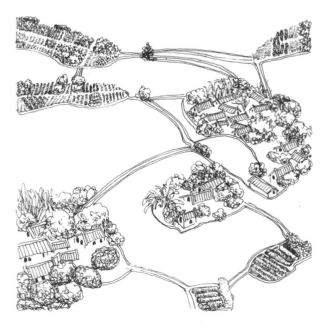

Tàng yóuyú 燙魷魚

Blanched Squid with Garlicky Dipping Sauce

SOUTHERN FUJIAN AND TAIWAN • SERVES 4 TO 6

A specialty of the best seafood stalls in Taiwan when I lived there, this dish is easy to make once you learn how to slice and blanch the squid into tender, frilly blossoms. And after that, you may incorporate it into a variety of dishes, like Kung Pao Scallops (page 276).

You can buy cleaned squid bodies, or you can clean a whole squid yourself and use both the tubes and the tentacles. To prepare the squid, peel off the thin skin, cut the tentacles off below the eyes, squeeze out the beak, and then cut between the tentacles, slicing them lengthwise in half, if necessary.

The sauce below is merely one suggestion. You can just as easily use another chili sauce (page 438 or 439, for example) and add soy sauce, vinegar, sugar, garlic, or whatever you like before thickening it slightly so that it clings to the slippery squid.

SAUCE

3 tablespoons peeled and finely minced fresh ginger
4 cloves garlic, finely minced
2 tablespoons regular soy sauce
6 tablespoons mild rice wine
2 teaspoons sugar
Freshly ground black pepper
2 teaspoons cornstarch mixed with 2 tablespoons water

SQUID

4 large squid tubes (6 to 8 inches long), cleaned
    and skinned
4 cups boiling water
Ice water, as needed, optional

1. First, cook the sauce: in a small pan, bring all of the ingredients quickly to a boil, stir until smooth, and then scrape the sauce out into a clean serving bowl. This can be done up to a couple of hours ahead of time if you cover and refrigerate the sauce. Don't make it too far ahead, though, as the garlic will turn gassy and overwhelm the other flavors. Taste and adjust the seasoning, adding chopped chilies or whatever else you like.

2. Defrost the squid tubes, if necessary, and clean them out, removing any bits of skin or membrane on the outside, and then drain the tubes. (For directions on how to cut "squid blossoms," see the diagram to the right.)

3. In a medium saucepan, bring the water to a full boil over high heat and have a slotted spoon and a bowl of ice water ready if you plan to serve your squid later. If you want to eat it warm, skip the ice water, have a rimmed plate ready, and serve immediately.

4. Drop no more than a handful of the squid into the boiling water and cook them only until they turn opaque, which should take just seconds. Do not under any circumstances overcook them, as this short blanching is what makes the squid so tender. As soon as the squid pieces turn from translucent to white, they are done. Scoop them out with the slotted spoon and toss them either in the ice water or onto the rimmed plate, and bring the water to a boil again before tossing in the next handful. This goes pretty quickly, so if you are planning to eat the squid right away, have everyone sitting at the table by the time the last handful has been thrown into the pot. Drain off the excess water and serve your squid with the dipping sauce. If you have cooked the squid in advance, bring a large pot of water to a full boil just before serving, toss in the squid, and after about 2 seconds, dump them into a colander placed in the sink. Serve posthaste.

CUTTING SQUID "BLOSSOMS"

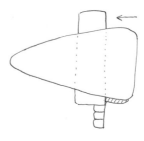

❶

Drain the tubes and slice them lengthwise in half so that you have 8 triangular pieces.

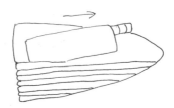

❷

Working on 1 triangle at a time, lay a piece on a cutting board with its interior face up and its pointed end at 3 o'clock; if you're left-handed, have the tip pointed at 9 o'clock. Use a very thin, sharp knife to make shallow cuts all the way down the length of the inside. The cuts should be about ⅛ inch apart. Be careful not to cut all the way through the body.

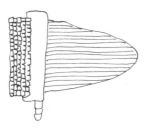

❸

Turn your knife to a sharp diagonal slant (30 to 45 degrees) and make shallow cuts across the width of the piece—again about ⅛ inch or less apart—to create a frilly surface.

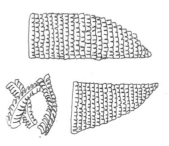

❹

A To make "book" slices, alternate one shallow and then one deep cut that goes all the way through as you make the diagonal slashes in Step 3, so that the piece will open up like a book.

❹

B To make larger pieces, cut the squid crosswise into strips 1 inch wide or so. These will curl up when they hit a hot wok. Whichever version you choose, repeat until all of the squid has been cut. You can cut the pointy ends off the triangles after they have been frilled and use them in whatever you are cooking.

Bìfēngtáng chǎoxiè 避風塘炒蟹

Typhoon Shelter Crab

HONG KONG · SERVES 4 TO 6

This stunning recipe from Hong Kong's boat people is deservedly famous among dining cognoscenti. The sweetness of the shellfish contrasts beautifully with a crunchy layer of garlic studded with chilies and black beans. This dish does not even have to involve crab: shrimp or prawns work equally well. Vegans could use deep-fried bean curd and it would still be fantastic, because the element that draws diners back time and again is not the protein but that brittle, spicy, garlic-laden blanket.

The traditional way to prepare this delicious sauce is to fry up a bunch of chopped garlic, season it, and serve it on top of the crab. This requires an exhorbitant amount of garlic in order to cover the crab, however, and its flavor becomes overwhelming. To resolve this dilemma, I mix fried garlic with *panko*, or Japanese dried bread crumbs. This lightens up the topping while maintaining its crispy texture. And here's another tip: if you are going to use a whole lot of chopped garlic, rinse it in a bowl of water after you chop it, as this gets rid of the stickiness that makes the garlic clump together.

Finally, when you fry garlic, don't overdo it. Garlic quickly turns from aromatic to acrid in hot oil, so fry it over a fairly low temperature until it is a light golden brown, then scoop it out with a fine sieve and let it cool down fast in a wide work bowl. It will continue to cook in the residual heat, so err on the side of undercooking. Then, if you find you still need to cook it a bit more, just return it to the oil.

CRAB

2 pounds crab (1 large Dungeness or a few smaller crabs), shrimp or prawns with the shell on; or about 1 pound deep-fried bean curd

¼ cup cornstarch

THE CRUNCHY STUFF

1 cup coarsely chopped fresh garlic

2 cups peanut or vegetable oil

3 tablespoons fermented black beans, rinsed and very finely chopped

1 or more jalapeño peppers, very finely chopped

1 cup dried bread crumbs (Japanese *panko*)

½ cup very finely chopped green onions

2 teaspoons (or more) coarsely ground dried chilies

½ teaspoon sea salt

1 teaspoon sugar

1. Clean and prep the crab(s) by removing the top shell and the legs (for directions on how to prepare a crab, see page 456). Clean out the body with your fingers, but leave any roe or tomalley you might find. Rinse the body well and chop both it and the legs into bite-sized pieces. Drain well in a colander. Just before cooking, toss the crab with the cornstarch, being especially careful to coat the cut edges that expose the flesh. If using shrimp or prawns, prepare as directed in Steps 1 and 2 on page 457, and then toss with the cornstarch. If you are using bean curd, just have it hot and ready, and skip the frying in Step 5. Keep the crab or other shellfish chilled.

2. Put the chopped garlic in a medium work bowl and cover it with cool tap water. Rinse the garlic thoroughly in a fine sieve and then dump it out onto a couple sheets of paper towels to dry completely.

3. Have a fine dry sieve set over a dry work bowl next to the stove. Set a wok over high heat and pour in the oil. Add the drained garlic, and when the oil starts to bubble around the edge of the pan, reduce the heat to low or medium-low, and stir often so that the garlic browns evenly. Don't rush this step, since gently fried garlic is the most important component in this dish. When the garlic turns a pale brown and floats to the surface—which means that all of the juices have transferred from the garlic into the oil, making the garlic nice and crunchy when it has cooled—empty the garlic and oil into the sieve. You will be left with about ½ cup fried garlic. Shake the oil off so that the garlic drains completely and turns crispy. You will have extra garlic oil by the end of this recipe, which is a *mingyou* (finishing oil) that is delicious in lots of other dishes.

4. Place the oil-slicked wok over medium-high heat and immediately add the black beans, jalapeños, bread crumbs, and ¼ cup of the garlic oil. Toss these together, drizzling just a little more of the garlic oil around the edge of the crumbs, if needed, to keep them from sticking and to ensure that they fry up an even, crispy brown. The secret to making this topping truly great is to add very little oil, so that the bread crumbs do not soak it up and turn heavy—you want to have nothing but light, crispy, super-crunchy flakes. Once this has been achieved, toss in the fried garlic and green onions, fry these together for a few seconds to incorporate them, and add the ground chilies, salt, and sugar. Taste and adjust the seasoning, then empty the topping back into the work bowl.

5. Immediately rinse out the wok, dry it over high heat, and then add about ¼ cup of the garlic oil. Quickly stir-fry the crab (or shrimp or prawns) until the shells turn a rosy pink and the flesh turns opaque; do not overcook the shellfish. Pour off any oil left in the wok, dump all of the garlicky crumbs back in, toss everything together to combine, and then immediately plate on a large serving platter. Serve right away with lots of napkins and an empty bowl or two for the shells. If you are using bean curd, simply toss it with the garlic mixture and serve.

Some people serve this with the same topping that is used on Cod with Crispy Bean Sauce (page 269).

HONG KONG HAD A THRIVING FOOD culture in the 1970s. I could rarely afford the major dining palaces then, but that did not mean that great food was out of reach. Some of the best food of all, like Typhoon Shelter Crab, came from the little boats, which doubled as floating restaurants, anchored in the many harbors ringing Hong Kong Island. Whenever a major hurricane threatened the area, fishermen would pull into safe harbors and hunker down over some good simple food like this until the storm passed—thus the dish's romantic name.

Prior to the 1990s, Hong Kong's boat culture thrived. These people gave birth, lived, and died on their boats, rarely setting foot on land. They had their own wedding traditions, food customs, accent, and way of life that set them apart from the land dwellers. Sampans and punts crowded the tight harbors of places like Shau Kei Wan on Hong Kong Island, and these fisherfolk cooked up the day's catch for their customers on the most minimal of stoves.

This way of life has vanished. But fortunately for us, many of the foods these people created have survived. One of the best is Typhoon Shelter Crab.

Dàliáng chǎo níunǎi 大良炒牛奶

Stir-Fried Milk with Crab

PEARL RIVER DELTA • SERVES 4

Many Chinese people have difficulty digesting milk, but it is hard to say whether lactose intolerance is the reason that dairy products never gained a foothold in China. Grazing land has always been in short supply there, and cattle require large expanses of grass for fodder. Whatever the reason, milk has never been a part of most Chinese cuisines, which is why lard has always been favored over butter.

But there are exceptions to this rule: in southwestern China, whole milk is formed into dried "milk fans" (see page 247), which have a texture similar to bean curd skins and soy batons. Out in the arid regions of western China, the yogurt and kefir of Central Asia has made its way into the local cuisines. In fact, the best yogurt I've ever tasted (page 414) was in Xinjiang's capital, Ürümqi.

The Pearl River Delta is one of the few places in China where milk is eaten fresh, though it is consumed with a distinctly Chinese twist. In the Daliang area, for example, dairies have traditionally flourished, and so milk is used in various local dishes, including Ginger Milk Pudding (page 230), the egg custard known as double-skinned milk (*shuāngpínǎi* 雙皮奶), and its strange but delicious stir-fried milk. There are different interpretations of this recipe in the Pearl River Delta—some feature shrimp or pork or chicken, for example—but I love this crab- and almond-studded version.

ALMONDS

1 tablespoon (or so) peanut or vegetable oil
¼ cup slivered blanched almonds

MILK

½ cup whole milk
1 tablespoon cornstarch

CRAB

1 cup crabmeat (fresh best, frozen second, and canned a very distant third place)
3 tablespoons peanut or vegetable oil, divided into 1 tablespoon and 2 tablespoons, plus more if needed
Sprinkle of sea salt
½ *lop chong* (sweet Cantonese sausage)
5 large egg whites
¼ teaspoon mushroom powder or fish sauce (see Tips)

1. First, toast the almonds: place a wok over medium heat and film the bottom with the oil. Add the nuts and toss, adjusting the heat as necessary, until they are golden and smell toasted. Scoop them out onto a plate covered with a paper towel.

2. Bring the milk to a boil (either in a saucepan on the stove or in a measuring cup in the microwave), let it cool down until just warm to the touch, and stir in the cornstarch until smooth.

3. Pick over the crabmeat carefully, removing any shells or cartilage but keeping the meat in pieces as large as possible. Place in a medium work bowl, add 1 tablespoon of the oil and the salt, and toss to mix.

4. Cut the *lop chong* into a small (⅛-inch or smaller) dice. Place the pieces in a wok or pan without any oil and fry them over medium heat until they render their fat and are lightly crispy. Remove them to a plate covered with a paper towel and wipe out the wok.

5. Lightly beat the egg whites in a medium work bowl until they are broken apart and only very slightly foamy. Stir in the milk mixture, crab, fried *lop chong*, and mushroom seasoning or fish sauce. Place a serving bowl or small individual bowls next to the stove, warming them first if possible.

6. Heat the remaining 2 tablespoons oil in the wok over medium heat until it starts to shimmer and then pour in the crab mixture. Use a silicone or wooden spatula to stir the crab gently over the heat, making sure to run the spatula along the bottom of the wok to keep the milk from burning. As the liquid heats, it will start to form curds. Drizzle in a bit more oil around the edge if it starts to stick. As soon as the liquid has turned into curds, immediately scoop the mixture out into the bowl(s); if there is extra liquid, drain it off and enjoy it yourself, since it tastes great but just doesn't look very nice. Sprinkle the crab with the toasted almonds and serve with spoons.

If you were wondering what to do with the crab body meat leftover from the Savory Crab and Cellophane Noodles on page 192, this is a great option.

One change I've made to the original recipe is the addition of toasted almonds instead of the traditional tropical kernels called Indian olives, or *lǎnrén* 欖仁, which come from the *Terminalia catappa* tree. I have done this only because it's difficult to find Indian olives in the United States, and slivered almonds work well as a substitute.

If you want, roasted duck, bits of ham, or mushrooms can be substituted for the *lop chong*.

EVEN THOUGH ARCHAEOLOGISTS HAVE discovered remnants of grape wine from 4,600 years ago, viniculture never really took hold in China until the past couple of decades, although it occasionally pops up as an unusual ingredient in a few ancient dishes, such as Consort's Chicken Wings (page 12).

This has a lot to do with China's flavor spectrum, which for the most part has always been governed by deeply fermented seasonings such as soy sauce and savory pastes. Grape wine rarely pairs well with these, or with the strong *xianwei* layers of the country's many dried and cured ingredients—its overt fruitiness conflicts too strongly with the deep aromas and powerful flavors of things like black mushrooms, dried seafood, pickles, and charcuterie. On the other hand, these local flavors do marry remarkably well with China's white liquors (see page 197), rice wines (see page 114), and beers. The reason for this is that the country's brews have invariably been based on grain, rather than fruit.

But the problem remains: if you love grape wine, how do you properly complement it with a culinary aesthetic that is, in many ways, diametrically opposite to that of Europe's cuisines? Noted wine connoisseur and author Gerald Asher spoke to me about this one afternoon at his home in San Francisco and offered a few rays of hope to the dedicated oenophiles among us. Asher pointed out that wines with aromatic esters—like Manzanilla sherry, vin jaune, and Tokaji—are not fruity and so would not overwhelm the subtler flavors of Chinese dishes. "No wine," explained Asher, "should ever be an intrusion, just as the food should never overpower the wine."

When I asked him about some of the usual default varietals—generally sweet and pale—he countered with a smile, "I don't subscribe to the idea that you can avoid the whole issue and just drink white wine as if it were a substitute for rice wine." Rather than reach for the Gewürztraminer, he says that we "need wines with a little

more character" when we savor them alongside the majority of Chinese foods.

Asher considers dishes as a whole before deciding what to drink with them and says the foods of China require singular reflection: "Most Chinese dishes that I've eaten have seemed to be both intricate and balanced. To my palate, a Chinese dish always has everything it needs within it." Nevertheless, for something on the order of a flavorful northern meat dish, he suggests a wine "with some backbone," like a Bordeaux. The connoisseur believes wines that act as a delicious foil for Moroccan food can also be considered here—something on the order of a young Zinfandel, or even a California Chardonnay or Pinot Noir.

As China's nascent viniculture begins to take hold in such areas as Shandong, Xinjiang, and Ningxia, varietals may yet be created that take the unique flavors of China's foods into account. Until then, when all else fails, a cold glass of beer can be the perfect alternative.

Pángxiè fěnsī bào 螃蟹粉絲煲

Savory Crab and Cellophane Noodles

HONG KONG • SERVES 4

I grew up near San Francisco and, as a result, my idea of a crab dinner was invariably a plate of cold steamed Dungeness. But Chinese crabs are smaller and have thinner shells than San Francisco's, and they are usually whacked apart with cleavers and then stir-fried with seasonings.

This dish is all about the flavor of crab, and yet the most difficult thing here is ensuring that the cellophane noodles are cooked properly. They are notorious for dissolving into gummy clumps, but if you follow these directions closely, you should be fine.

This recipe calls for Dungeness crab, and because Dungeness crabs are generally sold already cooked, I've designed the recipe to account for this. However, if you are lucky enough to have your own live local crabs, I have included instructions in the Tips section for preparing them.

4 bundles cellophane noodles

2 tablespoons dried shrimp

2 pounds cooked Dungeness crab legs (the legs of 2 crabs) or 1 whole Dungeness crab (about 2 pounds)

2 large shallots, thinly sliced (about ½ cup)

¼ cup peeled and finely chopped fresh ginger

2 green onions, trimmed and finely chopped, white and greens in separate piles

2 tablespoons toasted sesame oil

2 tablespoons regular soy sauce

2 teaspoons sweet soy sauce (page 439), or regular soy sauce with a bit of sugar to taste

¼ cup mild rice wine

Freshly ground black pepper

10 tablespoons peanut or vegetable oil, divided in half, plus more as needed

1. First, soak the cellophane noodles in warm water for 10 minutes. Then rinse them in a colander under cold tap water to immediately stop them from softening any further. Shake all of the water off the noodles and them dump them onto a clean tea towel. Lightly pat the noodles all over to get rid of the rest of the moisture and let them sit uncovered while you prepare the other ingredients. (This step is most important, because it ensures that the noodles will have the right chewy texture.)

2. Rinse the dried shrimp well, cover them with hot water, and let them soak until soft. Drain the shrimp, clean them as needed, and chop them finely.

3. If you are using only crab legs, separate the large lower (and middle, if needed) sections from the rest of the legs. Keep the meatier top sections whole and unshelled, but lightly crack them all over. Remove the meat from the lower sections, working over a bowl to catch all the juices and tiny flakes of crab (see Tips), and discard these shells. You should end up with about half of the crab legs whole and the other half shelled. If you are using a whole crab, crack and separate the legs into manageable lengths and completely remove all of the shells and cartilage from the body, which will also leave you with about half unshelled crab and half shelled. Keep the carapace intact, if you like, to decorate the final dish. Place the parts of the crab that are still in the shell (including the carapace, if you're using it) in a heatproof dish and steam over high heat for 5 minutes (see page 49).

4. Prep the shallots, ginger, and white parts of the onions and add them to the shrimp. Mix the sesame oil, soy sauce, sweet soy sauce, rice wine, and pepper in a small bowl. Cut the cellophane noodles into pieces approximately 2 inches long. Have a medium sandpot or casserole ready for serving.

5. Place a wok over medium-high heat, and when it is hot, add half of the oil and swirl it around. Sprinkle in the shallot mixture and fry it until it starts to brown. Lower the heat to medium, add the rest of the oil, and when the oil is hot, toss in the noodles. Stir-fry the noodles carefully, being sure to scrape up any that stick to the bottom of the wok; if needed, add a bit more oil. Fry the noodles for 2 or 3 minutes, until they start to become transparent. Add the crabmeat and the crab in its shell plus half of the seasonings; toss these together until the noodles have absorbed all the sauce and then add the rest. Toss a bit longer, taste and adjust the seasoning, and sprinkle the crab with the onion greens. Toss once more and pour into the prepared sandpot or casserole. Decorate with the crab carapace, if desired. Serve hot.

As you check over the Dungeness crab legs, use the butt of your knife to crack any pieces that are still thick and solid. I tend to use a 3-inch paring knife to wiggle the meat out of the legs. It also allows me to work my way into the joints and scoop out every last bit of fat and meat.

If you are using smaller, live crabs, follow these directions: Start with Steps 1 and 2; omit Step 3. Kill and clean the crabs (see page 456). A good way to kill the crabs with a touch of mercy is to place them in a plastic bag and stash it in the freezer until the crabs have drifted off to sleep. Make sure you take them out before they are fully frozen, however. If the shells are relatively small, use a cleaver to chop the crabs into quarters so that each piece has a quarter of the shell and two legs. With raw crabs, dust all of the meaty cut edges with flour before frying. This will keep the meat from drying out. After the cut edges have browned, continue to fry the crabs until the shells have turned completely pink. Remove them and then proceed to Step 4.

Once you've mastered this dish, you will probably want to play with the seasonings a bit: add ginger or chilies, or use curry powder. Just make sure that you don't drown out the flavor of the crab.

Cháozhōu kǎoxiā 潮州烤蝦

Chaozhou Shrimp Skewers

CHAOZHOU · SERVES 4

The seasonings in this dish are classic Chaozhou: fish sauce mixed with garlic, chilies, and green onion. They provide the basis for the compound butter that bastes and seasons the shrimp as they bake. Bamboo skewers keep the crustaceans nice and orderly during the cooking process, and the shrimp come out looking stunning. The skewers have another purpose, too: they stop the shrimp from curling up and dumping out the butter.

These spicy shrimp are fantastic for any part of a meal; I like to use them as appetizers or bar snacks. The sauce is so delicious that I sometimes serve this dish with a bowl of rice on the side, so diners can avoid wasting a single drop.

SHRIMP

12 extra-large shrimp in the shell (26/30 size),
    with or without heads
½ teaspoon sea salt
1 tablespoon mild rice wine
1 tablespoon fresh peanut or vegetable oil

COMPOUND BUTTER

1 clove garlic
½ serrano pepper (or whatever pepper you like), seeded
1 green onion, trimmed
2 tablespoons unsalted butter, softened
1½ tablespoons fish sauce

Spray oil

1. Soak 12 short bamboo skewers in warm water for at least 30 minutes; this will keep them from burning up in the oven.

2. Clean the shrimp (for directions on how to prepare shell-on shrimp, see page 457), then cut them down the back about halfway through their bodies. Pat the prepped shrimp dry with a paper towel and place them in a small work bowl. Toss the shrimp with the salt, rice wine, and oil and let them marinate while you prepare the compound butter.

3. Finely chop the garlic, pepper, and green onion. Place them in a small work bowl and stir in the butter and fish sauce.

4. Place a rack in the oven (a toaster oven is perfect here) 2 to 3 inches from the heating element, then heat the oven to 450°F. Spray the bottom of a small baking pan with oil. Drain the shrimp. Hold a shrimp upside down in one hand and thread the skewer through the length of the body just behind the feet. Repeat with the rest of the shrimp and skewers until done. Fill the opening in the back of each shrimp with the compound butter. Arrange the filled shrimp on the prepared pan and place them in the oven. Bake the shrimp for 5 minutes and then turn each shrimp over. Bake for another 3 or so minutes, until the shrimp are pink and beginning to brown. Remove the shrimp to serving plates or a platter and serve immediately. Eat with the hands. The skewers are easily removed if you first twirl them slightly inside the shrimp.

Púguó jī 葡國雞 or *Galinha à Macau*

Portuguese Chicken

MACAU · SERVES 6 TO 8

This recipe most likely arrived in Macau via Goa, Portugal's former colony on the west coast of India. It might have been slightly altered along the way by a few cooks from another former Portuguese colony, East Timor, which lies next to Indonesia. The result of all this globe-trotting is a dish with a wonderful diversity of flavor.

I've played around with this recipe a bit, replacing the curry powder with Japanese curry cubes, which give the dish a more predictable flavor. Curry powders also vary in intensity to such an extent that it is challenging to prescribe a specific amount. The cubes add just the right amount of salt, and they give the sauce a nice texture. Of course, feel free to use curry powder or canned curry paste if you prefer, but be sure to adjust the seasoning and the thickness of the sauce, too.

½ chicken, 4 chicken thighs, or 2 chicken breasts
2 tablespoons (or so) cornstarch
3 tablespoons peanut or vegetable oil,
    divided into 2 tablespoons and 1 tablespoon
½ onion
2 small or 1 large potato (Yukon Golds are great)
2 tablespoons mild rice wine
2 cups water
2 cubes Japanese curry paste
1 can (13½ ounces) coconut milk
Spray oil

1. Chop the chicken into 1-inch pieces. (You can do this with or without the bones and skin in the mix.) Toss the chicken with the cornstarch, fully coating each piece. Heat 2 tablespoons of the oil in a wok over high heat, add the chicken, and stir-fry until browned and cooked through. Remove the chicken to a work bowl. Clean the wok.

2. Cut the onion into 1-inch cubes and then separate the cubes into single layers. Peel the potatoes, cut them into 1-inch cubes, and either microwave or boil them until tender. Heat the remaining 1 tablespoon oil in the wok over high heat, add the onion pieces, and stir-fry for a few minutes, until soft. Add the rice wine, stir quickly to evaporate the alcohol, and then add the water. Toss in the curry cubes and bring the sauce to a boil. Add the potatoes and return the sauce to a boil. Add the coconut milk and the chicken, then taste and adjust the seasoning, if necessary. The dish can be made ahead of time up to this point and refrigerated.

3. About 15 minutes before serving, place a rack in your oven about 4 inches from the heat element and heat the broiler. Spray a 10-inch round broiler-proof casserole about 2 inches deep with oil. Bring the chicken mixture to a boil in the wok or a saucepan and pour it into the casserole. Place the casserole under the broiler and brown the chicken; it is ready when lovely leopard spots cover the top. Serve hot.

The secondary ingredients in this dish can be played around with as you like. Some people like to add tomatoes and raisins and carrots. Others throw in shredded coconut or sprinkle Parmesan cheese on top.

Although this dish is often served with steamed rice, it sometimes appears in Macau with baguette slices on the side.

Báiqiē jī 白切雞

White-Cut Chicken

GUANGDONG • SERVES 8

The Chinese name of this dish and its English translation don't sound very exciting, which might be why such an iconic southern way of poaching chicken has remained a secret to many outsiders. It works like this: instead of actually cooking the chicken in water over an open flame, the bird is boiled for only ten minutes and then left to sit in the hot water for an hour or so. During that rest, the heat travels into the center of the chicken, slowly but fully cooking the flesh while preserving all the juices. The resulting chicken is served with two simple dipping sauces made of ginger and green onion.

CHICKEN

1 whole fryer chicken (3 to 4 pounds)
1½ tablespoons sea salt
1 tablespoon white liquor
Ice water and ice cubes, as needed
Toasted sesame oil

DIPPING SAUCES

3 green onions, trimmed
2 teaspoons sea salt, divided in half
2 inches fresh ginger, peeled
½ cup peanut or vegetable oil, divided in half

1. Start this recipe at least 10 hours or even a day before you plan to serve it. Remove all of the viscera stuck in the back ribs of the chicken, pluck out any stray pinfeathers, and remove any extra fat. Pat the chicken dry with paper towels and place it in a medium work bowl. Rub the salt and white liquor all over the outside and inside of the chicken. Cover the bowl with plastic wrap and let the chicken marinate in the refrigerator for 8 to 24 hours. Remove it from the fridge about 1 hour or so before you start to cook, then tie the chicken as directed on page 461.

2. Note that you should not refrigerate the chicken after cooking, so plan your cooking time accordingly. Select a pan that is wide enough to just hold the chicken and tall enough that the chicken can be covered by at least 3 inches of boiling water—a pasta pot is a good bet here. Fill it with water, bring it to a boil, and carefully lower the chicken into the boiling water, adding more water as necessary to cover it by at least 3 inches. Cover the pot with a close-fitting lid, boil the chicken over high heat for 10 minutes, and then turn off the heat. Let the chicken sit in the covered pot for 1 hour. Check to see that the chicken is cooked through by piercing the thickest part of the thigh. If the juices run clear, the chicken is ready. If the juices are pink, return the pot to a boil, turn off the heat, and let the chicken sit in the covered pot for 10 to 15 minutes, until the juices are clear.

3. Prepare an ice bath that is large enough to hold the chicken and place it next to the pot. Gently remove the hot chicken from the stock, drain off all of the hot liquid from the bird, and lower it into the ice bath. (Reserve the stock for something else.) Roll the bird around in the ice water until the skin cools and tightens. Drain the chicken well, pat it dry, lightly rub sesame oil all over the skin, and place on a rimmed plate. Cover the chicken lightly and place it in a cool spot. Don't refrigerate it unless it's absolutely necessary.

4. When the chicken is completely cool, you can prepare it a number of ways. If you are eating it at home with friends and family, serve it whole and let everyone rip off their own pieces (see Tips). Traditionally, however, the chicken is chopped into 1-inch pieces (for directions on cutting up a chicken properly, see page 460). If you are serving this at a fancier dinner, remove as many bones as possible without destroying the skin or shape of the chicken; the drumsticks and wings can keep their bones. Cut each boneless part into ¾-inch pieces and arrange the meat on a serving platter so that it looks like a complete bird. Place the wings and drumsticks in their appropriate positions.

5. To make the dipping sauces, cut the green onions as finely as possible, place them in a heatproof small bowl, add half the salt, and rub the salt into the onions. Grate the ginger as finely as possible, remove any long fibers, pile it into another small heatproof bowl, add the rest of the salt, and rub the salt into the ginger.

6. Heat the oil in a wok over high heat. When it starts to smoke, pour half of it over the onions and half over the ginger. Lightly stir each bowl, then serve these alongside the chicken.

I recommend that you serve the chicken whole and let diners cut off pieces at the table. I don't really like slicing up the bird before serving it because the bones are sometimes still a bit red, and there's nothing like blood leaking out of the marrow to ruin an appetite. When the meal is finished, the carcass can be tossed back in the pot to make a flavorful broth.

If you do decide to chop up the bird and run across some bloody parts, you can either quickly steam them or drop them back into the hot poaching liquid to quickly cook the marrow.

HARD ALCOHOL IS VERY DIFFERENT IN CHINA than in the rest of the world. It is referred to in English as "white liquor," which is a direct translation of the Chinese name *báijiǔ* 白酒, although some refer to these spirits as *báigār* 白乾兒 after an old variety traditionally made in Hebei. Except for a few varieties seasoned with herbs or other additives, these are almost always clear, hence their name.

White liquor is beloved as a cooking ingredient for the elusive flavors it lends to certain dishes, like smoked chicken (page 26), although the better ones are of course meant to be reserved for appreciative sipping. These are best served neat at room temperature in wide small porcelain bowls similar to the cups used for rice wine (see page 486), as this allows their aromas to be fully enjoyed. But then again, this is hard liquor—most of these spirits are 80 to 120 proof—and so they are in many ways more akin to vodka than the much milder rice wines of China.

These strong distilled spirits are mainly fermented out of cooked sorghum, wheat, barley, Job's tears, sticky rice, or even millet, with other ingredients like dried peas, therapeutic herbs, or even flowers occasionally lending unique aromas and flavors to the brew. As with rice wines' classifications, the names suggest the best pairings for these white liquors, for alcohol is meant—as always in China—to be enjoyed with complementary bar snacks.

A good example of this would be Guizhou's *maotai*, whose heavy "sauce aroma" (*jiàngxiāng* 醬香) formed by its pronounced ester compounds allows it to stand up to heavily seasoned foods. Sweeter dishes would pair better with something like *wuliangye* of Sichuan and its "strong aroma" (*nóngxiāng* 濃香), while more delicate ones would be complemented by the "light aroma" (*qīngxiāng* 清香) of something like Shanxi's ancient *fenjiu*. There is also the "rice aroma" (*mǐxiāng* 米香) of white spirits brewed from

rice, as well as white liquors with a sugary "honey aroma" (*fēngxiāng* 蜂香) and even the more complex brews boasting of a "layered aroma" (*jiānxiāng* 兼香).

Because these are clear spirits, the main difference among the seemingly endless varieties is whether they are seasoned in some way. Unflavored ones rely on the aroma of the grains and pulses used in their distillation to create their unique flavors. Others, though, go in the opposite direction and tickle the senses in different ways. For example, *meiguilu* ("rose dew") is a floral variety that works well as a seasoning in a number of dishes, particularly such rich sweets as moon cakes (page 236), where it adds an almost indefinable whiff of roses. One of the most famous of China's heady alcoholic brews is made in Gansu: Ng Ka Py. A type of sorghum white lightning flavored with a member of the ivy family, this is the drink that John Steinbeck in *East of Eden* described as having the taste of "good rotten apples."

Hǎinán jī fàn 海南雞飯

Hainan Chicken and Rice

HAINAN • SERVES 4

If you've ever been to Southeast Asia, you've probably tried Hainan Chicken and Rice. It is the most famous dish to have emerged from China's second-largest island, and it was most likely brought to the more tropical parts of Southeast Asia by Chinese immigrants. It developed out of another local specialty, *Wénchāng jī* 文昌雞 (Wenchang village chicken), a similar dish that is also popular on Hainan.

This recipe is basically the same as White-Cut Chicken (page 196), but it includes rice that has been cooked with the leftover chicken stock. As with White-Cut Chicken, the secret lies in the timing: the bird must be poached all the way through but not cooked so much that it begins to dry out. I recommend serving this with any—or even all—of the four dipping sauces described here.

CHICKEN

1 whole frying chicken (3 to 4 pounds)
1½ teaspoons sea salt
1 tablespoon white liquor
Boiling water, as needed
Toasted sesame oil

RICE

2 cups long-grain white rice, like jasmine
2 tablespoons peanut or vegetable oil
3 bay leaves
5 slices fresh ginger
2 green onions, trimmed and cut into 2-inch lengths
½ teaspoon sea salt (or to taste)
3 cups stock from the chicken (including the fat)

DIPPING SAUCES

A 2 tablespoons peeled and minced fresh ginger
4 cloves garlic, finely minced
2 tablespoons peanut or vegetable oil
1 tablespoon dark soy sauce

B 2 tablespoons sugar
1 tablespoon pale rice vinegar
1 tablespoon black vinegar
2 tablespoons peeled and minced fresh ginger
4 cloves garlic, finely minced

C 3 red jalapeño peppers, finely diced
1 tablespoon fish sauce
1 tablespoon fresh lemon juice or pale rice vinegar
2 teaspoons toasted sesame oil
Sugar to taste

D Fresh limes
Cilantro sprigs

1. Prepare the chicken as directed for White-Cut Chicken (page 196) up through Step 3. Do not cut it up yet and reserve the poaching liquid for cooking the rice.

2. Rinse the rice and drain it well. Heat the oil in a wok over high heat until it starts to shimmer. Add the bay leaves, ginger, green onions, and salt. Mix them around in the oil until you can smell their fragrance, then toss in the raw rice. Stir-fry the rice until it begins to turn opaque. Stir in the stock, bring the mixture to a boil, cover, and reduce the heat to very low. Slowly cook the rice for 17 to 20 minutes, until the stock has been completely absorbed and the rice is fluffy. Turn off the heat, cover the wok, and let the rice steam while you prepare the rest of the meal. Just before serving, pluck out and discard the bay leaves, ginger, and green onions.

3. You can make as many of the sauces as you like. To make sauces A, B, and C, combine all of their respective recipe ingredients in a small pan and cook lightly and quickly over high heat. You just want to take off the raw edge of the aromatics and seasonings, so as soon as they come to a boil, pour each sauce into a separate small heatproof bowl and taste and adjust the seasoning. To make sauce D, slice the limes and coarsely chop the cilantro. (Diners can squeeze the lime over the chicken and sprinkle the cilantro over top.)

4. If you want to serve the chicken cut into pieces, now is the time to do it (for directions on how to properly cut up a chicken, see page 460), but that's not how I like it. If you're like me and prefer to make this chicken even juicier, heat up the stock to a simmer, turn off the heat, and then place the whole chicken back in the stock for a minute or two to warm it up. Remove the chicken, reserving the stock, then place it on a rimmed plate. Pull off all the meat with your fingers and reduce the meat to bite-sized pieces. Cut the skin into thin shreds. Return the bones to the stock and serve this broth at the end of the meal.

5. Have ready 4 dinner plates, and a single rice bowl to use as a mold. To serve, scoop a quarter of the rice into the bowl, smooth off the top, and then turn the bowl upside down onto a dinner plate to unmold. Repeat with the rest of the rice and plates. Arrange the chicken alongside and on top of the rice. Serve while everything is still hot, and pass around whatever dipping sauces you're using.

HAINAN'S CULINARY CULTURE ENCOMPASSES the Leizhou Peninsula, which stretches from the Guangdong mainland down toward Hainan. In the port city of Zhanjiang, in particular, the foods and language show a distinct relationship with Southern Fujian and Chaozhou, rather than with Guangdong.

The original inhabitants of Hainan were most likely the Li people, who still constitute the largest minority on the island. Calling themselves the Hlai, they—like the native people of Southern Fujian—are probably descendants of the ancient Yue tribe (see page 291) who settled there millennia ago, and they retain remnants of their unique language, customs, and culture.

However, South Fujian and Chaozhou flavors are what define Hainan's foods. Pounded sticky rice, or *ciba* (page 306), is filled with crushed peanuts, sesame seeds, sugar, and coconut. Dough made out of sticky or regular rice is sometimes flavored with fresh coconut milk and the emerald green of aromatic pandan leaves (see page 233) to make luxurious treats.

Rice is beloved in savory dishes, too. Hainan's tamales, or *zongzi*, are stuffed with salted egg yolks, pork, and chicken, and the outer layer of sticky rice is scented with banana leaf wrappers, a stunning combination of tropical flavors mingled with the taste of a distant culinary homeland.

Until only a few decades ago, Hainan and its surrounding islets were administered as part of Guangdong Province, and that is probably why some of the local dishes, such as Hainan Chicken and Rice, have such a distinctly Cantonese cast. Chickens and goats do not require much in the way of care or grazing land, so they are the main food animals in the rain forests that cover much of the island.

Yánjú jī 鹽焗雞

Salt-Baked Chicken

HAKKA · SERVES 4 TO 6

Rarely available outside the homes of good Hakka cooks (read: grandmas), this is a dish to master and enjoy. Long ago a version of this dish was served to wealthy Hakka salt merchants, whose cooks would actually bury the chicken in hot salt, without any wrapper. They would then rinse off the chicken and serve it with a dipping sauce on the side. About two hundred years ago, someone came up with the clever idea of shrouding the bird in paper to keep the salt out and the juices in, and this is how the dish is still prepared today.

Some Hakka or Guangdong-style places will offer this dish on the menu, but I have rarely found an authentic version at a restaurant. This is probably because the dish requires a bit of work, and chefs know that the majority of their diners will be satisfied with White-Cut Chicken (page 196). However, baking the chicken in salt on a stove top gives it a completely different texture, one you will instantly recognize once you've tried the real thing. The most distinctive seasoning in this recipe is sand ginger, so be sure not to leave that out.

6 pounds coarse salt (ice cream salt—aka rock salt—is perfect)

CHICKEN AND DRY RUB
1 whole fryer chicken (3 to 4 pounds)
1 teaspoon dry-fried salt and pepper (page 440)
½ teaspoon five-spice powder (page 441 or store-bought)
½ teaspoon ground sand ginger
¼ cup thinly sliced fresh ginger
3 green onions, trimmed
Spray oil

OPTIONAL SAUCE
¼ cup rendered chicken fat or lard
1 teaspoon dry-fried salt and pepper
½ teaspoon ground sand ginger

1. Before you start prepping the chicken, place the coarse salt in a rimmed baking sheet and heat it in a 550°F oven—or as high as it will go. The salt should be red hot—so hot that you cannot hold your hand over it by the time you are ready to use it. Do not rush this step, as it is the secret to making this dish a success.

2. Wipe the chicken dry (inside and out) with paper towels. If you are using the giblets, pat them dry, too. Cut 2-inch-long incisions under each wing, and then poke the outer two segments of the wings into the body so that the wing drumsticks lie flush against the body (see page 461). Place the chicken breast-side up on a work surface and press down firmly on the breast to flatten it so the bird is as compact as possible. Mix the salt and pepper, five-spice powder, and sand ginger together in a small bowl. Sprinkle half into the chicken cavity and rub it around; stuff the giblets, sliced ginger, and green onions into the chicken, then tie the ends of the legs together with butcher's twine. Rub the outside of the chicken with the rest of the spices.

3. Spray a 30-inch-wide sheet of parchment paper with oil and have two 30-inch-wide sheets of foil ready. Place the chicken upside down on the oiled parchment paper and wrap up the chicken tightly in paper. Turn the bird right side up again and wrap it in a sheet of foil—sealing the edges as much as possible—before turning it upside down on the last sheet of foil and again sealing the edges to keep all the juices in and the salt out.

4. Scoot any children and pets out of the kitchen and turn off your phone before you start working with the hot salt. Select a large sandpot or covered casserole dish that easily holds the chicken with room to spare for the salt. Place a trivet in the bottom of the sandpot and *very carefully* pour about a quarter of the hot salt into the bottom. Arrange the wrapped chicken in the center (breast-side up) and *very carefully* cover it completely with the remaining hot salt. Cover the sandpot and place the pot on the stove; the heat under it should be between low and medium-low so that the salt stays hot and the chicken slowly bakes.

5. Cook the chicken this way for 1½ hours, remove the pot from the burner, and let it cool down until you can touch the pot and bird without being burned. Again, make your kitchen free of all distractions. When you open the pot up, pour off at least half the salt and then lift out the chicken to a rimmed plate.

6. Unwrap the chicken layer by layer, discarding any salt that is sticking to the wrappings. When you get to the parchment paper, carefully dust off any salt. There will be lots of juices in the final wrapper, so be sure to corral them all in the plate. Check if the chicken is done by piercing the thickest part of the thigh with a chopstick; the juices should run very clear. But don't worry, as any meat that is still pink can be cooked quickly in the last step with the sauce.

7. To make the optional but absolutely delicious sauce, melt the fat in a wok over medium-high heat and add the dry-fried salt and pepper and the sand ginger. Drizzle in any juices from the chicken and bring the sauce to a boil. The traditional way to serve this chicken is to cut off and hand-shred the meat and skin. Toss the meat and skin with the hot sauce until every piece is coated, then arrange these on the serving plate over the bones. Serve hot or very warm.

Fēizhōujī 非洲雞 or *Galinha à Africana*

African Chicken

MACAU · SERVES 4 TO 6

Like Portuguese Chicken (page 195), this dish could be considered a colonial casserole of sorts, as it pulls together influences from around the globe. African Chicken usually has a side of rice or French bread to soak up the tasty sauce. As my husband said when he first tried this recipe, "This does not taste Chinese." And it doesn't. It doesn't taste like it is from Africa, either. It tastes like Macau.

CHICKEN AND SPICE RUB

2 pounds boneless chicken (thighs are good)

1 teaspoon coarsely ground chilies (not too hot)

¼ cup finely chopped shallots (see Tip)

2 tablespoons sweet paprika

½ teaspoon five-spice powder (page 441 or store-bought)

½ teaspoon sea salt

Spray oil

¼ cup peanut or vegetable oil, plus more as needed

About 1 pound Yukon Gold potatoes

SAUCE

¼ cup unsalted butter

2 cups finely chopped shallots

¼ cup finely chopped garlic

2 red or orange bell peppers, seeded and finely chopped

2 tablespoons sweet paprika

1 can (13½ ounces) coconut milk

½ cup flaked or shredded unsweetened dried coconut

½ cup peanut butter, chunky or smooth

1 cup unsalted chicken broth (page 380)

2 bay leaves

Sea salt to taste

GARNISH

¼ cup finely chopped parsley

1. Pat the chicken dry, cut it into serving-sized pieces, and slash the thicker parts of the meat so that the seasonings can penetrate it. Mix together the chilies, shallots, paprika, five-spice powder, and salt in a resealable plastic bag. Add the chicken, seal the bag closed, and massage the seasonings into the chicken through the bag. Refrigerate for at least 2 hours and up to overnight.

2. Spray an 11-cup casserole with oil. Set a wok over high heat, and when it is hot, add the oil and swirl it around to coat the bottom and sides. Add the chicken pieces in small batches so that they fit on the bottom, drizzling in more oil as necessary. Turn the heat down to medium and brown the chicken on all sides until it is cooked through. Place the browned chicken pieces in the casserole as they are ready. Peel the potatoes and cut into thin wedges (no larger than ⅛ inch on the outside edge) and either microwave or simmer them until tender; drain and set aside. Place a rack in the middle of the oven and heat the oven to 450°F.

3. To make the sauce, clean the wok, return it to medium heat, and melt the butter. Add the shallots, garlic, and peppers, cover, and cook, stirring occasionally, until soft but not browned. Stir in the paprika, coconut milk, flaked coconut, peanut butter, stock, and bay leaves. Bring the sauce to a boil uncovered, stirring the bottom constantly. Reduce the heat to maintain a gentle simmer and cook until the sauce has reduced to the consistency of sour cream. Season with salt.

4. Add the potatoes to the casserole. Pour the sauce evenly over the chicken and shake the container gently to spread the sauce around everything. Bake the casserole uncovered for about 20 minutes, until the sauce has browned and turned very bubbly. Dust the top with the parsley and serve hot.

You will need about 12 ounces total of shallots for this recipe. A food processor is useful here to reduce the shallots, garlic, and bell peppers into a finely chopped state.

Wúzhōu zhǐbāojī 梧州紙包雞

Wuzhou Paper-Wrapped Chicken

SOUTHERN GUANGXI · SERVES 4

Southern Guangxi doesn't have many famous dishes of its own; for the longest time it was part of Guangdong. This delicious way with chicken is one of the few exceptions. Honored as one of China's finest dishes at a 1983 national competition, it is named after Wuzhou, a city near the Guangdong border. Wrapping seasoned chicken in paper before deep-frying it is popular throughout China, but this recipe is particularly seductive.

1½ pounds (more or less) chicken wings or other chicken parts, preferably with the skin on (see Tips)

AROMATICS

2 tablespoons peeled and coarsely chopped fresh ginger
2 cloves garlic, coarsely chopped
2 green onions, trimmed and coarsely chopped
1 star anise
1 teaspoon sand ginger pieces
1 piece (1 inch square or so) aged tangerine peel
1 teaspoon fennel seeds

MARINADE

3 tablespoons mild rice wine
2 tablespoons oyster sauce
2 teaspoons dark soy sauce
1 tablespoon regular soy sauce
1 teaspoon sugar
2 tablespoons peanut or vegetable oil

Peanut or vegetable oil for frying
Chopped cilantro or green onions for garnish, optional

1. Pat the chicken dry and remove any excess fat or bonier parts. Chop the chicken into bite-sized pieces (about 1 inch square) and place them in a resealable plastic bag.

2. Place the ginger, garlic, and green onions in a small blender or food processor and pulse until they are ground, scraping down the sides of the container as needed. Add the remaining aromatics and all of the marinade ingredients and whirl these together to mix. Taste and adjust the seasoning as desired. Empty this marinade into the bag holding the chicken, and squish everything together so each piece is coated. Seal the bag and refrigerate the chicken for at least 4 hours and up to a day.

3. Ready 8 sheets of parchment paper, each 8 by 12 inches, and 8 sharp, round toothpicks. Lay the parchment sheets on a clean work surface, with a point of each sheet aimed at you (see the diagram for Oyster Spring Rolls on page 169). Divide the chicken and marinade evenly among the sheets, and fold up the chicken in the paper to form a compact, fairly flat package. Squeeze out any extra air as you go so you end up with a neat rectangle. Secure each package with a toothpick.

4. Pour the oil to a depth of 2 to 3 inches into a wok and heat over medium-high heat. When the oil shimmers, add half of the packets and reduce the heat to medium-low to maintain a merry bubbling, with the largest bubbles around ¼ inch in diameter. Use tongs to turn the packets over every 5 minutes or so until the paper takes on a golden hue, which will take about 15 minutes. Lift each packet out of the oil and hold it horizontally as you transfer it to a rimmed serving platter. If you turn it this way and that, you will release lots of the juices. Unwrap the chicken in front of your guests, using the paper as nests. Dust each portion with the garnish, if desired.

Chopping up chicken wings will usually result in some bone shards, so use boneless thighs if you are serving this to children.

If you don't have parchment paper, clean brown-paper lunch bags can be cut up. Just make sure that whatever paper you use doesn't have any wax or plastic on it. Also make sure your toothpicks are strong enough to pierce the paper. Or, just use foil.

Sānbēijī 三杯雞

Three-Cup Chicken

TAIWAN'S MILITARY FAMILIES AND JIANGXI •
SERVES 6 TO 8

In Taipei, during the early 1980s, there was a strip of little dives at the upper end of Zhongshan North Road. This was in a neighborhood called Tianmu, a rather posh enclave where most of the foreigners lived. Unlike most of the area's other establishments, which catered to expats, these "beer houses," or *píjiǔ wū* 啤酒屋, had a solidly Chinese clientele. They served what can best be described as Asian tapas. These little shacks were decorated with folk art and bamboo paneling, and they offered lots of good beer. But the real draw was the food.

On Friday nights, my husband and I would sometimes meet friends at one end of the beer-house section and eat and drink our way up and down the hill. The dish I looked forward to the most was this Jiangxi recipe filtered through a Taiwanese lens. The bird was served on the bone with a sticky, savory sauce, as well as with plump garlic cloves, fresh chilies, green onions, chewy ginger slices, and a big handful of basil leaves.

2 pounds chicken wings

4 inches fresh ginger

16 cloves garlic

¼ cup peanut or vegetable oil

¼ cup oyster sauce or regular soy sauce

1 tablespoon rock sugar

¼ cup mild rice wine

1 tablespoon toasted sesame oil

4 green onions, trimmed and white parts cut into
    ½-inch-thick rounds and green parts diced

2 to 4 red jalapeño peppers or other red chili, trimmed
    and cut into thin rings or half-moons, optional

1 cup packed stemmed fresh basil leaves, large leaves
    roughly chopped, optional

1. Trim off the tip sections of the chicken wings (use these for stock) and cut the rest of each wing into 2 pieces. I also like to whack the wing pieces in half crosswise to make bite-sized morsels. Slice the ginger paper-thin; you should have about ½ cup. Peel the garlic cloves and trim off the hard ends but leave the cloves whole.

2. Pour the peanut or vegetable oil into a sandpot and set it over medium heat. As soon as the oil starts to shimmer, toss in the ginger slices and fry them, stirring often, until they are golden and crispy; use a slotted spoon to remove them. Add the chicken to the ginger-scented oil and stir as you fry it until the chicken is golden all over. Pour in the oyster sauce or soy sauce and the optional sugar, rice wine, and sesame oil and toss in the fried ginger and the whites of the green onions.

3. Bring the pot to a boil, cover it, adjust the heat to medium-low, and then simmer the chicken until it is tender and the sauce has been reduced by more than half. Add the garlic, re-cover, and continue to cook gently until only the oil remains at the bottom of the pot. The dish can be made ahead of time up to this point and reheated just before you add the final ingredients.

4. Taste the sauce and adjust the seasoning. Toss in the optional chilies and the green parts of the onions. Sprinkle the optional basil over the top, place the lid back on the pot, and serve immediately.

The Taiwanese seasonings here are oyster sauce, green onions, chilies, and basil. Jiangxi style calls for soy sauce and rock sugar in place of the oyster sauce.

Méigāojiàng bào páigǔ 梅糕醬爆排骨

Spareribs with Garlic and Plum Sauce

CHAOZHOU · SERVES 4 TO 6

Sweet-and-sour ribs are popular all over China, and each region has its own take on the master recipe. But this one from Chaozhou is right up there with the best. Its secret? Sour plums. The traditional recipe calls for the sauce in name, a Chaozhou mainstay called *meigaojiang*, literally "plum paste sauce." True *meigaojiang* is practically impossible to find in the United States at the time of this writing, so I've substituted bottled plum sauce combined with vinegar and a dash of soy sauce. Garlic and ginger are also thrown in here; you end up with a lovely sauce that is sweet, sour, and savory.

SPARERIBS AND MARINADE

2 pounds pork spareribs, left whole or cut in half
    lengthwise by the butcher if you like
1½ teaspoons sea salt
2 teaspoons sugar
2 tablespoons mild rice wine
2 tablespoons peeled and grated fresh ginger

FINISHING TOUCHES

2 cups peanut or vegetable oil
2 tablespoons chopped garlic
3 tablespoons Chinese plum sauce (see Tips)
1½ tablespoons pale rice vinegar
1½ tablespoons black vinegar
1 teaspoon regular soy sauce
¼ cup water
2 green onions, trimmed and chopped

1. Pat the ribs dry, then trim off any extra fat and discard. Cut the ribs apart between the bones. Place the ribs in a resealable plastic bag with the marinade ingredients, squeeze out most of the air, seal closed, and then massage the marinade into the ribs. Refrigerate for at least a few hours and up to overnight. Before frying the ribs, rinse them in a colander set in the sink to rid them of most of the salt. Drain the ribs and then pat them dry with paper towels so they don't send the hot oil flying when you deep-fry them.

2. Heat the oil in a wok over high heat until a chopstick inserted in the oil immediately begins to bubble all over. Add about half of the ribs (to keep the oil from cooling off too quickly) and shake and flip them as they cook so they brown evenly. Once they are nicely caramelized on the edges, use a slotted spoon to remove them to a platter covered with a paper towel. Repeat with the other half.

3. Pour off most of the oil, leaving only about 2 tablespoons in the wok. Heat the oil again over high heat, add the garlic, and stir-fry for about 10 seconds to release its fragrance. Add the plum sauce, vinegars, soy sauce, water, and the fried ribs and quickly stir-fry everything together until the sauce thickens and becomes a nice gloss on the meat. Toss the ribs with the chopped green onions and serve.

If you get your ribs at a butcher shop, you can ask the butcher to slice the whole side of ribs in half using a band saw—although eating them whole is fun, too, and just as tasty.

I like Lee Kum Kee brand plum sauce here, but taste the different varieties and find one that pleases you.

Chāshāo 叉燒

Char Siu

GUANGDONG · MAKES 3 POUNDS OR SO

Char siu can be found in almost every American Chinatown. But Guangdong-style delis in the United States rarely use good-quality pork, and the best *char siu* is all about the flavor of the meat. It's a simple dish to make: just get a good cut of heritage pork, slice it and marinate it correctly, and then let the oven do the rest of the work.

I've made a few modifications to the original recipe over the years. First, I like Fujian's red wine lees for their scarlet color and delicious aroma. Also, instead of sugar and maltose, I use agave syrup, which is much lighter and less sweet. It works perfectly to season the meat and give it that crispy charring.

3 pounds (or so) boneless pork shoulder,
    rolled into a roast by the butcher
¼ cup *char siu* sauce (see Tips)
1 tablespoon red wine lees (page 418)
½ cup agave syrup, sugar, or melted maltose
2 tablespoons catsup
1 tablespoon *meiguilu* or other white liquor
1½ teaspoons regular soy sauce
1½ teaspoons ginger juice (page 481)
1 teaspoon ground sand ginger, optional but good
Spray oil

1. Have a large work bowl and resealable plastic bag ready. Remove the strings from the pork and find a natural opening in the side of the roast. Use a sharp knife to cut the roast or an unrolled shoulder into long ¾-inch-thick strips nicely marbled with fat. Cut the strips into whatever lengths you want. Use a sharp fork or knife to stab them all over so that the marinade can penetrate the flesh easily.

2. Mix together the rest of the ingredients except the spray oil in the large work bowl and add the pork. Toss it gently in the marinade to coat it thoroughly. Dump the meat and marinade into the plastic bag, press out most of the air, and seal it. Place the meat in the refrigerator for 6 to 8 hours to give the flavors time to penetrate the pork. If you have the time, take the bag out every hour or so to massage the meat through the plastic and turn it over.

3. Place a rack in the center of your oven and heat it to 350°F. Prepare the bottom of a broiling pan or other large rimmed pan and a large cake rack that fits easily into the pan by spraying both with oil. Remove the pork from the marinade, but reserve any leftover sauce. Lay the slabs of meat on the cake rack so that they do not touch one another and roast the pork for about 15 minutes. Turn the pieces over, baste with some reserved marinade, and roast for another 15 minutes. Raise the heat to 400°F and pour a shallow layer of water into the pan so the marinade doesn't burn, but do not let the water touch the rack. Continue to roast the meat, turning it occasionally and brushing on more of the marinade each time, until the pork is lightly charred all along the edges, about 45 to 50 minutes more. Let it come to room temperature and slice it thinly before serving. Leftovers can be stored in a clean resealable bag in the refrigerator or frozen for later use.

The shoulder (sometimes labeled "pork butt") is the best cut. There's lots of good meat in the shoulder, as well as marbled fat, which keeps this dish moist. If you get a boneless shoulder already trimmed and rolled up for a roast, that is even better, because half of your work is done.

Pork ribs are great cooked this way, too: simply slash them diagonally on the meaty side, marinate, and roast as directed.

Look for Lee Kum Kee brand *char siu* sauce. Or, instead of store-bought *char siu* sauce, you can make hoisin sauce by heating together 5 tablespoons regular soy sauce, 1 tablespoon toasted sesame paste (page 413), 3 tablespoons agave syrup, 2 tablespoons sweet wheat paste, 1 tablespoon balsamic vinegar, 1 clove garlic (minced), 1 tablespoon toasted sesame oil, and 2 tablespoons chili oil (page 435). This makes around 1 cup.

Méicài kòuròu 梅菜扣肉

Pork Belly with Preserved Mustard Greens

HAKKA • SERVES 4 TO 6

This dish most likely originated around the Shaoxing area of Jiangsu, where it is still popular (see page 118), but this recipe uses pale Hakka-style "plum vegetable," or *meicai*, which it borrows from the Pearl River Delta. There is a darker, heavily seasoned version of *meicai* made in the Shaoxing style, but that requires a different way of cooking and seasoning and, as a result, cannot be used as a substitute here.

PORK

1 pound pork belly, with the skin on
Boiling water, as needed
1 tablespoon dark soy sauce
½ cup peanut or vegetable oil (used oil is all right
    if it smells fresh)

GREENS

6 ounces (or so) Hakka-style preserved mustard greens
3 green onions, trimmed and cut into 1-inch pieces
10 thin slices fresh ginger
2 tablespoons peanut or vegetable oil
6 tablespoons mild rice wine
2 tablespoons regular soy sauce
5 tablespoons (or so) agave syrup, or sugar as needed

1. You don't have to worry about any fine hairs, as they will be burned off later, but thick hairs on the pork belly should be plucked out (see page 459). Place the pork in a medium saucepan, cover it with water, and bring the water to a full boil over high heat. Lower the heat to medium and simmer the pork for about 10 minutes to remove any impurities. Drain the pork, rinse off any scum, and let it cool down.

2. To prepare the mustard greens, soak them in warm water until pliable and then cut them into small pieces (½ inch or less). Carefully rinse the mustard greens, squeeze them dry, place them in a medium saucepan, and cover with water. Cook the greens until they are completely tender and then boil down the water until only a slick of sauce remains.

3. Pat the cooled-down pork with a paper towel until it is totally dry. Rub the skin all over with the dark soy sauce. Heat a frying pan over medium heat, add the oil, and then carefully slide the pork skin-side down into the hot fat (don't fry the other sides of the meat). Fry the pork skin until it is a nice mahogany brown with bubbles and blisters all over the surface. Use a spatter screen to protect you from flying fat. Remove the pork to a cutting board and let it cool down a bit. With the skin-side down on the board, use a sharp knife to cut down through the meat and fat all the way up to—but not through—the skin, making ⅜-inch-wide slices. Place the pork skin-side down in a heatproof 4-cup bowl.

4. Stuff the pork slices with the greens, packing as much as possible into and around the meat. Arrange the green onions and ginger on top. Pour the oil, rice wine, and regular soy sauce over everything; if you like this dish slightly sweet (which I certainly do), add up to 5 tablespoons agave syrup. Seal the bowl with foil and peak it up in the center a bit so that the steam will roll off the top rather than trickle into the bowl. Place the bowl in a steamer (see page 49) and cook over medium heat for 4 hours, adding more water to the steamer as necessary.

5. Take the pork out of the steamer and carefully pour the sauce into a measuring cup. Remove most of the fat from the sauce, if desired. Taste the sauce and adjust the seasoning one last time. Invert a rimmed plate over the bowl and invert the bowl onto the plate; carefully lift off the bowl. Pour the sauce around and over the meat and serve immediately.

Lǔ ròu fàn 滷肉飯

Diced Braised Pork over Rice

SOUTHERN FUJIAN AND TAIWAN · SERVES 6 TO 8

Whenever I get homesick for Taiwan, I make this dish. It's the kind of home-style food that grandmas always seem to have bubbling on the stove over there. It's also not hard to make. The pork and sauce are served over a bowl of steaming rice with an egg, a sprinkle of chopped cilantro, and a couple of slices of that yellow Japanese pickled radish known as *takuan zuke*. This last fillip is probably an inheritance from Taiwan's colonial days, when the Japanese controlled the island.

BRAISED PORK

2 pounds boneless, skinless, nicely marbled pork,
    such as from the shoulder or neck
½ cup sliced shallots
½ cup chopped garlic
6 tablespoons peanut or vegetable oil

SAUCE

¼ cup peanut butter, chunky or smooth
1 teaspoon ground cinnamon
3 star anise
½ teaspoon five-spice powder (page 441 or store-bought)
Sea salt
1 teaspoon freshly ground black pepper
½ cup light soy sauce
¾ cup mild rice wine
Walnut-sized piece of rock sugar
4 cups boiling water, plus more as needed

FINAL TOUCHES

6 to 8 hard-boiled eggs, peeled (see page 461)
6 to 8 cups hot steamed rice
Japanese daikon pickle (*takuan zuke*), sliced
Fried sliced shallots (page 435)
Chopped cilantro

1. Start this dish at least a day before you want to serve it. Blanch the pork in simmering water for 10 minutes, discard the water, and cut the meat into small (½-inch) dice.

2. Fry the raw shallots and garlic in the oil until they are light brown. Add the pork and fry until it begins to brown, too. Stir in all of the sauce ingredients, topping them off with more boiling water as needed to cover. Bring the pot to a boil, reduce the heat to maintain a gentle simmer, cover, and let it cook for about half an hour.

3. Taste and adjust the flavor with salt, wine, and sugar as needed. Add the eggs, bring the pot to a boil again, and then let it simmer, uncovered, for about 30 minutes. Allow the sauce to come to room temperature, then cover and refrigerate it for at least overnight for the best flavor. Try to submerge the eggs so that they take on an even golden color.

4. The next day—or even better, after a couple of days—scrape most of the fat off of the top before bringing the pork and eggs to a boil again. Reduce to a gentle simmer and cook uncovered for about an hour, turning the eggs occasionally so that they tan evenly. Remove the eggs from the sauce and bring the pork and sauce to a boil to reduce the sauce to about ½ cup.

5. To serve, place about a cup of hot steamed rice in a large soup bowl, put an egg on top of the rice and a mound of the pork next to it, and then decorate the top with a couple of slices of pickled daikon and a healthy handful of fried shallots. Dribble a bit of the sauce over the pork and egg. Throw some chopped cilantro on top and serve.

Xiányú ròubǐng 鹹魚肉餅

Steamed Minced Pork with Salted Fish

GUANGDONG · SERVES 4

When making this dish, Guangdong cooks include a strip of salted fish on top of the minced pork. The fish acts as a seasoning, its rich flavors working their way into the pork. In general, I think of salted fish as a condiment: on its own it's pretty overwhelming, but if it's used in small doses, it can be a delicious addition to many savory dishes, like fried rice (page 222).

When I lived in Taiwan, the preferred garnish for this dish was brined egg yolks (page 422), not salted fish. Other families mixed in some chopped pickles (the *huagua* pickles on page 423 work well). The main aim—no matter what you use—is to provide a salty, *xianwei* contrast to the rich flavors of the pork.

1 pound ground pork (15 percent fat or so)
3 green onions, trimmed and chopped
2 or 3 cloves garlic, chopped
3 thin slices fresh ginger, peeled and chopped
1 teaspoon sugar
1 teaspoon mushroom powder
2 teaspoons regular soy sauce
3 tablespoons mild rice wine
2 tablespoons shallot oil (page 435)
1 slice (2 ounces or so) salted fish (see Tips)

1. Place the pork in a medium work bowl and mix in the green onions, garlic, ginger, sugar, mushroom seasoning, soy sauce, rice wine, and shallot oil. (Your hand is probably the best tool for this.)

2. Shape the meat into a patty and place it in a shallow bowl that fits easily into your steamer (see page 49). Smooth down the top of the patty and squish the salted fish into the center. Place the bowl in the steamer and steam the patty on high for about 35 minutes. Insert a chopstick into the center of the meat; if the juices run clear, it's done. Serve hot with steamed rice.

Oil-packed salted fish is often available in Guangdong-style grocery stores, but I've found that vacuum-packed fillets of salted yellow croaker work well as a fresher component for this dish. I put the croaker in a medium canning jar, submerge the fish in fresh oil, cover the jar with foil, and steam it for about an hour. When it has cooled, I replace the foil with the jar's cover (one that will not rust) and store the jar in the refrigerator, where it keeps well as long as the fish is covered with oil. Look for salted yellow croaker fillets in grocery stores specializing in southern Chinese foods.

Another delicious way of making this dish is to flake half of the salted fish, mix it in with the meat, and then place the rest of it on top.

If you opt for brined egg yolks, stick the whole or halved yolks into the pork just before steaming.

If you're going the pickle route and you don't want to make *huagua* pickles, pick up a jar of Taiwanese *yìnguā* 蔭瓜, which is often roughly translated on the label as "Oriental pickling melon." These are basically hard squashes prepared almost exactly like *huagua* pickles. Add some of the liquid from the pickles to the mix instead of the mushroom powder and soy sauce.

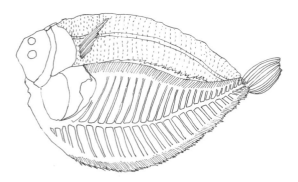

Fŭrŭ kōngxīncài 腐乳空心菜

Water Spinach with Bean Curd "Cheese" and Chilies

GUANGDONG · SERVES 6 TO 8

Fermented bean curd "cheese" looks sort of like feta cheese and has a similar tang from the brine it's soaked in. Its seasoning, though, depends on where it was made. Fujian Province has a gorgeous scarlet *dòufŭrŭ* 豆腐乳 (page 420) that is made with its local red wine yeast. Taiwan has a creamy sweet version that comes from the town of Sanxia. Guangdong and Guangxi have a couple of very funky versions, as well as some milder ones (page 248) and a few that are spiked with chili. They are all delicious—just think of them as cheese, rather than bean curd.

This recipe calls for the addition of a fresh chili to the "cheese," but if you'd rather have garlic in there, go right ahead. There are no set rules: the flavors can be adjusted depending upon what you like, what you're serving this dish with, and what kind of *doufuru* you're using.

1¼ pounds water spinach (about 3 fistfuls)
2 to 3 cubes fermented bean curd "cheese" (page 420 or 421 or store-bought), plus a few spoonfuls of the brine
3 tablespoons peanut or vegetable oil
10 thin slices fresh ginger, peeled and finely minced
1 green jalapeño pepper, diced
Splash of rice wine
Sugar, light soy sauce, or more fermented bean curd "cheese," if needed
1 teaspoon toasted sesame oil

1. Wash the water spinach carefully and trim off the ends, as well as any tough stems. Cut the bunch in half where the leaves start to grow more thickly.

2. Cut the bottom half of the stems into 2-inch pieces and put them into one pile; cut the leafy stalks into 2-inch pieces and set them in another pile. Place the bean curd "cheese," or *doufuru*, in a small bowl with the brine and mash it with a fork.

3. Heat the oil in a wok over high heat until it starts to smoke. Add the ginger and quickly stir-fry it until it begins to brown. Add the jalapeño pepper and then the water spinach stems and toss them in the hot oil until they turn a brilliant green. Add the leafy stalks and stir-fry the leaves quickly until they barely wilt. Pour the mashed *doufuru* into the wok and use the rice wine to rinse out the bowl into the wok, as well. Quickly toss everything together and taste, adjusting the flavor with more *doufuru* or a dash of sugar or soy sauce if needed. Sprinkle the sesame oil over the water spinach and serve hot.

Háoyóu jièlán 蠔油芥藍

Gailan with Oyster Sauce

GUANGDONG · SERVES 4 TO 6

Known as Chinese flowering kale in English and *jiè-láncài* 芥藍菜 in Mandarin, *gailan* is best served in spring when it is still young and tender. If you are a devotee of dim sum, you'll recognize *gailan* as one of the few green items regularly wheeled around the room. This recipe is a classic at teahouses and extremely easy to prepare.

First, the *gailan* is given a quick dip in boiling water with a bit of oil. After the stalks are blanched to a gentle crispness, they are stacked up parallel to one another and cut in half crosswise. A drizzle of oyster sauce is added as a final touch. When I make this dish, I also add some rice wine, sugar, and sesame oil. The vegetable can be steam-fried, as well; see Step 2 for directions on that.

1 pound tender young *gailan*
3 tablespoons peanut or vegetable oil
6 tablespoons rice wine
6 tablespoons oyster sauce or oyster-flavored sauce
3 to 4 teaspoons sugar
2 tablespoons toasted sesame oil

1. If the stalks need no more than a light trim on the bottom, take care of that and place the *gailan* in a colander; the stalks should be 6 to 8 inches long. If, on the other hand, they have thick skins, use a paring knife to peel the skin off, as well as any tougher leaves. Rinse the veggies under running water and lightly shake dry.

2. If you are blanching the stalks, bring a large pot of water to a boil and drizzle in a bit of oil. Dunk the *gailan* in the boiling water for only as long as it takes to turn them a brilliant emerald. Use a Chinese spider to pluck them out and drain. If you are steam-frying the *gailan*, heat the 3 tablespoons oil in a wok over high heat and add the veggies. Quickly stir-fry them until the color starts to change. Cover the wok with a lid or the colander and let them steam for a minute or two until they turn a bright green. However you've cooked them, center the veggies on a serving platter and arrange the stalks parallel to one another, with the leaves all pointing in the same direction. Cut them in half across the middle.

3. Add the rice wine, oyster sauce, sugar, and sesame oil to the wok and bring to a fast boil over high heat. Taste the sauce and adjust the seasoning. Pour the sauce over the *gailan* and serve hot.

When you go shopping for *gailan*, there are a couple of things to keep in mind, so check out the suggestions on page 481.

THE RECIPE FOR *GAILAN* HERE USES AN EXCELLENT CHINESE COOKING TECHNIQUE CALLED "steam-frying." A few tablespoons of oil are heated in a wok over high heat before the still-wet *gailan* is tossed in; the hot oil starts the initial cooking, and the steam formed by the water on the leaves finishes the job.

Start out by flipping the stalks around in the hot oil for a minute or so to coat every part of them. It's all right if there's a little searing going on, as this adds flavor. Then, cover the wok with a lid for a few quick minutes to steam the stalks until they are just this side of raw. Remove the *gailan* from the wok when it is a bright jade color. That's it.

Jǐucàihuā chǎo dòufǔgān 韭菜花炒豆腐乾

Garlic Chive Flowers with Pressed Bean Curd

HAKKA • SERVES 4

The Hakka are adept at making lovely meals out of simple ingredients, and this dish is particularly representative of their austere, yet comforting, cuisine. Garlic chive flowers, which are crisp, sweet, and slightly oniony, match up perfectly with the pressed bean curd. The dish is rounded out with salt as it is flash-fried in oil. Carnivores can substitute julienned pork for the bean curd; just marinate it in a mixture of rice wine and grated ginger before tossing it into the hot wok.

1 bunch garlic chive flowers (about 1 pound)
4 squares (about 8 ounces) pressed bean curd
3 tablespoons peanut or vegetable oil
1 teaspoon sea salt
2 tablespoons mild rice wine

1. Snap off or trim off any tough ends on the chive flowers, rinse, and then cut them into 1-inch lengths.

2. Rinse the pressed bean curd, then cut each square horizontally into slices about ⅛ inch thick. Cut the slices crosswise into julienne about ⅛ inch wide. They should be about the same size as the cut chive flowers (see the sidebar below).

3. Set an empty wok over high heat until it smokes, add the oil and salt, and swirl them quickly to melt the salt. Add the bean curd and toss it over high heat until it sears and browns lightly. Remove the bean curd to a plate, keeping as much oil in the wok as possible. Add the chive flowers to the wok and toss them quickly until all are lightly coated with the oil. Pour the rice wine over the chives, cover the wok, and let them steam-fry for about 30 seconds. When you remove the lid, the chives should be emerald green and tender. Toss in the bean curd, taste and adjust the seasoning, and serve hot.

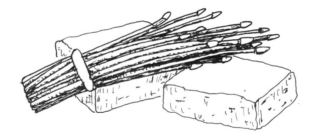

THE KEY TO MAKING MANY OF THESE DISHES successfully lies in properly prepping the ingredients. It is no coincidence that the recipe above asks you to cut the chives and the pressed bean curd into shapes that mirror each other. There are a few reasons for this.

First, the final dish will look more harmonious as a result. The similar shapes can mingle together and please the eye. Throughout this book, ingredients are often given complementary shapes and sizes, as with the thinly julienned items in Abalone Shreds with Mung Bean Sprouts (page 24), the squarish shapes in Chestnut Bean Curd (page 128), and the chunky bits in Fish Head Sandpot (page 94). This is one of the signatures of a Chinese cook's finesse.

Second, foods will cook more evenly if they possess similar forms. Hard ingredients like bamboo shoots work better in stir-fries when they're turned into fine shreds or thin shards, and the ingredients that accompany them should likewise be long and thin so they cook quickly. For braises and such, on the other hand, bamboo shoots (and whatever else is in the dish) should be given heftier shapes so that they can withstand longer cooking times.

And third, your diners will thank you: giving ingredients similar shapes and sizes allows each bite of a dish to convey different combinations of textures, flavors, and aromas.

Cuìzhá sīguā jiān 脆炸絲瓜煎

Crispy Silk Gourd Crêpes

CHAOZHOU • SERVES 6 TO 8

In the West, silk gourds mainly appear in their dried form, as loofah (or luffa) sponges. But when these squashes are still tender, they are soft, sweet, and wonderful when simply stir-fried with garlic, salt, and a splash of rice wine. In Chaozhou, silk gourds are given a special treatment that I haven't seen anywhere else: fried into crêpes with a handful of tasty condiments that play havoc with your taste buds.

CRÊPES

4 small or 2 large silk gourds (between 2½ and
    3 pounds total)
Peanut or vegetable oil for frying
¼ cup chopped dried salted radish
½ cup fried or toasted peanuts (page 411)
½ cup sweet potato starch
2 large eggs
½ cup water
2 green onions, trimmed and thinly sliced
2 teaspoons fish sauce or light soy sauce
2 teaspoons sugar
4 teaspoons toasted sesame oil
Freshly ground black pepper

GARNISH

Sea salt
Handful of cilantro, chopped

1. Remove the skin on the silk gourd with a potato peeler and cut off the stem and flower ends. Cut the squash into ¼-inch-thick slices. Place a large frying pan over medium-high heat and pour in about 3 tablespoons oil. Arrange a layer of the slices in the hot oil and fry on both sides until browned and soft (adding more oil as needed), then remove them to a small work bowl. Repeat this step with the rest of the squash. You should end up with about 2 cups cooked squash.

2. Rinse the salted radish in a sieve and shake it dry. Chop the peanuts into small pieces (less than ¼ inch across), about the same size as the radish. Mix together the sweet potato starch, eggs, and water to form a batter with the consistency of heavy cream. Stir in the peanuts, radish, fried squash (as well as any juices), green onions, fish sauce, sugar, sesame oil, and pepper.

3. Return the frying pan to medium-high heat and pour in about 3 tablespoons oil. Ladle a quarter of the batter into the pan and shake the pan to distribute the squash and crunchy bits evenly. Shake the pan again after about 20 seconds to loosen the crêpe and then turn it over when the underside is a golden brown. If you're like me and prefer the crêpe to have a crispier exterior, fry both sides until they are dark brown.

4. Transfer the cooked crêpe to a clean cutting board and sprinkle it lightly with salt. Repeat Step 3 with the rest of the batter until all of it has been fried. The crêpes can be made ahead of time up to this point and reheated in a 325°F oven until crispy right before serving. To serve, slice each crêpe into 4 to 6 wedges and garnish with the cilantro.

Yífŭ miàn 伊府麵

Yi Residence Noodles

GUANGDONG • SERVES 8

This dish is named for Yi Bingshou, the famous Qing dynasty calligrapher. One day, when Yi was stationed as a bureaucrat in Guangdong, he invited some guests over for dinner. As the story goes, his chef was running behind schedule and accidentally dumped some cooked noodles into a pot of boiling oil. There was no time to correct the error, so the chef poured some seasoned broth over the fried noodles and served them. The dish was a hit, and it became known as "noodles from the Yi residence," or *Yifu mian*.

This pasta is so easy to prepare that it is now credited as the precursor to today's instant noodles. The only challenge is finding good prepared *yifu* noodles, which can be difficult even in a busy Chinese supermarket. The good news is that *yifu* noodles can be made at home: all that is required is a simple egg dough, which can be cut as thickly or as thinly as you like. I prefer noodles about ¼ inch wide—sort of like fettuccine.

This dish also makes for a terrific bowl of birthday noodles: in China, the traditional celebratory dish is not cake and ice cream, but soup noodles with an egg on top. The egg symbolizes birth, and the noodles (which should be thin and as long as possible) signify longevity.

NOODLES

4 cups (more or less) peanut or vegetable oil
2½ to 3 pounds ¼-inch-wide whole egg
    dough noodles (page 389 or store-bought),
    cooked and drained

TOPPING

8 large shrimp, peeled and deveined (see page 457)
10 to 12 ounces firm white-fleshed fish fillets
¼ cup mild rice wine
1 pound yellow chives
3 tablespoons peanut or vegetable oil
¼ cup peeled and finely shredded fresh ginger

STOCK

6 cups unsalted chicken stock (page 380),
    divided into 4 cups and 2 cups
2 tablespoons regular soy sauce, divided in half
¼ cup mild rice wine, divided in half
2 tablespoons fish sauce, divided in half
2 tablespoons toasted sesame oil, divided in half
2 tablespoons sugar, divided in half
2 tablespoons black vinegar, divided in half
¼ cup coarsely chopped cilantro

1. Place a large platter next to the stove, cover it with parchment paper or paper towels, and have chopsticks and a Chinese spider ready. Place a wok over medium-high heat, add the oil, and when a chopstick inserted into the oil is immediately covered with lots of bubbles, grab a handful of the noodles and lower them gently into the hot oil. Immediately use your chopsticks to stir them around, as they will start to puff up and double in size. Turn them over and continue to fry them until they have hardened but not yet browned, then remove them to the platter to drain. Repeat with the rest of the noodles, continuing to fry them in small batches until all have been fried. The noodles can be cooled off completely and stored in resealable plastic bags in the refrigerator for up to a week or so.

2. About 30 minutes before serving this dish, prepare the toppings and the stock: cut the shrimp horizontally in half (so that you have 2 large shrimp-shaped pieces per shrimp) and slice the fish into pieces about ¾ inch wide. You can keep the skin on, if you like. Place the shrimp and fish in a small bowl and toss with ¼ cup rice wine. Pick over the yellow chives, removing any withered or slimy leaves, and then trim off the stem ends, wash carefully, and drain. Shake the chives dry and cut them into 1-inch lengths.

3. Set the wok over medium-high heat and add the oil. Swirl it around and add the ginger. Let the ginger sizzle for a couple of seconds until it smells great, then raise the heat to high, drain the shrimp and fish, and add them to the hot oil. Toss them in the oil for a few minutes until the shrimp is pink and the fish is opaque. Scoop them out into a medium work bowl, leaving most of the oil in the wok. Return the wok to high heat, add the chives, and toss them around until they are barely wilted. Scoop them out and place them on top of the shrimp and fish.

4. Without bothering to rinse out the wok, return it to high heat, add 4 cups of the stock and half each of the soy sauce, rice wine, fish sauce, sesame oil, sugar, and vinegar. Bring to a full boil and then add all of the fried noodles. Toss the noodles in the stock and cook them over high heat, stirring occasionally, for 5 to 10 minutes, or until the stock has been absorbed. Empty the noodles out onto a rimmed serving platter.

5. Put the remaining 2 cups stock in the wok along with the remaining soy sauce, rice wine, fish sauce, sesame oil, sugar, and vinegar. Bring to a boil and then add the shrimp, fish, and chives. Bring back to a boil, taste and adjust the seasoning, and then toss in the cilantro. Toss to mix well and pour over the noodles. Serve immediately.

Májiàng miàn 麻醬麵

Sesame Noodles

TAIWAN MILITARY FAMILIES AND BEIJING • SERVES 4

I have adored this simple street food ever since I took my first bite of it at a little stand on Nanhai Road, just a block or so away from my workplace. It was a very simple affair—just fresh noodles tossed with little more than toasted sesame paste, plus a dash of black vinegar, sugar, and soy sauce—but I always luxuriated over this quiet, solitary lunch.

Over the years I have messed around with this dish quite a bit, as I found it to be another one of those basic templates that ought to be tinkered with until you find your sweet spot. Peanut butter found its way into the mix to provide another layer of nutty creaminess and more complexity to the flavors. Garlic soon lent its fragrance, as did homemade chili oil with lots of goop, which can make this taste a whole lot like Sichuan's dandan noodles (*dāndānmiàn* 擔擔麵). Like stone soup, this just gets better as more delicious things are added.

2 tablespoons toasted sesame oil or chili oil plus goop (the recipe on page 436 is really good here)
2 tablespoons toasted sesame paste (page 413 or store-bought)
2 tablespoons peanut butter, crunchy or smooth
1 or more cloves garlic (I like 2 cloves), finely chopped
1 green onion, trimmed and finely chopped, white and green in separate piles
1½ tablespoons regular soy sauce
1 tablespoon dark vinegar
1 teaspoon sugar
8 ounces dried wheat noodles of any kind

1. First make the sauce: in a wok, mix together the sesame oil (or chili oil and goop), sesame paste, peanut butter, garlic, onion whites, soy sauce, vinegar, and sugar. Heat this slowly over medium-low heat, stirring constantly, until the sauce is slightly cooked through, then taste and adjust the seasoning.

2. Bring a saucepan filled with water to a boil, add the wheat noodles, and cook until barely done. Scoop out the noodles and add to the wok, reserving the pasta water. Toss the noodles until they are all well coated, adding some of the hot pasta water as needed to keep them from clumping up. (To be honest, this will take more water than you expect.) Divide the noodles among the bowls, sprinkle on the onion greens, and serve hot. I like to offer small bowls of the cooking water on the side as a simple soup that can be used to thin down the sauce as needed.

ONCE A STEPPING-STONE FOR SPANISH, Portuguese, and Dutch explorers—the red hair of some southern Taiwanese children still bears witness to a European sailor great-great-great-grandfather or two somewhere upstream—Taiwan is also home to fourteen recognized ethnic minorities, including the Atayal, Amis, Yami, and Paiwan, with most of them concentrated in the high mountain range that runs down the center of the island and others on the eastern plains and the small islands to the southeast. The Portuguese referred to Taiwan as *la ilha Formosa* (the pretty isle), and as a result Formosa was Taiwan's more common name until recently.

The indigenous people traditionally rely on taro and sweet potato as their main starches, although millet and sticky rice are common, as well. Many of them also prepare a dish called *zhútǒngfàn* 竹筒飯—or "bamboo cylinder rice"—in which rice is cooked in a section of freshly cut bamboo. The grains are allowed to soak for a couple of hours, one end of the bamboo is sealed with fresh leaves, and the container is then cooked over an open fire. The result is amber-colored rice scented with bamboo. Nowadays you can occasionally find this dish in Taiwanese villages with relatively large minority populations, such as Wulai, near Taipei. Variations are prepared as far away as Yunnan, and even down in Southeast Asia.

Chǎobǐng 炒餅

Stir-Fried Grilled Breads

TAIWAN'S MILITARY FAMILIES AND NORTHERN CHINA ·
SERVES 4 TO 6

As you can tell by these recipes, my favorites of all
the Taiwan Military Family dishes are their pastas.
Whenever stewed tilapia was on the museum's staff
lunch menu, I would usually opt to visit one of the little
stands down the road, where an elderly Mainlander
would whip up a small bowl of hot pasta like this,
along with a little saucer of blanched celtuce leaves.
Afterward I would take a walk through the nearby
botanical gardens and watch the turtles and dragon-
flies dart among the swaying lotuses. It was a magical
ninety-minute lunch break.

The pasta in this dish, called *làobǐng* 烙餅, looks
somewhat like a thick crêpe. It's cut into strips and
then stir-fried with vegetables and a bit of pork or eggs.
Nowadays, I much prefer this recipe with fresh black
mushrooms instead of pork, but it's all a matter of taste.

1 recipe grilled breads (page 396)
10 large black mushrooms, fresh or dried and plumped up,
    or 4 ounces fatty pork
¼ cup soy sauce
2 tablespoons mild rice wine
1 small bunch garlic chives (about 12 ounces)
1 pound mung bean sprouts
½ cup peanut or vegetable oil, divided in half
2 tablespoons peeled and finely julienned fresh ginger
4 large eggs, lightly beaten
2 tablespoons toasted sesame oil

1. Slice the grilled breads into pieces ½ inch wide and
keep them covered with a dry tea towel.

2. If using mushrooms, remove the stems and slice the
caps into thin pieces; for pork, thinly slice it against
the grain and then crosswise into matchsticks. Place
the mushrooms or pork in a small work bowl and toss
with the soy sauce and rice wine. While the mushrooms
or pork is marinating, prep the vegetables: trim off
the bases of the chives, rinse the stalks, and then cut
them crosswise into ½-inch lengths; shake the pieces
dry in a colander. Rinse the bean sprouts in another
colander and shake dry.

3. Place a wok over high heat, and when it is hot, add
half the oil plus the ginger. Drain the mushrooms or
pork, reserve the marinade, and add the mushrooms
or pork to the wok. Stir-fry the mushrooms until they
are slightly browned, or the pork until it turns white,
then toss in the chives and bean sprouts and continue
to toss over high heat to sear the vegetables. When the
bean sprouts are still crisp but do not taste raw, scoop
everything out into a clean work bowl.

4. Return the wok to high heat and add the remaining
¼ cup oil. Swirl the oil around in the wok and then
add the eggs. Tip the wok this way and that to form a
large omelet. Turn the omelet over to cook briefly on
the second side and then remove to a cutting board.
Slice the omelet into ½-inch-wide strips.

5. Add the sliced breads to the hot wok and toss them
without adding any extra oil, as this will crisp them
up a bit. When they are hot, toss in the contents of
the work bowl and the eggs, as well as the reserved
marinade and the sesame oil. Taste, adjust the seasoning, and serve.

Chángfěn 腸粉

Cheong Fun

PEARL RIVER DELTA · MAKES 6 ROLLS

This dish, with its soft rice sheets wrapped around fat, fresh shrimp, is a mainstay at most dim sum restaurants. Some places substitute shreds of roast duck, savory ground pork, or *char siu* for the shrimp, while others insert only a crispy Chinese cruller and call the dish *zháliǎng* 炸兩. I've always had a very difficult time deciding between the different versions, so in this recipe, I've gone all out and combined the sweet-savory flavors of a traditional meaty roll with the crunch of *zhaliang*. I've also added fried cellophane noodles, a sprinkle of almonds, and a sweet-salty sauce.

If you have a vibrant Vietnamese or southern Chinese community in your area, you might be able to substitute store-bought unsliced fresh rice noodles (*héfěn* 河粉). If not, these rice sheets, which are also often called *cheong fun*, are easy to make. It took me a long time to figure out the right way to do it because almost everyone says to use rice flour, which gives you mushy and grainy results. What you want are silky sheets, something that can be achieved only by grinding soaked rice into a soft slurry, with a touch of wheat starch and tapioca flour to bind everything together just right.

NOODLES

⅔ cup white rice soaked overnight in water to cover and then drained (about 1 cup soaked)

¾ cup cool water

2 teaspoons wheat starch

1 teaspoon tapioca flour

2 teaspoons canola or other flavorless oil

Pinch of sea salt

Spray oil

FILLING

1 cup shredded roast duck or char siu (page 206 or store-bought)

1 bundle cellophane noodles

Peanut or vegetable oil for frying

¼ cup slivered almonds, toasted

Cilantro or shredded green onion

SAUCE

¼ cup sweet soy sauce (page 439 or store-bought)

¼ cup peanut or vegetable oil

1. Rinse the soaked rice in a sieve, shake it dry, and toss it into a blender. Add the water, wheat starch, tapioca flour, oil, and salt. Blend on high speed until you have a very thin, smooth batter. Spray 2 pans (either 8 × 8 inches or 9 × 7 inches) with oil. Pour 3 or more inches water into a wide braising pot and bring the water to a boil. Place 1 of the oiled pans in the pot for a few seconds to heat up its bottom then remove pan from pot.

2. Measure out a scant ¼ cup of the rice batter, pour it into the heated pan, and swirl the pan around so that the batter completely and evenly covers the bottom. (The heat will set some of the batter and make it easier for it to grip the bottom.) Place the pan in the pot (no trivet is needed, for it will float like a little boat) and cover the pot. Steam the batter for a few minutes. It will be done when bubbles puff up from the bottom of the batter and the sides pull away from the pan. Use a dry towel or oven mitt to remove the hot pan from the pot. Place it on a heatproof counter. While it is cooling off slightly, repeat this step with the other pan.

3. While that second pan is cooking, loosen the edges of the cooked rice sheet with an offset spatula. Tilt the pan on its side, nudge one end, and the sheet should just roll up onto itself like a carpet. Remove the sheet, lay it out flat on a large plate, and let it cool off. If the sheet doesn't come out easily, the pan needs to be cleaned, dried, and oiled well before the next batch. Repeat with the rest of the batter until done. You should have 6 sheets total.

4. While the sheets are cooling off, prepare the duck or pork. If the meats are fatty or flabby, heat them in a 425°F oven on a rack to crisp up the skin and meat, and to melt off the extra fat. Cool the meat slightly, then shred or cut it into thin strips.

5. To fry the cellophane noodles, pour oil to a depth of 2 inches into a wok and heat over medium-high until the oil starts to shimmer. Break the noodles apart in large pieces in a paper bag so that they don't shoot out all over your kitchen. Line a large work bowl with a paper towel and have a Chinese spider or slotted spoon ready. Drop 1 noodle into the oil, and if it immediately puffs up, the oil is ready; if it browns, lower the heat. Fry the noodles in small handfuls, removing them to the prepared bowl as soon as they are puffy and white. (This step can be done ahead of time.)

6. Lay one of the rice sheets out on a flat work surface with the shiny side on the bottom and the dull side on top; if it is not a square sheet, have one of the shorter edges in front of you. Layer a sixth of the duck or pork along the closest edge, sprinkle on a sixth of the almonds and a bit of the cilantro or green onions, and place an inch-high layer of the fried cellophane noodles on top. Roll the sheet up as tightly as you can without crushing the noodles; the sheet should stick to itself by the time it is rolled up. Place it on a serving platter and repeat with the rest of the sheets and filling. Use kitchen shears to cut each roll into 3 or 4 pieces.

7. Heat the sweet soy sauce and oil together in a saucepan until they boil; pour this sauce over the stuffed rice sheets and serve.

ALTHOUGH THE EARLIEST RECORDS OF TEA being enjoyed in China date back to the first millennium BCE, it took a while before tea was provided to paying customers. The earliest such establishments opened up for business during the Northern and Southern dynasties (386–589). Refreshments like dim sum came much, much later. It was only about two centuries ago that tea snacks were finally offered in teahouses as a way to attract more customers. Popping up all across China, on both sides of the Yangtze River and even beyond the Great Wall in the far north, these teahouses provided their guests with more elegant surroundings so that they could better enjoy their tea and snacks.

Pastries, *baozi*, and other *dianxin* in North China tend to be hefty, as they are meant to satisfy hungry people in cold climates. It was in the south that tea snacks were transformed into the miniature works of art that we now know of as dim sum.

Shāchá níuròu chǎohé 沙茶牛肉炒河

Stir-Fried Rice Noodles and Satay Beef

CHAOZHOU · SERVES 2 AS A MAIN DISH,
4 AS A SIDE DISH

In this tantalizing dish, fresh rice noodles, called *hefen*, support rich slices of steak, crunchy mung bean sprouts, and the unmistakable sauce known as satay, or *shacha*, a staple of Chaozhou cuisine.

Here are my secrets for perfect *hefen*: First, the rice noodles should be really fresh and soft. Second, they must first be tossed in soy sauce; it is the soy sauce that browns in the wok, not the noodles themselves. Third, when the noodles are thrown into the wok, they must be seared quickly and with lots of oil. The oil can be poured off at the end, but it's important that there is plenty during the cooking process, so that the noodles can move freely.

STEAK

6 ounces flank steak or other good cut of beef

2 cloves garlic, minced

½ teaspoon cornstarch

2 teaspoons peanut or vegetable oil

NOODLES AND VEGETABLES

1 pound fresh rice noodles, cut into ½-inch-wide slices
    (see Tip, page 303)

1 tablespoon regular soy sauce

6 ounces mung bean sprouts

4 black mushrooms, fresh or dried and plumped up

½ cup peanut or vegetable oil

1 tablespoon peeled and finely chopped fresh ginger

2 green onions, trimmed and cut into 1-inch lengths

SAUCE

2 tablespoons mild rice wine

1 tablespoon regular soy sauce

2 teaspoons sugar

3 tablespoons satay sauce, or to taste

1. First prepare the steak: Cut the meat against the grain into thin slices, keeping any fat on. Place the meat in a small work bowl and add the garlic, cornstarch, and oil; toss and let the steak marinate while you prepare the rest of the ingredients.

2. Empty the rice noodles into a large work bowl and separate the strands as much as possible. Toss with the soy sauce. Rinse the sprouts and shake dry. Remove the stems from the mushrooms and save those for stock (page 381); cut the caps into ¼-inch-thick slices.

3. Set a dry wok over high heat. Have a clean plate next to the stove. Add about a third of the sprouts to the wok and toss them quickly until they sear but are still very crisp; remove them to the plate and repeat with the rest of the sprouts in two batches until all are cooked. (Cooking them without oil gives them great contrast to the rest of the ingredients.) Add the oil to the wok, and when it is hot, add the ginger and green onions and heat for about 10 seconds to release their fragrance. Toss in the mushrooms and steak and stir these quickly just until the meat has lost its pink color. Use a Chinese spider or slotted spoon to transfer the solids from the oil to the bean sprouts.

4. Mix together the sauce ingredients in a small work bowl. Return the wok to high heat and add the rice noodles. Toss them only until they start to brown, then drain off almost all of the oil. Add the sauce and toss with the noodles. Return the meat and vegetables to the wok and toss everything again. Serve immediately.

Bàozǐ fàn 煲仔飯

Crusty Rice with Charcuterie

GUANGDONG · SERVES 1 (SEE TIPS)

Written *baozi fan* (rice boiled in a little pot) in Cantonese and *làwèi fàn* 臘味飯 (charcuterie-flavored rice) in Mandarin, this one-pot wonder is a great winter comfort dish. In this recipe, I have added fresh black mushrooms and some white liquor, as well as a drizzle of sesame oil to hasten the browning. It's the rice that is the real treat: crunchy and golden, it fries up in the charcuterie drippings and sesame oil, emitting delicious aromas as it cooks.

½ cup jasmine rice
1 *lop chong* (sweet Cantonese sausage) (see Tips)
1 duck liver sausage (see Tips)
½ strip cured pork belly (see Tips)
1 black mushroom, fresh or dried and plumped up
2 teaspoons (or so) peeled and finely shredded
    fresh ginger
1 tablespoon white liquor
1 teaspoon regular soy sauce
1 cup water
2 teaspoons toasted sesame oil

1. Prepare a small covered sandpot, preferably one with a handle, by rinsing it out. Place the rice in a sieve, rinse under cool tap water, and drain.

2. Rinse the sausage and pork belly and pat them dry with a paper towel. Cut both sausages on a sharp diagonal into thin slices. Remove and discard the skin from the pork belly and slice the meat on a sharp diagonal, as well. Remove the stem from the mushroom and thinly slice the cap.

3. Place the rice in the sandpot and flatten it into an even layer. Place the meats and mushroom on top however you wish. Sprinkle the ginger over them and then pour in the white liquor, soy sauce, and water. Cover the sandpot, place it on one of the smaller of your stove's elements, and turn on the heat to high (see Tips). Bring the liquid in the sandpot to a boil, then cover the sandpot and lower the heat to the lowest setting. Set the timer for 17 minutes, then peek inside the cover to make sure the rice is fully cooked and the water has been absorbed. If not, cook 2 to 3 minutes longer and check again.

4. Pour the sesame oil into the center of the sandpot, re-cover, and raise the heat to medium-high. At this point you have to rely on your ears and nose to tell you when the rice is done: listen for the light crackling noises of the rice being fried to a crisp and keep your nose attuned to the smell of popcorn, which tells you that the rice has been toasted. When it sounds and smells ready, remove the sandpot from the heat and use a wide spoon to lift up one edge of the rice. It should be a toasty brown color. If not, return it to the heat and keep watch. Serve the dish while it is still hot and crackling.

This recipe is for one serving, but you can make as many as you wish. Just be sure to have a small covered sandpot for each person. Also, you will need a small stove burner for each sandpot, because large burners will focus too much of their heat around the edge of the pot and make it too hot to touch.

Jasmine rice is the preferred variety here. Basmati could be used in a pinch, but it has a looser texture.

Any sort of Cantonese charcuterie (see page 478) can be used here—whatever you like and is available will do.

If you have only two small stove burners and you want to make more than two servings, prepare your extra sandpots ahead of time up to Step 3 and keep them hot in a warm oven. Then, just before serving, brown the bottoms as in Step 4.

Xiányú jīlì chǎofàn 鹹魚雞粒炒飯

Fried Rice with Chicken and Salted Fish

GUANGDONG · SERVES 2 AS A MAIN DISH,
4 AS A SIDE DISH

Any number of fried rice dishes might appear on the menu of a Guangdong-style restaurant, but as far as I'm concerned, this one is the best. The salted fish adds a delicious edge to what might otherwise be a rather ordinary plate of chicken fried rice, deepening the flavors and amping up the *xianwei* factor. And then there is that handful of shredded lettuce: few cuisines would be able to take something so boring and turn it into a culinary star, but the chefs of Guangzhou make it happen. Drizzle a little sesame oil on top of everything and you're all set for a great meal.

2 cups cooked long-grain white rice, chilled, or 1 cup
    uncooked jasmine or other long-grain white rice and
    1½ cups water (or whatever your rice steamer calls for)
6 tablespoons fresh peanut or vegetable oil,
    divided into 1 tablespoon, 3 tablespoons,
    and 2 tablespoons
1 cup diced and gently shredded cooked chicken
1 slice salted fish in oil (see Tips, page 209, or
    store-bought), skinned, boned, and flaked
2 large eggs, lightly beaten
Sea salt or fish sauce to taste
2 cups finely shredded iceberg or romaine lettuce
1 green onion, trimmed and finely chopped
1 teaspoon toasted sesame oil

1. If you do not have 2 cups cold cooked long-grain white rice, make some fresh, either in a rice steamer or on the stove (page 383). Refrigerate it when it has cooled to room temperature. The rice can be made ahead of time and either refrigerated or frozen. Defrost it completely before proceeding, but be sure to make this with only cold rice.

2. Place a wok over medium-high heat, and when it is hot, add 1 tablespoon of the oil. Swirl the oil around before adding the chicken and fish. Fry these, stirring often, until they are golden brown. Scrape them into a small work bowl.

3. Pour 3 tablespoons of the oil into the hot wok and swirl it around. Break up any large clumps in the rice and add it to the wok. Toss the rice over medium to medium-high heat until it starts to steam and turn golden in places.

4. Make a well in the center of the rice, pour in the remaining 2 tablespoons oil and then add the beaten eggs to the oil. Let the eggs set for a moment, then cook them in this well until they look curdled and are about half done. Add the fried chicken and fish and toss everything together gently but thoroughly. Taste and adjust the seasoning with a sprinkle more salt or some fish sauce. Just before serving, add the shredded lettuce and green onion. Drizzle the sesame oil over the top, give the rice a final toss, and serve.

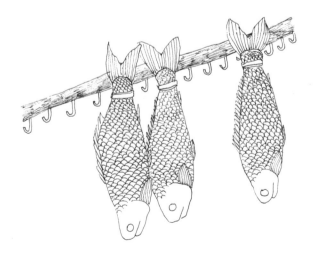

Hǎinán yùfàn 海南芋飯

Taro Rice

HAINAN • SERVES 4 TO 6

Whenever I serve this, my guests act like they're having dessert for dinner. This inspired combination of chewy rice, creamy taro, crunchy peanuts, rich coconut, and ample aromatics makes it seem like there's nothing else on the table.

2 cups long-grain sticky rice

1 mature taro (about 12 ounces)

1 cup unsweetened flaked or shredded dried coconut

3 or 4 cloves garlic

1 teaspoon sea salt

3 green onions, trimmed and finely chopped

½ cup fried or toasted peanuts (page 411)

1. Rinse the rice in a sieve and then soak it in cool water for about 2 hours, until it passes the fingernail test (page 480). Drain the rice and then steam in a steamer basket lined with cloth (see page 49) for about 40 minutes, adding more water if necessary, until tender but still nicely chewy.

2. While the rice is steaming, peel the taro and cut into 1-inch dice (wear gloves if you are allergic to raw taro). Steam the taro until it can be easily pierced. Turn the taro out onto a cutting board and coarsely chop it.

3. While both the rice and taro are steaming, spread the coconut on a small tray and toast in a toaster oven at 300°F just until it begins to turn golden and smells wonderful. Empty the coconut into a large work bowl to stop the cooking. Finely chop the garlic, add it to the coconut along with the salt and green onions, and then work all of the ingredients together, preferably with your fingers, to release their fragrances. Add the hot cooked rice and taro and toss together well. Scoop the rice out into a serving dish, sprinkle the peanuts on top, toss lightly, and serve immediately.

CHINA'S BEST ROAST MEATS AND POULTRY have traditionally come from Guangzhou. This has led to such local delights as pork ribs and meaty chunks being baked with sweet, reddish sauces (page 206), crispy-skinned piglets, and sweet-savory poultry of every flavorful persuasion that are part of the local way of cooking called *shāolà* 燒臘 (roasted meats and charcuterie).

On the sweet side, the city is known for baked goods: flaky tart crusts, crispy cookies, and savory crunchy pastries. These are all sold in bakeries and dim sum teahouses alongside traditional steamed goodies.

Noodles are unique in Guangzhou, partially because pasta is almost as popular as rice, but even more because of the inventiveness that has been used to create local specialties. Here the noodles are usually made with whole eggs, unlike the plain flour-and-water strands of the North. Flavors are often infused into the dough, too—things like shrimp roe or ground scallops or powdered fish—that then require only the simplest sauces of, say, hot oil or clear broth.

Egg pasta also fries up better and holds its shape well even when fried (page 214), and it has a more tensile bite to it. Sold fresh or dried, these noodles are especially popular in street stalls and simple restaurants, where they are eaten throughout the day, from breakfasts to late-night snacks.

Yóufàn, mǐgāo 油飯、米糕

Sticky Rice Two Ways

SOUTHERN FUJIAN AND TAIWAN · SERVES 8 TO 10

If you ever happen to be at a feast in southern Fujian or Taiwan, there is a good chance that a big bowl of savory sticky rice will appear. Bits of pork, black mushrooms, and crispy shallots mingle with seasoned rice in this dish, making it something like a deconstructed Chinese tamale. Molded sticky rice is almost the same thing, but it is normally served in individual portions as street food. You can, in fact, wrap either of these recipes in bamboo leaves (for directions on wrapping Chinese tamales, see page 385) and then steam them for the perfect *zongzi*, maybe even sneaking in a couple of brined egg yolks (page 422) as a special treat.

My favorite place to eat *migao* was at a little hole-in-the-wall in the Taipei suburb of Shipai, which was operated by a middle-aged Taiwanese lady. She seemed to make the best *migao* anywhere, and it is her recipe that I have attempted to re-create. She would steam the dish in bamboo cups that had been used for so many years that they were deeply saturated with layer after layer of soy sauce and oil. I bought cups just like hers in Taipei, but they cracked in the dry air of California. I've since devised a great substitute: glass jelly jars. They're cheap, perfectly sized, and you can use them for other things in between your sticky rice celebrations.

SAVORY STICKY RICE

4 dried black mushrooms
2 tablespoons dried shrimp
2 cups long-grain sticky rice
3 ounces pork belly, with the skin removed
1½ tablespoons dark soy sauce
2 tablespoons mild rice wine
Freshly ground black pepper
¼ cup shallot *mingyou* (page 435) or toasted sesame oil
¾ cup fried shallots (page 435)
½ cup stewed peanuts (page 412)
1 teaspoon sugar

MOLDED STICKY RICE

Above recipe for savory sticky rice except use only
    2 tablespoons oil and omit the stewed peanuts
Spray oil
8 (8-ounce) jelly jars

GARNISH

Chopped cilantro
¼ cup toasted or fried peanuts (page 411),
    crushed, for the molded sticky rice
Soy paste for the molded sticky rice

1. *For both recipes, use the following directions:* The night before you plan to make this dish, place the mushrooms and shrimp in separate bowls, rinse them with tap water, then cover each ingredient with cool water (use at least ½ cup water for the mushrooms). Let them plump up overnight. You may also prepare them the same day as the rice by covering them with boiling water.

2. Trim off the mushroom stems and reserve the soaking liquid; cut the caps into thin slices. Pick out and discard any shrimp that are discolored, drain off and discard the soaking liquid, and cut off any sandy veins that you see, but keep the shrimp whole.

3. Rinse the rice in a sieve and dump it into a medium work bowl. Cover with cool tap water and soak for about 2 hours, until it passes the fingernail test (see page 480). Drain the rice and then steam in a steamer basket lined with cloth (see page 49) for about 40 minutes, until tender but still nicely chewy. Remove the rice from the steamer. Cut the pork against the grain into thin slices and then crosswise into julienne. Place the pork in a small work bowl with the soy sauce, rice wine, and lots of black pepper and allow the meat to marinate while you work on everything else.

4. *If you are making molded sticky rice,* reserve 16 mushroom slices and 8 shrimp for garnish. Chop the remaining shrimp and add them to the rest of the mushroom slices. *If you are making the savory sticky rice,* chop all of the shrimp and add them to the mushrooms. Drain off and reserve the meat marinade.

5. Set a wok over medium-high heat and add the oil as soon as the wok is hot. Toss in the chopped shrimp and mushroom slices and stir-fry them for a couple of minutes to release their fragrance. Add the drained meat and fried shallots, continue to stir-fry until the pork is almost done, and then add half of the mushroom soaking liquid, the reserved marinade, and the steamed rice. Toss together well, allowing the liquid to loosen the clumps. Drizzle in the rest of the mushroom liquid when the rice becomes dry.

6. *If you are making the savory sticky rice,* add the stewed peanuts and toss to mix. Sprinkle on the sugar, toss again, and taste and adjust the seasoning. (The molded rice will be served with soy paste, so be sure not to oversalt it.) Pile the mixture into a serving bowl and sprinkle on some cilantro. Serve hot.

7. *If you are making molded sticky rice,* spray 8 jelly jars with oil. Place 2 mushroom slices and 1 shrimp in the bottom of each jar. Divide the rice among the jars and pat it down gently so that there are no air pockets. Steam (see page 49) for about 10 minutes, until heated through. Turn the jars over into individual rice bowls, sprinkle with the chopped cilantro and peanuts, and drizzle on soy paste to taste (about 1 tablespoon per serving). Serve hot.

8. Both recipes freeze well and can be steamed until piping hot before serving.

NORTHERN AND SOUTHERN FUJIAN ARE LIKE a pair of mismatched fraternal twins that seem related in name only. This cultural divide starts south of the provincial capital of Fuzhou, as the dialect known as Southern Fujianese (*Mǐnnánhuà* 閩南話, a close relative of Hokkien) begins to hold sway. As mentioned earlier (see page xiii), you eat what you speak, and nowhere is that more true than in Fujian. At the region's southernmost border with Guangdong, a Chaozhou variant of this dialect is spoken, and Chaozhou dishes are enjoyed; the inland mountains, meanwhile, are home to the Hakka language and cuisine.

As in Chaozhou, this diversity has much to do with Fujian's intensely rippled landscape. A Chinese expression describes the daunting topography well: "eight parts mountains, one part river, and one part field." In the past, those high peaks isolated scattered patches of civilization to such a degree that Fujian became one of China's most linguistically and culinarily varied provinces.

Three cities in Southern Fujian dominate the local culinary scene: Quanzhou, about halfway between Fujian's capital city of Fuzhou and its southern border with Guangdong; Xiamen, directly across the straits from Taiwan; and Zhangzhou, in a lush valley to the west.

Quanzhou used to serve as the easternmost edge of the Maritime Silk Route that once connected Fujian with the South Pacific, Africa, Arabia, and even Constantinople and Rome. So important was this city to the silk trade that the Arabs called it Zayton, a word that later morphed into "satin." In the 1800s, Quanzhou and Chaozhou served as treaty ports (see page 162), which explains why such foreign imports as Indonesia's satay wound their way into the local cuisines.

Xiamen is an island port famous for its poultry, seafood, and street snacks, and its recipes are mirrored almost exactly in Taiwan. As in much of the area, startlingly good sweet-savory combinations are employed, such as fried green onions with sugar or crushed peanut candy with cilantro.

Zhangzhou, near the border with Guangdong, shares many food traditions with nearby Chaozhou, such as *popia*, which are fresh spring-roll wrappers filled with a variety of delicious things, like fried sea moss (page 102), peanuts, stir-fried cabbage, and *char siu* (page 206). They are another example of the local penchant for inventive contrasts of salty with sweet, as well as crunchy with soft, raw with cooked, and vegetable with meat.

Guǎngdōng zhōu 廣東粥

Congee

GUANGDONG · MAKES ABOUT 4 QUARTS

There are as many recipes for congee as there are for good chicken soup. The first one here comes from a nurse friend who fell in love with the version served on the night shift when she worked in Guangzhou. The other variations are equally delicious. I realize that a gallon of anything might seem like a terrifying amount, but this is good stuff and it goes down quickly.

CONGEE

1 cup broken jasmine rice (see Tips)

¼ teaspoon sea salt

1 teaspoon peanut or vegetable oil

4 quarts plus 1 cup water

OPTIONAL SEASONINGS DURING THE COOKING

1 cup broken soy batons (see Tips and page 489),
    soaked in hot water and chopped

1 tablespoon mushroom powder,
    or regular soy sauce to taste

¼ cup mild rice wine

2 tablespoons peeled and finely minced fresh ginger

Unsalted stock (page 380 or 381) instead of water

GARNISHES (CHOOSE FROM ANY OR ALL, OR FOLLOW ONE OF THE VARIATIONS)

Lots of fried green onions (page 434)

Some oil from the fried green onions

Stir-fried mushrooms, vegetables, meat, poultry, or fish

Eggs fried sunny-side up or an omelet (page 179)

Shredded green onions, chilies, cilantro, and/or
    fresh ginger

Fried peanuts (page 411), slices of preserved eggs, or
    hard-boiled brined eggs (page 422), and/or fermented
    bean curd "cheese" (pages 420 and 421)

Regular soy sauce or chili oil, toasted sesame oil, and
    freshly ground black pepper

1. Rinse the rice in a sieve until the water runs clear, then place it in a large, heavy-bottomed pot. Mix the salt and oil into the rinsed rice and let sit for at least an hour, until the grains are gently seasoned and tenderized. This will smell fantastic.

2. Add the water and any of the optional seasonings to the pot, stir, and bring to a full boil. Lower the heat to a gentle simmer and cook, stirring occasionally and always scraping the bottom of the pan with a flat silicone spatula, for 40 minutes or so, until the grains have bloomed and the liquid has thickened. The congee will be ready when the grains have blossomed into soft little puffs. Don't overcook the rice to the point that it becomes gluey.

3. Divide the congee among 6 or more large soup bowls, leaving enough room for a generous assortment of garnishes. If you want, let people decorate their own bowls.

LOTUS LEAF CONGEE (*héyè zhōu* 荷葉粥)
This gorgeously scented rice porridge is a specialty of the Yangtze River area, and it is usually served cool or lukewarm during hot weather. Normally accompanied by little side dishes (see the appetizers selection on page 77 for some good ideas), it's an elegant and tasty way to beat the heat. A good alternative to the lotus leaves are bamboo leaves. Make the plain congee but add either 1 dried lotus leaf or 2 dried bamboo leaves that you have soaked until pliable and wiped clean. Remove the leaves before serving.

CHAOZHOU-STYLE CONGEE (*Cháozhōu mí* 潮州糜)
Follow the directions above for the basic congee, but only use 12 cups water, which will give you a thicker, glossier rice porridge that will serve around 4 people. (This is also the go-to recipe for people who are not feeling well.)

SWEET POTATO CONGEE (*hóngshǔ xīfàn* 紅薯稀飯)

This is a specialty of Southern Fujian and Taiwan, where whole restaurants are dedicated to nothing but this delicious congee and the small dishes that accompany it. Make the Chaozhou-style congee, but while the rice is cooking, peel 2 or 3 red sweet potatoes and cut them into large (1-inch) squares. Steam the sweet potatoes or simmer them in a small amount of water until they are barely cooked through, then add them to the congee 10 or 15 minutes before it is done; add more water if necessary to make the congee as thin or thick as you like it.

PORK AND PRESERVED EGG CONGEE
(*pídàn shòuròu zhōu* 皮蛋瘦肉粥)

Flavor plain congee with 1 tablespoon mushroom seasoning. Toast 2 Chinese crullers (*youtiao*) in a toaster oven until crisp. Meanwhile, heat ¼ cup toasted sesame oil over high heat and add ¼ cup peeled and julienned fresh ginger; fry the ginger until crisp and remove it to a small dish. Add ½ cup julienned pork to the hot oil and stir-fry until it has lost its pink color, then divide the pork and oil among 4 to 6 large soup bowls. Cut 4 preserved eggs into thin wedges and divide them among the bowls. Heat the congee until it almost starts to boil, then divide it among the bowls (extra congee can be added to the bowls halfway through the meal). Sprinkle the bowls with ½ cup finely chopped green onions and ¼ cup fried peanuts (page 411). Cut the crullers into thin rings and serve on the side as crunchy bits that diners can add to the congee as they eat. An even tastier way to make this is to shred roast pork (*siu yuk*, or *shāoròu* 燒肉) from a Cantonese deli and use that instead of the stir-fried pork.

SAMPAN CONGEE (*tǐngzǐ zhōu* 艇仔粥)

This version calls for good Guangdong-style deli meats. Flavor plain congee with 1 tablespoon mushroom seasoning. Divide ½ cup julienned braised pork stomach (*lǔ zhūdǔ* 滷豬肚), ½ cup julienned deep-fried pork skin (*zhá zhūpí* 炸豬皮), and either ½ cup julienned braised cuttlefish (*lǔ mòyú* 滷墨魚) or ½ cup blanched squid (page 186) among 4 to 6 large soup bowls. Soak 1 skein dried rice vermicelli in warm water until soft, chop it coarsely, and divide it among the bowls. Heat ¼ cup toasted sesame oil over high heat and add ¼ cup peeled and julienned fresh ginger; fry the ginger until crisp and remove it to a small dish. Warm the congee until it almost starts to boil and then divide it among the bowls (extra congee can be added to the bowls halfway through the meal). Sprinkle the bowls with ½ cup finely chopped green onions, ¼ cup fried peanuts (page 411), and the fried ginger and sesame oil.

ROAST DUCK CONGEE (*kǎoyā zhōu* 烤鴨粥)

Flavor plain congee with 1 tablespoon mushroom seasoning. Chop 3 stalks of Chinese celery (or 1 stalk Western celery and a small bunch of cilantro) into small pieces and divide among 4 to 6 large soup bowls; grind lots of black pepper into each bowl. Toast 2 Chinese crullers in a toaster oven until crisp. Meanwhile, heat ¼ cup toasted sesame oil over high heat and add ¼ cup peeled and julienned fresh ginger; fry the ginger until crisp and remove it to a small dish. Chop ¼ Guangdong-style roast duck into thin slices (bones and all), reserving the juices (the duck can be warm or cold; it doesn't matter). Warm the congee until it almost starts to boil and then divide it among the bowls (extra congee can be added to the bowls halfway through the meal). Arrange the duck across the top of each bowl, sprinkle the top with the ginger and oil, and drizzle on the reserved juices. Cut the crullers into thin rounds and serve alongside the congee to provide some occasional crunch.

Broken jasmine rice is one of the great pleasures of the Chinese grocery store. It is cheap, and because it has been broken up into small pieces during milling, it cooks down quickly into congee. It also has an unequaled fragrance and lends the dish a terrific perfume. Get the Thai brand with three ladies on it.

For the soy batons, I use the broken pieces at the bottom of the bag. You will always have these no matter how careful you are. If you don't have soy batons on hand, fresh or frozen soy skins are fine, too; just use an approximately equal amount.

Kèjiā bǎnzòng 客家板粽

Hakka Tamales

HAKKA · MAKES 24

The Dragon Boat Festival (see page 384) occurs on the fifth day of the fifth month of the lunar calendar. In Taiwan, signs of its imminence are unavoidable, for in the weeks leading up to the big event, there are always ladies sitting outside and assembling their own version of these tamales. For dessert, check out the sweet rice tamales on page 384.

WRAPPERS

24 large dried bamboo leaves, plus a couple of extras in case some split
24 long pieces (12 inches or more) dried grass ties (*zòngxiàn* 粽線) or kitchen string

MARINADE

5 tablespoons dark soy sauce
2 tablespoons mild rice wine
2 teaspoons sugar
1 teaspoon freshly ground black pepper
1 teaspoon five-spice powder (page 441 or store-bought)

FILLING

7 black mushrooms, fresh or dried and plumped up
3 gluten batons
12 dried Chinese toon leaves, optional
1 dried soy skin
6 pieces pressed bean curd
4 teaspoons unhulled or white sesame seeds
2 cups peanut or vegetable oil
½ cup stewed peanuts (page 412)
⅓ cup fried shallots (page 435)

RICE DOUGH

3½ cups sticky rice flour
½ cup Chinese flour (page 386)
1 teaspoon sea salt
About 2 cups water

FINAL TOUCHES

12 raw brined egg yolks (page 422 or store-bought), cut in half, or 24 whole raw brined egg yolks
Sweet chili sauce (page 439 or store-bought)

1. Wash the bamboo leaves carefully, being sure to avoid cutting yourself on their sharp edges (consider wearing rubber gloves). Cover the leaves (along with the grass ties, if you are using them) with very hot water. Mix the marinade ingredients together in a saucepan. Stem the mushrooms and cut the caps into ½-inch cubes. Cut the gluten batons into ¼-inch dice. Simmer the mushrooms and gluten in the marinade ingredients until the liquid is thick and syrupy. If you are using toon leaves, rinse and wipe them dry before crumbling them into a small bowl. Crumble the soy skin into smallish pieces in another small bowl. Cut the pressed bean curd into ¼-inch dice and set aside in yet another small bowl.

2. Dry-fry the sesame seeds (see page 413) in a wok over medium heat until they are just turning gold; remove them to a large bowl. Pour the oil into the wok and heat over medium heat. Separately fry the toon leaves for around 10 seconds, the soy skin until it puffs up, and the bean curd until it browns, scooping each one out with a slotted spoon or Chinese spider and adding them to the sesame seeds. Drain the mushrooms and gluten (reserve the marinade), add them to the hot oil, and cook until browned, then scoop them out and add them to the bowl, too.

3. Drain the oil out of the wok. Return the contents of the large bowl to the wok along with the peanuts, shallots, and about ¼ cup of the reserved marinade. Stir them over medium-high heat for about 5 minutes, until heated through, then let them cool down.

4. In another large bowl, mix together the rice flour, Chinese flour, and salt. Add the water in ½-cup increments, stirring in just enough water to form a barely damp dough. Knead the dough in the bowl until it is shiny, then divide the dough into 24 pieces and roll each piece into a ball.

5. Pat the bamboo leaves dry. Select the 24 nicest leaves, reserve any extra, and cover all of the leaves so they remain soft and supple. Drain and rinse the grass ties, if you're using them, and place them under the covering, as well. Before you wrap the tamales, add the filling and egg yolks to the rice dough ball as shown in

the diagram below, coating your hands with peanut oil as needed to keep the balls from sticking to your fingers. Then wrap the dough balls in the bamboo leaves as directed on page 385.

6. Bring the water in your steamer (see page 49) to a full boil and place the tamales in the steamer. Steam over high heat for about 10 minutes, then lower the heat to medium and steam for another 20 minutes.

7. Let the tamales cool until they are barely warm or even room temperature before unwrapping; this will help them keep their shape and not stick to the wrappers. Serve as is with some sweet chili sauce on the side for dipping. You can store the tamales in the refrigerator for about a week or freeze them for a longer period of time. Just steam them for about 15 minutes (30 minutes for frozen ones) and let them cool down again before serving.

FILLING HAKKA TAMALES

❶

Cover a baking sheet with a piece of plastic wrap or wax paper. Take a dough ball, make an indentation in it with your thumb, then quickly shape the ball into a thin-walled cup.

❷

Add about 1½ tablespoons of the filling to the cup, along with either a half or whole brined yolk.

❸

Close the dough over the filling and gently roll it between your hands to return it to a ball shape. It's all right if some of the filling pokes out.

❹

Place the filled ball of dough on the plastic wrap or wax paper. Repeat this with the rest of the dough and filling until you have 24 filled balls of dough.

Jiāngzhī zhuàng nǎi 薑汁撞奶

Ginger Milk Pudding

PEARL RIVER DELTA • SERVES 4

The name for this magical dish translates literally as "ginger juice bumping milk," because the fresh ginger juice used here actually causes the hot milk to congeal into a soft and creamy pudding. It's worth making this dish just to watch that fascinating process occur. It's also delicious, of course.

There are a few keys to making this dessert shine. First, you need to have fresh ginger juice. This is relatively easy to make: all you need is a coarse grater and a fine sieve. I love my bamboo ginger grater for this, and you can find your own in a Chinese hardware store, though any good grater will do. Second, use the best full-cream milk you can find; if possible, get something local and fresh. Finally, although this dish is served warm in traditional recipes, I recommend chilling it, as the pudding takes on a firmer texture in the fridge.

1 large finger fresh ginger, either young or mature
    (see Tips)
4 small pinches of sea salt
¼ cup agave syrup, plus more for the topping,
    or sugar to taste (see Tips)
2 cups organic full-fat milk

1. Grate the ginger and squeeze the pulp over a fine sieve placed on top of a small measuring cup until you have ¼ cup ginger juice. Set out 4 dessert bowls, each a little larger than ½ cup. Stir the juice and pour 1 tablespoon into each bowl.

2. Add a small pinch of salt and 1 tablespoon agave syrup or 1 teaspoon or more of sugar to each bowl.

3. Heat the milk in a microwave or on the stove until it almost boils, then, from 6 inches away, pour ½ cup hot milk into each of the bowls. Don't stir the milk, as it will automatically mix with the ginger juice and sweetener as it cascades into the bowl. Let the mixture set up into a pudding-like texture, which takes only a minute, and be sure not to stir or disturb it. Serve the puddings either warm or cold, with a swirl of agave syrup on top, if desired.

Select the plumpest, heaviest "hands" of ginger you can find: they will have the most juice. Hawaiian ginger is good and often organic.

Young ginger will have a mild heat, while older ginger packs more of a punch.

If for some reason your pudding doesn't set up, take heart, as it can be rescued. Sprinkle 1 envelope (2½ teaspoons) powdered gelatin on ½ cup cold milk and wait for 3 to 5 minutes until the gelatin blooms. Bring the ginger pudding mixture to a boil in a microwave or on the stove. Remove it from the heat, stir in the gelatin mixture until the gelatin completely dissolves, and then distribute the pudding among the bowls once more. Let cool and refrigerate until set.

Honey is tasty here, but it doesn't dissolve fast enough in the hot milk. And if you pour it on top of the cold or cool pudding, it seizes up into a sticky clump. Agave syrup behaves better.

Yēzi xīmǐ jú bùdīng 椰子西米焗布丁

Baked Coconut Tapioca Custard

GUANGDONG · SERVES 6 TO 8

Puddings and custards were not a big deal in Guangdong prior to the arrival of the British, but they have caught on since then and been altered by the local cuisine in interesting ways. This recipe has a distinctly Chinese bent to it, and the results are wonderful. Part of what makes this pudding special is its texture: chewy tapioca combines with creamy cubes of taro, all against a background of smooth custard.

TARO

1 mature taro, about 12 ounces

TAPIOCA

6 cups water
¾ cup small Chinese tapioca pearls

COCONUT CUSTARD

½ cup water
½ cup sugar
½ teaspoon sea salt
¼ cup unsalted butter
1½ cups coconut milk
2½ tablespoons cornstarch mixed with
    7 tablespoons water
1 large egg and 1 large egg yolk, lightly beaten

THE REST

About 1 tablespoon unsalted butter, cut into bits
½ to 1 cup sweetened red bean paste (page 442, with
    or without the chestnuts, or store-bought); if using
    canned red bean paste, fry it for a few minutes in
    about 2 tablespoons toasted sesame oil to rid it of
    any metallic edge

1. Peel the taro and cut into 1-inch chunks (wear gloves if you are allergic to raw taro). Place the taro in a saucepan, add water to cover, and bring to a boil over high heat. Reduce the heat to medium and simmer until the taro can be easily pierced. Drain, rinse the taro in cool water, and cut it into small batons about ¼ × ¼ × 1 inch.

2. To cook the tapioca, bring the water to a boil in a medium saucepan over high heat. Add the tapioca, stir until the water begins to simmer, and then lower the heat to medium and simmer, stirring occasionally, for about 20 minutes, until the tapioca is transparent. Remove the pan from the heat and drain the tapioca into a fine-mesh sieve.

3. To make the coconut custard, bring the ½ cup water to a boil in a medium saucepan and add the sugar. As soon as the sugar dissolves, stir in the salt, butter, and coconut milk. When the butter has melted, add the cornstarch slurry and stir constantly until the liquid has thickened. Remove the pan from the heat and whisk in the beaten egg and egg yolk and then stir in the cooked tapioca and taro.

4. Heat the oven to 450°F and place a baking sheet on the middle rack in the oven. Grease a 6-cup baking dish with butter. Pour in half the tapioca custard and spread it evenly over the bottom. Dot the custard with the bean paste and cover it with the rest of the tapioca mixture. (The custard can be made ahead up to this point, cooled down, covered, and refrigerated for up to a day. Gradually heat the chilled custard in the oven so the container does not break.)

5. Dot the surface of the custard with the butter, then place the casserole on the baking sheet in the oven. Bake the custard for about 20 minutes, until it is bubbling and the top is brown. If it doesn't brown readily but is nevertheless bubbling, brown the top with your broiler (if the container is broiler-proof) or a chef's kitchen torch. Serve the custard warm.

Lǎopó bǐng 老婆餅

The Wife's Cookies

CHAOZHOU · MAKES ABOUT 48

These filled cookies long ago traveled from their probable home, Chaozhou, to the teahouses and bakeries of Guangzhou. From there they were dispersed like dandelion seeds into the repertoires of many other southern cuisines, where they morphed into distinct but related pastries. For example, in Taiwan, winter melon jam filling has been replaced with a simple sugar center, creating the locally beloved Sun Cookies (page 234). The original cookie, though, is luscious evidence of Chaozhou's abiding love for sweets. The recipe takes a bit of time, but it can be spread over a day or two. A digital scale is helpful here for weighing out the pieces of dough and filling.

WINTER MELON JAM

About 1¾ pounds peeled, seeded winter melon
    (from a 2-pound melon)
¾ cup sugar
5 tablespoons lard or white shortening
1 teaspoon sea salt

FILLING

2 cups sticky rice flour
1 cup sugar
4½ tablespoons canola or other flavorless oil
¼ cup water
½ cup shredded coconut (sweetened or unsweetened)
¼ cup toasted sesame seeds (page 413)
½ teaspoon sea salt

DOUGH

1 recipe southern-style puff pastry (page 392)

TOPPING

2 large egg yolks, lightly beaten
Toasted sesame seeds

1. Use a food processor to puree the winter melon. If you don't have one, use a fine grater to reduce it to pulp. Dump the puree into a wide, heavy-bottomed saucepan and add the sugar, lard or shortening, and salt. Cover the pan with a spatter screen, bring the puree to a boil, and then reduce the heat to medium or medium-high so you maintain a steady simmer. Stir the puree occasionally with a silicone spatula, being sure to scrape the bottom to keep it from burning. As it reduces to a very thick jam, it will require almost constant stirring. When it is a deep yellow-green and the edges of the jam start to have what looks like white frosting on top, it should be thick enough for you to scrape down the center and see the bottom of the pan for a few seconds before the hot jam oozes back in. Scoop it into a wide bowl to cool off. You should have about 1⅓ cups jam.

2. To make the filling, first place the rice flour in a microwave-safe bowl and heat it in the microwave for 2 to 3 minutes, stirring every minute or so, to rid it of its raw taste. Try a tiny taste of the flour; it should have a neutral, pleasant flavor. Scoop it out into a wide work bowl so that it can quickly come to room temperature. Prepare the rest of the filling ingredients while the flour cools down.

3. Mix together the winter melon jam with the filling ingredients to form a light paste. Refrigerate the filling until it is slightly firm, then divide it into 48 balls, each weighing about 22 grams. Cover the balls with plastic wrap and refrigerate them if your kitchen is warm.

4. Place 2 racks in the center of the oven and heat the oven to 350°F. Line 2 baking sheets with nonstick baking mats or parchment paper.

5. To shape the cookies, make the puff pastry circles as directed in Steps 2 through 6 on page 393, working on 1 pastry at a time. Place a ball of the filling in the center of the pastry circle, then wrap the edges of the circle up and over the filling, pinch the edges together, and lightly and gently roll the filled pastry between your palms to smooth the surface. Place on a clean surface with the smooth side up and lightly roll out the cookie until it is about 2½ inches wide. Cover with plastic wrap and repeat with the remaining puff pastry and filling. Place as many of the cookies as will fit on the baking sheets so that they are about ½ inch apart (they won't spread); you will have to do this in a couple of batches.

6. Brush each cookie with the egg yolks and sprinkle with about 10 or so sesame seeds. Then, using a small knife, cut 2 slashes, about ½ inch apart and about ½ inch from the edges (see the illustration at left), down the middle of each cookie, cutting through the top layer of pastry to the filling. This will prevent the cookies from ballooning in the oven. Place the cookies in the oven and bake, rotating the sheets back to front halfway through the baking, for 20 to 25 minutes, until the tops are golden brown. Remove the cookies to a rack to cool, then store in a tightly covered container or in a resealable bag in the freezer.

Kèjiā jiǔcénggāo 客家九層糕

Hakka Nine-Layer Confection

HAKKA · SERVES 8

On the island of Hainan, fragrant pandan leaves are used instead of the dark sugar used here, giving this dish alternating layers of white and emerald green instead of ivory and warm brown. Note that the recipe calls for regular rice flour, which makes each bite melt on the tongue.

2½ cups Indica rice flour
2½ cups water
6 tablespoons white sugar
¼ teaspoon banana extract, optional
½ cup black or brown sugar
Spray oil

1. Mix the rice flour and water together in a large measuring cup until you have a smooth slurry. Pour 1½ cups of the slurry into a measuring cup and stir in the white sugar and optional banana extract. Stir the black sugar into the remaining slurry until the sugar is more or less dissolved.

2. Line the bottom of an 8- or 9-inch pan (round or square) with parchment paper and spray the inside of the pan lightly with oil. Place it in a hot steamer (see page 49).

3. When the pan is hot, pour ¼ cup of the dark slurry into it, moving the pan around so that the slurry coats the bottom evenly. Steam this for about 2 minutes. Pour 6 tablespoons of the white slurry evenly on top of the brown layer and steam for another 2 minutes. Repeat these two steps, alternating brown and white slurries, until you end up with 9 layers.

4. Steam the cake over medium-high heat for 15 minutes, cool, and cut it into diamonds. Serve warm.

Tàiyáng bǐng 太陽餅

Sun Cookies

TAIWAN • MAKES 36

Taiwan is famous for two local pastries: the pineapple-filled shortbread called *fènglísū* 鳳梨酥 and these delicious sweets. Like The Wife's Cookies (page 232), Sun Cookies feature Southern Chinese puff pastry wrapped around a sweet filling. The difference is that these cookies feature a slightly sticky center surrounded by an even shorter dough, resulting in lighter, flakier cookies. Their surface is not given an egg yolk wash, and so I stamp this whiteness with a decorative red mark (see Tips).

HIGH-FAT DOUGH

3½ cups pastry flour
1¼ cups white shortening or lard, at room temperature

LOW-FAT DOUGH

4½ cups plus 2 tablespoons Chinese flour (page 386)
1¼ cups white shortening or lard, at room temperature
¼ cup sugar
½ cup plus 2 tablespoons ice water

FILLING

¾ cup pastry flour, microwaved (see Tips)
½ cup maltose, warmed until runny
¾ cup powdered sugar
½ cup (1 stick) salted butter, softened
6 tablespoons powdered milk
½ teaspoon sea salt

DECORATION

1-inch piece carrot or radish
Few drops red food coloring

1. First make the high-fat dough: combine the flour and fat in a food processor and pulse until a smooth mixture forms. Divide it into 36 pieces (about 19 grams each) and roll each piece into a ball; chill the balls and keep them cold as much as possible while you make the cookies. (I do this by chilling the balls in a metal work bowl and covering it with a plate at all times.) You don't need to clean out the processor between the different doughs.

2. To make the low-fat dough, pulse together the flour, fat, and sugar until evenly mixed, then pour in the ice water and pulse to form a firm yet soft dough. Divide the dough into 36 pieces (about 29 grams each) and roll each piece into a ball; cover the balls with a piece of plastic wrap or a clean tea towel to prevent them from drying out.

3. To make the filling, pulse together all of the ingredients in a food processor until they clump together. Scoop the filling out, divide it into 36 even pieces (about 14 grams each), roll into balls, and cover with a piece of plastic wrap or a clean tea towel.

4. Place 2 racks in the center of the oven and heat the oven to 350°F. Line 2 baking sheets with nonstick baking mats or parchment paper. To create a stamp to decorate the tops of the cookies, cut the carrot or radish into a baton about ¼ × ¼ × 1 inch. Notch one end of the baton with a cross, and you will be left with a nifty little stamp that will decorate your cookies with four tiny squares. Place the red food coloring in a small bowl or even a bottle cap; be careful with it, as the coloring is concentrated and will stain everything that it touches.

5. To shape the cookies, using the low-fat and high-fat doughs, make the pastry circles as directed in Steps 2 through 6 for southern-style puff pastry on page 393, working on 1 pastry at a time and rolling out the first circle 3½ inches wide. Place a ball of filling in the center, then wrap the edges up and over the filling, pinch the edges together, and lightly and gently roll the filled pastry between your palms to smooth the surface. Place on a clean surface and roll out into a circle about 3 inches wide, turning the pastry over as it starts to curl to keep it flat. As the cookies are shaped, place them on the prepared baking sheets, spacing them about ½ inch apart, and cover them with plastic wrap to prevent them from drying out.

6. When you have filled a baking sheet with cookies, decorate them. Dip the carved end of your vegetable baton into the food coloring, gently tap off the excess, and then lightly stamp the center of each cookie.

7. Bake the cookies for about 20 minutes, until they puff up but not do not begin to color. The cookies should remain pale. Use a spatula to transfer them to a cooling rack. Repeat with the rest of the cookies until all have been shaped, decorated, and baked. Store the cooled cookies in sealed containers. They are very fragile, so I like to crumple up pieces of parchment paper between the layers and not pack more than 3 layers of cookies in a box. These cookies are at their best within 3 days of baking; refrigerate or freeze them if you must keep them longer.

It's always a good idea to decorate pure white foods like this with a touch of red, especially if they will be served to Chinese people. White is the color of funerals in China, and it's associated with bad luck. Red, on the other hand, is the sign of good fortune and happiness.

Cook the flour to remove its raw taste by microwaving it in 1-minute blasts until it has a pleasant flavor, but is not yet browned, about 2 to 3 minutes.

Mǎlāgāo 馬拉糕

Malay Sponge Cake

GUANGDONG AND HONG KONG • SERVES 8 TO 12

This fluffy confection looks very much like an English sponge cake, so it's my guess that Chinese cooks tweaked a European recipe to fit local tastes. Soy sauce gives the cake its rich color and adds a subtle suggestion of *xianwei* to this dim sum teahouse classic.

Spray oil
2 large eggs, at room temperature
6 tablespoons sugar
5 tablespoons peanut or vegetable oil
7 tablespoons milk (whole or low fat)
1 teaspoon vanilla extract
1 tablespoon regular soy sauce
1 cup cake flour
2½ teaspoons baking powder

1. Prepare a steamer (see page 49). Heat the water in the steamer to boiling, then reduce the heat to low. Spray an 8- or 9-inch round cake pan with oil and line the bottom with parchment paper.

2. Use a mixer to whisk the eggs until light and airy, and then slowly beat in the sugar until the mixture is light and lemon colored. Beat in the oil, milk, vanilla, and soy sauce. In a separate bowl, toss together the flour and baking powder and then beat them into the egg mixture until the batter does not have any lumps.

3. Pour the batter into the prepared pan and steam the cake for about 15 minutes, until a toothpick inserted in the center comes out clean. Cool the cake in the pan on a rack, then turn it out of the pan and cut it into wedges to serve.

Guǎngdōng yuèbǐng 廣東月餅

Guangdong-Style Moon Cakes

GUANGDONG · MAKES TEN 3-INCH MOON CAKES
OR THIRTY 1-INCH MINI CAKES

In Beijing and the rest of the north, moon cake pastry is white and flaky and known as *fānmáo* 翻毛, or "ruffled fur." In the areas around the Yangtze River, people make moon cakes out of puff pastry. And in the southern areas around Guangdong and even farther west, bakers prefer to use a cookie dough that is scented with caramel, as in this recipe.

Moon cakes are traditionally eaten during the major Chinese holiday known as the Mid-Autumn or Moon Festival. You can buy moon cakes in most Chinese markets, but they do not hold a candle to homemade ones.

2⅔ cups Chinese flour (page 386), plus more as needed
½ cup peanut or vegetable oil
¾ cup plus 1 tablespoon caramel syrup (page 446)
Sweet filling of any kind (pages 442–445)
Light glaze (page 446) or dark glaze (page 446)

1. To make the dough, place the flour in a medium work bowl. Make a well in the center and pour in the oil and caramel syrup. Mix these together gently to form a very soft dough. Sprinkle about 2 tablespoons flour on a smooth work surface and roll the dough into an even 20-inch rope; cut the rope into 10 pieces, each 2 inches long. If you are making mini cakes, roll the dough into an even 15-inch rope and cut it into ½-inch pieces. Roll each piece into a soft ball; cover the dough you are not immediately working on.

2. Place a rack in the upper third of the oven (to prevent the bottoms of the cakes from burning) and heat the oven to 325°F. Line 2 baking sheets with nonstick baking mats or parchment paper. Have 2 pastry brushes, a thin spatula, your moon cake mold, and

a pastry scraper ready. Dust the inside of the mold heavily with flour and knock out the excess.

3. *Large moon cakes:* Working on 1 pastry at a time, pat out 1 piece of dough into a 5- to 6-inch circle, making the center slightly mounded. Place a ball of filling of about 3 inch diameter in the center and wrap the dough around it (see page 229). Lightly roll the ball between your palms so the soft dough evenly covers the filling. Roll one side of the ball in some flour, then place the ball flour side down in the moon cake mold. Press lightly but firmly on the ball so it fills the mold. Turn the mold upside down and whack it on your counter to release the pastry; it may take a few tries before it comes loose. Transfer the pastry to the prepared baking sheet. Use 1 pastry brush to dust off any excess flour and the other to coat the moon cake all over with the glaze. Repeat this step with the rest of the dough, filling, and glaze until you have 10 moon cakes.

4. *Mini moon cakes:* Follow the directions in Step 3, but roll out the dough into circles about 3 inches wide and shape the filling into balls roughly 1 inch in diameter.

5. Bake the moon cakes, 1 baking sheet at a time, until they are golden brown, about 25 minutes for the small cakes and 35 to 40 minutes for the large ones. Let the pastries cool completely on the pans, and then cut into wedges to serve, preferably with cups of hot tea.

Liquor seasons the fillings for these pastries and also provides moisture that is easily evaporated as the moon cakes bake. If you don't want to use alcohol, add a little more caramel to thin out the yolk in the glazes and to bind the filling ingredients.

Store the moon cakes in resealable plastic bags. Try not to stack them, as they are easily squashed.

Moon cake molds—both big (3 inch) and small (1 inch)—can be found in Chinese kitchenware shops and online. Traditional molds are carved out of wood, but newer plastic molds have little plungers that make it easier to dislodge the filled cakes.

Mǎtígāo 馬蹄糕

Water Chestnut Gelée

GUANGDONG · SERVES 6 TO 8

I adore the delicate desserts of China's southern regions, particularly those of Guangdong. This might have something to do with the infamous sweet tooth my late father-in-law sported and all of the treats he introduced me to. He was a devotee, in particular, of thin black sesame candies, which he swore kept his hair black (though I'm pretty sure that was just an excuse to keep a stash handy). This cool, very gentle sweet was another favorite of his. With its crunchy bits of fresh water chestnuts and its subtle lavender or rose exterior, this light, translucent confection is great to serve at the end of a big meal or during an afternoon tea break.

Spray oil
16 (or so) water chestnuts, preferably fresh,
    but frozen and defrosted are all right in a pinch
1¾ cups water, divided into ½ cup and 1¼ cups
½ cup sugar
2 tablespoons unsalted butter or white shortening
¼ teaspoon sea salt
½ cup water chestnut flour
2 or more drops red food coloring, optional

1. Oil an 8- or 9-inch pan (square or round). Prepare a steamer (see page 49) that easily holds this pan.

2. Peel the water chestnuts, rinse, and coarsely chop them. You should have about 2 cups.

3. Place ½ cup of the water, the sugar, the butter or shortening, and the salt in a medium saucepan and bring to a boil. Whirl the water chestnut flour in a food processor until it is very fine. With the processor running, add the hot liquid mixture to the flour. Pour the mixture into the saucepan and stir over medium heat until a thick, bubbly batter has formed.

4. Add the water chestnuts to the batter. If you're using the food coloring, pour half of the batter into the pan and steam it for 5 minutes to set it. Add the food coloring to the remaining batter, mix well, pour it over the set layer, and steam it for another 30 minutes. If you're not using food coloring, pour all of the batter into the pan and steam it for 30 minutes.

5. Remove the pan from the steamer and let it cool. Cover with plastic wrap and chill for at least an hour. Cut the pudding into diamond shapes or squares and serve cold. Leftovers can be stored in the refrigerator in a covered container for a few days.

Fresh water chestnuts are becoming increasingly available in supermarkets. I strongly encourage you not to resort to canned ones, which taste more like can than water chestnut. Instead, hunt down frozen water chestnuts, or use jicama as a replacement.

Water chestnut flour is available in most Chinese markets and can be purchased online. Be sure to crush the flour in a food processor or blender because, right out of the box, it tends to have a crumbly texture that lumps when water is added.

I add a bit of red food coloring to one layer of this pudding because I think it's prettier that way, but the dessert looks good without it, too.

Qíngrén guǒ 情人果

Icy Green Mangoes

TAIWAN • SERVES 6 TO 8

The recipe is extremely easy if you can find green mangoes, which are often stocked in Chinese, Southeast Asian, and Filipino markets. My husband and I would often eat this dish at the restaurant Hǎibàwáng 海霸王, in Taipei and Tainan.

2 green mangoes (each 5 or 6 inches in length)
2 tablespoons plus ½ teaspoon sea salt,
    or more as needed
1 cup sugar
1½ cups water
Juice from ½ lemon

1. Wash, peel, and slice the mangoes (see the diagram below). Place the sliced mangoes in a colander, sprinkle the 2 tablespoons salt over them, toss well, and then let the bitterness leach out of the mangoes for about an hour. Rinse the mangoes well and drain. (If they are green-fleshed mangoes, repeat this step at least 2 more times.) Taste a slice of mango to ensure there's no lingering bitterness. If there is, salt and rinse the mangoes once again.

2. Combine the sugar, water, and the remaining ½ teaspoon salt in a medium saucepan and bring to a boil, stirring to dissolve the sugar. Remove from the heat and add the lemon juice. Taste and adjust the seasoning. Cool.

3. Add the mangoes to the cooled liquid and toss gently. Seal everything in a heavy-duty freezer bag and freeze it for a couple of hours. Squish the bag with your hands to break up the crystals a bit and freeze it again.

4. About 30 to 60 minutes before serving, remove the mangoes from the freezer, let them soften up a little, and then smack the bag once more. Serve the mangoes and slush in bowls with forks or toothpicks, and be sure to slurp the slush.

PREPARING GREEN MANGOES

❶
Use a vegetable peeler to remove the skin. Mangoes are slightly flat and have a large, flat pit inside. An unripe mango will be very hard, so you need to stabilize it before cutting. The way to do this is to slice off a piece of the thinnest side and set this flat part on your cutting board.

❷
Steady the mango with a heavy fork; this will keep your fingers firmly out of harm's way. Cut the fleshy sides of the mango off by slicing down both sides of the pit.

❸
You will be left with 2 mango halves and 1 pit surrounded by some flesh.

❹
Cut the flesh off of the pit before discarding it. Slice the mango halves crosswise (against the grain) into pieces no more than ⅛ inch thick.

Yēzhī xīmǐ lù 椰汁西米露

Sweet Coconut Soup

HAINAN · SERVES 8 TO 10

This has to be one of the most refreshing of all Chinese desserts. It is perfect for when the weather is hot and melons are at their best. You can use any type of melon you like, or even a mixture of them (green honeydew alongside orange cantaloupe and red and yellow watermelon, for example) to make this a riot of color. Or substitute another tropical fruit, like ripe mangoes.

My twist on this classic is to add a dash of coconut rum to kick up the tropical edge. Chill the soup for a couple of hours before serving, and thin it out with some ice water if it seems too thick.

3 cups water, divided into 2 cups and 1 cup

1 cup small Chinese tapioca pearls

½ cup rock or granulated sugar, or agave syrup to taste

1 cup ice water, plus more as needed

1 can (19 ounces) coconut milk

About 2½ pounds melon, peeled, seeded, and cut into matchsticks or small cubes (3 cups)

¼ cup coconut rum, optional

Ice cubes and mint sprigs, optional

1. Bring 2 cups of the water to a boil in a 3-quart saucepan. Stir in the tapioca pearls and keep stirring until the water comes to a boil again. Lower the heat to medium-low and stir the tapioca occasionally until it has swelled and the mixture is very thick. Add the remaining 1 cup water, which will turn the pearls translucent with little white centers. Bring the pot to a boil again, then remove from the heat. Add the sugar and stir until dissolved (or add the agave syrup to taste). Add the ice water to further shock the tapioca and loosen up the pearls, and then stir in the coconut milk, melon, and the rum, if desired.

2. Pour the soup into a covered container, let cool, and chill for a few hours before serving. If the soup is too thick, stir in some ice water until the desired consistency is achieved. On really hot days, float an ice cube or two in the soup, garnish with some mint, and get ready to feel refreshed.

Bōbàchá 波霸茶

Pearl or Bubble Tea

TAIWAN · MAKES 4 CUPS

Pearl tea was invented in Taichung, a big city in central Taiwan, but since then it has become an international hit. This drink is nothing more than sweetened tea and big, chewy balls of black tapioca called *boba*. The only thing you need in addition to the special tapioca is a fat straw, so you can suck up the tapioca balls.

Once you get the hang of this drink, you can make endless variations using fruit juice, milk, coffee, or even milkshakes instead of the sweetened tea. Play around with this recipe until you find the perfect mix. This version happens to be my favorite.

BOBA
½ cup uncooked *boba*
Juice from 1 can (16 or 20 ounces) lychees,
    or ¼ cup agave syrup

TEA AND THE REST
5 tablespoons lychee black tea leaves or any other
    fragrant black tea
6 cups boiling water, plus more for rinsing the leaves
½ cup (or more) finely chopped canned lychees,
    optional
Sweetened condensed milk to taste
Ice cubes

1. Cook the *boba* according to the package directions. (Many different varieties are now available; some are quick cooking and others take a bit of time. The label should tell you what to do.) Add the lychee juice or agave syrup to the hot tapioca and its liquid, stir, and let the *boba* soak up the flavor for a couple of hours.

2. Place the tea leaves in a sieve and rinse them with about 1 cup boiling water. Put the leaves in a large heatproof bowl and pour the 6 cups boiling water over them. Steep the tea for about 10 minutes, then strain the tea through the sieve into a pitcher. Chill for a couple of hours.

3. To serve, mix together the tea and *boba*. Add the lychees and condensed milk to taste. Put a few ice cubes in each glass and then distribute the tea, *boba*, and lychees evenly among them. Stick a fat straw and a long spoon into each glass and serve.

Boba pearls turn hard and powdery if they are chilled, so keep cooked *boba* at room temperature.

If you need to hold the cooked *boba* for longer than a few hours, refrigerate the pearls in their liquid. Then microwave the *boba* and liquid with short blasts until the pearls return to their desired texture.

Experiment with the different kinds of *boba* that are out there. Some are made with taro and have a warm, tropical flavor, while others are filled with liquid.

You can use small Chinese tapioca (see page 491) if you want a gentler texture. Little children in particular will handle these better than the large *boba*, which might be a choking hazard.

Hong Kong Milk Tea

HONG KONG · MAKES 4 CUPS

Milk tea is a product of England's colonial rule over Hong Kong, which lasted from 1841 to 1997. At its most basic, this drink is a mixture of good black tea and a drizzle of sweetened condensed milk. The traditional way of preparing the tea is to brew the loose leaves in a muslin bag. This makes the tea so well filtered that it is known locally as "silk stocking tea."

¼ cup black tea leaves (2 tablespoons loose-
    leaf Ceylon, 1 tablespoon loose-leaf *pu'er*, and
    1 tablespoon Keemun is a good mix)
4 cups boiling water, plus more for rinsing the leaves
Sweetened condensed milk to taste
Ice cubes, optional

1. Place the tea leaves in a sieve and rinse them with about 1 cup boiling water. Place the leaves in a muslin bag or mesh ball. Put the bag in a medium saucepan and add the 4 cups boiling water. Bring to a boil over high heat, cover, reduce the heat to the lowest setting, and simmer for about 5 minutes. Remove from the heat and let steep for 5 minutes.

2. To serve hot, distribute the tea evenly among 4 cups and offer condensed milk on the side. Each diner then stirs in the milk to taste.

3. To serve cold, add as much of the condensed milk as you like to the hot tea, then cool the tea to room temperature. Chill the sweetened tea and serve it over ice, if desired.

Some prefer evaporated milk and sugar instead of sweetened condensed milk. Fresh full-fat milk is good, too, though not traditional.

Yuanyang Tea

HONG KONG · MAKES 4 CUPS

Mandarin ducks, or *yuanyang*, are a symbol of marital bliss because they always appear in pairs. Conversely, because they traditionally constitute a pair of opposites—male and female—they are also used to describe foods that display stark contrasts. Whenever sticky rice dough, or *ciba* (page 306), is rolled up into layers of dark and light, for example, it is often referred to as *yuanyang*. So, too, is this drink, which is a mixture of Hong Kong Milk Tea and American black coffee.

Coffee is also used in some of Hong Kong's more inventive dim sum dishes (my favorite being deep-fried pork riblets that are coated with a sweetish coffee sauce). No coffee recipe, however, is more popular in Hong Kong culture than this beverage. If you have already made the milk tea, this one will be very easy to whip up.

2¾ cups Hong Kong Milk Tea (at left)
1¼ cups freshly brewed hot black coffee
    (dark roast is best)

1. Mix together the milk tea and coffee.

2. Serve hot or chilled.

THE CENTRAL HIGHLANDS

SICHUAN · HUNAN · YUNNAN · GUIZHOU · NORTHERN GUANGXI

Yangtze River

SICHUAN

• Chengdu

Chongqing •

Zigong •

Lake Dongting

• Changsha

GUIZHOU

HUNAN

Kaifeng •

Guilin & Yangshuo •

YUNNAN

NORTHERN
GUANGXI

"When it comes to eating chilies, the Sichuanese alone aim for the hottest ones, and moreover every single meal and every single dish has to be hot."

惟川人食椒，須擇其極辣者，且每飯每菜，非辣不可。

—XU XINYU, *A RECORD OF THINGS HEARD AND SEEN ON A TRIP TO SICHUAN*
(POSTHUMOUSLY PUBLISHED IN 1985)

Chili peppers made their way from the Americas to China several hundred years ago. In the landlocked Central Highlands, they have long since completely altered the way people eat. Raw, cooked, dried, pulverized, fermented in sauces, pickled in vinegar, or infused into oils, they unify the cuisines of the entire region. But not all of these cuisines use chilies in the same way. Sichuan's chilies are known for their numbing heat, Hunan's for their salty heat, Yunnan's for their sweet heat, Guizhou's for their sharp heat, and Northern Guangxi's for their raw heat.

Despite their popularity, chilies are rarely involved in the more refined banquets of the Central Highlands. Formal meals tend to feature restrained seasonings that reflect the ancestral tastes of the area's Han settlers. Originally hailing from the northern and eastern parts of China, the first of these immigrants arrived in the Central Highlands a little more than two thousand years ago. Their presence is still reflected in classically flavored dishes like Camphor Tea Duck (page 284) and Bean Curd Quenelle Soup (page 258).

What sets this region's cuisines completely apart from those of the rest of China, however, are the foods of its many indigenous peoples. Since prehistoric times, the Central Highlands have been home to a number of ethnic minorities, including the Zhuang, Buyei, and other Tai speakers, as well as the Miao, Yi, Dong, Yao, Bai, and many others. These were the original inhabitants of the Highlands, and they also settled much of what are now Thailand, Myanmar, Laos, and Vietnam. As a result, the foods of this region often display the hallmarks of Southeast Asian cuisines, including open-fire grilling and an abundance of raw, aromatic herbs.

The most renowned Central Highlands dishes come from Sichuan, a massive province perched on the Qinghai-Tibetan Plateau, right next to the headwaters of the Yangtze. We'll begin by looking at its cuisine, a member of both the Eight Great Cuisines (page 71) and the elite Four Great Cuisines (the North by Shandong, the East by Suzhou, the South by Guangdong, and the Center by Sichuan).

SICHUAN

Most of this province is composed of arid plateaus and mountains. The east, however, is fertile, humid, and densely populated. This is where most of Sichuan's cuisine evolved, and its cooking styles are aligned, more or less, with its three major cities: Chengdu, Chongqing, and Zigong.

At the far west end of the Sichuan Basin, near one of the Yangtze's many tributaries, is the capital city of Chengdu. Dishes here tend to be relatively refined and conservative, with subtle flavors balancing out the seasonings, as in Lotus-Wrapped Spicy Rice Crumb Pork (page 286). At the other end of the spectrum are the city's everyday foods and street snacks, which have a definite lip-numbing edge thanks to the Sichuan peppercorn. Mapo Doufu (page 268) and Wontons in Chili Oil (page 298) are good examples of this.

To the southeast of Chengdu is the vast metropolis of Chongqing, where an increase in heat is balanced by a more restrained use of the numbing peppercorn. Chongqing's kitchens love chilies, and the foods here have more of a swagger. The most popular dish here is the local fiery hotpot, slicked with chili oil and swimming with beef tripe, fish, or dog meat. Few places can match Chongqing for its range of complex flavors, as evidenced in Mouthwatering Chicken (page 255), Fish-Fragrant Prawns (page 274), and a very spicy version of Chili Chicken (page 279).

And then there is Zigong, an old salt-production center near the Fuxi River, a tributary of the Yangtze. The city's most famous culinary contributions are beef dishes devised by its salt workers. Water buffalo were used for over two millennia to extract salt from Zigong's deep saline wells, so beef has traditionally been a plentiful ingredient there. The toughness of the beef led to the creation of the "boiled" dishes of Zigong, which were little more than slices of meat cooked in a plain broth and seasoned with the local salt. Nowadays, though, any recipe with the characters *shuǐzhǔ* 水煮 ("boiled in water") in its name usually means that the meat will be cooked in a sea of searing chili oil.

HUNAN

Settlers and refugees formed the first wave of Han Chinese to set down roots in this south-central province. But as Hunan increased in wealth, its grand feast foods started to reflect the aesthetics of the Han elite, which helped this province become a member of the Eight Great Cuisines. Hunan's culinary prowess has given us alluring dishes like Honey Ham (page 288), which combines local charcuterie with Zhejiang's penchant for sweetness. Farther south, chilies reign supreme in everyday foods, though they are usually balanced by fermented black beans and/or garlic, as in Raw "White Jade" Bitter Melon (page 252) and the relatively modern Peng Family Bean Curd (page 265).

Hunan's celebrated foods mainly come from three areas: the capital city of Changsha, the northern fens of Lake Dongting, and the mountainous areas of western Hunan. Changsha is home to classic Hunan-style cooking, and its charcuterie (see page 289) ranks among the best in the country. To its north, the Lake Dongting area is known for dishes involving lotuses and water chestnuts, and for magnificent culinary inventions like Flash Fish Soup (page 260), in which translucent slices of freshwater fish are splashed with boiling stock at the dining table so that they appear to emerge out of the ether. The foods of the western mountains, meanwhile, reflect the tastes of the minorities who live in the region, including the Tujia, Miao, Dong, Yao, Zhuang, and Bai peoples.

YUNNAN

The third best-known cuisine in this region belongs to Yunnan, a name that means "south of the clouds." Stretching from the windswept steppes of Tibet down to the jungles that border Myanmar, Laos, and Vietnam, these mountainous lands are a gold mine of unique flora and fauna. Yunnan is anthropologically diverse as well, with more ethnic groups than any other region in China. For centuries, hill tribes such as the Dai, Bai, Yi, and Naxi have traversed their ancestral homelands on the once-amorphous border between China and its southern neighbors. As a result, fragrant combinations of herbs and spices have found their way into local dishes like Lemongrass Chicken (page 280), in which a whole bird is tied up with the citrusy plant before being grilled over a fire.

Other beloved aromatics include cilantro, Vietnamese coriander (*rau ram*), perilla leaves, and pandan fronds. Mushrooms are highly popular, too. Wild porcini, morels, black truffles, matsutake, "chicken fir" mushrooms that grow on termite mounds, tiger paws, and bamboo pith fungus (see page 263) are just some that local cooks use. And then, of course, there are the inevitable chilies, though the dishes here tend to have a sweet edge to them, which is another culinary tendril connecting this region to Indochina.

An introduction to the cuisine of Yunnan would not be complete without a mention of "milk fans." Invented by the Bai people (see page 256), this unique food is created by frying or braising the skin that forms on soured milk. Milk fans are often used to wrap other ingredients, like sweet bean paste.

GUIZHOU

Remote and subtropical, Guizhou is a land of extraordinary natural beauty. Nestled in the high ranges between Sichuan, Hunan, Guangxi, and Yunnan, its terrain is split by soaring peaks into complex mazes that leave little room for fertile flatlands. The intrepid farmers of Guizhou have nevertheless covered many of these mountains with undulating terraces of rice and tea. With so little arable land, the cooks of Guizhou have been forced to do more with less.

Some of the best local foods are therefore often simple delights, like Spicy Mung Bean Jelly Shreds (page 250), which contrasts cool jelly with the crunch of fried soybeans. Another great dish is Gold Hooks Hanging on Jade Plaques (page 264), in which chili powder is fried in hot oil and then made into a savory sauce that bathes bean sprouts and smooth bean curd squares. Simple, cheap ingredients like these make up the bulk of Guizhou's dishes, which favor local vegetables, rice, potatoes, pig blood, and snails, with the occasional dog, chicken, or pig reserved for major feasts. Like the other areas of the Central Highlands, Guizhou is also home to high-octane white liquors made from rice and sorghum, including *maotai* (see page 251).

NORTHERN GUANGXI

As noted in the section on the Coastal Southeast (see page 159), food from the southern half of Guangxi tastes like an extension of the food of Guangdong, while the dishes of mountainous Northern Guangxi have been influenced by the foods of its many indigenous peoples, particularly the Zhuang (see page 291). This is not a province per se, but an entity named after this ethnic group: the Guangxi Zhuang Autonomous Region. The culinary center of this area is the beautiful tourist magnet Guilin, which is famed for its spire-like hills. Guilin is best known for three ingredients: a white liquor called "three flowers" (*sānhuā* 三花), white bean curd "cheese" (page 421), and Guizhou fermented hot sauce (page 438).

The dishes of the mountainous northern area look and taste very much like what is prepared in Guizhou, Guangxi's northwestern neighbor. Red meats, especially pork, are thrown into the pot here, and the resulting broth is often enjoyed with a Chaozhou-style pasta, as in Guilin Rice Noodles (page 303). That Chaozhou connection is also evident in the sticky rice dough called Ciba (page 306), which is often folded around sweet fillings and wrapped in banana leaves before being steamed.

Like so many people of my generation, I first became interested in eating well thanks to Julia Child and her groundbreaking *The French Chef* series on PBS. I watched her show in high school, and I have to admit that if it were not for her, I probably never would have thought much about food at all. But if it were not for China, the Julia Child we know and love might never have existed. Nowadays we associate her almost exclusively with classic French cuisine, but she first discovered the joys of dining not in Europe, but in China's Central Highlands.

In the 1940s, Child worked for the Office of Strategic Services (the precursor to the CIA). During World War II, the OSS dispatched her to Ceylon—now Sri Lanka—and it was there that she first encountered foods like durian (which she described as smelling like "dead

babies mixed with strawberries and Camembert"). While in Ceylon, she worked with Paul Child, the man who would become her husband and partner in culinary exploration. Together, they were transferred to Yunnan's capital city, Kunming, where Child learned about a variety of Chinese cooking styles and fell in love with the country's cuisines.

Although she later spoke of her fondness for China's foods, she did not continue to study them in any serious way, perhaps because in the United States, in the early 1950s, there were few books and even fewer teachers who could have taught her much about them. Still, it's fun to imagine a parallel universe where Julia Child

somehow became our guide to China's food traditions, instead of France's. Just think of it: Julia Child on black-and-white television, whacking roasted ducks into pieces with a giant cleaver and frying bitter melons. I, for one, would have been entranced, and our culinary landscape would most certainly look a whole lot different today. ●

THE RECIPES

V = VEGETARIAN OR VEGAN OPTION

Guìzhōu liángfěn 貴州涼粉

Spicy Mung Bean Jelly Shreds

GUIZHOU · SERVES 6

Mung bean jelly is used all throughout south-central China and is another one of those ingredients prized for its texture rather than its inherent flavor. A vibrant sauce is necessary, therefore, to add to its allure. In Beijing, mung bean jelly is often draped with a subtle sesame paste dressing. But in this recipe from Guizhou, it's lashed with chili oil, ginger, and garlic to make one of my favorite things to eat.

MUNG BEAN JELLY

½ cup mung bean powder

3 cups water, divided into ½ cup and 2½ cups

SAUCE AND CONDIMENTS

1 tablespoon fermented black beans

1 tablespoon water

2 teaspoons peeled and finely chopped fresh ginger

2 teaspoons finely chopped garlic

½ cup chili oil (page 435), including the goop, or to taste

1½ teaspoons regular soy sauce, or to taste

1 tablespoon black vinegar, or to taste

2 to 3 tablespoon toasted sesame oil

1 green onion, green part only, finely sliced

Few tablespoons fried soybeans (page 410) or coarsely chopped fried peanuts (page 411) or a healthy sprinkle of toasted sesame seeds (page 413)

1. Prepare a square 4-cup pan by rinsing it out and setting it next to the stove along with a silicone spatula; also prepare a shallow bowl of cold water that is large enough to hold the pan, as this will be used as a bath to quickly cool down the jelly.

2. Mix the mung bean powder with ½ cup of the water to form a smooth, thin slurry. Bring the remaining 2½ cups water to a boil in a wide saucepan or very clean wok over medium heat. Stir the water with a whisk while you pour the bean slurry into it. Continue to stir the mixture as it quickly thickens and bubbles and regulate the heat to maintain a gentle bubbling. Cook the mixture for a minute, until it is glossy and translucent. Use the spatula to scrape it into the square pan. Shake the pan to settle the paste and then set the pan in the shallow bowl of cold water. When the mixture has cooled to room temperature, remove the pan from the water and place it in the refrigerator for about an hour, until it turns into an opaque jelly.

3. Turn the pan upside down onto a very clean cutting board and lift off the pan. Slice the jelly into thin pieces and then into long batons. You can also use a wavy-bladed knife to make it fancy or a Chinese-style grater to produce long ribbons. Arrange the jelly on a rimmed serving platter or wide bowl and keep it cool.

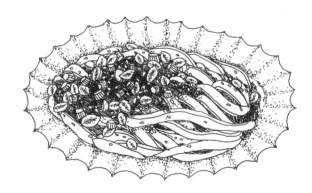

4. Coarsely chop the fermented black beans and place them in a clean wok with the water. Bring the water to a boil and stir the beans around in it to form a thin sauce. Add the ginger and garlic, mix them up quickly, and toss in the chili oil, soy sauce, vinegar, and sesame oil. Quickly bring the sauce to a boil once more, taste, and adjust the seasoning. Feel free to make it saltier with more soy sauce, sweeter with a dash of sugar, tarter with more vinegar, or spicier with a whole lot more chili oil. Pour the hot sauce over the cool jelly ribbons, garnish with the green onions and fried soybeans (or peanuts or sesame seeds), and serve. These ribbons are very slippery, so cradle them with a wide serving spoon as you pluck them up with the serving chopsticks. Toss them with the toppings before eating.

VARIATION

You can also use a northern-style sesame paste dressing that is pretty much identical to the one used in Manchurian Chicken Salad (page 11); just omit the mustard. Pour this over the jelly and then sprinkle it with toasted sesame seeds, chopped green onions, and cilantro.

Use a very clean wok (or pan) when making the jelly, because any blackened bits will mar it. Store leftover jelly in a plastic container in the refrigerator and use it by the next day.

Use a wire whisk to mix the paste.

TANGY FLAVORS SPARK THE DISHES OF Guizhou thanks to all sorts of chilies, like pickled red chili peppers (page 424), as well as vinegar and lemons, which are thought to stimulate appetites made sluggish by the heat. There is a saying in Guizhou that goes, "Three days without something tart to eat and you'll be dragging your feet."

Many believe that China's best chili peppers are grown here, and the local sauces and seasoned oils are generally based on handfuls of fresh or dried peppers. Most families make their own concoctions, combining the chilies with things like garlic, ginger, or fermented black beans, as can be tasted in Guizhou fermented hot sauce (page 438). Some of the best local foods are often the simplest, such as greens tossed with homemade chili oil and the delectable jelly shreds on this spread, which contrast the slithery, cool jelly with startlingly good spice and crunch.

As with just about every other square inch of the Central Highlands, rice is the staple food here. Probably the most beautiful of all the local rice dishes is the gorgeous "five color rice" (*wǔsè fàn* 五色飯) made by the Miao to commemorate their five ancestral clans. Traditionally colored black, white, purple, yellow, and red, this has to be one of the most dazzling ways to serve this grain.

This region, like others in the Central Highlands, is also home to high-octane white liquors made from rice and sorghum. The most famous of these is Guizhou's sorghum white lightning, *maotai*, which is so powerful that I once saw a guy kill a cockroach by flicking a single drop of the liquor onto its head.

Liángbàn báiyùkǔguā 凉拌白玉苦瓜

Raw "White Jade" Bitter Melon

HUNAN · SERVES 4 TO 6

Bitter melon gets a bad rap because it can be very astringent; bitterness is an acquired taste. When you select the right bitter melon, though—one that is gently sweet and very pale—it will not be that harsh. The best time to find one is during autumn. This is also the only time that the beautiful variety called "white jade" (*baiyu*) shows up in Chinese markets.

These melons are served raw in this wonderful appetizer. A subtle bitterness comes from the melon, of course, but everything else is found in the sauce, which features fermented black beans, soy sauce, vinegar, sugar, cilantro, jalapeños, and garlic. Traditionally offered at the beginning of autumnal banquets, this dish came to be one I adored whenever it was ordered by the director of the history museum as part of one of his memorable Hunanese meals.

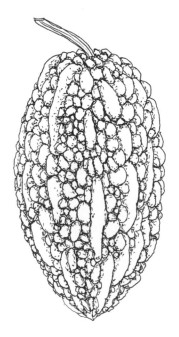

1 large bitter melon, the paler the better
1 red jalapeño pepper
2 cloves garlic
1 green onion
1 small bunch cilantro, optional
1 tablespoon fermented black beans
1 tablespoon regular soy sauce
1 tablespoon black vinegar
1 teaspoon sugar
1 tablespoon toasted sesame oil
Sea salt to taste

1. Wash the bitter melon, trim off the stem end, and cut the melon in half. Scoop out the seeds, saving the red coverings, if there are any.

2. Thinly slice the melon halves about ⅛ inch thick and either on the diagonal or straight cut, keeping the slices together so the shape of the melon is preserved. Lay them on a rectangular or oval platter and then fan them out slightly so they separate a bit. Cover the platter and chill.

3. Remove the stem from the pepper, cut it in half, and discard both the seeds and fleshy ribs. Cut the pepper into small dice (about ⅛ inch) and place in a small work bowl. Peel and finely chop the garlic. Trim the green onion and then cut it into very thin rounds. Add both the garlic and onion to the bowl. If you like cilantro, chop some finely and add that, as well. (You can make this dish an hour or two ahead of time up to this point, but don't add the cilantro until just before serving.) Cover and chill.

4. Rinse and lightly chop the fermented black beans. Place them in a small work bowl and add the soy sauce, vinegar, sugar, sesame oil, and salt. Mix well, taste and adjust the seasoning, and then add the pepper mixture and any red seed coverings you might have. Toss everything lightly, taste again, and tweak with whatever is needed. Pour the sauce over the middle of each melon half so that it drips attractively down the slices. Serve chilled.

Liángbàn hǎizhétóu 涼拌海蜇頭

Cold Tossed Jellyfish

HUNAN • SERVES 4 TO 6

The Chinese love jellyfish primarily for its texture. I recommend using "jellyfish heads" (*haizhetou*)—the fringy oral arms that cascade down from beneath the bowl-shaped hood—for this dish, because they have a wonderful crunch. The thin hood, which the Chinese refer to as "jellyfish skin" (*hǎizhépí* 海蜇皮), is a suitable option as well.

Jellyfish are usually sold cleaned, salted, and packed in clear plastic bags. Often there is no English description on the label—just "jellyfish"—but it's easy to figure out what is what: jellyfish skin is smooth, thin, and generally folded up, while the heads are fatter and look like beige cauliflower florets.

JELLYFISH AND CUCUMBERS
8 ounces salted jellyfish heads
About 4 cups boiling water

DRESSING
2 tablespoons toasted sesame oil
2 tablespoons peanut or vegetable oil
1½ tablespoons peeled and minced fresh ginger
2 cloves garlic, minced
1 red jalapeño pepper, seeded and minced
1 green onion, white part only, trimmed and minced
½ cup unsalted chicken stock (page 380)
2 tablespoons black vinegar
About 2 tablespoons sweet soy sauce (page 439)
    or 1 teaspoon sugar plus 1 tablespoon soy sauce,
    or to taste

GARNISH
2 Persian or other small, seedless cucumbers, unpeeled
½ teaspoon sea salt
1 red jalapeño pepper, seeded and finely chopped, optional
1 green onion, green part only, thinly sliced
2 tablespoons finely chopped cilantro, optional
2 tablespoons toasted sesame seeds (page 413)

1. Start this recipe 3 days before you plan to serve it. Rinse the jellyfish and place it in a container with at least 4 inches of headroom. Add water to cover by about 2 inches and refrigerate for 2 days, changing the water twice a day. On the third day, drain the jellyfish, arrange it in a single layer in a colander or sieve, and douse it with the boiling water, shaking the jellyfish around so that every bit is evenly blanched. When the fringes spread out, the jellyfish has cooked enough. Rinse and drain. Slice the spiky fronds into a thin julienne.

2. To make the dressing, set a wok over medium heat, pour in both oils, and swirl them around. Quickly fry the ginger, garlic, jalapeño, and onion whites until they sizzle, and then add the stock, vinegar, and soy sauce or soy mixture. Turn up the heat to high and bring to a boil. Taste and adjust the seasoning. Reduce the dressing until it is syrupy, then chill it.

3. An hour or two before serving, cut the cucumbers into thin shreds about the same size as the sliced jellyfish. Toss the cucumbers with the salt in a colander, wait until they are limp, and then squeeze them gently to remove most of the salt.

4. To serve, toss the jellyfish in a medium work bowl with the dressing, cucumbers, optional pepper, onion greens, and optional cilantro. Mound the jellyfish on 1 or 2 small serving plates and sprinkle with the sesame seeds. Serve chilled.

You can make whatever dressing you like for this dish, but I suggest one that is slightly tart, full flavored, and spiked with aromatics. Rich, smoother dressings will muffle the jellyfish's crunchy texture.

Gānpēng jīchì 乾烹雞翅

Dry-Fried Chicken Wings

SICHUAN · SERVES ABOUT 4

Most fried chicken has a thick coating, but these wings, simply dusted with cornstarch, offer a nice, light crunch. When making the sauce, be sure to caramelize the sugar properly: as soon as the vinegar has boiled down and large bubbles start to form, watch the sauce carefully and swirl it around so that it heats evenly. The sugar can burn easily, so this part of the process requires close attention. Once the sauce is done, it should be sticky and syrupy.

Middle sections from 12 chicken wings (see Tips),
    or 6 whole chicken wings
¼ cup cornstarch
2 cups (or so) peanut or vegetable oil for frying
6 cloves garlic, finely chopped
½ inch fresh ginger, peeled and finely chopped
2 green onions, trimmed and finely chopped
10 dried Thai chilies, or to taste, broken in half
    and seeds discarded, and/or smoked paprika
¾ cup pale rice vinegar
6 tablespoons sugar, or to taste
1 teaspoon toasted Sichuan peppercorn salt (page 440),
    or to taste
2 teaspoons regular soy sauce

1. Start this recipe at least 6 hours before you want to serve it. If you are using whole wings, cut off the tips and use them for stock, and then cut the wings between the first and second joints so that you have 12 pieces. Place the wing pieces in a work bowl and sprinkle the cornstarch over them. Toss the wings in the bowl until each piece is thoroughly coated.

2. Place a cake rack on a large plate or small baking sheet, then arrange the wings, not touching, on the pan. Refrigerate uncovered so the cool air slightly dries out the wings. Refrigerate for at least 6 hours and up to 1 day.

3. Pour the oil into a wok and heat over high heat until a wooden chopstick inserted in the oil is immediately covered with bubbles. Hold a spatter screen in one hand while using the other hand to carefully add half of the wing pieces to the hot oil. Cover with the screen to reduce the possibility of burns and mess. As soon as the wings are golden on one side, turn them over, adjusting the heat as necessary. Remove the wings to a large work bowl once they are nicely browned and cooked through (see Tips). Repeat with the other half of the wings.

4. Drain off all but 1 tablespoon of oil from the wok (or put 1 tablespoon of the oil in a saucepan), place it over medium-high heat, and add the garlic, ginger, onions, and chilies. (Smoked paprika can be used instead of, or in addition to, the chilies.) Toss them in the hot oil to release their fragrance, and then add the rest of the ingredients. Turn the heat to high and quickly boil down the sauce. Just before it turns syrupy and starts to caramelize, taste and adjust the seasoning. Once it is the consistency of maple syrup, remove from the heat. Toss the wings in the sauce to coat them completely. Arrange the wings on a serving platter and eat while hot.

My preference here is for the middle section of the wings, which offers a nice ratio of crispy skin to juicy chicken.

Chicken wings will generally take 10 to 15 minutes to cook through. The wings will be done when they are a lovely golden brown all over. Blood will seep out of the core if they are not completely cooked, so check them in the work bowl before you toss them with the sauce.

Thank you *Mission Street Food* for this dandy way to coat wings.

Kǒushuǐjī 口水雞

Mouthwatering Chicken

SICHUAN · SERVES 6 AS AN APPETIZER
OR 2 TO 3 AS A MAIN DISH

This dish is basically chilled poached chicken, but the sauce turns it into a genuine Chongqing classic. It features an inspired combination of spicy, sweet, tart, nutty, and savory flavors, along with an abundance of aromatics. Mouthwatering Chicken is great for a big dinner, as it comes together easily and is a stunning way to start off an evening. It's also perfect for family meals—sometimes I make a meal out of topping a green salad with the chicken, sauce, and crunchy tidbits.

CHICKEN
5 or 6 chicken thighs (about 1½ pounds)

SAUCE
¼ cup red chili oil with toasty bits (page 435),
    including the goop
½ teaspoon ground toasted Sichuan peppercorns
    (page 441)
2 tablespoons regular soy sauce
1 tablespoon mild rice wine
1 tablespoon pale rice vinegar
1 tablespoon black vinegar
2 tablespoons sugar
2 large cloves garlic, finely chopped
1 tablespoon peeled and finely chopped fresh ginger

CONDIMENTS
2 green onions, trimmed
¼ cup toasted peanuts (page 411), chopped
2 tablespoons toasted sesame seeds (page 413)

1. If the chicken thighs have not been boned and skinned, do so now and use the bones and skin for something else. Place the chicken in a pan, cover with water, and bring to a boil. Lower the heat and simmer for about 7 minutes, remove the pan from the heat, take out the chicken, and let it come to room temperature. Tear the chicken into thin shreds and then cover and chill it.

2. Mix together all of the sauce ingredients in a saucepan or wok and heat over medium-high heat until the mixture comes to a boil. Taste and adjust the seasoning.

3. Shred the onions into very fine strips. Toss the chicken with the onions and pile this mixture into a serving bowl or rimmed plate. Pour the hot sauce over the chicken and sprinkle the peanuts and sesame seeds on top.

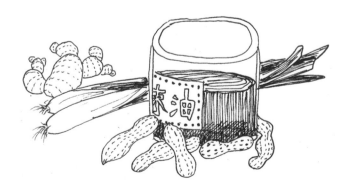

Dàbáopiàn 大薄片

Big, Thin Slices of a Pig's Head

YUNNAN · SERVES 8 TO 12

This was our favorite item at Yúnnán Rénhéyuán 雲南仁和園, a restaurant in downtown Taipei. Traditionally, this dish is made with an entire boned pig's head: face, snout, jowls, ears, and tongue. I prefer to make it with only the meaty jowls (i.e., the cheeks), however. Pig jowls come precleaned, which saves you a lot of hassle, and for my money they are the tastiest part of the head. The jowls look for all the world like a nice piece of pork belly: a thick cut of meat interwoven with white fat, with a good layer of skin on top. Most Chinese restaurants treat the jowls as if they were fresh bacon, just like the Italians do when making *guanciale*; you can even consider substituting pig jowl for pork belly in other recipes. It is generally cheaper because most people are not familiar with it, and it's just as delicious.

MEAT

1 pig jowl with the skin attached (2 pounds or so)

¼ cup white liquor

4 green onions, trimmed

¼ cup thinly sliced fresh ginger

½ teaspoon sea salt

2 teaspoons whole Sichuan peppercorns

1½ teaspoons fennel seeds

SAUCE

1 to 2 red jalapeño peppers

3 green onions, trimmed

6 cloves garlic

6 tablespoons regular soy sauce

6 tablespoons black vinegar

3 tablespoons toasted sesame oil

NO OTHER PLACE IN CHINA HAS AS MANY ethnic groups as Yunnan. This has to do with its history on the edge of an empire.

In the thirteenth century, Kublai Khan drew Yunnan into the imperial fold. It is believed that most of Yunnan's people were then still ethnically Bai. This minority still exerts great influence on the culture and cuisine of Yunnan and is credited with creating the area's unique "milk fans" (see page 247). Milk is not used as a beverage in either Mongolia or Yunnan but rather is fermented before being turned into a dried, cheese-like substance.

Another important minority are the Dai, who maintain a vivid food culture in the Central Highlands as well as in Myanmar and Thailand. They contributed fermented crunchy bean paste (see page 269) and Lemongrass Chicken (page 280) to the local cuisines. They also make something they call "sour meat" (*suānròu* 酸肉) by fermenting beef with cooked rice and seasonings.

The Pumi, meanwhile, have their own special form of charcuterie called *pipá zhū* 琵琶豬: a pig is opened up, flattened, and dried so it can be eaten over years, if necessary. And it is said that the Yi people, who live in an area northwest of the capital city of Kunming, raise the most famous of Yunnan's chicken breeds, a bird known as "the robust chicken of Wuding." This chicken is typically neutered—males and females both—to direct all of its energy into creating meat rather than into reproduction. The resulting birds are considered very flavorful; the capons sell for one-and-a-half times more than regular roosters, and the hens sell for twice the price of their unaltered sisters.

1. Rinse the jowl and pat it dry. If there are hairs poking out of the skin, wait until later to pull them out, as they can easily be dealt with once the pork skin has been cooked. Place the jowl in a medium saucepan and cover with water. Bring the water to a boil and simmer for about 10 minutes, then dump out the water and scum, rinse the jowl and saucepan, return the jowl to the pan, and cover the meat with water once again. Add the white liquor, green onions, ginger, and salt. Enclose the Sichuan peppercorns and fennel seeds in either some cheesecloth or a mesh ball and toss this into the pot, too. Bring the water to a boil, lower the heat to a gentle simmer, and cook the jowl, uncovered, for about 3 hours, adding more water as necessary. Check to see if the jowl is done by poking a chopstick through the skin into the meat. It should offer absolutely no resistance, but the meat and skin should not fall apart, either. Let the meat cool in the broth and then remove the jowl to a clean covered container. Refrigerate it overnight and for up to a couple of days. The broth can be strained, the solids discarded, and the broth used for something else.

2. Before you do anything else, pull out any hairs you find in the skin at this point, since they will now be easy to remove with either tweezers or a paring knife (see page 459). Once that is done, cut the jowl against the grain into very long, thin slices while it is still chilled and easy to handle. Arrange the slices on a platter and then let the meat and silky fat come to room temperature before serving.

3. While the jowl is gradually softening, prepare the sauce: stem and seed the peppers and cut them into tiny dice. Finely chop the onions and garlic. Place all of these aromatics in a small work bowl. Stir in the soy sauce, vinegar, and sesame oil. Adjust the seasoning and then either serve the sauce alongside the meat or pour it over the room-temperature slices just before serving.

Pig jowls are not always available in Western butcher shops, so if I want to make this, I ask my butcher to set them aside for me whenever he brings in a whole hog. You can, of course, use a whole boned pig's head here. But make sure you multiply the recipe ingredients by three, because you will have around 7 pounds of pork to contend with.

The white liquor, ginger, and spices work to tame the natural gaminess of the jowls. What you should end up with is a mildly flavored meat.

As with French headcheese, this dish benefits from a tart, aromatic sauce. The chili peppers can be as hot as you like. I'd caution against adding sugar to the sauce.

Dòufŭ yuánzi tāng 豆腐圓子湯

Bean Curd Quenelle Soup

SICHUAN • SERVES 4 TO 6

This recipe looks like it will take forever to make, but with the help of a food processor, it is not at all difficult, and it's a particularly excellent option when you want to serve something special for dinner. Be sure not to bring the soup to a full boil or the quenelles will disintegrate. The soup will still be delicious, just not very pretty.

NOODLES AND VEGETABLES

1 bundle cellophane noodles

2 black mushrooms, fresh or dried and plumped up, stemmed

1 small winter bamboo shoot, defrosted if frozen (see Tip, page 122)

1 bunch spinach, any tough stems discarded and cleaned (page 10)

QUENELLES

1 block (14 ounces or so) regular bean curd

5 ounces ground pork (15 percent fat)

1 tablespoon Shaoxing rice wine

1 tablespoon cornstarch

¼ teaspoon sea salt

Freshly ground black pepper

1 large egg

SOUP

1 tablespoon toasted sesame oil

2 tablespoons peeled and minced fresh ginger

2 tablespoons green onions, trimmed and minced

3 tablespoons Shaoxing rice wine

4 cups unsalted chicken stock (page 380)

Sea salt to taste

Freshly ground black pepper

IN SICHUAN, EACH MOUTHFUL OF FOOD IS A bite of history. Not many Chinese and even fewer Westerners know that the recipes of this enormous province were written in the wake of genocide.

In the mid-1600s, Zhang Xianzhong captured Sichuan and proclaimed himself emperor of the area. This murderous brigand known as the Yellow Tiger was a giant with a jaundiced complexion, a strong jaw, and an unquenchable thirst for killing. Millions of people were slaughtered at Zhang's command. Before long, Sichuan was nearly empty, and its culture was wiped clean.

This bloodthirsty tyrant had a short reign, though, and imperial troops were able to wrest Sichuan back into the fold. The central government in Beijing organized a vast influx of natives from more populous provinces to the south and east—mainly Hunan and Guangdong—to settle Sichuan's rich lands. As they put down roots, the immigrants shared their traditional cooking styles, creating a genuine fusion cuisine that changed the face and flavors of Sichuan forever.

One spice does remain the iconic flavor—or should I say sensation—of not only Sichuan, but the entire Central Highlands, as well as Tibet. In spite of its name, the Sichuan peppercorn, or *huājiāo* 花椒, is not related either to black or chili peppers, and so does not offer any sort of heat to a dish. Rather, it supplies a pine-like or even lemony scent that is particularly noticeable when these little red balls are dry-fried, which toasts the husks and releases their fragrant oils.

But it is their numbing nature that makes them so unique. As food science writer Harold McGee so eloquently described them in *On Food and Cooking,* "They produce a strange, tingling, buzzing, numbing sensation that is something like the effect of carbonated drinks or of a mild electric current." He went on to say that the chemicals in these seeds "appear to act on several different kinds of nerve endings at once, induce sensitivity to touch and cold in nerves that are ordinarily nonsensitive, and so perhaps cause a kind of general neurological confusion." And that is probably what makes chili peppers their perfect partners in the Central Highlands' addictively delicious form of culinary mayhem: one blows the fuses, while the other lights the fire.

1. Soak the cellophane noodles in cool water for at least 10 minutes, until soft, and then cut them into 3-inch (or so) lengths with kitchen shears. Slice the mushrooms and bamboo shoot into thin pieces; if you're using a fresh bamboo shoot, peel it before you slice it and then boil or steam it. Cut the spinach into 3-inch lengths.

2. To make the quenelles, cut the bean curd into large chunks and toss it into a food processor with the pork, rice wine, cornstarch, salt, a sprinkle of pepper, and the egg. Process until the mixture is light and fluffy, stopping the processor once or twice to scrape down the sides.

3. To make the soup, place a 6-cup saucepan over medium heat and add the sesame oil. When it begins to shimmer, add the ginger and green onions, stir-fry for a couple of seconds until fragrant, and then pour in the rice wine and stock. Bring to a boil and add the mushrooms and bamboo shoots. Reduce the heat and simmer the vegetables for about 5 minutes, until tender. Taste and adjust the seasoning with salt and pepper.

4. A few minutes before you are ready to serve, drop the noodles and spinach into the saucepan and bring the soup to a bare simmer. Make golf-ball-sized spheres out of the bean curd mixture (to make the balls using the "tiger's mouth" technique, see the diagram below), gently dropping each ball into the soup as it is made. Serve as soon as the balls float to the top.

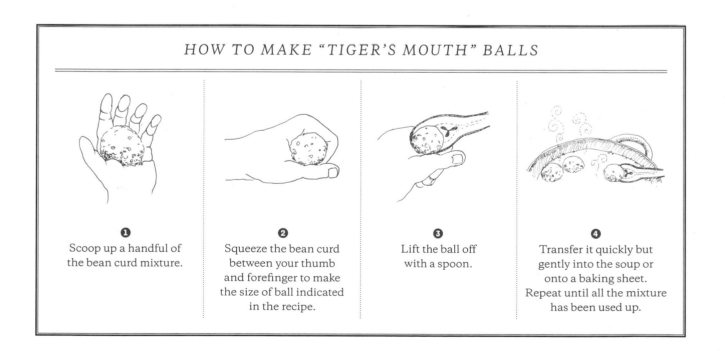

HOW TO MAKE "TIGER'S MOUTH" BALLS

❶ Scoop up a handful of the bean curd mixture.

❷ Squeeze the bean curd between your thumb and forefinger to make the size of ball indicated in the recipe.

❸ Lift the ball off with a spoon.

❹ Transfer it quickly but gently into the soup or onto a baking sheet. Repeat until all the mixture has been used up.

Shàngtāng yúshēng 上湯魚生

Flash Fish Soup

HUNAN • SERVES 6 TO 8

Raw fish doesn't make a whole lot of appearances on Chinese dinner tables (see page 164 for a delicious exception), but this brilliant soup from the northern reaches of Hunan is one occasion where it does—briefly. At first, the fish hovers in the background, carefully arrayed along the inside of the tureen, hiding behind greens and toasted Chinese cruller slices. But then, at the dining table, boiling hot broth is poured over everything, and the fish appears in a flash, as if conjured into being.

FISH AND GARNISHES

4 ounces fish fillets, skinned (grass carp is best, but other candidates include any number of mild but tasty fish with a firm texture, including snapper, butterfish, and amberjack)

1 tablespoon Shaoxing rice wine

1 Chinese cruller, fresh or frozen and defrosted

3 black mushrooms, fresh or dried and plumped up

2 romaine lettuce leaves, trimmed

1 small bunch cilantro, picked over

BROTH

4 cups unsalted chicken stock (page 380)

1 inch fresh ginger, smashed

2 tablespoons rendered chicken fat

¼ cup Shaoxing rice wine

Sea salt to taste

1½ teaspoons pale rice vinegar

Freshly ground black pepper

1 teaspoon toasted sesame oil

HOW TO SERVE FLASH FISH SOUP

❶

Arrange the fish slices around the inside of the tureen. Place them next to one another in a single layer so that they completely line the bowl.

❷

Sprinkle the lettuce and cilantro in the center of the tureen.

❸

Arrange the toasted cruller slices on top. Grind lots of pepper over the greens but not over the fish, which should be kept as invisible as possible. Drizzle the sesame oil on top of the greens.

❹

Pour the soup into the tureen in front of your guests and quickly stir everything together so that the fish suddenly appears.

1. Chill the fish in the freezer for about 10 minutes, until very firm. This will make it easier to slice thinly. Using a sharp knife, cut the fish against the grain and on the diagonal into razor-thin slices, plucking out any tiny bones you find along the way. Place the slices in a pretty, thin-walled, 6-cup serving tureen, add the rice wine, and toss to mix well. Let the fish marinate at room temperature while you prepare the rest of the ingredients.

2. Slice the cruller into ¼-inch-thick rounds, scatter the rounds on a baking sheet, and toast them at 275°F until golden and crispy. (A toaster oven is perfect for this.) Remove the stems from the mushrooms, and cut the caps into ¼-inch-thick slices. Trim the lettuce, then finely shred against the grain. Trim the cilantro and coarsely chop; you should have about ¼ cup.

3. To make the broth, bring the stock to a boil in a saucepan over high heat and add the ginger, chicken fat, rice wine, and salt. Add the sliced mushrooms, turn down the heat to medium, and simmer for 10 minutes. Remove and discard the ginger. Add the vinegar to the stock and taste and adjust the seasoning.

4. While the broth is simmering, arrange the fish in the tureen (for directions on arranging everything, see the diagram to the left) and sprinkle with black pepper and the sesame oil. Keep the bowl in a cool place, but do not refrigerate, as this would make the soup cool down too quickly in Step 5 and the fish would not cook.

5. Taste the broth one last time. Place the tureen and a serving ladle on the dining table, along with individual soup bowls and spoons, close to where you will stand to prepare the dish in front of your guests. The crullers will become soggy if you hesitate during this performance, so have everything ready, then bring the broth to a full boil, carefully rush it to the dining table, and dramatically pour it into the tureen. Make a quick swirl with your ladle and immediately serve the soup.

Zhàcài ròusī tāng 榨菜肉絲湯

Shredded Pork and Pickle Soup

SICHUAN • SERVES 2 AS A MAIN DISH OVER NOODLES,
4 TO 6 AS A SOUP COURSE

This is one of those dishes that's great as is or over a bowl of noodles. The only real variable is the saltiness of the pickled tuber, or *zhacai*. After it's been blanched for the first time, give it a taste and make sure it's not too salty. Traditionally, pork shreds are added to the simmering pickles; I've substituted black mushrooms for half the pork to provide some extra *xianwei*. Because the meat is so lean, I stir-fry it in oil with garlic and ginger, which gives the soup more depth and a luxurious texture.

4 ounces lean, boneless pork

½ head Sichuan pickled tuber

4 large black mushrooms, fresh or dried and plumped up

3 tablespoons peanut or vegetable oil

2 or 3 cloves garlic, finely chopped

1½ tablespoons peeled and finely chopped fresh ginger

¼ cup mild rice wine

1 teaspoon toasted sesame oil

1 green onion, thinly sliced on the diagonal

Large handful of fresh noodles, or 2 bundles cellophane noodles, optional

1. Place the meat in the freezer for about 30 minutes to make it easier to slice.

2. Rinse the pickled tuber under cool running water, pat it dry, cut it into slices ⅛ inch thick, and cut the slices into matchsticks. You should have about ½ cup. Place in a medium saucepan, add about 4 cups water, and bring to a boil over high heat. Turn down the heat to a simmer and cook for about 10 minutes. Taste both the broth and the pickled tuber. If either is too salty, discard half of the water and add 2 more cups water to the pan; bring the broth to a boil again and then slowly simmer the pickles while you prepare the rest of the ingredients, adding more boiling water as necessary to bring the pan back up to 4 cups liquid.

3. Slice the meat very thinly against the grain and remove any fat or gristly pieces. Cut the slices into a julienne the same size as the pickles. Remove and discard the mushroom stems and julienne the caps.

4. Place a wok over medium-high heat until hot, and add the oil. When the oil is shimmering, toss in the garlic and ginger and fry them for about 10 seconds to release their fragrance. Add the pork and mushrooms and stir-fry until the meat starts to brown. Scrape the pork mixture into the broth, add the rice wine, and bring the soup to a boil. Lower the heat and simmer for about 5 minutes. Taste and adjust the seasoning and then sprinkle on the sesame oil and green onions. Serve very hot.

5. If you are serving the soup over noodles, bring a pot of water to a full boil, add the fresh noodles, stir, cook until barely done, and drain. If using cellophane noodles, soak them in cool water to cover until just softened and drain. Divide them among the soup bowls, and ladle the finished soup over the top.

Yěgū Yúntuǐ tāng 野菇雲腿湯

Yunnan Ham and Wild Mushroom Soup

YUNNAN • SERVES 8

I like to make this soup with as many different mushrooms as possible: porcini, morels, the netlike bamboo pith fungus (see below), hen-of-the-woods, and whatever else I can find. In Yunnan, chefs pair all of these fungi with a local ham, but at the time of this writing, true Chinese hams are impossible to find in the United States. Until that beautiful charcuterie makes its way into our markets, I recommend prosciutto or Hunan-style charcuterie (see page 289).

SOUP

2 tablespoons rendered chicken fat

2 tablespoons peeled and finely julienned fresh ginger

3 to 6 tablespoons (depending upon its saltiness) finely julienned dry-cured ham (see headnote)

6 tablespoons mild rice wine

8 cups unsalted chicken stock (page 380)

2 cups (or so) assorted fresh mushrooms (preferably wild, or a mixture of wild and farmed), or rehydrated dried mushrooms of any kind plus their soaking liquid

4 or more long pieces dried bamboo pith fungus, soaked in hot water until soft

Sea salt to taste

Freshly ground black pepper

1 tablespoon sugar, or to taste

1 teaspoon pale rice vinegar, optional

GARNISH

3 to 6 tablespoons finely julienned Chinese-style ham

Slivered green onion or chopped cilantro

1. Melt the fat in a 4-quart pot over medium-low heat and add the ginger. Slowly brown the ginger before tossing in the ham. Stir the ham around in the fat to release its fragrance, then immediately pour in the rice wine, bring to a boil, and add the stock. Bring the stock to a full boil and then lower the heat to a simmer.

2. While the stock is simmering, cut or tear the mushrooms into bite-sized pieces: about ¼ inch wide for porcini, morels, and other thick mushrooms, or into separate "feathers" for hen-of-the-woods, oyster, and other stemmed mushrooms. If you are using rehydrated mushrooms, cut them into slightly smaller pieces, since they will be chewier, and be sure to strain their soaking liquid and add it to the stock. Rinse the bamboo pith fungus, cut off the tough bottoms and fringed tops, and chop the stalks crosswise into 1-inch pieces. Add all these mushrooms to the stock and simmer the soup for about 20 minutes, until the thickest mushrooms are tender. Taste and adjust the seasoning with salt, pepper, and sugar. If you'd like to add a slight edge, stir in the rice vinegar just as you take the soup off of the heat. Toss in the chopped ham and sprinkle on the green onions or cilantro. Serve immediately.

BAMBOO PITH FUNGUS IS ONE OF THE MOST BEAUTIFUL INGREDIENTS around. It is also one of the strangest. It starts out like pretty much any other mushroom, growing out of the ground and forming a cap and stalk. *Phallus indusiatus* proceeds to grow a filigree skirt (that is what *indusium* means) under its cap, and then the outside covering dries off and flakes away, leaving a skeleton that looks like muslin netting. At this stage, it's collected, dried, and packaged in bundles.

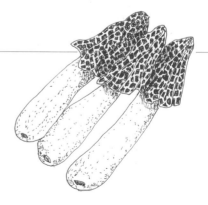

Jīn'gōu guà yùpái 金鈎掛玉牌

Gold Hooks Hanging on Jade Plaques

GUIZHOU · SERVES 4 TO 6

Because Guizhou has traditionally been a province with relatively low incomes, cheap proteins like bean curd and bean sprouts play a significant role in its cuisine. This classic Central Highlands dish combines the two ingredients perfectly, with the chewy texture of the bean curd acting as the ideal foil for the crunchy bean sprouts. But it's the sauce that truly distinguishes this dish.

BEAN SPROUTS AND BEAN CURD

5 to 6 ounces very fresh soybean sprouts

1 block (14 ounces or so) medium-firm bean curd

1 cup water

1 teaspoon sea salt

SAUCE

2 green onions, trimmed and very thinly sliced

1 tablespoon toasted sesame oil

¼ cup peanut or vegetable oil

1½ tablespoons ground dried chilies

1½ tablespoons ground toasted Sichuan peppercorns (page 441)

1 tablespoon regular soy sauce

1. Pluck off the hairy ends from the soybean sprouts (see page 450). Remove any skins clinging to the seed ends, but leave on the yellow heads, as these are your "gold hooks." Rinse the sprouts and drain.

2. Trim any tough edges off the bean curd and cut the block into even quarters to form the "jade plaques." Slice each quarter into 5 even tiles, for a total of 20 pieces.

3. Place the bean sprouts in a wide pan and add the water and salt. Bring the pot to a boil and then lower it to a simmer. Cook the sprouts for about 5 minutes, layer the bean curd tiles on top, and gently swish the pan (don't stir it or flip the bean curd, as it will break) for about 3 minutes, until the bean curd is cooked. Carefully drain off all of the water and arrange the sprouts and bean curd on a serving platter.

4. While the sprouts are cooking, place the sliced green onions and the sesame oil in a heatproof measuring cup that will hold the sauce. Place a wok over medium-high heat and add the peanut or vegetable oil. When the oil is barely shimmering, turn down the heat to low. Sprinkle in the dried chilies and ground peppercorns and slowly cook the spices for about 2 minutes, until their fragrance has been released. Remove the wok from the heat and stir in the soy sauce, which will boil and bubble. Pour this spicy oil and all of the crumbly bits into the measuring cup and stir. Taste and adjust the seasoning as needed before scraping the sauce into a small bowl.

5. Serve the dish while both parts are still hot. To eat, pick up a square of bean curd along with a couple of sprouts and dip them lavishly into the sauce.

Péngjiā dòufǔ 彭家豆腐

Peng Family Bean Curd

HUNAN · SERVES 4 TO 6

A relatively new recipe in Hunan's canon, Peng Family Bean Curd was created by Hunanese chef and restaurateur Peng Changgui at his restaurant Peng's Agora Garden, in Taipei. When I would eat there with folks from the National Museum of History, we would order things like Honey Ham (page 288) sandwiched in Lotus Leaf Buns (page 408), smoked pork charcuterie with green garlic, and Flash Fish Soup (page 260); this dish, though, was a favorite on visits with my husband, when we would gravitate toward food that was more homey than fancy.

1 block (14 ounces or so) firm bean curd

2 to 3 ounces pork loin, shredded against the grain

1 tablespoon mild rice wine

1 teaspoon cornstarch

1 tender leek, cleaned (see page 450), or
    2 green onions, trimmed

¼ cup peanut or vegetable oil (used oil is all right if it
    smells fresh)

2 cloves garlic, coarsely chopped

2 or more red jalapeño peppers, seeded and cut
    into thin shreds

2 tablespoons fermented black beans,
    rinsed and lightly chopped

½ cup hot water

1 tablespoon regular soy sauce

1 teaspoon sugar

1 teaspoon cornstarch mixed with 1 tablespoon water

1 teaspoon toasted sesame oil

1. Cut the bean curd block in half lengthwise and then cut crosswise into squares ¼ inch thick. Place them in a single layer on a clean tea towel and pat the tops with the towel. Let them drain while you prepare the rest of the ingredients.

2. Place the pork in a small work bowl and toss it with the rice wine and cornstarch. Cut the leek or green onions on the diagonal into ½-inch-wide strips.

3. Place a wok over medium-high heat, and when it starts to smoke, add the oil. Swirl the oil around in the wok and then lay in half of the bean curd squares in a single layer. Cook these until they are golden brown on one side, shake them loose, and then flip each one over and cook the other side. Remove the now-golden squares to a plate, leaving as much oil in the wok as possible, and repeat with the other half of the bean curd. Pour out about half of the oil.

4. Raise the heat under the wok to high. Add the leeks (or green onions) and garlic to the hot oil and stir-fry for about 10 seconds to release their fragrance. Toss in the pork and its marinade and stir-fry until the meat is no longer pink. Add the peppers and black beans, stir them quickly to heat them through, and then pour in the hot water, soy sauce, and sugar. Toss everything together and then scoot the vegetables up the side of the wok.

5. Arrange the browned bean curd squares in the sauce, cover, reduce the heat to medium-low, and simmer for about 5 minutes. Turn the squares over, drizzle the cornstarch mixture around the edges, and then gently shake the wok to mix everything together while the sauce thickens. Toss in the sesame oil and serve on a rimmed platter.

Chicken can be used instead of pork—or both can be left out if you prefer this meatless. Black mushrooms are a good substitute.

Zhuàngjiā niàng dòufǔ 壮家酿豆腐

Zhuang-Style Stuffed Bean Curd Balls

NORTHERN GUANGXI · SERVES 6 TO 8

In the West, you rarely hear much about the Zhuang people of southern China, but they are the largest minority in the country, numbering around 18 million. Most of them live in the mountains of Guangxi's northern half, or in eastern Yunnan. Zhuang dishes tend to be heavily seasoned with chili peppers; this mild dish is an exception. What makes this recipe so remarkable, though, is the way it stretches a small amount of meat into a meal big enough for a large family.

BEAN CURD

1½ blocks (20 to 24 ounces total) firm bean curd
½ teaspoon sea salt

MEATBALLS

8 ounces lean pork (either 15 percent fat ground pork
    or a boneless pork chop)
4 black mushrooms, fresh or dried and plumped up
1 tablespoon peeled and finely minced ginger
2 green onions, trimmed and finely chopped
Sprinkle of sea salt
1 tablespoon regular soy sauce
2 tablespoons rendered pork, duck, or chicken fat
Freshly ground black pepper
2 tablespoons cornstarch

FOR FRYING

Peanut or vegetable oil, as needed
    (used oil is all right if it smells fresh)
About 1 cup cornstarch

SAUCE

1 tablespoon peeled and finely minced fresh ginger
1 cup water
1 teaspoon regular soy sauce
1 tablespoon mild rice wine
1 tablespoon rendered pork, duck, or chicken fat
1 teaspoon toasted sesame oil
1½ teaspoons cornstarch mixed with 2 tablespoons water

GARNISH

Chopped green onions and cilantro

1. Wet a fine piece of muslin or cheesecloth and drape it over a colander set in the sink. Put the bean curd in the cloth, break it apart with your fingers, and then squeeze it into a fine mush. Sprinkle the salt over the bean curd, toss it around, and then let it drain while you work on the meatballs.

2. If your pork isn't already ground, chop it finely. To do this by hand, chill the meat, cut off any tendons or silver skin, thinly slice the meat and fat, and then chop it with a sharp, heavy knife (see page 458). Otherwise, use a food processor to chop the chilled pork. Place the meat in a medium work bowl. Stem the mushrooms and finely chop the caps. Add them to the meat along with the rest of the meatball ingredients. Stir the mixture in one direction until it's bouncy (see page 458).

3. Roll the meat mixture between your palms into marbles about ½ inch in diameter. The best way to form these meatballs is to use the "tiger's mouth" method (see the diagram on page 259). You should end up with 45 balls, more or less. Keep them in a cool place.

4. Next it's time to wrap each meatball in the mashed bean curd (see the diagram below). This is a lot easier than it sounds, since the bean curd actually behaves pretty well if it has been properly squeezed and drained. It should feel sort of like mashed potatoes at this point.

5. Once the bean curd balls have been formed, heat about ½ inch of oil in a wok over medium-high heat until a chopstick placed in the oil is immediately covered with bubbles. Place the cornstarch in a small work bowl and coat each ball just before you fry it. Gently slide the balls into the hot oil, frying them in small batches to prevent them from sticking to one another. Shake the wok once the bottoms are fried so the balls roll around; continue to do this until they are a golden brown all over. Remove the fried balls to a clean plate and repeat with the rest until all have been fried. You can prepare the dish ahead of time up to this point. Let the balls cool to room temperature and then refrigerate in a covered container.

6. About 15 minutes before you want to serve this dish, make the sauce. Combine the ginger, water, soy sauce, rice wine, fat, and sesame oil in a medium saucepan or the wok and boil over high heat until the liquid thickens. Taste and adjust the seasoning. Add the fried balls to the sauce, return the sauce to a boil, and then lower the heat to a simmer. Stir in the cornstarch slurry and adjust the seasoning.

7. After about 5 minutes, use a slotted spoon to transfer the meatballs to a heatproof rimmed serving plate or bowl that fits easily in your steamer (see page 49). Any scrappy-looking fried bean curd balls should be placed at the bottom of the serving dish, with the pretty ones piled on top. Steam the balls over high heat for about 10 minutes, until they puff up a little. Bring the reserved sauce to a boil and then lower to a simmer. Stir the sauce occasionally to keep it smooth, and taste and adjust the seasoning. Remove the bean curd balls from the steamer, pour as much of the sauce over them as you wish, and sprinkle with the chopped green onions and cilantro.

WRAPPING A FILLING WITH A SOFT OUTER LAYER

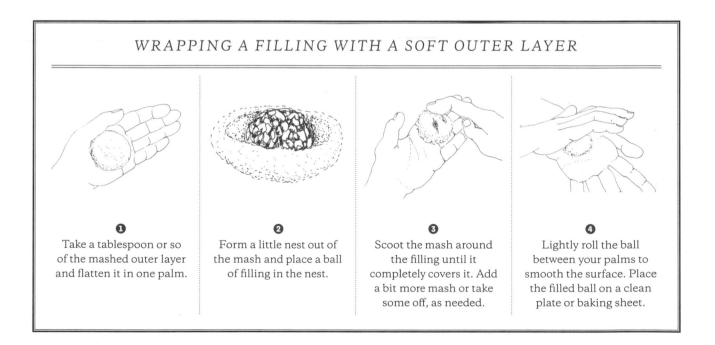

❶
Take a tablespoon or so of the mashed outer layer and flatten it in one palm.

❷
Form a little nest out of the mash and place a ball of filling in the nest.

❸
Scoot the mash around the filling until it completely covers it. Add a bit more mash or take some off, as needed.

❹
Lightly roll the ball between your palms to smooth the surface. Place the filled ball on a clean plate or baking sheet.

Mápó dòufǔ 麻婆豆腐

Mapo Doufu

SICHUAN · SERVES 4 TO 6

More than a century ago, a pockmarked woman (which is what *mapo* means) named Chen invented this bean curd dish at her stand outside the northern gates of Chengdu. The dish quickly caught on, and because it could be cooked so fast, it became something like the fast food of its time. Travelers and local workers filled up on the widow's specialty before entering the capital city's gates. The dish was so famous that it even attracted the local literati, who willingly rubbed elbows with the working class in order to eat at Chen's stand.

BEAN CURD

1 block (14 ounces or so) soft bean curd,
    cut into ½-inch cubes
4 cups boiling water
2 teaspoons sea salt

MEAT AND SAUCE

4 ounces ground beef
3 tablespoons peanut or vegetable oil
1 tablespoon peeled and finely chopped fresh ginger
¼ teaspoon sea salt
1 tablespoon fermented black beans, coarsely chopped
3 tablespoons Sichuan hot bean sauce
1 teaspoon finely ground dried chilies
1 cup unsalted stock of any kind (page 380 or 381)
1 leek, cleaned (see page 450) and thinly sliced
    on the diagonal
About 2 teaspoons sweet soy sauce (page 439),
    or 2 teaspoons regular soy sauce
    plus ½ teaspoon sugar
1 tablespoon toasted soybean flour (page 410)
    or cornstarch mixed with ¼ cup water

GARNISH

1 teaspoon ground toasted Sichuan peppercorns
    (page 441)
1 green onion, green part only, thinly sliced

1. Place the bean curd in a small saucepan, cover with the boiling water, and add the salt. Bring the water to a boil again and then lower the heat to a gentle simmer and cook the bean curd for about 10 minutes to heat it and prevent it from falling apart. Gently transfer the bean curd to a colander set in the sink and let drain thoroughly.

2. Place the ground beef on a cutting board and use a heavy knife to chop it until it is light and fluffy (see page 458). Heat a wok over high heat and add the oil. When the oil shimmers, swirl it around and then toss in the beef and the ginger. Stir constantly as the beef cooks so that it does not stick to the wok. As it starts to brown nicely, season it with the salt and then scoot the meat up the side of the wok.

3. Add the black beans, bean sauce, and chilies to the hot oil at the bottom of the wok and fry them together for a few seconds to release their fragrance. Toss the beef with the bean sauce in the wok and pour in the stock. Add the bean curd, leek, and sweet soy sauce (or soy sauce and sugar) to taste. Bring the bean curd and sauce to a full boil.

4. Reduce the heat under the wok to medium. Thicken the sauce by adding the soybean or cornstarch slurry in three parts: the first time, the sauce will absorb the slurry, but the bean curd will continue to release water, so add the slurry a second time. After each addition, do not stir the ingredients. Instead, shake the wok gently yet firmly over medium heat, as this will mix in the thickener without breaking up the bean curd. Add the slurry a third time to stabilize the texture.

5. Remove from the heat, sprinkle on the ground peppercorns and green onion, and then transfer to a rimmed dish or a bowl. Serve hot.

Dòusū xuěyú 豆酥雪魚

Cod with Crispy Bean Sauce

YUNNAN · SERVES 4 TO 6

The basic ingredients for the bean sauce used here are the smashed, dried, and salted beans known as *dousu*, or "crispy beans." They are directly related to the Burmese fermented soybean disks called *tua nao*. This crunchy, deeply savory sauce is an instant hit whenever it is served, and I have come to pile more and more of it onto the fish as the years have gone by just to make people happy.

FISH

1½ pounds cod fillets or steaks, skin removed

1 teaspoon sea salt

1 tablespoon mild rice wine

SAUCE

7 ounces dried crispy soybeans or store-bought prepared sauce (see Tips)

¾ cup peanut or vegetable oil

1 tablespoon peeled and finely chopped fresh ginger

1 tablespoon coarsely ground dried chilies, or to taste

2 cloves garlic, finely chopped, optional

2 tablespoons sugar (use half if you are reserving half of the sauce for later)

GARNISH

2 green onions, trimmed and finely chopped

1. Rinse the fish and pat it dry. Place it on a heatproof plate, rub it all over with the salt, then sprinkle the wine over it. After you have prepared the rest of the ingredients, steam the fish while you prepare the sauce, allowing 10 to 20 minutes for it to cook depending how thick it is and how hot your steamer (see page 49) is. If the fish is done before the sauce is ready, cover it lightly to keep it warm.

2. If you are using packaged dried crispy soybeans, first make a small slit in the plastic bag so the vacuum is released, then break up the soybean brick into smaller parts inside the bag. Use the handle of your cleaver to crush the soybeans into a powder; it's all right if there are clumps left, as these will fall apart as they're fried.

3. About 10 minutes before you wish to serve this dish, put the oil into a cold wok and add the ginger and chilies. Slowly heat the oil over medium heat so that the ginger and chilies can season the oil without burning. As soon as the ginger has fried to a pale tan and the chilies are not yet browned, add the dried crispy soybeans and optional garlic. If you want, remove half the sauce as soon as the beans absorb the oil and set it aside for another day. It will keep well if refrigerated in a covered jar. If you are using store-bought sauce, simply add it to the wok along with the garlic.

4. Raise the heat to medium-high and fry everything until the beans are brown and crispy. Sprinkle the sugar over the beans and stir it in. Taste the sauce and adjust the seasoning. Pour off and discard any liquid surrounding the fish, then drizzle it with the sauce, which should cause a delectable popping sound. Sprinkle the green onions over the dish and serve it immediately with a spoon.

Nowadays, you can often find dried *dousu* already crushed into a powder. There is even a bottled version that requires you to do nothing more than fry the *dousu* before serving. The best product is Master brand's Fried Crispy Soy Bean from Taiwan.

The most common way of serving this sauce is over steamed cod, but you can serve it with other foods, as well. It's delicious over a plain omelet or steamed soft bean curd. For the omelet, simply cook 4 beaten eggs into a round omelet, plate, and pour half of the sauce over the eggs. For the bean curd, cut it into large cubes and steam it until it is heated through, being careful to pour off as much water as you can before adding the sauce.

This recipe makes a lot of sauce, but it's easy to scoop out half just after you have added the ground beans and save it for later.

Shēngxūn yú 生薰魚

Smoked Whole Fish Hunan Style

HUNAN • SERVES 6 TO 8

The Chinese name for this way of cooking says it all: *shengxun,* or "raw smoked." In most smoked Chinese dishes, the animal is first cooked—usually by steaming or braising—and then gently smoked. In those cases, the smoking simply flavors the meat. This dish is one of the few in which the smoke actually cooks the fish. Wood chips are used here in the initial smoking because they burn more slowly. The second smoking seasons the fish with tea, sugar, and rice.

FISH

1 whole fish (about 2½ pounds); pick one with a buttery texture, like a small amberjack or yellowtail
2 tablespoons peeled and grated fresh ginger
2 tablespoons finely chopped green onions
1 tablespoon whole Sichuan peppercorns
2 teaspoons sea salt
1 tablespoon Shaoxing rice wine

FIRST ROUND OF SMOKING

Spray oil
2 large handfuls of applewood (or other sweet wood) smoking chips

SECOND ROUND OF SMOKING

¼ cup raw rice of any kind
¼ cup dry tea leaves of any kind
¼ cup sugar of any kind
2 tablespoons sea salt

FINISHING TOUCHES

2 tablespoons peeled and finely grated fresh ginger
¼ cup black rice vinegar
½ bunch cilantro, chopped
¼ cup chili oil (page 435)
2 tablespoons very tasty salt with a good texture, like *fleur de sel*
¼ cup toasted sesame oil

COMMUNALLY DINING ON A WHOLE FISH armed with little more than chopsticks and a serving spoon may seem like a challenging task, but it's not hard, if you know the rules.

The whole fish (and any other main dish) is usually positioned in front of the guest of honor, so that he or she can be served first. If you are such a guest, you should try to offer the first servings to those next to you, especially if they're not relatives. Use the serving chopsticks—never your own—to gently hold the fish down while scooping off a portion with

the spoon. Try to skim the spoon over the bones in order to proffer a boneless serving, and then scoop a bit of the sauce on top. When it comes to serving yourself, nick off pieces from the back or near the tail, rather than the fat belly, if you want to appear very polite.

When you get to the skeleton, the easiest and most acceptable way to remove it is to press down on the bones with the back of the serving spoon, as this loosens the flesh. Then, use the serving chopsticks to lift up the tail while maneuvering off any flesh that clings to the skeleton. When you

get to the head, snap the skeleton off at the neck and set it to one side. The head often contains interesting bits and pieces, so you don't want to toss it away.

One of the most beloved parts of the fish is the cheek, which is located underneath a plate below the eye. Called *hétáoròu* 核桃肉 (walnut meat), it has a firm texture and is considered a delicacy, so be sure to offer it to others before attempting to claim it as your own.

1. Start this dish a couple of hours before you plan to serve it. Clean and scale the fish, remove the gills and fins (leave on the head and tail), and rinse it thoroughly under cool running water. Pat it dry with a paper towel and then either slash the fish in the "willow leaf" pattern (page 23) or make 2 long gashes down each side parallel to, and about 1 inch from, the backbone.

2. Mix together the grated ginger, green onions, Sichuan peppercorns, and salt. Rub a third of this mixture on the inside of the fish and the rest all over the outside, paying particular attention to the gashes. Place the fish in a large resealable plastic bag and pour the wine inside the bag, streaming it down both sides of the fish. Seal the bag, place it on a plate, and refrigerate it for 2 or more hours to marinate.

3. Prepare your smoker (see page 27): spray the rack that rests over the center of the smoker with oil. For the first round of smoking, which will cook the fish, scatter the dry wood chips in an even layer on top of the foil. Place the covered smoker to the rear of your stove, turn the fan on high, open some windows for cross-ventilation, and turn your burner up to high.

4. While the smoker is heating up, remove the fish from the bag and knock off all of the aromatics from both inside and outside the fish, including from the gashes. When the smoker starts to emit steady tendrils of smoke, place the prettiest side of the fish face up on the rack, immediately cover the smoker, and lower the heat to medium-high. Smoke the fish for 25 to 30 minutes, until it is almost—but not quite—done.

5. For the second round of smoking, which will further season the fish, mix together the rice, tea leaves, sugar, and salt. Remove the rack with the fish on it and sprinkle the rice mixture over the embers in the smoker. Return the rack with the fish to the smoker, cover it, return it to smoke for another minute or two at medium-high heat, and then immediately take the smoker off the heat. Let the smoker cool down with the lid on and the fish inside it, which will allow the fish to be slowly seasoned by the tea smoke. The fish can be prepared up to this point ahead of time, cooled to room temperature, and refrigerated. When you are ready to serve it, warm the fish in a 275°F oven until it is heated through.

6. While you are waiting for the fish to smoke, prepare the various condiments: combine the ginger and vinegar in a small bowl, and use other bowls or saucers to hold the cilantro, chili oil, and salt.

7. Remove the fish to a serving platter. Just before serving, heat the sesame oil in a wok until it starts to smoke, then pour the hot oil all over the fish. Serve it with the condiments. To eat, use chopsticks to pluck off chunks of the fish and dip them in the various seasonings as desired.

Dòufǔ dòubàn yú 豆腐豆瓣魚

Fish and Bean Curd in Fermented Bean Sauce

SICHUAN • SERVES 4

A favorite place of my husband and mine to eat on the outskirts of Taipei was a Sichuan-style restaurant near the river port town of Tamsui. It was always packed, and almost everyone ordered this dish, which was the house specialty. Before we ate, though, we had to walk over to the restaurant's aquarium and select the fish that would end up on our plate. When I first started doing this, it felt rather grisly, but as time went on, it made me more fully appreciate the origins of my meal.

Those in the know would finish their fish and send the plate back to the kitchen with most of the sauce still on it. The kitchen would return the plate with a second round of either regular white bean curd or with "red bean curd" (see the sidebar to the right).

To my mind, there is no fish recipe more quintessentially Sichuanese than *doubanyu*. It's traditionally made with a whole fish, but because it is sometimes hard to find whole fish in American markets, I've come to rely on the occasional salmon fillet, which is perfectly tasty here and firm enough to stand up to a simple braise.

FISH

1 whole freshwater fish (about 1 pound), preferably grass carp or something with a similar texture, or about 12 ounces thick fish fillets (see headnote)

¼ cup peanut or vegetable oil

2 tablespoons finely chopped fresh ginger

3 green onions, white parts only, trimmed and coarsely chopped

3 cloves garlic, coarsely chopped

BEAN CURD

1 pound firm bean curd or very fresh coagulated pork, chicken, or duck blood, or 8 ounces each bean curd and blood

Boiling water, as needed

1 tablespoon sea salt

SAUCE

3 tablespoons Sichuan hot bean sauce

¼ cup lees (solids) from fermented rice (page 415)

2 tablespoons liquid from fermented rice

About 1 tablespoon sweet soy sauce (page 439), or about 1 tablespoon regular soy sauce and 1 teaspoon sugar

¾ cup unsalted chicken stock (page 380)

1½ teaspoons black vinegar

1 teaspoon cornstarch mixed with 2 tablespoons water

GARNISH

½ teaspoon ground toasted Sichuan peppercorns (page 441)

3 green onions, green parts only, coarsely chopped

1. If using a whole fish, clean and scale the fish, remove the gills and fins (leave on the head and tail), rinse thoroughly under cool running water, and pat dry. Slash the sides in one of the patterns on page 23. If using fillets, leave the skin on and cut the fish against the grain into strips as wide as you want them.

2. Place a wok over medium-high heat, add the oil, and swirl it around before adding the ginger. As soon as it is fragrant, lower the heat to medium and place the fish skin-side down in the oil. Leave the fish to brown, and as soon as it moves easily when you shake the wok (see page 454), turn the fish over and add the whites of the onions and garlic to the oil. When the second side is lightly browned, remove the fish and aromatics to a plate.

3. While the fish is browning, cut the bean curd and/or blood into 16 pieces. (I like batons or rectangles, but it's up to you.) Place the bean curd and/or blood in a small saucepan, cover with the boiling water, and add the salt. Bring the water to a boil again and then lower the heat to a gentle simmer. Cook the pieces for about 5 minutes and gently drain into a colander in the sink.

4. Remove all but about 2 tablespoons oil from the wok. Set the wok over medium-high heat and add the bean sauce. Stir for about 30 seconds to get the sauce hot and smelling terrific and then add the fermented rice lees and liquid, sweet soy sauce (or soy sauce and sugar) to taste, and the stock. As the mixture comes to a boil, add the bean curd and/or blood and simmer for 5 to 10 minutes, until they are cooked and flavorful. Make a well in the center of the wok and nestle the fish and its aromatics in the well. Heat the fish on both sides in the sauce, then swirl in the vinegar; taste and adjust the seasoning. Dribble the cornstarch slurry around the bubbling edges of the sauce, swirl the wok around to mix it in, and then plate the fish, with the white or red cubes decorating the sides. Dust the top with the Sichuan peppercorns and green onions and serve immediately.

BLOOD FINDS ITS WAY INTO MANY CHINESE dishes, from the mahogany pillows that decorate banquet dishes like this one to Taiwan's rice blood pudding (*zhūxiěgāo* 豬血糕), which is cut into large batons, threaded onto Popsicle sticks, coated with soy paste, and then dipped in crushed peanuts and cilantro.

In China, the most popular types of blood come from ducks, chicken, and pigs.

It is sold already coagulated, in little plastic boxes alongside things like chicken livers and pork kidneys. Good-quality blood will be dark red, rather than bright red or brown.

It is difficult to find places that sell excellent-quality blood from free-range birds and heritage pigs. It's a dilemma that has no easy solution, though you can sometimes special-order blood from butchers or sausage-supply companies.

Blood is one of the most fragile of all proteins, so purchase it just before you plan to use it. Treat it just like the best bean curd: cover the coagulated blood with chilled fresh water and keep it refrigerated at all times. It is great in braises like the one described here, but one of the most popular ways to cook it is in a stir-fry with garlic chives or garlic chive flowers.

Yúxiāng duìxiā 魚香對蝦

Fish-Fragrant Prawns

SICHUAN · SERVES 4 TO 6

The sauce for this dish is called *yuxiang* in Chinese, which literally means "fish aroma." Some cookbooks say that it got this name because it's often used for fish, which is not a bad explanation. But I've found that the traditional recipe for *yuxiang* included chilies fermented with crucian carp, which gave the sauce a deep, anchovy-like flavor; hence, perhaps, the name.

I emphasize using pickled chilies here, which can be easily prepared at home or purchased in a Chinese market. They have a purity of flavor that is hard to beat, although some Chinese chefs now rely solely on Sichuan hot bean sauce. I use only a dab of the bean sauce in addition to the chilies to give the sauce good color and body.

PRAWNS

1 pound fresh or frozen and defrosted prawns
 or extra-jumbo shrimp (16/20 or larger),
 peeled or unpeeled, with tail segments intact
1 large egg white, lightly beaten
¼ teaspoon sea salt
2 teaspoons cornstarch
2 cups peanut or vegetable oil (used oil is all right if
 it smells fresh)

VEGETABLES

4 fresh or frozen water chestnuts
4 black mushrooms or wood ear fungus,
 fresh or dried and plumped up
2 to 8 pickled red chili peppers (page 424 or store-bought)
8 cloves garlic
4 green onions, trimmed
2 tablespoons peeled and finely chopped fresh ginger

SAUCE

5 teaspoons sugar
4 teaspoons black vinegar
2 teaspoons regular soy sauce
½ cup water
2 teaspoons cornstarch
2 teaspoons Sichuan hot bean sauce

SICHUAN LITERALLY MEANS "FOUR RIVERS," and so is named after the waterways that crisscross the province and empty for the most part into China's two greatest rivers, the Yangtze and the Yellow. These are the paths that early humans probably forded into this lush land back when history was yet to be written.

Once Sichuan had been claimed for the Qin dynasty around 2,000 years ago, bureaucrats, merchants, and military officers soon followed, settling in Chengdu and Chongqing. Much, much later, massive numbers of other Chinese arrived, bringing with them tidal waves of flavors and ideas that shaped Sichuan's cuisine into its present form.

As a result, the snacks and street foods in Sichuan are some of the best in China. The adoption of North China's wheat flour led to an astounding variety of stuffed breads (*baozi*), filled pasta (*jiaozi*), raised breads, noodles, cookies, pastries, and cakes, in addition to the seemingly endless invention that is called into play whenever rice flour is used instead.

As with so many of China's best places to eat, Muslims have played a huge role in creating so many of these dishes. Beef and lamb dishes, for instance, probably wound their way down south into Sichuan from Gansu, and the local variations on recipes like Lanzhou Beef Noodle Soup (page 328) are so stellar that they are classics in their own right.

Chili peppers originated, of course, in the Americas, and they blazed their way into China's heartland via either Portuguese merchant ships or trade routes from India and Southeast Asia. Only then did Central Highland dishes come to be sparked with their now iconic red seasoning.

1. Peel the prawns, if necessary, leaving the tail segments intact, and then devein them (see page 457). Pat them dry with a paper towel, place them in a medium work bowl, add the egg white, salt, and cornstarch, and toss to coat. Let the prawns marinate while you prepare the rest of the ingredients.

2. Trim the water chestnuts. Remove and discard the stems and hard bits from the mushrooms or wood ears. Chop these ingredients into fine (⅛-inch) dice and place them in a small work bowl. Slice the pickled chilies into thin rings and chop the garlic into very small pieces. Slice the white parts of the onions into thin rings and place these and the ginger in a small work bowl. Cut the green parts of the onions into thin rings and keep them separate, as they will be added to the prawns at the last minute.

3. To make the sauce, mix the sugar, vinegar, soy sauce, water, and cornstarch together in a small bowl, but don't add the bean sauce yet.

4. Have ready a Chinese spider or slotted spoon, a heatproof bowl for the hot oil, a small work bowl to hold the cooked prawns, and a small serving platter. Place a wok over high heat, add the oil, and when it shimmers, swirl it around and then add the prawns. Stir them in the hot oil for a minute or two until their tails are pink and their bodies have turned opaque. (Don't overcook them, as they will continue to cook from the residual heat and will also cook a tiny bit more when added to the sauce.) Remove the prawns from the oil with the spider and place them in the work bowl.

5. Drain off all but 2 tablespoons of the oil from the wok. With the heat still on high, add the chilies, garlic, whites of the onions, and ginger and stir-fry them for a few seconds to release their fragrance. Toss in the Sichuan hot bean sauce and mix everything together for a few seconds until the sauce boils and cooks through. Add the water chestnuts and mushrooms or wood ears. Quickly toss these until the mushrooms start to look cooked, then add the prawns and sauce. Working very fast, stir them over the heat until the sauce thickens, which should take only a couple of seconds. Taste and adjust the seasoning. Add the green parts of the onions, toss once, and arrange the prawns on your serving platter. Serve immediately.

This classic preparation works with any number of main ingredients. Try this sauce with shredded pork, which can be julienned, briefly stir-fried, and then added to the sauce.

For a fantastically delicious meatless version of this dish, use eggplant: Cut the eggplant into batons, salt them, and then drain them in a colander. Deep-fry or roast the eggplant (see page 43), or else blanch them for a few minutes in boiling water until barely cooked through. Proceed with the rest of the recipe as directed above. The fried or roasted eggplant will taste and feel meaty, while the blanched eggplant will be soft and delicate.

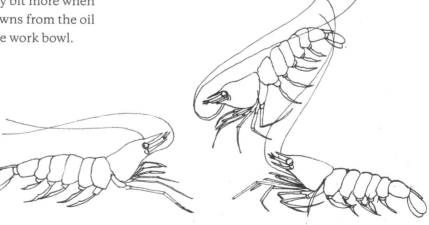

Gōngbǎo gānbèi 宮保干貝

Kung Pao Scallops

SICHUAN • SERVES 4

Kung pao chicken is standard fare at most American Chinese restaurants, but that doesn't necessarily mean that it is lacking in merit. I don't believe chicken is the best candidate for the recipe, though: it's too bland, and doesn't match the vibrancy of the sauce. To my mind, something with a bit more personality is needed, which is why I love to use fresh scallops in this dish.

Small bay or big diver scallops work great here (see the ingredients list for other suggestions). I also add fresh black mushrooms to deepen the seasoning that the Chinese describe as having a lychee flavor; you can heighten this fruity suggestion by adding a bit more sugar. Homemade sweet soy sauce (page 439) works well, too. You can use twice the amount of scallops and eliminate the mushrooms if you like, or vice versa, if you want to go the meatless route.

SCALLOPS

1 pound shelled scallops, fresh or frozen and defrosted
    (or squid, peeled and deveined shrimp,
    or boneless chicken)
2 tablespoons regular soy sauce
2 tablespoons Shaoxing rice wine
4 teaspoons cornstarch

AROMATICS

12 black mushrooms, fresh or dried and plumped up
4 stalks Chinese celery
3 tablespoons peeled and finely minced fresh ginger
4 cloves garlic, thinly sliced
6 green onions, trimmed
½ cup dried Thai chilies, broken in half, seeds shaken out
    and discarded, and caps removed

SAUCE

About 1½ tablespoons sweet soy sauce (page 439),
    or 1½ tablespoons regular soy sauce
    and 1½ teaspoons (or more) sugar
2 tablespoons black vinegar
2 teaspoons cornstarch

THE REST

½ cup peanut or vegetable oil, or as needed
2 heaping tablespoons whole Sichuan peppercorns
½ cup fried or toasted peanuts (page 411)

CHILIES AND SICHUAN PEPPERCORNS (see page 258) are the defining flavors of Sichuan, as seen in the region's two main schools of cooking: Chongqing's and Chengdu's. Chongqing's seasonings tend to be a bit hotter, while Chengdu's are a tad more numbing.

Chengdu's cuisine is called the "upriver gang." As befits a culinary capital, dishes here are more traditional and refined, favoring textbook-perfect renditions of classic Sichuan-style dishes over new ideas. This is thus the place to enjoy the almost idiosyncratic dishes of this province, like Camphor Tea Duck (page 284) and roast suckling pig.

To the east is Chongqing. Its cuisine, along with that of Dazhou, almost directly to its north, is known as the "downriver gang." The forerunners of this branch cuisine were the rough-and-tumble foods made in the street stalls and by the barge haulers who worked along the docks of the Yangtze, physically towing boats upriver with long, thick ropes.

During the middle third of the twentieth century, strong influences from Jiangsu made their way into the local foods, brought by people who came to make Chongqing their new home in wartime China. The tastes of the Huai Yang area (page 72) started seasoning

Chongqing's food with more soy sauce and oil than are used in other Sichuan cities and, in the process, invigorated the local dishes with ingredients like rice cakes (see page 136) and salted mustard greens (see page 426).

This last influx rebounded, leading to a rather short-lived but delectable way of cooking called *Chuān Yáng cài* 川揚菜. When the Nationalists left the Mainland for Taiwan, they brought this fusion cuisine with them, and by the 1970s, some of Taipei's finest restaurants featured eastern Chinese dishes crossed with Sichuan sensibilities.

1. Clean the scallops, leaving bay scallops whole and slicing diver scallops horizontally into 3 or 4 pieces. (If using squid, use the "blossom cut" on the bodies as directed on page 187, and then cut them into 1 × 2-inch rectangles; cut the trimmed tentacles into bite-sized clumps. Leave medium shrimp whole or cut large ones in half horizontally through the back to increase their surface area and make them easy to eat. Cut the chicken into ¾-inch cubes.) Place the scallops (or other main ingredient) in a small work bowl. Mix together the soy sauce, rice wine, and cornstarch, toss with the scallops, and let marinate while you prepare the rest of the ingredients. Discard the marinade just before Step 4 and allow the scallops to drain in a sieve set in the sink. (Having them relatively dry will allow them to sear quickly, rather than stew.)

2. Stem the mushrooms, then tear or cut the caps into pieces that are about the same size as the scallops. Remove the strings and leaves from the celery and cut the stalks into ½-inch lengths. Combine the ginger and garlic in a small bowl. Cut the green parts off the green onions, chop them into ¼-inch pieces, and save as a garnish. Cut the white parts of the onions into ¼-inch-wide rounds and add them to the ginger and garlic. Place the chilies in a sieve, rinse, and shake them dry.

3. Mix the sauce ingredients together in a small bowl or measuring cup, adding the sweet soy sauce (or soy sauce plus sugar) to taste.

4. Place a wok over medium heat and pour in the oil when the wok is hot. Swirl the oil around and add the Sichuan peppercorns. When the peppercorns have toasted to a very dark brown, use a slotted spoon to remove and discard them. Turn up the heat under the wok to high. Add the chilies to the oil, fry them until they start to brown, and add the ginger, garlic, and whites of the green onions. Stir-fry these for a few minutes to release their fragrance.

5. Add the mushrooms and stir-fry them until they start to brown, and then add the celery and toss it with the mushrooms. Fry only until the raw edge of the celery is gone. Scoot the vegetables up the side of the wok. Add the scallops (or other protein) and fry them quickly in the oil at the bottom of the wok until they barely brown, adding more oil as needed to keep them from sticking to the wok. Toss them with the vegetables.

6. Pour the sauce ingredients around the edge of the scallops and vegetables. Toss these together quickly until the sauce thickens and forms a sheen over all of the ingredients. Taste and adjust the seasoning. Toss in the onion greens and peanuts and then serve immediately.

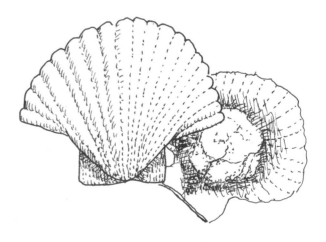

Qìguōjī 氣鍋雞

Steampot Chicken

YUNNAN · SERVES 4 TO 6

Yunnan steampots are found throughout most of south-central China. They're made of smooth clay, with a funnel-shaped opening on the bottom (see the diagram to the right). The steampot is filled with meats, vegetables, seasonings, and broth and then placed over a pan of boiling water. The steam moves through the funnel and into the pot, creating a flavorful stock while cooking the meats and vegetables.

Traditional recipes call for a very large steampot and a whole chicken, but I prefer to use a smaller, 6-cup-capacity steampot and boneless chicken. If you don't have a steampot handy, simmer the soup in a large covered sandpot or casserole and add another cup or two of unsalted stock as the broth cooks down.

10 ounces boneless, skinless chicken breast

6 thin slices Chinese-style ham

1 large winter bamboo shoot, defrosted if frozen and peeled and blanched if fresh (see Tip, page 122)

8 black mushrooms, fresh or dried and plumped up, stemmed

1 inch fresh ginger, thinly sliced

4 green onions, trimmed and cut into 2-inch lengths

2 tablespoons wolfberries, rinsed

1 cup mild rice wine

Freshly ground black pepper

1 cup unsalted chicken stock (page 380), boiling hot, plus more as needed

1 teaspoon light soy sauce, or to taste

GARNISH
Toasted sesame oil
Shredded green onions or chopped cilantro

1. Remove any silver tendons that run through the chicken, then cut the meat into 1-inch pieces. Bring a large saucepan filled with water to a boil, drop in the cubed meat, and stir so that none of the pieces stick together. Simmer for about 2 minutes to blanch the chicken, removing any scum. Drain and discard the water, rinse the meat under running water, and allow it to drain.

2. Prepare the steampot and the pan that will provide the steam (for directions on setting up a steampot, see the diagram to the right).

3. Slice the ham into a thin julienne and cut the bamboo shoot into 1-inch chunks. Evenly place the blanched poultry pieces in the steampot and layer on the ham, bamboo shoots, mushrooms, ginger, green onions, wolfberries, and rice wine. Grind some fresh black pepper over everything. Pour the hot stock and a bit of soy sauce on top, leaving at least an inch of the pot's funnel showing so that the soup won't flow out through the funnel.

4. Cover the steampot, bring the water in the saucepan back to a full boil, lower the heat to medium, and let the soup steam for about 2 hours. Try not to open the lid too often while the chicken is cooking, so that the steam doesn't escape. When everything is tender, the soup is ready. Taste and adjust the seasoning as necessary. Sprinkle on a bit of sesame oil and either some shredded green onions or cilantro.

5. Fold a towel into a square and place it on a large plate. The towel will help keep the pot steady and prevent burns. Use 2 potholders or a thick towel to remove the steampot from the saucepan and place it on the folded towel before carrying it proudly to the dining table. Remove the lid with a flourish and ladle out the soup into individual bowls.

This dish can be varied to include whatever vegetables are in season. Consider it a template rather than a strict recipe.

SETTING UP A STEAMPOT

❶
Since you want to direct as much steam into the steampot as possible, line the edge of the saucepan with a couple of strips of cheesecloth or gauze. Fill the bowl half full with water.

❷
Nestle the steampot firmly into the top of the saucepan, pushing down slightly so that it fits snugly.

❸
Bring the saucepan to a full boil and cover the steampot. After a few minutes, check around the edges of the steampot to find any steam coming up through the cloth. Use a paring knife to poke these holes closed. After a minute, check again: you should have all of the steam directed straight into the pot where it belongs. Turn down the heat to medium.

❹
When adding stock, leave about an inch of clearance around the tip of the funnel so that the stock does not drain out of the steampot and into the pan.

Làzi ji 辣子雞

Chili Chicken

GUIZHOU • SERVES 4

This dish is popular throughout the Central Highlands, but my favorite version comes from Guizhou.

CHICKEN AND MARINADE
½ fryer chicken
2 tablespoons mild rice wine
2 tablespoons or more Guizhou *ciba* chili paste (page 438)
2 tablespoons regular soy sauce
¼ cup cornstarch
½ cup peanut or vegetable oil, or as needed

SAUCE
2 tablespoons or more Guizhou *ciba* chili paste
About 2 tablespoons sweet soy sauce (page 439),
      or about 2 tablespoons regular soy sauce
      and 2 teaspoons sugar
¼ cup water
1 medium leek, cleaned (see page 450) and cut
      into 1-inch lengths, or 3 green onions, trimmed
      and cut into 1-inch lengths

1. Chop the chicken into bite-sized pieces no larger than 1 inch square, place in a work bowl, and toss with the rice wine, chili paste, and soy sauce. Marinate the chicken for at least 2 hours, then drain and toss with the cornstarch.

2. Place a wok over high heat, swirl in the oil, and brown a handful of the chicken at a time, adding more oil as needed.

3. For the sauce, pour out the oil and return the wok to medium heat. Stir in the chili paste and then the sweet soy sauce (or soy sauce and sugar) and water. Bring this rapidly to a boil. When the sauce has reduced, adjust the seasoning and then toss in the leeks (or green onions) and chicken. Serve as soon as the leeks wilt.

Xiāngmáocǎo kǎojī 香茅草烤雞

Lemongrass Chicken

YUNNAN • SERVES 4 TO 6

This recipe comes from the Dai people of southern Yunnan. The Dai live near the headwaters of the Mekong River; they are closely related, both culturally and culinarily, to the Shan people of Myanmar, Laos, and Thailand. As a result, this dish tastes a lot like the cooking of Southeast Asia. The chicken is partially boned, which allows it to cook quickly before the meat dries out; most of the flavor comes from the long fronds of citrusy lemongrass.

1 small fryer chicken (about 2½ pounds)
Spray oil
1 bunch (4 ounces) lemongrass
2 tablespoons regular soy sauce
½ cup chopped cilantro
2 green onions, trimmed and chopped
1 teaspoon peeled and finely chopped fresh ginger
1 teaspoon finely chopped garlic
1 teaspoon (or more) coarsely ground dried chilies
¼ cup rendered chicken fat, lard, or vegetable oil

1. Trim off the extra fat around the chicken's cavity and render it (follow the directions for rendering pork fat for lard on page 482), if you like, to use for basting the bird later on. Remove the neck, giblets, and wing tips and use those for something else. If you are barbecuing the bird, start your fire so that the coals will be ready and spray the grill with oil. Otherwise, place an oven rack about 4 inches from the broiler, turn on the broiler, and spray a wire rack with oil and set it in a rimmed baking pan (see Tips).

2. Remove and discard the bulbs of the lemongrass, then rinse the lemongrass carefully, paying special attention to the grooves at the bottoms of the fronds. Dry each piece with a paper towel to get rid of any grit still clinging to the leaves. Pick out the palest leaves in the center and chop them finely until you have 1½ cups. Leave the rest of the leaves whole.

3. Place the chopped lemongrass in a medium work bowl and add the soy sauce, cilantro, green onions, ginger, garlic, and chilies. Toss them and add more seasoning if you wish, then let the flavors of this marinade mingle while you prepare the bird.

4. Remove the breastbone, back, and ribs from the chicken (see page 460).

5. Pat the lemongrass marinade inside the bird in a thick layer and fold the breast meat over the filling. Select your longest lemongrass leaves and tie them around the body, starting with the circumference of the thighs and legs and then tying the wings and body. Turn the bird 90 degrees and tie more leaves around the body from the neck to the tail. Keep tying leaves around the chicken until it's completely wrapped in lemongrass.

6. Lay the chicken on the barbecue grill or wire rack. Cook it on both sides, occasionally brushing the top with the rendered fat or oil, until it's roasted through, about 40 to 50 minutes. Remove the chicken from the heat, let it rest for about 10 minutes, and then cut off the blackened lemongrass. Chop the chicken into pieces of any size and serve.

Lemongrass is found in the produce section of most Chinese and Southeast Asian markets. If you live in a warm area, consider growing lemongrass: simply root the base of the lemongrass and plant it in rich, moist soil.

A broiler pan can be used instead of a cake rack set in a baking pan, but I prefer the latter because it allows the heat to circulate under the chicken as it cooks.

Huíguō ròu 回鍋肉

Twice-Cooked Pork

HUNAN AND SICHUAN · SERVES 4 TO 6

When we lived in Taipei, my husband and I would visit our favorite home-style Hunan restaurant, Tiānréntái 天仁臺, at least once a month. Located across the street from South Gate Market—a collection of food stalls, homemade-charcuterie places, and produce stands—this restaurant was old-school, and it made the best Twice-Cooked Pork around.

This dish was originally created to use up the cooked square of pork offered two times a month to the gods and ancestors. In addition to the fresh bacon, Tianrentai also included thinly sliced pressed bean curd, which was the perfect complement to the meat.

4 ounces (or so) pork belly, with the skin removed, chilled

2 squares pressed bean curd

½ sweet red pepper

1 large leek

2 tablespoons peanut or vegetable oil

1 tablespoon peeled and finely chopped fresh ginger

2 cloves garlic, thinly sliced

3 tablespoons toasted sesame oil

1 tablespoon bean sauce

1 tablespoon Sichuan hot bean sauce

About 2 teaspoons sweet soy sauce (page 439),
    or about 2 teaspoons regular soy sauce
    and ½ teaspoon sugar

1. Cut off and discard any skin, tough tendons, and stringy fat on the meat. Slice the pork thinly against the grain, then cut it into pieces no larger than 1 inch square. Lay the pressed bean curd on a cutting board and slice the squares horizontally into very thin pieces; cut these into pieces about the same size as the pork. Remove the seeds from the pepper and cut it, too, into pieces about the same size as the pork. Trim the leek carefully, being sure to wash out all the sand that lurks in the bottoms of the leaves (see page 450), and then cut into 1-inch lengths.

2. Heat a wok over high heat and add the oil. When the oil shimmers, add the ginger and stir-fry it for a few seconds to release its fragrance. Add the pork and move it around in the hot oil to sear the edges and brown it a little and then scoot it up one side of the wok. Toss in the bean curd, stir-fry until lightly browned, then push it up the side of the wok to join the pork. Add the red pepper and quickly brown it before sidling it up against the bean curd. Finally, toss in the leeks and garlic and quickly wilt them. Scrape the meat and vegetables into a clean work bowl, leaving any extra oil in the wok.

3. Set the wok over high heat, add the sesame oil, bean sauce, and hot bean sauce, then drizzle in the sweet soy sauce (or soy sauce and sugar) to taste. Stir everything around for a few seconds and adjust the seasoning. Return the meat and veggies to the wok and toss everything together over high heat until all the surfaces are slicked with sauce. Taste again, adjust the seasoning as desired, and serve.

The prepared sauces here have wildly varying levels of saltiness, so start with a smallish amount—you can always add more. As with all bottled sauces, be sure to cook the sauce in some fat to remove the canned flavor.

There are endless variations on this recipe. The rendition from Chongqing is one of my favorites. It ramps the heat way up with a handful of fresh chili peppers and reduces the sweetness.

Dōngān jī 東安雞

Dongan Chicken

HUNAN • SERVES 6 TO 8

In 712 CE, three elderly women ran a restaurant in a small town in southern Hunan. One evening, some tradesmen came by looking for dinner, but the restaurant had run out of food. The owners quickly bought two chickens and decided they'd try something new. They briefly poached and boned the birds, then tossed them in a spicy sauce. The tradesmen loved it, and word of the chicken eventually reached the county chief. He came to the restaurant, ordered the dish, found it delicious, and soon it was named after the county where they lived: Dongan.

CHICKEN AND POACHING LIQUID

½ teaspoon ground toasted Sichuan peppercorns (page 441)

1 tablespoon dark soy sauce

2 tablespoons Shaoxing rice wine

1 tablespoon rock sugar (a piece about half the size of a walnut)

Boiling water, as needed

1 whole fryer chicken (about 3 pounds)

EVERYTHING ELSE

3 to 6 small dried chilies, or to taste

1½ teaspoons ground toasted Sichuan peppercorns, or 2 teaspoons whole Sichuan peppercorns

¼ cup peanut oil

2 tablespoons peeled and finely julienned fresh ginger

2 tablespoons black vinegar, or to taste

2 tablespoons Shaoxing rice wine

1 teaspoon sugar, or to taste

¼ cup poaching liquid (from Step 2)

1 teaspoon sea salt, or to taste

1 teaspoon cornstarch mixed with 2 tablespoons stock or water

3 green onions, trimmed and cut into 1-inch lengths

2 teaspoons toasted sesame oil

SOME OF HUNAN'S MOST DEFINITIVE DISHES were already being created as early as the third century CE, and even today the area's delectable Dongan Chicken displays nothing less than an ancient sensibility: many centuries before chili peppers had wiggled their way into the Chinese heartland, sophisticated Hunanese diners were enjoying something similar to this iconic dish.

Since tart flavors wake up the senses, one of the protocols for formal banquets back in the Han dynasty decreed that the fifth course must be the one called "the chicken opens the mouth," which stimulated the appetite through the addition of vinegar. Nowadays, banquet dishes are generally mild, like Honey Ham (page 288), but the rustic dishes of Hunan are often lashed with dried and fresh chilies, sometimes with liberal handfuls of fermented black beans tossed in for a delectably savory note.

When meat makes an entrance in Hunan's everyday foods, it is often as charcuterie (see page 289). Both domestic animals and wild game are preserved with curing and smoke in ways that have been practiced for millennia. The ancient *Book of Changes* includes mention of early techniques, explaining that "charcuterie is that which has been dried with the sun and placed over the fire."

1. Start this recipe a couple of hours—or even a day or two—before you plan to serve it. Put the ground Sichuan peppercorns, soy sauce, rice wine, and sugar in a 2-quart pot, add about 1 cup boiling water, and swish this mixture around. Add the chicken, breast-side up. Pour in enough boiling water to cover the chicken, then place it on the stove over high heat. As soon as it boils, reduce the heat so that you have a lively simmer and let the chicken cook for 20 to 30 minutes, until a chopstick inserted into the thickest part of the thigh goes in very easily. Let the chicken sit in the stock; when it has cooled to lukewarm, carefully remove it to a rimmed platter and let it cool off until it's easy to handle. Reserve the poaching liquid in the stockpot.

2. Place another large plate or platter next to the chicken. If the head, neck, and/or feet are still attached, remove them and toss them into the poaching liquid. Cut off the wing tips and back and put them in the stockpot. (As you break down the chicken, you can leave the skin attached to the meat if you wish, or add it to the stockpot along with the bones.) Remove the bones from the wings, legs (pull out the tendons), and thighs. Leave the meat in chunks as large as possible and place them on the clean plate. Slice that meat crosswise as needed to make pieces about ½ inch wide, then remove the meat from the rest of the carcass and cut it to the same size. Toss the rest of the bones into the stockpot. Bring the stock to a boil, then simmer it uncovered for about an hour; strain and discard the solids. Reserve about ¼ cup of the stock for this dish, and use the rest for something else. The recipe can be made ahead of time up to this point. Chill the chicken and the reserved stock.

3. Before you assemble the sauce, break the chilies in half and discard the seeds and stem ends. Crumble or chop the chilies into smallish pieces. If you're using whole Sichuan peppercorns, place them on the cutting board and crush them with the side of a wide Chinese knife, pressing down on the blade so that they break open.

4. Set a wok over medium-high heat until it barely begins to smoke, then add the oil and swirl it around before adding the ginger and chilies. Quickly stir-fry them before adding the chicken to the wok. Gently toss the chicken over the heat for a minute before adding the ground or crushed peppercorns, vinegar, rice wine, and sugar. Continue to gently toss everything together for another minute before adding the poaching liquid and salt. Cover the wok and let the flavors combine for about 2 minutes, by which time most of the stock will have cooked off.

5. Uncover the wok and pour off any excess oil. Taste and add more salt, vinegar, or sugar as needed. Return the wok to medium-high heat. Drizzle in the cornstarch slurry and toss the chicken until the cornstarch has evenly coated it and is cooked through. Sprinkle in the green onions and sesame oil. Serve immediately.

Zhāng chá yā 樟茶鴨

Camphor Tea Duck

SICHUAN · SERVES 4 TO 6

Camphor Tea Duck was a favorite of the Qing royal family—Ding Baozhen, the Qing official responsible for the proliferation of kung pao dishes, is believed to have popularized it. Ding served under the last three emperors, as well as the Dowager Empress Cixi; this duck is thought to be the invention of one of his chefs, Huang Jinlin of Chengdu, who adapted a traditional smoked duck recipe for the royal family by adding smoldering camphor leaves and twigs.

In 1911, when the imperial family was deposed, Huang's recipe returned with him to his hometown. It became a local classic there, and it's still popular in Chengdu today. The dish is seasoned with Sichuan peppercorns, which lend it a piney, dry heat. The flavors are amplified by the fragrant camphor leaves and tea smoke. I have added a bit of pink salt, too, which colors the meat and elevates its flavors.

DUCK AND DRY RUB

1 whole duck (about 5 pounds), fresh or frozen
    and defrosted, feet removed but including the
    head, if you like
¼ teaspoon pink salt, optional but very good
3 tablespoons toasted Sichuan peppercorn salt (page 440)
3 tablespoons Shaoxing rice wine
3 green onions, trimmed and cut into 1-inch lengths
12 thin slices fresh ginger
Spray oil

FUEL FOR THE SMOKER

½ cup dried camphor leaves (or cedar needles or
    camphor sawdust), coarsely crumbled or chopped
    (see Tips)
¼ cup dry tea leaves of any kind
2 tablespoons brown sugar

SAUCE

1 teaspoon toasted sesame oil
½ cup bean sauce or sweet wheat paste
Sweet soy sauce (page 439), or regular soy sauce and sugar,
    as needed

TO DEEP-FRY

Peanut or vegetable oil (used oil is all right if it smells fresh)

TO SERVE

1 teaspoon toasted sesame oil
20 lotus leaf buns (page 408), steamed and kept hot
2 or 3 green onions, trimmed and julienned

1. Start this recipe at least 1 day before you wish to serve it. First, marinate the duck: clean out the viscera, remove any large pieces of fat around the cavity and neck, and cut off the wing tips. Pat the bird dry inside and out with paper towels. Put the duck on a chopping board breast up and press down firmly on the breast to flatten it, working your way up and down the body to crack the ribs. Place the duck in a medium work bowl. If you are using the pink salt, toss it well with the toasted Sichuan peppercorn salt in a small bowl. Rub the rice wine all over the skin and in the cavity, then immediately rub the salts inside and outside the duck, paying special attention to the thicker parts so that they're seasoned well. Stuff the cavity with the green onions and ginger. Cover the bowl with plastic wrap and refrigerate for at least 24 hours and up to 48, turning the bird over a couple of times whenever you think of it.

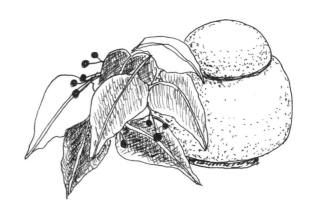

2. Prepare a smoker as described on page 27 and oil its rack. Mix together the camphor leaves (or other smoking materials), tea leaves, and sugar in a small bowl, then pile these in the bottom of the smoker. Turn the heat to high, and when billows of white smoke emerge from the vents, place the duck, breast-side up, on the oiled rack, being sure to flatten it firmly in the smoker in order to set its shape. Turn the heat to low and smoke the duck for about 10 minutes, then turn off the heat. Leave the duck in the covered smoker for another 20 minutes or so and then remove it to a clean plate. (Do not heat the smoker for any longer than this, as the sugar will turn acrid and sour the smoking flavors.)

3. Next, steam the duck: prepare a steamer (see page 49) and bring the water in it to a full boil. Put the duck breast-side down on a deep rimmed plate. Place the plate with the duck on it in the steamer, cover, and steam the duck for about 1 hour, checking it every 15 minutes and using a turkey baster to remove the juices if they threaten to overflow the plate. The bird is done when you can pierce the thigh and no pink juices appear. Remove the duck and place it on a rack to cool completely. When it can be handled easily, drain off the juices and discard the seasonings in the cavity. Reserve the juices for something else and pat the inside of the duck with a paper towel. Place the duck in front of a small table fan for an hour or two to dry the skin (see page 26). Turn the duck over after a while so that both sides can dry off. It's ready when the skin feels tacky.

4. Prepare the sauce: place a wok over medium heat, pour in the sesame oil, and swirl it around. When the wok is hot, add the bean sauce or sweet wheat paste. Season this with a bit of sweet soy sauce (or soy sauce and sugar) as needed (see Tips). When the sauce starts to bubble, scrape it out into a small serving bowl.

5. Pour about 3 inches of oil into a hot wok and deep-fry the duck until it's an even golden brown (follow Steps 2 and 4 on page 111). Remove the browned duck, drain it completely, and place the bird on a cutting board.

6. Lightly rub the skin with the teaspoon of sesame oil to give it a nice sheen. Cut off the wings, legs, and thighs, and chop them into 1-inch pieces (see page 460); the head may also be chopped in half if you like. Use a cleaver or heavy sharp knife to first cut the duck down the middle and then down the sides so that you have 4 large pieces. Chop these crosswise into clean 1-inch-wide pieces. Rearrange the duck on a platter in an attractive manner. (Traditionally, it should be put together so that it looks like a whole duck.)

7. Serve the duck while it is still very hot, accompanied by the steamed lotus leaf buns, slivered green onions, and prepared sauce. Your diners should stuff the meaty pieces into the buns along with a bit of the green onion and sauce, and eat the bonier pieces with chopsticks. The latter can also be dabbed with sauce and draped with a strand or two of green onion.

VARIATIONS

If you omit the smoking step, you will have a dish that is popular in Sichuan and Beijing: fragrant crispy duck (*xiāng sū yā* 香酥鴨); serve it the same way. Fragrant and crispy chicken (*xiāng sū jī* 香酥雞) is another classic, and it's cooked just like fragrant and crispy duck.

If you can't get your hands on a camphor tree, use some apple or almond wood chips.

The amount of sugar and soy sauce used should be adjusted based on the flavors of the bean sauce or sweet wheat paste. Be sure not to use chili sauce, as it would overpower the nuances in this dish.

The preparation of the duck can be spread over several days. Just be sure to fry it at the last minute.

Héyè fěnzhēngròu 荷葉粉蒸肉

Lotus-Wrapped Spicy Rice Crumb Pork

SICHUAN · SERVES 6 TO 8

I ate many versions of Sichuan- and Hunan-style rice crumb pork when I lived in Taiwan. Some were terrific, such as the insanely spicy version at Old Zhang's Dandan Noodles, where the pork was piled onto small bamboo steamers (see Tips).

The dish consists of spicy pork chunks covered in the coarsely ground rice known as *zhēngfěn* 蒸粉, or "rice crumbs." It's great for parties, because it can be made far in advance; you can even cook it completely and freeze it.

If you leave out the chilies, you will have something more in the style of northern Hunan's Lake Dongting cuisine. Milder iterations of this dish are very popular along the lower Yangtze, as well, and are often served at banquets; spicier renditions are sold at street stalls and mom-and-pop restaurants.

PORK AND MARINADE

14 to 16 ounces boned pork shank with the skin on or other fatty cut (see Tips), or about 12 pork back ribs, cut in half

¼ cup liquid from white bean curd "cheese" (page 421) or red fermented bean curd "cheese" (page 420), or ¼ cup mild rice wine

¼ cup sweet soy sauce (page 439), or ¼ cup regular soy sauce and 4 teaspoons sugar

2 tablespoons finely minced fresh ginger

2 green onions, trimmed and finely chopped

4 cloves garlic, finely chopped

2 tablespoons sweet wheat paste

6 tablespoons solids from Hunan-style chili paste (page 437), or hot bean paste, or to taste, optional

RICE CRUMBS AND LOTUS LEAVES

2 cups rice crumbs (page 383), made from sticky rice

4 dried lotus leaves, soaked in hot water until pliable

1. Rinse the meat and pat it dry with paper towels. If there is skin attached, be sure to remove all the hairs with tweezers (see page 459). Cut the meat, including all of the fat, skin, and any tendons, into thin slices. If you are using ribs, cut evenly between the bones. Chop any particularly tough bits—especially loose fat—into even smaller dice.

2. Mix the marinade in a medium work bowl; taste and adjust the seasoning (see Tips) to fit your taste, menu, and guests. Add the meat to the bowl, toss, and let it marinate while you prepare the rest of the ingredients. This can be done up to 8 hours in advance.

3. Set up a deep steamer and bring a couple inches of water to a boil underneath it (see page 49). Pour the rice crumbs into the marinating pork and toss well.

4. Prepare the lotus leaves and roll up the pork and crumbs in them (for directions on cleaning the leaves and wrapping the pork, see the diagram below). Place the leaf packets in a single layer in the steamer baskets. Steam them for about 3½ hours, until the meat is very tender. You can either serve them immediately or cool the packets down, put them in a resealable freezer bag, and freeze. They do not have to be defrosted prior to resteaming. To serve, either portion out the packets on individual plates or serve directly from the steamer baskets.

To steam the pork without the lotus leaves, use small bamboo steamers like the ones found in dim sum restaurants. Spray their insides well with oil and then pile the pork inside; it should come up to the rim. You can place thick slices of red sweet potato or pumpkin in the bottom of the steamer to soak up the flavors of the pork and marinade. This is what they did at Old Zhang's.

Any nice cut of pork works for this recipe, so see what looks good to you. Pork butt (shoulder) and pork belly with skin are two good options. If you select ribs, have the butcher saw them into pieces no longer than 2 or 3 inches. Then cut them apart so that each bone is surrounded by meat and fat.

For a mild dish in the style of northern Hubei, substitute a seasoned oil (pages 434 and 435) for the chili oil. If you want it to be spicier, add a tablespoon or two of Sichuan hot bean sauce and leave out the sweet wheat paste. If the hot bean sauce is very salty, omit the sweet soy sauce. If you want, you can even toss in chopped fresh chilies.

HOW TO MAKE LOTUS-LEAF PACKETS

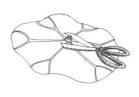	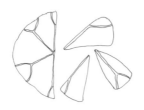		
❶	**❷**	**❸**	**❹**
Wipe the 4 lotus leaves dry with a clean towel and cut off the hard stem section in the center.	Cut each leaf in half and then cut each half into 3 even triangles, for a total of 24 triangles.	Divide the pork into 24 portions and place these small mounds near the bottom of each triangle.	Fold the long edges over each mound of pork, then roll the leaf up from the wide end to the pointy tip (it should form a tight packet). Set the packet tip down in the steam basket to keep it from unrolling.

Mìzhī huǒtuǐ 蜜汁火腿

Honey Ham

HUNAN · SERVES 4 TO 6

Because authentic Chinese ham cannot be imported to the United States, most Chinese markets sell something that they typically label "Smithfield ham." This is an American dry-cured pork leg, and it is what I usually rely on to give a nice hammy seasoning to many of the dishes in this book. But when the main ingredient in a Chinese dish is ham, a country-style ham will not work because it is too hard and salty. What I have discovered is that Hunan-style charcuterie happens to work perfectly. It is moist enough to cook through easily, and its cure will not overwhelm the dish.

Every Hunan cookbook I've ever looked at says that sliced ham should be steamed only with simple rock sugar. On occasion, a writer might say that lotus seeds can be added. But I have added some extra elements: Chinese brown slab sugar, Shaoxing rice wine, and ginger juice. These ingredients make the dish much more layered and interesting, while still preserving the traditional flavor. I recommend sandwiching the finished ham in lotus leaf buns.

6 tablespoons dried lotus seeds

Boiling water, as needed

1 pound Hunan-style cured pork (see charcuterie, page 478)

2 whole pieces Chinese brown slab sugar, or 2 walnut-sized pieces of rock sugar

2 tablespoons Shaoxing rice wine

2 tablespoons ginger juice (page 481)

20 lotus leaf buns (page 408), steamed and kept hot

1. Soak the lotus seeds in boiling water and then clean them (see the diagram to the right).

2. Remove the skin from the smoked pork (use it for something else, like stock), and slice the meat against the grain into very thin pieces, keeping as much fat on as possible but removing any tough membranes.

3. Arrange the meat slices in an overlapping pattern in the center of a rimmed heatproof plate so they look like flower petals. Pile the cleaned lotus seeds around the edge of the plate to form a white fringe. Arrange the 2 pieces of slab sugar on top of the ham, and then pour the rice wine and ginger juice over everything.

4. Prepare a steamer (see page 49) and bring the water in it to a full boil. Place the plate in the steamer and steam for about 1 hour, until the meat is very tender and the lotus seeds are soft. Taste a lotus seed to ensure that it is cooked through. Remove the plate from the steamer and carefully pour the sauce off into a wok or pan. Bring the sauce to a boil and reduce it until it is thick and bubbly, then pour it over the meat and lotus seeds. Serve with the hot steamed lotus buns. Have each diner open up a bun and insert a slice or two of the meat. These are to be eaten like tiny sandwiches; the lotus seeds can be picked up with chopsticks and eaten as a garnish.

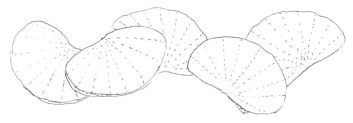

PREPARING LOTUS SEEDS

❶ Place the lotus seeds in a small heatproof bowl and cover them with boiling water. Let the lotus seeds sit in the water until it has cooled completely.

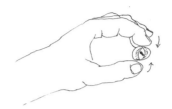

❷ Squeeze open each softened seed.

❸ Pluck out any green spouts (these are bitter).

❹ Rinse again and drain.

HUNAN'S CHARCUTERIE AND SMOKED foods are some of the best in the country. Pork, poultry, fish, and even bamboo are prepared in three steps—marinating, drying, and finally smoking—to give them a deep mahogany sheen. The process is usually underway by early winter so that these specialties will be ready in time for Chinese New Year, but many people enjoy these foods all year-round.

Pigs are butchered when they are at their fattest and the chilly northeast winds start to blow. Long strips of fresh bacon, chunks of shoulder and thigh, and other favorite parts are soaked in a heavily seasoned marinade for around six days, after which the curing salts will have done their magic. The meat is then rinsed well and any hairs are removed before it is hung out to dry under the eaves for a few days in the cold wind. Finally, it is moved to a smoker.

When made by someone with experience, Hunan-style charcuterie is simply stunning. Large whole fish are butterflied, chickens and ducks are spread open with thin bamboo strips so that every morsel dries and smokes evenly, and thin sausages hang like aromatic meat bouquets from the rafters of a master *charcutière*. My favorite place to hang out at South Gate Market (see page 281) in Taipei was near the charcuterie stands, where these animals ended up looking as if they were made of the finest polished wood. Deep brown plaques with the names of each variety hung next to the charcuterie and glistened with oil after decades of use, while the air was filled with the perfume of smoke and meat.

Gānbiān kǔguā 乾煸苦瓜

Dry-Fried Bitter Melon

SICHUAN · SERVES 4 TO 6

I am a big fan of raw bitter melon. Every year I get excited when an especially pale variety surfaces for a few short weeks in autumn, which means I can finally enjoy Raw "White Jade" Bitter Melon (page 252). I was never very interested in cooked bitter melon, however, until I tried this dish. It's a very simple recipe: all you have to do is fry the melon slices in peanut or vegetable oil and sprinkle them with salt. The completely edible seeds fry up, too, offering a nutty, textural contrast to the juicy melon rounds, which take on a sweet edge as they sear.

2 pale green bitter melons, 10 to 12 inches long
Peanut or vegetable oil
Sea salt

1. Rinse the bitter melons and trim off both ends, as well as any bruises. Cut the melons crosswise into ½-inch-thick rounds but do not remove the seeds. If the seeds have bright red coverings, so much the better (see page 477).

2. Place a wok or flat-bottomed frying pan over medium-high heat until it starts to smoke and then drizzle in a tablespoon or so of the oil to barely slick the surface. Put in only as many melon slices as will cover the bottom. Fry the slices until they are browned and speckled, shake them loose, and then turn them over to cook the other side. Remove to a serving plate and repeat with the rest of the melon slices until they are all cooked. Serve hot with a sprinkle of salt.

Báiguǒ qíncài chǎo bǎihé 白果芹菜炒百合

Ginkgo Nuts, Chinese Celery, and Lily Bulbs

NORTHERN GUANGXI · SERVES 4 TO 6

In Northern Guangxi, the beautiful yellow beads called ginkgo nuts are matched perfectly with two other ingredients: fresh lily bulb petals and Chinese celery. When combined in a simple stir-fry, this trio of Chinese vegetables offers up the perfect contrast of color, flavor, and texture. The celery turns jade green as it cooks and emits salty and herbal aromas. The fresh lily petals, which are pale ivory and shaped like little cups, offer a gentle sweetness. And, finally, the golden ginkgo nuts ground everything, adding a starchy element to the dish.

You can use Western-style celery here, of course, but it is not as flavorful as the Chinese variety.

2 sterile bags (3½ ounces each) prepared ginkgo nuts
6 stalks Chinese celery
Boiling water, as needed
8 fresh lily bulbs (about 2 packages),
    or 8 fresh water chestnuts, peeled and sliced
¼ cup peanut or vegetable oil
1 teaspoon sea salt

1. Place the ginkgo nuts in a small saucepan and cover with boiling water. Bring to a boil again, turn the heat down to a simmer, and cook for 10 minutes, to plump them up and freshen their taste. Drain and rinse the nuts. Taste one—it should be creamy and have a faint bitter edge.

2. Remove the strings from the outsides of the celery stalks to make them tender and trim off the leaves. Cut the celery into pieces about the same length as the ginkgo nuts. Place the celery in a saucepan and cover with boiling water. Bring to a boil again and then lower the heat to a simmer. Simmer the celery until the rawness has been cooked off but it is still crispy. Drain the celery in a colander and immediately shock it with cool water to stop the cooking.

3. Trim and clean the lily bulbs (see page 450), and then shake them dry in a colander or salad spinner.

4. Heat a wok over high heat and add the oil and salt. Swirl them around so that the salt melts a bit. Add the ginkgo nuts and brown them very lightly. Scatter in the celery and toss everything around for a few seconds until the stalks are coated with oil. Sprinkle in the lily bulbs or water chestnuts. Toss the vegetables together quickly over high heat for only a minute or so, just until the lily bulbs turn from white to opaque, or as long as it takes the water chestnuts to be barely cooked through. Taste and adjust the seasoning. Serve immediately.

NORTHERN GUANGXI IS AN ALMOST unbroken undulation of mountains completely covered with rain forest, and most of the people who live here belong to one of a dozen or so vibrant minorities, with the Zhuang being the most populous group. The Zhuang outnumber China's Hui Muslims by a ratio of two to one—which makes the almost nonexistent effect their cuisine has had on China's eating traditions, compared to the immense impact of the Hui (see page 317), an interesting puzzle.

Sticky rice is the mainstay here, whether made into fat, round noodles called *mǐfěn*

米粉 or sliced into the flattened ovals known as *qiēfěn* 切粉. These are either covered with hot broth or stir-fried much in the way they are in Chaozhou (page 220). The local Zhuang beverage, called *dǎyóuchá* 打油茶, is similar to the "pounded tea" (*léichá* 擂茶) of the Hakka: tea leaves are fried and then simmered with fried rice crusts before being garnished with a variety of savory and crunchy bits.

Freshwater fish and shrimp are enjoyed in different parts of Guangxi, as are wild game, homegrown vegetables, and more exotic things like snakes, snails, lizards, insects, horse, and dog.

The love for dog meat is practically ingrained in many areas of China; the dog has been considered a prime source of meat since at least Neolithic times. During the reign of King Goujian of Yue (496–465 BCE), he encouraged his people to bear many children by giving them a pig for each daughter and a dog (which was then more valuable) for each son. It should be noted, though, that those Chinese who do not grow up in dog-eating environments often get as upset about the idea of eating one as any dog-loving Westerner.

Dòuchǐ chǎo lúsǔn 豆豉炒蘆筍

Black Bean Asparagus

HUNAN • SERVES 4

Asparagus is not native to China, but it has been adopted to such an extent that the country now produces more asparagus than any other nation. There are countless ways of cooking the vegetable, but this is the method I like best. The flavor of the asparagus is not drowned in seasonings, and very little oil is used. I like to include fresh ginger or garlic, but you can experiment with other aromatics, such as fresh chili peppers.

I have served this dish in the past with the thinnest possible stalks, and with larger stalks shredded with a vegetable peeler to create a satiny texture. It works either way.

1 bunch asparagus (about 1½ pounds), thick or thin stalks
2 tablespoons peanut or vegetable oil
2 tablespoons peeled and finely chopped fresh ginger
     or coarsely chopped garlic
2 tablespoons coarsely chopped fermented black beans
A splash of rice wine, optional

1. Rinse the asparagus and then snap off and discard the tough ends. If the asparagus is thinner than a chopstick, cut each stalk into 2-inch lengths. If the asparagus is fat, you may roll cut it (see page 449), slice it on a sharp diagonal, or use a vegetable peeler to shred it into confetti.

2. Place an empty wok over high heat and pour in the oil once it is hot. Immediately add the ginger or garlic as well as the chopped beans. Stir-fry these for about a minute, until the ginger or garlic just begins to brown. Scoot everything up the side of the wok and toss in the asparagus. Stir-fry the asparagus until barely tender and then toss with the aromatics. (If the asparagus is very thick, splash in some wine to speed up the cooking.) Taste and adjust the seasoning and serve immediately.

If you want to ramp up the seasonings for this dish, use 3 tablespoons of both the ginger or garlic and the black beans.

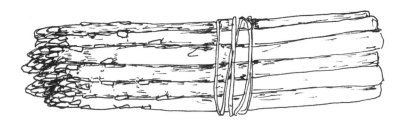

Guāhuā niàng 瓜花酿

Stuffed Squash Blossoms

NORTHERN GUANGXI · SERVES 6

When you mention stuffed squash blossoms, most people think of the Italian dish, which features ricotta cheese, herbs, and garlic. But the Chinese rendition, which comes from the tropical mountains of Northern Guangxi, features a savory meat or mushroom filling instead. This dish originated in the county of Yangshuo, which is known for its eighteen stuffed dishes (everything from lotus roots to chilies to bitter melons); this version is my favorite. The blossoms turn crunchy on the outside as they fry, and the meatballs inside become deliciously juicy.

SQUASH BLOSSOMS AND FILLING

12 very fresh squash blossoms

1½ cups finely chopped pork or fresh mushrooms

2 cloves garlic, finely chopped

4 green onions, trimmed and finely chopped

1 large egg, lightly beaten

2 teaspoons regular soy sauce

1 red jalapeño pepper, diced, optional

TO FRY

1 large egg, lightly beaten

Cornstarch, as needed

Peanut or vegetable oil, as needed

GARLIC AND CHILI SAUCE, OPTIONAL

2 tablespoons peeled and finely chopped fresh ginger

4 cloves garlic, finely chopped

2 to 4 red jalapeño peppers

¼ cup peanut or vegetable oil

¼ cup mild rice wine

2 teaspoons light soy sauce

2 teaspoons sugar

2 teaspoons black vinegar

DIP, OPTIONAL

Dry-fried salt and pepper (page 440)

1. Carefully rinse and pat dry the squash blossoms. Cut out the thick stamens in each one and trim off any green calyxes at the bottom of each blossom.

2. Mix together the filling ingredients and stuff the mixture into the squash blossoms. Close the petals over the filling by lightly squeezing them together. Dip each blossom in the beaten egg before rolling it in the cornstarch. Shake off any extra cornstarch and arrange the blossoms on a plate next to the stove.

3. Pour an inch of peanut oil into a wok and set it over medium heat until a wooden chopstick inserted in the oil is immediately covered with bubbles. Fry about 4 of the squash blossoms at a time, being careful not to crowd them. The petals will cook faster than the bases, so as they turn golden, tip them up against the side of the wok to keep them out of the heat. Once the bases of the blossoms are a golden brown, too, remove them to a serving platter with the petals facing outward and the bases snuggled up against one another, so that the dish looks like a sunflower.

4. To make the optional ginger and chili sauce, pour all but 2 tablespoons of the oil out of the wok. Set the wok over medium-high heat and quickly stir-fry the ginger, garlic, and peppers for about 20 seconds. Add the rest of the sauce ingredients, and as soon as they come to a boil, pour the sauce over the bases of the squash blossoms; this will help keep the petals crisp. Serve immediately.

5. If you're using the seasoned salt dip rather than the sauce, just serve a few tiny bowls of it alongside the freshly fried squash blossoms.

Jīyóu jiècài 雞油芥菜

Mustard Cabbage with Schmaltz and Ginger

HUNAN · SERVES 4

Hunan is home to many dishes that are heavy on charcuterie and fatty cuts of meat. But it also offers many dishes like this that act as nice foils, cleansing the palate and refreshing the senses.

When preparing your large green heads of mustard cabbage, be sure to slice them deeply on the angle. This is the key to the entire recipe. If you cut across the tough fibers in just the right way, you will be left with very tender stems that absorb the schmaltz (chicken fat), salt, and ginger. Vegetarians and vegans can use some other seasonings here, such as a seasoned oil (pages 434 and 435) plus mushroom stock.

1½ pounds large mustard cabbage

3 tablespoons rendered chicken fat

½ teaspoon sea salt

3 tablespoons finely shredded fresh ginger

2 tablespoons Shaoxing rice wine

½ cup unsalted chicken stock (page 380)

½ teaspoon sugar, optional

1. Rinse the mustard and shake it dry. Trim off the leaves and use them for something else. Cut the stems into thin slices (see page 450).

2. Set a wok over high heat until it is hot and then add the fat and salt. Swirl them around and add the ginger. When the ginger is slightly browned, add all of the mustard slices and toss them quickly to coat them with the fat, salt, and ginger. As they turn ever so slightly bright green on the edges, add the rice wine, stock, and sugar. Cover the wok and let the mustard steam for about 30 seconds. Uncover, toss the mustard, cover again, and cook only until the fat bases of the vegetable have turned a brilliant green. Plate and serve immediately.

You can also soak and steam dried scallops, crumble them into fine shreds, and add them to the wok along with the rice wine. Use less salt if you do this.

Zìrán kǎo mǎlíngshǔ 孜然烤馬鈴薯

Cumin Roasted Potatoes

SICHUAN • SERVES 3 OR 4

The farther west in China you go, the more you encounter cumin. It's a wonderful companion to chilies, garlic, and onions, and it plays a major role in this dish. The interesting thing about this recipe is that most of its main ingredients are not traditionally Chinese: the potatoes, the chilies, and the cumin are all imports, adopted by their new home with such enthusiasm that they've become Chinese by association.

This dish features my favorite style of preparing potatoes. They are steamed thoroughly, tossed with oil and aromatics, and finally baked. This last step crisps up the skin and fluffs up the insides. It also infuses the oil with all the flavors of the spices and garlic and onions. A healthy dose of salt rounds out the flavors and gives everything a nice sharp edge.

POTATOES AND SEASONING

Generous 1 pound small new potatoes (any variety)

3 tablespoons peanut or vegetable oil

1 green onion, trimmed and finely chopped

1 clove garlic, finely chopped

1 teaspoon ground toasted Sichuan peppercorns
    (page 441)

1 teaspoon ground cumin

1 teaspoon coarsely ground dried chilies, or to taste

1 to 2 teaspoons sea salt

GARNISH

1 green onion, trimmed and finely chopped

Few cilantro sprigs, optional

1. Scrub the potatoes and then steam them for about 15 minutes, until tender.

2. Heat the oven (a small toaster oven works fine) to 350°F. Place the potatoes in a small baking pan and toss them with the oil. Mix together the green onion, garlic, Sichuan peppercorns, cumin, chilies, and salt and sprinkle the mixture over the potatoes. Roast the potatoes for 15 to 20 minutes, until browned, tossing them occasionally as they cook.

3. Garnish the potatoes with the extra chopped green onion and optional cilantro. Serve hot.

Use whatever ratio of spices and aromatics you like. Ginger is a good addition, and if you love chili, add extra. Smoked paprika goes very well here, too.

If you are serving this with something salty or fried, use less salt. On the other hand, use more salt if you want to have these little potatoes as a bar snack or as a savory side for something like steamed fish.

Sìchuān liángmiàn 四川涼麵

Spicy and Numbing Cold Noodles

SICHUAN • SERVES 4 AS A MAIN DISH

In traditional Chinese medicine, it's thought that eating spicy food helps cool you down. This might seem counterintuitive, but the idea is that chilies release heat from the body through perspiration, thereby lowering one's temperature. No one abides by this prescription more than the people of Sichuan, who eat hot peppers all through the muggy summer months.

One of the best spicy Sichuan summer meals is this one: *liangmian*, or "cold noodles." It's nothing more than cooked, chilled pasta piled on top of blanched bean sprouts, which end up making the dish exceptionally refreshing. It's topped with lots of other vegetables and either pressed bean curd or poached chicken strips, and everything is dressed with the spicy sauce known as "strange flavor" (*guàiwèi* 怪味).

THE FOUNDATION

1½ pounds (about 4 cups) mung bean sprouts

1 pound fresh hot-water, cold-water, or whole egg noodles (page 386, 387, or 389 or store-bought wheat noodles)

SUGGESTED TOPPINGS (ANY OR ALL)

1 cup shredded poached chicken or julienned pressed bean curd

2 or 3 green onions, trimmed and shredded

2 Persian or other small, seedless cucumbers

1 carrot, peeled and shredded

½ sweet red pepper, seeded and julienned

1 large stalk Chinese celery, trimmed and julienned

Handful of blanched snow pea pods, julienned

Just about any other vegetable you'd like here (see Tips)

SAUCE

10 to 12 tablespoons goop from citrus chili oil with black beans (page 436) or other chili oil

6 to 8 tablespoons citrus chili oil or other chili oil

2 to 3 tablespoons sweet soy sauce (page 439), or 2 tablespoons regular soy sauce and 2 teaspoons sugar

¼ cup black vinegar

6 tablespoons toasted sesame oil

2 tablespoons toasted sesame paste (page 413), or peanut butter

2 teaspoons ground toasted Sichuan peppercorns (page 441)

1. Blanch the bean sprouts by putting them in a 2-quart saucepan, covering them with water, and bringing the pot to a boil. The sprouts are ready when they have lost that beany flavor but are still crisp; do not overcook them. Immediately dump the pot into a colander placed in the sink and run cold water over the sprouts to stop them from cooking any further. Drain and shake the sprouts to get rid of most of the water. Divide the cooked sprouts among 4 large noodle bowls.

2. Fill the saucepan halfway with water and bring it to a boil. While it is heating up, ready the toppings and run your fingers through the noodles to break up the clumps. (I dump them in a big bowl if they are particularly tangled up and then work the knots loose.) Add the noodles to the boiling water in small handfuls, stirring as you sprinkle them in. Stir occasionally until the water comes to a boil again, and then lower the heat to medium. The noodles will cook quickly, and you should start tasting them as soon as they rise to the surface. When they have cooked through but are still chewy, pour the water and noodles into a colander placed in the sink and run tap water over them until they are cool. Shake them dry and divide the noodles among the 4 bowls.

3. Once the noodles have been divvied up, arrange the toppings in the bowls in a decorative manner, doing your best to alternate the colors.

4. Mix the sauce ingredients together until smooth, adding as much sweet soy sauce (or soy sauce and sugar) as you like. Taste and adjust the seasoning. Pour an equal amount over each bowl and serve. Let your diners toss the noodles themselves.

Fresh noodles taste best here, but dried can be substituted.

Things like tomatoes don't work well in this recipe because of their assertive flavor and soft texture, but carrots, cucumbers, green onions, celery, and sweet red peppers get along quite well with the noodles and bean sprouts.

If your sesame paste or peanut butter has hardened, microwave it in short bursts and stir.

Hóngyóu chǎoshǒu 紅油炒手

Wontons in Chili Oil

SICHUAN · SERVES 6 TO 8 AS A SIDE DISH,
OR 4 TO 6 AS A MAIN DISH

Wontons appear all over southern China. In the United States, we most often see them served Guangdong-style, as shrimp and pork packets floating in a pork broth. Near the Yangtze, wontons are much larger and usually served in pale broths with shreds of omelet, laver seaweed (nori), and green onions. This particular preparation from Sichuan is my favorite. It's basically a street food, and I have very fond memories of eating it in busy alleys, sitting on a bamboo stool, and watching the world bustle by. As in most Sichuanese dishes, the chili-laden sauce packs a punch, but here it is sensuously tempered by the juicy wonton filling.

FILLING

2 inches fresh ginger, more or less
1½ cups unsalted chicken stock (page 380),
    divided into ½ cup and 1 cup
1½ pounds boneless pork shoulder or any other
    30 percent fat cut of pork, chilled
Sea salt to taste
2 large eggs, lightly beaten
2 tablespoons light soy sauce
3 tablespoons mild rice wine
2 teaspoons sugar
3 green onions, white parts only, trimmed and finely minced
1 tablespoon toasted sesame oil
1 teaspoon freshly ground black pepper

WONTON WRAPPERS

1 package (16 ounces) thin wonton wrappers
Flour for dusting

SAUCE (MAY BE DOUBLED)

3 tablespoons red chili oil with toasty bits (page 435),
    or to taste
3 tablespoons light soy sauce, or to taste
3 tablespoons toasted sesame oil, or to taste
2 cloves garlic, finely minced, optional
Sugar to taste

GARNISH

3 green onions, green parts only,
    trimmed and cut into thin rounds
Ground toasted Sichuan peppercorns (page 441)

1. Cut the ginger into roughly ½-inch pieces, then whirl it in a blender or food processor with ½ cup of the stock. Strain the liquid, squeezing out every last drop of ginger-flavored stock into a bowl before discarding the fibrous mass left behind.

2. Chop the pork finely by hand (see page 458). If you wish to use a food processor, cut the chilled meat into 1-inch cubes and pulse it.

3. Place the minced pork in a large work bowl and use your hand as a paddle to beat in the ginger-flavored stock, salt, eggs, soy sauce, rice wine, sugar, the whites of the green onions, sesame oil, and the black pepper. Slowly add the remaining 1 cup stock in small increments so that the pork absorbs all of the liquid (see page 458). It will be light and fluffy at this point. Chill the filling for an hour or longer, if you have the time, as this will firm it up and make it easier to wrap.

4. Before you start wrapping the wontons, place 2 baking sheets next to your work area, cover them with clean tea towels, and dust these with some flour; have a couple of extra towels on the side to cover the filled wontons. Place a couple of tablespoons of cool water in a small bowl next to the filling bowl, as well as a flat piece of wood or a small blunt knife. (You'll use both to wrap the wontons; see the diagram below.) If you are going to cook these right away, pour water (at least 8 cups) into a large pot and bring it to a boil just before you are ready to cook.

5. Wrap the wontons; you will end up with 80 to 90. You can prepare uncooked wontons ahead of time: place them in a single layer on the towel-covered pans and place in the freezer for a couple of hours, until frozen solid. Transfer the wontons to a freezer bag. They do not need to be defrosted before cooking.

6. Mix together the sauce ingredients, taste and adjust the seasoning as desired, and divide the sauce among as many bowls you wish; double the amount of sauce if you really enjoy spicy flavors.

7. To cook the wontons, drop them in small handfuls into the boiling water while stirring with a wooden spoon. As soon as the water returns to a boil, pour in about 1 cup cold water. Bring the pot to a boil again and pour in another cup of cold water. When the pot boils a third time, the wontons should be floating gracefully.

8. Use a Chinese spider or slotted spoon to gently remove the wontons into the prepared bowls, draining off as much of the water as you can. Toss them lightly in the sauce and sprinkle with the chopped green onions and the ground toasted Sichuan peppercorns to taste. Serve immediately.

WRAPPING WONTONS

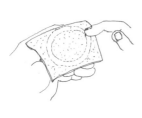			
❶	❷	❸	❹
Curl the fingers of your nondominant hand into a loose fist and place a wrapper on top of the circle formed by your forefinger and thumb. Wet a finger on your other hand and draw a circle on the wrapper. Scoop up about a tablespoon of the filling and place it in the center.	Fold one corner up over the filling to form a triangle and seal the edges.	Lightly wet one of the bottom angles of the wonton wrapper and then bring both bottom angles together.	Seal these two ends by pressing them together. Now your wonton is complete. Place the filled wonton on a flour-dusted towel and cover it with another towel.

Méicài ròu bāo 梅菜肉包

Pork and Preserved Mustard Green Baozi

SICHUAN · MAKES 16 (3-INCH) FILLED BUNS

The filled steamed breads known as *baozi* are as popular in Sichuan as they are throughout the rest of China. The *baozi* in this recipe feature a savory pork filling that is seasoned with crisp *meicai*, the Chinese name for salted and slightly fermented mustard greens that have been dried in the sun. Because Huizhou-style *meicai* (see page 485) is a Hakka ingredient, it's likely that this dish was created in the village of Luodai, near Chengdu, where many of the Hakka in Sichuan live.

WRAPPERS

1 recipe fast steamed bread (page 400), through Step 4

FILLING

6 to 7 ounces Hakka-style preserved mustard greens
1 pound boneless pork shoulder or other fatty cut, chilled and chopped into ¼-inch dice
2 to 3 tablespoons regular soy sauce (depending upon the saltiness of the preserved vegetable)
2 tablespoons mild rice wine
2 tablespoons peanut or vegetable oil
1½ tablespoons peeled and minced fresh ginger
2 green onions, trimmed and chopped
1½ tablespoons sugar
1 tablespoon cornstarch mixed with 2 tablespoons water

1. Make the bread dough for the wrappers and cut it into 16 even pieces before you begin the filling. Cover the dough pieces with a slightly damp cloth or plastic wrap. Also have 16 pieces of steamer paper on hand, and a steamer set up with at least 2 steamer baskets (see page 49). Place the baskets and cover on the steamer, bring the water underneath to a boil, and then turn the heat off so that the baskets are ready to go when you are.

2. Soak the mustard greens in a bowl of warm water set in the sink and swish them around after a few minutes. Dump out the water and repeat this soaking until there is absolutely no sand in the bottom of the bowl. Cut out the cores of the greens and discard them, and then cut the stems into ¼-inch dice. Chop the leaves finely, without worrying about being too precise.

3. Place the chopped pork in a medium work bowl with 2 tablespoons of the soy sauce and the rice wine. Toss the meat and let it marinate for about 10 minutes. Set a wok over medium-high heat, then add the oil, swirl it around, and add the ginger. Brown it lightly before tossing in the green onions and the meat and all of the marinade. Stir-fry the meat until it has lost all of its pink color. Add the sugar and the chopped greens and cook everything for about 5 minutes to heat the greens through. Stir in the cornstarch slurry, toss until the juices have thickened, and finally taste and adjust the seasoning, adding more soy sauce if you think it's needed. Scoop the filling out into a clean work bowl where it can cool down. The filling can be made ahead of time up to this point and refrigerated.

4. Use the cold filling and the risen dough to stuff and shape the *baozi* (see pages 406 to 407). Let them rise again for about 5 minutes, then place them at least 2 inches apart in the warm steamer baskets. Steam over high heat for 15 minutes. Turn off the heat under the baskets and let the *baozi* rest for about 5 minutes, as this will help stabilize the risen dough and keep the bread fluffy. Serve hot—no dipping sauce is needed.

Note that this recipe calls for fat, greenish Hakka-style preserved vegetable, not the dark, chopped version made in Zhejiang.

Mǐ dòufǔ 米豆腐

Rice "Bean Curd"

GUIZHOU · SERVES 4 TO 6

Rice paste is a major staple of south-central China's cuisine. It has a smooth, silky texture and is traditionally made by pounding cooked sticky white grains. All throughout the Central Highlands and even up into Southern Fujian and Taiwan, it is served as freshly made thick rice noodles, dried thin rice noodles, crêpes, and filled balls of cooked rice paste called *ciba* (page 306). Only in certain areas like Guizhou, though, will you often find it made in this fashion: formed into a soft brick that looks like bean curd.

In this dish, the cooled rice paste is cut into pieces with a lusciously spongy texture that makes them particularly enjoyable in the summer. I like to drape them with a rich and spicy sauce and finish the dish with something crunchy, like fried soybeans. I'm particularly proud of how I've turned this dish into a supereasy recipe and hope you will make it part of your hot-weather repertoire, too.

3 cups sticky rice flour
3 cups water
Sauce of some sort (the one on page 250 is highly
 recommended)
Fried soybeans (page 410) or fried peanuts (page 411),
 optional
Chopped green onions, optional

1. Start this recipe the day before you plan to serve it so that it has time to chill. Pour the rice flour into a large heatproof bowl, preferably a big measuring cup with a handle that will protect your hands. Whisk in the water, smashing any lumps you come across.

2. Place the bowl in your microwave and cook it uncovered on high for 4 minutes. Stir the mixture thoroughly with a silicone spatula. Microwave again on high for 4 minutes, stirring it every minute or so. The paste should be thick and malleable at this point. Take a taste: if you detect any raw flavor, microwave it again for another minute or two. (If you do not have a turntable in your microwave, cook the paste for a minute at a time, stirring after each blast.)

3. Remove the bowl from the microwave. Rinse out an 8-inch-square cake pan or a standard loaf pan with cold water. Use your spatula to scrape the boiling-hot paste into the pan. Rinse the spatula with cold water and smooth it across the surface. Let the paste come to room temperature. Cover with plastic wrap and refrigerate overnight. Empty the chilled rice paste onto a cutting board. Slice it into cubes, squares, or rectangles, cutting off and discarding any tough or hard edges.

4. Arrange the rice dough on a serving platter. Top with whatever sauce you like. Something tart and spicy is perfect, along with a handful of crunchy bits, like fried soybeans or peanuts and a sprinkle of chopped green onions. Or, you can fry up some shredded pork with sweet peppers seasoned with soy sauce and cover the rice paste with that—just about anything deeply savory would be good.

If your knife is sticking to the paste while you're slicing, rinse it clean, dry it well, and rub sesame or peanut oil over the dry blade.

Store any unsauced leftover pieces in the refrigerator. They will keep for at least a couple of days. If they start to change color or leak lots of water, toss them.

Guòqiáo mǐxiàn 過橋米線

Crossing-the-Bridge Rice Noodles

YUNNAN · SERVES 4 AS A MAIN DISH

This dish was invented by a woman from Yunnan during the Qing dynasty. Her husband, a scholar, had holed himself up on an island to prepare for his imperial examinations. She wanted to bring him his meals, but because she had to cross a long bridge to reach him, she was never able to keep his food warm during the journey. Eventually, she discovered that if she coated his soup with a layer of chicken fat before leaving the house, she could maintain the heat as she crossed the bridge—hence the name.

This is one of Yunnan's most famous dishes. It is unusual in that raw ingredients are set out on the table for diners to add to the boiling-hot soup. Like Hunan's Flash Fish Soup (page 260), it relies on the extreme heat of the broth to cook the ingredients quickly while preserving their tenderness and fresh flavor. That generous amount of chicken fat lends the broth a nice richness.

THE BASICS

12 ounces or so fresh round rice noodles (see Tip)
6 cups unsalted chicken stock (page 380)
¼ cup mild rice wine
4 slices fresh ginger
Sea salt
6 tablespoons or so rendered chicken fat
4 cups water
1 bunch spinach or 6 ounces bok choy or
    other leafy green vegetable

CHICKEN AND MARINADE

1 boneless chicken breast, frozen slightly until firm
1 tablespoon regular soy sauce
2 tablespoons mild rice wine
1 tablespoon ginger juice (page 481)

OTHER POSSIBLE PROTEINS (SELECT 1 OR 2)

8 fresh or frozen and defrosted large shrimp or prawns,
    peeled and deveined (see page 457) and sliced in half
    lengthwise
4 ounces grass carp fillets, fresh or frozen and defrosted,
    scaled if necessary, and thinly sliced
4 ounces squid, cleaned and very thinly sliced
8 to 12 quail eggs, hard-boiled and peeled

GARNISHES

8 black mushrooms, fresh or dried and plumped up,
    stemmed and thinly sliced
3 soy batons, soaked in hot water and cut into small pieces
Large handful of snow pea pods, trimmed and blanched

DIPPING SAUCE

Any good chili oil (page 435 recommended)
Regular soy sauce and/or sweet soy sauce (page 439)
    to taste
Toasted sesame oil to taste
½ cup chopped cilantro and/or green onions

1. Separate the noodles in a large bowl, fluff them up gently, and cover with plastic wrap to prevent them from drying out. Heat the chicken stock to boiling in a 2-quart pan, add the rice wine and ginger, and lower the heat to a simmer. Add salt to taste and then add the chicken fat; keep the stock warm.

2. Bring the water to a boil in a saucepan. Clean the spinach or leafy vegetable you are using, shake dry, remove any tough bits, and cut into roughly 3-inch lengths. Blanch the vegetables briefly in the boiling water, drain into a colander, rinse with cool tap water, and divide among 4 large soup bowls.

3. Thinly slice the chicken breast crosswise and arrange on a plate. Mix together the soy sauce, rice wine, and ginger juice and drizzle a bit over the chicken breast. Arrange the other protein(s) and the garnishes on individual plates. Drizzle the remaining marinade over the protein(s) on the table.

4. Combine the chili oil, soy sauce, and sesame oil as you like for a dipping sauce, adjust the seasoning, and divide it among 4 small rice bowls. Set a bowl of sauce at each place along with chopsticks and soupspoons.

5. Remove the ginger from the stock and bring the stock to a boil. Divide the rice noodles and chicken breast among the soup bowls and have your guests arrange whatever proteins and garnishes they want on top of their noodles. Set the bowls where you can reach them easily, as you are going to pour lots of boiling-hot stock on top of them. Have your guests stand back as you divide the hot stock among the 4 bowls. Everything should cook instantly in the broth, and your guests should immediately stir their bowls with their chopsticks.

The best place to find fresh rice noodles is at an Asian grocery store with lots of Southeast Asian customers. Where I live, the Vietnamese make marvelous versions for *pho* and *hefen*. These noodles are usually packed on disposable trays and displayed in a lightly refrigerated area so that they stay soft but don't spoil. If possible, get the noodles the day you are going to eat them.

Guìlín mǐfěn 桂林米粉

Guilin Rice Noodles

NORTHERN GUANGXI · SERVES 2 AS A MAIN DISH

This is one of the most famous dishes to emerge from Guilin, that extraordinarily scenic city in northeast Guangxi, with shimmering emerald rice paddies clustering around those strangely beautiful, parabola-shaped hills. It's a perfect balance of soft, slightly sweet noodles, savory meat, tart beans, spicy peppers, and crunchy nuts. Usually made with pork, this dish is also fantastic with braised beef.

1 pound fresh round rice noodles
Boiling water, as needed
½ cup (or so) chopped pickled long beans (page 428 or store-bought) or other pickled vegetables, rinsed with boiling water
10 (or more) thin slices braised beef shank (page 14), plus some of the braising liquid
Large handful of coarsely chopped cilantro
2 green onions, trimmed and finely chopped
Finely ground chili peppers, to taste
¼ cup fried soybeans (page 410) or peanuts (page 411)

1. Place the rice noodles in a wide colander and separate them as much as possible. Put the colander in the sink and run boiling water over them. Shake the colander to fluff up the noodles and then divide them between 2 large soup bowls.

2. Arrange the pickles and beef slices on top of the noodles and drizzle in about ¼ cup of the braising liquid. Pour enough boiling water into each bowl so that about an inch of the noodles is peeking out. Taste and adjust the seasoning. Divide the cilantro and green onions among the bowls and sprinkle on some ground chili peppers and soybeans or peanuts, if you like. Toss and eat.

Hóngzǎo bíqí bǐng 紅棗荸薺餅

Water Chestnut Pastries with Red Date Filling

HUNAN AND ELSEWHERE • SERVES 8

The Chinese have two names for water chestnuts: *biqi*, which just means "water chestnuts," and *mǎtí* 馬蹄, or "horse hooves" (because their leaves suggest hoof imprints). Water chestnuts straddle the line between vegetable and fruit—they can even be squeezed for their juice, much as sugarcane is. In this dish, ground fresh water chestnuts are turned into little pastries. Once they're fried, they end up looking like fresh water chestnuts once again—but with a sweet filling hidden inside.

FILLING

4 ounces dried Chinese red dates

Boiling water, as needed

2 tablespoons toasted sesame oil

1 tablespoon sugar

¼ teaspoon sea salt

PASTRIES

2½ pounds (about 40 whole) fresh water chestnuts

1 cup sticky rice flour

Peanut or vegetable oil

SAUCE

Red date juice (from Step 1)

Water chestnut juice (from Step 2)

¼ cup rock sugar

2 tablespoons osmanthus blossom syrup, optional

4 teaspoons cornstarch mixed with
    2 tablespoons water

1. First make the red date filling: place the dates in a heatproof bowl and cover with boiling water. When they have plumped up and softened a bit, cut out and discard the pits and stems. Place the dates back in the bowl, add 1 cup boiling water, and steam them for 30 minutes or so, until they're completely soft. Cool the dates slightly, reserve all the juice in the bowl for the sauce, place the cooked dates in a food processor, and puree. Pour the sesame oil into a wok, add the puree, sugar, and salt, and cook the dates over medium heat until the paste has thickened. It will be done when all the oil has been absorbed and the paste is glossy. Scrape the paste into a small work bowl and cool it to room temperature; you will have about 10 tablespoons. Roll the filling into 40 small balls.

2. Next make the water chestnut pastries: peel the water chestnuts, rinse, and then chop them coarsely. Place them in a food processor and chop them very finely. Remove most of the moisture by wrapping fistfuls of the puree in cheesecloth and squeezing out the juice (the puree should feel somewhat powdery), capturing the juice for the sauce. Mix the water chestnut paste with the rice flour, return this to the food processor, and puree until a dough forms. Divide the dough into 40 pieces and roll them into balls.

3. Working on 1 ball of dough at a time, flatten it lightly in the palm of one hand and then place a ball of filling in the center (see page 267). Wrap the dough around the filling and then roll the ball between your palms to smooth it out. Repeat with the rest of the dough and filling.

4. Pour 2 inches of oil into a wok and place a small (8-inch or so) rimmed platter, a small plate, a wok spatula, and a Chinese spider or slotted spoon next to the stove. Set the wok over medium heat, and when a chopstick inserted in the oil is immediately covered with bubbles, fry only as many of the pastries as will fit without touching one another. Shake the wok gently with one hand as you add the water chestnut pastries, as this will help keep them from sticking. Fry the pastries until they are golden brown on both sides. Remove the pastries to the small plate, flatten each one lightly with your spatula to break them ever so slightly open, and then transfer them to the platter. Repeat with the rest of the pastries until done. Keep the pastries warm.

5. To make the sauce, mix together the date juice and water chestnut juice, sugar, and optional osmanthus blossom syrup in a saucepan and bring to a full boil. Stir in the cornstarch slurry, and when the sauce thickens, pour it into either the center of your serving platter or offer it on the side in a small pitcher; serve immediately. You can also serve these pastries on individual rimmed dessert plates or in bowls.

Don't use canned water chestnuts here, which taste mostly of the can and have little character or texture.

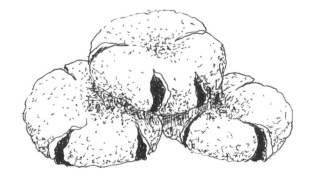

Guìhuā shānyào 桂花山藥

Raw Chinese Yam with Osmanthus Syrup

GUIZHOU • SERVES 4 TO 6

Chinese yams are unusual tubers. They grow to impressive lengths, and their oddly hairy, flesh-colored skins sort of resemble human legs. And then there are the insides, which are white and sweet and gooey. But if you can get past this superficial weirdness, you can do a lot with these vegetables. This dish from Guizhou demonstrates one of the simpler ways to prepare them: all you do is drizzle raw batons of Chinese yam with osmanthus syrup and serve. It's a soothing, refreshing, and sweet way to end a spicy meal.

1 large Chinese yam, about 2 × 10 inches
Osmanthus blossom syrup or local honey

1. Use a potato peeler to remove all the skin from the yam. It's easiest to do this if you work on the yam under a slow stream of cold water, as this keeps the gooeyness to a bare minimum. The tuber will become intensely slippery as more and more of the skin is removed, so either grip it with a clean towel or stick a large fork in it to keep it steady.

2. Cut off the ends and slice the tuber lengthwise down the middle, which will help stabilize it as you slice it further. Use a sharp knife to shape it into batons about ½ × ½ × 3 inches, and then submerge them in cold water and refrigerate until you are ready to serve them.

3. Drain the yam pieces well. Stack the batons like logs on individual plates and pour as much osmanthus syrup or honey as you like over the top of each serving. Provide small forks, as well as some extra syrup on the side.

Cíbā 糍粑

Ciba

ALL OVER SOUTHERN AND CENTRAL CHINA ·
MAKES AROUND 60

It seems that each cuisine from Sichuan to Guizhou and up into the Hakka territories has its own way of preparing these filled balls of cooked rice paste. Some *ciba* are rolled in sandy coatings (such as in this recipe) and others are filled; some are sweet, while others are savory; some are formed into a smooth dough that is wrapped in leaves and others are fried and crispy. *Ciba* are traditionally served around the Chinese New Year and the Dragon Boat Festival. Pounding the steamed rice used to be such an arduous undertaking that an entire village would have to help. Nowadays there's a much easier shortcut: all you need is a microwave. In this way, the modern recipe is a close cousin of the one for Rice "Bean Curd" on page 301.

¾ cup toasted or fried peanuts (page 411)
6 tablespoons toasted sesame seeds (page 413)
¼ cup brown sugar
¼ teaspoon sea salt
3 cups sticky rice flour
3 cups water

1. First make the coating for the rice balls: grind the peanuts in a mini processor until they are relatively fine, then add the sesame seeds, sugar, and salt. Process until a sandy texture forms. Taste and adjust the seasoning. Pour into a wide bowl.

2. To make the rice paste, pour the rice flour into a large microwave-safe bowl, preferably a big measuring cup with a handle that will protect your hands. Whisk in the water, smashing any lumps you come across.

3. Place the bowl in your microwave and cook it uncovered on high for 4 minutes. Stir the mixture thoroughly. Microwave again on high for 4 minutes, stirring every minute or so. The paste should be thick and malleable at this point. Take a taste: if you detect any raw flavor, microwave it again for another minute or two. (If you do not have a turntable in your microwave, cook the paste for a minute at a time, stirring after each blast.)

4. Remove the bowl from the microwave. Rinse out a baking pan of any size with cold water. Use a silicone spatula to scrape the boiling-hot paste into the pan. Rinse the spatula with cold water and use it to smooth the surface. Let the paste cool until it is easy to handle. Set out a small bowl of water, a small spoon, a pair of chopsticks, a couple of baking sheets, and about 60 cupcake liners.

5. The top of the rice paste will form a skin as it cools, so pat some water over it as you work your way through the dough; this will make the paste sticky enough to pick up the coating. Wet the spoon and the fingers of your nondominant hand. Scoop up a scant tablespoon of the paste, nudge it off the spoon into the coating with your moist fingertips, and use your chopsticks to form it into a lumpy ball. Use the chopsticks to transfer the *ciba* to a cupcake liner. Repeat with the rest of the paste. Serve within a couple of hours for optimum flavor and texture and keep the *ciba* covered at all times.

You will have leftover coating. Save it in a covered jar to sprinkle on your morning oatmeal.

Zuì bāxiān 醉八仙

Drunken Eight Immortals

SICHUAN · SERVES 4 TO 6

Named after the Eight Immortals of Taoist folklore, this dish is considered "drunken" because of the fermented rice that seasons the broth.

3 tablespoons Job's tears or pearled barley

2 tablespoons wolfberries or raisins

Boiling water, as needed

1 fresh lily bulb, or 3 fresh water chestnuts

¼ cup small rice pearls (page 144), uncooked

2 teaspoons water chestnut flour (whirl in a mini processor or spice grinder until smooth)

4½ cups cool water, divided into ½ cup and 4 cups

Rock sugar, as needed

Pinch of sea salt

4 kinds of fresh seasonal fruit (see Tip), finely diced if larger than the wolfberries

1 cup fermented rice, both lees and liquid (page 415 or store-bought)

1. Soak the Job's tears or barley for a couple of hours until they pass the fingernail test (see page 480). Drain, place in a saucepan, and cover with fresh water. Bring to a boil, lower the heat to simmer, cook until tender, and drain. While the grains are soaking, cover the wolfberries or raisins with boiling water and let them plump up.

2. Prepare the lily bulbs (see page 450). If using water chestnuts instead, peel and finely dice them.

3. Bring a small pan of water to a boil and simmer the rice pearls until just cooked. Mix the water chestnut flour with ½ cup of the cool water until smooth.

4. Bring the remaining 4 cups water to a boil in a saucepan and toss in the rock sugar and salt. Add the seasonal fruits, wolfberries or raisins (plus their soaking liquid), Job's tears or barley, rice pearls, and the fermented rice lees and liquid. When the mixture comes to a boil again, stir in the water chestnut slurry to thicken the soup slightly. Taste and adjust the seasoning and serve hot.

The fruits can be switched around with utter abandon so seasonal fruits are used. Apples, oranges, bananas, and mangoes can find themselves called upon in winter, while melons, mangoes, strawberries, and blueberries will make a colorful summer dessert. You can even serve this dish chilled as a hot-weather treat. In that case, I'd suggest using *boba* tapioca (see page 477) instead of the rice pearls, which really taste better hot.

Làbāzhōu 臘八粥

Winter Congee with Eight Treasures

HUNAN AND ELSEWHERE • SERVES 8 TO 12

This warming dish is traditionally made during the last lunar month, known as *Làyuè* 臘月. It is basically a bowl of congee filled with sticky rice and dried fruits and nuts. The red dates and longans swell up in the congee, growing juicier and lending the dish an almost caramel edge. I've made this for years, and winter just wouldn't be the same without it. If you happen to live in the southern hemisphere, where *Layue* occurs during the late summer, turn this sweet congee into Popsicles—they're unusual and delicious.

¼ cup dried red beans

¼ cup raw peanuts

1 cup round sticky rice

¼ cup broken or chopped walnuts

Boiling water, as needed

4 cups cool water

¼ cup rock sugar or black sugar

1 teaspoon sea salt

¼ cup slivered blanched almonds

¼ cup dried Chinese red dates

¼ cup dried longans

¼ cup raisins

¼ cup wolfberries

1. Start this recipe a day before you want to serve it. Rinse the beans and peanuts separately and soak in water to cover in different bowls until they pass the fingernail test (see page 480). Place the beans and peanuts in separate saucepans, cover with water, and cook until barely tender, then drain the beans and peanuts. While the beans are soaking, cover the rice with water and let it soak until it passes the fingernail test; drain the rice. Place the walnuts in a bowl and cover with boiling water. When the water has cooled, drain the walnuts and rinse them well.

2. Bring the cool water to a boil in a saucepan and add the beans, peanuts, and rice. Stir in the sugar and salt and then add all of the nuts and fruits. Return the mixture to a boil and then lower the heat to a gentle simmer. Stir the congee occasionally and cook it until it's thick and creamy, adding more boiling water if you like. Taste and adjust the seasoning. To reheat, use a microwave or steamer so that the rice doesn't become too mushy.

Xìngrén nián 杏仁粘

Candy-Coated Almonds

ALL OVER CHINA · MAKES 1 POUND

Chinese New Year calls for lots of sweets and red envelopes (those little presents of folding money wrapped up in crimson paper called *hóngbāo* 紅包). You're on your own when it comes to preparing cash for children and unmarried young adults, but I have a deliciously crunchy snack that those kids and all adults will love: Candy-Coated Almonds.

This is so easy that I am not going to go into great detail here. You start with deep-fried almonds, moisten them in an easy sugar syrup, and then toss them with powdered sugar. Couldn't be simpler.

1 pound raw almonds
3 cups or so peanut or vegetable oil
3 tablespoons water
¼ cup sugar
Pinch of sea salt
½ cup powdered sugar, sifted

1. Fry the almonds in the oil as described for fried peanuts on page 411. Pour off the oil and allow the nuts to drain on some paper towels.

2. Have ready a clean medium work bowl. Wipe the wok clean, add the water, sugar, and salt to it, and bring to a boil over medium heat. As soon as the sugar water has turned into a syrup (you will see big bubbles and the liquid will have thickened), remove the wok from the heat, add the almonds, and use a metal spatula to toss them thoroughly in the syrup. Each nut should be evenly coated. Sprinkle the powdered sugar on top of the nuts and immediately toss the nuts again until they are evenly coated. Remove the nuts to the work bowl and allow them to cool completely.

3. Shake off any excess powdered sugar. Store the cooled nuts in a covered container. If not using immediately, keep them in the refrigerator, where they will last longer if hidden well.

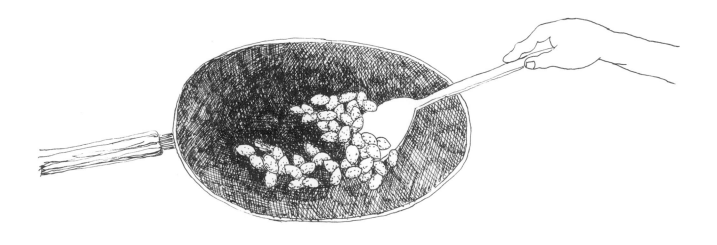

Huāshēng nǎilù 花生奶露

Peanut Milk

ALL OVER CHINA • SERVES 4

This beverage tastes like melted peanut butter ice cream. I worked on a number of versions over the years, but it never tasted perfect. Then I discovered that red dates were the missing element—they provide a delicious fruity edge, which balances out the drink's sweet, nutty flavors. It's a very subtle touch, but it makes all the difference in the world. If you have Popsicle molds or an ice-cream maker, consider making this drink into a frozen treat.

8 dried Chinese red dates

8 ounces raw peanuts, preferably skinned

Boiling water, as needed

2 tablespoons raw white rice

6 cups cool water, divided into 4 cups and 2 cups

Rock sugar to taste (about the size of a small egg)

Pinch of sea salt

1 teaspoon vanilla extract (not traditional, but good)

1. Soak the dates and peanuts the night before you want to serve this. Place the dates in a small heatproof bowl and cover with boiling water. When the dates are plump, slit each one open and discard the pit; reserve the soaking water. If the peanuts are not skinned, put them in a medium heatproof bowl and cover them with boiling water. Wait for 5 minutes, drain the peanuts in a colander, rinse with cool tap water, drain again, and dump them out onto a terrycloth towel. Rub the peanuts in the towel to remove the red skins. Place the peanuts back in the work bowl, cover them with tap water, and let them soak overnight. The next day, drain and rinse them in a colander.

2. Put the pitted dates, peanuts, rice, 4 cups of the cool water, and the date soaking liquid in a blender and pulverize the mixture on high for a few minutes to make it as smooth as possible. Strain the mixture into a medium saucepan. Return the solids to the blender, pour in the remaining 2 cups water, and repeat this step to extract as much flavor from the peanuts as possible.

3. Add the rock sugar and salt (and vanilla, if using) to the saucepan and bring the liquid slowly to a boil over medium heat before lowering the heat to maintain a gentle simmer. Cook the peanut milk for a few more minutes until it is thick and tastes fully cooked, stirring the bottom often with a silicone or wooden spatula. Taste the peanut milk and add more sugar, if necessary, then remove the pan from the heat. Serve the peanut milk immediately or let cool to room temperature and chill it for a couple of hours. Add chilled water to the chilled peanut milk to thin it as needed before serving.

Huāchá 花茶

Floral Tisanes

ALL OVER CHINA

Flower teas—also called floral tisanes—are hot infusions that generally contain only fragrant blossoms, rather than tea leaves. Because of this, they go especially well with light pastries and fresh fruit. Some of the more popular ones are the Chrysanthemum Tea (page 151) of Hangzhou and an infusion of little rosebuds, but many others are enjoyed throughout much of China. According to *The Book of Tea* (*Chápǔ* 茶譜), written by Gu Yuanqing in the Ming dynasty, the blossoms that can be used for floral tisanes include "osmanthus, Arabian jasmine, fragrant roses, multiflora roses, fragrant orchids, orange blossoms, gardenias, Lady Banksia roses, and plum blossoms." Floral tisanes are almost always brewed in large covered cups or glass pots. Glass teapots are better if you're brewing tea for a group: they allow everyone at the table to watch the blossoms swell in the water and change color.

FOR A SINGLE CUP

3 to 4 larger flowers, or about 2 teaspoons tiny blossoms
Boiling water, preferably spring or filtered

1. Rinse the flowers with boiling water. This can be done one of two ways. You can place them in a sieve and rinse them over the sink, after which the blossoms can be placed in a covered cup, or you can add them directly to the cup along with the boiling water. Angle the lid against the cup in order to discard the first dousing while reserving the flowers.

2. Next brew the tisane: pour fresh boiling water over the flowers and cover the cup immediately. Let the flowers steep for 3 to 5 minutes, which will give them enough time to plump up and release their fragrance. Angle the lid against the cup as you sip to keep the flowers from entering your mouth, or gently blow the blossoms out of the way before each sip.

3. Refill the cup with water that has been boiled and then cooled down for a few minutes to about 200°F, as the flowers will have completely opened and not need super-high heat for the second brewing. The fragrance of most blossoms will last only 2 rounds before it dissipates.

FOR A 4-CUP GLASS TEAPOT

10 to 12 larger flowers, or about 3 tablespoons tiny blossoms
Boiling water, preferably spring or filtered

1. Follow the directions above for a single-cup serving, rinsing the flowers off inside a teapot with a perforated plate at the base of the spout (keep the blossoms loose, rather than in a mesh ball, so you can enjoy their appearance), discarding the water, and then filling the pot again with fresh boiling water.

2. Cover the teapot and wait until you see the flowers fully expand before pouring. Refill a second time with the slightly cooler water.

THE ARID LANDS

SHAANXI · SHANXI · GANSU · THE NORTHWEST · INNER MONGOLIA · TIBET

THE NORTHWEST

INNER
MONGOLIA

Hohhot •

The Great Wall

Gobi Desert

Taiyuan •

Ürümqi •

XINJIANG

Taklinakan Desert

QINGHAI

NINGXIA

SHANXI

Yellow River

Xining •

GANSU

Lanzhou

Xi'an •

SHAANXI

TIBET

• Lhasa

Mount Everest

PREVIOUS SPREAD:
The color white and the tiger
symbolize the West.

"Where the food is meat and the drink is whey."

以肉為食兮酪為漿。

—PRINCESS LIU XIJUN, *THE SONG OF THE YELLOW CRANE*
(CIRCA 107 BCE)

The Arid Lands cover a dry, sparsely populated territory encompassing the far north and west, one so immense that it constitutes nearly half of China's landmass. It stretches from the vast prairies of Inner Mongolia to the shimmering sand dunes of Xinjiang and down toward the eternally frozen mountains of Tibet. It's home to Hui Muslims, Uyghurs, Kazakhs, Mongolians, and Tibetans, who all dine primarily on wheat, lamb, dairy, and warm spices, instead of the pork, soy sauce, rice wine, ginger, and fermented ingredients that define Han cuisine.

The foods of Tibet in particular have been greatly influenced by the cuisine of Mongolia, which first spread across the region in the thirteenth century, as the armies of Genghis Khan moved south. Meanwhile, near the southwestern border, Indian spices made their way over the Himalayas, along with the teachings of the Buddha. And from the New World, a little later, came the chilies, potatoes, peanuts, and tomatoes that are featured in most of the region's cuisines.

It is no coincidence that China's former capital, Chang'an (literally "lasting peace," and now called Xi'an, meaning "peace in the west"), was located in the Arid Lands. In Shaanxi Province, on the southeastern edge of what was then the limits of the Chinese empire, the city served as a bulwark against foreign incursions. Chang'an eventually grew into a wealthy metropolis with a burgeoning Han population. To this day, the city serves as a culinary mecca.

SHAANXI

When you eat in Shaanxi, you are dining at a crossroads of ancient and modern influences. Eastern Chinese cooking methods bump up against Central Asian traditions here, and northern Chinese sensibilities wrap around chili-laden flavors that echo the Central Highlands. It is a place that almost shimmers with vibrant aromas. Shaanxi was a cradle of early Chinese man; it later became the seat of empire and anchored a major stop on the Silk Road, which turned it into a confluence of history and appetite.

The culinary heart of Shaanxi has been and always will be the timeless imperial capital now called Xi'an. Like China's other great imperial cities—Beijing, Luoyang, and Nanjing—this metropolis's wealth and power attracted chefs from all over the country. Even today, its foods reflect a diverse array of influences. Central Asian flavors are present in such recipes as Rose-Scented Lotus Patties (page 371), while dishes like Sweet-and-Sour Squid Blossoms (page 334) gesture toward the cuisine of Sichuan, and Muslim sensibilities are manifested in dishes like Lamb Soup with Biscuits (page 326). And devotees of street foods love this place best for its Spicy Biangbiang Noodles (page 354) and other lively pastas and breads.

SHANXI

The Yellow River snakes down the western border of Shanxi, dividing it from neighboring Shaanxi.[1] Shanxi is the easternmost province in this region, merely 300 miles from Beijing, but it is included here since it is dry and landlocked like the rest of the Arid Lands. Shanxi is almost exclusively inhabited by Han Chinese, so pork is its default meat. However, feuding tribes have fought over this area for so many centuries that

its cuisine features a mixture of food traditions. This is particularly evident in the vibrant seasonings at work in Sesame Lamb (page 325) and Buddha's Hand Rolls (page 342).

Shanxi's traditional cuisine has been deeply affected by the Mongolian flavors that seep down through its northern border. So many varieties of noodles are made here that a local saying proudly proclaims, "All of the world's pastas can be found in Shanxi alone." The province is also renowned for its aged black rice vinegar, which plays a central role in sweet pickled garlic cloves (page 433). Han tastes are especially evident in Shanxi's delicate sweets, such as Sweet Pear Soup with Silver Ears (page 372), in which wood ear fungus jelly is ornamented with fresh and dried fruits.

GANSU

In Gansu, the tail end of the Great Wall crumbles into a land of measureless sand dunes and windblown steppes. Running through this province is the 620-mile-long Hexi Corridor, a string of oases that for

---

[1]. These two provinces have different first characters but similar romanizations because of the change in the first vowel sound. Shanxi is pronounced *shan shee*, with two high, flat tones, while Shaanxi is pronounced with a low dip in the *a*.

almost three thousand years was one of the few passages between Central Asia and Chang'an. Today, Gansu functions as the point at which traditional Han culture begins to be supplanted by the culture (and food) of the Hui Muslim people, who graze their sheep and goats along the headwaters of the Yellow River.

Muslim origins are celebrated here in dishes like Stuffed Muskmelon (page 373) and Lanzhou Beef Noodle Soup (page 328), which features hand-pulled pasta and braised red meat. In addition to its beef noodle soup, the city of Lanzhou, in southern Gansu, is renowned for its roses. But the local plant that has made the most indelible contribution to the country's cuisine is the lily bulb. Both the orange-flowered plants and their bulbs are referred to simply as "lilies" in Chinese (*bǎihé* 百合). Their sweet and delicate bulbs are celebrated in local dishes like Lily Bulbs and Wolfberries (page 348).

THE NORTHWEST

The defining flavors in this region are chilies, meats, breads, and cumin. Up here, Muslim-inspired cuisines hold sway. Lamb is the meat of choice, and the people of Xinjiang, Qinghai, and Ningxia[2] prepare it in many different ways.

In the province of Xinjiang, foods reflect the tastes and cooking styles of Uyghurs, Hui Muslims, Tibetans, Mongolians, Tatars, Kazakhs, and even the descendants of Persians and Russians. Yogurt (page 414), lamb kebabs (page 346), and baked breads (page 362) are central to the local cuisines. Han flavors waft through dishes like Chicken with Walnuts and Lotus Root (page 337), while Xinjiang's Big Plate of Chicken (page 338) celebrates more nomadic aesthetics. Noodles are enjoyed all over, and culinary ties to the Near East are evident in dishes like Uyghur Pilaf (page 369).

Qinghai dishes are not well known outside its borders, probably because a relatively small number of people live there. The three largest ethnic groups in Qinghai are Hui Muslims, Tibetans, and Han Chinese.

The Huis in the north cook more traditionally halal foods—what the Chinese call *Qīngzhēn cài* 清真菜 (Muslim cuisine) and *Huízú cài* 回族菜 (Hui peoples' cuisine). The Tibetans in the south tend to rely on yak meat and the toasted barley flour called *tsampa*, or *zánbá* 糌粑, which is usually mixed with liquid and butter. In Qinghai's few cities, where the Hans generally live, the local foods reflect sensibilities from all over China.

Ningxia is a desert area populated mainly by the Hui Muslim people. The majority of its dishes are halal, and so the traditional emphasis here is on lamb, breads, and pastas. Ningxia is one of the main sources of the world's wolfberries, also known as *gouqi* (in Chinese) or *goji* (in Japanese) berries. Both the delicately astringent leaves and the sweet red fruits are used in local dishes like Lamb with Wolfberry Buds and Berries (page 347).

INNER MONGOLIA

Politically speaking, there are two Mongolias: Inner Mongolia, which is one of China's autonomous regions, and the separate nation known as Mongolia, which was a Chinese territory referred to as Outer Mongolia until the Chinese Revolution of 1911. When it comes to food, both Mongolias share pretty much the same short list of ingredients: lamb, wheat, and hard cheese.

2. When discussing their country's lands, the Chinese refer to these three areas plus Gansu and the western part of Inner Mongolia as "the Great Northwest" (*Dàxiběi* 大西北). However, they possess such unique food traditions that here they are considered as separate cuisines.

True Mongolian barbecue[3] is meat pure and simple, and it is generally reserved for celebratory spreads. Whole animals—including goats, sheep, cows, horses, camels, yaks, *khainag* (a cross between yak and cattle known as the *dzo* in Tibetan), and even marmots—are usually cooked with little seasoning at all.

Everyday meals center on soups, ground meats, and other filled pastas and breads, such as *jiaozi*-like *buuz* (page 364). The area near the Inner Mongolian capital of Hohhot is home to many people of Shanxi ancestry, and this has led to local hybrid specialties like Oat Honeycomb Rolls (page 368).

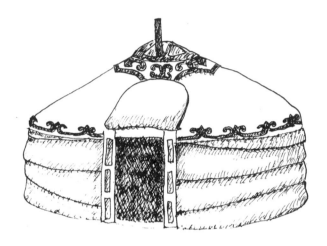

TIBET

Tibet's foods fit in well with the cuisines of this region, particularly Inner Mongolia's. Although the two areas share no borders, their cultures have vividly impacted each other over the centuries. Mongolian forces first invaded Tibet in 1240, when Genghis Khan's troops stormed through the Tibetan Plateau, and they invaded again in the seventeenth century. These military conquests spurred cross-pollination: Tibetan Buddhism came to be practiced in Mongolia, and Mongolian sensibilities worked their way into Tibetan cuisine.

Mongolian flavors are particularly evident in Lamb Noodle Soup (page 330), which has been tempered with Tibetan seasonings like fenugreek, turmeric, and

cumin. Nearby India is responsible for most of the spicy elements in Tibet's lively foods. As in Indian cuisine, seasonings like fenugreek are lightly fried in oil or butter before they are added to a dish. While wheat is enjoyed in Mongolian cuisine, Tibet relies on *tsampa* (see page 317), an ancient grain that has been farmed in this region since the fifth century. Dairy is important in Tibet, as it is throughout the Arid Lands; yak milk here is turned into fresh and dried cheese called *chhurpi* in Tibetan and *byaslag* in Mongolian. It's also used to produce the butterfat for Butter Tea (page 374) and the dairy for yogurt.

I never really grasped the sheer scope of China's lands and cultures until my husband and I visited the Arid Lands in 2001. Like most people who have visited or lived in China, I had spent almost all of my time in its modern eastern metropolises. As wonderful as those cities are, they make it easy to forget that China is at least five thousand years old and home to more than fifty ethnicities. I felt nothing short of culture shock when I walked into two-thousand-year-old Han tombs and visited the ancient frescoes of Dunhuang and Bezeklik, and when I watched Kazakh women racing horses across the grasslands of Xinjiang.

The foods of this region were unlike anything I had ever tasted in China: rich yogurt, roasted lamb, and the scent of freshly baked breads lured us down tiny alleys. We ate pulled noodles that were made mere moments before they were cooked. None of these foods fit into my previous understanding of China's culinary heritage.

It became clear to me that very few people were talking or writing about these cuisines, even in China. Most Chinese culinary discussion was preoccupied with the Eight Great Cuisines of the Han people, which meant that many of China's most fascinating and ancient cuisines were not receiving the attention they deserved. This realization, as much as anything else, spurred me to write the book you are now holding, which I hope properly honors all of the many food traditions of the Chinese people. ●

---

3. What we know of as Mongolian barbecue in the West is actually a Taiwanese invention that is similar to Japanese *teppanyaki*.

THE RECIPES

V = VEGETARIAN OR VEGETARIAN OPTION

Sānsī shēngcài 三絲生菜

Lettuce with Three Shreds

SHAANXI · SERVES 4 TO 6

Lettuce does not appear in China's cuisines too often, but when it does, the results are usually startlingly good. In Guangzhou and Hong Kong, for example, iceberg lettuce is often blanched and then tossed with warm oyster sauce and oil, or added to fried rice (page 222). In the desert regions, lettuce is treated a bit like a delicate relative of the cabbage family. In this dish, it is salted first so that the excess moisture can be squeezed out; then it is seasoned, piled on a plate, and dusted with threads of Thai chilies, black wood ears, and ginger. This is all doused with hot sesame oil to make a light yet tantalizing first course.

1 pound (more or less) iceberg or romaine lettuce
1 teaspoon sea salt
3 dried Thai chilies
1 tablespoon dried wood ear fungus threads,
    or 1 large dried or fresh wood ear fungus
Boiling water, as needed
1 tablespoon black vinegar
½ teaspoon sugar
2 tablespoons peeled and finely shredded fresh ginger
¼ cup toasted sesame oil
2 tablespoons toasted sesame seeds (page 413)

1. Clean the lettuce and shake it dry. Cut the leaves into a fine (⅛-inch) julienne. Place the lettuce in a colander set in the sink and toss with the salt.

2. Break the chilies in half, shake out the seeds, and remove the caps. Place the chilies in one small work bowl and the dried wood ears in another, and cover both with boiling water. When the chilies have plumped up, drain and cut them into very fine threads, making certain that there are no fiery clumps sticking together that will startle your diners. Slice the wood ears into thin pieces, if they are not already julienned. If you are using a fresh wood ear, trim it and slice it into fine shreds.

3. Squeeze the lettuce and discard the excess water. Put the lettuce in a work bowl and toss it with the vinegar and sugar before tasting and adjusting the seasoning. It should not be sweet, but rather refreshing, with a gently tart edge.

4. Pile the lettuce loosely in a wide serving bowl. Sprinkle the chili, wood ears, and ginger threads over the top. Heat the sesame oil until it barely starts to smoke, and pour this evenly over the threads to release their fragrance. Scatter the sesame seeds over the top, bring the bowl to the dining table, and toss before serving.

Labu dangtsel

Vegetable Confetti Salad

TIBET · SERVES 4 TO 6

This is a simple, colorful Tibetan dish. The key here is to cut the vegetables so that their shapes complement one another. As is true of most recipes in this book, shapes and sizes matter (see page 212). Here, for example, the vegetables are cut into long, thin strips, and draped gracefully around one another so each bite includes a taste of every ingredient.

2 cups finely julienned Korean or Chinese radish (see Tips)
2 carrots, peeled and finely julienned
1 Roma or other fleshy, ripe, tasty tomato
Juice from ½ lemon, or pale rice vinegar to taste
Sea salt and freshly ground black pepper to taste
¼ cup cilantro, in 1-inch lengths

1. Start this dish about an hour before you want to serve it. Place the radish and carrot threads in a medium work bowl. Cut the tomato in half and squeeze out and discard the seeds and juice. Cut the tomato flesh into a fine julienne and add it to the radish and carrots. Add the lemon juice or vinegar, toss everything together, and add salt and pepper. Cover and refrigerate the salad for about an hour.

2. Just before serving, toss in the cilantro, adjust the seasoning, and serve.

The best radishes for this are the Korean ones that are shaped like little footballs and at their absolute best in the cold months, when they are as sweet and crisp as apples. Second best are Chinese radishes of any kind or color. If all else fails, use tiny Western radishes, which are a bit hotter but still good.

Any kind of fresh tomato will do here as long as it is red and full flavored. I specify Romas because you won't need to waste much tomato juice with them, but you can, of course, enjoy the juice as a cook's treat.

Add the cilantro right at the end so that it is crunchy and lively when you serve the salad. If it sits in the salt and lemon juice, it will wilt and become a sad excuse for a vegetable.

TIBET'S FOOD HAS BEEN INFLUENCED BY many cuisines over the centuries, located as it is at the edge of many great ancient Asian crossroads. The Silk Road itself never made it through Tibet, which is bordered by the natural barriers of the earth's highest mountains to the west and south, and the Kunlun and Nanshan Ranges to the north. This forced the Silk Road to split off into northern and southern routes, bypassing the massive ring of peaks around Tibet's great central plain.

Tibet began to grow into a great empire under the rule of Songtsän Gampo (604–650), who was powerful enough to marry a daughter of the renowned Taizong emperor of China during the Tang dynasty. As the Tibetan Empire grew in strength, Buddhism wound its way north from India and over the narrow passes into the Tibetan heartland. But eventually the empire declined to such an extent that by the tenth century, its people had closed themselves off.

Nearly a thousand years later, in the late nineteenth century, only Chinese officials and a few other foreigners were allowed into the Tibetans' hidden world, and so the Tibetan people sent traders down the winding passes into their neighbors' territories to obtain whatever ingredients could not be locally grown or made.

Because Tibet is nestled up at some of the highest elevations on the planet, water boils at a much lower temperature there than at sea level, and so slow stews take the place of roasts and stir-fries. Trees are in short supply, which means that traditionally pots and homes have generally been heated with the most plentiful fuel around: dried yak dung.

Chéncù huāshēng 陳醋花生

Peanuts with Pickled Garlic

SHANXI • MAKES 1 CUP

One of the genuine pleasures of a Chinese banquet is the moment when an array of little dishes is served. This occurs before the real feast gets under way, just as everyone is settling in and pouring themselves tea or something else to drink. The dishes usually involve braised and pickled ingredients, and they're often presented in a decorative way—sometimes even in the shape of a peacock or a landscape.

Peanuts with Pickled Garlic, which is similar to the northern-style dish called Spinach and Peanuts (page 10), is a more relaxed example of one of these little dishes. This is a recipe you truly need to master—which will take all of ten minutes—because it goes with practically anything. It's especially good with smoked meat or fish.

1 cup peanuts with their skins on
Peanut or vegetable oil, as needed
3 to 4 tablespoons sauce from sweet pickled garlic cloves (page 433)
10 or so cloves sweet pickled garlic (page 433)
Chopped cilantro, for garnish

1. Place the peanuts in a cool wok and cover them with unheated oil. Turn on the heat under the wok and cook the peanuts over medium heat so they barely simmer. As soon as they start to split and smell toasted, taste one to make sure it has no raw taste, and then drain the peanuts in a sieve set over a heatproof bowl. Let the peanuts come to room temperature, by which time they should be crunchy. Refrigerate until cool.

2. Put the fried peanuts in a small serving bowl and toss them with the sauce and pickled garlic cloves. Sprinkle with the cilantro and serve.

There is a skill to frying nuts, but it's not hard. Just follow the directions and remove them from the heat and the hot oil the moment they're barely done. The residual heat in the nuts will continue to cook them for a few minutes as they cool down. Overcooked nuts will taste dry and bitter, so practice with a small amount of nuts until you get the hang of it.

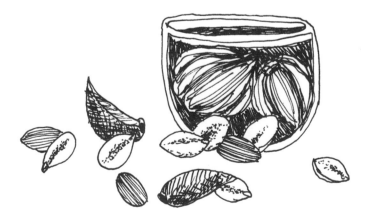

Huāshēngmǐ bàn xiāngcài 花生米拌香菜

Tossed Cilantro and Peanut Salad

THE NORTHWEST · SERVES 4 TO 6

I put this traditional Northwest salad together one evening when I realized that the colors in my dinner of Xinjiang-Style Lamb Kebabs (page 346) and Uyghur Pilaf (page 369) ranged from brown to beige. Something colorful—and preferably bright emerald—was needed to enliven the meal. This beautiful dish seemed like the perfect solution. Into the mixing bowl went everything and out came the most startlingly delicious salad I'd tried in a long time.

½ cup fried or toasted peanuts (page 411)

1 bunch very fresh cilantro (see Tip)

½ red sweet pepper

About 1½ teaspoons sweet soy sauce (page 439),
    or 1½ teaspoons regular soy sauce
    and ½ teaspoon sugar

¼ teaspoon sea salt

2 tablespoons any kind of seasoned oil, but shallot oil
    (page 435) is highly recommended

1 tablespoon toasted sesame seeds (page 413)

1. If you have not prepared the peanuts yet, cook them and let them cool completely before mixing them with the rest of the ingredients.

2. Rinse the cilantro carefully in cold water, shake it dry, and remove any less-than-stellar leaves and stalks. Trim off the ends and cut the cilantro into 1-inch pieces before placing them in a work bowl. Prepare the pepper by removing the cap, inner ridges, and seeds. Cut the pepper into pieces about the same size as the peanuts, and then add these to the cilantro along with the cooled cooked peanuts. (The salad can be made ahead of time up to this point, covered, and chilled. Add the dressing just before serving.)

3. Toss the cilantro, pepper, and peanuts with the rest of the ingredients. Taste and adjust the seasoning. Serve as an appetizer or side salad.

Use the freshest bunch of cilantro you can find. The stalks should be really crisp and tender.

Xīfēng chá chúndàn 西風茶鶉蛋

West Wind Tea Quail Eggs

SHAANXI · SERVES 4 TO 6

This romantic-sounding dish gets its name from a white liquor called West Wind. One of China's oldest liquor varieties, West Wind is made in Fengxiang county, which lies almost directly west of Xi'an in Shaanxi. Excavations have shown that a thriving brewing culture has existed in Fengxiang for at least three thousand years. West Wind is made mainly from sorghum grown in the area, but barley and dried peas give it a distinctive flavor.

In this dish, the white liquor is used as a flavoring. Because West Wind is still hard to find outside of China, feel free to use any good white liquor as a substitute; *gaoliang* or *meiguilu* (see page 492) are good options. Pigeon eggs are traditionally used, but quail eggs are much easier to hunt down in the United States.

Make these eggs three to five days before you want to serve them. As with all tea eggs or braised eggs, they need considerable resting time in the fridge for the flavors to seep all the way down to the yolks.

EGGS

30 quail eggs

BRAISING LIQUID

4 cups boiling water

3 tablespoons green tea leaves

4 slices fresh ginger

2 green onions, trimmed

1 tablespoon whole Sichuan peppercorns

1 large piece aged tangerine peel

2 teaspoons fennel seeds

1 tablespoon rock sugar

7 tablespoons regular soy sauce,
    divided into 5 tablespoons and 2 tablespoons

7 tablespoons good white liquor (see headnote),
    divided into 5 tablespoons and 2 tablespoons

1. Simmer the eggs for about 3 or 4 minutes while stirring them (see page 461); the time doesn't matter much, as they're going to be cooked further in the braising liquid, and you just need to get the whites hard enough to withstand the cracking of the shells. Empty out the water, fill the pan with cold tap water, and let the eggs cool down completely. Gently crack them all over by tapping them with the back of a spoon—but don't peel them—and let them drain in a colander.

2. Pour the boiling water into a medium saucepan and add the tea leaves, ginger, green onions, Sichuan peppercorns, tangerine peel, fennel seeds, sugar, and 5 tablespoons of both the soy sauce and the white liquor. Bring the braising liquid to a boil and then simmer it for an hour or two, until the liquid has been reduced by half. Add the unpeeled eggs, bring the liquid to a low boil again, and then lower it back to a simmer. Be sure not to cover the pan. After about an hour, turn off the heat and let the eggs come to room temperature. Add the remaining 2 tablespoons each soy sauce and white liquor and adjust the seasoning.

3. Place the eggs and the braising liquid in a tall covered container; the liquid should cover all or most of the eggs. Refrigerate the eggs, and, whenever you think of it, lightly shake them in the liquid so that they get a good dunk in the flavorings.

4. After 3 days and up to a week later, peel the eggs just before serving. I like to rinse them in the braising liquid in case there are any tiny bits of shell clinging to the whites. Serve these little marbled eggs at room temperature or slightly chilled.

Zhīmá yángròusī 芝麻羊肉絲

Sesame Lamb

SHANXI • SERVES 4 TO 6

In the farthest reaches of northern Shanxi, Mongolian influences usually take precedence over Han Chinese flavors. Historically, this area has been home to both ranching and farming families—some Mongolian and some Han. Sesame Lamb reflects the cooking styles of both groups. It combines lamb with the famed local black vinegar, white liquor, toasted sesame seeds, chili peppers, soy sauce, and a touch of sugar. Because it is served at room temperature, this dish makes a wonderful hot-weather entrée as well as an appetizer.

LAMB AND MARINADE

1 pound boneless lamb shoulder or other boneless, fatty cut of goat, lamb, or mutton

2 tablespoons dark soy sauce

2 tablespoons white liquor or mild rice wine

GARNISH

3 red jalapeño peppers or 6 dried Thai chilies (plus boiling water), or to taste

¼ cup peanut or vegetable oil

¼ cup peeled and finely shredded fresh ginger

2 green onions, trimmed and finely shredded

2 tablespoons black vinegar

1 teaspoon sugar

¼ cup unsalted butter or lard

½ cup toasted sesame seeds (page 413)

1. Place the lamb in the freezer for about 30 minutes, as this will make it easier to slice. Cut the lamb against the grain into very thin (⅛-inch) slices, and then turn these into 3-inch-long shreds. Put the lamb into a medium work bowl and toss with the soy sauce and white liquor or rice wine.

2. If you are using fresh chili peppers, remove the caps and seeds and then slice them into very thin julienne. If using dried peppers, break each pepper in half, shake out the seeds, remove the caps, and then cover the peppers with boiling water. Once the peppers have softened, drain them and slice into thin threads.

3. Place a wok over high heat, and once it is hot, add the oil. Swirl the oil around to coat the inside of the wok. Drain the lamb (reserve the marinade) and carefully sprinkle it into the hot oil. Stir-fry the lamb, using chopsticks to separate the strands, until the meat has browned. Remove the lamb to a clean plate and drain out all of the oil except for whatever is slicking the bottom.

4. Turn down the heat to medium-high and add the ginger, green onions, and chili peppers. Toss and fry them until they have lightly browned and then add the lamb, reserved marinade, vinegar, and sugar. When most of the sauce has been absorbed, taste and adjust the seasoning. Finally, toss in the butter or lard along with the sesame seeds until each piece of lamb is coated. Serve warm or cool.

Yángròu pàomó 羊肉泡馍

Lamb Soup with Biscuits

SHAANXI · SERVES 4 TO 6 AS A MAIN DISH

This dish has been around for over a thousand years; it was a staple on the dry, windswept plains above Xi'an. What makes this soup unique are the savory pieces of biscuit that take the place of the more common noodle. Traditionally, these biscuits are as tough as hardtack, but I prefer them this way: softer and a little bit like English muffins.

SOUP

1½ pounds boneless lamb, mutton, goat, or beef stew meat

10 cups meat stock (page 381)

1 teaspoon fennel seeds

1 teaspoon whole Sichuan peppercorns

2 star anise

1 small stick cinnamon

2 or 3 dried Thai chilies, optional

2 inches fresh ginger, smashed with the side of a cleaver

5 green onions, trimmed and lightly smashed

1 teaspoon sea salt, or to taste

BISCUITS

A little over 2 cups Chinese flour (page 386), divided into ¼ cup, 1½ cups, and 6 tablespoons

⅔ cup water

1 teaspoon active dry yeast

FINISHING TOUCHES

2 bundles cellophane noodles, soaked in cool water until soft

¼ cup dried wood ear fungus, soaked in hot water for at least 1 hour

Handful of cilantro, chopped

Sweet pickled garlic cloves (page 433) plus some of the liquid, or black vinegar

Hunan-style chili paste (page 437) or chili oil (page 435), or to taste

CHINA'S DESIRE TO QUASH PERSISTENT RAIDS by its nomadic enemies led in a roundabout way to its discovery of the West: about two thousand years ago, the great Han dynasty emperor Wudi grew so irritated by the Huns that he sent the explorer Zhang Qian out west to find allies who could help him eliminate them once and for all. His emissary failed at this, but he brought back the first news China ever had of the great Persian and Roman civilizations.

Zhang also told his emperor of the powerful "heavenly horses" bred by Greek descendants in the fertile Fergana Valley (called Dayuan in Chinese, it is located at the eastern edge of present-day Uzbekistan). These horses would change the face of warfare in East Asia, for China had until then depended upon the sturdy beast known as Przewalski's horse, a stocky, dun-colored animal that is now the only truly wild horse left in this world. More important to our tale, though, Zhang also reported back on the wonderful grains being grown in Dayuan.

Even though China has grown different grains (including wheat) for millennia, some believe that exceptional strains of wheat originating in the Fergana Valley changed the edible landscape of China forever, so much so that they came to form the bedrock of all of the Arid Lands' cuisines, from Shanxi in the east all the way out across the deserts and steppes to the highest settlements in the Himalayas.

Zhang brought back news about grapes as well, but viniculture never really took root in China until recently. This might be due to the strongly fermented flavors of things like soy sauce and the strong *xianwei* layers of China's dried ingredients, which do not marry well with most grape wines (see page 191).

1. A pressure cooker is recommended here, but a regular saucepan is fine, too. To make the soup, cut the meat into pieces no larger than 1 inch square. Place them in a pressure cooker or pan, cover with water, and bring the water to a boil. Simmer the meat for around 10 minutes, dump out the water and the scum, rinse the meat in a colander, and rinse out the pressure cooker or pan. Return the meat to the pressure cooker or the pan and cover with the stock. (If your pressure cooker or pan is relatively small, use less stock and add the rest when the soup is finished.) Place the fennel seeds and Sichuan peppercorns in a mesh ball or tie them in a piece of cheesecloth; add this to the stock with the star anise, cinnamon, chilies, ginger, green onions, and salt. If you're using a pressure cooker, cover and bring it to a boil over high heat, then cook with high pressure for about 45 minutes, until the meat is very tender. Otherwise, simply cook the meat until tender, adding more water as necessary to keep the meat submerged. Taste the meat and soup and adjust the seasoning. This step can be completed ahead of time and the soup either refrigerated or frozen. As with most soups, it is better the next day; the hard fat can be scraped off easily before the soup is reheated. About 10 minutes before serving, chop the softened noodles in half and add to the soup. Drain the wood ears, cut into smaller pieces if needed, and add them to the soup. Bring the liquid to a boil, then lower the heat and simmer for 10 minutes.

2. While the meat is cooking, start the biscuits: place ¼ cup of the flour in a medium work bowl and stir in both the water and the yeast. Cover the bowl with plastic wrap and let the yeast rise for about an hour. The batter should be bubbly. Stir in 1½ cups of the flour to form a stiff dough. Turn the dough out onto a smooth surface. Knead in about 6 tablespoons flour; the dough will be ready when it is very firm and no longer tacky. Cover the dough and let it rest for at least 20 minutes and up to an hour.

3. Lightly knead the dough and cut it into 6 equal pieces. Shape each piece into a ball and use a rolling pin to roll each ball into a circle about 3½ inches wide; no extra flour should be necessary but sprinkle on a bit if the dough sticks. Heat a large nonstick or cast-iron frying pan over medium heat until drops of water flicked onto it hiss into steam. Place as many of the biscuits in the pan as will fit rather loosely. I usually do this in 2 batches. Cover the pan and let the biscuits cook over medium heat for 3 or so minutes, until the bottoms are golden. Flip the biscuits over, cover, and cook the other sides until golden, too. Test one with a wooden skewer to ensure that it's cooked all the way through; the skewer should come out clean. Remove the biscuits to a plate and cover with a tea towel. Repeat with the rest of the biscuits.

4. Serve the soup in individual (2-cup) soup bowls with the biscuits on the side. Sprinkle the bowls with the cilantro and offer the garlic or vinegar and chili paste or oil on the side as condiments. To eat, break off small bits of biscuit into the soup and scoop them up with some broth before they get too soggy.

Lánzhōu níuròu miàn 蘭州牛肉麵

Lanzhou Beef Noodle Soup

GANSU · SERVES 4 AS A MAIN DISH

It is believed that a Lanzhou restaurant was the first to serve some combination of beef soup over *lāmiàn* 拉麵, or "pulled noodles." One legend holds that this dish was invented around a thousand years ago, during the Tang dynasty. It was described as having "a clear and mirror-like broth, aromatic and tender meat, and refined, thin pasta." Others, though, believe that this dish has a shorter history and was created a mere hundred years ago by a local Hui Muslim chef named Ma Baozi.

Whatever its origins, this noodle soup is the most famous dish Lanzhou has ever produced. Most people prefer to eat true pulled noodles in restaurants, because they are difficult to make at home. However, you can always make this dish with easier homemade pastas, like *biangbiang* (page 354), shaved noodles (page 356), or rolled noodles (page 388).

SOUP

1 boneless beef shank (1¼ to 1½ pounds, see Tips)
3 tablespoons peanut or vegetable oil
¼ cup thinly sliced fresh ginger
1 large leek, cleaned (see page 450), split in half lengthwise, and cut into 1-inch lengths, or 1 medium yellow onion, cut into eighths
3½ tablespoons bean sauce
¼ cup mild rice wine
1 tablespoon rock sugar
1 tablespoon regular soy sauce
1 pound (or so) Chinese radish, peeled and cut into 1-inch (or so) chunks
2 carrots, peeled and roll cut (see page 449) into 1-inch lengths, optional
3 ripe tomatoes (fresh or canned), peeled, seeded, and coarsely chopped, optional
10 cups unsalted beef stock (page 381)

SPICES

1 small black cardamom pod
2 teaspoons fennel seeds
1 tablespoon whole Sichuan peppercorns
1 teaspoon whole white peppercorns
3 pieces sand ginger
3 pieces licorice root
1 piece aged tangerine peel, about the size of a quarter
1 stick cinnamon
5 star anise

NOODLES

About 2 pounds fresh noodles of any kind (see headnote or use store-bought)

GARNISH

Spinach leaves, finely chopped leeks, and/or cilantro
Chili oil (page 435)
Black vinegar

1. This soup is a million times better the second or third day after you make it—letting it sit deepens the flavors and eliminates much of the bitterness present in some of the seasonings—so start it at least 24 hours before you wish to serve it. Pat the beef very dry. Set a pressure cooker or a wok over medium-high heat, add the oil when the wok is hot, and then add the whole beef shank and the ginger when the oil starts to shimmer. Brown the shank on both sides and then add the leek, tossing it so that it browns along the edges. Scoot the meat and leek to one side, tip the pan so that the oil collects at the other side, and add the bean sauce, frying it for about 30 seconds to release its fragrance. Pour in the rice wine before adding the sugar and soy sauce. Arrange the radish, carrots, and tomatoes around the shank and cover them with 6 to 10 cups of stock, depending upon the size of your pan.

2. Crack the black cardamom pod open by pressing down on it with the side of a wide Chinese knife. Tie it up along with the other spices in a cheesecloth bag, or in a large mesh ball, and add them to the pan. Cover and seal the pressure cooker, or simply put a lid on the wok. Bring the soup to a full boil and pressure-cook it over medium heat for about 1 hour, or about 3 hours if it's a stove-top braise, adding more stock as necessary.

3. Check the meat: it should be extremely tender, and the tendons should be soft and gummy. If they are not, cover and pressure-cook the soup for another 15 minutes or so, or simmer it for another 30 minutes. If you haven't added all the stock to the pan, do so now and bring the soup to a full boil. Taste and adjust the seasoning. Remove the shank and let it cool. Refrigerate both the soup and the shank and skim the fat off the soup before you heat it again.

4. About 10 minutes before you wish to serve the soup, cook the fresh noodles in boiling water until they float. Use a Chinese spider to remove them to large individual soup bowls. While the noodles are cooking, slice the cold shank against the grain into pieces about ¼ inch thick. If you are serving the soup with spinach, quickly blanch the leaves in the noodle water and divide them among the bowls. Fan the meat out attractively on the noodles, pour the soup over them, and garnish as desired. Offer chili oil and black vinegar on the side, and serve immediately; if you have leftover broth, top off the bowls when everyone is about halfway through.

Any good cut of beef that can put up with braising or contains lots of tendons is a candidate for this dish. Brisket is a good bet, as are short ribs. If the meat comes with bones, even better—the marrow will add more flavor to the dish. Just buy about twice the amount listed here (2½ to 3 pounds bone-in meat). Lamb is also good.

THE NORTHWEST TAKES DELIGHT IN FINDING ingenious ways to work dough into pastas. Some are shaved (page 356), clipped with shears (page 357), or rolled into the little gnocchi called "cat's ears," which recall the Italian *orecchiette*. Others have more exotic names—like "pasta warts" (*miàn gēda* 麵疙瘩), "brushed maggots" (*mǐnqūqū* 抿蛆蛆), and slithery little dough "flicked fish" (*bōyúer* 撥魚兒)—that owe a serious debt to the Chinese sense of humor.

Shanxi is home to the petals called "clutched noodles" (*jiūmiàn* 揪麵) and the super-lengthy "longevity noodles" (*chángshòumiàn* 長壽麵) served at birthday celebrations (page 214); Shaanxi, in turn, boasts *biangbiang* noodles (page 354), a type of pulled noodle. Qinghai is known for pasta squares called *miànpiàn* 麵片, while Uyghur cooks in Xinjiang stretch out incredibly long noodles called "pulled strands" (*lātiáozi* 拉條子) from oiled coils of dough.

The earliest known mention of pulled noodles is in a Ming dynasty book called *Sòngshì yăngshēng bù* 宋氏養生部, and over the centuries dozens of different styles have been perfected. Lanzhou's version could best be described as performance art. There, chefs fling skeins of dough into the finest threads imaginable. Dough that started out soft and passive is teased into resiliency by repeated pulling and folding; this strengthens the gluten and forms tiny teeth on the outside of the noodles that grab at sauces and seasonings.

Few people make pulled noodles like this at home; sort of like baguettes in France, they are considered best left to the experts, who do nothing but make the same edible masterpieces day after day.

Guriltai shul and *Gyatuk*

Lamb Noodle Soup

INNER MONGOLIA AND TIBET · SERVES 4 AS A MAIN DISH

Lamb Noodle Soup is one of those dishes that shows how much the cuisines of Tibet and Mongolia have intermingled. It features many Tibetan spices, like fenugreek, turmeric, and cumin, but if you leave them out, it becomes a Mongolian-style soup. Any good cut of stewing lamb or goat can be used, but I recommend that it have tendons running through it, because they lend the broth extra body. You can also substitute beef for the lamb with equally delicious results.

SOUP

2 tablespoons peanut or vegetable oil

1 teaspoon fenugreek seeds, optional

4 cloves garlic, smashed

1 teaspoon ground turmeric, optional

1 teaspoon ground cumin, optional

5 thin slices fresh ginger

1 bone-in lamb or goat shank

2 teaspoons mushroom powder, optional

1 tablespoon regular soy sauce (about 2 tablespoons if no mushroom seasoning is used)

8 cups water

NOODLES AND VEGETABLES

2 Roma tomatoes, thinly sliced

2 carrots, peeled and thinly sliced

1 pound rolled noodles (page 388), biangbiang noodles (page 354), or store-bought fresh pasta

2 to 4 cups coarsely chopped greens, optional

¼ cup shredded green onions

1. Ideally, start this a day or two ahead of time to give the flavors time to develop. To make the Tibetan version, warm the oil and fenugreek seeds together over medium heat in the bottom of a pressure cooker (see Tips if you don't have one) until the seeds turn a nut brown. Add the garlic, turmeric, cumin, ginger, and lamb or goat shank and brown the meat until it is golden all over. If you are going for a more Mongolian flavor, simply brown the garlic, ginger, and lamb shank in the pan until golden. Sprinkle the mushroom powder and soy sauce into the pan before pouring in the water. Cover the pressure cooker, seal, and cook the soup on high for 25 minutes, until the meat is very tender. Release the steam and let the soup cool to room temperature before refrigerating. The next day, discard the bone and slice the meat against the grain. Remove the fat from the stock before heating it up again.

2. About 10 or 15 minutes before serving, bring a pot of water to a boil. While you are waiting for it to boil, add the tomatoes and carrots to the soup. As soon as the carrots are barely done, taste and adjust the seasoning. Add the noodles to the pot of boiling water and cook them until they are barely done, then scoop the noodles into 4 large soup bowls. Blanch the optional greens and divide them among the bowls. Arrange the slices of meat on top of the noodles. Add the green onions to the soup at the last minute, then divide it among the bowls. Serve this soup very hot.

If you don't have a pressure cooker, stew the lamb uncovered for 2 to 3 hours, until the meat is very tender. Be sure to top off the broth with boiling water as it evaporates.

Although barley paste, or *tsampa* (see page 317), is the most common accompaniment to meals in Tibet, noodles are popular, too.

Níngxià yángròu fĕn tāng 寧夏羊肉粉湯

Ningxia Midwinter Soup

THE NORTHWEST · SERVES 2 AS A MAIN MEAL

The longest night of the year is a time for celebration in China. The winter solstice usually occurs on December 21 or 22, according to the lunar calendar; my husband and his family always look forward to bowls of rice balls (like the ones on page 144) that evening, but others see this as a time to enjoy some *jiaozi* (page 45) or lamb soup.

Ningxia puts a special spin on this custom, with celebrations centering around a spicy lamb soup with thick batons of mung bean jelly (or *liangfen*, page 250) floating among mushrooms and tomatoes. I have to tell you, the *liangfen* is a touch of genius: the cubes turn into enticing, gently textured pillows that really stand out against the rich bits of lamb.

SOUP

3 or more ounces boneless lamb or goat meat

1 teaspoon regular soy sauce

½ teaspoon dark soy sauce

2 tablespoons peanut or vegetable oil

2 tablespoons peeled and shredded fresh ginger

3 green onions, trimmed and julienned,
    whites and greens in separate piles

1 teaspoon coarsely ground dried chilies, or less if you are
    chili-adverse

½ teaspoon five-spice powder (page 441 or store-bought)

4 black mushrooms, fresh or dried and plumped up,
    stemmed and thinly sliced

4 whole canned Roma tomatoes, cut into
    ¼-inch-thick slices

2 teaspoons black vinegar, or to taste

4 cups unsalted mushroom stock (page 381) or water

l recipe mung bean jelly (page 250), through Step 2

Sea salt and freshly ground black pepper to taste

TO SERVE

Handful of cilantro, coarsely chopped

Grilled breads (page 396) or any other raised breads from
    this region

1. Cut the lamb into strips about ¼-inch thick and wide, and 1 to 2 inches long. Place them in a small work bowl and toss with both kinds of soy sauce. While these are marinating, prepare the rest of the ingredients. If you have any bones or fat on the meat, consider tossing them into the stock for extra flavor; remove them before you pour the stock into the vegetables.

2. Set a wok over medium-high heat and add the oil when the wok is hot. Swirl it around and add the ginger and onion whites. As soon as they are fragrant, sprinkle in the lamb and marinade and toss these around until the lamb is barely done. Scoop them out into a clean work bowl, but drain the oil back into the wok.

3. Over medium heat, add the chili powder and five-spice powder to the oil and swirl them around before raising the heat to medium-high and adding the mushrooms. Toss these quickly to release their fragrance, then add the tomatoes and vinegar. Pour in the stock or water and bring it to a boil before lowering the heat to a simmer. The soup can be made ahead of time up to this point.

4. Cut the mung bean jelly into fat batons around ¾ inch wide and an inch or so long, or whatever size you like. Slide these into the soup and simmer them gently for about 10 minutes to heat through; they will turn from an opaque white to almost translucent when ready. Add the lamb, then taste and adjust the seasoning with salt and pepper and whatever you like. Ladle the soup into large bowls, top with the finely chopped onion greens and coarsely chopped cilantro, and serve with the bread, which may be torn into smallish pieces and tossed into the soup.

Xīnjiāng kǎoyú 新疆烤鱼

Northwestern Roasted Fish

NORTHWEST • SERVES 4

In China's desert areas, freshwater fish is traditionally barbecued in a way that resembles Xinjiang-Style Lamb Kebabs (page 346). Here's a modern interpretation.

1 whole mild fish (about 1 pound), like branzino, grass carp, or bass
¾ teaspoon sea salt
Spray oil
Extra virgin olive oil, as needed
2 teaspoons cumin seeds, divided in half
2 cloves garlic, finely chopped, divided in half
2 red jalapeño peppers, seeded and finely chopped, divided in half

1. Heat the oven to 500°F or its highest setting. Scale, gut, and clean the fish, then remove the gills. Slash the sides in the "willow leaf" pattern (see page 23). Butterfly the fish by opening it up completely along the belly, laying it skin-side up, and flattening it by pressing along its backbone. Massage the salt into both sides of the fish and let it marinate for about 10 minutes.

2. Spray a baking sheet with oil. Rub some olive oil on both sides of the fish, being careful to hit every spot. Lay the fish flesh-side up on the baking sheet and sprinkle it with half of the cumin, garlic, and chili peppers. Roast the fish for about 8 minutes, until the flesh begins to brown. Remove the fish from the oven, turn it over, and coat it thoroughly with olive oil and the rest of the cumin, garlic, and chili peppers. Roast for another 3 to 5 minutes or so until the skin is golden and crispy. Plate the fish and pour the drippings from the broiler pan over it before you serve.

Gōngfū dùn yú 功夫燉魚

Kung Fu Fish

THE NORTHWEST · SERVES 6 TO 8

In this dish, steamed fish is accompanied by a chili-flecked broth of chicken stock, a little black vinegar and rice wine, and a bit of seasoning. Traditionally, this recipe—which comes from a landlocked region—calls for freshwater fish, like grass carp. But use whatever kind of fish you like, as long as it's not super oily or strongly flavored (like mackerel). Small amberjack, rock cod, or another similarly firm-fleshed fish will work well. I also use a bit of butter to fry the chilies; it gives the sauce a silky texture.

1 whole mild fish (see headnote, about 2 pounds)
1 teaspoon sea salt
3 tablespoons peanut or vegetable oil
1 teaspoon coarsely ground dried chilies, or to taste
2 tablespoons unsalted butter
2 tablespoons black vinegar
1 tablespoon mushroom powder
¼ cup mild rice wine
2 cups unsalted chicken stock (page 380)
Freshly ground black pepper
¼ cup chopped cilantro or green onions

1. Clean the fish, removing the guts and gills, and then scale it; leave the head, tail, and fins attached. Pat the fish dry with a paper towel and deeply slash both areas on an angle (see page 23). The slashes should be about an inch apart, so that the fish will cook evenly and absorb all the flavors in the sauce. Rub the salt all over the fish, especially in the slashes, and set the fish aside in a work bowl to marinate briefly while you prepare everything else.

2. Place a wok over medium-high heat, then add the oil when the wok is hot. Swirl the oil around and sprinkle in the ground chilies. Fry the peppers until they turn from red to brown and then add the butter, vinegar, mushroom powder, rice wine, and stock. Bring the mixture to a full boil, taste and adjust the seasoning, and remove from the heat.

3. Set up a steamer (see page 49). Rinse the fish again to get rid of the salt and pat it dry with a paper towel. Find a bowl or wide-rimmed deep plate that fits easily in your steamer. Lay the fish down flat on the bowl or plate, or curl it up—whatever fits and looks nice is fine—and then pour the sauce over and around it. Grind black pepper over the fish and place it in the steamer.

4. Steam the fish over medium heat until it flakes easily but is not overcooked. While the fish is steaming, baste it occasionally with the sauce. Remove the bowl or plate from the steamer, decorate it with the cilantro or green onions, and serve hot.

Tángcù yóuyújuǎn 糖醋鱿魚卷

Sweet-and-Sour Squid Blossoms

SHAANXI · SERVES 4

Fish and crustaceans from the Pacific have only recently made their way—fresh and frozen—to the markets of the vast Northwest. Dried seafood, on the other hand, has almost always been around. This Sichuan-style dish features dried squid, which can be very funky or very mild, depending on how old it is and how it was dried.

Like beef tendons and shrimp eggs, dried squid may sound odd and slightly off-putting at first, but I strongly encourage you to try it. The Chinese have loved dried squid for many years, and there's a good reason why: it's delicious.

At first it will look like you're making an enormous amount of squid, but reconstituted squid casts off much of its liquid while it's cooking and shrinks dramatically. The addition of almonds here is a personal touch. I think their subtle crunch provides a nice complement to the aromatic sauce and the squid's tender yet slightly chewy texture.

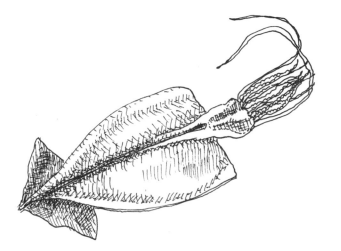

SQUID

2 large or 4 medium dried, flattened squid
    (around 5 ounces), the bigger the better
    (see page 490 and Tips)
2 teaspoons baking soda

SAUCE

4 dried Thai chilies
Boiling water, as needed
2 tablespoons peeled and finely minced fresh ginger
4 green onions, white parts only, trimmed and finely minced
4 cloves garlic, finely chopped
¼ cup black vinegar
2 tablespoons light soy sauce
3 tablespoons sugar

THE REST

½ cup peanut or vegetable oil, divided in half
4 green onions, green parts only, coarsely chopped
½ cup toasted slivered blanched almonds (see Tips)
    or toasted peanuts (page 411), coarsely chopped

1. Start this recipe at least a day before you plan to serve it. Place the squid in a large work bowl or casserole, cover it with cool tap water, and soak it for around 3 hours. (Do not use hot water anywhere in this step, as it will toughen the flesh.) Discard the water, then cover the squid with fresh cool tap water, sprinkle the baking soda over it, and soak it for another 3 hours. Thoroughly rinse the alkaline water off the squid and container. Cover the squid with clean cool water and store it overnight in the refrigerator. Drain and pat the squid dry before proceeding.

2. Remove the dark membrane from each squid body, as well as any discolored areas and hard bits around the mouth. Pull the tentacle section from the body, separate the individual strands, and cut them into 1-inch lengths. The area at the top of the tentacles that lies inside the body is perfectly edible and should be cut against the grain into thin strips. Remove the clear plastic-like cuttlebones from the bodies. Cut off the tips of the bodies and then slice the bodies in half before cutting them into "blossoms" (see page 187). Score the tips of the bodies the same way. Rinse the squid blossoms and tentacles, as well as the work bowl, and return the squid to the bowl.

3. To make the sauce, first prepare the chilies: break them in half, shake out the seeds, remove the caps, and then place them in a small, heatproof work bowl. Cover the chilies with boiling water for about 10 minutes, then drain and slice them into fine threads. Mix the chilies with the rest of the sauce ingredients.

4. Place a wok over medium-high heat; when it is hot, swirl in ¼ cup of the oil. Carefully toss the squid into the wok and stir-fry it only until the pieces curl up. Remove the cooked squid to a clean bowl and discard any milky liquid that was cast off.

5. Place the wok over high heat and add the remaining ¼ cup oil. Pour in the sauce and bring it to a rapid boil. Taste and adjust the seasoning. As soon as the sauce has thickened and is completely covered with bubbles, add the squid. Toss it around in the sauce until each piece is evenly covered. Add the green onions and nuts, toss a final time, and serve immediately.

If you cannot find dried squid in your area, fresh or frozen squid works perfectly here, too. No soaking is necessary in this case. Just prepare the squid as directed on page 186.

To toast the almonds, heat a toaster oven to 350°F. Spread the almonds on a shallow tray and bake them in the oven, stirring them now and again, until they turn a pale gold. The almonds can also be fried; use the recipe for fried peanuts on page 411.

WHEN YOU ARE A STRANGER IN A STRANGE land—and you also look completely different from the locals—you soon find that you represent your homeland, for better or worse. This all takes various forms. At times it pops up as misinformation, such as when a museum coworker demanded to know why American women smoke and drink to excess, which she said was true because this always happened in Hollywood movies. I told her that despite such evidence to the contrary, this wasn't the norm, and we didn't have extraterrestrials or zombies roaming around the countryside, either.

Most times, though, being an American was a load of fun, as my favorite night market memory demonstrates. Taipei is chockfull of these great places that sprout up stands along otherwise quiet alleys as the sun sets. Night markets are places where you can always get a delicious snack of some sort, shop for Taiwan's amazing variety of fresh fruit, sip on a glass of freshly squeezed sugarcane juice, and paw through tarps covered with masses of DVDs, cheap clothes, and fashionable accessories. These night markets are always packed, and I've never understood why they are not the norm everywhere else in the world—what better way to enjoy a warm evening than satisfying a case of the munchies while wandering around with friends and stocking up on Hello Kitty knickknacks?

So what happened was, I was meandering through the Shilin night market on the outskirts of Taipei the evening that the original space shuttle returned to Earth. Television sets arranged in the various stalls had their sound turned up, and everyone gathered around the nearest ones, anxious to see whether the *Columbia* would successfully land after its trip into outer space.

All action in the market came to a standstill as the plane approached the runway. There was a collective intake of breath when its wheels brushed the tarmac, and then absolutely everyone turned to me and applauded. I gave them my best curtsy, waved graciously, and demurred that, really, it was nothing, nothing at all.

Lǒngnán qīngzhēng jī 隴南清蒸雞

Steamed Chicken Southern Gansu Style

GANSU · SERVES 3 TO 4

The headwaters of the Yellow River flow through Gansu, and this vital source of fresh water sets the foods of this province apart from those of its neighbors in these otherwise dry western lands. On the banks of the river in southern Gansu is one stretch where Han Chinese often congregate to enjoy more eastern-style foods.

Steamed Chicken Southern Gansu Style is flavored by an unusual ingredient: the thin salted bamboo shoot tips called *yùlánpiàn* 玉蘭片, or "magnolia petals." A delicious side effect of their preservation is transformation of the naturally grassy flavor of the bamboo into something much more savory.

CHICKEN

¼ cup dried wood ear fungus

¼ cup small salted bamboo shoot tips (see headnote)

Boiling water, as needed

1½ pounds chicken wings (see Tips)

3 green onions, trimmed

1 inch fresh ginger, thinly sliced

1 teaspoon ground toasted Sichuan peppercorns (page 441)

Sea salt, as needed

SPINACH

4 cups packed spinach leaves, washed carefully (see page 10)

1 small bunch cilantro, picked over

2 tablespoons mild rice wine

1 tablespoon cornstarch

1 tablespoon seasoned oil of any kind (pages 434 to 436), or toasted sesame oil

1. Place the wood ears and the dried bamboo shoots in 2 small work bowls and cover with boiling water. After about 15 minutes, empty the water and use fresh boiling water to cover the shoots and wood ears again. Let them steep a while longer until they're fully plumped up.

2. While the bamboo shoots and wood ears are soaking, cut the wings into three segments, saving the wing tips for something else. Place the chicken in a medium heatproof bowl. Drain the shoots and wood ears. If they're in large pieces, shred them into thin julienne (shredding the bamboo shoots with the grain so they don't disintegrate) before adding them to the chicken. Add the whole green onions to the bowl along with the ginger and ground peppercorns. Place the bowl in a steamer (see page 49) and steam the chicken for about an hour, adding more water to the steamer as necessary.

3. Remove the chicken from the steamer. Pick out and discard both the green onions and the ginger. Pour the remaining juices and vegetables into a wok, boil them down over high heat until you have about ½ cup left, then taste and adjust the seasoning, adding more salt if necessary. Add the spinach and quickly toss the leaves in the hot juices until they wilt. Use a slotted spoon to remove the spinach to a rimmed serving plate or bowl. Form a nest out of the greens and then nestle the chicken in the center. Top the chicken with the cilantro. Mix the rice wine with the cornstarch, add to the wok, and stir until the sauce thickens. Add the seasoned oil and pour the sauce over the dish. Serve hot.

If you prefer to use a whole chicken, cut it into smallish pieces and double the rest of the ingredients.

When steaming the chicken, make sure that there is at least a 1-inch clearance between the bowl and the steamer cover, so that the steam can circulate easily.

Jiàngbào táorén jīdīng 醬爆桃仁雞丁

Chicken with Walnuts and Lotus Root

THE NORTHWEST · SERVES 4 TO 6

This dish combines chicken, crisp lotus root, chilies, and crunchy walnuts in a sauce seasoned with sweet wheat paste. Walnuts are probably more popular in the vast Northwest than anywhere else in China. Although originally from the Middle East, traders traveling along the Silk Road brought them here long ago, and they're featured in many local recipes, like Rose-Scented Lotus Patties (page 371). Fresh chilies are traditionally used in this dish, but I've come to prefer the more subtle heat provided by dried Thai ones. These dried chilies seem to sidle up especially well to the toasted walnuts, echoing and amplifying their flavor.

CHICKEN

1 pound boneless chicken, with or without skin,
    bones removed
½ teaspoon sea salt
2 tablespoons mild rice wine
1 large egg white
1 teaspoon cornstarch

THE REST

1 cup walnuts, in large pieces
Boiling water, as needed
1 lotus root (4 to 6 ounces)
1 teaspoon pale rice vinegar
10 or so dried Thai chilies
¼ cup peanut or vegetable oil
2 tablespoons peeled and minced fresh ginger
2 green onions, trimmed and chopped
2 cloves garlic, finely chopped
2 tablespoons sweet wheat paste
1 tablespoon toasted sesame oil

1. Cut the chicken into ¾-inch cubes, place in a small work bowl, and toss with the salt, rice wine, egg white, and cornstarch. Allow the chicken to marinate while you prepare the rest of the ingredients.

2. Pick over the walnuts to make sure there are no shells, then place them in a small work bowl. Cover the walnuts with boiling water for at least 10 minutes to remove any bitterness. While the walnuts are soaking, peel the lotus root, wash it carefully inside and out (see page 451), and drain. Cut the lotus root into ¾-inch cubes, place in a small work bowl, cover with water, and add the vinegar to keep the flesh white. Break the chilies in half, shake out the seeds, discard the caps, and cut into ¼-inch pieces. Drain the walnuts, rinse in a colander, and pat dry.

3. Place a wok over medium-high heat and add the oil. Fry the walnuts in the oil, tossing the whole time, until they are toasted and smell wonderful. Remove the fried walnuts to a clean medium work bowl, but keep the oil in the wok. Fry the chilies in the hot oil until they are dark red and then transfer them to the work bowl with the walnuts. Drain the lotus root cubes, rinse them under tap water, shake them as dry as you can, and add the lotus root to the wok. Stir-fry the lotus root for a minute or so to barely cook it through, then remove it to the work bowl. Add the chicken and marinade to the wok and stir-fry the chicken until it barely starts to brown, then remove it to the work bowl. Pour any oil in the work bowl back into the wok.

4. Heat the wok over high heat and add the ginger, green onions, and garlic. Stir-fry these for a few seconds to release their fragrance, then add the sweet wheat paste and about ¼ cup boiling water. When the liquid comes to a boil again, return everything in the work bowl to the wok and quickly toss over high heat until the water has evaporated. Sprinkle on the sesame oil, toss again, adjust the seasoning, and serve hot.

Xīnjiāng dàpán jī 新疆大盤雞

Xinjiang's Big Plate of Chicken

THE NORTHWEST · SERVES 4

This dish was created by Sichuanese cooks who immigrated to Xinjiang toward the end of the last century. They wanted to make a meal that would satisfy the appetites of people who worked with their hands all day long, and this is what they came up with. You can, of course, use a chopped-up half chicken here, bones and all, but I tend to use boneless meat. The chicken tastes great if it's marinated for a day or two before cooking—which also makes for a really fast dinner later in the week. Consider marinating it one day, cooking it the next, and serving it a day or two later, so that the potatoes have enough time to absorb all the flavors.

CHICKEN

1 pound boneless (or 2 pounds bone-in) chicken

¼ cup mild rice wine

¼ cup regular soy sauce

EVERYTHING ELSE

1 pound potatoes (Yukon Gold recommended)

1 mild green pepper

4 or more dried Thai chilies

¼ cup peanut or vegetable oil, or as needed

2 tablespoons whole Sichuan peppercorns

½ teaspoon sea salt

3 green onions, trimmed and chopped

2 tablespoons peeled and finely chopped fresh ginger

3 cloves garlic, finely chopped

1 cup water

1. Cut the chicken into ¾-inch cubes. Use a cleaver if the chicken has bones. Place the chicken in a medium work bowl and toss with the rice wine and soy sauce. Marinate the chicken for about 30 minutes, or cover and refrigerate it for a day or two.

2. Peel the potatoes if you like, then cut them into ¾-inch cubes. Place the cubes in a medium work bowl and cover with cool tap water to keep them from browning. Remove the seeds from the mild green pepper and cut it into ¾-inch cubes. Break the dried chilies in half, shake out the seeds, discard the caps, and cut into ¼-inch-wide rings.

3. Place a wok over medium-high heat. When the wok is hot, add the oil and then the Sichuan peppercorns. Make a seasoned oil by frying the peppercorns in the oil until they turn dark, then strain them out with a slotted spoon and discard. Next, fry the dried chilies in the seasoned oil until they're dark, then remove them to a clean work bowl. Raise the heat under the wok to high, add the salt, green onions, ginger, and garlic, and fry these for a few seconds to release their fragrance. Toss in the chicken and marinade and stir-fry until the chicken is lightly browned. Remove the chicken and aromatics to a clean work bowl but keep the oil in the wok.

4. Place the wok over high heat and add the green pepper. Quickly stir-fry the pepper to remove its rawness, then remove it to the bowl with the chicken. Drain the potatoes and stir-fry them—adding a bit more oil, if necessary—until the pieces are lightly browned.

5. Return the chicken and peppers to the wok and pour in the water. Scrape off the crust at the bottom of the wok to help it dissolve in the liquid. Cover the wok and reduce the heat to a gentle simmer. Stir every once in a while, adding more water as necessary, until the potatoes turn creamy, which will take about 15 minutes. When the potatoes are done, reduce the sauce if needed before tasting and adjusting the seasoning. Serve hot.

Suānlà lǐjí 酸辣里脊

Hot-and-Sour Pork

GANSU AND THE NORTHWEST · SERVES 4 TO 6

Hot-and-Sour Pork probably first emerged during the Warring States Period, over two thousand years ago. The heat of the chilies is certainly fairly new, but the numbing edge of the Sichuan peppercorns and the gentle tang of the vinegar are traditional seasonings for meats in this area.

This dish is most popular in Tianshui, Gansu's second largest city. Tianshui is known as the birthplace of the fabled ancestors of humanity: Fuxi and his sister, Nüwa. During the Time of Myths, a great flood wiped out mankind, and so, as the story has it, the siblings climbed up legendary Kunlun Mountain and breathed life into a new race molded out of clay.

PORK

12 dried Thai chilies

Boiling water, as needed

1 pound boneless pork loin (or boneless pork chops)

2 tablespoons toasted sesame oil

2 tablespoons regular soy sauce

2 tablespoons peeled and minced fresh ginger

2 teaspoons ground toasted Sichuan peppercorns
 (page 441)

2 tablespoons cornstarch

SAUCE

1 cup water

2 teaspoons cornstarch

2 tablespoons regular soy sauce

2 teaspoons sugar

THE REST

4 cloves garlic

6 green onions, trimmed

¼ cup black vinegar

2 cups peanut or vegetable oil (used oil is all right
 if it smells fresh)

1. Break the chilies in half and discard both the seeds and caps. Cover the chilies with boiling water and let sit until soft; drain and coarsely dice. If the pork is not already sliced, cut it into ¾-inch-thick slices, then cut each slice into ¾-inch (more or less) cubes. Put the pork in a medium work bowl and toss with the chilies, sesame oil, soy sauce, ginger, Sichuan peppercorns, and cornstarch.

2. To make the sauce, gradually stir the water into the cornstarch so that there are no lumps. Add the soy sauce and sugar.

3. Peel the garlic cloves and cut them into thin slices. Cut the green onions on a sharp diagonal into 1-inch lengths, keeping the whites and greens in separate piles. Measure out the vinegar.

4. Place a wok over medium-high heat, and when the wok is hot, add the oil and swirl it around. As soon as the oil starts to shimmer, add the pork and stir it so that the cubes don't stick to one another. Fry the pork until it's a golden brown. Remove it to a clean work bowl and strain the oil through a fine-mesh sieve into a heatproof container. Rinse out the wok, as the cornstarch mixture will most likely be caked on the bottom.

5. Return the wok to the stove, this time over medium heat. When it is dry and hot, add about ¼ cup of the frying oil. Toss in the garlic and the white parts of the onions and fry these until they turn a golden color. Raise the heat to high and add the vinegar. As soon as it bubbles, pour in the sauce mixture and fried pork and bring to a full boil. Taste and adjust the seasoning. Toss in the onion greens and serve hot.

Mùxī ròu 木樨肉 or *mùxū ròu* 木須肉

Osmanthus Blossom (Moo Shu) Pork

ALL OVER NORTH AND NORTHWESTERN CHINA •
SERVES 3 TO 4

Beloved throughout China's northern regions and thus known by many names (including "clover pork," or *mùsù ròu* 苜蓿肉), this dish is often called "moo shu pork" in the West. Its Chinese name, *muxi rou*, translates as "osmanthus blossom pork," not because there are flowers involved, but because the yellow egg curds are thought to resemble the tiny blossoms of an evergreen bush called *Osmanthus fragrans* or "sweet olive," which has been revered in China since ancient times for its intensely fruity perfume. This dish is so popular in Shandong and Beijing that many think it might have originated on the eastern coast of China. Others say it hails from the Northeast, and still others credit Shanxi for its creation. Wherever it came from, it's genius when done right.

There are a couple of secrets to making this correctly. First, don't use soy sauce because it will dull the colors in the dish, and part of the appeal of Osmanthus Blossom Pork is its amazing color palette. The eggs in particular should stay bright yellow, and the lily flowers or carrots should remain orange. Instead of soy sauce, use just a touch of salt and then dab sweet wheat paste sauce on the wrapper (you should underseason the stir-fry itself, because this sauce is very salty). Make sure, too, to stir-fry the meats and vegetables in separate small batches so they cook up quickly and evenly before tossing them together at the last minute. The mung bean sprouts, in particular, should be rapidly seared; otherwise, they'll release all of their juices into the wok.

SAUCE

2 tablespoons toasted sesame oil
¼ cup sweet wheat paste
2 teaspoons regular soy sauce
2 teaspoons sugar

PORK

4 ounces boneless pork tenderloin
    (or beef or pressed bean curd)
½ teaspoon sea salt

THE REST

¼ cup salted dried bamboo shoots, 1 large winter
    bamboo shoot (fresh or frozen and defrosted),
    or 8 ounces mung bean sprouts
¼ cup shredded dried wood ear fungus,
    or 3 fresh wood ears
Boiling water, as needed
¼ cup dried daylily flowers, or 1 small carrot
2 green onions, trimmed
3 large eggs
6 tablespoons toasted sesame oil or peanut or
    vegetable oil, divided
2 cloves garlic, minced
2 tablespoons mild rice wine
1 teaspoon sugar

TO SERVE

8 thin wheat wrappers (page 394),
    or 8 (8-inch or so) soft flour tortillas, warmed
2 green onions, trimmed and finely shredded

1. First make the sauce: heat the sesame oil in a wok over medium heat and mix in the sweet wheat paste. Stir together until smooth and then add the soy sauce and sugar. When the sauce bubbles, taste and adjust the seasoning and then scrape the sauce into a small bowl. Rinse out the wok.

2. Place the meat in the freezer for about 30 minutes to make it easier to cut, then slice it against the grain into ¼-inch-thick pieces. Cut into batons about ¼ inch wide. Put the batons in a small work bowl and toss them with the salt. (If you are using pressed bean curd, cut it into thin julienne before tossing it with the salt.)

3. If you are using dried bamboo shoots, soak them in hot water until they're soft, then rinse, trim, and shred them. A fresh bamboo shoot should be peeled (see Tip, page 122), julienned, and then blanched until barely done, while a frozen one needs only to be defrosted and then julienned. The bean sprouts should be rinsed and spun very dry in a salad spinner.

4. Soak the shredded dried wood ear fungus in boiling water until pliable, then rinse it and drain it in a colander. Fresh wood ears should be rinsed before they're trimmed and cut into a thin julienne. Cover the dried daylily flowers with boiling water until soft, then drain and tear them into strips. If you are using a carrot instead of the daylilies, peel and then cut it into a very thin julienne. Cut the green onions into thin shreds.

5. Lightly beat the eggs in a small work bowl. Place the wok over medium heat, and when it is hot, swirl in about 2 tablespoons of the sesame oil. Toss in the garlic and lightly fry it until it smells wonderful. Add the eggs and scramble them, breaking up any large curds into pieces ½ inch or smaller. When the eggs are barely done, scrape them into a clean medium work bowl.

6. Raise the heat under the wok to high. Pour another 2 tablespoons of the oil into the hot wok and quickly stir-fry the meat until it's browned before scraping it into the eggs. Return the wok to high heat. Stir-fry the bamboo shoots with a little bit more oil, then add the wood ears and either the daylily flowers or carrot and cook these until they are barely done before tossing them into the bowl with the meat and eggs. If you're using the bean sprouts, place the wok over high heat, swirl in a tiny bit of oil, and quickly stir-fry the sprouts until they're just beyond raw but still very crisp before adding them to the bowl with the other cooked ingredients.

7. Place the wok back over high heat, pour in any remaining sesame oil, and add the green onions, all of the cooked meat and eggs and vegetables, and the rice wine and sugar. Toss these quickly together for a few seconds, taste and adjust the seasoning, and plate in a bowl or on a rimmed platter. Serve hot with the sauce, wheat wrappers, and shredded green onions. Have each diner spread about 2 teaspoons of the sauce down the center of a wrapper, sprinkle on some raw green onions, and pile on about ½ cup of the meat mixture. Fold the bottom edge of the wrapper up over the meat mixture, then fold one side over the center before rolling up the rest of the wrapper from the opposite edge. Eat with your hands.

Tángcù Fóshǒu juǎn 糖醋佛手卷

Buddha's Hand Rolls

SHANXI · SERVES 4 TO 6

These little stuffed omelets look something like bear-claw pastries. They get their name from the slices cut halfway through each roll to form five "fingers." Some regions have their own version of Buddha's Hand Rolls, but this one from Shanxi is particularly wonderful. Although pork is the traditional filling here, I have used ground turkey quite successfully, too. Just make sure that you have a slightly fatty meat in there—that is, dark meat rather than white—so that these omelets are juicy.

This recipe uses a very refined method for seasoning the meat: instead of chopping the ginger and green onions, you whirl these two aromatics with a shot of rice wine then strain out the solids. This leaves you with a beautiful green juice that blends elegantly with the meat.

SEASONED WINE

2 green onions, trimmed

1 inch fresh ginger

¼ cup mild rice wine

PORK

1 pound ground pork (15 percent fat, or relatively fatty turkey, beef, or chicken)

Freshly ground black pepper

½ teaspoon sea salt

1 large egg, lightly beaten

OMELET WRAPPERS

7 large eggs, lightly beaten

¼ cup cornstarch

1 teaspoon flour mixed with 2 teaspoons water

¼ cup peanut or vegetable oil, or as needed, divided

SAUCE

4 teaspoons peeled and finely minced fresh ginger

¼ cup pale rice vinegar

¼ cup black vinegar

¼ cup sugar

4 teaspoons regular soy sauce

6 tablespoons water

2 teaspoons cornstarch mixed with 2 tablespoons water

GARNISH

2 green onions, green parts only, trimmed and thinly sliced

1. First make the seasoned wine: chop the green onions and slice the ginger into fine pieces. Place these in a mini-chopper or blender, add the rice wine, and whirl them together until they're completely pureed. Strain through a fine-mesh sieve into a bowl, pressing down on the solids to get every last drop, and then discard the solids.

2. Place the pork in a medium work bowl. Mix in the seasoned wine, pepper, salt, and egg. Beat the mixture in one direction with your hand until the meat is light and fluffy (see page 458).

3. To make the omelet wrappers, beat the eggs and cornstarch together in a measuring cup until you have a fairly smooth batter. Put a plate next to the stove to hold the finished omelets. Place a very clean but well-seasoned wok over medium heat. Lightly film the bottom quarter of the wok with some oil—this is easily done by pouring some oil onto a paper towel and wiping the inside of the wok with it. Pour a quarter of the batter into the wok and then swirl it around so that it forms an even omelet about 8 inches wide. Cook it on one side until the edges start to loosen and the center turns a bit dull. Use a wok spatula to carefully lift the omelet out and place it onto the plate. Wipe the wok again with the oiled paper towel and repeat 3 more times to create 4 omelet wrappers.

4. Place an omelet wrapper on a cutting board. Slice the omelet down the middle to form 2 half circles, fill with the filling, and seal with the flour-water mixture (for directions on making the Buddha's hands, see the diagram below).

5. Heat the wok over medium heat, add about 1 tablespoon of the oil, then slowly fry about one-fourth of the omelet packets at a time until they are a golden brown on one side. Flip them over and fry the other sides. Remove the fried packets to a rimmed serving plate and repeat with the rest of the oil and packets until all are done.

6. Immediately place the sauce ingredients in the wok and bring to a boil while stirring so that the cornstarch doesn't form lumps. Taste and adjust the seasoning. Pour the sauce over the rolls, sprinkle with the green onions, and serve.

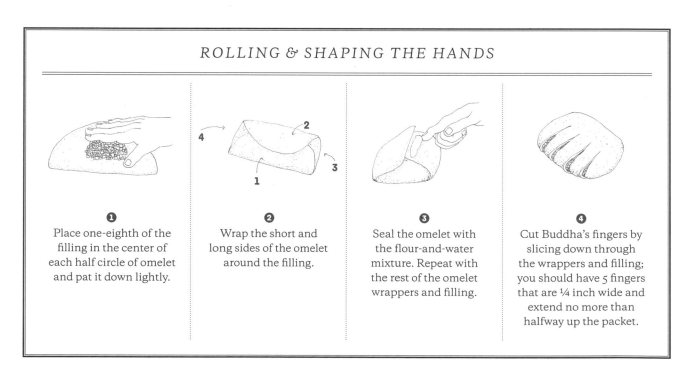

ROLLING & SHAPING THE HANDS

❶ Place one-eighth of the filling in the center of each half circle of omelet and pat it down lightly.

❷ Wrap the short and long sides of the omelet around the filling.

❸ Seal the omelet with the flour-and-water mixture. Repeat with the rest of the omelet wrappers and filling.

❹ Cut Buddha's fingers by slicing down through the wrappers and filling; you should have 5 fingers that are ¼ inch wide and extend no more than halfway up the packet.

Báobǐng jiān níuròu 薄餅煎牛肉

Silk Road Fajitas

THE NORTHWEST • SERVES 4

As a California kid, I practically grew up on Mexican food. However, I have to admit that as much as I adore the Mexican way with steak and tortillas, I think I prefer this version of fajitas from China's Northwest. The two styles have so much in common—flour wrappers, grilled steak, barely cooked vegetables, cilantro, cumin, garlic, and a pinch of salt—that they almost seem like mirror images of each other. But the green onions, rice wine, and ginger let you know that this dish is a Xinjiang special.

BEEF

12 ounces boneless beefsteak of any kind

2 tablespoons mild rice wine

½ teaspoon sea salt

½ teaspoon ground toasted cumin

½ teaspoon (more or less) finely ground dried chilies

2 tablespoons peanut or vegetable oil

WRAPPERS

1 recipe wheat wrappers (page 394),
    or 16 small store-bought flour tortillas

VEGETABLES

2 tablespoons peanut or vegetable oil

2 cloves garlic, finely chopped

1 tablespoon peeled and finely minced fresh ginger

1 sweet red pepper, seeded and cut into thin strips

3 green onions, trimmed and julienned

1 cup coarsely chopped cilantro

1. Trim the fat and any gristle off the steak before cutting it against the grain into thin slices. Cut these slices to form strips less than ¼ inch thick. Place the steak strips in a small work bowl and toss with the rice wine, salt, cumin, chilies, and oil. The steak can be prepared earlier in the day up to this point, covered, and refrigerated to give it extra time to marinate.

2. When it is close to mealtime, prepare the wheat wrappers and grill as directed on page 394, Step 4, or heat store-bought tortillas on an ungreased griddle until they puff up lightly. Place them in a clean tea towel and fold it around them to retain their heat. Just before serving, peel the homemade wrappers apart into thin crêpes if you wish, or leave them as is.

3. About 10 minutes before serving, heat a dry wok over high heat. Toss in the steak and all of the marinade. Sear the steak before flipping the strips over. When most of the pink has disappeared and the meat has a good brown sheen, drizzle the oil around the edge of the meat and then add the garlic, ginger, and red pepper to the wok. Toss these together over high heat. As soon as the peppers start to wilt, remove the pan from the heat and toss in the green onions and finally the cilantro. Taste and adjust the seasoning. Serve alongside the warm wrappers.

Shabril

Tibetan Meatballs in a Yogurt Sauce

TIBET · SERVES 4 TO 6

In the arid lands that stretch from Inner Mongolia in the north to Tibet in the southwest, leafy vegetables are in short supply. Grazing lands are seasonal and sparsely covered with hardy grasses, and sheep and goats are the main sources of meat. As a result, you see many dishes like this one, which features creative and tasty ways to use the products those animals provide.

Also evident in this dish is Tibet's relationship with its Kashmiri neighbors to the south. This can be seen most clearly in the dish's warm spices—fenugreek and turmeric are found elsewhere in China only in ready-made curry powders, rather than as individual flavorings, as they're employed here.

MEATBALLS

1 pound ground lamb or goat
½ teaspoon fenugreek seeds
5 tablespoons peanut or vegetable oil,
    divided into 1½ tablespoons and 3½ tablespoons
2 medium yellow onions, chopped
½ teaspoon ground turmeric
4 cloves garlic, chopped
4 teaspoons peeled and finely chopped fresh ginger

VEGETABLES AND SAUCE

12 large black mushrooms, fresh or dried and
    plumped up, stemmed and sliced
12 small red radishes, sliced
2 tablespoons regular soy sauce
½ cup water
1 cup full-fat yogurt (page 414 or store-bought)
2 green onions, trimmed and finely chopped

1. Place the ground meat on a cutting board and chop it until it is fine and fluffy (see page 458). Form the meat into 12 small meatballs. Place the fenugreek and 1½ tablespoons of the oil in a wok or frying pan and toast over medium heat until the seeds turn a golden brown. Add the onions and turmeric and cook, stirring frequently, until the onions are also browned. Remove the onions to a work bowl and add the garlic, ginger, and the remaining 3½ tablespoons oil to the wok. Stir these around over the heat to release their fragrance before adding the meatballs. Fry the meatballs while swirling the wok around so that they brown all over. Scoop them out and place them in the bowl with the onions.

2. If you have lots of oil in the bottom of the wok, pour off all of it except for a light film. Toss in the mushrooms and radishes and quickly fry them until the mushrooms are lightly browned. Pour in the soy sauce and water and use them to deglaze the caramelized juices at the bottom of the wok. Return the meatballs and onions to the wok, bring the sauce to a boil, and then cover the wok and reduce the heat to medium-low. Simmer the meatballs with the vegetables for about 15 minutes.

3. Bring the wok to a full boil and then remove it from the heat. Stir in the yogurt and adjust the seasoning. (Do not boil the sauce once the yogurt has been added or it will separate.) Pour the meatballs into a serving dish, sprinkle with the chopped green onions, and serve.

Fenugreek and turmeric can be found in some Western-style grocery stores, but I like to get mine from busy Indian markets whenever possible.

If you like, try growing fenugreek in your backyard. The seedlings smell like maple syrup.

Xīnjiāng yángròu chuàn 新疆羊肉串

Xinjiang-Style Lamb Kebabs

THE NORTHWEST · SERVES 4

Kebabs are beloved from Morocco to North China. The differences in their preparation are relatively minimal and depend on the type and cut of meat, as well as the seasonings. You can easily imagine this skewered lamb dish from Xinjiang being prepared by Uzbekis, with lemon juice, onions, cilantro, coriander seeds, and garlic, or by Persians, with olive oil, saffron, and onions. But in Xinjiang, it's seasoned with a simple dry rub of ground chili peppers, garlic, salt, and ground cumin.

The traditional recipe calls for oil to be mixed in with the meat; I have found, though, that the fat in the lamb is enough to baste the meat as it cooks, while providing a buttery flavor. Also, if you are cooking indoors, adding oil will often lead to billows of smoke in your kitchen, so try this dish without oil first and see if you like it. You can vary the spices, adding more chili pepper or tossing in some minced ginger. I like to use freshly ground cumin seeds, which are much more aromatic than the powdered stuff.

1 pound boneless lamb shoulder (see Tip)
4 to 6 cloves garlic
2 tablespoons ground cumin, toasted or untoasted
2 tablespoons coarsely ground dried chilies
2 teaspoons sea salt

1. Start this recipe at least 6 hours before you wish to serve it. Use 8 small or 4 large metal or bamboo skewers for the kebabs. I like long forked bamboo skewers, as the tines help keep the meat from sliding around, and the sharp ends make threading the meat relatively easy. If you are using bamboo skewers, soak them in warm water for a few hours before you cook the meat.

2. Trim off and discard any silver skin on the lamb but leave on the fat. Cut the meat in long, thin strips against the grain—the length of the strips doesn't matter, but the meat should be about ¼ inch thick. Place the strips in a resealable plastic bag or container.

3. Mix the garlic, cumin, chilies, and salt together, then use this as a dry rub for the meat. Toss the seasonings with the meat and lightly massage them into each piece so that the lamb is well seasoned. Close the bag or container and refrigerate for at least 6 hours and up to 5 days, depending upon your fridge. (This prepped meat also freezes well.)

4. Prepare either a ridged grill pan for indoor cooking or an outdoor barbecue for grilling. Thread the meat onto the skewers, but don't compact it too tightly, as the heat must circulate freely so the meat cooks evenly. Grill the meat over medium heat. Allow one side to char a bit before turning the skewers over. The lamb will be ready when the second side is also lightly charred. Let the meat rest for about 10 minutes before serving.

I like lamb shoulder because the meat is cheap, flavorful, and tender. If you buy a whole shoulder, you can divide it into smaller portions and freeze whatever you're not using.

Yángròu gǒuqǐyá 羊肉枸杞芽

Lamb with Wolfberry Buds and Berries

THE NORTHWEST · SERVES 4 TO 6

Most of the world's wolfberries, also known as *gouqi* or *goji* berries, are grown in Ningxia. In addition to enjoying the fruits, the Chinese prize wolfberry leaves as a tonic and vegetable. The leaves have a slight bitterness that can easily be tamed with a short ice-water bath, and their brilliant emerald color lends beauty to any dish. I am particularly fond of tossing them into dishes like Guangdong-style soups (use them instead of the dried vegetable in the recipe on page 173), where their subtle flavor can be appreciated against a simple gingery meat broth.

MAIN INGREDIENTS

1 pound lamb or goat loin
½ cup wolfberries
Boiling, cool, and ice water, as needed
2 tablespoons whole Sichuan peppercorns
3 tablespoons finely chopped fresh ginger
1 bunch fresh wolfberry leaves (about 1 pound),
    or 2 bunches watercress, tough stems removed

BATTER AND SAUCE

2 large egg whites, lightly beaten
2 tablespoons cornstarch
¼ cup peanut or vegetable oil, plus more as needed
1½ teaspoons sea salt, or to taste
3 green onions, trimmed and cut on the diagonal into
    1-inch lengths
¼ cup unsalted chicken stock (page 380)
2 tablespoons seasoned oil (pages 434 and 435;
    Sichuan peppercorn oil is recommended)

1. Trim any silver skin and fatty lumps from the meat. Freeze the loin for about half an hour to firm it up.

2. Cover the wolfberries with boiling water to plump them up. Put the Sichuan peppercorns and ½ cup cool water in a blender and pulverize the peppercorns. Pour the water through a fine-mesh sieve into a large (16-ounce or so) measuring cup. Divide this peppercorn water in half to use in the marinade and in the stir-fry. Place the ginger and ¼ cup cool water in the blender, pulverize, and pour the juice through a fine-mesh sieve into the measuring cup. Reserve to use in the stir-fry.

3. Cover the stemmed wolfberry leaves with ice water for about 15 minutes to get rid of some of the bitterness and then drain well.

4. Cut the meat against the grain into thin slices and then marinate with the ¼ cup peppercorn water for about 20 minutes. Pour off any excess water, add the egg whites to the meat, then stir in the cornstarch to make a thin batter that thoroughly coats each slice. Heat a wok over high heat, then add the oil; as soon as it starts to shimmer, lower the heat to medium. Add half of the meat and cook it gently while tossing it in the oil until it is almost cooked but not browned. Remove the cooked meat to a clean work bowl, repeat with the rest of the meat, and then pour off most of the oil, leaving about 1 tablespoon in the wok.

5. Turn the heat under the wok to high. As soon as the oil starts to smoke, toss the salt and green onions into the hot oil and then add the wolfberry leaves or watercress and stir-fry them until they begin to wilt. Pour in the combined Sichuan peppercorn and ginger water, as well as the stock; check the seasoning and add salt as needed. Bring to a boil and add the meat before bringing the sauce to a boil again, then toss in the plumped-up wolfberries with their juices. Toss everything together quickly; as soon as the sauce has thickened, plate the dish. Drizzle it with the seasoned oil and serve hot.

Bǎihé chǎo gǒuqǐ 百合炒枸杞

Lily Bulbs and Wolfberries

GANSU · SERVES 4 TO 6

Of all the lovely dishes my husband and I ate in Lanzhou, this one was the most memorable. It was set before us at a Buddhist restaurant on the banks of the Yellow River, just before we visited a shrine upriver in Gansu Province. Everything there was cooked according to strict Buddhist vegetarian principles: there was no meat, garlic, chilies, onions, or ginger. Because of this, the natural flavors of the few ingredients included stood out starkly.

The sweet, crunchy lily bulbs are difficult to find outside of China. They come into season only in late fall, and they have to be imported from Lanzhou, the capital of Gansu Province. They are available dried, but the desiccated bulbs are starchy rather than juicy and relatively tasteless. If you see the fresh ones in a Chinese market, snap up as many as you can. Plant the bulbs that have roots clinging to the bottom and use the rest for this dish. Lily bulbs grow easily in almost any temperate climate, and soon you'll have your own private source.

¼ cup wolfberries
Boiling water, as needed
4 fresh lily bulbs, 10 to 12 ounces total (see Tips)
1 tablespoon peanut or vegetable oil
½ teaspoon sea salt, or to taste

1. Place the wolfberries in a medium heatproof bowl and cover them with boiling water. Let the berries plump up while you prepare the rest of the ingredients.

2. Prepare the lily bulbs by using a paring knife to trim off any roots or discolored areas (see page 450).

3. Drain the wolfberries, capturing the soaking liquid in a measuring cup. If you have less than ¼ cup liquid, add just enough water to reach that mark.

4. Set the wok over high heat and add the oil and salt. Swirl the oil to dissolve the salt before adding the wolfberries, the soaking liquid, and the lily bulb petals. Quickly stir-fry them over high heat until the liquid boils. Taste one of the petals: it should be cooked and sweet but still crisp. Serve hot or warm.

Use only Lanzhou lilies for this dish. Do not substitute another kind of lily, because not all lilies are edible.

If you cannot find lily bulbs, use peeled and thinly sliced fresh water chestnuts or even jicama instead.

Jīnbiān báicài 金邊白菜

Golden-Edged Cabbage

SHAANXI • SERVES 4

To the Chinese, cabbage generally means only one thing: napa cabbage. Grown and beloved throughout all of northern, western, and central China, this is a cold-weather vegetable that stores well. The plant's wide, white stalks are crisp and juicy, and they are responsible for giving napa cabbage its Chinese name: "white vegetable."

This dish is one of my favorite renderings of napa cabbage. It contrasts the inherent sweetness of the vegetable with dried chilies and tart vinegar. The result is a refreshing cool-weather dish.

1½ pounds napa cabbage (about ½ large head or
    1 small head)
5 dried Thai chilies
2 tablespoons peanut or vegetable oil
1 tablespoon peeled and finely chopped fresh ginger
1½ tablespoons black vinegar
1½ teaspoons regular soy sauce
½ teaspoon sugar
1 teaspoon toasted sesame oil

1. Rinse the cabbage carefully, removing any damaged leaves. Shake it dry and then cut out the core. Separate the leaves into stacks of 3 or 4 and place them curved-side down on a cutting board. Use the side of a wide knife to lightly whack the stems, as this will serve to gently break them open so that they can absorb some of the sauce. Cut them lengthwise and then crosswise into pieces approximately 2 × 1 inch, a shape that Chinese chefs call "dominoes," or *gǔpáipiàn* 骨牌片. (If you are serving this at a fancier dinner, use only the stems and save the leafy parts for something else.)

2. Break the chilies open and discard both the seeds and the stem ends. Cut them into smallish pieces. Set your wok over high heat and swirl in the oil when the wok is hot. Immediately add the chilies and fry them quickly until they have crisped up. Toss in the ginger and the cabbage, and stir-fry them over high heat. As soon as the cabbage has wilted, add the vinegar, soy sauce, sugar, and sesame oil. Taste and adjust the seasoning. Continue to toss the cabbage until all of the edges are a golden brown. Serve hot.

Add more chilies to this if you like, and adjust the sweet-and-sour notes to fit your own taste.

If you want to thicken the sauce with a cornstarch slurry, mix 1 teaspoon cornstarch with 1 tablespoon water and add it to the sauce a few minutes before the cabbage is done, so the cornstarch has a chance to cook fully and lose its starchy flavor.

Kǎo hóngshǔ 烤紅薯

Roasted Sweet Potatoes

SHANXI · MAKES AS MANY AS YOU WANT

Back when I lived in Taipei, gray clouds covered the city basin from early November through April. One of my favorite vendors during those cold months was an old Shanxi gentleman who rolled a heavy concrete barrel down the city streets. This container was shaped sort of like a traditional tandoor oven; there was hot charcoal in the bottom of the barrel, and orange sweet potatoes hung on hooks around the rim. His potatoes would slowly bake over the coals, their skins turning a crispy black.

The potatoes in this recipe will ooze with juices as you cook them. The juices will first caramelize and then burn on the baking pan, making the kitchen smell like cotton candy. If you remove the potatoes while the juices are still brown, they will form sugary strings that have the texture of real caramel. If you wait a bit longer to pull them out, the caramel will turn black, but the potatoes will be even juicier. You can't lose either way.

Red sweet potatoes, preferably on the thin side and of approximately uniform size so that they cook evenly

1. Heat your oven to 375°F; a toaster oven works perfectly for small amounts. Scrub the sweet potatoes well, since you'll probably end up at least nibbling on the skin. Cover a baking sheet with foil for easy cleanup. Trim off any soft or bruised areas, but don't worry about pricking or oiling the skin.

2. Place the potatoes on the baking sheet in a single layer with a bit of space between them. Bake for 1 to 1½ hours, depending upon your oven and the size of the potatoes, until the potatoes are squishy soft and the caramel is either oozing around them or burned to a crisp. Serve as hot as possible with no adornment.

SWEET POTATOES ARE BELOVED BY CHINA'S poor. These tubers and another plant native to the Americas, maize, are the staples that have kept them alive during times of famine. But as in any fairytale worth its salt, this tremendous gift came with an unexpectedly devastating price. Hard as it may be to believe, the disastrous cycles of flood and drought along the Yellow and Yangtze Rivers over the past few centuries can be traced directly to these two imported plants.

According to Charles C. Mann (*1493: Uncovering the New World Columbus Created*), since both plants could be grown in China's drier areas, far away from its fertile river valleys, countless farmers moved into the country's hitherto unpopulated forest highlands, where they ripped out the trees to make fields. This caused massive erosion that silted up the rivers down below, instigating the tragic cycle of flooding and drought that has killed millions ever since.

It was a political and economic disaster as well as a human one, for it—along with the unbelievable corruption described so compellingly in such records as *A Factual History of the Ming* (*Míng shílù* 明實錄)—hobbled China just as the rest of the world was modernizing, making the country an easy target for those who dreamed of its colonization.

Dàn chǎo jiǔhuáng 蛋炒韭黃

Stir-Fried Yellow Chives and Eggs

SHAANXI • SERVES 4 TO 6

Yellow chives are nothing more than garlic chives grown under tarps or pots to prevent them from turning green in the sunlight. This coddling also diminishes their oniony flavors, leaving them with a subtler aroma. Yellow chives are wonderful in *jiaozi* (page 45) and in the Yangtze area's Freshwater Eels with Yellow Chives (page 109)—or they can simply be stir-fried, as in this dish. Serve these chives over steamed rice at any time of the day for an easy, perfect meal.

1 pound yellow chives
6 tablespoons peanut or vegetable oil
    (or use half unsalted butter and half oil)
1 teaspoon sea salt
4 large eggs, lightly beaten

1. Rinse the chives and pat them dry. Trim off any dry ends or less-than-perfect leaves. Either finely chop the chives if you like them particularly tender, or cut them into 1-inch lengths if you prefer a crunchier texture.

2. Place a wok over high heat, and when it's hot, add the oil and salt. Swirl the oil to dissolve the salt, and then add all of the chives. Quickly toss the chives until they wilt and a few strands start to brown.

3. Scoot the chives to one side and add a bit more oil if you don't see any at the bottom of the wok. Pour the eggs in and stir them around as they curdle. As soon as most of them have formed large curds, chop them up with your spatula and then toss them with the chives. Taste and adjust the seasoning. Plate and serve immediately.

There are many variations on this dish. Instead of eggs, try julienned pressed bean curd, shredded pork or chicken, little shrimp, or even thin strips of fresh black mushrooms. Or, instead of the yellow chives, chop up some garlic chive flowers (page 478), which will serve as a sweeter, crispier companion to the eggs.

See page 478 for more information on selecting and storing yellow chives.

Xihóngshì chǎo jīzǐ 西紅柿炒雞子

Tomatoes and Eggs

THE NORTHWEST · SERVES 4 TO 6

While the areas along the lower Yangtze are home to a vibrant Buddhist food culture, China's desert lands pose a challenge for those who prefer meatless meals. This dish is one of the more popular vegetarian options around.

There are a few secrets to making it work. First, the tomatoes have to be deliciously ripe, and the eggs should be fresh. Second, the tomatoes should be in large enough pieces that they do not mush up. Third—and this is where most restaurant versions fail—the tomatoes should be fried in oil with aromatics and a touch of sugar until they almost caramelize. Their juices should concentrate into a thick marmalade; it's this juice that coats each yellow egg curd and makes the dish stand out. Finally, season this dish with salt rather than soy sauce to keep the flavors sharp and the colors bright. If you love *jiaozi* (page 45), consider using this as an especially wonderful filling.

1 pound very tasty red tomatoes of any kind (see Tip)

5 tablespoons peanut or vegetable oil,
    divided into 3 tablespoons and 2 tablespoons

½ teaspoon sea salt

1 tablespoon peeled and finely chopped fresh ginger

2 green onions, trimmed and finely chopped,
    whites and greens in separate piles

½ to 1 teaspoon sugar

Freshly ground black pepper

4 large eggs, lightly beaten

1. Cut the tomatoes into pieces about 1 inch wide and ½ inch thick. If you are using cherry or plum tomatoes, cut them in half. (An easy way to cut a bunch of tiny tomatoes in half is to place them on a plastic rimmed lid, cover them with another lid of the same size, and then run a sharp chef's knife or bread knife between the two lids.) Taste a tomato—if it is very sweet, use ½ teaspoon sugar in Step 2; otherwise, use 1 teaspoon.

2. Place a wok over high heat, and when it is hot, swirl in 3 tablespoons of the oil and the salt. Fry the ginger and the whites of the onions until they are golden, and then add the sliced tomatoes. Lower the heat to medium-high and fry them, shaking and turning them over every 30 seconds or so. When the juice reduces to a few tablespoons, sprinkle on the sugar and pepper, and toss the tomatoes. Continue to cook them until you can smell the sugar and bits of caramel have formed on your spatula. Scrape the tomatoes out onto a plate.

3. Return the wok to medium-high heat and swirl in the remaining 2 tablespoons oil. Stir the onion greens into the eggs and pour the eggs into the wok. Flip the eggs over as they solidify and brown until they have formed a soft, golden omelet. Chop up the omelet with your spatula and then toss in the cooked tomatoes. Serve hot.

VARIATION

Some people like to make a creamier dish, where the eggs turn custardy rather than form large curds. To do this, keep the tomatoes in the wok at the end of Step 2 and stir the beaten eggs and onion greens into the tomatoes. Lightly toss everything together until the eggs have cooked through.

Cherry and plum tomatoes are my favorites here, because they keep their shape well.

Shogog khatsa

Curried Potatoes

TIBET · SERVES 4

At first glance, Curried Potatoes might be mistaken for an Indian dish. But the size of the potato slices and the subtle flavors let you know that this is a Tibetan recipe. In addition to the Indian aromatics, there are three American imports here: potatoes, tomatoes, and chilies. It's hard to imagine Tibetan food without potatoes, which were introduced by multiple groups—French missionaries, the Chinese, and the Bhutanese—more than two hundred years ago. They have since become so integral to Tibetan cuisine that they seem almost native to the Himalayas.

VEGETABLES

1 pound thin-skinned potatoes, like Yukon Gold

½ large or 1 small yellow onion

4 cloves garlic

1 Roma or other meaty tomato

¼ cup peanut or vegetable oil

1 teaspoon peeled and finely minced fresh ginger

3 dried Thai chilies

CURRY

1 tablespoon peanut or vegetable oil

½ teaspoon fenugreek seeds, toasted

3 tablespoons unsalted butter

1 teaspoon paprika

1 teaspoon ground turmeric

½ teaspoon ground cumin

3 tablespoons water

1. Rinse the potatoes and cut them into wedges about ½ inch thick. You don't have to peel them unless you want to. Place them in a medium saucepan and cover with water. Bring the water to a boil over high heat and then lower the heat to a gentle simmer. When the potatoes are cooked through but not falling apart (it should take 15 to 20 minutes), drain them in a colander and cover with a clean tea towel to keep them warm.

2. While the potatoes are cooking, cut the onion into roughly ½-inch dice and lightly mash the garlic cloves. Cut the tomato in half, then squeeze out and discard most of the seeds before cutting the flesh into about ½-inch dice. Place your wok over medium heat, swirl in the oil, and add the ginger, chilies, onion, and garlic. Fry these gently until they just begin to brown and then add the tomato and continue to cook everything until the tomato is soft. Place these vegetables (but not the potatoes) in a small food processor or a blender and puree them.

3. Rinse out and dry the wok. Heat the oil and fenugreek seeds over medium heat until the seeds have turned a nut brown. Add the butter, paprika, turmeric, and cumin and gently fry until the spices smell wonderful. Pour in the water and the puree, mix well, and then fold in the potatoes. Gently warm the potatoes in the sauce until they are heated through. Serve hot.

Be sure to toast the fenugreek first, or the seeds will be hard and bitter. Also, keep a close eye on the ground spices to keep them from burning. I do this by never raising the heat above medium and stirring the spices almost constantly. As soon as they are toasty and fragrant, remove them from the heat.

Fenugreek is called *húlúbā* 葫蘆巴 in Chinese. It is possible that this name came from the Yemenite Jews, who refer to it as *halba* or *hilbeh*, which would give us yet another cultural postcard from the travelers who once passed through China.

Yóupō làzi biángbiángmiàn 油潑辣子 *biángbiáng* 麵

Spicy Biangbiang Noodles

SHAANXI • SERVES 2 AS A MAIN DISH OR
4 AS A SNACK

The Chinese name for these noodles contains one of the most complicated characters in the Chinese language (see the illustration below). This character is so unorthodox that it's not included in any Chinese dictionary or software, at least at present. It's pronounced *biang* (now sometimes written as 奤—"big" over "noodles"—in simplified Chinese), and it is used only to describe this way of making pasta.

Known as one of the "ten strange things of Shaanxi"—probably because of that weird character rather than the noodles themselves—this pasta is similar to the pulled noodles of Lanzhou (see page 329). It's made of nothing more than Chinese flour, water, and salt. *Biangbiang* noodles are usually flattish and chewy, rather than stretched into fine strands. In this dish, they are coated with a light yet sensuous sauce that's made from green onions, chilies, black vinegar, soy sauce, and hot oil.

NOODLES AND SPINACH

2 cups Chinese flour (page 386), plus more as needed
2 teaspoons sea salt
¾ cup warm water, plus more if needed
Peanut or vegetable oil, as needed
4 cups spinach leaves, washed carefully and drained

SAUCE

½ cup fresh peanut or vegetable oil
1 teaspoon finely ground dried chilies, or to taste
2 tablespoons toasted sesame seeds (page 413)
2 green onions, trimmed and thinly sliced
2 teaspoons black vinegar
2 teaspoons regular soy sauce

1. Mix the flour and salt together in a medium work bowl and stir in the water to form a soft dough. Turn the dough out onto a flat surface and knead it until it is smooth and supple, adding more flour or water only if absolutely necessary. You want to end up with a very soft dough that does not stick to your hands or the board. When it is no longer tacky, roll it into a ball, place it in a bowl, and cover the bowl with plastic wrap. Let the dough rest for at least 20 minutes, until it is fully relaxed. Knead the dough again without adding any more flour, if possible, and then cover it and let it rest. Repeat this process at least 3 times.

2. Pour some oil into your hands and generously coat the ball of dough with it. Use a Chinese rolling pin to roll the dough out into a fat 10-inch square. Cut the dough into strips about an inch wide, and then cut these strips in half. Cover the dough one final time and let it rest for at least 20 minutes and up to an hour.

3. Prepare a couple of baking sheets by covering them with clean tea towels and then lightly sprinkle them with flour. Bring a large pot of water to a boil, set out the bowls for the noodles, and have a pair of chopsticks and either a Chinese spider (ideally) or a large slotted spoon next to the stove along with the bowls.

4. Next, shape the noodles; see the diagram below.

5. When the water is at a rolling boil, toss in the spinach and blanch it only until it is barely wilted. Use chopsticks and a spider to remove the spinach and then press your chopsticks down lightly on it to get out most of the water before you divide it among the bowls. Then pick up small handfuls of the noodles—being careful not to compress them—and lower them into the boiling water. Stir the noodles to keep them from

sticking to one another as you add them to the pot. Keep stirring them occasionally until the water comes back to a full boil. Taste a noodle, and as soon as they are cooked through but still chewy (this will be only a few seconds after the water has returned to a boil), use the chopsticks and spider to transfer the pasta to the waiting bowls.

6. Pour the oil into a small pan and set it over high heat until it starts to shimmer. While the oil is heating up, sprinkle the bowls of noodles with equal amounts of the ground chilies, sesame seeds, green onions, vinegar, and soy sauce. As soon as the oil is very hot, pour it over the bowls and serve the noodles immediately. Each diner should toss their noodles well. Offer more vinegar and soy sauce on the side for those who like it tarter or saltier.

HOW TO SHAPE BIANGBIANG NOODLES

❶
Take 1 strip of dough and lay it horizontally on a cutting board in front of you. Use your rolling pin to press down the center until you end up with 2 long ridges.

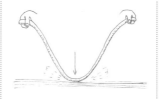

❷
Pick up the strip at either end and pull it until it is 3 feet long. Then whack it lightly on the board.

❸
As you stretch the noodle, you will notice that both ends start to split near where you are holding them.

❹
You can encourage this division by working your fingers into the split, resulting in 2 thin noodles. Lay the finished noodle down on the prepared tea towel and repeat with the rest of the noodles.

Shaved Noodles with Meat Sauce

SHANXI · SERVES 6 TO 8 AS A MAIN DISH

Shaved noodles are one of my favorite pastas from this region. We have nothing like them in the West. To make them, you hold a block of firm dough with one hand and shave off inch-wide strips with the other. Some people use a specially made curved blade for this, but I have found that a good, thin, and very sharp knife works just as well. Some pronounce this dish *dāoxuèmiàn* 刀削麵, but most people I know say *daoxiaomian*. Either way, it means pretty much the same thing: "knife-shaved noodles."

The idea here is to have long, thin strips of pasta, and there are a few keys to making this happen. First, the dough has to be kneaded until it is glossy and then allowed to rest; this prevents the gluten from fighting with the knife. Second, your knife must be as sharp as a razor. I've had the best success shaving noodles with thin Chinese chef's knives (see Tips). And finally, you need to practice, practice, practice.

NOODLES

2½ cups Chinese flour (page 386)

¼ cup sticky rice flour, optional

1 teaspoon sea salt

1 cup cool water, plus 2 tablespoons if using the rice flour

SAUCE

½ cup peanut or vegetable oil

1 carrot, peeled and chopped

1 medium yellow onion, chopped

2 star anise

2 bay leaves

1 small stick cinnamon

2 teaspoons ground toasted Sichuan peppercorns (page 441)

1 teaspoon fennel seeds

3 tablespoons Sichuan hot bean sauce

1 pound ground pork (15 percent fat)

3 green onions, trimmed and chopped

2-inch piece fresh ginger, peeled and chopped

6 cloves garlic, chopped

¼ cup oyster sauce

½ cup regular soy sauce

2 tablespoons black vinegar

½ cup water

1 small bunch cilantro, chopped

1. Toss the flours and salt together in a medium work bowl. Use chopsticks to stir in the water to form fat flakes. Turn the dough out onto a smooth board and knead it until it is stiff, shiny, and no longer the least bit sticky. Cover and let rest for about 20 minutes.

2. While the dough is resting (or even a day or two beforehand), set your wok over medium heat, add the oil when the wok is hot, and then toss in everything listed from the carrots through fennel. Slowly cook these until they have browned. Stir in the Sichuan hot sauce. Use a slotted spoon to remove the solids, but don't worry about any crumbs at the bottom of the wok.

3. Raise the heat under the oil to medium-high and add the meat, green onions, ginger, and garlic. When these have turned fragrant and lightly brown, add the oyster sauce, soy sauce, vinegar, and water, then cover. Bring to a boil, lower the heat, and simmer for about 15 minutes, adding more water as needed to keep the sauce from drying out. Taste and adjust the seasoning.

4. Bring a large pot of water to a boil. Use a very sharp, thin knife to shave the noodles either onto a baking sheet or, if you've practiced enough, directly into the boiling water. (For directions, see the diagram at right.) Stir, and use a Chinese spider or slotted spoon to remove the noodles as soon as they're barely cooked. These noodles can be cooked in batches, or you can make them ahead of time, freeze them in a single layer on plastic wrap–covered baking sheets, pack them into freezer bags, store them in the freezer, and then cook them without defrosting.

5. Just before serving, divide the pasta among noodle bowls, top with the sauce, and garnish with cilantro.

VARIATION

Clipped noodles (*jiǎnzi miàn* 剪子麵) use the same dough as shaved noodles. Let the dough rest as directed, and then use kitchen shears to clip off noodles that are about ¼ inch thick in the center and around 2 inches long (see the diagram below). Serve with a sauce or in soup.

Special knives designed for shaving dough are occasionally available in Chinese groceries or kitchen-supply stores. The most traditional noodle shaver is a thin, slightly bent piece of steel that has one sharp side and another curled side, which forms the handle.

Whatever kind of noodles you make, if you are not cooking them immediately, toss with flour to keep them from sticking to one another and cover with a tea towel.

HOW TO MAKE SHAVED NOODLES

❶ Shape the dough into a smooth oval. Lightly moisten the bottom and place it on a small cutting board.

❷ Prepare a very sharp, thin blade. A Chinese chef's knife works well—just hone it until it is razor sharp. Hold the dough in your nondominant hand. Position the knife at the top of the oval at a slight angle.

❸ As you shave the dough, angle the handle side of your knife down to cut off the noodle.

❹ For the next noodle, set your knife next to the groove from the previous cut and shave down again. If your first noodles don't come out well, you can knead them back into the dough.

HOW TO MAKE CLIPPED NOODLES

 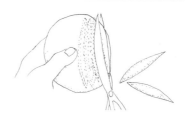

❶ Hold a ball of dough in one hand and kitchen shears in the other.

❷ Snip around the ball to form sturdy, pointed bits of pasta.

Khuushuur

Grilled Layered Lamb Pastries

INNER MONGOLIA, NORTHERN CHINA,
AND THE NORTHWEST · SERVES 4

Popular throughout China's northern areas, the *khuushuur* is basically a meat pie. Traditionally made with lamb in Inner Mongolia, there's also a beef version that's popular farther south. Sometimes these appear as deep-fried crescents, and at other times they're round; some people make them on the smaller side, while others make them big and cut them into wedges. My favorite version is the following one, known as "1,000-layer pastries" (*qiāncéngbǐng* 千層餅) and commonly served in Beijing. This recipe boasts 7 layers, which leaves us, oh, about 993 short. But never mind. These 7 layers are still pretty darned good.

FILLING

1 pound ground lamb or beef (15 percent fat)
1½ tablespoons peeled and finely minced fresh ginger
2 green onions, trimmed and finely chopped
2 teaspoons regular soy sauce
½ teaspoon sugar
⅛ teaspoon pink salt, optional
Freshly ground black pepper
1 clove garlic, finely minced

WRAPPERS

1 cup Chinese flour (page 386), plus more for dusting
6 tablespoons boiling water
2 to 3 tablespoons cool water

Peanut or vegetable oil, as needed
Black vinegar or chili oil, optional

1. The day before you make these pastries, combine all of the filling ingredients except the garlic, place in a covered container, and refrigerate for at least 8 hours so that the meat has time to marinate. Just before filling the pastries, stir in the garlic, which would overpower the filling if left in there too long. Divide the filling into 8 even lumps, as each of the 4 pastries will require 2 portions of the meat.

2. To make the wrappers, place the flour in a small work bowl and use chopsticks to stir in the boiling water until large flakes form. Then mix in just enough of the cool water to form a soft dough. Knead the dough on a lightly floured smooth surface until it is supple and as soft as an earlobe. Cover the dough with plastic wrap and let it rest for 20 to 30 minutes, then divide it into 4 even pieces.

3. See the diagram below for directions on filling and forming the pastries. Be sure and cover the filled pastries with plastic wrap to keep them from drying out.

4. The pastries can be either immediately cooked or frozen at this point. To freeze them, put them in a single layer on a baking sheet lined with plastic wrap; as soon as they have frozen solid, pack them in a resealable freezer bag. The frozen pastries can either be defrosted first or fried while still frozen. If you opt for the latter, cook over medium-low heat so the filling has time to cook through.

5. To cook the pastries, heat a flat seasoned frying pan over medium heat and then film it with a tablespoon or two of oil. Lay as many pastries in the pan as you wish, being careful they do not touch one another, and cover the pan. Gently fry the pastries until they are golden brown on the first side and then flip them over and fry the other side. Remove the cover for the final few minutes of frying so that the pastries crisp up on the outside. Cut into pieces if you like and serve as is or with black vinegar or chili oil for dipping.

FILLING & FORMING GRILLED LAYERED LAMB PASTRIES

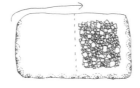

❶
Working on one piece at a time, and keeping the rest of the dough covered, roll out the dough on a lightly floured smooth surface into a thin 10-inch square.

❷
Spread one-eighth of the filling evenly over the lower half of the square, keeping the edges clean so they can be sealed later. Fold the top half over the filling and lightly pinch the open edges closed. Spread another one-eighth of the filling evenly over the right half of the pastry, still keeping the edges clean.

❸
Fold the left half over the right like a book. Firmly crimp the open edges closed to seal in the juices. Repeat with the rest of the dough and filling until you have 4 filled pastries.

Dàbǐng 大餅

Coiled Bread

THE NORTHWEST AND NORTH CHINA •
MAKES 1 (8-INCH-WIDE) ROUND LOAF

Easily one of the most beloved of China's homemade breads, Coiled Bread is as pleasing to the eye as it is to the palate. I've had this bread any number of ways—thick or thin, flavored with minced dried shrimp or ground Sichuan peppercorns—and found each version to be wonderfully tasty. The dough in this recipe is seasoned with little more than salt and green onions; it's great as a side for breakfast, lunch, or dinner, and it's nice to have lying around as a snack, too. It also can be made ahead of time and frozen.

1½ cups Chinese flour (page 386)
About ½ cup cool water, plus 1 teaspoon
1 green onion, trimmed and finely chopped
½ teaspoon sea salt
Freshly ground black pepper
1 tablespoon toasted sesame oil
2 tablespoons peanut or vegetable oil, divided in half

1. Mix together the flour and about ½ cup of the water to form a soft dough. The amount of water will vary depending upon the room temperature and the age of the flour. Knead until the dough feels like an earlobe when pinched. Cover and let it rest for at least 20 minutes and up to an hour.

2. Mix together the green onion, salt, and a little pepper.

3. On a lightly floured smooth surface, roll out the dough into a rectangle measuring about 18 × 10 inches, adding only as much flour as necessary to prevent the dough from sticking to the board or your rolling pin. Keep the long edge farthest away from you clean as you smear the sesame oil over the rest of the dough. Sprinkle evenly with the green onion mixture. Roll the dough into an even rope and pinch the clean edge into the roll to seal it, then pinch both ends closed.

4. Now comes the fun part: roll and gently pull on the coil until has a (more or less) even ¾ inch diameter. Then press down softly on one end as you wrap the rope around this end to form a fat coil. Lightly flour both sides of the bread and gently roll it out to just under 8 inches in diameter. Cover the bread. The bread can be frozen at this point, if you wish.

5. Heat a seasoned 8-inch-wide cast-iron frying pan over medium heat until it is hot, smear about 1 tablespoon oil on the bottom to create a light film, and then add the bread. Shake the pan gently to scoot the bread around in the oil and then fry it uncovered—shaking the pan now and then—until it is a light brown on the first side. Flip the bread over and fry the other side the same way. Then add the remaining 1 teaspoon water and immediately cover the pan tightly, as this will steam the center of the bread.

6. When the water has completely evaporated, uncover the pan, add the remaining 1 tablespoon oil, and fry both sides of the bread again until they are crispy golden brown. Cut into wedges before serving.

Zhīmá dàbǐng 芝麻大餅

Grilled Sesame Breads with Green Onions

THE NORTHWEST AND NORTH CHINA • SERVES 4 TO 6

One of the best parts about dining in Chinese Muslim restaurants is their selection of homemade grilled breads. I love this one most because of its texture: crunchy toasted sesame seeds on the outside contrast with wisps of flaky bread on the inside. And then, of course, there are the moist green onions that season every bite. If you've made bread before, you'll find this very easy indeed.

DOUGH

¾ cup warm water

1 teaspoon active dry yeast

1 teaspoon sugar

1¾ cups Chinese flour (page 386), plus more as needed

1 teaspoon peanut or vegetable oil

1 teaspoon baking powder

SEASONINGS

2 tablespoons toasted sesame oil

¾ teaspoon sea salt

¾ cup finely chopped green onions

½ cup raw white sesame seeds

1. Place the water in a bowl or cup and sprinkle the yeast and then the sugar on top. Gently mix the yeast into the water and give it about 20 minutes to foam. Put the flour in a medium work bowl. Stir the yeast mixture into the flour to form a soft dough. Knead the dough until it no longer sticks to your hands, adding a bit more flour as necessary. Form the dough into a ball. Coat the inside of a clean work bowl with the oil, place the dough in the bowl, cover, and let it rise until it has doubled in size.

2. Sprinkle the baking powder on a smooth work surface. Punch down the dough, form it into a ball, and place it on the baking powder. Knead these together until smooth. When the dough is as soft as an earlobe, cover it and let it rest for around 20 minutes.

3. Cut the dough in half and roll each piece into a 10 × 12-inch rectangle. Rub the sesame oil all over the surface of both pieces and then evenly sprinkle on the salt and green onions. Fold the top and bottom thirds of each piece over the middle like a business letter. Then fold the left and right sides over the center to form a square packet. Cover the dough and let it rest for about 20 minutes.

4. Form each half of the dough into circles by gently rolling them out from the center toward the edge until they are about 8 inches in diameter.

5. Pour the sesame seeds into a rimmed dish. Lightly moisten the top of 1 dough circle with water, and then press the circle upside down on top of the sesame seeds. Moisten the other side of the circle and press this side, too, into the sesame seeds. Repeat with the other dough circle. (The bread can be made ahead of time up to this point and frozen. Defrost the bread before cooking it so it can rise properly.) Place 1 circle in a cool, clean, nonstick frying pan and the other on a baking sheet, cover both, and let the dough rise for 15 to 20 minutes.

6. Place the pan over medium-low heat, cover, and slowly grill the bread until it is browned on the bottom and the seeds begin to pop, 10 to 15 minutes. Carefully flip the bread over, cover again, and fry the second side until it, too, is golden. Remove to a cutting board, slice the bread into wedges, and serve. Repeat with the other bread. To reheat, grill lightly on both sides or toast in a small oven, but, as with all breads, do not microwave it.

Baked Round Uyghur Bread

THE NORTHWEST · MAKES 4 SMALL LOAVES;
SERVES 6 TO 8

This bread, sometimes called *nang*, is a very close relative of the bread that feeds most of Central Asia, naan. As far as the Chinese are concerned, it is definitely a culinary import; the people from the northern plains refer to it as *húbǐng* 胡餅, or "foreign bread." Always round and always rimmed like a pizza, Baked Round Uyghur Bread is usually adorned with decorative pricks, which are made with a special nail-like tool.

These breads vary greatly in size—some are a few inches across, while others are about 16 inches in diameter. What makes them truly special, though, are the ovens they're baked in. Often referred to in the north as "*nang* pits" (*nángkēng* 饢坑), these heavy clay jars look much like the tandoor ovens of India. They have a slow-burning fuel at their base, and their clay walls serve as their cooking surface. Raw rounds of raised dough are moistened and then slapped onto the vertical walls of the hot oven. The dough sticks to the clay the instant it touches it, preventing the baking breads from falling into the hot charcoal.

I wish I had a tandoor oven, but because I don't, I have adapted this simple bread recipe for a conventional oven. I've found that using a large clay pizza tile on the bottom rack will give your *nang* that recognizable crunch, as will giving the loaves light baths of plain water while they are rising and just before they hit the heat. I use white Chinese flour here, which has just the right amount of gluten to produce the requisite chewiness, but I also throw in some wheat germ to add more flavor and color.

1¼ cups warm water, plus more for brushing the loaves
1½ teaspoons active dry yeast
1 teaspoon sugar
1 tablespoon peanut or toasted sesame oil
1 cup wheat germ, optional
2½ cups (more or less) Chinese flour (page 386)
2 tablespoons unsalted butter, softened
Optional toppings: about 1 teaspoon per loaf of
    toasted sesame seeds, nigella seeds, fennel seeds,
    freshly ground black pepper, coarsely ground
    dried chilies, coarse sea salt

1. Pour the water into a medium bowl and sprinkle the yeast and sugar over it. Stir the yeast into the water and then give the yeast about 20 minutes to completely foam.

2. Stir in the oil, optional wheat germ, and about 2 cups of the flour to form a loose dough. Turn the dough out onto a floured board and knead it until it is soft and no longer tacky, adding more flour as needed only to keep it from sticking. Form the dough into a smooth ball. Rinse out and dry the bowl and then rub the inside of it generously with the softened butter. Place the ball of dough back into the bowl and toss it around to thoroughly coat it. Cover the bowl with plastic wrap and a towel, and let the dough rise in a warm place until doubled, which will take about an hour. Remove the towel and plastic wrap and punch the dough down, then fold the edges of it onto the top. Flip the dough over, cover it with the plastic wrap and towel, and let it rise again until doubled, 30 to 45 minutes.

3. Lightly knead the dough and cut it into 4 equal pieces. Form each piece into a ball. Let the dough rest for about 15 minutes to relax the gluten and then use a rolling pin to roll each piece out on a board lightly dusted with flour, forming circles about 7 inches in diameter. Place the circles on lightly dusted baking sheets and brush each circle with some water. Cover with the plastic wrap and tea towel, and let rise for about 30 minutes, until puffy.

4. Place an oven rack as low as it will go, set your clay tile on the rack, and heat the oven to about 500°F. While it's heating up, shape the circles into *nang*: Wet one hand and lightly pat the inside of each circle, leaving a rim around the edge about 1 inch wide so it looks like a pizza. Use a dough prick or sharp fork to thoroughly perforate the inside of the circles up to the rim. Lightly brush the circles with water and sprinkle on the optional toppings. Depending upon the size of your tile, bake 1 or 2 of the breads at a time. Use a pizza peel or a rimless baking sheet to slide the dough onto the tile. Bake the breads for about 7 minutes, until they are golden brown around the edges. Serve hot or warm.

Momo and Buuz

TIBET AND INNER MONGOLIA · SERVES 3 TO 4

Momo and *buuz* are two iconic dishes of Tibet and Mongolia, respectively. No cookbook about either cuisine would be complete without including a recipe for them. That said, the following recipe is a bit of a new take on these traditions. At their most basic, both *momo* and *buuz* are steamed filled pastas, much like the *jiaozi* on page 45. In Tibet and Inner Mongolia, they are generally stuffed with seasoned ground lamb or beef. Mongolian *buuz* are usually heftier, with thick wrappers that have a braided fold on top, while *momo*, which are popular throughout the Himalayas, tend to have lighter wrappers that are often given triangular folds (see the illustration) or shaped like *xiaolongbao* (page 132).

Normally, these wrappers are made with water, but I prefer to use hot stock, which produces a lighter pasta. This all started when I was reading Liu Zhenwei's collection of early twentieth-century food memoirs called *Gùxiāng zhī shí* 故鄉之食 ("Hometown Foods")—the source of many of the stories recounted here in this book—and came across his discussion of filled pasta in a chapter on Inner Mongolia. Mr. Liu noted that those skins "were rolled out very thinly, and after they have been steamed, they appeared translucent, reflecting the brown of the filling, with a circle of white folds on top." And so I went to work trying to re-create these delicate steamed packets of long ago. In the process of fooling around with my food (a practice I heartily endorse), I used hot stock instead of water to make the wrappers. The results are ethereal. If you are more of a traditionalist, though, check out the variations at the end of the recipe.

One more thing: I became excited all over again when I started putting two and two together and came up with eight. The reason? Tibetans make a dipping sauce out of tomatoes, fresh chilies, green onions, garlic, salt, and cilantro. To a dyed-in-the-wool Californian, that was nothing less than a recipe for salsa. And the Tibetan name for this salsa?: *tsal.*

FILLING

1 pound ground lamb (or beef), preferably at least 20 percent fat

1 tablespoon peeled and finely minced fresh ginger

2 cloves garlic, finely minced

5 green onions, trimmed and finely minced

¼ cup finely chopped celery

¼ cup finely chopped cilantro

3 tablespoons peanut or vegetable oil

2 tablespoons unsalted stock (page 380 or 381)

2 teaspoons sea salt

4 large black mushrooms, fresh or dried and plumped up, stemmed and finely chopped

2 teaspoons cornstarch

DOUGH

1½ cups Chinese flour (page 386), plus extra flour as needed

5 tablespoons boiling-hot unsalted chicken stock (page 380)

TIBETAN SALSA (TSAL), OPTIONAL

3 or 4 ripe red tomatoes

1 fresh red chili pepper, finely chopped, or to taste

2 cloves garlic, finely minced

2 green onions, trimmed and finely chopped

¼ teaspoon sea salt

1 tablespoon peanut or vegetable oil

1 small bunch cilantro, coarsely chopped

FOR THE STEAMER BASKETS

Spray oil, steamer paper, or napa cabbage leaves

OPTIONAL DIP

Black vinegar

1. Start this recipe at least 4 hours before you want to serve it to give the filling time to chill. Mix together the filling ingredients and stir them rapidly in one direction until they are light and fluffy (see page 458). Place in a container, cover, and refrigerate.

2. While the filling is chilling, make the dough by placing the flour in a medium work bowl and using chopsticks to stir in the boiling chicken stock. As soon as it forms clumps, empty the dough onto a smooth surface and knead it until it is smooth and bouncy, adding flour only if it is truly necessary to keep the dough from sticking to your hands or the board. Cover the dough and let it rest for at least 20 minutes.

3. Next, make the optional salsa by chopping the tomatoes into ½-inch dice. Place them in a small work bowl. Add the chili pepper, garlic, green onions, salt, and oil but not the cilantro. Toss the salsa, cover, and refrigerate until serving time. Taste and adjust the seasoning just before serving.

4. Roll the dough out into a rope 36 inches long and cut the dough into 1-inch pieces. See page 46 for directions on filling and forming *jiaozi*. You can make the edges of the seals frilly, if you like, by pinching the edges until they are thin and lacy. What you have made is, in effect, seasoned hot-water dough (page 386).

5. Spray 2 steamer baskets with oil (or line the bottoms of the steamers with steamer paper or cabbage leaves, if you prefer) and place them over boiling water for about 5 minutes to warm them up (see page 49). Arrange as many of the filled packets as fit comfortably in the baskets without touching, stack and cover the baskets, and steam them for about 15 minutes. (Do this in 2 batches if necessary.) If you have made the salsa, add the cilantro; otherwise, have some black vinegar ready for dipping. Serve everything immediately.

VARIATION: *MOMO*

To make traditional *momo*, double the amount of flour and add enough hot water to form a soft dough. Knead it and let it rest, then cut the dough into 36 pieces. Roll each piece out into a circle about 3 inches wide and then form a triangular packet by bringing the edges together at 0, 120, and 240 degrees, and then sealing the seams (see the illustration at left). Or shape into little *baozi*, as with *xiaolongbao* (page 132). Steam as directed above and serve with the sauce.

VARIATION: *BUUZ*

To make traditional *buuz*, double the amount of flour and add enough hot water to form a soft dough. Knead it and let it rest, then cut the dough into 36 pieces. Roll each piece out into a circle about 5 inches wide and then make an oval packet by pinching the top seam together in a braided pattern (see the illustration at left). Steam as directed above and serve without a sauce.

YOU MAY HAVE NOTICED THAT THE NAMES of certain things in this cookbook are different from those used elsewhere, such as "black mushrooms" and "bean curd" instead of the Japanese names shiitake and tofu. I stick with the Chinese terms because these items originated in China, and also out of respect for Chinese feelings about Japan's actions in the last century.

I have also scrupulously avoided any mention of "dumplings" when discussing *jiaozi* (page 45), rice tamales (*zongzi*, page 384), and so on. We often use the word as a shortcut when referring to anything that is both Chinese and either starchy and small or wrapped in some way, whether it is rice or bread or pasta. There's nothing wrong with that, but it could lead to confusion in a book like this, where so many things thought of as "dumplings" are introduced.

To wit, in addition to the *momo* and *buuz* described above, and the *jiaozi* and rice tamales pointed to earlier in this sidebar, you can look elsewhere to find various dim sum (page 218), *baozi* (page 405), *xiaolongbao* (page 132), wontons (page 298), and filled omelets (page 34).

By referring to these dishes either by their Chinese names or in ways that offer a more accurate picture of what they are, I hope to give you a clearer introduction to all of these glorious members of the "dumpling family" that are yours to enjoy.

Jiānbǐng juǎn tǔdòusī 煎餅捲土豆絲

Crêpes and Chili Potatoes

SHAANXI • SERVES ABOUT 2

Xi'an is primarily known as the home of the Terracotta Army, but it's also a wonderful, unpretentious place filled with good things to eat. One of my favorite dishes from this capital city is Crêpes and Chili Potatoes. It's a study in austerity: there's no meat, fancy vegetables, or sauces. The main ingredients are flour and potatoes. And yet you end up with some astoundingly delicious wrappers that are filled with seasoned potatoes and a vibrant chili sauce.

CRÊPES

1 cup Chinese flour (page 386)

½ teaspoon sea salt

1 cup plus 2 tablespoons warm water

FILLING

2 medium Yukon Gold potatoes or similar variety

2 green onions, trimmed

4 tablespoons (or so) peanut or vegetable oil

1 to 3 finely ground dried chilies, or to taste (see Tip)

1 teaspoon sea salt

SAUCE

2 tablespoons garlic chili sauce,
    such as Guizhou *ciba* chili paste (page 438)

1 tablespoon soy sauce

4 tablespoons toasted sesame oil

1. First make the crêpe batter: place the flour in a medium work bowl. Stir the salt into the warm water until it dissolves, and then mix the salt water into the flour to form a thin batter with the consistency of cream. It's quite all right if there are some lumps in there. Let it sit while you prepare the rest of the ingredients.

2. Next, prepare the vegetables. You may peel the potatoes or leave them unpeeled; rinse them and pat dry. Slice off 1 edge of the long side of a potato so that it lies flat on your cutting board (see page 449). Then cut the potato into very thin slices before cutting the slices into very thin matchsticks. Repeat with the other potato. (Do not grate the potatoes, as they will then mush up as they cook.) Cut the green onions into 2-inch pieces, flatten them slightly with the side of a heavy knife, and cut them into thin matchsticks, too.

3. Place a wok over medium-high heat, swirl in the oil, and add the chili powder and salt. Let the chili powder heat up and slowly turn from red to brown. Turn the heat to high and immediately toss in the potatoes and green onions. Stir-fry these quickly until the potatoes have lost their rawness but are still slightly crisp. Cover the wok, remove it from the heat, and let it sit while you cook the crêpes.

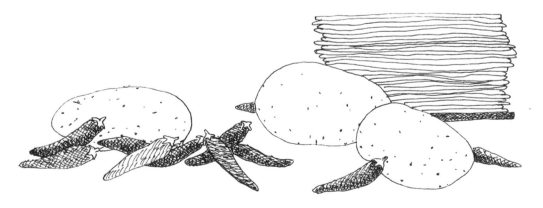

4. Cook the crêpes (for directions, see the diagram below).

5. Make the chili sauce: heat the garlic chili sauce and soy sauce together in a small pan until bubbly. Remove from the heat and pour in the sésame oil, taste, and adjust the seasoning. Scrape this sauce into a small bowl.

6. Serve the crêpes and potatoes hot alongside the sauce, and have diners fill and roll their own, dribbling a bit of the sauce inside as they go. Eat with chopsticks from the top of the roll, with one hand steadying the bottom.

Use as much or as little finely ground chilies in the potatoes as you like. It's hard to give an exact amount because chilies and palates differ so much. If the filling is not hot enough, you can always add more zip with the sauce.

HOW TO MAKE CRÊPES

❶ Use a flat-bottomed frying pan about 8 inches in diameter. Place the pan over medium-high heat and lightly oil it using a piece of paper towel dipped in oil. (If you add more oil than that, the crêpe will move around in the pan.)

❷ When the oil starts to smoke, pour in about one-sixth of the batter and swirl the pan around so that the batter covers most of the bottom.

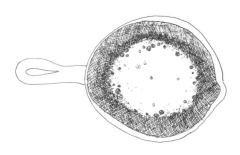

❸ Cook the crêpe, adjusting the heat as necessary, until the edges start to curl up and the top has some bubbles and is fairly dry.

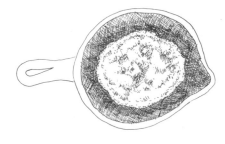

❹ Flip the crêpe over and cook for a few seconds. Remove to a plate and cover with another plate. Repeat with the rest of the batter until you have 6 crêpes.

Yóumiàntuīwōwō 莜麵推窩窩 and *Kǎolǎolǎo* 栲栳栳

Oat Honeycomb Rolls

SHANXI AND INNER MONGOLIA • SERVES 4 TO 6

Few people think of oats when they consider the foods of the cold Chinese North. But along the border between Shanxi and Inner Mongolia (and even in parts of northern Hebei, for that matter), flour made from oat groats (*youmian*) is used in some very interesting ways. This recipe is a visually spectacular example: the tiny, clustered rolls of the oat dough look like a honeycomb or a wasps' nest. It's also a delicious and satisfying meal. I like to serve it with nothing more than julienned cucumbers and a bowl of chili oil, but it goes particularly well with any sort of Northwest-style lamb soup (try page 331). This method of preparing oat groats is called "thrice-cooked" (*sānshóu* 三熟) because the oats are first toasted, then blanched, and finally steamed. This process may look complicated, but it's actually very easy. I use two 6-inch-wide bamboo dim sum steamer baskets, which allow the little bread rolls to cook quickly and evenly.

2 cups organic oat groats (see Tips)
1¾ cups boiling water
Spray oil

1. Place the oat groats in a dry wok and toast them over medium-high heat, stirring them with a wok spatula, until they start to pop and are gently toasted. Pour the toasted groats into a work bowl and let them cool to room temperature.

2. Grind the groats in a blender or food processor until they are very fine. Do this in 2 or more batches if necessary. Put the groat flour into a heatproof bowl and stir in the boiling water. When a dough has formed, knead it on a smooth surface until smooth.

3. Next form the little rolls. Break off bits of dough to create balls about an inch across. Cover any dough you are not working on with a damp towel or some plastic wrap. Have 2 small dim sum steamer baskets ready and spray them with oil. Working on 1 piece at a time, form each ball into a cigar shape and then use a rolling pin to roll it out into a rectangle about 6 × 2 inches. Cut the rectangle in half lengthwise (giving you 2 strips each about 6 × 1 inch). Starting from a short edge, roll up each strip into a cylinder and place them cut-side down in a steamer basket. Fit the rolls right next to one another, as they will not expand as they steam. Repeat with the rest of the dough until all of it has been shaped and packed into the steamers (see Tips).

4. Stack and cover the steamer baskets and place them in a steamer (see page 49). Steam the honeycomb rolls for about 15 minutes and serve immediately.

Oat groats are not the same as rolled oats. They are also called oat berries, and can be found in health food stores or online.

The rolls can be packed fairly tightly in the steamer baskets; there is no leavening, so they will not swell up. However, they will stick to one another as they cool off, so I usually serve one basket at a time and keep the other one covered and gently steaming.

If you have any leftover dough, you can make "oat groat fish," or *yóumiànyúyú* 莜麵魚魚: cut the dough into thin 3-inch by ¼-inch strips and then roll them so that the middle is fat and the ends are tapered. Steam these just like the honeycomb rolls.

Uyghur Pilaf

THE NORTHWEST · SERVES 4 TO 6 AS A SIDE DISH

Fragrant rice medleys are common throughout Asia. There's the pilaf of Armenia, the *pilav* of Turkey, and the Persian *polow*, not to mention the takes on this dish that appear in Russia, India, and Afghanistan. In the Northwest, the Uyghurs refer to this easy meal as *polo*, while in Chinese the dish usually goes by *zhuafan*, or "grabbed rice," meaning it is meant to be picked up with the fingertips, rather than with chopsticks.

This pilaf is the ideal accompaniment to any of the Uyghur lamb dishes in this book, such as Xinjiang-Style Lamb Kebabs (page 346). Most standard recipes call for a variation on fried rice, but I've adjusted things a bit, giving this dish a slightly more Middle Eastern edge. For example, I gently brown the onions, lamb, and raw rice first. I also use a combination of oil and butter instead of lamb tail fat (lamb tails are rather hard to find around my neighborhood, regrettably). Finally, I add the raisins and carrot later on so they keep their personality.

3 tablespoons peanut or vegetable oil

½ medium yellow onion, cut into ½-inch dice

4 ounces boneless lamb shoulder, cut into ½-inch dice

½ teaspoon sea salt

Freshly ground black pepper

2 tablespoons unsalted butter

1 cup long-grain rice (see Tips)

Boiling water, as needed

½ cup moist golden raisins

1 medium carrot

1. Place a wok or large frying pan over medium-high heat, and when it is hot, add the oil and swirl it around. Add the onion, lamb, salt, and pepper to the shimmering oil, lower the heat to medium, and fry the onions and lamb until they just start to turn brown on the edges. Scoot the meat and onions up the side of the wok or pan, away from the heat.

2. Raise the heat to medium-high, add the butter, and when it has melted, pour in the rice. Stir the rice until it starts to brown and smell nutty. Toss the toasted rice with the lamb and onions. Pour in 1 cup boiling water and stir it into the rice. Lower the heat to medium-low and gently cook the rice uncovered, stirring once in a while and adding more boiling water if the pan is dry before the rice is cooked.

3. While the rice is cooking, rinse and drain the raisins. Peel the carrot, cut it lengthwise into thin strips about the width of the raisins, and then cut the strips crosswise to create pieces about the same size as the raisins.

4. When the rice is almost done, toss in the raisins and carrots so that the carrots will be just barely cooked by the time the rice is ready. Taste and adjust the seasoning, adding more butter if you like. Cover the pan, remove it from the heat, and let the rice steam from the residual heat for about 10 minutes before you serve it very hot.

Any cut of lamb can be used here as long as it is of good quality. Remove any sinews or silver skin.

Vegans and vegetarians can, of course, eliminate the lamb and include mushrooms instead.

Use long-grain rice, not short grain, which is too starchy for this dish. I really like brown jasmine or basmati rice here, because it adds an extra level of nuttiness to the pilaf.

The amount of water used and the cooking time vary according to the type of rice used, the heat of the stove, and so forth, so keep an eye on the pilaf as it cooks and add a bit more boiling water as needed to keep the rice moist and fluffy.

Boortsog

Fried Cookies

INNER MONGOLIA · SERVES AT LEAST 20

I like to enjoy these cookies alongside a nice cup of hot black tea or, even better, some Butter Tea (page 374). You don't need to serve them with the traditional sides of honey and some fresh farmer's cheese, but why not make a feast of it?

½ cup (1 stick) unsalted butter, melted

¾ cup sugar

1 teaspoon salt

1 cup water

About 4½ cups Chinese flour (page 386),
    divided into 4 cups and ½ cup

Peanut or vegetable oil for frying

Powdered sugar, optional

1. Mix together the melted butter, sugar, salt, and water in a work bowl. Stir in 4 cups of the flour to form a soft dough. Sprinkle the remaining ½ cup flour on a smooth surface, turn the dough out onto it, and knead the dough until smooth, adding more flour as needed to keep it from sticking. Cover and let rest for 30 minutes.

2. Divide the dough into 4 pieces and work on 1 piece at a time; cover the dough you are not immediately working on. Roll out each piece about ¼ inch thick and cut it into 1 × 3-inch strips.

3. Cut a slit down the middle of each strip of dough, stopping about ½ inch from either end. Gently insert 1 end of each piece through the slit 2 times, which will make the long edges twist (see the diagram below).

4. Warm at least 3 inches of oil in a wok or saucepan over medium-high heat until a chopstick inserted in the oil is covered with bubbles (around 375°F). Cover a baking sheet with a couple of paper towels, have some chopsticks ready, and prepare a large platter. If you want to sprinkle powdered sugar on the hot cookies, have ready a small sieve, a spoon, and the powdered sugar.

5. Slide a few cookies at a time into the hot oil. Leave them alone for at least 20 seconds, so that they harden a bit and keep their shape, and then gently move them in the oil to keep them from sticking. When medium brown, use your chopsticks to pluck them out of the oil and place them on the paper towels. Arrange the cookies on the platter and sprinkle with powdered sugar, if you want.

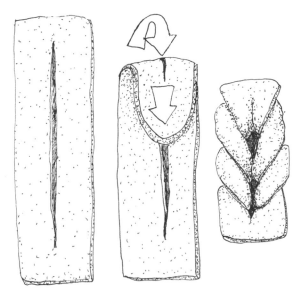

Shuǐjīng liáncài bǐng 水晶蓮菜餅

Rose-Scented Lotus Patties

SHAANXI · SERVES 4 TO 6

In this sweet from Shaanxi, balls of ground fresh lotus root are stuffed with a delicate filling of walnuts and roses and then fried. I have, as usual, played around with this recipe a bit. For example, I use rose petal jam, which is much more fragrant than plain dried roses. (I find it tastier than rose water, too.) I've also used honey instead of the thickened sugar water that is usually called for in the sauce. Serve these lotus patties in the afternoon, accompanied by hot, unsweetened black tea.

LOTUS ROOT PASTE
1 pound (more or less) lotus roots
1 teaspoon fresh lemon juice
2 tablespoons cornstarch

FILLING
2 tablespoons unsalted butter
¼ cup lightly toasted, chopped walnuts
1 tablespoon wolfberries, soaked in boiling water until
    plumped up and drained
2 tablespoons rose petal jam (see Tip)
¼ teaspoon sea salt

Peanut or vegetable oil for frying

SAUCE
½ cup boiling water
¼ cup honey
¼ cup rose petal jam
1 tablespoon cornstarch mixed with 2 tablespoons water

1. Peel the lotus roots, trim off the ends, and wash them thoroughly inside and out (see page 451). Shake them dry, chop them coarsely, and then pulse the lotus roots in a food processor until finely ground. Add the lemon juice and cornstarch and pulse only until the mixture is smooth. Chill the puree, divide it into 20 pieces, and then roll the pieces into balls.

2. Rinse and dry the food processor, add the butter and walnuts, and chop together. Add the wolfberries, rose petal jam, and salt and pulse everything a few times to combine into a paste. Chill the filling, divide it into 20 pieces, and then roll each piece into a ball. The recipe can be made ahead of time up to this point.

3. Poke a hole in one of the lotus paste balls and insert one of the balls of filling (see page 267). Close the lotus paste around the filling and lightly roll the ball between your hands. Repeat with the rest of the lotus paste and filling until you have 20 filled balls.

4. Place a wide frying pan over medium heat and add at least an inch of oil. As soon as it is hot, remove the pan from the heat before carefully sliding in the filled balls. Add only as many as can bob around comfortably in the oil without sticking to one another. Return the pan to the heat and fry the balls on both sides until golden. Remove them to a large rimmed plate. Repeat until all the balls have been fried.

5. Empty the oil out of the wok and wipe the wok with a paper towel. To make the sauce, pour the water, honey, and jam into the wok and bring to a full boil. Stir in the cornstarch slurry until the sauce thickens and then pour the sauce over the lotus patties. Serve immediately.

Rose petal jam can be found in Middle Eastern markets.

Yínĕr tiánlí tāng 銀耳甜梨湯

Sweet Pear Soup with Silver Ears

SHANXI AND ALL OVER CHINA • SERVES 8 TO 10

Harvested from tall cliffs in Southeast Asia by death-defying climbers, birds' nests are prized ingredients in China. These nests, made by swiftlets, are composed mainly of salivary cement, and the best ones are insanely expensive. They have little taste, and are valued instead for the lovely gelatinous quality they lend to sweet and savory soups.

Although it's not exactly the same, you can closely mimic the texture of birds' nests by using the jelly fungus known in Chinese as silver ears (or white wood ears or snow ears). I never really liked the texture of silver ears much until I learned the key to preparing them: they have to soak for three days, and only then can you slowly simmer them until they become gelatinous. You will end up with a delicious, vegetarian, and affordable birds' nest alternative that leaves the little birds and their nests alone.

2 large heads silver ear fungus

3 quarts boiling water

1 piece of rock sugar about the size of a large egg

2 teaspoons ginger juice (page 481)

3 tablespoons wolfberries, rinsed

2 tablespoons osmanthus blossom syrup

1 large Chinese pear of any variety, peeled, cored, and cut into small dice

Fresh lemon juice to taste, optional

1. Start this recipe at least 4 days before you wish to serve it. Rinse the silver ears and place them in a large work bowl. Cover the fungus with at least 2 inches of cool tap water, adding more water as needed to keep the silver ears submerged, and refrigerate. Change the water twice a day for 3 days. On the second day, you can trim the silver ears by placing them in a colander set in the sink for easy cleaning. Use a paring knife to trim off the hard cores and any dark yellow spots, then separate the heads into individual petals (they do not have to be the same size), being sure to rinse off any detritus you find.

2. Rinse the silver ears once again in a colander and then place them in a slow cooker, if you have one, or in a 4-quart pot with a heavy bottom. Add the boiling water, return the water to a boil, and then cover and simmer very slowly for 6 to 8 hours, until the silver ears are completely translucent but have not started to break apart. About 1 hour before they are done, add the sugar, ginger juice, wolfberries, and osmanthus blossom syrup. The soup may be made ahead of time to this point and refrigerated; just heat it up before proceeding to the next step.

3. When the silver ears are soft and tender, remove the insert from the slow cooker or the pan from the heat. Add the pears to the hot soup, then taste the soup and add lemon juice or more sweetener if you wish. Serve the soup hot, or let it cool to room temperature, chill it, and enjoy it cold.

Niàng zuìguā 酿醉瓜

Stuffed Muskmelon

GANSU • SERVES 8 TO 10

The melons and grapes of China's far west are justly famous. Eaten fresh, while still warm from the late summer sun, or chilled until refreshingly cold, they're the perfect end to a big local meal. This recipe for stuffed melon comes from the city of Lanzhou, and it features many traditional ingredients from the area, like wolfberries, raisins, and nuts. Everything is bound together with sticky rice and a gently sweet syrup. I have updated the preparation quite a bit, cutting down on the sweetness, hollowing out the melon so that it is much easier to eat, and substituting Taiwanese *boba* tapioca pearls (page 240) for the jelly-like cyanobacteria called *gěxiānmǐ* 葛仙米—known in the West by wonderful names like "star jelly," "troll's butter," or "rot of the stars"—which I've never been able to find.

¾ cup dried lotus seeds
1 teaspoon baking soda
Boiling water, as needed
1½ cups round sticky rice, soaked for 1 to 2 hours
¼ cup *boba* (big black pearl tapioca), regular or instant
1 piece of rock sugar about the size of a large egg
1 cup cool water
2 tablespoons osmanthus blossom syrup
2 tablespoons wolfberries
3 tablespoons raisins
¼ cup lightly toasted walnuts, roughly chopped
2 tablespoons toasted sesame seeds (page 413)
1 Persian or similar melon, about 10 pounds

1. This dish is best prepared a day in advance to give the melon and stuffing time to chill thoroughly. Place the lotus seeds and baking soda in a small work bowl and cover with boiling water. Soak them until the water has cooled down a bit and the seeds have become pliable, and then squeeze each seed open and remove any green sprouts that you find inside (see page 289). Place the very slippery lotus seeds in a sieve and rinse them thoroughly under tap water before transferring them to a heatproof bowl. Cover them once again with boiling water and then steam the seeds for about 20 minutes (see page 49), until they are plump and tender. Drain the seeds and place them in a large work bowl.

2. Drain the rice and spread it out in a cloth-lined steamer basket. Steam it over high heat for about 20 minutes, until it is tender but still chewy. Combine the rice with the lotus seeds and toss lightly.

3. Prepare the *boba* tapioca pearls according to the package instructions, drain, and add them to the rice. Combine the rock sugar and cool water in a pan and simmer until the sugar melts. Remove from the heat and add the osmanthus syrup, wolfberries, and raisins. When the mixture has cooled down a bit, add it to the rice along with the walnuts and sesame seeds and gently toss everything together.

4. Wash the melon carefully with soap and water before patting it dry. Slice off about ½ inch from both the stem and blossom ends so that both melon halves will stand upright. Cut the melon in half around its equator using a zigzag pattern. Discard the seeds and membrane. Use a sharp serving spoon to scoop out the melon flesh, leaving a roughly ¼-inch-thick layer of flesh on the rind and being particularly careful not to cut through the flattened ends.

5. Chop the melon flesh into ¼-inch dice and toss it with the rice mixture. Stand the melon halves on their ends so they look like large, fringed bowls. Using the serving spoon, pack the rice mixture into the melon halves, adding only as much of the syrup as will fit. If there is some leftover rice mixture, set it aside as a cook's treat. Cover the melon halves with plastic wrap and chill, preferably overnight.

6. To serve, bring the stuffed melons to the dining table and slice into wedges.

Boeja and *Suutei tsai*

Butter Tea

TIBET AND INNER MONGOLIA · MAKES ABOUT
6 CUPS

¼ cup (or so) Chinese fermented compressed tea
(*pu'er* or *tuocha*, see page 150), broken into
smallish pieces
6 cups boiling water, divided into 1 cup and 5 cups
1 to 4 tablespoons best-quality salted butter
Pinch of sea salt
1 cup heavy cream

This is an approximation of a tea that is enjoyed
in Tibet and Inner Mongolia. In Tibet, it is usually
foamed up with a churn—much like the *molinillo*
used to make hot chocolate in Mexico—while in
Inner Mongolia, the milk is foamed by repeatedly
lifting ladlefuls high over the pan and pouring
them back in. This is pretty much the same concept as India's "pulled tea" (*teh tarik*), which is
poured back and forth between two containers.

I use whole cream instead of milk, which prevents the fat from separating. Then I add a touch
of salted butter. I tend to put more tea leaves in the
brew—around 6 tablespoons—than is traditional
because I like this drink to have a very bitter edge.
The amount of tea, water, butter, and cream you
use, however, is ultimately a personal preference.

1. Place the tea in a saucepan, cover it with 1 cup of
the boiling water, and let it soak for about 3 minutes
to loosen the leaves, and then discard the water.
Drain the tea leaves, return them to the pan, add
the remaining 5 cups boiling water, and return the
water to a boil over high heat. Lower the heat to a
simmer and simmer for about 10 minutes, then
strain the tea into a blender.

2. Cut the butter into small pieces and add it to
the tea along with the salt and cream. Blend the
tea, starting on low and gradually increasing the
speed to high in order to make the tea foam. Serve
the tea in small bowls, preferably wooden.

Bābǎochá 八寶茶

Eight Treasure Tea

THE NORTHWEST · SERVES 1 (CAN BE MULTIPLIED
INFINITELY)

This is most likely a Hui Muslim tea, but other areas of
China have their own versions. The base of the drink
is green tea, which is seasoned with rock sugar, red
dates, wolfberries, dried longans (dragon eye fruit),
walnuts, apricot pits, chrysanthemum blossoms, and
raisins. Other herbs and flowers are sometimes used,
but there must always be eight ingredients total.

In Sichuan, this tea is made with local green tea,
ginseng, rock sugar, licorice root, wolfberries, raisins,
red dates, and both jasmine and chrysanthemum blossoms. In the Central Highlands, it is sometimes made
with black tea or even dark compressed teas like *pu'er*.
The recipe here is basic and can be tinkered with. The
one thing to remember is that you need to use a good-
quality tea for this drink to come out well. Try to hunt
down the small yellow chrysanthemums that are grown
in Hangzhou, Zhejiang Province (page 151), too; their
fragrance is particularly clean and fresh.

1 teaspoon high-quality green tea leaves
1 large or 2 small dried Chinese red dates
1 teaspoon wolfberries
1 teaspoon apricot pits
2 dried longans
1 walnut half, lightly crumbled
3 dried chrysanthemum blossoms
1 teaspoon raisins
Boiling water, as needed
1 teaspoon rock sugar

1. The traditional way to prepare this tea is to place
the tea leaves, dates, wolfberries, apricot pits, longans,
walnut, chrysanthemum blossoms, and raisins in an
8 to 12 ounce covered cup before dousing them with
enough water to rinse them off. The cover is then
angled against the cup as this water is poured off and
discarded. Or, you can simply rinse the ingredients in
a small sieve before steeping the tea.

2. Pour boiling water over the ingredients, add the
sugar, and cover the cup. Wait for a few minutes before
sipping.

THE FUNDAMENTALS

BASIC RECIPES · TECHNIQUES & HANDY ADVICE · GLOSSARY & BUYING GUIDE
SUGGESTED MENUS

BASIC RECIPES

If you are looking to discover the key to creating great Chinese food, welcome to my secret stash. These are the recipes that form the delectable foundation for many of the dishes featured throughout this book, as well as the little bits of sleight-of-hand that allow you to create some pretty amazing things to eat.

Take a simple thing like chili oil. Yes, you can buy that in the store, but I guarantee you that nothing you purchase will come close to the taste, aroma, and quality of homemade. Besides that, it's dead simple and costs only pennies.

Raised breads and pasta are easy to learn, as well, and these are the sorts of things that will make your reputation as a good cook. Few things will bring as much joy—to my life, at least—as looking in the freezer and finding stuffed *baozi* and juicy potstickers that can be cooked at a moment's notice. Once you master these, roll up your sleeves and make puff pastry. I guarantee that it is much easier than the French version, and it also freezes well.

Fermented and salted ingredients are key to just about all of China's finest dishes, and as with everything else here, whatever you make at home will be fresher, more delicious, much healthier, and always many times cheaper than anything you can buy. Salted Shanghainese greens can be mastered in ten minutes. Yogurt is a snap. Fresh pickles can be put together even by children. And once you get a well-honed taste for the delicious things sailing out of your kitchen, set up your own crock for traditional fermented Sichuan-style pickles—you'll be blown away by how good they are.

THE RECIPES

V = VEGETARIAN OR VEGAN OPTION

Stocks give classic Chinese dishes their depth and savory xianwei flavors. There is simply no substitute for great stock as the base for many of the best sauces.

Use whatever kind of stock best fits the dish—unsalted chicken stock is the default foundation—and discover what a world of difference this makes. If you find yourself without good homemade stock, use an organic stock packaged in an aseptic box. These are great to have on hand and are terrific time-savers. But homemade is always best.

Simmer chicken and meat stock uncovered at very low heat to ensure a crystalline liquid. If you prefer it milky, add more skin and boil it with the cover slightly askew.

Jī gāotāng 雞高湯

Chicken Stock

MAKES ABOUT 3 QUARTS

2 quarts assorted chicken parts (necks, backs, wings, and carcasses, but no livers)
½ cup rice wine of any kind, optional
8 slices fresh ginger, optional
4 green onions, trimmed, optional
1 tablespoon whole black peppercorns, optional
Sea salt to taste, optional

1. Place the chicken parts in a large stockpot. Add water to cover by about 1 inch and bring the pot to a full boil. Then dump out the water and rinse the scum off of the chicken. Rinse out the pot, too.

2. Return the chicken parts to the pot and add the same amount of water as in Step 1. Bring the water to a boil and add any of the optional ingredients you like. Lower the heat to maintain a very gentle simmer and cook the stock uncovered for about 1 hour; more than that and the chicken will start to break down and muddy the stock, which is all right if that is what you are aiming for, as in the recipe for Mock Shark Fin Soup (page 16).

3. Strain the stock, discard the solids, skim off as much fat as you want, and either use the stock immediately or chill it. The stock and fat can be refrigerated in separate containers for a few days or frozen in resealable freezer bags, if desired.

Duck stock can also be made with this recipe. Duck is much fattier than chicken, so be sure to remove most of the fat after the stock has cooled.

Ròu gāotāng 肉高湯

Meat Stock

MAKES ABOUT 3 QUARTS

Pork skin will add a considerable amount of collagen to this stock, which gives it body and texture. However, it will also tend to make the liquid more opaque, so take that into consideration when selecting cuts of meat.

2 quarts pork, beef, or lamb bones with some meat on them (necks, trotters, and tails are great; have your butcher split any large bones)
¾ cup rice wine of any kind, optional
12 slices fresh ginger, optional
6 green onions, trimmed, optional
1 tablespoon whole black peppercorns, optional
Sea salt to taste, optional

1. Place the bones in a large stockpot. Add water to cover by about 1 inch and bring the pot to a full boil. Then dump out the water and rinse the scum off of the bones. Rinse out the pot, too.

2. Return the bones to the pot and add the same amount of water as in Step 1. Bring the water to a boil and add any of the optional ingredients you like. Lower the heat to maintain a very gentle simmer and cook the stock uncovered for about 3 hours. Let the bones and the stock cool down naturally.

3. Strain the stock, discard the solids, skim off the fat, and either use the stock immediately or chill it. The stock can be refrigerated for a few days or frozen in resealable freezer bags, if desired.

Xiānggū gāotāng 香菇高湯

Mushroom Stock

MAKES ABOUT 8 CUPS

1 quart dried black mushroom stems (see Tip) or sliced or whole dried black mushrooms
½ cup rice wine of any kind, optional
5 slices fresh ginger, optional
3 green onions, trimmed, optional
Sea salt to taste, optional

1. Start this the day before you wish to use it. Rinse the stems or mushrooms and cover with cool water. Let them sit overnight to slowly plump up. (They can also be covered with boiling water if you need to do this quickly. The flavor will not be quite as rich, but it's fast.)

2. The next day, swish the mushrooms around in the water to loosen any detritus and then scoop them out into a large stockpot. Pour the liquid through a fine-mesh sieve into the stockpot and add enough water to cover the mushrooms by at least 1 inch. Bring to a full boil and season with any or all of the optional ingredients. Lower the heat to maintain a very gentle simmer and cook the stock uncovered for an hour or two.

3. Strain the stock, discard the solids, and either use it immediately or refrigerate it. It also can be frozen in resealable freezer bags, if desired.

I always save the stems of both fresh and dried black mushrooms and then let them dry in a plastic strawberry box I have set up on the kitchen counter. When they are completely dry, they get tossed in a large jar and stashed in the pantry. It's amazing how quickly these add up, and a jar full of these stems is a wonderful thing to have on hand for making rich and flavorful stocks.

In most of China, rice is what the Chinese people turn to as the cornerstone of almost every meal. But this being China, inventiveness has been called into play even with this most basic of foods, allowing these simple starchy grains to range from the chewy to the tender, from the satiny to the rough, and from the filling to the ethereally light.

One of the reasons for this is that there are simply so many varieties of rice. The most common of all is plain, short-grain, white rice (also called níanmǐ 粘米 [黏米], or Indica), which is very similar to what we know of as sushi rice: it's polished, meaning the bran and brown exterior have been removed, and that is what makes it just sticky enough to be successfully maneuvered into the mouth with chopsticks.

Long-grain rice is used mainly in southern China; its texture is fluffier and less tacky than short-grain, which makes it perfect for things like fried rice, as the seasonings thereby get a chance to attach themselves to every tiny morsel.

Sticky rice, on the other hand, forms a soft coating as it cooks, and that is what makes it, well, sticky. It is sometimes erroneously referred to as "sweet" or "glutinous" rice (see page 486), but the Chinese have an even more elegant moniker: "creamy rice," or nùomǐ 糯米. Chinese sticky rice tends to be white, although some people prefer it brown or even purple.

Raw rice can be ground into flour and turned into noodles, or the cooked grains can be pounded into paste. When steamed grains are fermented, they turn into wine. At other times savory pastes and sauces are created out of combinations of rice and other ingredients—like wheat and beans—that are carefully allowed to mold. It's hard to imagine the foods of China without this remarkable grain.

Zhēng báifàn 蒸白飯

Steamed Rice

When it comes to automatic rice steamers, the Japanese have it nailed. The best one on the market at the time of this writing is the Zojirushi "Neuro Fuzzy" rice cooker, which also has to win some sort of prize for the strangest name. Rice cookers are fully automatic, so if you cook a lot of rice, buying one is something to seriously consider. Just follow the directions that come with the steamer.

If you are old-school, you can also steam rice in bamboo steamer baskets. The main thing to remember is that the rice has to be soaked before steaming. Some people advise that you soak it for 8 hours or overnight, but it really depends upon the type of rice and how fresh it is. I tend to soak white rice for about 3 hours and then use the fingernail test (see page 480) to know when it's ready to be cooked. Check out the directions for fermented rice (page 415) if you want detailed directions on making steamed rice the old-fashioned way.

Shŭizhŭ báifàn 水煮白飯

Stove-Top Rice

MAKES ABOUT 3 CUPS

I did not have an electric rice steamer even after almost three decades of living with a Chinese guy simply because I had always worked in tiny kitchens with limited counter space. I served rice many times a week by simply cooking it on the stove. When done right, it's foolproof.

Although this is not technically steamed rice, what you end up with is virtually indistinguishable from the real deal. Brown rice cooks up perfectly this way, too. Lots of rice producers will have directions printed on the package, and that is the perfect place to start because each brand and variety of rice is different. Don't add any salt or oil, even if the package tells you to, as this is just not done in East Asia.

This is the recipe I have used since forever.

1 cup plain white short-grain rice
1½ cups water

1. Rinse the rice in a sieve until the water runs clear. Dump the rice into a 4-cup saucepan, preferably with a heavy bottom and a clear lid. Pour in the water and swirl the rice around in it to loosen up any clumps.

2. Bring the water to a full boil and then turn the heat down to low. Cover the pan and let the rice slowly cook for 17 to 20 minutes. Remove the pan from the heat and let the rice sit covered for another 10 minutes. Fluff the rice up with chopsticks or a fork and serve.

For brown rice, use 2 cups water and cook the rice for 45 minutes, or follow the package directions.

Zhēngfěn 蒸粉

Rice Crumbs

MAKES ABOUT ½ CUP

Commercial rice crumbs are called *zhēngròufěn* 蒸肉粉 ("steamed meat powder") and are usually found in the spice or dried-foods aisle of a Chinese grocery, but homemade crumbs will be fresher, lighter, and much, much tastier.

Most rice crumb recipes call for raw plain rice, but once in a while sticky rice is needed, so be sure to check. If the recipe calls for plain rice, I always use broken jasmine rice. This is the same thing I use in Congee (page 226), and the beauty of it is that you don't need to grind it, as it's already the perfect size.

½ cup white rice of any kind
2 petals star anise, ground to a fine powder, optional
1 teaspoon ground toasted Sichuan peppercorns
    (page 441), optional

1. Measure out the rice. If you are using broken jasmine rice, proceed directly to Step 2. If you are using whole grains, pulverize them in a spice grinder, mortar, a food processor, or a blender. Pulse the rice until it is broken down to between half and a quarter of its original size. Do not grind it into dust.

2. Place the broken rice in a dry, unoiled wok along with the optional spices. Cook the rice over medium-high heat, tossing constantly, until the grains turn from translucent to white and then to a very slightly toasted golden brown. Cool the rice before using. If you want to prepare it ahead of time, it can be refrigerated in a sealed plastic bag.

Dòushā zòng 豆沙糭 (or 豆沙粽)

Sweet Rice Tamales with Bean Paste

MAKES 16 TAMALES

Dragon Boat Festival is one of the three great traditional Chinese celebrations, the other two being the Mid-Autumn Festival and Chinese New Year. Most people use this summer holiday to honor the poet and official Qu Yuan (340–278 BCE), as well as to celebrate China's national symbol, the dragon. Even today, more traditionally minded Chinese say that they are the descendants of that mythical creature, for many of China's most ancient gods, such as Fuxi and Nüwa (see page 339), had bodies that were at least partially dragon-like.

As the festival's English name tells you, dragon boat races are a big part of the celebrations. They share an origin story with these tamales: it is said that Qu Yuan drowned himself in a river after his king, under the influence of corrupt advisors, banished him from the court, and that the commoners who witnessed the act used their boats to try to save him and then threw bundles of rice into the river so that the fish would not touch his body.

This practice of making tamales and racing boats has continued to modern times, a celebration of patriotism and dragons, of food and culture, of fun and sacrifice . . . just a few of the puzzle parts that make up the wonderful world that is China.

16 large dried bamboo leaves,
    plus a couple of extras in case some split
1½ cups round sticky rice
2 tablespoons toasted sesame oil
1 cup sweetened red bean paste
    (page 442 or store-bought)
½ teaspoon sea salt
½ cup chopped walnuts, optional
4 quarts cold water
Boiling water, as needed

1. Wash the bamboo leaves carefully, being sure to avoid cutting yourself on the sharp edges (consider wearing gloves). Cover the leaves with very hot water until soft and green. Trim off about an inch from both ends and then wipe both sides of the leaves with a towel; cover the leaves to keep them moist. Place the rice in a sieve and rinse it under running water; drain.

2. Heat the sesame oil in a wok over medium-high heat until it begins to smell fragrant and then add the bean paste, salt, and optional walnuts. Simmer the bean paste if it is canned to remove any metallic taste and to lend the beans a nice creaminess; if it's homemade, cook it just until it absorbs the oil. As soon as the paste is gently bubbling, scrape it out into a small work bowl and let it cool down to room temperature. Divide the cooled paste into 16 pieces and roll each one into a ball.

3. Bring the cold water to a boil in an 8-quart pot while you are busy wrapping the tamales.

4. Wrap the tamales as shown in the diagram to the right.

5. When all of the tamales have been filled and tied, lower them gently into the boiling water, cover the pot, and boil them for about 5 minutes to set their shape. Then remove the cover, lower the heat to a simmer, and gently cook the tamales for about 2 hours. Add more boiling water as needed to completely submerge the tamales, and check them at 15-minute intervals to make sure they don't need a bit more water.

6. Remove the tamales from the boiling water and drain well. Eat them right away or cool them down and store them in a plastic bag in the refrigerator. To reheat, steam them until heated through.

WRAPPING TAMALES

1

Take a trimmed leaf with the shiny side facing you and fold it into a cone.

2

Be sure to have a small fold at the bottom of the cone, as this is the secret to preventing the rice from escaping.

3

Scoop a spoonful of rice into the cone and then place the filling on top.

4

Place another scoop of rice on top of the filling.

5

Fold the leaf ends over the cone, allowing about ½ inch of slack in the fold so the package has room for the rice to swell. Shake the tamale a bit. You should hear a rattling noise that signals it's been wrapped perfectly.

6

Give the wrapper a bit more slack as you tie it up, so that the fold is made a tiny bit longer, since this will also help keep the leaf from breaking open as the rice swells.

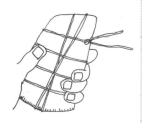

7

For the same reason, wrap the string around the bundle as gently as if you were wrapping it around a baby's wrist, but make the leaf lie flat against the tamale.

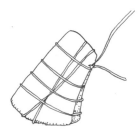

8

Keep one end of the string around a foot long so that you can tie the tamales into bundles of 6 or more for cooking.

Miànfěn 麵粉

Chinese Flour

The main difference between the breads and pasta of China and the United States lies in their white flours. Here in the States, we use flour with a high amount of gluten, and this in turn makes our breads and pastas chewier. There's nothing inherently wrong with that, of course, but it does cause considerable confusion when you try to make recipes that originate in other countries.

If you have access to Asian markets, you can use Korean flour, which tends to be of excellent quality. Korean flour is usually available as both all-purpose and pastry (that is, medium- and low-gluten) white flours, but at the time of this writing, no manufacturer is bothering to use English on the packages, so you will need to find someone in the market who speaks Korean and English in order to get the right one.

To deal with this problem, I monkeyed around with the ratios of American all-purpose and pastry flours, and these proportions turned out to be ideal.

The beauty of this is that it allows you to easily make Chinese breads and pastas even if you don't have an Asian market in your neighborhood. You can use organic flours instead of highly processed ingredients, and such things as whole wheat and non-wheat flours can be substituted for the white in certain recipes, though not for pastry. (My favorite combination for some pasta and raised dough recipes is unbleached all-purpose with whole wheat pastry flour, by the way.)

2 parts unbleached all-purpose flour
1 part unbleached pastry flour

Tàngmiàn miàntuán 燙麵麵糰

Plain Hot-Water Dough

MAKES ABOUT 2¼ POUNDS

In almost any situation where breads or pastries will be steamed or panfried—in other words, where they are not directly dunked into boiling water—the dough I like to use best is made with boiling water. This brilliant idea courtesy of northern Chinese home cooks heats up the flour, expands each tiny fleck, and moistens the flecks completely so that I end up with something more supple and tender than anything made with cool-water dough. Please note that if you try to steam *jiaozi* (page 45) made with cold-water wrappers, the dough will have a dry, pasty center, and it will ruin both your appetite and your meal.

6 cups Chinese flour (at left), plus more
    for kneading and rolling out the dough
2 cups boiling water
¾ cup cool water

1. Follow the directions for plain cold-water dough (page 387), but mix the boiling water into the flour first to form fat flakes. Only then should you add the cool water, which will turn the mixture into a soft dough.

One of the best places to roll out dough or knead bread is the underside of a pull-out chopping board. Most people use one side to cut things on and forget that there is a nice, unblemished surface underneath. If you are lucky enough to have such a board, place a damp cloth on your counter (or on a table if you're on the shorter side) to keep the board from moving around and set the board on top of that. When you're done, make sure that you turn the board right side up before you put it away in order to protect its smooth surface. If both sides are banged up, sand one side down until it is smooth, oil it with some mineral oil, and be sure to yell at anyone who tries to cut on your nice, smooth surface.

Lěngshuǐ miàntuán 冷水麵糰

Plain Cold-Water Dough

MAKES ABOUT 2¼ POUNDS

This is the dough to use when you want to make either boiled *jiaozi* (page 45) or rolled noodles (page 388). Cold water plus flour makes something that is strong enough to withstand the punishment of being tossed into a vat of hot water and stirred around without falling apart. And if you make it with Chinese flour, rather than American all-purpose, your dough will be delicate enough to melt in your mouth.

The problem with making Chinese pasta with American all-purpose flour was driven home for me when I had some nice folks from Xi'an over to my house, and they wanted to demonstrate the way to make a particular kind of noodle. I set out my bag of Korean flour, they went to work, and they quickly became thrilled at the suppleness of the dough. They had tried to use American all-purpose flour before, they said, and had found it terribly hard to work with.

Color can be added to the dough courtesy of vegetables, spices, or even food coloring. When I have *jiaozi* parties during the Lunar New Year, I offer a variety of fillings and mark each one clearly with brightly hued dough wrappers: spinach juice for green, carrot juice for orange, beet juice for magenta, turmeric for yellow, and even the occasional squid ink for black. Just substitute the juice for about half of the water, or add a teaspoon or more of turmeric and squid ink. (Both beets and turmeric will stain anything they come into contact with, so I strongly suggest making those doughs in a machine and kneading them on marble or some other nonporous surface.)

6 cups Chinese flour (page 386), plus more
    for kneading and rolling out the dough
2¾ cups cool water

1. Whirl the flour and water together in a food processor or stand mixer with a paddle attachment, either of which takes mere seconds. If you are using a machine, place the flour and water in the bowl and either process it with a metal blade or beat it with the paddle attachment until the dough forms a ball and no longer sticks to the bowl.

2. Scrape the dough onto a floured flat surface (see Tip, page 386), sprinkle more flour on top, and knead the dough until it is soft and satiny. At this point, the dough should not stick to either your hands or the board, and when pinched between the fingers, it will feel like an earlobe. Form the dough into a ball, dust it liberally with flour, and place it in a plastic bag. It may be prepared up to this point a few days ahead of time and refrigerated; allow the dough to return to room temperature before shaping the dough.

3. If the dough has been chilled, knead it gently on a lightly floured board to soften it a bit; ideally it should not need more than a mere sprinkling of flour, so only add as much as is absolutely necessary to keep the dough from sticking to your hands or board. Cut the dough into fist-sized chunks and knead them one at a time until the dough is supple again, using a tea towel to cover whatever dough you are not working with so that it stays moist. Proceed as directed in individual recipes for shaping noodles and wrappers.

4. To make noodles, set the dough on a lightly floured surface and dust with flour. A fun way to do this is to use your 12-inch Chinese rolling pin to shape it into a rectangle that is no more than 8 inches wide, so that both ends of your pin remain free (see Step 1 in the Rolled Noodles diagram on page 388). Wind the dough around the pin (Step 2). Roll the pin back and forth evenly and gently using your arm pressure to stretch the pasta sheet out against the pin into a thin, silky sheet. Whatever method you use, it is the right thickness when you can see your fingers through the dough. Create a nice pile of pasta sheets by slicing down through the dough without nicking the wood (Step 3). Then, slice these into whatever width you like (Step 4).

ROLLED NOODLES

❶ Use a Chinese rolling pin to shape the dough into a rectangle.

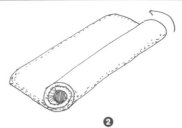

❷ Dust the dough with flour and roll it around the pin. Gently roll it back and forth.

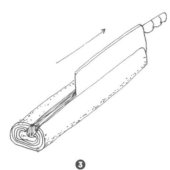

❸ Cut gently down through the length of the roll without nicking the rolling pin.

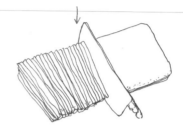

❹ Slice these layers of dough however you wish.

DRYING PASTA

❶ To dry noodles in long lengths, drape them over the back of a chair or a wooden hanger until they become brittle; refrigerate in sealed plastic bags.

❷ To make noodle nests in single serving sizes, shape them into neat mounds on a clean kitchen towel and turn them over occasionally until they are fully dried and brittle. Store in the refrigerator.

Quándàn miàn 全蛋麵

Whole Egg Dough

MAKES 2½ TO 3 POUNDS

This recipe makes excellent southern-style noodles. Tensile and golden, they are great in just about any kind of soup. They are also the basic pasta for the remarkable dish called Yi Residence Noodles (page 214), in which the cooked strands are fried into puffy tangles that then settle down into spongy pillows when the sauce is poured over them.

4 large eggs
7 tablespoons warm water
4 cups Chinese flour (page 386), plus more
    for kneading and rolling out the dough

1. Lightly beat the eggs in a large work bowl, add the water, and then use chopsticks to mix in the flour. You can also use a stand mixer or food processor for this step. Turn the dough out onto a lightly floured board and knead it until smooth. Cut it into 4 even pieces, cover the dough with a damp cloth, and let it rest for about 20 minutes.

2. Working on 1 piece of dough at a time, roll a piece out into a rectangle about 9 × 12 inches. Dust the dough thoroughly with flour and roll it up loosely around the rolling pin, gently cut it into sheets, and then slice the sheets into noodles anywhere from ⅛ to ½ inch wide (see the diagram to the left). Toss these lightly with flour so they do not clump up and then cover with a towel. Repeat with the rest of the dough until all of it has been turned into noodles. The pasta can either be cooked immediately or frozen or dried in small nests. (For directions on how to dry pasta, see the diagram to the left.)

3. To cook the noodles, bring a large pot of water to a boil and have ready 2 colanders set in the sink, a large work bowl, chopsticks, and a Chinese spider or slotted spoon. Shake a large handful of the raw noodles to separate them and knock off most of the flour and then add them to the boiling water. Stir the noodles continuously to keep them from sticking to one another, and as soon as the water is about to boil again, use your chopsticks and spider to remove them to the large work bowl. Dump the noodles into a colander set in the sink, run cold tap water over them to cool them down, and then toss them into the other colander to drain completely. Repeat with the rest of the noodles until all have been cooked, cooled, and drained. Shake the colander a couple of times to remove as much water as possible.

Běifāng yóusūpí miàntuán 北方油酥皮麵糰

Northern-Style Puff Pastry

MAKES ENOUGH DOUGH FOR ABOUT 16 *SHAOBING*

Chinese puff pastry is not well known in the West, but this is something that should change as soon as news of this lighter-than-air approach to baked goods gets around. Until recently, the Chinese have never been all that excited about butter or cream, and so Chinese pastries taste and smell a whole lot different than, say, Viennese or Parisian ones.

But what I love about Chinese pastries is exactly that reliance on flavors other than butter and cream to make a sweet statement. I think it is pure genius that two kinds of dough are folded over each other to make what seems like zillions of thin layers that taste of nothing but good flour, yeast, and a touch of sesame. Quite simple once you get the hang of it—which will take no more than one time if you pay attention to the directions—this is the secret behind such delicious creations as North China's *shaobing* pastries (page 56).

The principle is easy: an oily dough is wrapped inside a flour-and-water dough and then rolled out and folded a few times until simple mathematics takes over and these layers—water, oil, water—are multiplied into superthin strata. Then, after the puff pastry is either baked or fried, the layers made with water form steam that billows up between the oily ones, and the oily ones in turn crisp up in the heat. It's delicious magic.

WATER DOUGH

1 teaspoon active dry yeast
¾ cup plus 2 tablespoons warm water
1 tablespoon sugar
2 cups Chinese flour (page 386)
½ teaspoon sea salt

OIL DOUGH

2 cups Chinese flour (page 386)
½ cup neutral-tasting oil like canola, or peanut oil if you
    want to emphasize this flavor
3 tablespoons toasted sesame oil

1. Follow the directions in the diagram to the right.

1

First make the water dough: stir the yeast into the warm water, add the sugar, and give the yeast about 20 minutes to bloom (meaning that it will bubble up and froth if fresh; if this doesn't happen, toss out the yeast and buy some more). Mix the flour and salt together in a medium work bowl and stir in the yeast mixture. Empty this out onto a smooth board. Knead briefly until it does not stick to your hands.

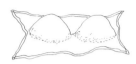

2

Divide the dough in half, roll each half into a ball, and cover them with a moist tea towel.

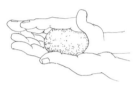

3

Now make the oil dough: mix together the flour and oils in a medium work bowl until they form a smooth ball. Divide the oil dough in half and roll each half into a ball.

4

Pat 1 ball of the water dough out into a fat circle and place 1 ball of the oil dough in the center. Pull the edges of the water dough up and around the oil dough so it completely encloses the oil dough.

5

Pinch the opening closed and pat the fat ball out on a lightly floured surface into a fat disk about 5 inches wide.

6

Use a Chinese rolling pin to roll the disk out into a rectangle about 10 × 15 inches.

7

Fold the rectangle in thirds like a business letter. Roll it out again into a long strip about 5 × 16 inches.

8

Starting at a long edge, roll up the strip to form a baton 16 inches long and then pinch the long edge into the roll to form a solid rope. Cover the finished dough with a damp tea towel while you repeat this step with the other halves of the doughs. Cut the ropes crosswise into pieces as directed in the *shaobing* recipe (page 56). The dough can be prepared up to this point and frozen in a single layer until hard and then stored in a freezer bag. Defrost the dough under a damp tea towel.

Nánfāng yóusūpí miàntuán 南方油酥皮麵糰

Southern-Style Puff Pastry

MAKES ABOUT 4½ POUNDS DOUGH, ENOUGH FOR
ABOUT 4 DOZEN COOKIES

Southern-style puff pastry is richer than what is made in the North. Because of this, roll out this dough without additional flour so that it stays light and flaky. If my board or rolling pin sticks in the least, I lightly oil the wood, rather than adding the usual dusting of flour.

The other big difference is that each southern-style pastry is individually shaped using the two kinds of dough. It sounds difficult, especially when you get to the part about weighing each piece, but I've found that my hands and eyes quickly learn to recognize the difference between 10 and 11 grams. (Metric definitely has the upper hand here because the small gradations make all the difference between just right and too much or not enough. You'll need a small metric scale for this recipe.)

Here are a few more tips for making these pastries fast and hassle-free:

- Keep the high-fat dough and any high-fat fillings chilled, especially in hot weather, so that they roll out easier and the short dough won't squish out of the sides.
- Cover the dough at all times when you aren't working with it, as it dries out quickly, especially in dry climates. Breakage leads to squishing.
- Measure out one kind of dough at a time so that your hands and eyes rapidly recognize the correct weight.
- Whole wheat flour does not work here as well as unbleached refined flour. Although whole wheat pastries are tasty, the dough dries out quickly and tears easily, so whole wheat is not recommended for either the high- or low-fat dough.

LOW-FAT DOUGH

2¼ cups plus 2 tablespoons Chinese flour (page 386)
2 tablespoons sugar
5 tablespoons white shortening or lard
½ cup cool water

HIGH-FAT DOUGH

½ cup plus 2 tablespoons white shortening or lard
3 cups unbleached pastry flour

Sesame or vegetable oil, as needed, if the dough sticks

1. Follow the directions in the diagram to the right.

SOUTHERN-STYLE PUFF PASTRY

❶

A food processor makes life easier for this recipe, so if you have one, use it for both kinds of dough. If not, use an electric mixer or make it by hand. First make the low-fat dough by mixing together the dry ingredients, then work in the shortening or lard, and lastly add the water to form a soft dough. Work it lightly in the machine or on a board, cover it tightly with plastic wrap, and let it rest for at least 20 minutes. To make the high-fat dough, mix the fat into the flour until it is fully incorporated and you have a soft dough. Cover it tightly with plastic wrap and refrigerate for at least 20 minutes; keep the dough chilled whenever you aren't working with it.

❷

Divide the dough into as many pieces as you need; for example, if you are making 48 cookies, divide the low-fat dough into 48 pieces, or about 12 grams per piece. Roll the pieces into balls and cover with plastic wrap. Then, divide the high-fat dough into another 48 pieces, which will be about 10 grams per piece. Roll each piece into a ball, cover with plastic wrap, and refrigerate again if the kitchen is warm. To form the individual puff pastries, work on 1 pastry at a time and keep the rest of the dough covered. Roll out a piece of the low-fat dough into a circle about 3 inches wide and place a ball of high-fat dough in its center.

❸

Wrap the low-fat dough around the ball, making sure there are absolutely no cracks or holes.

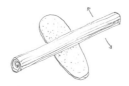

❹

Gently roll the filled ball around between your palms. Place it on a clean board (oil it lightly if the dough begins to stick) and use a Chinese rolling pin to roll it out into a strip 5 to 6 inches long.

❺

Roll the strip up into a cigar and then curl the ends toward each other to form a ball.

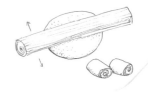

❻

Again use your rolling pin to roll out the ball into a circle about 3 inches wide. Repeat with the rest of the dough pieces until all of the puff pastries have been formed. The basic puff pastry circles can be frozen in a single layer on plastic wrap, then placed in a resealable freezer bag for later; defrost them under a sheet of plastic wrap before using.

Héyèbǐng 荷葉餅 *or jiānbǐng* 煎餅

Wheat Wrappers (Chinese Flour Tortillas)

MAKES 8 THICK OR 16 THIN (5-INCH) WRAPPERS

This is the sort of bread that is very often enjoyed in the northern half of China. Part of this is due to the consequent simplicity of the meal, since anything stir-fried in small shreds can be wrapped inside—Silk Road Fajitas (page 344) and Osmanthus Blossom Pork (page 340) are two classic examples. Much like Mexican flour tortillas, these wrappers are best fresh off the grill and lose much of their magic when reheated. So, make them ahead of time and freeze, if need be, and then grill them just before serving.

Both thin and thick wrappers make their way into northern cuisines. More elegant dinners, of course, require the presence of thin wrappers, while street foods and home-cooked meals favor the thicker ones. When made even thicker, they turn from wrappers into breads, reaching a delicious pinnacle in Grilled Breads (page 396).

1 cup Chinese flour (page 386), plus more if needed
6 to 7 tablespoons boiling water
1 tablespoon (or so) peanut or vegetable oil

1. Place the flour in a medium work bowl and stir in just enough boiling water so the flour forms flakes and all of the water is absorbed into a soft dough. Empty the dough onto a smooth surface and knead it until smooth, adding more flour as necessary to keep it from sticking. When it is as soft as an earlobe, cover the dough with plastic wrap and let it rest for about 20 minutes.

2. Divide the dough into 16 even pieces and roll each piece into a ball before flattening these balls with the palm of your hand. Use a pastry brush to lightly brush the surface of half of the circles with oil, and place the other half of the circles on top of the oiled ones to create 8 dough sandwiches.

3. Roll each sandwich out into an even circle. The best way to do this is to use a Chinese rolling pin in one hand and to turn the circle with the other (see Step 3, page 406); roll the circles out into flat tortillas about 5 inches wide. Keep the dough covered when you are not working with it. The wrappers can be prepared ahead of time up to this point and frozen in plastic wrap. Be sure and separate each wrapper with plastic wrap to keep them from sticking, and then pack them in a resealable freezer bag.

4. Heat a seasoned yet unoiled cast-iron frying pan over medium heat. When the bottom is hot, add 1 wrapper and slowly cook it on one side until the bottom is spotted brown and the top starts to puff up. Turn the wrapper over and briefly cook it on the other side, then transfer it to a clean tea towel and cover it so that it steams slightly. Repeat with the rest of the wrappers until all are cooked and you have a stack of warm tortillas in your towel. At this point you will be able to peel them apart, if you wish, for very thin wrappers, or keep them as is for thicker ones.

BASIC DIRECTIONS FOR RAISED DOUGH

❶

Mix your liquid and dry ingredients with chopsticks until flakes appear and the dough starts to come together. Prepare a clean, smooth surface where you can knead and work the dough. (The underside of a pull-out cutting board is perfect.) Dump the dough out and use a hand and a pastry scraper to knead it into a smooth mass.

❷

Knead the dough, adding flour only if necessary, until it is smooth and elastic. It is done when you can pinch a piece and it feels like an earlobe. Shape the dough into a smooth ball. Rinse out the bowl, wipe it dry, and coat it with a bit of oil. Place the ball of dough in the bowl, turn it over a couple of times to coat it with the oil, and then cover the bowl with plastic wrap or a damp tea towel. Set it aside to rise.

❸

When the dough has doubled in size, punch it down and fold the edges into the center. Flip the dough over in the bowl so it is smooth on top, cover, and let it rise a second time. It is ready when it has doubled once again. If you poke it with your fingers at this point, the holes will not collapse.

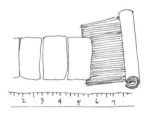

❹

Lightly flour your kneading board and place the dough on it. If you are adding baking powder or soda, knead it in at this point. Let the dough rest covered for 10 to 20 minutes and then roll it out into a rope. The easiest way to divide the dough is to roll it out into a length that makes it easy to divide accurately. For example, if you need 16 pieces of dough, roll the dough into an even rope that is 16 inches long, line a ruler up against the rope, and then use a pastry scraper to cut the dough into sixteen 1-inch pieces.

❺

Toss the pieces of dough with some flour so that they do not stick to one another and cover them with a towel. Let them rest for about 10 minutes so that they are easier to work with.

Làobǐng 烙餅

Grilled Breads

MAKES 6 (7-INCH) FLATBREADS

We have nothing like this in the West that I know of, but this recipe is beautifully simple, easy to make, and very versatile. Unleavened dough patties are grilled (meaning that they are fried without oil) on both sides, and the result is a chewy, extravagantly satisfying bread. These can be eaten as any other bread, wrapped like a taco around a juicy sausage, or shredded into noodle-like strips that are then stir-fried (page 217).

The secret to this is, as always, using lower gluten flour and boiling water. All-purpose flour will result in a tough bread, while cold water will leave the center doughy and unpleasant. I have also discovered that covering the pan while it grills allows the water in the dough to turn into steam, which then cooks the bread from the inside out while the crust bakes on the hot pan. Always best fresh from the fire, this dough can be made ahead of time, if you like. Grill the defrosted frozen breads, rather than reheat them.

2 cups Chinese flour (page 386), plus more if needed
1 teaspoon sea salt
¾ cup plus 2 tablespoons boiling water

1. Place the flour and salt in a medium work bowl and make a well in the center. Stir in just enough of the boiling water to form fat flakes. Empty the dough onto a smooth surface and knead it until smooth, adding more flour as necessary to keep it from sticking. When it is as soft as an earlobe, cover with plastic wrap and let rest for about 20 minutes.

2. Divide the dough into 6 even pieces and roll each piece into a ball before flattening these balls with the palm of your hand. Roll each flattened ball out into an even circle. The best way to do this is to use a Chinese rolling pin in one hand and to turn the circle with the other (see Step 3, page 406); roll the circles out into flat disks about 7 inches wide. Keep the dough covered when you are not working with it. The breads can be prepared ahead of time up to this point and frozen in plastic wrap; be sure and separate each disk with plastic wrap to keep them from sticking, and then pack them in a resealable freezer bag.

3. Heat a seasoned yet unoiled cast-iron frying pan over medium heat. When the bottom is hot, add 1 disk and slowly cook it on one side until the bottom is spotted brown and the top starts to puff up, adjusting the heat as needed to get the bread to rise and brown easily. Turn the bread over and briefly cook it on the other side, then transfer it to a clean tea towel and cover it with the towel so it steams slightly. Repeat with the other breads, grilling only as many as you plan to eat immediately.

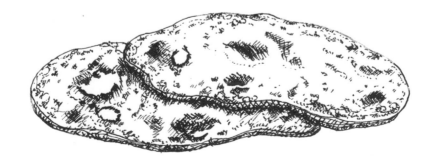

Huājuǎn 花捲

Flower Rolls

MAKES 16 BUNS

Flower Rolls are a popular and beautiful way to form steamed dough, and it seems like just about everyone has a unique way of making them. The following approaches are the most traditional and among the most delicious.

1 recipe traditional or fast steamed bread
  (page 398 or 400), through Step 4

NORTHERN-STYLE FLOWER ROLLS
¾ toasted sesame paste (page 413 or store-bought)
1 teaspoon or so dry-fried salt and pepper (page 440),
    or toasted Sichuan peppercorn salt (page 440)
¼ cup dark brown sugar, optional but very good

SOUTHERN-STYLE FLOWER ROLLS
Green onion oil (page 434) or other seasoned oil
4 green onions, trimmed and thinly sliced
1 teaspoon or so sea salt

1. Make the dough as directed, and when it has rested, lightly dust your work surface and pat the dough out into a squarish shape. Then use a Chinese rolling pin to roll it out into a rectangle 32 inches long and about 10 inches wide.

2. For directions on how to fill and shape these rolls, see the diagram to the right. If you are making northern-style flower rolls, spread an even layer of the sesame paste all over the surface of the dough, leaving the top 1-inch edge clean so that you can seal the rolls later on; sprinkle the salt and pepper over the paste and then the optional sugar. For southern-style flower rolls, spread a thin layer of oil evenly over the dough, again leaving the top 1-inch edge clean, and then sprinkle on the green onions and salt.

3. Prepare the steamer baskets as directed in the steamed bread recipes (page 398 or 400). Place the filled rolls on oiled steamer paper and let them rise once more before steaming as directed.

FLOWER ROLLS (*Huajuan*)

❶
Follow the diagram on page 395 up through Step 3. Roll out the dough and layer on the filling as directed. Starting from one of the long edges, roll up the dough gently so the filling does not get squeezed out.

❷
Pinch the long edge of the dough into the cylinder to seal it. Gently roll the length of dough to even it out.

❸
Cut off the two ends (you can steam these two raggedy pieces and reserve them as a cook's treat) and then slice the dough crosswise into 32 even pieces.

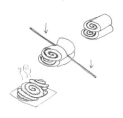

❹
To create a flower roll, stack 2 slices, place a chopstick or skewer lengthwise on top of the stack, and press down firmly to stick the slices together. Repeat with the rest of the dough until you have 16 double flower rolls.

Chuántóng mántóu 傳統饅頭

Traditional Steamed Bread, or Traditional Mantou

MAKES 16 BUNS

This bread and wheat pasta are the staple foods of North China. Simple to make, tasty, and filling, authentic *mantou* also serves as almost Proustian foods for many people of a certain age, because their taste and scent seem different now than they did back in the good old days.

The reason is that in most metropolitan areas, yeast has taken the place of the starter (or *levain*) long used in China. Just like in the West, wheat flours are being processed and bleached into mere shadows of their former selves, but it is hard to deny the ease that active yeast provides the average family cook when making *mantou* from scratch.

However, it's also hard to argue with tradition once you have tasted steamed breads made with the wild yeasts that multiply with incredible enthusiasm on your kitchen counter, turning plain old flour and water into an almost fruit-and-wine-scented froth. If you use the great organic wheat flour that is sold in health food stores nowadays, these breads become stellar.

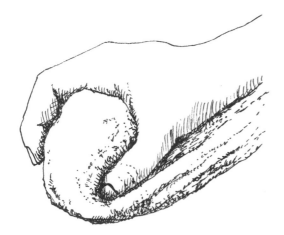

I realized what was missing only recently when I was talking about bread making with an acquaintance who had grown up in rural Jiangxi. She recalled how *mantou* and other raised breads had been made regularly in her Hakka family during the days before they were allowed to move to the great metropolis of Guangzhou, and I asked her what kind of leavening she used. She looked at me very surprised and said, "Why, *levain* [*miànzhǒng* 麵種], of course!" The starter would sometimes stay buried in a sack of flour for a long time before the family got around to digging it out again, and it would need only to be soaked in warm water to come alive, much like today's active yeast.

The recipe here will provide you with enough starter (about 6 cups) to make two batches of steamed buns, with extra left over to keep as a starter for next time. This is an easy and delicious way to turn pro.

STARTER
1 cup Chinese flour (page 386)

FIRST RISING
1 cup starter
2½ cups warm water
5 cups Chinese flour (page 386)

SECOND RISING
2 cups starter
½ cup warm water
½ teaspoon active dry yeast
2 tablespoons sugar
1 teaspoon sea salt
2½ cups Chinese flour, plus more as needed (page 386)
2 teaspoons baking soda
Spray oil, optional

1. Make the starter at least 2 weeks before you make steamed bread, as this will give it enough time to develop a good population of yeast and, even more important, excellent taste. In fact, the longer you keep and feed your starter, the better its flavor will be. Begin by placing the flour in a resealable clean container of some sort (a large glass jar with a cover or a plastic basin with a lid), and then mix in just enough warm water to create a thick batter, as if you were going to make pancakes. Cover the container with a thick-weave cloth to keep out dust and fruit flies and place it in a warm place. Stir the batter once a day and keep it covered. It should start to form bubbles within 3 to 5 days, depending upon how warm it is and what kind of yeasts you have wandering around your kitchen. When it is nice and bubbly, cover the container and refrigerate it until needed. To replenish the starter, mix whatever is left after making your bread dough with more flour and water to form a thick batter, let it form bubbles as before, and then refrigerate. This will happen faster and faster as your starter matures. Be sure and keep it fed, just like a pet. If you don't use it at least every couple of weeks, pour out all but ¼ to ½ cup and repeat the feeding steps.

2. About 18 hours before you plan to make the buns, measure out 1 cup of the starter into a 1-quart work bowl for the first rising. Thin it out with the warm water and then stir in the flour. Cover the bowl with plastic wrap, place it in a warm place, and let the mixture rest for about 16 hours, stirring it once at the halfway point.

3. Stir this mixture again and measure out 2 cups of the batter into a 2-quart work bowl for the second rising. Pour the rest of the starter (about 4 cups) into a covered container and refrigerate for something else. Stir in the warm water, yeast, and sugar and let it rest for about 30 minutes to let the yeast wake up. Then add the salt and about 2 cups flour to form a soft dough. Turn this out onto a work surface and knead it with more flour as needed (start with ½ cup and add more if necessary) until it is soft and only a tiny bit sticky.

4. Cover the dough with the plastic wrap and let it rest for an hour or so, until it has doubled in size. Poke 2 fingers into the middle of the dough; if the holes are still there after 5 minutes, the dough has finished rising. Sprinkle the baking soda on the dough and knead it in completely, adding a small amount of flour as needed.

5. Cut the dough into 16 pieces (see Step 4 on page 395), shape as desired (see page 401), dust lightly with flour, and let it rest covered for about 15 minutes. While the dough is resting, wet 2 large squares of coarse-weave cheesecloth, wring them out, and arrange them inside 2 steamer baskets, or use steamer paper or cupcake liners and spray with oil. Fill the bottom of the steamer with water (see page 49) and bring it to a boil. Arrange as many of the dough pieces in the steamer as will fit comfortably with about 2 inches between them, as they will rise more during the steaming; keep the rest of the dough pieces covered (see Tips).

6. Steam the buns for about 15 minutes, turn off the heat, and let them sit in the covered baskets for another 5 to 10 minutes so they don't deflate suddenly when the cover is removed. Repeat with the rest of the dough until all of the buns have been steamed. Either enjoy them while they're hot or let them cool down completely. They can be refrigerated in resealable plastic bags, or they can be frozen in a single layer on plastic wrap and then placed in resealable freezer bags. You can then steam them directly from the refrigerator or freezer.

A bamboo steamer works best for all steamed breads because the steam drips off more easily and is absorbed by the basket. Metal steamers tend to collect water around the edges and on the buns, which can make some of the buns wet on the bottom. If a metal steamer is the only kind you have, use a steamer liner of some sort—paper or cloth—and then remove the steamed buns to a clean towel, flipping them over so the wet bottoms are on top. They will dry out quickly as they cool.

Keep any finished buns covered and in a very cool place if they need to wait a while before being steamed, as this will prevent them from rising too quickly. If your kitchen is hot, place them in your refrigerator.

Jiǎnyì mántóu 簡易饅頭

Fast Steamed Bread, or Fast Mantou

MAKES 16 BUNS

For a long time, this was my go-to recipe for steamed bread. And it is pretty darned good, if I do say so myself. My ample pride in this recipe was corroborated by the unexpected praise I received from the daughter of a famous northern warlord: when she came over for dinner a long time ago, I served her these breads shaped into Flower Rolls (page 397) alongside a big plate of Beijing-Style Smoked Chicken (page 26). Delighted at their taste, she asked for the recipe, and I can't think of higher praise than that.

2 teaspoons active dry yeast
2 tablespoons sugar
1¼ cups warm water
3 cups Chinese flour (page 386), plus more for kneading
1 teaspoon sea salt
Peanut or vegetable oil for bowl and dough
2 teaspoons baking powder
Spray oil, optional

1. These rolls can be prepared up to 3 days in advance if they are refrigerated after steaming, or up to a few weeks in advance if frozen. Dissolve the yeast and sugar in the warm water. Allow the yeast to expand for about 20 minutes. If it is not foaming at this point, discard it and get some fresher yeast.

2. Refer to the Basic Directions for Raised Dough on page 395 as you work from this point through Step 5. Stir the flour and salt together in a large work bowl. Use chopsticks or a wooden spoon to mix in the yeast solution until fat flakes form. Turn the dough out onto a lightly floured smooth surface and use a pastry scraper and your free hand to scrape and knead the dough. When the dough is elastic and no longer sticks to the board, check the texture: a pinch of the dough should feel like an earlobe. Form the dough into a ball.

3. Clean the work bowl, dry it, and lightly oil both the bowl and the ball of dough. Transfer the dough to the bowl, cover tightly with plastic wrap, place the bowl in a warm place, and let the dough rise until doubled in size, about an hour. Punch down the dough and fold the edges in on the ball. Cover the bowl and let the dough rise again until it has doubled in size.

4. Turn the dough out onto a clean, smooth work surface and sprinkle with the baking powder, which will give it a bit of extra lift. Lightly knead the baking powder into the dough, cover the dough with the plastic wrap, and let it rest for about 10 minutes.

5. Lightly dust the board and then roll the dough into an even rope 16 inches long. (Use a ruler at this point for accuracy.) Cut the rope into 1-inch pieces. If you like, you can shape each piece into a ball by popping it out through your thumb and forefinger to form a perfect sphere (see below).

6. When all of the buns have been shaped, line 2 Chinese basket steamers with either steamer paper or cupcake liners and then spray the paper with oil. Alternatively, rinse coarse-weave cheesecloth with water, wring it out, and use it to line the baskets. Leave about 1 inch between the buns as you fill each basket with 8 buns. Set up your steamer (see page 49).

7. Steam the buns over medium heat for 10 to 15 minutes, until they have fully risen and are cooked through. Turn off the heat and allow the buns to sit in the covered steamer for about 10 minutes to prevent them from deflating once the steamer is uncovered. Enjoy them while they're hot or let them cool down completely. They can be refrigerated in resealable plastic bags, or they can be frozen in a single layer on plastic wrap and then packed into resealable freezer bags. You can then steam them directly from the refrigerator or freezer.

STEAMED BREADS (*Mantou*)

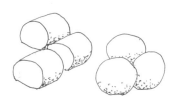

❶

Cut the dough as directed in Step 4 of the diagram on page 395. The dough can now be shaped any number of ways. The easiest is to leave the cut pieces as they are, so each one looks like a little loaf. They can also be shaped into balls.

❷

To make a smooth, round bun, pop the dough out from your fist between your thumb and forefinger, which is what the Chinese call the "tiger's mouth" (*hŭkŏu* 虎口), much like what is shown on page 259.

❸

Place each piece on oiled steamer paper or an oiled cupcake liner and let rise once more before steaming.

Fried Sesame Rolls

MAKES 16 ROLLS

Yeast breads have traditionally played a big part in the cuisines of North and West China. The reason is simple: Muslim traders settled down in these areas centuries ago, after following the Silk Road that stretches through Persia to today's Xi'an in Shaanxi Province. They brought new ideas and new art and new religions, as well as the foods of the Middle East and Central Asia.

Sesame seeds were another one of their imports. They became so beloved that they quickly and indelibly colored many of China's culinary traditions, most often in the form of the toasted sesame oil that now shows up in almost every corner of the nation.

I find these sesame buns, which are a specialty of Sichuan, particularly scrumptious. They offer a lovely contrast of crunch and softness, nuttiness and yeastiness. That they're exceptionally pretty makes them even more of a delight.

1 recipe traditional or fast steamed bread
   (page 398 or 400), through Step 4
3 tablespoons sugar
¼ cup hot water
Spray oil
1 cup raw white sesame seeds
About 2 cups peanut or vegetable oil

1. These rolls can be prepared up to 3 days in advance if they are refrigerated after steaming, or they can be frozen and fried at the last minute. Make the dough as directed.

2. Mix together the sugar and hot water and let cool to room temperature while you are working on the next step.

3. Lightly dust a clean, smooth work surface with flour, roll the dough into an even rope 16 inches long, and cut the dough into 1-inch pieces (see Step 4 on page 395). Cover the rest of the dough with plastic wrap while you work on each piece. Roll each piece into a smooth ball by popping it out through your thumb and forefinger to form a perfect sphere (see page 401), and cover it with the plastic wrap.

4. When all of the rolls have been shaped, line 2 Chinese steamer baskets with either steamer paper or cupcake liners and spray the paper with oil. At one end of your work surface, line up the balls of dough, the sugar water, a wide bowl filled with the sesame seeds, and finally the lined steamer baskets. Set up your steamer (see page 49).

5. Working with 1 roll at a time, use one hand to dip it into the sugar water and shake off any excess. Lightly toss the roll in the sesame seeds with your dry hand, gently knocking off any loose seeds, and place it on the steamer paper. Leave about 1 inch between the rolls as you fill each basket with 8 rolls.

6. Steam the rolls over medium heat for 10 to 15 minutes, until they are cooked through. Turn off the heat and allow the rolls to sit in the covered steamer for about 10 minutes to prevent them from deflating once the steamer is uncovered.

7. About 20 minutes before you want to serve the rolls, heat the oil in a wok over medium heat until a pinch of flour tossed in the oil immediately foams. Have a plate lined with paper towels next to the stove. Add a few rolls to the oil at a time and fry them on all sides until golden. Repeat with the rest of the rolls until done, keeping the fried rolls in a warm oven, if necessary. Serve hot.

Kǎofū 考麸

Raised Gluten

MAKES ABOUT 8 OUNCES

1 teaspoon active dry yeast
2 cups warm water
2 cups gluten flour (see Tip)
Spray oil

Back when my husband and I were vegetarians, raised gluten was a bit of a lifesaver. It was definitely meatless, but with just a little coaxing it could be turned into dishes that tasted and felt almost meaty. The problem was that my Chinese grocery stores here in California sometimes carried it, and sometimes not, and I was always a bit leery about how fresh it was and how many preservatives had been used, because raised gluten does not sit around well. In fact, I recommend freezing it if you do not use it the day it's made.

When I first went looking for recipes to make my own, none could be found in Chinese or in English. So I fiddled around and found to my delight that it was not that hard at all.

I like to make a batch of this, let it cool, and then tear it up into bite-sized hunks, the raggedier the better. The thin edges fry up crisply and contrast with the spongy centers. Plus, if you have these already prepped and in the freezer, a delectable dish of Jiangsu-style Four Happiness Gluten and Vegetables (page 124) can be tossed together in a matter of minutes.

1. Dissolve the yeast in the warm water and let stand for about 20 minutes, by which time you should have a good head of foam on top of the liquid.

2. Place the gluten flour in a medium work bowl, make a well in the center, and pour the liquid into it, using a silicone spatula to scrape out all of the yeast. Mix the liquid thoroughly into the gluten flour so it is completely moistened. You should have a spongy mass.

3. Spray a 9-inch round or 8-inch square cake pan with the oil. Scrape the dough into the pan and gently flatten the top as much as possible. Let the gluten rise until doubled in size. Place the pan in a boiling steamer (see page 49), cover, and steam for about 15 minutes, until a toothpick inserted into the center comes out clean. Remove from the steamer and let the gluten come to room temperature. Do not be alarmed if it collapses, as this is to be expected. Turn the pan over onto a work surface and lift off the pan. Tear the gluten into ragged pieces (different sizes are the tastiest, as some will crisp up and others will turn meaty), and store either in the refrigerator or freezer in a resealable bag.

Gluten flour is available in most health food stores; Bob's Red Mill is a good brand.

Red Date Steamed Buns

MAKES 16 BUNS

This is a Chinese New Year treat from the North, often made as one or two large steamed breads with fat red dates arrayed in a ring around the top. Making them as individual buns with baby dates is also beautiful for the holidays; they end up looking like a cross between alien spaceships, deep sea mines, and Christmas ornaments.

Remove the pits if you are serving these to children or people who have problems dealing with things like olive pits and crab shells. I like to make the buns in this recipe with all white flour so there's a dramatic contrast between the red and the white. This decoration uses nine dates per bun, which is a lucky number especially around the New Year because it conveys wishes that you get everything you want (*jĭurú* 九如).

1 recipe traditional or fast steamed bread
    (page 398 or 400), through Step 4
144 small dried Chinese red dates, with or without pits
    (about 13 ounces)

1. Make the dough as directed, and when it has rested, lightly dust your work surface, pat it out into an even rope 16 inches long, and cut the rope into 1-inch pieces. Roll each piece into a ball (see Step 2 in the diagram on page 401) and cover with a towel while you prepare the dates and the steamer.

2. Rinse the dates and pat them dry. Remove any small stems you find, as well as any odd-looking dates. Just make sure you have 144 dates when you're through.

3. Now comes the fun part: shaping the buns (see the diagram to the right). Cover the finished buns with a towel to let them rise a bit.

4. Prepare the steamer baskets and steam the buns as directed in the steamed bread recipes (pages 398 and 400). These can be frozen and reheated.

RED DATE STEAMED BUNS
(Hongzao Mantou)

❶ Form each ball into a half-dome shape by setting it squarely on a lightly floured work surface. Then, pinch a ½-inch-wide band from the left all the way over the top to the right.

❷ Use a paring knife to cut an incision through the band at the very top and slip a date through so that it is held by the tiny band of dough. Then, make a cut near the left and right sides of the band and slip dates into those, as well.

❸ Halfway up each side of the dome, cut 2 more holes and add 2 more dates.

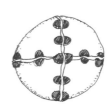

❹ Turn the bun 90 degrees and pinch a new band up both sides almost to the top; make incisions near the bottom and halfway up the sides so you can add 4 more dates to the bun, giving you a total of 9 dates per bun.

Bāozi 包子

Filled Steamed Buns, or Baozi

MAKES 16 BUNS

Baozi (also called "bao" in the West) are popular just about everywhere in China where steam is used to prepare food. They are found more often in street stalls and small restaurants than in homes, and they are popular for breakfast and afternoon snacks.

Baozi can be filled with all sorts of things depending upon the locale. North China has a serious love affair with pork-filled buns, the filling of which is pretty much identical to what you find in the many varieties of *jiaozi* (page 45) up there. The North is also where sweet bean paste and sweet date paste find their way into *baozi*. All of the buns are usually large.

Diners in the Yangtze River region tend to prefer smaller, thinner wrappers, such as those found on the popular, soupy little *baozi* called *xiaolongbao* (page 132). Rather than being made of raised dough, these are usually wrapped in unleavened plain hot-water dough (page 386), which gives the requisite tensile quality to each little parcel.

South China—especially Guangzhou—is the other place where *baozi* seem particularly divine (see the sidebar on page 219), although Sichuan certainly has its moments (see page 300). The teahouses in Guangzhou

and in Hong Kong have turned these *baozi* into combination pork-and-chicken buns, sweet mounds filled with bright yellow custard, and such iconic creations as the sweet roast pork buns called *char siu bao* (see Char Siu, page 206). Guangzhou's street stalls are also home to large buns designed especially for the working class. Because these were traditionally sold very cheaply, bones would be left in the chicken *baozi* so customers could be assured that they were indeed made out of poultry, rather than something much furrier that had been caught in a back alleyway.

A quick note on the nomenclature: although these buns are often referred to as bao in English, in Chinese they are almost invariably called *baozi* or something-something-*bao*—such as *xiaolongbao* or *char siu bao*, rather than plain old bao.

1 recipe traditional or fast steamed bread (page 398 or 400), through Step 4
2 cups any *jiaozi* filling (pages 45 and 47), potsticker filling (page 50), or sweet fillings (pages 442 through 445), the recipe on page 300, or just about anything you like that is not too soupy

1. Make the dough as directed, and when it has rested, lightly dust your work surface, pat it out into an even rope 16 inches long, and cut the dough into 16 equal pieces (see Basic Directions for Raised Dough on page 395). Roll each piece into a ball (see Step 2 in the diagram on page 401) and cover with a towel to let them rest while you prepare the filling and steamer (see page 49).

2. Lightly flour your work surface and place one of the balls of dough in front of you, keeping the rest covered. Flatten the ball with the palm of your hand. For directions on how to shape and fill *baozi*, see the diagram on pages 406 and 407.

3. Prepare the steamer baskets as directed in the steamed bread recipes and steam the *baozi* for 20 to 25 minutes. They can be frozen and reheated as directed in those recipes, too.

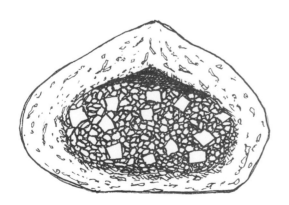

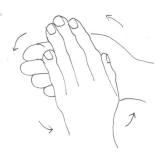

❶

Work on 1 piece at a time and keep the rest of the dough covered so it does not dry out. Lightly roll the piece into a ball between the palms of your hands.

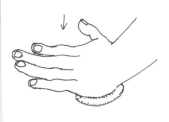

❷

Press down on the ball with the palm of your hand to flatten it into a disk.

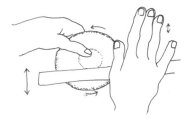

❸

Lift up a side of the disk with one hand and use a Chinese rolling pin in the other to roll the disk out into a thin circle. Do this by rolling down one edge of the disk from just below the center outward to the edge. Turn the disk counterclockwise (or clockwise, if you are left-handed) about 45 degrees and roll it out again; you will do this 8 times before you get back to the starting point and end up with a fairly even circle. Keep rolling and turning the dough until you have a circle of the desired diameter.

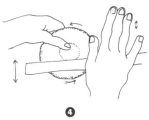

❹

As you roll out your dough, leave the exact center alone so you end up with what looks like an egg fried sunny-side up.

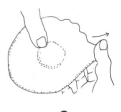

❺

The best *baozi* have an even layer of bread around the ball of filling, so it is important to make the top as thin as possible. However, you are going to be pleating that dough, which ends up making it pretty thick, so lightly pull the edges all the way around before folding them, which will thin them out and give the final circle the look of a sombrero.

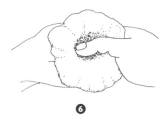

❻

To fill the *baozi*, make a cup shape with your left hand and poke the dough disk into that cup, so the base of the dough is cuddled up against your middle finger.

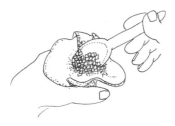

❼

Carefully place your filling inside the center of the dough. *Do not get any filling on the edges,* as the oil in the filling will make the dough impossible to seal.

❽

Pleat the top of the *baozi* closed: do this by using the thumb of your left hand to poke down the filling while you start to pinch the dough closed with the thumb, pointer finger, and middle finger on your right hand.

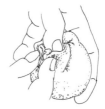

❾

Work your way around the edge, keeping the filling away from the pleats.

❶❶

If you keep all of the pleats tight, you will end up with a pointed top.

❶❶

If you release the pleats as you go along, you will end up with a little depression in the top, which is also pretty. Place the filled *baozi* on oiled steamer paper and let them rise once more before steaming.

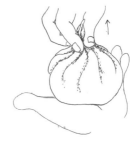

❶❷

For things like Chinese Hamburgers (page 52), follow the directions for filled steamed buns. Pleat the top as in Step 10 so that you have a pointed top. Pull the top up and away from the bun, and then nip off this tip at its base.

❶❸

Lightly roll the filled bun between your hands to smooth the pleated side a bit and ensure that it is well sealed.

Héyè juǎn 荷葉卷 and *guābāo* 刮包 (written as 刈包 in Taiwan)

Lotus Leaf Buns and Guabao

MAKES 20 BUNS

Made from basically the same recipe for steamed bread (page 400) that appears throughout most of North China, these are split half-moons that are as gorgeous to look at as they are delicious to eat.

The name comes, obviously, from their shape. And although they appear impossibly beautiful, they are a snap to make. All you need to do is whip up some Chinese steamed bread dough. Taiwan's version is even simpler and can be just as pretty.

I've played with this recipe, like I do with just about every Chinese classic, to produce more of the flavors and colors and textures that I enjoy. Here, I've added powdered milk and baking powder to the dough for a number of reasons. First, the milk adds a lovely aroma and gentle sweetness, and the baking powder gives the dough a head start on the rise so the buns turn out light and slightly chewy. The milk also does something that I really like: it adds tan speckles to the breads, making them more leaflike than ever.

Use Chinese flour here, as always; you will notice the difference as soon as you take a bite. In Chinese restaurants, these buns are generally made with low-gluten flour, which makes them rise quickly and saves time, but those breads always end up sticking to the teeth. On the other hand, regular American all-purpose flour is too hard, which gives the buns an unbecoming toughness.

Buns like these are traditionally served with things like Camphor Tea Duck (page 284) or Honey Ham (page 288). But even if you offer a simpler stuffing, like a crispy omelet (page 179), you will be rewarded with a dish that has been elevated from good to ethereal.

Offer a sweetish sauce (like the one on page 284) and some shredded green onions on the side, as these add more flavors and textures to this beautiful way of transporting good food from plate to mouth. Then, show your guests how to open up a bun and dab a bit of the sauce and onion in there before tucking in a piece of the main attraction. Use your hands or your chopsticks to pick up the sandwich and enjoy.

LOTUS LEAF BUNS (Heyejuan)

❶

Use a small rolling pin to roll a piece of the dough out into an oval about 4 inches by 3 inches.

❷

Paint half of the oval with some of the extra oil and then fold the other half on top to form a half circle. If you stop shaping it at this point, it is called a *guabao* and is used wherever rich meats are turned into sandwiches.

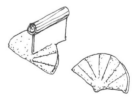

❸

To decorate the lotus buns, use a pastry scraper to lightly mark the half circle with radiating spokes so it resembles a leaf. You can even pinch the middle of the folded edge so it has a bit of a stem.

---

1 cup warm water

2½ teaspoons (1 envelope) active dry yeast

2 teaspoons sugar

1 teaspoon sea salt

3 tablespoons powdered milk (any kind, see Tips), optional

2 tablespoons peanut or vegetable oil (see Tips)

2¾ cups Chinese flour (page 386), plus more as needed

1 teaspoon baking powder

Peanut or vegetable oil for bowl

1. Pour the water into a food processor. Sprinkle the yeast over the warm water and add the sugar. Allow the yeast to wake up and foam, which will take about 20 minutes. Add the salt, optional powdered milk, oil, and flour and process until the ingredients come together in a nice smooth ball. You can also mix the ingredients together by hand in a medium work bowl. Oil a work bowl, place the dough in the bowl, turn the dough over a few times to coat it with the oil, and then cover the bowl with a tea towel or plastic wrap. Let the dough rise until it has doubled in size, which should take about an hour. It will be ready if when you poke your fingers into the dough, the impression stays there.

2. Lightly flour a clean, smooth work surface. Dump the dough onto the surface, knead it lightly, work in the baking powder, and shape it into a thick, even rope 20 inches long. Use a pastry cutter to cut the cord into 20 even pieces (see Step 4 in the diagram on page 395). Lightly dust the dough pieces with a bit of flour and cover any you aren't immediately working on with a dry tea towel.

3. Use a small rolling pin to roll a piece out into an oval about 4 inches by 3 inches (see the diagram to the left) and shape as directed. Place the finished buns on a clean towel and cover them with a second towel. Let the dough rise for about 15 minutes.

4. You will most likely have to steam these buns in batches, as most regular steamer baskets (see page 49) will hold only about 5 buns at a time. Steam the buns for about 15 minutes, until they have fully risen and are puffy. Remove the steamer from the heat and serve the buns hot. These can be made ahead of time and frozen. Just place the steamed buns in a single layer on a baking sheet lined with plastic wrap, freeze them, and then transfer them to a resealable freezer bag. To serve, steam them again until hot.

Experiment with different types of powdered milk here, if you like, as they will give you different results. Powdered nonfat milk is tasty and has a sweet aroma. Goat milk is slightly gamier, but I like it too, as it makes the buns' flavor more assertive.

Use whatever oil you like. Do note that peanut oil will give a slight peanut flavor to the finished buns, so use a more neutral oil if you think this might conflict with whatever you are using as the filling.

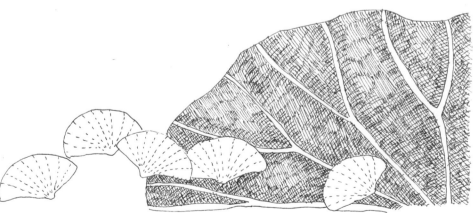

Zhá huángdòu 炸黄豆

Fried Soybeans

MAKES 1 CUP

Try these instead of peanuts when you need a bit of crunch in your life.

1 cup dried soybeans
Peanut or vegetable oil as needed (used oil is all right if it smells fresh)
Sea salt, optional

1. Soak the soybeans overnight until they are plump. Drain, rinse thoroughly, and then pat very dry with a towel.

2. Place the beans in a medium to large saucepan and cover with cool oil. Bring the oil to a simmer over medium heat, reduce the heat to low, and stir the beans now and then as they slowly cook. You will need to pay attention to the beans as they fry, since the oil will foam up as the water in the beans evaporates. As soon as the foaming begins to settle down, keep an even closer eye on the beans; they'll now begin to crisp up. Once the beans are a light golden brown, drain them in a sieve over a heatproof bowl.

3. Return the oil to the saucepan and turn the heat up to medium-high. When the oil starts to shimmer, carefully slide the beans back into the oil and fry them for a minute, until they are brown and taste nutty. Drain the beans once again and let them cool before eating. Note that they will crisp up as they cool. Store in an airtight container.

The best soybeans are found in good health food stores with a high turnover. Old soybeans get hard and musty, so shop at a busy place.

The beans are fried twice: first to evaporate the water and cook the beans, and then to crisp them up.

Huángdòufěn 黄豆粉

Toasted Soybean Flour

MAKES ABOUT ½ CUP

Chinese cooks often rely upon this to provide a subtly flavored coating for sticky things, like Rolling Donkeys (page 60), or as in Mapo Doufu (page 268), as a tasty thickener.

¾ cup fried soybeans (at left)

1. Use a paper towel to wipe off as much of the oil on the cooled beans as possible, then grind them (in a spice grinder, blender, or food processor) until reduced to a powder.

2. Store in a closed container in the refrigerator.

Zhá huāshēngmǐ 炸花生米

Fried Peanuts

MAKES ABOUT 3 CUPS

Every Chinese person (and just about everyone else) I know loves peanuts. There are a lot of Chinese recipes that call for fried or roasted peanuts, too, so I've tried just about everything to make the perfect peanut. But it wasn't until I figured out this method that I hit the jackpot. It's so easy that it seems almost silly to focus a recipe around it, but sometimes it's just a simple little thing, like starting with cool oil.

3 cups (or so) vegetable or peanut oil (used is all right if it smells fresh)
1 pound raw peanuts, with or without the skins
Sea salt, optional

1. Pour the oil into a wok and add the nuts. Place the wok over medium-high heat until the oil begins to bubble and then lower the heat to medium. Stir the nuts often as they cook. The heat must be high enough so that white foam forms around the nuts, but not so hot that the nuts burn. Stir and cook until the nuts are toasted and golden brown. Taste one to make sure: it should be nice and toasty with a touch of bitterness.

2. At this point the nuts are done, even if they are not crunchy, because that won't happen until they cool down. Use a slotted spoon or Chinese spider to scoop the nuts out of the hot oil into a work bowl lined with a couple of paper towels. Shake the nuts around in the bowl so most of the oil gets sponged up by the towels. Sprinkle on salt to taste while the nuts are still hot. To store, let cool completely and pack into an airtight container.

Kǎo huāshēngmǐ 烤花生米

Toasted Peanuts

MAKES ABOUT 3 CUPS

Another no-fail way to achieve perfect peanuts.

1 pound raw peanuts, with or without the skins

1. Heat the oven or a toaster oven to 275°F. Place the peanuts in a baking pan large enough to hold them in a single layer—the bottom of the broiler pan that might have come with your oven works well. Put the peanuts in the oven.

2. Slowly roast the nuts for about 1½ hours. Because the edges of your pan will be hotter than the center, you'll want to shake the pan once in a while and stir the nuts occasionally. When the peanuts start to smell cooked and begin to split along the center, taste one; if the rawness seems to have disappeared, taste a couple more from different parts of the pan just to be sure. It doesn't matter if the nuts are crisp yet, as that will happen once they cool down.

3. Pour the peanuts into a wide, heatproof bowl and let them come to room temperature. Store in a sealed container.

Běifāngshì lǔ huāshēng 北方式滷花生

Stewed Peanuts

MAKES ABOUT 2 CUPS

Peanuts may have originated in the New World, but they have become so beloved throughout China that they seem to have always been a part of its cuisines. No matter where you travel, from the extreme north to the most tropical south, peanuts are a vital part of the local offerings, present in everything from street foods to the most refined banquets. And with little wonder: they are delicious in just about every dish, savory or sweet.

We're all familiar with fried and roasted peanuts, but here you will find another treatment that acknowledges their innate bean nature. Cooking peanuts in liquid is a revelation: their taste, texture, and aroma are unlike anything else. And nobody does this method better than North China.

Slowly stewed in a classic broth of soy sauce and aromatics with just a touch of sweetness, these nuts are sheer perfection. This is also one of the simplest dishes you can toss together: just put everything in a pan and simmer away until the peanuts are barely soft and full of flavor.

Once you've tried this, you'll be tempted to make larger batches. Give in to this temptation. Stored in the refrigerator in a glass jar, these peanuts will keep for many days, thanks to the salt in the soy sauce.

2⅓ cups (12 ounces) skinned raw peanuts
¼ cup regular soy sauce
¼ cup mild rice wine
2 tablespoons sugar
3 star anise
¼ stick cinnamon
1 tablespoon whole Sichuan peppercorns
3 slices fresh ginger
Toasted sesame oil, optional

1. Rinse the peanuts and place them in a saucepan with the soy sauce, rice wine, sugar, star anise, cinnamon, Sichuan peppercorns, and ginger. Add water to cover the peanuts by about ½ inch.

2. Bring to a boil over high heat and then lower the heat to medium. Simmer the peanuts for about 10 minutes, skimming off any scum that rises to the surface.

3. Lower the heat to medium-low, so that the pan is barely simmering. Cook the peanuts slowly, adding water as needed to cover them. After about 45 minutes, start testing the peanuts every 5 minutes to see whether they're done yet. When ready, they will have no raw taste and will crumble easily; be sure not to overcook them until mushy.

4. Immediately raise the heat to high and boil down the liquid until only about ¼ cup remains. Cool the peanuts to room temperature and either serve with a little dribble of sesame oil, if you wish, or refrigerate them in a covered container.

I like to use peeled peanuts, rather than ones with their skins on, but this is a matter of personal taste.

Freshness is key here, so buy your peanuts from a health food store or a busy Chinese market.

Vary the seasonings to suit your tastes, adding or omitting spices, using green onions or garlic, and tossing the cooked peanuts in any of the seasoned oils on pages 434 to 436.

Keep an eye on the amount of liquid in the pan, as the peanuts will burn if the water boils off.

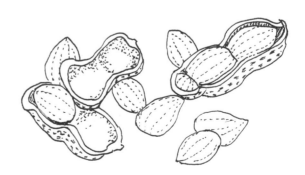

Kǎo zhīmá 烤芝麻

Toasted Sesame Seeds

MAKES 1 POUND

Toasting raw sesame brings out the flavor of these otherwise very mild, gently bitter seeds. Because they are so small, the seeds are dry-fried (that is, fried without any oil) until they start to burst like popcorn. The resulting toasted seeds are indispensable as a garnish for many dishes, and they can also be easily turned into toasted sesame paste (at right).

1 pound raw **sesame seeds** (white, unhulled, or black, depending upon your preference)

1. Pour the sesame seeds into a cool wok, place the wok over medium-high heat, and toss the seeds with a wok spatula the whole time. When the seeds start to pop and smell delicious, lower the heat a little to keep them from burning.

2. As the popping noise slows down, wet a fingertip, pat it on the toasted seeds, and take a taste. As soon as the seeds become fully toasted, pour them into a wide heatproof bowl and let them cool down to room temperature. Keep the toasted seeds in a covered container in a cupboard if you use them often, or stash them in the refrigerator for longer storage.

Májiàng 麻醬

Toasted Sesame Paste

MAKES ABOUT ¾ CUP

Unlike the Middle East, which prefers its sesame paste raw, Chinese people like it toasted so that the full flavor of the seeds comes to the forefront. You can buy sesame paste in any Chinese market, but unless you get the right brand, you'll most likely find it mixed with cottonseed oil or sugar or other unnecessary ingredients.

The solution? What else? Make it yourself.

Raw sesame seeds are available in health food stores, where the bulk bins make it easy to smell and taste whether the seeds are fresh. But go to an Asian market to find Japanese toasted sesame oil, which tends to be of the highest quality. Again, though, do your homework and read the label: it should say "100 percent sesame oil."

1 cup toasted sesame seeds (at left)
5 tablespoons or so toasted sesame oil
Sea salt, optional

1. Use a small food processor or a good-quality blender. Pour in the seeds and add a few tablespoons of the oil.

2. Puree the seeds on high, gradually adding the rest of the oil until you have a relatively smooth paste. Season the sesame paste with salt, if you plan to use it like peanut butter, but for Chinese recipes it is best to leave it unsalted. Store the paste in a covered jar in the refrigerator.

Xīnjiāng suānnǎi 新疆酸奶 or *Xīnjiāng yōugé* 新疆優格

Xinjiang-Style Yogurt

MAKES ABOUT 1 QUART

From eastern Europe out to China's western lands, yogurt is invariably part of the culinary landscape. I've long been a big fan, and so when my husband and I visited Xinjiang, I was eager to try the local yogurt. After all, who makes it better than nomadic people surrounded by cattle and sheep?

My opportunity came when our tour group went out for a dinner of whole roasted lamb in Ürümqi, Xinjiang's capital city. My husband and I were vegetarians at the time and so we bugged the waiters to bring us big bowls of yogurt to act as our very own protein course. They happily complied.

It turned out to be the richest, most delicious yogurt we'd ever tasted, and it took me quite a while to figure out how to make it back home. For one thing, my yogurt starter was never quite right; it tasted either too acidic or too bland or just not nutty enough. It was only when I started looking at a map and connecting the dots that I realized Bulgarian yogurt would be my key.

Keep in mind that China's Uyghurs are ethnically Turkic and speak a language that is related to Turkish. Now look to Bulgaria: there, too, the food has been colored by its massive neighbor on the right, Turkey. And so it makes sense that the yogurt we enjoyed in Ürümqi (the name even looks Turkish) would share the same yeasty mothers as that made by the folks who live on the edge of the Black Sea.

The yogurt we had was rich, almost like crème fraîche in texture and flavor. When I tried to replicate it, I found that heavy cream was too buttery and whole milk too thin, so half-and-half was the logical next step. And there we had it: yogurt just like the stuff Xinjiang moms make.

1 quart half-and-half
½ cup Bulgarian-style yogurt

1. Pour the half-and-half into a 2-quart heatproof container. Heat it in a microwave on high for 90 seconds to warm it through. Stir the liquid and give it short bursts (15 seconds or so) of heat until it reaches about 100°F; it should feel about body temperature when you hold the container against the inside of your wrist. Use a whisk to mix in the yogurt. When no lumps can be seen, cover the container with plastic wrap and place it in a warm area (see Tips).

2. Let the yogurt rest without stirring or moving it for at least 8 hours. At that point it should be nicely coagulated and completely solid. Check by lightly shaking the container: if the yogurt doesn't move at all, it's done. If the center is still liquid, leave it alone for another few hours.

3. Taste the yogurt; if you prefer it tarter, return the yogurt to its warm place for a few more hours to develop its flavor. When the yogurt is to your liking, chill it, still covered. It will stay fresh and tasty for about 5 days and can be used like any other yogurt, crème fraîche, or sour cream.

Use whatever Bulgarian-style yogurt you prefer. I have come to like an organic brand called White Mountain that is available in health food stores.

Organic half-and-half is—to my mind, at least—tastier than supermarket brands. Under no condition use "fat-free half-and-half," which is basically nothing more than a mixture of nonfat milk and sugar.

The best environment for growing your own yogurt is somewhere out of the way, warm, and still. I always turn to my oven for this. Either the pilot light in a gas oven or the light in an electric oven should provide just the right temperature for fast growth of the yeast. If your oven is too hot, you can also wrap the warm container from Step 1 in a couple of thick towels and place it in a warm part of the house.

Jiǔniàng 酒酿·

Fermented Rice

MAKES 1 LARGE JARFUL

The first time I heard about Chinese fermented rice was from a fellow American student in Taipei. She told me with singular excitement that she had just seen people eating rice wine soup for breakfast, that she had tried a bowl, and that it was really, really good.

Intrigued at the thought of enjoying a hot toddy sometime between getting up and yet another day of slogging through my impenetrable Chinese textbooks, I sped down to the alley she'd described and ordered a big bowl of *jiǔniàng dàn* 酒釀蛋, or fermented rice with a poached egg floating inside. Sweet, perfumed, and definitely alcoholic, this was sheer heaven. I broke out in a sweat and turned up for class with a shiny red face, happier than usual, and very sure of where I was going to dine the next morning.

I soon discovered that this dish could be served in a number of other ways: with little rice pearls (page 144) at a Beijing-style shop, or with sliced rice cakes (*nian'gao*, page 136) at the stand run by a guy from Ningbo, or with larger rice balls stuffed with ground black sesame at the Shanghainese place. Once I had gotten over the sheer novelty of this spectacular winter breakfast, I noticed that the locals usually clutched something crunchy in one hand while spooning up the sweet soup with the other. Yes, of course, I thought— hard with soft, crunchy with chewy, plain with sweet, cool with hot. All the Chinese principles of yin and yang right there before 8 a.m.

When my husband and I returned to the States, one of my first orders of business was to make big crocks of this fermented rice throughout the cold months. Warmed to our toes and chock-full of what must have been massive amounts of alcohol-induced endorphins, we ate this hot, sweet soup morning and night, and I also began to use it in dishes like Fish and Bean Curd in Fermented Bean Sauce (page 272).

What is particularly endearing about homemade fermented rice is that it is incredibly easy and cheap.

The only unusual ingredient is the yeast, which you can get from almost any Chinese grocery store, and which keeps practically forever as long as you close it up in a zip-top bag and freeze it. (Do note that if it's kept outside, such as in a pantry or cupboard, it will often turn buggy. Check the yeast carefully before you buy it, and only take it home if it's pure white, with no suspicious dust clinging to the bottom of the bag.)

Of course, you can probably buy *jiuniang* already made in the refrigerated section of your favorite Chinese grocery store. But it's expensive that way and never as good as homemade. Besides, if you have a big batch of it sitting in your fridge, you will have many more good reasons to enjoy it.

Having made this for years, I have finally perfected the technique. When I started out, every Chinese recipe I read informed me in no uncertain terms that the rice should be fermented v-e-r-y s-l-o-w-l-y. I did what they said and watched as batch after batch lost out in the race of yeast against mold. My secret is this: get the yeast off to a roaring start and there will be no contest at all. Once the yeast has taken over the jar—preferably in less than 24 hours—the rest of the fermentation process is pretty much clear sailing.

The way I get the yeast to take off so quickly and subdue any errant mold spores is threefold:

- First, I use a bit of cornstarch and sugar, so that the yeast can have something to feed on immediately, without waiting for the rice to break down into manageable bites.
- Second, I use boiled water, so that my rice mixture stays clean, clean, clean.
- And finally, I put the inoculated rice in a very warm place for the first 24 hours to encourage the fermentation to begin.

The other instruction I can't stress enough is that everything that touches the fermented rice must be absolutely clean. If there is even a whisper of oil or contamination anywhere along the way, the whole batch can go south in an instant. Wash every utensil thoroughly, including your bamboo steamers, your

continued

cheesecloth, and of course your hands. If some steamed rice hits the counter instead of the jar, just eat the wayward grains rather than risk corrupting the rest of the rice.

Once the rice has started to exude liquid, it will smell faintly yeasty and fruity, but not yet alcoholic; that will take a couple more days of fermentation. As the yeast grows, it will release lots of carbon dioxide, which will create bubbles and cause the mass of steamed rice to float. Your jar will need a safety valve to keep from exploding. For this reason, I put a couple layers of cheesecloth and a sheet of plastic wrap between the jar and the lid. This also keeps any curious fruit flies from invading my precious rice.

I encourage you to double or triple this recipe once you get the hang of it. The directions are very detailed, but you will find that it's not at all hard after the first time around. This is a great recipe to master; you'll look incredibly competent once you're cooking away with your own homemade hooch.

3 pounds round or long-grain sticky rice
1 Chinese wine yeast ball
2 cups boiling water cooled to room temperature
    (for fermenting), divided into ¼ cup and 1¾ cups
Lots of boiled water cooled to room temperature
    (for rinsing)
2 tablespoons sugar
1 tablespoon cornstarch

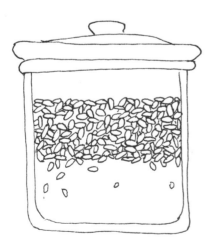

MODERN METHOD

1. You will need a very clean 2-quart glass jar with a lid plus an electric rice cooker. Start by scrubbing the jar and the insert for the rice cooker with soap and water, pouring boiling water over them, and allowing them to air-dry.

2. Rinse half of the rice 3 times in running water and drain the rice well in a sieve. Do not soak the rice. Fill the cooker using the cup that came with it, add the amount of water the cooker suggests, cover, and turn on the cooker. When the rice is fully cooked, repeat with the other half of the rice. (Do note that the measuring cups that come with rice cookers do not hold 1 standard cup, but rather contain around ¾ cup. To avoid confusion, just follow the directions on your rice cooker and use the cup that came with it.)

3. While the rice is cooking, place the yeast ball in a small, clean bowl and pour in ¼ cup of the cooled water designated for fermenting. Allow the yeast to soften, then place a very clean sieve with medium holes in the sink. Dump one portion of cooked rice into the sieve and rinse it under cool tap water to break up any clumps. Shake off the water and pour some of the cooled, boiled rinsing water over the rice. Drain the rice again and put it into the clean jar. Repeat this step with the rest of the rice until all of it has been rinsed.

4. When all of the rice has been placed in the jar, sprinkle the sugar and cornstarch on top. Mash the softened yeast ball with a clean spoon and add it to the jar. Use the remaining 1¾ cups cooled water to rinse out the bowl before pouring this water into the rice, too, so you get every last bit of the yeast. Wash your hands thoroughly and use one hand to gently toss the rice together with the other ingredients. Pat the rice into a more or less smooth layer, and then form a well in the center, giving the wine a place to gather the first day.

5. Clean off the top and insides of the jar with a clean paper towel, cover the jar with a piece of clean cheesecloth and plastic wrap, and then put the lid on loosely enough to allow air to escape but securely enough to keep any insects out. Use a felt pen to write the date on the jar so you'll know when you made this batch.

6. Wrap the jar with a kitchen towel and place it in a very warm place, like a gas oven with only the pilot light on or an electric oven with just the oven light on. Let the jar sit undisturbed for 24 hours. Check it after that time. There should be liquid in that well you made, and the top of the rice should be free of mold. (If mold forms on the rice, it was either contaminated somewhere along the line or wasn't fermented in a warm enough place. Take a deep whiff of what's inside your jar: if it has the aroma of wine, swish the liquid over the top of the rice, as the alcohol will kill any errant mold spores. Do this a couple of times a day until there is absolutely no sign of spoilage. If it smells bad, though, toss it and start over.)

7. Remove the jar from the oven and place it in a relatively warm place, like on the kitchen counter, so that you can watch the wine formation occur. After 2 or 3 days, the mass of rice will be floating on top of the wine. It will be ready in about a week, but it only improves as the wine ages. Sniff it now and then—you can even take a taste with a really clean spoon—to keep track of its progress and make certain the flavor is sweet and alcoholic. When you're pleased with the taste, store the fermented rice in the refrigerator to keep it from fermenting any more and turning sour.

TRADITIONAL METHOD

1. You will need a very clean 2-quart glass jar with a lid, very clean cheesecloth, and very clean steamer baskets (metal is best, since you can easily get rid of any oil and contaminants). Four baskets are needed to steam the rice all at once; if you have fewer baskets, you can steam the rice in batches, but be careful not to make your rice layers too thick, or the rice will cook unevenly and take forever. (I know this from personal experience, since I'm always looking for shortcuts.) Start by scrubbing the jar and baskets with soap and water, pouring boiling water over them, and allowing them to air-dry. Launder the cheesecloth if it isn't brand new, rinse it out well, place it in a clean colander, and pour boiling water over it before letting it air-dry, too.

2. Rinse the rice 3 times in running water and then cover it with cool water by at least 2 inches; allow the rice to soak for 8 hours and up to overnight. If you are not going to steam it right away, place the soaked rice in a clean container and refrigerate.

3. Prepare a pot or an old wok to hold your baskets and fill it partway with water (see page 49). Have ready a pot of boiling water and a very clean slotted spoon.

4. Line your baskets with at least 2 layers of the clean cheesecloth, so there is enough to go up the sides all around and even drape over the edges; this will keep the rice from dribbling out. Drain the rice.

5. Use the slotted spoon to layer the rice into each basket, spreading it out in an even layer about ½ inch thick. Fold the cheesecloth over the top of the rice and repeat with the rest of the rice in your other baskets. Stack the baskets, cover, and steam the rice for about 20 minutes. Reverse the position of the baskets, so that the top basket is on the bottom and so forth. Pour a pot of boiling water over the top layer of rice; this will filter down through the other baskets and help the rice plump up, as well as fill up the bottom of your steamer. Cover and steam the rice for another 15 to 20 minutes, until the rice is cooked but not soggy. Remove the baskets from the steamer and let them cool off for about 10 minutes.

6. Starting from Step 3, follow the Modern Method directions to the end.

Hóngzāo 紅糟

Red Wine Lees

ABOUT 3 CUPS WINE AND ABOUT 1 POUND
RED WINE LEES

Nothing symbolizes Northern Fujian-style cooking more than its red wine lees, called either *hongzao* in Mandarin or *ang chow* in the Northern Fujian dialect. Made in much the same way as fermented rice (page 415), this local concoction is flavored and colored by a remarkable ingredient called red yeast rice, or *hóngqúmǐ* 紅麴米, a type of rice grain coated with *Monascus purpureus*.

The Chinese have enjoyed the health benefits of this cholesterol-lowering mold for countless years, but the West has only recently started to pay attention to red yeast rice as a medicine. Few outside of China know how good it tastes when brewed the right way. You could even be forgiven if you made it just for its deep crimson hue and winey aroma.

Red wine lees can sometimes be found already fermented and ready to use in their paste form, usually in the refrigerated section of a Chinese grocery store. However, if you enjoyed making your own fermented rice, you'll find that this recipe is a snap.

1 pound round or long-grain sticky rice
2 ounces red yeast rice
Lots of boiling water cooled to room temperature
1 tablespoon sugar
1 Chinese wine yeast ball
1 tablespoon cornstarch

1. Complete Steps 1 and 2 of this recipe the day before you plan to steam the rice. Rinse the rice under running tap water, and then place it in a medium work bowl. Cover the rice with cool tap water by about 2 inches. Leave the rice to soak for 8 hours and up to overnight.

2. While the rice is soaking, place the red yeast rice in a very clean 2-quart jar with a lid. Cover it with 3 cups of the cooled boiled water, add the sugar, and stir. Cover the jar and let it sit for 8 hours and up to overnight to wake up the mold.

3. The next morning, steam and rinse the sticky rice as in fermented rice, using either the modern (page 416, Step 2) or traditional (page 417, Steps 3 to 5) method.

4. While the sticky rice is steaming, place the wine yeast ball in a small bowl and barely cover it with cooled boiled water so it can soften. After the sticky rice has been steamed and rinsed, smash the wine yeast ball with your fingers or a fork. Add the sticky rice, the smooshed yeast ball and its soaking water, and the cornstarch to the jar with the red yeast rice and its soaking liquid. Stir the ingredients together with a very clean wooden spoon. Cover the jar loosely so carbon dioxide can escape but insects can't get in (see page 417). Place the jar in a warm place as directed in the fermented rice recipe (Step 7) and stir or shake it once a day for a week to evenly distribute the yeast and its food.

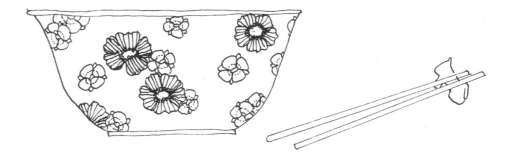

5. After a few days, check the jar. If it smells alcoholic and the rice has formed a raft that floats on top of the wine, move the jar to a cool area out of direct sunlight, keeping the lid loosely screwed on.

6. When the rice has broken down enough to form a much thinner raft on top of the wine, it's time to strain out the solids. It will have taken a month or longer for this to happen, depending upon the heat of your kitchen. Place a few layers of very clean, fine cheesecloth in a very clean sieve over a bowl. Carefully ladle the rice and wine into the cheesecloth, giving the wine a chance to dribble down into the bowl before adding more. When all of the wine has been decanted into the bowl, bring the corners of the cheesecloth together and tie the ends. Place a small plate on top of the cheesecloth bundle and then put a can that weighs about a pound on top of the plate to gently press down on the lees and extract as much wine as possible. Cover everything with a clean towel to keep out insects, and leave the lees to slowly drip for a couple of hours. The lees should end up being moist but not wet, with the consistency of fairly dry mashed potatoes.

7. Empty the drained lees into a very clean jar, label it, cover the jar, and refrigerate. They will keep for a long time this way, but you can mix in a bit of salt if you want to keep it for more than a few months. The wine can be decanted into very clean bottles. Discard the solids at the bottom of the bowl, or use them in any dish that calls for red wine lees.

The only unusual ingredient here is that red yeast rice, but it is becoming more available nowadays in the dried-foods sections of Chinese markets, usually near the beans or herbs. Whenever you run across it, snag a bag or two and store in the freezer or refrigerator, along with any Chinese wine yeast balls that are left over from your last wine-making session.

As with fermented rice, the main requirement for success with this recipe is that absolutely everything be spanking clean. Use only freshly cleaned utensils and containers, making sure that oil never touches anything.

Patience, too, is key. It takes months to develop the flavor of the lees. You can keep them up on your shelf while they ferment, however, enjoying their color as they take their sweet time to mature.

The liquid you decant will age into a nice cooking wine. It will keep a long time—even improving as it ages further.

Nánrǔ 南乳

Red Fermented Bean Curd "Cheese"

MAKES ABOUT 1 PINT

I've had an indiscreet love affair with the stuff called *nanru* for nigh on three decades now. If you want to taste something that, in its natural state, is beyond your wildest imagination, then have I got a gift for you. After waiting six months for fermentation, with only occasional tastes along the way, I recently opened up a jar that had waited so patiently for my attentions and discovered ambrosia. I devoured it with singular pleasure and instantly regretted that I hadn't made a couple of additional gallons of this brined wonder.

The magical transformation that took place in that jar is hard to relate; bits of the bean curd actually sparkled on my tongue. Fermentation was still going on, and as I scooped the *nanru* into my mouth, tiny bubbles of carbon dioxide were exploding on my taste buds. That is one reason why this is the best recipe ever.

Of course, making any kind of fermented bean curd is nothing less than an act of faith. Those slimy squares of rotting curd look dangerous, like they could cause severe gastric distress, if not death.

But you will find that when your bean curd hits the perfect state of moldiness—what Andrea Nguyen (*Asian Tofu*) called the "3S criteria": slime, splotches, and stink—that the bean curd actually smells pretty good. My last batch brought a breadlike, yeasty bloom to the air, and when I sampled one of the moldy squares (yes, I am insane), it tasted like a soft Camembert.

Here is the recipe, one that more or less follows Andrea's wonderfully precise directions, which she says were influenced by *Florence Lin's Chinese Vegetarian Cookbook*, a work written by my good friend and mentor. Their method gives the bean curd just the right environment to mold perfectly. The brine and some of the other techniques here and in the next recipe, of course, are the result of lots of guesswork

and good luck and memories of what my mother-in-law told me, too.

By the way, I always multiply this recipe by six. I know; I should be in a twelve-step program.

1 block (13½ ounces or so) extra-firm bean curd (see Tips)
1½ tablespoons sea salt
3 tablespoons red wine lees (page 418)
½ cup wine left over from red wine lees (page 418),
   or a mild rice wine (see Tips)
½ cup or so boiling water cooled to room temperature
Sugar

1. Wash your hands and cutting board and everything else so that there is absolutely no oil or contamination.

2. Cut the bean curd in half horizontally and then into pieces that are more or less an inch square. Lay a tea towel (something with a smooth weave, rather than terry cloth) in a clean rimmed pan on your kitchen counter and then place the bean curd squares on top of the towel so they don't touch. Lay another towel on top of the squares, place a smaller pan on top of that, and then weight the whole thing down with 2 to 3 pounds of cans, pans, or whatever. This will gently squeeze most of the moisture out of the bean curd. The squares will feel relatively dry after a couple of hours.

3. Have a glass baking dish ready—one that is (as always) super clean. Place the squares in the dish so that they don't touch one another, as this gives each side more of a chance to grow mold. Cover the pan with plastic wrap and use a toothpick or skewer to punch about 10 holes in the plastic so the gases can escape and the molds soaring around in your kitchen can work their way into this welcoming platter of food.

4. Place the dish in a warm place away from breezes (an unheated oven with the door cracked open is handy), and wait for about 2 days, until the bean curd is barely covered with yellowish spots. Remove the plastic wrap and reserve for the next step.

5. Carefully clean a 1-pint jar and lid, and then rinse them out with boiling water, turn them upside down, and let them air-dry. Prepare a clean fork or a couple of toothpicks for handling the bean curd. Use these to carefully pick up each square and place it in the jar; broken pieces can go in the center, where no one will be the wiser. When all of the squares have been transferred to the jar, lightly cover it with the reserved plastic wrap and return it to the warm place until the bean curd is completely covered with yellowish mold, looks very moist, and has a yeasty smell. The time it takes for the bean curd to mold perfectly will vary according to your kitchen temperature but usually takes about one to three days. Check on it daily, and when it's ready, proceed immediately.

6. Spoon the salt and wine lees on top of the bean curd squares and then pour in all of the wine and enough of the cooled water to almost reach the top of the jar. Cover the jar tightly with the lid and gently rotate the jar back and forth like a seesaw to distribute the solids and liquids. Untwist the lid a bit so that gases can escape as the bean curd ferments. Label the jar with the date before placing it in a cool place, like the pantry or even the refrigerator. After about a month, add a tablespoon of sugar to the jar and then lightly reseal and return it to a cool spot. After another month, add another tablespoon of sugar. By the third month, take a very clean spoon and taste the sauce; if it still needs a bit more sugar, add it (see Tips).

7. By the fifth or sixth month, your fermented bean curd cheese will be ready. Always use a very clean spoon to remove the squares as needed and store the jar in the fridge. It will keep for a very long time, and the sauce can be used again in your next batch, or in any dish that calls for red fermented bean curd.

WHITE BEAN CURD "CHEESE"

Dòufǔrǔ 豆腐乳
Makes about 1 pint

Follow the preceding directions using the following ingredients:

1 block (13½ ounces or so) extra-firm bean curd (see Tips)
1½ tablespoons sea salt
½ to 1 teaspoon chili flakes, and/or 1 teaspoon ground
    toasted Sichuan peppercorns (page 441), and/or
    ½ teaspoon toasted fennel seeds
½ cup mild rice wine
½ cup or so boiled and cooled water

Use extra-firm bean curd here, not firm or anything softer. The reason for this is that the curd will become incredibly soft as it molds, and extra-firm is the only type (in my experience, at least) that keeps its shape relatively easily. Don't worry, though, as the fermented result will still have the consistency of custard.

I always recommend organic, non-GMO (not genetically modified) bean curd. For that matter, your corn, soy, and anything that is made with them should always be non-GMO for your health and for the planet's. End of speech.

If you don't have any wine left over from your red wine lees expedition, use a mild rice wine like Taiwanese rice wine (Taiwan *mijiu*). Shaoxing's flavor will fight too much with that of the Fujian lees.

How much sugar you use depends on two major things: the flavor of your red wine lees and your palate. The sugar will help feed the yeast and form those delightful bubbles, but don't overdo it. When it tastes right, stop.

Good *nanru* is most traditionally served as a side dish with Congee (page 226), and I love it that way. But even better is when a single cube is placed on top of a bowl of freshly steamed rice (get the best you can) or slathered inside of a split *mantou* (pages 398 and 400). You see, just as with ripe Western cheeses, *nanru* pairs well with things that possess a starchy sweetness and welcomes a bit of blandness to play against its salty pungency. Of course, if you are a serious addict like me, you might find yourself nibbling on a spoonful while staring mindlessly out the window, licking bits off the spoon, letting them dissolve in a shimmer of bubbles on your tongue and lips, and then going back for more until, with little warning, the jar is empty.

Xiándàn 鹹蛋

Brined (Salted) Eggs

MAKES 1 DOZEN

Brined eggs, or "salted eggs" as they are known in China, are a staple throughout much of the country. We adore them in our family as a side dish for Congee (page 226), atop a steamed Taiwanese ground pork patty with pickles (page 209), tucked inside moon cakes (page 236), as delicious little morsels hidden within Hakka Tamales (page 228), and as the "golden sand" (page 123) that gilds certain Shanghainese stir-fries. This is definitely a recipe worth getting to know on a close personal basis.

1½ cups sea salt

6½ cups boiling water

12 large fresh chicken eggs that have no cracks
     or other damage to the shells

1 inch fresh ginger, thinly sliced

2 star anise

1 tablespoon whole Sichuan peppercorns

3 dried Thai chilies

3 cloves garlic, lightly smashed

2 tablespoons Shaoxing rice wine

1. Clean a tall 2-quart jar and its lid. Find a disposable plastic lid (from restaurant takeout or a plastic yogurt container, for example) that is about the same diameter as the jar; wash it carefully and drain.

2. In a large pitcher or bowl, dissolve the sea salt in the boiling water. Allow the water to cool down completely to room temperature before proceeding. (You don't want to cook the eggs at this point; they must be brined while still raw.)

3. Gently lower the eggs one by one into the jar. Add the rest of the ingredients, and then fill the jar with the salted water to within about 1 inch of the rim. Toss out any extra salted water.

4. Squeeze the plastic lid into the jar so that it keeps the eggs submerged in the brine. It's all right if the lid is at an angle; the only thing that matters is that the eggs are completely submerged.

5. Cover the jar and place it in a cool place. Check 1 egg after about 3 weeks by cracking it into a bowl. The yolk should be dark orange and hard, while the white should be clear and very salty. If the egg is cured enough, remove the rest of the eggs from the brine and store them in a closed container in the refrigerator until you want to use them. If they haven't cured completely, continue to brine them, testing an egg every couple of days.

6. Eggs that are not to be eaten within a couple of weeks should be hard-boiled (see page 461).

7. You can keep the brine and use it again; just store it in the fridge. Or, make a new batch with different flavors. This brine is so cheap that you can afford to be wasteful here.

Traditionally, brined eggs are made with duck eggs, whose large shells turn an even lovelier shade of blue during their weeks in the salted water. But since duck eggs are relatively hard to find, I've substituted large chicken eggs. The taste is similar except that duck yolks tend to be a bit more buttery.

One nice thing about making your own brined eggs is that you can use any variety of egg you like. You can also flavor the egg whites, something I've never seen done by Chinese cooks.

Don't flavor the brine if you plan to use the yolks in a sweet recipe, like the one for moon cakes.

Huāguā 花瓜

Huagua Pickles

MAKES ABOUT 1 CUP

3 Persian or Japanese cucumbers
4 tablespoons regular soy sauce
2 tablespoons sugar
2 tablespoons pale rice vinegar
1 piece slice dried licorice root

Few pickles have the distinctively Taiwanese taste that these little guys do. For the longest time, the only way we could ever enjoy *huagua*, or "flower squash," was in jars or cans direct from Taiwan. Whenever my husband would get a craving, I would find him lingering in front of the pickle shelves at the local Chinese grocery store, trying to decide among the different brands.

I've always liked these pickles for the lovely piquancy they add to many Taiwanese ground pork dishes. Simple and luscious, they make for an inspired combination. But I could rarely get too excited about the pickles by themselves; they always tasted too much like the container from which they'd just emerged, and there was a strong undercurrent of preservatives with names too long to pronounce. The Chinese have a word for this kind of flavor: *mèn* 悶, or "stale."

If you've ever had a good deli pickle out of a barrel—crispy and garlicky and still just a tad raw in the center—you know what I'm holding up as my personal gold standard, which I've tried to match here.

1. Rinse the cucumbers, pat dry, and trim off the ends. Slice the cucumbers into ¼-inch-thick rounds. Place the rounds in a small saucepan and add the rest of the ingredients.

2. Bring everything to a boil for exactly 1 minute and then remove from the heat. Allow the cucumbers to cool to room temperature and then pour the cucumbers and marinade into a clean jar. Poke the pickles down into the jar so that the marinade covers them completely; this will help keep them from turning bad. Cover the jar and chill the pickles overnight. Use within a week or two and keep refrigerated. Use a clean pair of chopsticks or a fork to pluck them out to cut down on contamination.

Persian or Japanese cucumbers are the perfect size for these pickles, and they do not have to be peeled first. So-called pickling cucumbers are tougher skinned and much thicker, while salad cucumbers are just wrong in every way. Hold out for the slender ones here.

Licorice root is said to have all sorts of medicinal properties, but the small amount used here is just for flavor, as a simple background note, one that is very subtle yet very authentic. If you can't find any, a pinch of fennel or anise will be a close enough match.

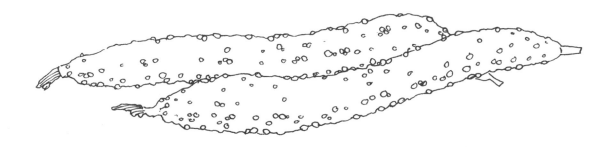

Pào hónglàjiāo 泡紅辣椒

Pickled Red Chili Peppers

MAKES ABOUT 1½ PINTS

As with so many easily canned items, this condiment can often be found on a Chinese grocery shelf. And many of those pickled peppers are quite good. But none are as stunning as the ones you can make yourself.

When you have a jar of pickled chiles made from truly fresh ingredients, the taste is a couple of thousand times more wonderful than anything a commercial producer can make. Plus, you can pick exactly the ingredients you like, mix up aromatics to suit your palate, and play with the salt-sugar-vinegar ratios until the wheels come off.

That's precisely what I did. I was wandering around a huge Chinese market in San Francisco, poking through the vegetable displays and feeling very uninspired, when I noticed net sacks full of Thai chilies. To call these chilies red is sort of an understatement. These were the true scarlet of fire engines, and I immediately knew what they were destined to become.

The thing that bothers me about many commercial pickled chilies is that they are so one-note. There's intense heat, of course, but not a whole lot of flavor. So I've added Sichuan peppercorns for their fresh piney aroma, star anise to bring a relatively indefinable spicy note to the brine, and Chinese brown slab sugar to make things a little more pleasant and aromatic. The results are delicious—and gorgeous.

This is a truly simple recipe, one you could put together while watching an old movie or a ballgame. If you have sensitive skin, wear disposable gloves and resist the temptation to rub your face. And under no circumstances should you touch your eyes if there is chili juice on your hands.

The aromatics in here can be adjusted at will. These are just guidelines, and loose ones at that.

8 to 10 ounces fresh or frozen and defrosted red Thai or serrano chilies
4 cups water
1 piece slab brown sugar, or 2 ounces (about 6 tablespoons) light brown sugar
1½ ounces sea salt (about 7½ teaspoons)
2 star anise
1 teaspoon whole Sichuan peppercorns
1½ tablespoons white liquor

1. Clean and sterilize 3 half-pint canning jars and lids, or one 1-pint and 1 half-pint jar and lids. Have 2 or 3 plastic spoons cleaned and ready.

2. Wash the chilies and pat them dry. Remove the stem ends by pulling them off and trim away any less than perfect parts. Pack the chilies vertically into the prepared jars, with the cut sides on top as much as possible.

3. Pour the water into a very clean saucepan and add the sugar, salt, star anise, and Sichuan peppercorns. Bring to a boil over high heat, cover, lower the heat, and simmer until the sugar and salt have dissolved. Remove the pan from the heat and let the brine come to room temperature.

4. Pour the brine over the chilies and distribute the whole spices more or less equally among the jars. (If you're using 3 jars, do this by pulling some of the petals off of the star anise.) The chilies will float to the top; to keep them submerged, place a plastic spoon inside the jar where it curves in toward the lip, and then break or bend the handle so the whole thing can be slipped into the jar and used to hold down the chilies (see Tips).

5. Pour ½ tablespoon of the white liquor into each half-pint jar or 1 tablespoon into the pint jar. Cover the jars loosely so gases can escape, wipe them clean, and label them. Place the jars in a cool, dark place so that the contents can ferment. The peppers will be ready as early as 2 weeks later, but they improve with age; tighten the lids when the peppers have fully fermented. Check the jars occasionally to ensure the chilies remain submerged. If any mold forms, remove it, wipe down the inside of the jar with a paper towel dipped in white liquor, and add a bit more liquor to the jar. When the chilies are just as you like them, store the jars in the fridge or process them in a hot-water bath for 10 minutes.

Fresh red chilies are best at the beginning of autumn when they have just been harvested, but they are commonly available at other times of the year as well. Check with your greengrocer or farmers' market.

Frozen Thai chilies are often sold in Chinese markets and can be of very good quality. Just defrost them and use them right away, since they will rot quickly if not immediately processed.

Have a couple of very clean plastic spoons at the ready the first time you try this method, as sometimes they break at awkward times. I've found that spoons without ridges along the edges are more flexible. Of course, forks, knives, and sporks can be used, too.

Pàojiāo lián'ǒu 泡椒蓮藕

Pickled Lotus Root

MAKES ABOUT 2 CUPS

Nowadays, lotus roots can be found in Chinese markets most of the year, but they are at their best in fall and early winter when the sugars in the roots reach their peak.

LOTUS ROOT AND AROMATICS

1 plump lotus root (6 to 7 inches long)
½ teaspoon sea salt
3 green onions, trimmed and cut into ¼-inch-thick rounds
2 plump cloves garlic, thinly sliced
1 tablespoon peeled fresh ginger, finely chopped
10 or more pickled red chili peppers (page 424 or store-bought)

BRINE

2 tablespoons vinegar from the pickled chilies
¼ cup pale rice vinegar or good cider vinegar
¼ cup sugar
2 teaspoons sea salt

1. Peel the lotus root and remove both ends. Rinse the root thoroughly under running water (see page 451). Cut it lengthwise in half and then into ¼-inch cubes. Place the cubed root in a small saucepan, add the salt, and cover with water. Bring the pan to a full boil and then reduce to a simmer. Cook the root for about 5 minutes, until it is just barely tender but still has a crunchy texture. Drain and rinse with cool water to stop the cooking.

2. Place the cooked root in a 3-cup container with the green onions, garlic, ginger, and pickled chilies. To make the brine, mix together the vinegars, sugar, and salt and then pour it over the vegetables. Top them off with just enough water to barely cover them. Cover and refrigerate for at least 24 hours, shaking the container now and then. The pickles will stay crispy and tasty for at least 5 days.

Xuělǐhóng 雪裏紅 or 雪裏蕻

Salted Shanghainese Greens

MAKES ABOUT 2 CUPS CHOPPED GREENS

One of the classic flavors of the lower Yangtze River area comes from fresh mustard greens quickly cured with nothing but salt. Often available in Chinese supermarkets nowadays, these salted greens can be found either in refrigerated plastic bags or canned. However, you can make them at home with minimal effort, and they are infinitely fresher and tastier that way.

I have always loved the unique heat of the mustard family's volatile oils. With salting, though, this nose-tickling tendency gets tamped down, providing a really delicious hit of flavor that turns almost buttery when the greens are chopped and fried.

Summer and autumn are the times when true *xuelihong* mustard greens appear in Chinese markets, their long stems and wrinkled leaves offering perfect counterpoints of crunchiness and softness when salted. Just about any variety of mustard will do, though, and I have even made these from Chinese radish greens when I couldn't find any mustard that grabbed my fancy.

The only caveat is that many greens—and especially radish greens—can be terribly gritty, and just a single microscopic grain will ruin your enjoyment of these sensuous salted vegetables, so wash and wash and wash them until every speck is gone. I usually soak the fresh greens in a big basin of warm water, which softens the dirt and makes it easy to dislodge (see page 10).

2 pounds (more or less) fresh *xuelihong* or other
    mustard greens or fresh Chinese radish greens
2 tablespoons coarse sea salt

1. Rinse the greens thoroughly and shake them dry. Tear the greens in half or thirds and dry them either in a salad spinner or by wrapping them in a dry tea towel. Cut the thick stems lengthwise in half.

2. Place the greens in a large work bowl and sprinkle them with the salt. Lightly rub the salt into the greens for a few minutes. Let the greens sit in the bowl, tossing them every 5 minutes or so, for about 20 minutes, and then let them rest in the bowl for another 40 minutes, until the leaves and stems are limp.

3. Use your hands to squeeze out and discard the liquid from the greens, handfuls at a time, and place the greens in a resealable plastic bag. Close the bag and refrigerate the greens for a day or two, then chop the leaves and stems into approximately ¼-inch pieces. Return the greens to the bag and keep them refrigerated. Rinse the greens under cool tap water and squeeze them dry just before using. Use them within a week for optimum flavor and texture.

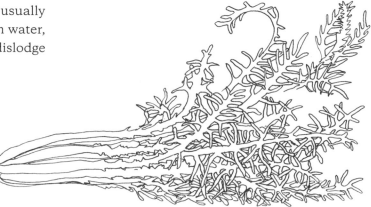

Tángcù jiècài 糖醋芥菜

Shanghai Mustard Pickles

MAKES ABOUT 1 QUART

Jackson Street in San Francisco's Chinatown used to have a little hole-in-the-wall called the Star Cafe. It was my kind of place. Star Cafe was only wide enough to squeeze in a semblance of a kitchen on the right, run a counter down the middle, and stuff a couple of worn tables and chairs in the back.

But what this little dive lacked in refinement it more than made up for in flavor and price. And what I really loved there were its Shanghai mustard pickles. A huge glass jar of them stood in an old cooler, the pickles nicely crisp and cold, just the way I like them. My husband and I would order a bowl to munch on while we perused the menu, and I'd usually commandeer the lion's portion before washing them down with a glass of cold, sweetened, homemade soymilk (page 64).

One day, we tromped over there for another meal only to find the doors locked and a sign saying the owners were away on a trip to China. That trip turned into years while the storefront stayed empty and I longed in vain for my pickles, as no other place I knew ever offered them. Then I ran across a recipe for Mustard Stems Pickled in Sweet Rice Vinegar in the wonderful Bruce Cost book _Asian Ingredients_. With a little tweaking, his pickles were soon transformed into the ones that haunted my dreams.

MUSTARD

5 medium heads Chinese mustard cabbage

2 tablespoons sea salt

BRINE

3 cups pale rice vinegar

2¼ cups sugar

2 tablespoons sea salt

8 dried Thai chilies

5 cloves garlic, crushed

10 thin slices fresh ginger

Boiling water, as needed

1. Start this recipe a couple of days before you plan to serve it. Trim any flimsy leaves off of the mustard cabbage and use them for something else, like a stir-fry. Cut the heads in half (see page 450), and then cut each half into pieces no more than ½ inch wide. Rinse the mustard cabbage carefully, shake it dry, and place it in a colander. Sprinkle the salt over the veggies, lightly rub it in, and let them sit for an hour or so to remove most of the excess water.

2. Clean a quart-sized glass jar and lid, making sure that there's no oil or soap residue in there, as this could cause the pickles to mold. Rinse the jar and lid with boiling water and turn them upside down to drain.

3. Bring the vinegar to a boil in a medium saucepan. Add the sugar, salt, chilies, garlic, and ginger and then simmer for a few minutes until the sugar has dissolved. Shake the excess salt and water off of the mustard cabbage and place it in the jar. Pour the boiling brine over the vegetable and toss lightly, adding a bit of boiling water as needed so that the liquid almost reaches the top of the cabbage. Taste and adjust the seasoning as desired. Stir the cabbage every 5 minutes or so as it cools so that it turns from emerald green to an even olive. As the vegetable turns color, it will shrink, and the brine should soon cover it. Add a little more water as needed to keep the cabbage submerged.

4. When the jar is cool, cover and refrigerate for at least 2 days. Use a very clean pair of chopsticks or fork to remove the pickles. They'll last for at least a month if kept clean and cold.

If you like sausages, try stir-frying sausage slices with onions and this pickle for a piquant and utterly divine dish.

Chuántóng Sìchuān pàocài 傳統四川泡茶

Traditional Fermented Sichuan-Style Pickles

MAKES ABOUT 1 QUART

As I've delved deeper into the traditional ways of making some of the best pickled and fermented ingredients that China has to offer, I've discovered some truly delicious things along the way. One is naturally fermented pickles.

Even better, the following recipe allowed me to make my own slightly tart and intensely flavored long beans. Yes, you can get them sometimes in Chinese markets, but they've invariably been around for a long time, cooked enough to survive in a vacuum pack, and left with none of the appetizing green color or terrific crunch that I love so much. This recipe lets you add a bunch of long beans to the pickling crock. These pickled beans are wonderful when rinsed, finely chopped, and stir-fried with little more than dried chilies and minced pork for the Sichuan home-style dish called *ròumò jiāngdòu* 肉末豇豆, or "ground meat long beans."

No vinegar is involved in the making of these naturally fermented pickles. Instead, the veggies are paired with nothing but a seasoned brine, and nature does the rest. It's taken a while for me to work out the bugs and ensure perfection every time, but it's all been worth it.

What are the advantages of making your own pickled vegetables this way? First of all, if you get a really good crock with a moat around the top, the pickles will let out farts as they cure. I'm not kidding. The crock that is sitting on my kitchen counter tends to cut the cheese when I come downstairs to start the day, and then I inevitably begin to laugh, which is always a good way to greet the morning. It's a nice, muffled, wet sort of explosion, the kind that sounds like someone sitting in a bath. Check out the label on page 430, which I'd encourage you to photocopy onto red paper and tape onto your crock. It says it all in Chinese calligraphy—"fart jar"—and is courtesy of Zhou Guiyuan.

Despite the sound, there is no fermenting smell if you use something like the crocks that the Chinese have used for countless years. They have a cup-shaped lid, and that moat around the top ingeniously lets the carbon dioxide out while acting as a barrier to outside air, insects, and contamination, which is why you get those lovely sounds.

Farting aside, these pickles are outstandingly good: crisp, crunchy, flavorful, and just bursting with the authentic taste of perfect fermentation.

My late mother-in-law used to make something like them back in Taiwan (she excelled at the salted and fermented stuff, while my father-in-law made the daily meals), and so the sight of a crock full of things pickling away in the dark makes my husband very happy, reminding him as it does of his childhood days.

Vegetables that are slowly pickled via fermentation also have incredible health benefits: they aid in digestion, and are especially recommended for people who are middle-aged and older, as the stomach's hydrochloric acid diminishes over time, which is why so many people eventually suffer from heartburn and indigestion (in addition to overeating and general dissipation at the dining table, of course).

Enjoy these pickles every day and see whether symptoms don't improve; they are healthier and definitely much tastier than antacid tablets. And there's something just terribly comforting about seeing a glazed pot on the counter filled with good things to eat, farting away without shame, and promising excellent meals in the days ahead.

SEASONED BRINE

9 cups water

5 ounces sea salt

1 tablespoon whole Sichuan peppercorns

6 star anise

6 bay leaves

2 tablespoons white liquor

Rock sugar to taste (start with about 3 tablespoons)

2-inch piece fresh ginger, peeled and thinly sliced

6 cloves garlic, cut in half

2 to 6 red jalapeño peppers or other fresh chilies to taste, trimmed and halved

VEGETABLES

1 head firm, sweet, round cabbage

Any or all of the following (see Tips):

1 Chinese or Korean radish, peeled and thinly sliced

2 or 3 carrots, peeled and thinly sliced on the diagonal

1 bunch long beans, as tender and as thin as possible, trimmed and kept whole; use kitchen twine to tie them loosely together at one end

1 or 2 kohlrabi, peeled and thinly sliced

1. Boil the water and salt together to dissolve the salt. Let the salted water come to room temperature.

2. While the water is cooling, carefully scrub out a large (8- to 12-cup) crock (see Tips), including its lid, and rinse it thoroughly under running water. Give the crock and lid a good dousing of boiling water, turn them over on a clean towel, and let them dry. Then pour the salted water into the crock, cover it, and let it sit in the crock by itself for a week. What you end up with is something the Chinese call "old salt water," or *lǎo yánshuǐ* 老鹽水, and it sets the stage for successful fermented pickles.

3. After a week, tie the Sichuan peppercorns and star anise in either a very clean small cloth bag or a mesh ball and add them to the salted water. Then add the bay leaves, white liquor, sugar, ginger, garlic, and chilies.

4. Clean your vegetables and pat them dry. Let them air-dry for a couple of hours, if possible, to keep any fresh water from entering the pickling crock. Cut off and reserve 2 large leaves from the outside of the cabbage. Slice the cabbage in half, core it, and tear it into pieces about 2 inches square. Prepare the other vegetables as desired and add them to the crock.

5. Place the 2 large cabbage leaves on top of the other veggies. Carefully lower a very clean weight on top of the cabbage leaves (see Tips). If the brine does not cover the vegetables by at least 1 inch, make up more salted water using the same ratio as before. Cover the crock (see Tips), place it in a cool place, and let the vegetables ferment for a couple of days. Check the crock to ensure that no mold has formed; if it has, pour a couple more tablespoons of white liquor into the pickles, gently swish the crock around, and then cover it again. The pickles will be ready in 2 to 4 weeks, depending upon the temperature, vegetables, and so on.

6. Use very clean chopsticks to remove the pickles from the brine (see Tips). As soon as they're done to your liking, remove them to a clean jar without adding any brine and refrigerate. You can reuse the brine to pickle more vegetables; the flavor will improve over time. Add more salted water as needed, and if the flavor needs a boost, add more spices, aromatics, sugar, or white liquor.

Chinese pickle crocks are hard to find at the time of this writing, but oddly enough, eastern Europe has crocks with similar designs. These are available online.

Store your crock in a very cool area, like a basement or a shady kitchen corner, as the pickles need to ferment slowly in order to develop their flavor.

If you are using a crock with a moat, be sure to check the water level daily around the lid, adding more water as needed.

A plain large glass crock can be used instead, as long as the lid does not have a plastic rim that seals the crock shut, since you want to give the gases an escape route. With this sort of crock, place a thin sheet of cheesecloth over the top before covering with the lid. As with ceramic crocks, clean and sterilize both the crock and the lid (as well as the cheesecloth) before using.

Doughnut-shaped, unglazed ceramic disks that are split in the middle—this aids in their insertion and removal—serve as good pickle weights here. They can be found online, but you can also go the more traditional route and place a very clean plate on top of your pickles and then balance a (very, very clean) rock on top of the plate; if you do that, get a rock that has a flat side, so that it doesn't roll around and either break the crock or disappear into the pickles. Wrap the rock with very clean string or cheesecloth so you can get a firm grip on it.

Use only firm vegetables that are not at all juicy here. Things like cucumbers and tomatoes should not be added, as they will spoil.

Add as much sugar to the crock as you like, and change the seasonings, too, if you prefer. Sichuan pickles traditionally have fresh ginger, garlic, and chilies, as well as Sichuan peppercorns, but use whatever flavors you like.

Keep a clean pair of chopsticks tucked away for nothing else but your pickles. This will prevent contamination.

Calligraphy by Zhou Guiyuan

Jiǎnyì Sìchuān pàocài 簡易四川泡茶

Fast Sichuan-Style Pickles

MAKES ABOUT 1 QUART

Delicious and easy, this is a recipe worth memorizing. It is much lighter in flavor than traditionally fermented pickles, since vinegar is used. This sort of pickle goes with just about anything, including stir-fries (just sear some meat, toss in these pickles to barely warm them through, and season to taste) and sandwiches.

1 pound Chinese or Korean radishes
1 pound carrots
1 large, firm, round, sweet cabbage
1 tablespoon sea salt
2¼ cups pale rice vinegar
1½ cups sugar
1½ cups water
5 to 10 small fresh or dried chilies, or to taste
1 tablespoon whole Sichuan peppercorns
2 tablespoons peeled and thinly sliced fresh ginger

1. Start this recipe up to 4 days before you wish to serve it. Peel the Chinese or Korean radishes, halve them lengthwise, and cut each half into thin slices. Peel the carrots and slice them on the diagonal into thin slices. Core the cabbage, cut it in half through the stem end, and then tear the leaves into pieces about 2 inches wide. Separate any leaves that are stuck together and place the cabbage, radishes, and carrots in a large colander. Set the colander in your sink and toss the vegetables with the salt. Let them sweat out excess moisture for about 2 hours, at which point they should be slightly firm and not at all limp.

2. While the vegetables are sweating, mix the vinegar, sugar, water, chilies, peppercorns, and ginger together in a medium nonreactive saucepan and bring the pickling solution to a boil. Reduce the heat to a simmer and gently cook for about 20 minutes; taste and adjust the seasoning. Remove the pan from the stove and let the pickling solution come to room temperature.

3. Grab small handfuls of the vegetables and gently squeeze out and discard most of the moisture, but don't rinse them. Place the squeezed vegetables in a 1-quart bowl, pour the cooled pickling solution over them, and refrigerate covered for up to 4 days. When serving, drain only as many pickles as you wish to use and serve them chilled.

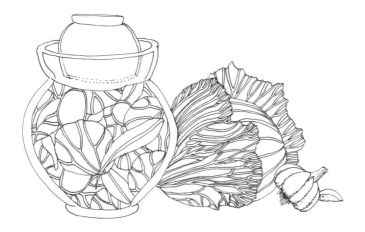

Suānlà huánggguā 酸辣黄瓜

Spicy Pickled Cucumbers

MAKES ABOUT 1 QUART

Variations on this hot fresh pickle abound in Central China, starting with Jiangxi on the eastern edge of the region and traveling all the way to Sichuan, where it is called *qiàng huánggguā* 熗黄瓜. Although Jiangxi's food is often very mild, it has a serious hot streak in many of its homestyle dishes and street snacks, making it the spiciest of the Yangtze River Valley's cuisines. For that reason, many people group its food with that of Hunan, another charter member of the chili-loving club.

Unlike in the West, fresh pickles are served as often as preserved pickles in China. Fresh pickles like these adorn the dining tables of the high and low, offering quick refreshment between bites, stimulating the appetite before a banquet, and sometimes appearing as complements to other, blander ingredients, such as jellyfish or poached chicken breast.

Because they are fresh, their flavors and colors are brighter, and they can be made on the spur of the moment, although they are almost always better the next day, after they have had a chance to mellow a bit. Eat pickles like this within a day or two of making them, while their texture is still at its best.

CUCUMBERS

1 pound Persian or other small, seedless cucumbers
2 teaspoons sea salt

SAUCE

2 cloves garlic, finely minced
2 tablespoons water
2 tablespoons regular soy sauce
2 tablespoons whole Sichuan peppercorns
5 thin slices fresh ginger
3 tablespoons peanut or vegetable oil
1 tablespoon sugar
2 tablespoons black vinegar
3 tablespoons of any chili paste or oil (pages 435 to 438)
2 teaspoons toasted sesame oil

1. Start this recipe a day before you plan to serve it. Clean the cucumbers and trim the ends. Slice the cucumbers lengthwise in half and then once again into quarters, and then once again across the middle to make batons about 3 inches long. Place the cucumbers in a colander set in the sink, sprinkle the salt on them, and toss them lightly. Let the excess water drain out for at least 15 minutes while you prepare the rest of the ingredients.

2. Place the garlic in a small bowl. Add the water and soy sauce and let the garlic soak for 15 to 30 minutes.

3. Put the peppercorns and ginger in a wok along with the oil and fry over medium heat until the ginger is browned. Scrape the oil, peppercorns, and ginger into a medium work bowl. Add the sugar to the hot oil and stir until the sugar dissolves. Add the vinegar, chili oil solids, sesame oil, and the garlic mixture. Taste and adjust the seasoning.

4. Lightly squeeze the water out of the cucumbers and add them to the work bowl. Toss well, cover, and refrigerate overnight. Taste again and adjust the seasonings, as they will taste a bit different when chilled. Serve cold.

Tángsuàn 糖蒜

Sweet Pickled Garlic Cloves

MAKES 8 HEADS

One of the highlights for me of northern-style Chinese hotpot dinners (see page 20) has always been the tawny brown heads of sweet pickled garlic plunked down with the plates of pickled cabbage and boiled peanuts. Fixed this way, garlic turns from bitingly hot to mellow and sweet, with the vinegar and salt providing a deliciously cleansing edge. I like my garlic exotically dark, so I use very dark brown sugar and a tasty but cheap balsamic vinegar, which also lends a lovely tang to the little cloves.

But the real prize in this recipe is the sauce. It has everything you could ask for, in a perfect balance. Sweet, sour, salty, and garlicky, this is one ingredient I prize so highly that I never give it away. Instead, I hoard it like a miser and serve it dribbled over tidbits only when I'm certain that it will be appreciated. Selfish? Undoubtedly. Reserve judgment until you taste it, though, and then you'll understand.

Like so many of China's greatest culinary master-pieces, this dish is understated, simple, and requires only a modicum of ingredients and preparation. But it does demand patience. These lovely heads of garlic have to settle quietly into the sweetened and gently salted vinegar for a couple of months—or even longer, if you can bear it—before they surrender their fire and become mellow enough to be eaten just the way they are. Then and only then should you pluck out a sweetly drowned clove, surreptitiously licking your fingers, and squeeze it out of its jacket and into your mouth.

If you find these as intoxicating as I do, consider preparing a batch every three months or so and having jars continually mellowing away in the pantry or on the shelf. I label my crocks and keep them in regular rotation. As summer draws near, you will find plenty of use for that luscious sauce, which is great in salads and drizzled over things like fresh, flavorful tomatoes. I get hunger pangs just thinking about a Brandywine tomato still warm from the vine, sliced into wedges, lightly salted, and oozing with this loveliest of vinegar sauces.

GARLIC AND BRINING LIQUID

8 large heads garlic
½ cup sea salt
6 cups hot water

MARINADE

3 cups black vinegar
2¼ cups dark brown sugar
1 cup water
2 tablespoons dark soy sauce

1. Clean the heads of garlic, but don't break them apart. Peel off most of the outer layers, leaving only a layer or two of skin over the garlic cloves. Carefully scrub the root end and cut off as much of it as possible without cutting into the cloves or breaking the heads.

2. Dissolve the salt in the hot water and let it cool. Place the garlic heads in the cool salted water and let them soak for about 24 hours to remove some of their harshness and to make them as clean as possible.

3. Place the vinegar, sugar, water, and soy sauce in a medium saucepan, bring to a boil, and stir until the sugar dissolves. Allow the marinade to cool down to room temperature.

4. Remove the garlic from the salted water and place it in a clean jar or crock without rinsing the salt off. Pour the cool marinade over them, place a plate on top of the garlic to help submerge it in the marinade, and cover the container. Lightly stir the garlic every day or two for a week and then store it in a cool place for about 2 weeks before using. Taste a clove to see whether its flavor is sweet and relatively gentle. As soon as the garlic is pickled to your liking, pack it in small jars or plastic containers and store it in the refrigerator; it will keep for a long time that way.

Cōng yóu 蔥油

Green Onion Oil

MAKES ABOUT 1½ CUPS

12 green onions
1½ cups peanut or vegetable oil

1. Clean and trim the green onions, pat them dry (this is important, since you don't want them to spatter in the oil), and then slice them into either thin rounds or on an angle into long, thin ovals.

2. Line a plate with a paper towel and place it next to the stove along with a slotted spoon. Set a wok with the oil in it over medium-high heat. When the oil just begins to shimmer, add a few pieces of the onion. What you want is for the onions to gently bubble, so adjust the heat as needed and then add the rest of the onions. Stir them every minute or so, letting them slowly cook and giving them a chance to release their fragrance and gradually dry out. As soon as they start to smell toasty and a few begin to brown, stir them almost constantly so they brown evenly.

3. Once almost all of the onions are a light brown and crispy, remove them from the oil with the slotted spoon and place them on the paper towel. Set the wok with the hot oil aside if you're going to use it immediately; otherwise, let it cool and pour the oil into a squeeze bottle or jar. The fried green onions can be used as a garnish for just about anything, especially soft, bland foods like fried eggs, cold bean curd, and noodles (page 134).

Huājiāo yóu 花椒油

Sichuan Peppercorn Oil

MAKES ABOUT 1 CUP

¼ cup whole Sichuan peppercorns
1 cup peanut or vegetable oil

1. Pour the oil into a 2-cup saucepan and add the Sichuan peppercorns. Bring the oil to a boil and then immediately reduce the heat to low so the oil gently bubbles; do not cook the peppercorns over higher heat, as they will burn rather than color the oil and infuse it with their fragrance.

2. Keep slowly simmering the oil and peppercorns until they have a vivid aroma. The peppercorns will begin to turn a dark brown; don't let them blacken and burn.

3. Remove the saucepan from the heat and let it sit overnight. Pour the oil into a jar and store it in a cool, dark place like the refrigerator. Use within a couple of weeks for optimum flavor and freshness.

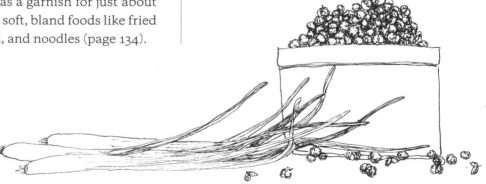

Yóucōng sū 油蔥酥 *and hóngcōng yóu* 紅蔥油

Fried Shallots and Shallot Oil

MAKES ABOUT 1 CUP FRIED SHALLOTS
AND 3 CUPS SEASONED OIL

12 ounces shallots, peeled
3 cups peanut or vegetable oil

1. Slice the shallots crosswise and separate them into individual circles.

2. Place the cool oil and sliced shallots in a saucepan or wok and slowly raise the heat to create a gentle bubbling around the shallots. You want them to slowly cook and release their flavors into the oil, but do this carefully so that the sugars in the shallots do not burn. Stir the shallots occasionally, and when they are a uniform golden brown, drain them in a sieve over a work bowl.

3. Wick off any extra oil in the shallots by placing them on a paper towel. Refrigerate both the oil and the shallots if you are not using them soon.

Málà hóngyóu 麻辣紅油

Red Chili Oil with Toasty Bits

MAKES ABOUT 3 CUPS

2 cups peanut or vegetable oil
¼ cup toasted sesame oil
½ cup finely ground dried chilies
¼ cup coarsely ground dried chilies
¼ cup whole Sichuan peppercorns
1 whole dried orange peel (just remove the peel from an orange in a single long strip and air-dry it until hard)

1. Pour the oils into a 4-cup saucepan and add all of the chilies and the Sichuan peppercorns. Bring the oil to a boil and then immediately reduce the heat to low so that the oil gently bubbles; do not cook the chilies over higher heat, as they will burn.

2. After about 10 minutes, place the orange peel in the oil. I found through trial and error that the best way to cook the chili oil to perfection is to simmer the peppers over low heat for another 15 to 20 minutes or so, until the orange peel has turned brown. At this point the peppers will be crispy but not burned, and the oil will have a gentle smokiness and will still be bright red.

3. Remove the saucepan from the heat and let it sit overnight. You can either discard the orange peel or chop it finely and add it to the oil for a subtle citrusy perfume. I like to strain out a portion of the red oil and keep it in a squeeze bottle next to the stove, while the rest can be poured into a clean jar along with the toasty bits and spooned out as needed. Either way, store the oil in a cool, dark place; if you don't use it every day, you'll find that it will keep longer in the refrigerator. Use within a couple of weeks for optimum flavor and freshness. Try it on anything that could use a little pizzazz.

Júxiāng dòuchǐ làyóu 橘香豆豉辣油

Citrus Chili Oil with Black Beans

MAKES ABOUT 1½ CUPS

Homemade chili oil that has a good layer of ground ingredients lurking at the bottom of the jar is—in my little universe, at least—the sign of an excellent Chinese restaurant, one that pays attention to the little details and doesn't just scoop a sour sauce out of a generic can.

The road to this recipe started when I came across the late Barbara Tropp's second and final work, *China Moon Cookbook*, which includes favorites from her restaurant of the same name.

The recipe that struck me between the eyes was for her China Moon Chili-Orange Oil. It had all of the components I was seeking, plus a vibrant citrus note that took this condiment to stratospheric levels. In the twenty years since then, I have fooled around with it, adding more savory things, halving the oil (I am a sucker for the lovely goop at the bottom of the jar, after all), and amping up the aromas with a whole bunch of ginger and garlic. The resulting recipe is one that I am proud to call my own, developed over the years into a personal favorite. Use the oil as you would any bright oil, and savor the goop as a dipping sauce, in marinades, and in stir-fries. It goes with just about anything, and it will prove highly addictive.

3 medium oranges
1 Meyer or other lemon
7 or 8 cloves garlic
4 tablespoons fermented black beans (see Tips)
1 cup peanut or vegetable oil
2 tablespoons toasted sesame oil
2 tablespoons peeled and finely minced fresh ginger
½ cup coarsely ground dried chilies (see Tips)

1. Scrub the oranges and lemon before patting them dry (see Tips). Remove the zest (just the colored part) with a potato peeler, and then dice it finely. Use the flesh of the fruits for something else.

2. Smack each garlic clove and peel it, but leave the peeled cloves more or less whole (see Tips). Rinse the fermented black beans and coarsely chop them.

3. Pour both oils into a small frying pan or saucepan, add all of the other ingredients to the cool oil, and then place the pan over medium heat until the oil starts to bubble (see Tips). Lower the heat and simmer the sauce for about 20 minutes, stirring occasionally. Cook the sauce until the oil is a Day-Glo orange, the chilies are dark brown, and the garlic cloves are soft. Remove from the heat and cool. Store in a covered jar in a cool place, preferably in the fridge if you are not going to use it up within 2 weeks.

Use the black beans that come in plastic bags or in jars and don't have any sauce. They should be plump and dark, rather than shriveled and gray.

Experiment with different types of dried chilies, adding more if you love the heat. The chilies can be very coarsely ground with the seeds still whole, or you can use a sifted variety that has the seeds removed. I like the varieties available at Korean grocery stores, where the offerings tend to be both varied and of terrific quality.

Scrub the oranges and lemons well to remove any dust that might have worked its way into their pores. Use hot water and a brush to clean off any wax. Dry the fruit well before zesting them, as any water will explode in the hot oil.

Keeping your garlic cloves whole protects them from cooking too quickly and burning. This way they will slowly poach in the oil and remain luscious. After cooking, smash the garlic with your spoon.

Starting the sauce off by adding the dry ingredients to the cool oil will prevent them from cooking too quickly. This slow simmer gives the aromatics a chance to release their oils and flavors before they brown, making the oil a gorgeous orange hue and the goop at the bottom a crunchy, chewy obsession.

Xiāngshì làjiàng 湘式辣酱

Hunan-Style Chili Paste

MAKES ABOUT 1½ CUPS

Hunan-style chili paste is one of my absolute favorite things to have around the kitchen. It smells terrific; the nutty and spicy aromas act as some sort of potent pheromone, as far as I'm concerned. And oh, the taste: a light heat, a gentle chewiness, a subtle saltiness, and an amazing depth of flavor makes this a great basic chili concoction that goes with just about everything short of cheesecake. Now that I think about it, I'm pretty sure it would be good there, too.

Even though this paste is from Hunan, it is not incredibly hot. Rather, the coarse, relatively seedless dried chilies create a warm base that vibrates gently on the tongue. This base contrasts perfectly with the chopped fermented black beans, which serve to tantalize the taste buds with their salt and that savory, meaty flavor the Chinese call *xianwei*.

Binding everything together is another ingredient, something I have come to positively adore: toasty tea oil. Pressed from the seeds of the camellia species that produces tea leaves, *kǔcháyóu* 苦茶油 (bitter tea oil) is a nutty amber liquid used throughout Hunan and Jiangxi for cooking and tossing with pickles. Not every Chinese grocery store carries it, but places with Taiwanese products sometimes do, and it should be snapped up with no hesitation. Be sure to get the Taiwanese variety, which (from what I've tried, at least) tastes unadulterated. It's not especially cheap—around six dollars for about 600 ml—but it is worth it.

Tea oil also has a very high smoke point, making it great for deep- and stir-frying. Again, that gentle nuttiness acts as an extra layer of seasoning, so I generally use it to fry lightly flavored ingredients. Strangely enough, though, it holds its own against the dried chilies and fermented black beans here. I think this is because it is so totally different in flavor from them that it hits some different sensory receptors. Or maybe it's just me.

A warning: if you end up loving this as much as I do, you will find yourself eating the goop as is, or else loading so much of it on your food that it's a bit embarrassing. I will make scrambled eggs and drown them in this delicious crunch, letting those full flavors find the perfect partner in the soft yellow curds on my plate. My husband tends to butter his toast at moments like this and raise his eyebrows at my obscenely laden eggs. To each his own, I guess.

Since I am such a fan of that goop, you will find a very large ratio of solids to oil here. If you want to turn this into a seasoned oil, add another ½ to 1 cup to the recipe. Store the paste in the fridge if you don't plow through it as fast as I do. Mine never gets old enough to turn stale.

1 cup oil, preferably tea oil but any flavorful vegetable oil will do
1 cup coarsely ground dried Korean chilies with very few seeds
½ cup fermented black beans, rinsed, dried, and coarsely chopped

1. Pour the oil into a cold wok. Add the chilies and black beans. Turn the heat to medium or a bit higher and cook this trio, stirring every once in a while as it starts to bubble.

2. When the chilies start to brown and the oil is a deep red, stir pretty much constantly to keep the chilies from burning. It is very important that you toast the chilies and black beans long enough for their characters to change, as the chilies have to turn from slightly sour and soft to toasty and crunchy, and the beans need to release their aromas into the oil and the chilies.

3. After about 15 minutes, when the chilies are very dark and taste nutty, remove the wok from the heat. Be careful, as you do not want the chilies to burn. You will know they are ready when they sound gravelly as you stir them; they will also smell insanely delicious. Scoop the oil and solids into a heatproof bowl or clean jar, let them come to room temperature, and cover. Refrigerate the paste, or can it for longer storage.

Cíbā làjiāo 糍粑辣椒

Guizhou Ciba Chili Paste

MAKES ABOUT 1 CUP

When I first looked at the ingredients for this sauce, I did not have an inkling of how amazing it would turn out to be.

1 cup dried Thai chilies, stem ends removed
¼ cup coarsely chopped garlic
¼ cup peeled and coarsely chopped ginger
1 teaspoon sea salt
Freshly ground black pepper
1 cup peanut or vegetable oil, divided in half

1. Cover the chilies with warm water by about 2 inches and let them soak until they have softened completely. Drain them in a colander and shake dry. Place the softened chilies in a blender or mini food processor and pulse in the garlic, ginger, salt, black pepper to taste, and ½ cup of the oil.

2. Pour the remaining ½ cup oil into a cool wok and add the chili paste. Slowly cook the paste over medium heat, stirring often, until the chilies have turned from red to a mahogany hue—about 30 minutes. When the paste is ready, the garlic will taste mellow and there will be a yellowish foam on top of the sauce. Cool to room temperature and refrigerate.

Guìzhōu làjiāojiàng 貴州辣椒醬

Guizhou Fermented Hot Sauce

MAKES ABOUT 3 CUPS

8 ounces fresh red chilies (about 1 cup; mild or hot, depending upon your preference)
1 cup (4 ounces) fermented black beans
1 cup garlic cloves (7 ounces or about 50 cloves)
2 tablespoons sea salt, or to taste
White liquor to cover

1. This sauce takes about 1 month to ferment. Sterilize and air-dry a quart crock or jar and its lid; use non-rusting materials for both. Rinse and dry both the chilies and beans. Trim the chilies and garlic cloves, and then coarsely chop these and the beans. Mix them in a work bowl with the salt, which will make the chilies and garlic sweat. Taste and adjust the seasoning: it should have a nice, salty punch to it.

2. Pour the mixture into the sterilized container. After a couple of hours, pat the chopped ingredients into a firm layer and wipe down the inside of the container with a clean paper towel moistened with some white liquor. Then, cover the mixture with at least a ½ inch more of white liquor, which will soon be absorbed by the aromatics. Store the container (don't tighten the lid, so that gases from the fermentation can escape) in a cool place for at least 2 weeks, but longer is much better, as the flavors will continue to mellow and mature. When you like the flavor, tighten the lid and chill.

Tiánlàjiàng 甜辣醬

Sweet Chili Sauce

MAKES ABOUT 2 CUPS

½ to 1 teaspoon dried chili powder
1 or 2 red jalapeño peppers, seeded and minced
1 clove garlic, finely minced
¼ cup sugar
3 tablespoons catsup
2 tablespoons pale rice vinegar or cider vinegar
1¾ cups water
2 tablespoons cornstarch mixed with ¼ cup water

1. Mix the chili powder, jalapeños, garlic, sugar, catsup, vinegar, and water together in a small saucepan. Bring to a boil over medium-high heat and stir in the cornstarch slurry. Stir the sauce constantly as it comes to a boil and then lower the heat to a simmer. Keep stirring as the sauce slowly cooks for the next 5 minutes; this will eliminate the raw cornstarch flavor. Remove the pan from the heat.

2. If you are going to refrigerate this, cool the sauce down before pouring it into small, clean glass jars. If you are canning the sauce, do not cool the sauce, but rather pour it, still boiling, into sterile glass jars. Cover and seal in a hot-water bath for about 10 minutes. Cool the jars, label, and store in a cool cupboard.

Tiánjiàngyóu 甜醬油

Sweet Soy Sauce

MAKES ABOUT 2 CUPS

Homemade sweet soy sauce has a stronger flavor and is saltier than the store-bought kind, so adjust how much you use accordingly.

1½ cups sugar
¾ cup water, divided into ¼ cup and ½ cup
1 bottle (500 ml) regular soy sauce
1 teaspoon whole Sichuan peppercorns
2 slices licorice root
2 star anise
2 cloves garlic, lightly crushed
5 thin slices fresh ginger
Boiling water, as needed

1. Place the sugar in a heavy stainless saucepan and moisten it with ¼ cup water. Caramelize the sugar (see page 454) over medium-high heat, and then cool the pan down slightly.

2. Pointing the pan away from you, pour the remaining ½ cup water into the caramelized sugar, as it will sizzle and boil. Add all the other ingredients and bring the liquid to a full boil as you stir it to melt the hardened caramel. When a fine foam forms on the surface, watch it closely so that the sauce does not boil over. Reduce the sweet soy sauce to a molasses-like consistency, which will take 20 to 25 minutes.

3. Strain the sauce into a measuring cup and add boiling water to bring the sauce to 2¾ cups. Cool the sauce completely and refrigerate it if you do not use it often.

Hújiāo yán 胡椒鹽

Dry-Fried Salt and Pepper

MAKES ½ TO ¾ CUP

This is the go-to dry dip for fried things in just about every part of China. Make up a batch and store it in a jar next to your stove. If you're like me, you will find yourself sprinkling it on all sorts of things. It's the dry-frying that changes the character of both the black pepper and the salt, mellowing them out and making them taste so much more aromatic.

2 to 4 tablespoons whole black peppercorns
½ cup sea salt

1. Place the peppercorns and salt in a dry wok and stir them over medium heat until the salt turns tan. The mixture should smell fragrant at this point, and the peppercorns should smoke a little. Remove the wok from the heat, pour the salt and pepper into a dry work bowl, and let the mixture come to room temperature.

2. Use a mini blender or spice grinder to pulverize the toasted peppercorns and salt until they have the texture of talcum powder. Pour the powder into a small container and store it with the lid tightly closed.

Tellicherry black pepper is delicious. You can also use whole white peppercorns here for a slightly subtler flavor and appearance.

Huājiāo yán 花椒鹽

Toasted Sichuan Peppercorn Salt

MAKES ¾ TO 1 CUP

A numbing variation on the recipe for dry-fried salt and pepper (at left), this uses Sichuan peppercorns instead. A higher ratio of peppercorns to salt gives this dry dip a lot of zing. Sprinkle it on things like fried fish or chicken, or toss it into marinades for smoked foods, as on page 26 or 284.

½ to 1 cup whole Sichuan peppercorns
½ cup sea salt

1. Place the peppercorns and salt in a dry wok and stir them over medium heat until the salt turns tan and the peppercorns start to pop. The mixture should smell fragrant at this point, and the peppercorns should smoke a little bit. Pour the mixture into a small work bowl and let the ingredients come to room temperature.

2. Pulverize the toasted peppercorns and salt with either a spice grinder or mini-blender. They should have the texture of talcum powder, so grind them as finely as you can. The powder can then be shaken through a fine sieve, as the hard pits of the peppercorns are very gritty.

3. Store the peppercorn salt in a tightly capped jar and keep it in a cool, dark place.

Huājiāo fěn 花椒粉 or *huājiāo miàn* 花椒麵

Ground Toasted Sichuan Peppercorns

MAKES A FEW TABLESPOONS

Toasting heightens and softens the flavor of Sichuan peppercorns, elevating the aromas of this spice while mellowing its bitterness. I always have a jar of this ground spice next to the stove. If you don't use it that often, toast only a small amount of peppercorns so that the volatile oils don't dissipate.

¼ cup whole Sichuan peppercorns

1. Pour the peppercorns into a dry wok and stir them over medium heat until the seeds start to pop and send out fine tendrils of fragrant smoke. Remove the wok from the heat and pour the peppercorns into a small work bowl to cool off.

2. When the peppercorns are at room temperature, grind them finely with a spice grinder or mini-blender. You want them as fine as possible, since the seeds are very hard and can be unpleasant to crunch down on. I like to shake the powder through a fine sieve just to be sure that no surprises await my molars.

3. Pour the ground peppercorns into a jar and keep them in a cool, dark place. Making this ground toasted spice in small amounts guarantees its perfume stays lively and seductive, but of course make more if you love it as much as I do.

Wǔxiāngfěn 五香粉

Five-Spice Powder

MAKES A FEW TABLESPOONS

The cuisines along China's southern coast would not be the same without the tantalizing mixture called five-spice powder. The ingredients can be added or subtracted as you like, in order to fit your taste buds and the dishes you'll be seasoning. (There are never any chili peppers in this mixture, by the way.)

½ stick cinnamon or cassia bark, crumbled
2 teaspoons fennel seeds
2 star anise, crumbled into petals
2 whole cloves
4 slices sand ginger

OPTIONAL ADDITIONS OR SUBSTITUTIONS
1 black cardamom pod, crushed with the side of a blade
4 green cardamom pods, crushed with the side of a blade
2 teaspoons whole Sichuan peppercorns
2 teaspoons whole black peppercorns

1. Place the spices in a cool wok and set them over medium heat. Stir the spices as they warm up until their aromas are released and you hear faint popping noises. Remove the spices to a small work bowl and let them come to room temperature; they tend to clump up if they are ground while even the least bit warm.

2. Pour the spices into a clean spice grinder or a mini-blender and reduce them to a fine powder. If any hard bits remain, pass the powder through a fine sieve.

3. Store the five-spice powder in a closed container away from the sunlight. Use within a month for maximum flavor. Whenever the flavor starts to taste dull, toss your powder out and start over.

You can also add dried ginger, coriander seeds, aged tangerine peel, and/or licorice root, to taste.

All of the filling recipes that follow are enough for either 10 large (3-inch) or 30 small (1-inch) Guangdong-Style Moon Cakes (page 236).

Students of Chinese will note that while both date paste and red bean paste are referred to as ní 泥, or "mud," the other two fillings are correctly called róng 蓉, which everywhere else means a type of mallow or hibiscus. In the Cantonese dialect, however, it is often used in names for fluffy foods, as can be seen in that old American Chinese classic egg foo yung (fúróng dàn 芙蓉蛋), or in minced chicken (jīróng 雞蓉).

Dòushā lìzi 豆沙栗子

Red Bean Paste with Chestnuts

MAKES ABOUT 2½ CUPS

Scant 1 cup dried small red or adzuki beans (6 ounces)
4 ounces vacuum-packed peeled chestnuts
6 tablespoons unsalted butter
¼ teaspoon sea salt
⅓ cup packed dark brown sugar

1. Soak the beans in water to cover for 8 hours and up to overnight. Drain, add water to cover, and cook them until very soft, at least 1 hour. Drain, let cool a bit, and then mash as desired.

2. While the beans are cooking, prepare the chestnuts: keep them more or less whole for large moon cakes, or break them up a bit for the small ones.

3. Place the cooked, mashed beans in a wok with the butter, salt, and sugar. Stir constantly over medium-high heat with a silicone spatula until the bean paste is dark and thick. Taste and adjust the seasoning. You can add more brown sugar or even caramel syrup (page 446) to heighten the sweetness, but if you do, be sure to cook the paste down again until it is thick and glossy. There should be absolutely no moisture in this bean paste, as any liquid will soak into cooked moon-cake pastry and make it soggy.

4. Cool the bean paste in a work bowl and then chill. Roll the bean paste into 10 large or 30 small balls of even size. Distribute the chestnuts evenly among the bean paste balls and scoot them into the paste, covering them completely.

Hétáo zǎoní 核桃棗泥

Date Paste Filling
with Toasted Walnuts

MAKES ABOUT 2½ CUPS

8 ounces pitted Chinese red dates
¼ cup unsalted butter
¼ cup toasted sesame oil
½ cup caramel syrup (page 446)
¼ teaspoon sea salt
⅓ cup packed dark brown sugar
1 cup chopped walnuts

1. Soak the dates for 8 to 24 hours in cool water. Steam the dates and their soaking water (see page 49) for 45 minutes, until the dates are very soft. Drain off the liquid (save it for something else; see Tips). Run the dates through the fine holes of a food mill (or a coarse sieve), discarding the skins.

2. Pour the date puree into a wok and add the rest of the ingredients except the walnuts. Bring the puree to a boil and then lower the heat to medium in order to achieve a steady simmer. Use a silicone spatula to continuously scrape the bottom of the puree; this will keep it from sticking and release the steam that would otherwise cause it to boil and spit.

3. When the puree has been reduced to a thick paste with the consistency of mashed potatoes, continue to stir and cook it until it changes from a mahogany color to a dark reddish brown. There should be absolutely no moisture left in the paste. When it's ready, you will be able to draw your spatula down through the paste to the bottom of the pan while the paste stays put. At this point, pour it into a bowl to cool completely. The filling can be made weeks ahead of time and stored in the refrigerator. If you are keeping it for longer than that, freeze it to avoid spoilage.

4. Before you use it to fill moon cakes, check the moisture of the date paste once again. It should feel slightly oily without a trace of wetness, and it should look super glossy. If it fails any of these tests, fry it again without adding any other ingredients. (Moisture will ruin your moon cakes by seeping into the cooked wrappers and making them soggy, hence the attention to this detail.)

5. Pick over the walnuts and remove any shells. To dry-fry the walnuts, place them in a cold wok and turn the heat under the wok to medium-high. Continually stir the walnuts as they toast to keep them from burning; no additional oil will be necessary. When the nuts are evenly toasted, pour them into a bowl to cool. Mix the toasted walnuts evenly into the date paste. Divide the paste into 10 large or 30 small pieces and roll them into balls of even size; moistening your hands will make this a whole lot easier.

Chill the date paste before rolling it into balls. Even then, bits of date will squish their way out and peek through the filling, making for a marbled effect that I think is actually quite pretty. All that sugar will ensure that the paste is thick enough not to melt, even when it's exposed to the heat of your oven.

Reserve the water in which the dates steamed, as it will be incredibly delicious (see page 151). Drink it as is, cold or hot, or add it to other things like oatmeal or tea.

Coconut Filling

MAKES ABOUT 3 CUPS PACKED

14 ounces (about 5⅓ cups) sweetened flaked coconut
¼ cup unsalted butter, at room temperature
¼ teaspoon sea salt
½ cup powdered sugar
¼ cup coconut rum

1. Shake the coconut into a large work bowl and break apart any lumps.

2. Add the rest of the ingredients and stir.

3. Let the filling sit for at least 30 minutes so all the rum is absorbed. Chill and then roll the filling into balls.

Coconut rum is used here to heighten the rum flavor; Malibu is a good brand. However, you can use any other liquor here to fit your taste.

Fruit and Nut Filling

MAKES ABOUT 2½ CUPS

1 heaping cup (about 25 large) dried Chinese red dates
1 cup water
½ cup hulled pumpkin seeds
¼ cup dried cranberries or golden raisins
¾ cup chopped toasted walnuts
½ cup toasted sesame seeds
½ cup sliced almonds
¼ cup *meiguilu* liquor
2 tablespoons caramel syrup (page 446)
1½ tablespoons unsalted butter, softened
¼ cup packed dark brown sugar
¼ teaspoon sea salt
1 tablespoon flour
1 tablespoon sticky rice flour

1. Cook the dates in the water until they are soft and the water has been absorbed. Remove the dates from the heat, drain them (use the liquid for something else—see Tips, page 443), and when they are cool enough to handle, pit them. Carefully chop them into a fine paste, removing any pits or shards that you come across.

2. Place the date paste in a medium work bowl. Add the rest of the ingredients and mix well.

Liánróng sōngzi dànhuáng 蓮蓉松子蛋黃

Lotus, Pine Nut, and Salted Yolk Filling

MAKES ABOUT 2½ CUPS

6 ounces (about 1½ cups) dried lotus seeds

¼ cup unsalted butter, at room temperature

¼ teaspoon sea salt

¼ cup powdered sugar

¾ cup caramel syrup (page 446)

5 tablespoons *meiguilu* liquor, divided into 3 tablespoons and 2 tablespoons

1 teaspoon rose water (optional)

4 ounces (heaping ¾ cup) toasted pine nuts

10 raw brined egg yolks (page 422)

1. Soak the lotus seeds for at least 8 hours and up to overnight. Drain. Place the seeds in a heatproof bowl and steam them (see page 49) for about 30 minutes, until very tender. Remove from the steamer and let come to room temperature.

2. Remove the bitter green sprouts that will appear in many of the seeds (see page 289).

3. Place the lotus seeds in a food processor (see Tips) and pulse until the seeds are reduced to a fine gravel. Add the butter, salt, sugar, caramel syrup, and 3 tablespoons of the *meiguilu* and then whiz them together to make a fine paste. Dump the paste into a medium work bowl; taste and adjust the seasoning, adding the rose water if desired. Stir in the pine nuts until evenly distributed. Chill the filling.

4. While the filling is in the refrigerator, place the egg yolks on an ovenproof plate and sprinkle them with the remaining 2 tablespoons *meiguilu*, as this will remove some of their gaminess. Bake them at 375°F for about 7 minutes to soften and cook them. This will also release some of the oils in the yolks and turn them creamier. Remove the yolks from the plate and let them come to room temperature. Or, if you wish, you can use the yolks as is, especially if you are using chicken eggs rather than duck eggs. Cut each one into thirds if you are making small moon cakes.

5. Divide the lotus filling into 10 large or 30 small pieces, and roll each piece into a ball. Moistening your hands occasionally makes this a lot easier. Push 1 yolk into each ball and then cover the yolk with the lotus filling.

6. When wrapping moon cakes with this filling, pinch off a ½-inch marble of each cake's dough and set it aside while you use the rest of the dough to wrap the filling as usual. When you press the filling into your mold, you will usually see the yolk poking through the bottom, since it is harder than both the filling and the dough. Use that little piece of leftover dough as a patch and then smooth it down.

I like to add a bit of Cortas brand rose water to the lotus paste to heighten the suggestion of roses in the *meiguilu* liquor. You can't really taste the roses—I don't want pastries that smell like Nana anyway—but the rose water provides a subtle undercurrent. This is, of course, totally optional.

Shelled pine nuts can be used either raw or toasted in this recipe. I prefer toasted ones for their heightened nut flavor and color contrast. You can buy the pine nuts toasted or toast them yourself in the oven or a dry wok. The main thing to look for is freshness, so check the expiration date. Store your pine nuts in the freezer if you don't use them often, as this will keep their oils from going rancid.

During the cold months, raw brined yolks can be found prepackaged (without the whites) in many Chinese markets, usually in the same case as the other eggs. Make sure they are from the United States rather than China. Refrigerate any leftover yolks in a sealed bag and use them within a week or two. Discard any that look or smell wrong.

Don't try using a food mill on the lotus seeds; they are much too dry. A food processor works perfectly, though.

Hēi tángjiāng 黑糖漿

Caramel Syrup

MAKES ABOUT 1½ CUPS

2½ cups powdered sugar
1 cup water, divided in half
3 tablespoons pale rice vinegar or cider vinegar

1. Place the powdered sugar and ½ cup of the water in a stainless-steel pan so that you can easily see the sugar change color. Bring the mixture to a boil over high heat, cover for a few minutes so that the steam washes down the sugar crystals, and then uncover. Add the vinegar and bring the pan back to a boil without stirring. Briskly boil the sugar syrup for about 10 minutes, until it starts to turn amber and caramelize.

2. When the syrup is an even golden brown, lower the heat to medium-high and then add the remaining ½ cup water. Be careful, as the caramel will boil furiously at this point, so direct the pan away from your face. As the boiling starts to simmer down, stir the caramel with a silicone spatula until the syrup is smooth.

3. Pour the caramel into a heatproof measuring cup and let it cool to room temperature; refrigerate in a closed container if you're not using it immediately.

Shēnsè dànshuǐ 深色蛋水

Dark Glaze

ENOUGH FOR 20 LARGE OR 30 SMALL MOON CAKES

1 large egg yolk
2 teaspoons *meiguilu* liquor or vodka
1 tablespoon caramel syrup (at left)

1. Mix all the ingredients together in a small bowl. Brush the glaze lightly over the tops and sides of unbaked pastries.

2. Store any leftovers covered in the refrigerator for not more than a day, as the yolk will start to dry out.

Dànsè dànshuǐ 淡色蛋水

Light Glaze

ENOUGH FOR 20 LARGE OR 30 SMALL MOON CAKES

1 large egg yolk, lightly beaten
2 teaspoons milk
1 tablespoon caramel syrup (at left)

1. Mix the ingredients together in a small bowl. Brush the glaze lightly over the tops and sides of unbaked pastries.

2. Store any leftovers covered in the refrigerator for not more than a day, as the yolk will start to dry out.

TECHNIQUES & HANDY ADVICE

One of the true joys of learning to cook like a great Chinese chef is that very soon you will end up with some pretty amazing things on the dinner table. I am talking about dishes that you cannot find even in good restaurants.

But China's kitchen arts involve much, much more than assembling a recipe correctly; they require mastery of a number of ancient skills. Do not be alarmed—this mastery is in fact downright fun, and will make what you do seem to the uninitiated almost like sleight-of-hand. The Chinese have been using these techniques forever to make life in the kitchen a genuine pleasure, and you will look very sophisticated as you swirl around the kitchen, following in their footsteps.

I am talking here about things like buying only the best ingredients, selecting the perfect vegetables and cooking them correctly, knowing how to cut apart a chicken and clean a shrimp, using a Chinese chef's knife as if it were an extension of your hand, looking at water on the stove and knowing exactly how hot it is, and understanding how to use the handle and the back of your cleaver to mash foods into a paste and tenderize meats.

This mastery also extends to dining like a proper Chinese person, and possessing the proper gravitas as you work your way from appetizers to the final cup of tea. It all adds up to unmitigated dining pleasure—to enjoying every step from purchasing ingredients to pushing back from the table with a satisfied smile.

Here, then, are the keys to my Chinese kitchen, and the doorway to eating the best food in the world.

First, a Word about Ingredients

Before you begin to cook, you need to have a firm grip on what quality ingredients are and where to find them.

As you search around for the freshest vegetables, peak seasonal fruits, tastiest meats and seafood, and most reliable Chinese materials, keep track of which places sell the best items and start to nurture relationships with these merchants. I have found that repeat business will be rewarded, and you will soon be able to special-order things, to grill the managers on their sourcing, and to ask them to keep you in mind when they are out stocking up for the day's offerings.

Also notice what brands of prepared Chinese ingredients please you the most. I like Taiwan's Wan Ja Shan soy sauce and make a point of searching out its organic labels. Likewise, I stock up on the Shaoxing rice wine produced on the island and sold by the government entity called TTL (aka Taiwan Tobacco and Liquor, which used to be called the monopoly bureau, until someone wised them up to the fact that "monopoly" doesn't sound especially nice).

Wander around the little stores that dot the alleys and strip malls in your nearest Chinatown whenever you can, and try new things. Keep business cards with products you purchased and liked written on the back, so you can either visit again or call them up to send you more. If you like, take this book along with you so that you can point out the Chinese words for whatever it is you'd like to find. Look online for ingredients and equipment if you don't live near a Chinese community.

Vegetables, Hard and Soft

Vegetables in every Chinese cuisine (with the exception of vegetarian cooking, of course) tend to act as side dishes, supporting players, and ample garnishes for the entrées. Nevertheless, the Chinese eat them at almost every meal. Produce is prized in China and is cooked with care so as to best celebrate its natural flavors and textures.

DON'T USE CANNED VEGETABLES

One of the most frightful things about some Chinese restaurants in America is the dependence upon canned vegetables. Yuck. I never, ever buy canned water chestnuts, bamboo shoots, baby corn, or mushrooms, as I would rather not use them if I cannot find them fresh. Tinned veggies taste of the can and should be avoided. (I've never understood the attraction of baby corn, actually, and can only picture Tom Hanks nibbling on one in *Big*.)

When my husband and I lived in Taiwan, and in our visits to mainland China and Hong Kong, it seemed that every cook loved fresh veggies as much as we do. There is zero need to use less than stellar ingredients in your cooking; use the best or omit.

This is one of the core concepts of the classic Chinese cooking traditions. A green onion right out of the earth will be springy and have a bright aroma, as well as a satisfying crunch when sliced; an onion that has hung around for a few days will be flaccid, radiate a gassy stink, and have lost its green color. If you are going to the trouble of cooking with something, buy small amounts of the finest quality and use them up as quickly as possible.

CORRECTLY PREP AND STORE YOUR FOODS

Certain vegetables need to have their outer layers removed before use, like Chinese radishes, carrots, lotus roots, and water chestnuts. Once this is done, you should place them in a bowl of cold (and sometimes acidulated) water if you are not going to immediately prep them further, as this helps prevent them from drying out or discoloring. This bath will also crisp them up a bit.

Other vegetables need only the bottom parts of their stems peeled or cleaned, such as asparagus and Chinese flowering kale (gailan), and the woody ends discarded. Celery must have its tough strings removed and the bases of each stalk carefully scrubbed to get rid of lumps of mud. Leafy greens are often notoriously gritty and will also benefit from a quick chill after a gentle bath. The best way to do it is to wrap them in a clean tea towel and refrigerate them in a plastic bag for a few hours. Even the most fragile leaves will become crunchier as a result.

PREPPING HARD VEGETABLES

SMACKING OPEN CUCUMBERS
This does not require a whole lot of force.
Use a wide knife; a distance of a couple of inches
should provide enough momentum to break
the cucumber open without mashing it.

ROLL CUTS
Steady a long, cylindrical vegetable—like a carrot
or Chinese radish—with one hand, and use that
same hand to roll the vegetable back and forth
while cutting on an angle. This opens up the
maximum amount of surface area and allows
the vegetable to cook quickly and evenly.

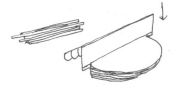

SLICING ROUND VEGETABLES
To keep things like potatoes from rolling around, first
cut off one slice from a long side. Put this cut side
down on the board and start to slice the vegetable.

JULIENNE, MATCHSTICKS, AND BATONS
Thin strips are created by first slicing the ingredient,
and then cutting it crosswise. Julienne strips are very fine,
matchsticks are larger, and batons are anywhere
from ¼ to ½ inch wide all around.

PREPPING LEAFY VEGETABLES

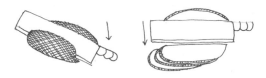

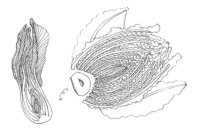

For things like pea shoots, pinch off the
tender stems and discard anything fibrous.
For vegetables like gailan, separate the leaves from
the stem, and then peel the stem if it is edible.

Members of the cabbage family, like bok choy
and napa cabbage, have the leaves attached to
a core. Remove the core if it is tough, or else
clean carefully in the crevices at the base.

LILY BULBS

1 Cut off any discolored areas, including any rotting in the center.

2 Separate the bulb into "petals," trim away any brown areas, and rinse in a colander.

BEAN SPROUTS

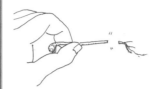

1 Remove the root ends by pinching them off just where the stalk starts to narrow.

2 If you are not using the heads, snap them off with your fingertips.

MUSTARD CABBAGE

1 Trim off the floppy leaves and cut off the larger hard leaves, which should be sliced crosswise at a deep angle.

2 Hold the head with the stem end on top and slice down vertically through the head at an angle.

LEEKS

1 Cut off the dark green leaves and discard, but leave the root end on.

2 Slice the leek vertically down the middle and then carefully rinse out all of the grit at the base of the leaves. Cut off the root end and slice the leek as directed.

THE TECHNIQUE MUST MATCH THE MATERIAL Lotus roots, Chinese radishes, carrots, and other roots have uniform, dense textures that lend themselves to carving, slicing, and dicing, as these vegetables will retain their shapes up to the point of being cooked to near-death. Restaurants will often include carrots and bamboo shoots in their stir-fries for the carrots' color and sweetness and for the bamboo shoots' texture. These will always appear as thin slices—either simple strips or cut into fanciful shapes, if the restaurant is really kicking out the jams—that allow the vegetables to cook quickly and evenly. The best cooks will cook these ingredients separately, according to their individual thicknesses and textures, and then combine them just before serving.

Whenever you stir-fry these kinds of vegetables, the secret to having them crisp yet cooked is to add a couple of tablespoons of liquid—things like water,

❶ Use a potato peeler to remove the skin and trim away the hard root ends, as well as any bruises.

❷ Cut open the root as directed in the recipe and wash out any mud. If you are using a whole lotus root, a chopstick can be used to dislodge dirt deep within the holes.

rice wine, or stock—to the wok just as the outside of the thinly sliced veggies become slightly browned. Immediately cover the wok and let them steam in the rapidly evaporating liquid. When most of the liquid has boiled off, remove the cover and check the vegetables; they should be perfectly done.

Another way to guarantee that harder vegetables cook quickly and evenly is to blanch them before tossing them into a wok. In fact, if you are having people over for dinner and want to have as many things ready as possible before your guests arrive, blanch the heftier vegetables until they are cooked but still crisp, rinse them quickly in a colander with cool tap water, and then place them in a work bowl covered with ice water. You will have brilliantly colored, perfectly textured, and fully flavorful veggies nearly ready that way. All you have to do is drain and heat them quickly in whatever sauce you're using.

The starchiest vegetables are often braised rather than stir-fried. Potatoes, taro, carrots, Chinese yams (*shanyao*), pumpkins, winter melon, lotus roots, onions, meaty mushrooms, and bamboo shoots in

particular are delicious when slowly cooked in a flavorful liquid that seeps into their flesh and gives them a totally new dimension.

To braise vegetables, first brown some ginger and/ or green onions in oil, then add the braising liquid of your choice (a combination of soy sauce, rice wine, and rock sugar will make this a red-cooked dish) as well as your vegetables. Braised veggies should be cut thickly—as slices, batons, or in roll cuts—so that they do not disintegrate during the slow cooking process. If you are using more than one vegetable, make sure that your cooking times take this into account. You might place black mushrooms, onions, and bamboo shoots in the pot first, before later adding lotus roots, pumpkin, and carrots. If in doubt, simply blanch your vegetables first, give them a quick braise, and (if time allows) let them sit in the sauce overnight so that they can fully absorb the flavors.

The most important step in prepping hard vegetables is cutting them into pieces that will allow them to cook evenly. However they are trimmed, keep in mind the shapes of the other ingredients in your dish— visual harmony is just as important as any other criteria (see page 212).

The diagrams on page 449 show you how to properly prepare hard vegetables the Chinese way.

SOFTER VEGETABLES

Leafy, tender greens like water spinach and Chinese chives need only a flash in a hot wok to cook evenly; other vegetables with an even more fragile cellular structure will dash from raw to cooked in a matter of seconds. Tomatoes, for example, are uniformly soft once their skins and seeds are removed, and therefore should either be very briefly heated through or allowed to dissolve into a smooth mush.

Greens are generally cooked very simply to preserve their color, flavor, and texture. The optimum amount of heat is one that will nudge the vegetable over the line from a raw state into barely cooked, as this keeps it bright green, crisp, and sweet.

Vegetables like Chinese mustards and cabbages, as well as some tougher leafy vegetables such as spinach, are made up of many parts that have different flavors, textures, and colors. For this reason, most cooks will separate the leaves from the stems and the tender parts from the tougher areas, removing the skin where necessary, and try to make each part as uniform in size and texture as possible, in order to allow the pieces to be cooked quickly and evenly.

As you clean your vegetables and carefully remove any foreign matter, observe the structure of their leaves and stems: they'll tell you what needs the most attention. The bases of bok choy stems, for example, are cupped and grow close to the soil, and so dirt becomes stuck to their bases. Spinach likewise attracts grit in its tightly wound bases.

What you need to do before you wash them, then, is to make the dirty parts accessible. Bok choy can be left whole if you have immature heads that are very clean, but otherwise it should be sliced lengthwise in half, quarters, or smaller sections so that the base of each leaf is exposed. Spinach needs to be separated into individual stems so that its sand can be dislodged. The easiest way to clean leafy vegetables is to soak the leaves and stems separately in a basin of warm water (see page 10). This softens any dirt quickly, and the warm water is soothing to the hands, so the cook is more willing to swish those veggies around and rinse out all of the foreign matter. As you dump out the water, notice how much grit is in the bottom of the basin. Rinse the vegetables again until the water is clear. The leaves should then be shaken dry in a colander or salad spinner, so only tiny drops of water remain on the vegetable.

This water is important because it will allow for a small amount of steam to be produced during the vegetables' time in the wok. This will help cook the leaves quickly and evenly. In fact, if your vegetables are going to be served alongside dishes that already have more than their share of fat, leafy vegetables can even be flash-fried without any oil at all, with the water on their leaves taking the place of the usual dollop of oil. A good example of this would be pea shoots flash-fried with just a sprinkle of salt in a dry wok and then used to surround a platter of Dongpo Pork (page 114).

The main requirement for greens in a Chinese kitchen is that they be super fresh. That is the first secret to preparing perfect leafy vegetables, because with fresh produce all the cook needs to do is prep them and then quickly toss them over high heat.

Leafy vegetables do need to be prepped correctly, however. Those with delicate and tender stems, like pea shoots and water spinach, must have their fibrous bits removed. The rest of the stems can stay attached, as shown on page 449. Each variety of leafy vegetable has an individual structure that should be understood in order to get the most out of it. Every part of the plant might need to be cooked a different way in order to preserve its flavor and texture. With certain leafy vegetables, Chinese cooks often flash-fry the leaves but braise the tougher stems.

WHAT IS FLASH-FRYING?

This is cooking a relatively small amount of vegetables in a wok over very high heat, using little more than a slick of oil (or no oil at all) and a sprinkle of salt. Here are the keys to achieving a great flash-fried dish.

First, your wok should always be placed on high heat without any oil, so that the iron itself becomes very hot. No oil should be added before the wok has heated up; the only thing that should be in there is the thin film of oil that remained after the wok was last rinsed out. When the wok is hot enough, this oil film will begin to smoke a tiny bit, so wait until that happens.

Second, if you are now adding oil, swish it around to cover at least the lower half of your wok. Sprinkle in your salt so that it has a chance to melt a bit. Toss in whatever aromatics you might be using, such as chopped garlic, ginger, or green onions. If your arms are strong enough, toss the aromatics around by holding the wok above the stove and shaking it (see Tossing Ingredients in a Wok, page 454); otherwise, use a wok spatula.

At this point the wok should still be red hot, so add your leafy vegetables. How much to add depends upon your stove. If you have a good Chinese propane wok burner, you can probably stir-fry just about anything in there because the heat is so good and so even. Those who have only regular gas stoves or even electric burners, though, can still flash-fry with exceptional results if only small amounts of food are added at a time. This prevents the wok from cooling down quickly. If you have a wimpy stove (see page 468), simply scoot the aromatics up the side of your wok, out of the heat, and then add a handful of leafy vegetables (or whatever else you're cooking) to the bottom of the wok so that they can cook quickly. As soon as the leaves are wilted (or the shrimp are pink, or the chicken is lightly browned), push these up the sides of the wok, too, and then fry your next handful.

As you stir-fry, you might find that your ingredients are sticking to the bottom of the wok. All you need to do then is drizzle a little bit of oil around the edge of the food, so that it heats up quickly as it flows to the bottom. Alternatively, you can pour in a bit of some other liquid, such as water, rice wine, or stock. Tossing the ingredients with this new addition should stop the sticking, at least until the food is cooked or the liquid has evaporated. Just a touch of oil will coat your ingredients with a thin film and help to evenly transfer the heat from the wok; too much will make the food deep-fried or soggy.

As soon as your ingredients have barely lost their rawness, remove your wok from the heat and scoop the food out onto a platter. The residual heat from the cooking will continue to change its character, especially with vegetables, so serve your flash-fried dish immediately.

COMMON VEGETABLE SIDES
ACCORDING TO REGION

Just about any vegetable can round out a meal, no matter the cuisine. However, the following is a list of favorites that seem to go especially well with this book's individual regions:

- The North & Manchurian Northeast: Napa cabbage, spinach, mung bean sprouts, soybean sprouts, Chinese radishes, eggplants, carrots, mushrooms, wood ear fungus, garlic stems, gourds, yellow chives, tomatoes, cucumbers, and potatoes.
- The Yangtze River & Its Environs: Pea sprouts, bamboo shoots, bok choy, *tatsoi*, yellow chives, Chinese aster (*mălántóu* 馬蘭頭), shepherd's purse (*jìcài* 薺菜), water-shield (*chúncài* 莼菜),[1] edible ferns, watercress, fava beans, lotus roots, bitter melons, and taro.
- The Coastal Southeast: Water spinach, garlic chives, garlic chive flowers, yellow chives, mushrooms, mung bean sprouts, celtuce leaves, sweet potato leaves, various mustards, flowering kale, Chinese celery, bitter melon, kelp, and taro.
- The Central Highlands: Spinach, mustard cabbage, asparagus, soybean sprouts, lily bulbs, Chinese celery, potatoes, sweet potatoes, peppers, mushrooms, bitter melon, cucumbers, and Chinese yams.
- The Arid Lands: Spinach, yellow chives, lily bulbs, carrots, wolfberry leaves, napa cabbage, potatoes, peppers, eggplants, tomatoes, and cilantro.

Chinese Chef Moves

China's role as one of the world's oldest continuing food cultures has led to an accumulation of thousands of years of observation, experience, and sophisticated techniques. A whole book could (and should) be written about them, but here are a few of my personal favorites.

TOSSING INGREDIENTS IN A WOK

My favorite James Bond quote is, "I'll do anything for a woman with a knife." He was also right about shaking, not stirring, especially when it comes to cooking with a wok. A good cook will know how to shake a wok to toss ingredients, rather than moving things around with a spatula.

A northern-style wok, with its long handle, works especially well for this; you can train your dominant arm (or both arms) to lift it up while deftly shaking and tossing its contents over a high flame. Ingredients mingle more easily and quickly when tossed, and tenderer things will not get mashed up.

---

1. These three relatively unusual vegetables are presently available frozen in some Chinese markets.

TOSSING INGREDIENTS IN A WOK

1

Practice this with some small wet sponges in a cold empty wok. Gently but firmly tug the wok toward you, which will slide the sponges in your direction.

2

Do this with force so that the sponges come all the way up the side nearest you and then skate to a stop near the handle.

3

Quickly jerk the wok away from you while swirling the outer edge up, which will make the sponges glide to the far edge of the wok and then fly back toward the handle.

4

As the sponges cartwheel over the wok like little gymnasts, their bottoms will automatically flip over. Once you feel comfortable with this, switch to actually frying things like sliced mushrooms and firm bean curd.

BROWNING FOODS

1

First, heat the wok or pan and only then add the oil. Carefully lay the meat or other foods down on the hot iron. Don't move the food once it has hit the wok.

2

Wait until the bottom of the food has caramelized and started to separate from the wok, and then jerk the pan toward you (see above) to release the foods before flipping them over.

This does require a few preparatory steps. One, your wok has to be well seasoned, with a smooth, cooked-on oil patina that makes it almost nonstick. (I do not recommend woks sold with so-called nonstick surfaces; a well-made wok will become nonstick naturally.) Second, your wok must be so hot that the iron instantly cooks the sugars on the surface of your ingredients, forming a crust that allows them to release easily from the wok. The best way to achieve this is to set your empty, dry wok over a high flame, let the iron heat up, and only then add oil. This has the added advantage of exposing your oil only briefly to high heat, which would otherwise break down the fats. (See "Stir-Frying on a Wimpy Stove" on page 468 for more tips on this.)

And third, you need to practice lifting a heavy pan to get these moves down. You will develop some serious arm, wrist, and hand muscles as time passes, and it is amazing how confident it will make you feel. See the diagram to the left for a good way to practice.

MULTIPLE TECHNIQUES
IN ONE DISH

Most Chinese dishes require at least two—and sometimes many more—different ways of cooking ingredients. Although this might seem fussy, it actually helps make things simple. When a recipe calls for firm vegetables to be quickly blanched before being flash-fried, for example, it allows the vegetables to be partially cooked a couple of hours before being served, when a quick turn in the wok will complete the prep. With some dishes you can space your labor over as much as a day or two, while also addressing the individual character of each of your ingredients.

Take good fried rice (pages 138 and 222). You need cold steamed rice (first step), which is then stir-fried (second step). You might want to add some shrimp or pine nuts or veggies or eggs, which are best fried separately or in a well at the bottom of the rice (third step), and only then combined with it. Get these steps coordinated and fried rice comes together quickly and easily, giving you light, fluffy grains seasoned with savory bits.

Or, consider Oyster Spring Rolls (page 168): the raw oysters are first poached, the other ingredients are stir-fried, and then they are tucked into wrappers together and deep-fried. Each step is necessary for the dish to come together correctly; the oysters have to be cooked through, and the best way to retain their juiciness and shape is to gently poach them. The meat and vegetables likewise require individualized cooking, so that they don't end up raw in the center. By cooking them separately ahead of time—even a day or so in advance, if you like—the only thing left to do when you're ready to eat is to roll everything up and slide the packets into the hot fat.

In the end, what this means is that most of China's greatest dishes can be casually assembled over days. A tour-de-force dinner party can be a relaxed affair for the chef, because you do not have to do everything at the last minute.

PREPPING MEATS, POULTRY,
AND SEAFOOD

In China, meat and poultry are rarely cooked as is. One of these four things will generally be done first to leach out unnecessary moisture, tighten any skin and flavor the flesh:

- Blanching. A quick, hot bath will cause all sorts of nasty scum to appear, stuff that would otherwise cloud your sauce and muddle its flavors. Blanching gives blood and other things a chance to quickly exit muscles and bones. After that, just rinse off the flesh and the pot and then proceed with your recipe.
- Browning. Nothing can equal the depth of flavor and color that this brings to meat, chicken, and mushrooms as it transforms their sugars into a sticky, caramelized crust. Be sure to let your ingredients rest against the cooking surface until that crust has formed; if you move them around, they will steam rather than caramelize. Properly browned ingredients will flip over easily and no longer stick to the pan once that caramelization is complete; this is the most accurate indication that they are ready to be turned.

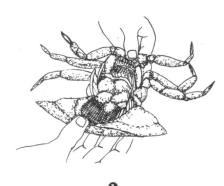

❶

If the crab is alive, put on heavy gloves and hold the crab from the back. Scrub the crab clean, and then kill the crab by either pulling off the top shell from the back or removing the abdomen flap and stabbing the crab in the hole down there. Reserve any orange roe, green tomalley, and pale fatty "butter" that you find, as these are full of flavor.

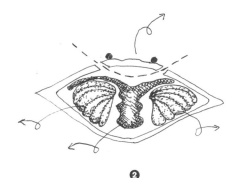

❷

On the interior of the top shell, trim off and discard the feathery gills along the side. Cut off the mouth and brain area and discard the organs.

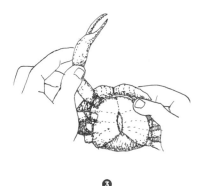

❸

Remove the legs and chop the larger ones apart along their joints as needed.

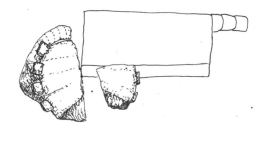

❹

Use a cleaver to chop the body in half, or into quarters, or as desired.

There are two types of browning. The first involves simply adding your ingredients—marinated or not—to your hot oil; this is what is done most of the time in stir-fries, braises, and so forth. The other way is to blanch your ingredients first, rinse and dry them off, and then sear them in hot oil. This works best for big chunks of meat destined for soups and stews.

· Marinating. If you're cooking flesh without the use of a stock or sauce, consider infusing it with a few other flavors first. Proteins that are particularly strong smelling—like liver, kidneys, oily fish, and so forth—become much tastier when bathed in things like rice wine, salt, and/ or soy sauce, as this gives them the opportunity to expel their impurities and off-flavors.

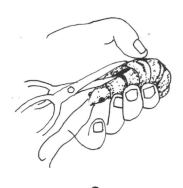

❶

If you are leaving the head and shell on, use kitchen shears to cut down the back of the shrimp through the shell and down as far as the sandy vein.

❷

Trim off the long antennae and the pointy end of its nose. If you are going to deep-fry the shrimp, lop off the eyes, too, to prevent them from exploding.

❸

To remove the shell, insert a finger or two into the body between the rows of legs and work the shell off, which will also get rid of the legs. You can leave the tail on or remove it, depending upon the recipe.

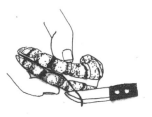

❹

Remove the vein and rinse out the back, and then pat the shrimp dry with a paper towel.

Marinades will also help tenderize flesh and insert other layers of flavor into your final dish. Pour off your marinades (rinsing the meats, if they are really gamy) and pat the ingredients dry with a paper towel if your main purpose in marinating is to lighten their aromas.

· Salting. Ingredients are often salted to remove excess liquid, as well as for seasoning, especially when soy sauce and other savory ingredients will not season the final dish. Chinese radishes, cucumbers, and fish are good examples of things that truly benefit from this extra step, as it will firm them up, concentrate their flavors, and keep too much liquid from diluting the seasoning.

CHOPPING MEAT BY HAND UNTIL FLUFFY

❶

To prepare the meat in the traditional manner, first lay a wet kitchen towel under a heavy chopping block.

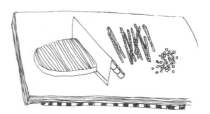

❷

Place the meat on the chopping block and cut it into small dice.

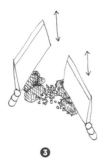

❸

Use the back of one or two cleavers to pound the meat into a fine mince, pausing now and then to remove any white tendons from the meat.

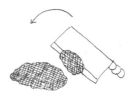

❹

Lift and turn over the meat with your cleaver and then pound it in different directions to turn it into a tender paste.

MIXING FORCEMEATS BY HAND

❶

Place the finely chopped meats and other ingredients in a wide work bowl set on a kitchen towel, which will keep it from sliding around.

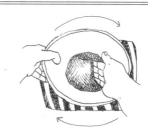

❷

Hold the bowl while using your dominant hand as a paddle to whip the forcemeat in one direction, which will make it light and tensile.

REMOVING PIG HAIRS & PINFEATHERS

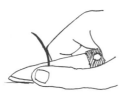

❶

Use Chinese kitchen tweezers or a small paring knife to pull out thicker hairs or feathers, which have deep roots and so should not be simply burned off. To use a knife for this, place the blade against one side of the hair and your thumb on the other and then pull up sharply. This is easiest to do when the pork has already been cooked, as this softens the skin.

❷

Smaller hairs can be burned away with a chef's kitchen torch.

BONING A PORK SHANK

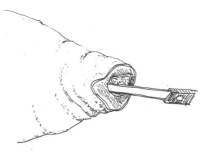

❶

Slide a long, thin blade around both ends of the bone and direct the sharp edge toward the bone as you scrape away the flesh and tendons.

❷

When you have cut the bone free, you will be able to pull it out, leaving behind a nice meaty pyramid.

CLEANING A BEEF HEART

❶

Use a very sharp knife to trim off any silver skin and fat on the outside of the heart.

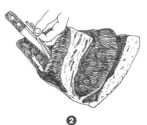

❷

Cut the heart open like a book. Remove the fat, arteries, and silvery connective tissue; rinse with cool water.

CHOPPING UP A WHOLE BIRD

1

Slice off the whole legs where the thighs join the back, keeping as much of the skin attached to the meat as possible. Slice through the cartilage in the joint between each leg and thigh to give you two pieces; the thigh meat can be carved lengthwise to make bite-sized pieces.

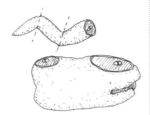

2

Cut off the wings through the joint that connects the wings to the breast, and then separate each wing into three pieces.

3

Slice down on both sides of the breastbone to loosen the meat and then run your knife all the way around it to separate it from the bones. Cut the breast meat crosswise into bite-sized pieces. (If you want to serve the back, cut out the spine and then chop the ribs into bite-sized pieces, too.)

4

To serve a cut-up cooked chicken, reassemble the pieces so that the bird looks almost whole. The messy pieces and the back can be hidden under the breast meat.

PARTIALLY BONING A BIRD

1

Place the bird on its back and slice down on either side of the breastbone. Cut around the wishbone at the collar and remove it.

2

Use a boning knife to remove the rib cage, scraping along the bones, and leaving the skin and meat as much attached to the chicken as possible.

3

Cut down around the back ribs and remove the top half of the bones in the back, severing the spine just at the bottom of the ribs.

4

The bird will now be nice and floppy, except for the legs and wings, and you will be able to fold the breasts over the body and tuck the wings under to form a compact package.

PREPPING A BIRD FOR COOKING

1

Pat the chicken (and giblets) dry, then remove any extra fat around the neck and bottom cavities.

2

Pull out the pinfeathers and any viscera clinging between the back ribs. Cut off the wing tips, if you want.

3

Tuck the wings underneath the drumstick joint, or cut small holes in the "armpit" area under the wing and stick the outer two joints inside the bird's body.

4

Tie the bottoms of the legs tightly together.

5

If you are going to either deep-fry or poach the whole bird, tie kitchen twine snugly around the body underneath the wings and add a loop on both sides so you can lift it from the top.

6

Tie loops around both sides of the ankle knot to lift the bird upside down. (This diagram shows the wings stuck into the body cavity.)

HARD-BOILING EGGS

1

Use room-temperature eggs, preferably free range and about a week old. Punch a hole in the round end of each egg with a sharp pin or tack. This will prevent the air sac from expanding in the hot water and breaking the shell.

2

Bring the water slowly to a boil over medium heat. Since the eggs will be starting out at room temperature, the water will boil fairly quickly, but it won't be fast enough to surprise the air sacs into exploding.

3

Stir the eggs every 30 seconds or so as they come to a boil. This will center the yolks inside the whites. Cook to desired doneness.

4

Immediately submerge the eggs in cold water and then tap them all over to crack the shells, if needed.

In the world of perfume, aromas are said to have high, middle, and low notes; this applies to the world of food, as well. The high notes are things like the fresh, grassy flavors of celery, the sweetness of a carrot, the piquancy of lemon juice. In the middle are the flavors released after the first bite, like juicy chicken or braised pork or cooked onions.

Underlying all of these is another layer, a savory stratum of complex flavors and aromas that the Chinese call *xianwei*, which translates as "fresh flavor," and which the Japanese refer to as umami. It is this sense of *xianwei* that is usually responsible for making a Chinese dish extraordinary.

China has what has to be the greatest stockpile of fermented, salted, pickled, dried, and cured ingredients known to man. These give a special edge to many of the country's most delectable dishes. Natural fermentation via a helpful family of molds has given us soy sauce, sweet wheat paste, a wealth of bean pastes, wines, and dry-cured ham, and this fermentation—along with a battery of other deeply aromatic ingredients like dried shrimp, scallops, and black mushrooms—is the major reason why Chinese dishes are best complemented with grain-based beverages like rice wine, white liquor, and beer, rather than with grape wine (see page 191).

USE STOCK AND SOAKING LIQUID

Traditionally, chefs in China have relied on aromatic stocks to give dishes a flavor boost that sends diners into sensory overload. Good things are never wasted in a Chinese kitchen, and so scraps of meat, poultry, and vegetables tend to get tossed into a stockpot simmering at the back of the stove, which in turn sends out lovely aromas that make the cook (that is, you) feel exceptionally virtuous.

But I don't always have a pot of stock boiling away, so I trim the stems off of black mushrooms and let them dry out on the kitchen counter before storing them in a pantry jar. These are then hauled out for special occasions when I want an intense burst of *xianwei* in my stocks, and they never let me down. Backs and wings of ducks can also be frozen until I have a nice stockpile from which I can create fresh duck stock within the hour.

If you don't have a stockpot going at all times either, do not despair, for there are some excellent organic broths out there now in aseptic paper boxes; just look for the unsalted or very lightly salted ones. I always have at least a half-dozen boxes of free-range, organic chicken broth on hand, because so many savory dishes taste better with it hiding in the background. If you love MSG, by all means sprinkle it on—it's said to be safe for most people. I'm just not much of a fan.

Another easy source of *xianwei* is the soaking liquid from certain unsalted dried ingredients, like red dates. If you are unsure whether a soaking liquid will augment or distract from your dish, take a tiny sip.

STEAM

Steam will make a huge difference in how your fried pastries, vegetables, and meats turn out. The easiest and simplest way to introduce it is to cover your pan as the food cooks, which traps any moisture inside and turns it into steam. This in turn will speed up the cooking without the dish becoming too browned. You will see this technique called for often throughout this book.

In some cases, additional liquid will be required. If the pan is covered quickly after the liquid is added, an enormous amount of steam will be produced, which cooks things like firm vegetables and the dough on the top of potstickers to a perfect state of doneness.

Regardless of steam's benefits, though, certain things should almost always be cooked uncovered. First and foremost are stocks. Covering a stock will turn it milky, so if you want to obtain a beautifully crystalline broth from your bones, leave the cover off. Cook poultry stocks for only about an hour; after that the cartilage and skin will start to break down and you'll lose that lovely clear sheen.

Second are cabbages. Be very careful when cooking any kind of cabbage with a lid on; sulfuric gases may form and cause foul aromas.

NOT ALL SUGARS ARE CREATED EQUAL

As you cook your way through this book's recipes, you will learn to employ three types of sweetener that are particularly wonderful: rock sugar, caramel syrup, and black sugar.

Rock sugar is composed of large crystalline lumps that can be smashed into smaller chunks as they melt. This ingredient is beloved in China because it leaves no sour aftertaste, a quality that becomes especially apparent in things like a sweetened dessert soup (see page 372 for an example). But it goes beyond that. Rock sugar also lends a smoothness and a definite richness to braises; red-cooked meats become glossier when rock sugar is used, and the flavors turn mellower. Get the yellowish type of rock sugar—white ones tend to be bleached—and prepare to be hooked.

Rock sugar has another side that is revealed when it is simmered in a bit of oil: the crystals crack, crumble, and finally melt into glorious caramel. Honestly, I cannot think of a more delicious edge to a dish than this mahogany goo. It is easy to make (see page 115, Step 4), and will transform rich stocks.

Dark brown sugar is the final member of this sweet triad, with a color so deep that the Chinese refer to it as *hēitáng* 黑糖, or "black sugar." In addition to its hue, it has a depth of flavor and a very substantial edge that easily acts as a seasoning. The best I've found comes from South Korea in plastic bags.

MAKE THESE DISHES YOUR OWN

Although I have done my best in this book to preserve the traditional tastes and dishes of China, there is no single standard national recipe for anything, and everyone in China knows that their grandma is the best cook in the world. Yes, there are gastronomes who have penned opinionated guides to their favorite dishes, but not one is considered the be-all and end-all of culinary instruction.

That being said, some little touches, like browning, make all the difference in the world. Browning your ginger before anything else will turn it golden and chewy and sweet, infusing your oil with its warm essence. The aromatics I'm always going on about are simply astounding if treated right, and one of the best ways to feature their perfume is to gently brown them to create a seasoned oil (pages 434 to 436) that can be used at the beginning or end of a recipe. And browned bits of garlic, green onion, shallots, and ginger can be used to decorate the final dish.

Feel free to incorporate new ingredients and equipment, too. Food processors, pressure cookers, and mini-blenders, for example, are permanent members in my *batterie de cuisine*, and things like agave syrup and aseptic boxes of good stock are quite tasty and convenient. I also take my personal tastes into account. I prefer desserts that are not overly sweet, I cut back on the salt if it is overpowering the other flavors, and I reduce the fat if it gets in the way of my enjoyment of a dish. Lots of times I add extra Shaoxing rice wine out of love for its mushroomy aroma, or double the amount of green onions because I can't get enough of their silky texture against certain meats. This is always done with respect for tradition, but every family has its own take on the great foods of China, including mine.

Mark up this book with notes on what you like so that you remember to add a dash more salt, say, or to cut the garlic in half. Once you have mastered your favorite recipes here, you can start to improvise. Do not be afraid to substitute ingredients, as long as the switch makes sense to you. Add more garlic or rice wine to a dish and see what happens. Use duck instead of pork, or try Chinese yams instead of potatoes, or substitute a dab of bean sauce for sweet wheat paste. As long as you make sensible swaps of similar ingredients (such as that duck for pork substitution, which ensures you're still using a sweet, rich meat), you will soon be enjoying your very own creations.

MINOR MOVES THAT MAKE A BIG DIFFERENCE

When Chinese chefs want to taste soups or sauces, a bit is ladled out into a little soup bowl, from which the chefs sip before adjusting the seasonings in the pot. This is really quite brilliant: not only do these chefs not have to keep coming up with clean spoons all the time, but the liquid cools off very quickly in the bowl, so lips and tongues don't get scalded. All you need is a ladle—a Chinese one that has the bowl flush with the handle is easier to use than Western dippers—and a porcelain bowl. The bowl should not be metal, to protect your hands and lips, nor should it be plastic, since soup can be, after all, very hot. (I also keep a jar of little spoons and bamboo chopsticks next to the stove for adding to, and tasting, thicker sauces or solid things.)

Cooking chopsticks are great to have, too. These should be made of sturdy plain bamboo or wood, so that they can be dunked into boiling oil and then tossed into the dishwasher. Don't use ones with paint or lacquer that can dissolve in hot oil, and avoid plastic.

USE UP EVERYTHING

When you start to look at meaty ingredients in the Chinese way, you will notice that almost every part of them is completely edible—or at the very least usable. For Westerners, especially, there may be a yuck factor that has to be addressed and overcome, but I am here to proselytize the beauty of the animal, every square inch of it. After all, most of the tasty bits of a beast or bird include a variety of muscles, organs, and tendons; these parts may have different textures and different flavors, but once you transcend the weirdness of eating the grisly bits and learn how to clean things properly, a whole new world opens up.

Take a leg of beef, for example; in most American kitchens, the edible stuff below the knee, though delicious, is pretty much ignored. Or consider the beauty of beef tripe. Feathery book tripe and beautifully patterned honeycomb tripe have totally unique textures and tastes. Once you try book tripe cooked to an absolute state of tenderness and tossed in a spicy sauce, or tender slices of braised honeycomb tripe seasoned with warm spices in a rich sauce, you will wonder why the whole world doesn't worship these gorgeous cuts of beef the way the Chinese do.

A Note about Stance and Hands

Chinese cooks hold themselves differently. Their feet stay flat on the ground, held either in parallel or perpendicular to each other, much like a ballerina in third position, with the heel of one foot near the arch of the other.

Although this may feel odd at first, you will find that you stand steadier as a result and have the ability to turn your body smoothly without shifting your feet. Your knees remain slightly bent as you prep and cook, which helps straighten the spine. Always maintain an inch or two between the work area and the body; this helps keep your apron clean, and provides you with even more freedom of movement.

Chinese cooks grasp the hilts of larger knives with their middle, ring, and little fingers; the thumb and forefinger are used to keep the blade steady and direct it with absolute precision (see the diagram on page 466). Again, this may take a bit of getting used to, but the logic behind it is impeccable: with that grip, you can wield a knife with great flexibility and turn it in almost any direction.

Chopping the Chinese way takes time and practice. It's not about showmanship, but rather about giving your knife the opportunity to do its job with the least effort. Try to bring the sharp edge down perpendicular to the cutting surface in a light, even pattern, one that does not dull the blade by banging it against your cutting board. Most of the cut's force should be spent by the time your knife has passed through its target.

As you do this, check your progress: Are your cuts unevenly sized? Are they connected along one edge? Are some segments mushed, rather than cut cleanly? Any of these suggest that you need to slow down, sharpen your knife, and get your technique straightened out before you continue.

The fingers of your non-knife hand should, of course, be kept out of harm's way. When that hand is being used to hold something you're chopping, keep the fingers gently curled, so that your knuckles can guide the blade safely past your skin. If you are working on a bunch of vegetables, like Chinese chives or green onions, hold the bunch so that your forefinger and thumb form a straight collar around them, and then use this collar to both guide your blade and protect your fingers.

Basic Equipment

If you have nothing more than a sharp knife and a frying pan, you'll still be able to create almost any type of Chinese cuisine. However, here are a few things that will make life easier for you, especially if you suspect you'll often be cooking from this book.

CHINESE KNIVES

See the diagram on page 466 for information on a variety of Chinese knives. The thin and wide blade known as a "vegetable knife" (*càidāo* 菜刀) is especially useful, as is a cleaver, which is thick and heavy enough to whack through bones. Hang your knives on the wall or store them in a specially made slot so that they don't get banged up.

WOK

A good-quality wok (*guō* 鍋 or 鑊) that is about 24 inches in diameter and made of hand-beaten carbon steel or cast iron is an extremely worthwhile purchase. It will improve with proper use and should last you a lifetime.[2] You want a pan you can lift without endangering yourself even when it's filled with food or hot oil. Avoid nonstick coatings.

Southern-style woks have two looped handles at the top, while northern ones have a long wooden handle. Either kind works well, but I prefer the northern style—it's easier to hold on to, and I can shake it with one hand while using chopsticks or a spatula in the other. If you have an electric stove or flat gas burners, get a wok with a flattened bottom so that it can sit steadily on your stove. Make sure it has a cover that fits well.

WOK SPATULA

A shovel-shaped wok spatula fits the curvature of a wok and is very useful as a result. The best ones are made of a single piece of steel, with no rivets to shake loose. Get a *guōchǎn* 鍋鏟 that has a good handle, preferably wood rather than screwed-in plastic.

Perhaps the most important use for my spatula, though, comes when I'm adding seasonings to a dish.

You can pour things like soy sauce or rice wine into the spatula first, eyeballing the amounts as you go; it slows you down a bit and forces you to be more accurate. Then drizzle what you need around the edges of the food in your wok, so that the seasoning heats up before being incorporated.

SANDPOT

Unglazed on the outside, these pottery casseroles usually have a brown interior and lid, and almost always have a wire cage knotted around the body. When you buy a *shāguō* 砂鍋, ask the salesperson to fill it with water to ensure that there are no hairline cracks. Wash these pots by hand and air-dry to avoid mildew. Sandpots are cheap, so buy extra, as gluing them when they do eventually crack is unsafe.

STEAMER

Chinese basket steamers (*zhēnglóng* 蒸籠) are available in steel and bamboo. Both have their advantages and both are cheap, so I have a couple of sets of each kind on hand. Steel steamers usually come with a pot to hold the steamer's water, but bamboo steamers need to be placed on a wok wide enough to hold them comfortably, with no gaps for the steam to escape. (Make sure that the wok you use for steaming is not going to also be used for stir-frying, since its patina will be boiled off.)

Steel is good for steaming things like rice, because the baskets can be scrubbed clean of any oil; bamboo, on the other hand, will soak up oil and gradually turn nonstick. Both sorts of steamers should be lined when in use, either with steamer cloth, specially made steamer paper, cupcake liners, napa cabbage leaves, or even greased lotus leaves. Coarse-weave cheesecloth will also work. Bamboo steamers need to be hand-washed and then air-dried thoroughly so that they do not mildew.

Larger steamers can be improvised by placing a trivet inside a wide pan that is then filled with an inch or two of water and covered (see page 49).

To make sure your steamer water hasn't boiled away, toss a couple of pennies into it. As long as you can hear the coins rattling around, things are going

---

2. For selecting and seasoning your wok, there is no better guide than Grace Young and Alan Richardson's *The Breath of a Wok*.

CHINESE KNIVES

The best of these blades have metal extending all the way through the handle, which allows you to use the bottom of the handle to pound things like garlic. Keep your blades sharpened and stored properly, and always hand-wash them. That way, they'll last you a lifetime.

The most useful of all is the standard Chinese knife, which is light and has a wide, 6 × 3-inch blade.

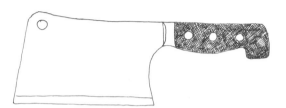

Cleavers are about the same size, but are much thicker and heavier, so save these for whacking through hard things like bones.

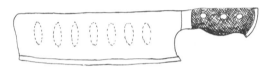

For light work, a small vegetable knife comes in very handy, as its 6 × 1½-inch blade is easy to maneuver.

A small, 4-inch paring knife is indispensable for the most delicate work.

HOW TO HOLD A KNIFE

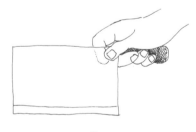

❶

Grasp the hilt of the blade with your middle, ring, and little finger, but place your thumb and forefinger on either side of the blade itself.

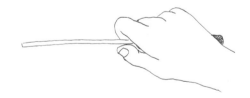

❷

Your wrist should be above the handle, so that your thumb and forefinger pinch the top half of the metal.

great. As soon as they start slowing down, pour in some boiling water. If they've gone quiet, things will start burning soon.

These are basically inch-wide dowels that are about a foot long. You can make a *gǎnmiànzhàng* 擀麵杖 yourself or get one from a Chinese market. Before the first use, smear yours well with mineral oil and wipe it dry after the oil has seeped into the wood. Wash the rolling pin by hand and dry it immediately after use.

The *zhàolí* 笊籬 is a stiff round net on a long bamboo handle that is used much like a slotted spoon, which can of course be used in its stead.

Nièzi 鑷子 are used often in my kitchen for pulling out the hairs from pig skin and the pinfeathers of ducks and chickens. Cosmetic tweezers don't work too well in the kitchen, so use industrial-sized tweezers or needle-nose pliers and a small knife (see Removing Pig Hairs & Pinfeathers, page 459) instead.

This is one of my favorite pieces of Chinese cooking equipment; I would be sure to bring it with me if I were ever marooned on a tropical desert isle festooned with wild ginger.

A *zhújiāngmó* 竹薑磨 is simplicity itself: rows of super-sharp bamboo teeth tacked together in a frame. Fresh ginger can be scraped across the teeth to form a mush that is then squeezed to produce ginger juice. A box grater or wheatgrass juicer can be used instead, but these bamboo tools cost only a few bucks, so get one. Just don't run your knuckles across those unforgiving teeth.

* * *

Those are the essentials; everything else is just gravy. Get a spatter screen to protect yourself, and consider buying both a food processor and a pressure cooker. If you already have a well-stocked kitchen, you will be able to use Western-style equipment for most Chinese dishes, and you can add to your *batterie de cuisine* as the mood strikes you.

Exquisite Knife Techniques

One of the details that sets Chinese cooking apart from the rest of the world's is the way in which ingredients are cut. Dicing, slicing, and mashing will be employed in much the same way they are everywhere, of course, but those skills are only the beginning. In a Chinese kitchen, a skilled chef will turn a cucumber into a frilled coil that summons up images of a sleeping dragon, or employ a few diagonal cuts on a slice of bean curd to give it the distinctive latticework pattern known as "orchid flowers." Some chefs specialize in creating entire floral bouquets out of things like radishes and carrots, with fragile vegetal butterflies poised on the petals, or froufrou landscapes with all the over-the-top detail of Louis XIV marquetry. But that is not what we are going to encourage here.

The true value of good knifework is in the way it opens up an ingredient to the cooking process. Vegetables or meats that are simply whacked into pieces will end up in different states of rawness, with varying textures and a decidedly slovenly appearance. Good Chinese chefs will consider the nature of their ingredients as they go to work with their blades, matching up like or contrasting textures, colors, and flavors.

In some of this book's recipes, as in Sister-in-Law Song's Fish Chowder (page 93), ingredients are cut into fine pieces—not mashed or haphazardly chopped—which permits them to easily fold around one another in the thickened broth. Each tiny sip you take of the resulting dish encompasses a spectrum of flavors and textures, while tender petals of egg white slip in and out of the darker hues to provide visual pleasure. In Molded Ham, Chicken, and Bean Curd Shreds (page 126), the sliver-cut style allows the savory ham and chicken to thoroughly season the mild bean curd, even though they constitute only a small proportion of the dish.

Whole poultry is never carved at the table in China; usually the bird will be chopped up into clean squares in the kitchen with a heavy cleaver that uses the weight of the blade to sever the bones.

Stir-Frying on a Wimpy Stove

My husband and I have been renting our home for many years, and I love this place, but the stove . . . ah, the stove is something else. It's electric, it's one of those glass-top deals, and it's an energy saver. But we're stuck with it and an overhead fan that takes little more than delicate, ladylike sniffs of whatever I'm cooking, so that the rest of the smoke can billow around the kitchen. In other words, I'm less than delighted with this three-foot-square area where I cook our meals.

But that doesn't mean that I don't get to stir-fry. It means only that I've learned to adapt, in the way of the iguanas in the Galapagos Islands. Consider me a Darwinian study in cooking.

Here are my secrets to stir-frying when you have nothing stronger to work with than I do.

PROBLEM NUMBER ONE:
MAKING THE WOK HOT ENOUGH

This is the main complaint that electric stove users have. Gas is great for stir-frying, especially if you can get one of those ferociously hellish rings that shoot flames up the sides of the wok and give a dish that lovely smokiness that Grace Young refers to as *wok hay*, "the prized, elusive, seared taste that comes only from stir-frying in a wok." Yes, one of these days I'm going to have one of those stoves and a restaurant-grade fan. But for now it's just me and that stupid glass-top.

The first thing you have to do is make sure that you're using a flat-bottomed wok or pan. Round-bottomed woks are traditional, yes, but they're meant for gas stoves, where they can sit on a ring and have their little round bottoms pressed up against the flames. My first wok was given to me in high school by my wonderful friend Wendy, and I was thrilled to pieces at my first piece of authentic Chinese cooking equipment. However, I soon got so frustrated trying to get it hot enough that I had the brilliant idea of wrapping the stove ring with foil to close up all the holes and concentrate the heat. I quickly blew out the coil on my mother's General Electric stove top, a sin that was never quite crossed off her list of Major Transgressions. So, find yourself either a flat-bottomed wok that is specifically designed for electric stoves or just use a good frying pan.

Next, figure out which one of your burners is the hottest. If you're not sure, put a cup of water to boil on each burner and see which one boils first. That is your designated wok burner, so treat it with love.

If your stove is on the verge of pooping out and you can't get a new one, consider a portable induction cooker or an electric wok. I still have the beaten-up old Westbend electric wok I got back in high school after the infamous Stove Incident, and now that it's old enough to qualify as an antique, I use it as the heating element for my stacked steamers, which frees up my lousy burners for other things. You can often find pretty good electric woks at your neighborhood Goodwill, and portable induction cookers can be bought for well under a hundred dollars (especially at Chinese supermarkets), so they're worth considering.

PROBLEM NUMBER TWO:
GETTING THINGS TO FRY QUICKLY
RATHER THAN STEAM

We've all tried to stir-fry things only to end up with a plate of soggy vegetables and flabby meat. This has a lot to do with that Chinese principle of *huǒhòu* 火候, or "fire and time" (see page 67). For example, stir-frying strips of beef requires a superhot wok and a very short cooking time, so that the outside of the meat is seared and crispy while the inside stays tender and juicy. Therefore, when you are planning to stir-fry on a wimpy electric stove, this is what you should do:

- Don't move the food around. Yes, this is called "stir-frying," but when you are faced with an electric stove of questionable ferocity, you should toss your ingredients only after they have browned and skip the stirring until you get toward the end and add your sauce. This allows the meats to caramelize on the hot metal; once they build up that delicious brown exterior, they won't stick to the pan so much and their juices will stay locked inside where they belong, which means you won't have a lot of moisture to contend with.

- Salt or marinate foods that are too wet. Eggplant is one of those vegetables that will drown in its own juices if given half a chance, so salt the cut-up slices and allow them to exude as much moisture as possible before patting them dry and stir-frying. Better yet, deep-fry or bake these nuggets to get some great caramelization going, so that all they need is a quick toss in the sauce.

  Chicken, which sometimes is pumped full of water, may poach rather than fry, so if you are in doubt, marinate it for about half an hour first. If it exudes lots of liquid, dump that out and season the meat again. Defrosted seafood, meanwhile, will often behave as a sponge, so salt or marinate it before cooking and then discard the diluted marinade.

- Dry off your ingredients. If you marinate meat or seafood before stir-frying it, or if you have salted any ingredients, drain them thoroughly and pat off as much moisture as possible.

  Greens should be rinsed thoroughly before cooking, of course, but try using a salad spinner to remove any water clinging to the leaves. Another good tip comes from my mother, who would wash greens, wrap them in a tea towel, and then store them in the fridge, where they became crispy and dry. It's an excellent way to prep your veggies ahead of time.

- Cook things in small amounts and combine them at the end. Small portions will cook many times faster over high heat than larger ones, which increases your odds of frying rather than steaming and of getting a good brown exterior in the process. Caramelization is always delicious.

  If you want to practice this, the best ingredient I've found is fresh mushrooms, particularly black mushrooms. Remove the stems, slice them thickly, and experiment with frying different-sized amounts. First, fry a small handful; if you heat the wok up to the point at which it smokes, add your oil, swish it around, put in the mushrooms, and let them sear before flipping them around, you'll notice that they'll take very little time to brown and cook. Now slide them out of the wok, heat it up again, and add new oil before putting in two large handfuls of uncooked mushrooms. You will find that your fungi won't brown as well, as the additional liquid within the extra mushrooms will keep the batch from frying quickly.

  Always add ingredients in small amounts, as well. Adding anything will immediately lower the heat in your wok, as your new addition absorbs it; to keep the heat up as high as possible, add only small increments, so that the heat can recover very quickly.

- Many recipes in this book call for "scooting" ingredients up the side of your wok, which frees up the hottest part of the pan—the very bottom—while keeping cooked ingredients warm up on the sides. A wok's slanted edges are angled just enough so that most things can get a grip on the iron while still letting oils and liquids dribble back to the bottom. As you season your dishes, take care to pour liquids like rice wine and soy sauce directly onto the hot iron, where they can quickly sizzle, burn off their raw taste, and become incorporated. If you pour liquids over your other ingredients, they'll have to find a way to dribble down to the wok surface before they can heat up enough to fuse with everything else.

- You should, though, use very little liquid in stir-fries. You want food to fry at as high a heat as possible, without giving it a chance to boil. Things like wine and soy sauce should be added in small enough portions and over high enough heat for them to evaporate almost at once, leaving only a tantalizing layer of fragrance and taste. If you notice a few table-spoons of liquid at the bottom of your pan, push your other ingredients over to the edge or up the side to get them away from the heat and then rapidly boil down the sauce. This technique is called *shōutāng* 收湯, or "collecting the liquid."

- If your stove is truly on the edge of burning out, try covering your pan while the food sears. This will increase the temperature inside and speed up the searing time.

A long time ago, I was told the following story of a famous gourmet who had a foolproof method for testing cooks applying for the position of chef at his residence. Instead of allowing them to whip up fancy meals replete with exotic ingredients, he asked these cooks to prepare two dishes: fried rice and stir-fried pork with bell peppers.

Sounds easy, but the simplest dishes are often the ones that trip people up. With the pork dish, the pork and peppers had to be stir-fried separately and combined just before they were served. That way the pork would be seared and succulent while the peppers would still be crispy and barely cooked. This is the correct way to stir-fry if you want each of your ingredients to shine. It's especially important with an electric stove, since controlling the heat and timing there is particularly difficult.

I know the feeling: you want to just plunge in and start cooking, prepping your veggies along the way and searching through your cupboards as you go, certain that there must be a jar of sweet wheat paste in there somewhere.

The Chinese have a saying that pretty much sums up this situation: *shǒumáng jiǎoluàn* 手忙腳亂, or "busy hands and confused feet." Cooking that way slows things down and gives you lots of room for error. For the best results, you should have everything ready to go before you even think about turning on the stove. The French rely on what they call *mise en place*, the practice of setting out everything you'll need—all of your ingredients, flavorings, and equipment—before you start to cook. The Chinese teach the same concept, and especially with stir-frying, this is without question the way to do it. If you're cooking a meal with more than one dish, it's best to have everything for all your dishes set out beforehand; that way you can chop all of your onions at the same time, measure out your oils in one swoop, and so forth. It will all look so reassuring when you're finally ready to turn on the stove.

Some recipes in this book will tell you to prep one or two ingredients well ahead of the others; certain items might require more time to marinate or defrost or plump up. What this all means is that you should slow down, prep everything that will require more time, place all of your ingredients and flavorings and equipment within reach of the stove, read through the directions one more time, and then plunge in. You will find that it makes cooking so much easier and much more fun.

How to Dine like a Chinese Person

All right, now we get to the best part of the meal: eating.

I am assuming that you know how to use chopsticks. If not, go online and watch a video. There is a whole tradition of etiquette built up around these clever utensils, and knowing the rules will make you look less like a rube, which will allow your Chinese dining companions to relax.

Clasp the chopsticks as high up on their handles as is comfortable. Use a relaxed grip, as it looks a whole lot nicer, sort of like grasping a fork, and will give you more flexibility, as well. The Chinese believe that educated people can be discerned by the way they hold their sticks, so the right grip gives you a definite cool vibe as you dine.

The eating ends of disposable bamboo chopsticks need to be rubbed against each other to remove any slivers. Break them apart and file away so that the dust falls on the floor, not the table. If you like, you can fold their wrapper into a stylish little chopstick holder; see

CHOPSTICK HOLDERS, THREE WAYS

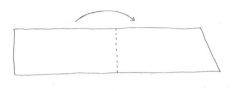

①

If the chopsticks are not disposable and come in a stiff paper sheath, first fold the paper in half down the middle to form a short rectangle.

②

Crease the rectangle down the center to make a roof shape. Push in the ends so that it pops up into a tent.

①

The simplest way to fold disposable chopstick covers is to turn one long edge over to make a thin strip.

②

Tie this into a loose knot, flatten gently, and you're done.

①

This is a more complex holder, but it's stunning and gives you something to do while you wait for your food to appear. First, make a long strip by folding the wrapper lengthwise in half.

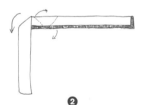

②

Make a 90-degree valley fold about one-third of the distance from the left end. Then, fold the right edge back over itself at a 90-degree angle two more times to form a square end.

③

This next part "braids" the two strands together: fold whichever strand is on the bottom up into a 90-degree valley fold and fold the top strand behind itself at a 90-degree angle until you run out of paper.

④

Even up the ends, if needed, and flatten it lightly with your hand. With any luck, your meal will have been served by now.

the illustrations on page 471 for some examples. This is another cool move.

Never plunge your chopsticks into the food and leave them there; doing that gives many Chinese people a serious case of the willies, since incense sticks are stuck into the food meant for ancestors and ghosts in order to summon them. Making your dish look like an offering for the dead is therefore a definite no-no.

Make sure there is no food on your chopsticks when you remove them from your mouth. Rice grains that are glued on need to be inconspicuously nibbled off before the sticks head back toward the table.

When they're not in use, rest your chopsticks at the side of your bowl or plate or on your handy chopstick holder. When you're done eating, lay them parallel to you on the far side of your dish.

When dining with family and close friends, you can get away with using your own chopsticks to reach into the serving dishes; shared cooties are okay if everyone is on the same page. Some people are fastidious, though, so watch what your fellow diners are doing and then follow suit. Oftentimes dishes will have serving spoons or chopsticks (the latter are called *gōngkuài* 公筷, or "communal chopsticks," and you can ask for them in restaurants); use them if they're available.

BASIC RULES FOR DINING ANYWHERE

Whether you're eating alone or dining at a major banquet, a few things are worth mentioning in order to help you save face.

Do not use your hands to pick up food unless it is clearly finger food. If you can't use chopsticks, ask for a fork or carry one with you.

This goes double for removing bones and other things from your mouth. Just as in the West, whatever got that food up to your mouth should carry the remains back to the plate. Take small bites, particularly of things with shells or bones or gristle, and daintily remove anything inedible with your chopsticks or fork and set it unobtrusively on one corner of your plate. Some people have even more finesse and cover their detritus with a leaf or a particularly large shell to make their plate attractive. I will never forget eating orange wedges with a famous writer in Taipei who carefully arranged the peels on his plate into an orange fan as he ate—it was such a refined touch.

Chinese people have been known to slurp their noodles, but only in cheaper joints, and so it's best not to be too obnoxious about this. Feel free to drink directly from soup bowls if the meal is not a fancy one; otherwise, look for the ceramic soupspoon. In China, soup is traditionally served at the end of the meal so that its delicious heat can work its way into the digestive system and help comfort swollen tummies.

BASIC RULES FOR DINING WITH OTHERS

As in the West, you should strive to eat with your mouth closed, wait for your host to start before diving in, and be considerate of the people around you. But here are some additional clues that will make you fit in at the dinner table as if you grew up in China.

If you are a guest, wait to be told where to sit. Chinese etiquette places the guest of honor—or the oldest person—at the seat farthest from the entrance, so that they face out. Pay attention next time you see a large party of Chinese people being seated, as there will often be some polite tussling going on as everyone tries to avoid being so honored; self-effacement is a treasured characteristic. Try to maneuver the eldest person into that seat. Couples are usually not split up at Chinese dining tables, unless everyone is a close friend, so keep Mr. and Mrs. Li seated together.

Hands (but not elbows) belong on the table. Rest your less dominant hand at the edge of the table for much of the time; people like to know what you are up to. Leave your napkin in front of you, as well, rather than in your lap, so that you can use it as needed. If it gets dirty, fold it so that the clean side faces up.

Take small portions from serving plates. My first year in Taipei, I watched in horror as a male student piled his plate high whenever the lazy Susan passed something new in front of him. It was like he was at a buffet line and the closing bell had sounded. Finally, one of the other students (me) cleared her throat and asked him to please leave something for the rest of us. He finally looked up from his eating frenzy, saw the relatively empty plates in front of us, and then noticed the glares of the other eternally starving guys we went to school with.

What he should have done was to take one (or, at the most, two) spoonfuls of each dish. You can always have seconds once everyone has been served, but you should never polish off any one dish unless it's at the end of the meal, and others have stopped helping themselves. Even then, try to tempt others with it before sighing regretfully and taking the final helping.

By the same token, a very gracious thing to do at any meal is to serve others, particularly those sitting on either side of you, before yourself. Chinese people might protest that this is not necessary, but such avowals are nothing more than polite reactions. You should ignore them—unless they are emphatic, as in "I don't eat pork, thank you"—and serve them the best parts of each dish, even if that means not eating the meatiest cuts or prettiest leaves yourself. Assume that your fellow diners will return the favor, plying you with food when the next dish rolls around.

If this is a feast, pace yourself. Wedding banquets in particular are designed to impress, so take small portions and save room for the best stuff, which generally shows up toward the end.

Rice and other starches are usually not served during fancy dinners, as the host wants you to fill up on delicacies, so don't ask for or expect them. If a rice or noodle dish does appear, compliment your host by refusing another bite and claiming you are way too full, or by taking a small nibble at the most. If the rice is on a plate rather than a bowl, use a fork to scoop it up; chopsticks will get you nowhere fast.

Eat whatever is offered, even if you don't recognize something, unless you have medical or religious or moral constraints. Sometimes you will be offered things that are just downright wrong, such as carp deep-fried but with the head still moving; things like that are obscenities, as far as I am concerned. I will also refuse raw crustaceans because of parasites and pollution, and rabbits because we have pet bunnies running around our house. In cases like these, a simple but firm "No, thank you" will do. You should not feel compelled to eat something on a dare. If in spite of your protests you are served things you don't want, just push them delicately to the side of your plate and ignore them. Whenever possible, I warn my hosts of these quirks of mine ahead of time so that no one is embarrassed.

Tea and liquor should also be served to others before you fill your own cup. Always, always, always. If you do not want a particular beverage, hold your hand over your cup or glass and say "No, thank you" (*búyòng, xièxiè* 不用，謝謝).

A warning: beware of competitive drinking, especially if you are young and/or female, for this can quickly devolve. That's why, if I don't know the people I'm dining with, I steer clear of the liquor.

When it comes to nice dinners, toast the host, if there is one, with the first glass of whatever it is you're drinking. A little bit later, toast other people at the table; if there are couples, toast them as a couple. The correct way to do this is to hold the cup with the fingers of both hands as you raise it in front of you. Say something simple, like "thank you" (*xièxiè* 謝謝), while rising slightly out of your chair if the person is of higher status or much older than you, and bow your head just a bit to show respect. At the end of the meal, repeat the toast and thanks. Leave the meal with a promise to invite them out for another meal in the near future, and call or write the next day with your repeated thanks.

In the end, though, dining with the Chinese is like dining with just about anyone else in the world: it all comes down to relaxing at the table, enjoying good conversation, and luxuriating in delicious food.

Fortunately for the Chinese, they mastered all of this centuries ago, and it's been my incredible good fortune to have lived all of my adult life among them. Few things make me happier than eating well on the incredible foods of this ancient and beautiful culture. Life doesn't get much better than that, and I hope that I've been able to share some of this passion with you.

Mànyòng 慢用, *bon appétit*, and let's eat! ●

GLOSSARY & BUYING GUIDE

M any of the items in this book may seem unusual, but as more people become interested in the cuisines of China, the demand for authentic ingredients should grow, even outside of areas with large Chinese American populations. I take heart when I remember that back when *Mastering the Art of French Cooking* was first released in 1961, unsalted butter, freshly roasted coffee, spring mix lettuces, extra virgin olive oil, and organic flours were virtually unheard of, and yet here we are today with farmers' markets and artisanal-food companies, as well as crème frâiche and fresh herbs in our grocery stores.

A major problem when shopping for Chinese ingredients pops up when it comes to their English labels, which vary greatly in accuracy. For example, you will rarely find the English words "sweet wheat paste" on the label of a jar of *tiánmiànjiàng* 甜麵醬 (see page 490). Instead, something totally incorrect—like "bean paste"—will almost always be slapped on. This glossary should help. When in doubt about whether you're buying the right thing, show the relevant entry below to a knowledgeable employee or customer at a Chinese store and ask for assistance.

Abalone; *bàoyú* 鮑魚. Get sustainably farmed fresh or frozen ones, if at all possible, and trim off the tough foot before using. Some canned ones are good but very expensive. A good and much cheaper substitute is canned "top shell" conch meat.

Alum; *míngfán* 明礬. Potassium alum is a fine white powder that is occasionally used in Chinese cooking, mainly to firm up pickles and cured meats. A small package should last you forever. Store in a closed container or bag in the pantry.

Apricot pits, sweet; *nánxìng* 南杏. These ivory kernels have a strong almond scent and flavor. Bitter apricot pits (*běixìng* 北杏) are also very fragrant; a few are usually used in combination with a large amount of sweet apricot pits to create traditional almond-flavored sweets. The bitter ones contain traces of cyanide, so use caution. Both can be purchased in Chinese markets and herbal stores.

Arhat fruit; *luóhànguǒ* 羅漢果. The dried fruit of the *Siraitia grosvenorii* plant is close to three hundred times sweeter than cane sugar. The Chinese have long used this as a natural sweetener and a way to deal with diabetes. The fruits are hard, dark brown balls that weigh very little. They're mainly grown in Guangxi and Guangdong, and they can be purchased at Chinese herbalist shops or grocery stores. Store them in a closed container in a dark cupboard. They can be easily broken apart into smaller pieces as needed. Sometimes translated as "monk fruit." Use rock sugar (see entry) to taste as a substitute.

Asparagus; *lúsǔn* 蘆筍. When shopping for this vegetable, first look at the tips, which should be tight and not in the least bruised. Purplish tips are the best. The cut ends should be plump and healthy. Store the asparagus in the fridge with the cut ends in water and a plastic bag over the tips. Or even better, use them as soon as you get home, while they still smell of spring rains and warm earth. If you are going for thin stalks, try to get the really slender ones that appear in spring. They have a wonderful grassy flavor and are very tender. If you get thick asparagus, cut them on the angle in order to maximize the cooking surface for each stalk. It doesn't matter whether they are roll cut (see page 449) or simply sliced on a sharp diagonal.

Bamboo leaves; *zòngyè* 綜葉 (糭葉). Big bamboo leaves come from a special variety of large tropical bamboo called *Dendrocalamus latiflorus*. You can find them wrapped in plastic bags in most Chinese groceries and dried-foods stores. Keep the leaves dry and bug-free, and they'll be usable for a long time. To prepare, soak them in hot water until they are pliable and then wipe both sides carefully to remove any grime. Beware of the leaves' sharp edges.

Bamboo shoots, dried and salted; *sǔngān* 筍乾 (dried bamboo shoots) or *yùlánpiàn* 玉蘭片 (magnolia chips). Most dried bamboo shoots can be used interchangeably, although they might have different aromas and degrees of saltiness. To plump up these shoots, cover them with boiling water and let them soak for a few hours. Discard the water, trim off any hard or discolored pieces, and then shred the shoots into smallish strips. Cut the strips into whatever length you like. Fully dried bamboo shoots will keep forever if they're kept completely dry and stored in a dark cupboard. Slightly moist bamboo shoots will be shrink-wrapped and need to be refrigerated once the package is opened.

Bamboo shoots, fresh or frozen; *chūnsǔn* 春筍 (spring bamboo shoots) and *dōngsǔn* 冬筍 (winter bamboo shoots) are the main varieties available in the States at present. Spring bamboo shoots are long and thin, while winter bamboo shoots are short and chubby. Spring shoots are grassier and more delicate and should be cooked gently. Winter shoots have a heavier texture and are great for braises.

Select fresh shoots that are firm all over; the sheaths should have no sign of mold or mildew. If the tips are not green, it means that the shoot was harvested while it was still underground and it's likely that its sugars have not had a chance to turn bitter. Look for shoots that have freshly cut bases; shrinkage around the bases tells you that the shoots are drying out. Store them in the refrigerator in their sheaths and use as quickly as possible. Peel and blanch them if you need to keep them a while longer (see Tip on page 122). Frozen ones keep well, but they should be used before they get freezer burn.

Bay leaves; *xiāngyè* 香葉 or *yuèguìyè* 月桂葉. These are the same bay leaves that are used in Western cuisines. They are generally used in braises and stews. Keep the leaves dry, store them in a jar in a dark cupboard, and use them within a year. Discard them if their scent has dissipated.

Bean curd, egg; *dàn dòufǔ* 蛋豆腐 or *yùzi dòufǔ* 玉子豆腐. This is a smooth custard that is made of eggs, rather than soybeans, and it is used in place of soft bean curd in some dishes. The second name is Japanese (*yuzi* means "egg"), but it has been adopted in some areas of coastal China, particularly Taiwan and Hong Kong. A recipe for this can be found on page 178.

Bean curd, firm; *bǎndòufǔ* 板豆腐 and *lǎodòufǔ* 老豆腐, among many other local names. Firm bean curd is, obviously, firmer, but it's also slightly more ivory in color, has a stronger bean flavor, and contains less water than soft bean curd. Its tougher texture allows it to withstand things like frying and braising. Refrigerate uncooked bean curd in a closed container with water; change the water daily, and discard the bean curd if it smells sour. In the West, all types of bean curd are also referred to by their Japanese name, tofu.

Bean curd, pressed; *dòufǔgān* 豆腐乾. Pressed bean curd is created by weighting down firm curd until almost all of the moisture is squeezed out, leaving a leathery, chewy layer of bean curd. Most pressed bean curd varieties can be used interchangeably, although the texture will vary. Refrigerate pressed bean curd in a closed bag and use within 4 or 5 days once it's opened. Discard if it smells sour or feels slimy.

Bean curd, silken; see Bean curd, soft.

Bean curd, soft; *nèndòufǔ* 嫩豆腐. Slightly firmer than soy custard (see entry), soft bean curd has a smooth texture and breaks easily. It is sometimes called "silken bean curd." Soft bean curd is coagulated using refined plaster rather than brine. The silky white squares are often sliced and added to sauces at the last minute, so that they barely heat through before being served. They can also be lightly breaded and fried.

Bean curd "cheese"; *dòufǔrǔ* 豆腐乳. This "cheese" is made by fermenting molded bean curd and then preserving it in a mixture of rice wine, salt, and seasonings. See the recipes on pages 420 and 421.

Beans, crispy; *dòusū* 豆酥. Soybeans that are cooked, smashed, salted, lightly fermented, and dried are turned into this distinctive Yunnan-style seasoning. Crispy beans are directly related to the Burmese fermented soybean disks called *tua nao*, and so these most likely are an invention of one of the area's ethnic minorities. These are sometimes found in the dried seasonings aisle as hard bricks in vacuum-packed plastic bags, but they appear more often as finished sauces in a jar; Taiwan's Master brand Fried Crispy Soy Bean is reliable. Traditionally, the beans are sold as tan balls about the size of duck eggs, but this form has yet to appear on Western shores.

Beans, mung; *lǜdòu* 綠豆. These small dried legumes play a large role in China's cuisines. Available either skinned (*lǜdòurén* 綠豆仁) or with their skins on, they can be purchased in most Chinese grocery stores, as well as in health food stores. Plain mung beans (which have their green skins still attached) need to be picked over for small stones and then soaked in cool tap water. They

are then drained and simmered until they "bloom," or explode open. Skinned mung beans are often dyed bright yellow, so rinse them in a sieve with cool tap water until the water runs clear. Usually boiled, they will dissolve into a silky yellow mush when done.

Bitter melon; *kǔguā* 苦瓜. This member of the squash family grows on long climbing vines and can easily be grown in warmer areas. Chinese bitter melons have smooth bumps, while Indian melons are spiky. The paler the melon is, the less astringent it will be. Select melons that have a slight "give" when pressed—this means they are ripe. Pass over melons with bruises or black spots. Keep them refrigerated in plastic bags with a paper towel to absorb any moisture. Very ripe bitter melons will have red pith around the ripe brown seeds; this pith is rather sweet and surprisingly tasty. If you live in a warm climate, try growing these beautiful vines from your collected seeds.

Black beans, fermented; *dòuchǐ* or *dòushì* 豆豉. To make these, black or tan soybeans are boiled and allowed to mold. These are then fermented with a combination of salt, rice wine, and aromatics. Fermented black beans are usually packed in little paper drums or plastic bags, and they can be found in just about any Chinese grocery store. Rinse the whole beans before using them, and chop them coarsely to release their flavor. Keep them in a covered container.

Boba or pearl tapioca; *bōbà* 波霸. Also called *fěnyuán* 粉圓 or *zhēnzhū* 珍珠, *boba* are most often used in sweet drinks. They are available in most Chinese grocery stores, both as instant and regular *boba*. Follow the package directions and store in a sealed container.

Bok choy, dried; *báicàigān* 白菜乾. These small leafy cabbages are sun-dried and then sold in bunches. A specialty of Guangdong and Hakka areas, dried bok choy can be found in dried-foods shops, as well as most Chinese supermarkets. Soak them in warm water until the stems

have plumped up, and then rinse the stalks and leaves carefully.

Cabbage, napa; *báicài* 白菜. Sometimes called celery or nappa cabbage, this is the standard cabbage variety in North China. It has a large football-shaped head and wide white stems. Select heads that are tight and pale and don't have split stems. If the weather has turned warm, check the center of the vegetable to ensure that the cabbage has not started flowering, as this will result in a hard core. Refrigerate these cabbages unwashed in closed plastic bags; if the leaves are wet, add a paper towel to discourage spoilage. The name "napa" comes from the Japanese word for the vegetable, *nappa* 菜っ葉, not the city of Napa in Northern California.

Cardamom, black; *cǎoguǒ* 草果. This variant of cardamom has large seedpods and a smoky scent. It's mainly used in braises or ground up as part of five-spice powder (page 441). Store the seedpods whole in a sealed container to maximize their shelf life. They're available in traditional herb stores, as well as Chinese groceries. They do not have to be ground or chopped before using, but should be cracked open with the side of a blade to release their flavor.

Catsup; *fānqiéjiàng* 蕃茄醬. Heinz is a good brand, but many tasty artisanal varieties are becoming more available. Store it in a cool pantry if you use it often. Otherwise, put it in the refrigerator. Also spelled ketchup.

Celery, Chinese; *qíncài* 芹菜. Longer, more slender, and more flavorful than the Western variety, Chinese celery is worth seeking out. Buy heads with the roots attached so that you know they're still fresh; you can also cut off the roots about 1 inch from the base and plant these for your own homegrown celery. Get heads that are firm and have bright leaves. Clean the bases of the stems carefully and remove the strings on the stalks if they are tough; the leaves are generally trimmed off because they have a strong flavor. Refrigerate in a closed plastic bag.

Cellophane noodles; *fěnsī* 粉絲 or (in Taiwan) *dōngfěn* 冬粉. Cellophane noodles go by several other English names, including bean thread noodles, Chinese vermicelli, glass noodles, and mung bean threads. They are processed out of many different starches, including mung beans, potatoes, and yams. My favorite brand is Taiwan's Long Kow Vermicelli Bean Thread (*Lóngkǒu fěnsī* 龍口粉絲); get the ones that are packed in small skeins or bundles, as these are much easier to work with than the large bags. Soak the dried noodles in cool water until they soften and then cut them with kitchen shears, if needed. They cook very quickly, so do not use hot or boiling water to rehydrate them. Store in a sealed bag in a pantry.

Charcuterie; *làwèi* 臘味. Meats, poultry, and fish are marinated and hung in a cool place to dry to make these cured products. The most common are cured pork charcuterie, or *làròu* 臘肉.

Guangdong's cured pork, which most often consists of pork belly with the skin attached, also includes the rosy sweet sausage known as *lop chong* (*làcháng* 臘腸), as well as duck's liver sausage (*yāgāncháng* 鴨肝腸). These tend to be the sweetest types of China's charcuterie and are made with sugar, salt, spices, and/or soy sauce and pink salt. The cured meats of Hunan (*Húnán làròu* 湖南臘肉) generally have a deeper flavor, since they are smoked (see page 289). Guangdong- and Hunan-style charcuterie can be found in most Chinese grocery stores, with the widest variety showing up in winter.

Charcuterie will come in shrink-wrapped plastic; refrigerate after opening and use before it gets moldy. Many excellent cured meats are now made in the United States, and I've come to rely on a number of brands, especially Orchard, Hsin Tung Yang, and Kam Yen Jang. See also Chinese-style ham.

Chestnuts; *lìzi* 栗子. Because chestnuts are so popular in a variety of regional cuisines, Chinese markets often offer both dried and frozen ones that are already shelled and skinned. Dried chestnuts come in small plastic bags and need only to be soaked before use. Store these in a closed container in the pantry. Frozen chestnuts are also sold in plastic bags and should be defrosted before cooking. For both types, use a paring knife to remove any of the mahogany skin still attached to the tiny folds on the surface. Vacuum-packed chestnuts are peeled, cooked, and ready to eat.

Chilies, dried; *gānlàjiāo* 乾辣椒. The most common dried chili in this book is the 2-inch Thai chili, although you may certainly use whatever you like. These are usually rinsed and patted dry before use, and then any stem ends and misshapen chilies are discarded. If the chilies are not used whole, break them in half and shake out the seeds, then cut the chilies as desired or specified. Store in a closed container in a cool place.

Chilies, ground; *làjiāo fěn* 辣椒粉 and *làjiāo miàn* 辣椒麵. Dried chilies are pulverized either finely or coarsely to make this spice. Finely ground chilies will usually have no seeds, while coarsely ground ones may or may not have the seeds sifted out. These come in a range of heat, from mild to fiery. The best selections can be found at busy Korean grocery stores and Latin American markets. Each type of chili has its own flavor, so opt for what pleases you. Store in a closed container in the pantry. Mexican spice mixes that include such things as cumin and dried garlic are not acceptable substitutes.

Chinese angelica root; *dāngguī* 當歸. Dried slices of *Angelica sinensis* root are used in medicines and soups in various parts of China. Purchase small amounts from a Chinese herbalist and store them in a closed container in a cool place. Also referred to by its Cantonese name, *dong quai*; not to be confused with Dahurian angelica root (see entry).

Chinese-style ham; *huǒtuǐ* 火腿. The traditional salted, cured, and pressed hams of China are most often used as a seasoning. Brined or canned ham should not be substituted. At the time of this writing, meat cannot be imported from China, so American country-style hams (usually labeled "Smithfield") are the best substitutes.

Select a piece that has a nice rosy color and feels slightly soft—but not at all sticky—when you press it. It should smell fresh and smoky. If you find any black mold on the skin, just scrape it off. Keep the ham completely dry and refrigerated in an airtight bag; it will keep well for weeks this way. Cut off the amount you wish to use and rinse it carefully under tap water. Pat it dry with a paper towel, and trim off any bones or skin; these can be tossed in soups. Other acceptable substitutes include Hunan-style charcuterie (see page 289), as well as prosciutto.

Chive flowers, garlic; *jiǔcàihuā* 韭菜花. These flowering stems are in season between late spring and midsummer. Unlike garlic stems (see entry), these little flower heads can be eaten as long as the buds are tight. Check for tenderness at the base of the stem by using the fingernail test (see entry). If you find any stalks that are tough, use only the tender tops. Wrap the flowers in a damp paper towel and refrigerate them in a plastic bag, where they will keep for a couple of days.

Chive flowers, salted garlic; *yān jiǔcàihuā* 醃韭菜花. To make these, chive flowers are minced, salted, and then lightly fermented. Purchase jars at a busy Chinese grocery store, check the expiration date, and refrigerate after opening.

Chives, garlic; *jiǔcài* 韭菜. These members of the onion family have wider and flatter leaves than Western chives but possess a similar taste. Select bunches with stiff, bouncy leaves and check the bases of the leaves for signs of desiccation or rot. Refrigerate them wrapped in a paper towel and plastic bag. Use them within a day or two. Trim off the tough bases and then rinse carefully before using. These are easy to grow from seed or divisions. Also called Chinese chives.

Chives, yellow; *jiǔhuáng* 韭黃. Yellow chives are garlic chives that have been completely shielded from the sun. Select bunches that show no sign of spoilage and use them as quickly as possible. Wrap the yellow chives in paper to cut down on moisture and refrigerate in a plastic bag. Trim off the bases of the strands and carefully remove any imperfect leaves before rinsing.

Chrysanthemum blossoms, dried Hangzhou; *Hángzhōu júhuā* 杭州菊花. This specialty of the city of Hangzhou in Zhejiang Province is famed for its fragrance and honeylike flavor. Sold in Chinese herbal shops, dried-foods stores, and some groceries, these blossoms should be compressed into a little brick and wrapped in tan paper. Select blossoms that have a powerful scent and store them in a closed container.

Cilantro; *yuánsuī* 芫荽 or (in Taiwan) *xiāngcài* 香菜. The leaves should be bright green and bouncy, the stems green and firm; avoid any bunches that show yellowing or flowers. Refrigerate the cilantro wrapped in a paper towel and plastic bag. Rinse just before using, trim off the tough ends, and chop as desired. This herb is easy to grow from seed. Some people refer to both cilantro and parsley as *xiangcai*, which can lead to confusion. Also known as coriander or Chinese parsley.

Cinnamon; *ròuguì* 肉桂. This fragrant bark lends warmth and spice to many Chinese dishes, and is often used whole. For the best flavor, grind the curled bits of bark sold as cinnamon sticks into a powder, rather than purchasing it already ground. The softer and milder variety from Sri Lanka known as canela can be substituted. Store cinnamon in a closed container in a cool area. Also known as cassia bark.

Coriander; see Cilantro.

Cruller, Chinese; *yóutiáo* 油條. These are foot-long pieces of fried dough that are airy and bland. They can be made from scratch, but frozen ones are convenient and often quite tasty. Crullers can also be purchased from a Chinese deli, especially

on weekends. Crisp them up in a toaster oven before eating. Freeze in a plastic bag for storage.

Cucumbers, Persian or Japanese; *xiǎohuángguā* 小黄瓜. A thin cucumber with seeds so undeveloped it is often called "seedless," this vegetable is used in many Chinese cuisines for its fresh flavor and crunchy texture. Select cucumbers that are firm and have no shriveling at the stem end. These are rarely peeled and never need to be seeded unless they have grown to a large size; if they are overgrown, cook them Chinese style as peeled chunks in a clear pork broth. Refrigerate cucumbers in an open bag with a paper towel so that they do not sweat and rot quickly. Use them within a couple of days, if at all possible.

Cumin; *zīrán* 孜然. These tiny, thin, curved seeds are an integral part of cooking in the Northwest. However, they are so unfamiliar elsewhere in the country that their name doesn't appear in most Chinese dictionaries. Not to be confused with caraway (its close relative, along with fennel, anise, and parsley), cumin can be used whole or ground. The seeds don't need to be toasted first, but as with so many warm spices, it doesn't hurt. I suggest purchasing the seeds whole and then toasting and grinding them just before they are going to be used.

Curry paste, Japanese. I like the Japanese curry brand called S & B Golden Curry, which comes in various degrees of heat, preferably the one marked "medium hot," which has a green box. This ingredient is great for making all sorts of curry dishes. Other types of curry paste or even curry powder can be substituted; just adjust the seasoning and thickness accordingly.

Dahurian angelica root; *báizhǐ* 白芷. A variety of angelica that is native to northeastern Asia, these dried roots are used in Chinese medicine and cookery. Purchase small amounts as needed from a Chinese herbalist and store them in a closed container in a dark cupboard.

Daikon pickle, Japanese; *Rìběn pàoluóbó* 日本泡蘿蔔. The yellow pickle called *takuan zuke* 沢庵漬け in Japanese can be purchased whole or already sliced, and is often used as a condiment in Taiwanese cooking. These are vacuum-packed in plastic and can be found in the refrigerated section. Korean brands are often quite good.

Dates, Chinese red; *hóngzǎo* 紅棗. Also known as jujubes, red dates are prized throughout China, but especially in the North. Dry rather than juicy when fresh, these fruits possess a light apple fragrance and white flesh. Their skin is a pale green-yellow, but it becomes spotted with mahogany as it begins to dry; when they are completely dried, the skin will be fully red.

Dried dates can be purchased throughout the year in Chinese herbal shops and busy grocery stores. Large ones are especially meaty, but the smaller ones known as "chicken hearts" (*jīxīnzǎo* 雞心棗) have good flavor, as well. Black dates (*hēizǎo* 黑棗) are smoked and always sold dried. Refrigerate fresh dates in a plastic bag; dried ones will stay tasty if stored in closed containers.

Daylily flowers, dried; *jīnzhēn* 金針 (golden needles) or *huánghuācài* 黄花菜 (yellow flower vegetable). The unopened buds of the fragrant, golden, nocturnal Chinese daylily plants are unusual, tasty vegetables. They are almost always sold dried, although fresh ones are beginning to appear in some local Chinese markets.

Try to find buds that feel slightly moist and supple and are a light color; dark, brittle buds have likely been sitting around too long and will taste sour. The bright orange ones have been dyed, so I avoid those. Revive the flowers by soaking them in hot water for about 10 minutes and then trim off the hard stem ends as needed. These flowers should be tied into knots for braises to prevent them from disintegrating. Shorter blossoms can be saved for other dishes; they can also be hand-shredded into strings. Refrigerate the dry flowers in a sealed bag and discard them if they become stiff. This variety of daylily can be grown easily in the garden from corms. In many dishes, thinly shredded carrot can be substituted.

Dry-frying; *gānchǎo* 乾炒. This involves frying something (e.g., spices, sesame seeds, or salts) without any oil in order to toast it.

Eggs, brined or salted; *xiándàn* 鹹蛋. When fresh raw eggs (traditionally duck) are soaked in a heavy brine, their quality and flavor are entirely altered. The whites absorb the flavors of the brine and the yolks become solid. Brined eggs can be used in pastries or savory dishes. The eggs can also be boiled in their shell until firm. See the recipe for brined eggs on page 422. If you buy or make brined duck and goose eggs, they will tend to be a bit gamy and sometimes have a fishy flavor. In that case, cut their yolks in half, sprinkle them with white liquor (see entry) or rice wine, and steam them for about 5 minutes. If you plan to mash the yolks, cool them first.

Eggs, preserved; *pídàn* 皮蛋. Preserved eggs are an iconic part of China's cuisines. To make them, duck eggs are coated in clay mixed with alkali and then rolled in rice hulls. These coated eggs are then allowed to rest for several weeks until the whites turn amber and the yolks become greenish-black and golden in the center. The best preserved eggs at the time of this writing come from Taiwan. Their yolks are soft and creamy and the whites often have crystalline "pine blossom" (*sōnghuā* 松花) or "snowflake" (*xuěhuā* 雪花) patterns under their shells. Preserved eggs are almost always used raw. Store refrigerated, covered in plastic wrap, and use within a month or so. Also known as thousand-year eggs, century eggs, and so on.

Fat, rendered chicken or duck; *jīyóu* 雞油 and *yāyóu* 鴨油. Rendered chicken fat is usually made at home, as is rendered duck fat. They are prepared and stored in the same way as lard (see entry). Unsalted butter can sometimes be substituted.

Fennel seeds; *huíxiāng* 茴香. Smelling delicately of licorice, these seeds are used throughout much of China as part of five-spice powder (see entry). They are also used whole in braises. Buy them at a busy health food or spice store, preferably in the bulk bins where you can smell their fragrance. Store the whole seeds in closed jars and use them within a year.

Fenugreek; *húlúbā* 葫蘆巴. These hard ocher seeds are mainly used in Indian cuisine, but have also been introduced to Tibet (see page 318), where their gentle aroma flavors many stews and braises. These can be found in Indian grocery stores and some Western supermarkets. Fry the seeds in a bit of oil before using them or they will become bitter little rocks in your food. Store fenugreek in a closed container.

Fermented rice; *jiǔniáng* 酒釀 or *lǎozāo* 老糟. Sticky rice is steamed until barely soft, and then combined with Chinese rice wine balls (see Yeast balls), water, and sometimes a bit of sugar and corn-starch. The yeast then gradually turns the starches and sugars into alcohol. See the recipe on page 415. Refrigerate in a covered, nonreactive container.

Fingernail test. Used for things that need to be soaked until even the center is soft enough to break apart with just a bit of pressure. To see whether rice is ready for cooking, for example, a cook will place a soaked grain on a finger and gently press down on it with a fingernail. If it crumbles easily, it has passed the fingernail test and can be cooked with confidence. Vegetables can also be submitted to this test to determine whether they are tender by piercing the stem with a thumbnail.

Fish, salted; *xiányú* 鹹魚. The southern coastal areas of China have many varieties of fish that are preserved with salt and then dried. Dried fish—most often the desiccated flatfish called *dàdìyú* 大地魚—are sold in dried-seafood stores, as well as in Chinese groceries. Other dried varieties, including yellow croakers and mackerel, are also steamed in oil and then

packed in jars; they are available in most Chinese supermarkets, but see the recipe for making them at home on page 209. Refrigerate oil-packed fish after opening.

Fish sauce; *xiāyóu* 蝦油. Called "shrimp oil" in Chinese and *nước mắm* in Vietnamese, this clear amber liquid is usually made from smaller fish, like anchovies, that are layered with salt and then left to ferment. Fish sauce is highly concentrated and seasons dishes—especially along the southern coast—with that wonderfully deep flavor that the Chinese call *xianwei* (see page 56). Most brands come from Southeast Asia. I have used the one with a pink label and three blue crabs for decades and find it reliable. Store it closed in a pantry, and it will remain tasty for years. Light soy sauce can be substituted to a certain extent, but the flavor will not be the same.

Five-spice powder; *wǔxiāngfěn* 五香粉. Usually made from a combination of ground cinnamon, fennel, Sichuan peppercorns, star anise, and cloves, this spice mixture can also contain ginger, black cardamom, and so forth. See the recipe on page 441 for more ideas. Unless you have a great spice store that can sell you small amounts, make your mixture fresh every once in a while and store in a closed jar in the pantry.

Flour, Chinese; *Zhōngguó miànfěn* 中國麵粉. Wheat flours in East Asia have a lower protein (i.e., gluten) content than American flours. In order to achieve the correct texture in Chinese bread, pasta, or pastry, you must have the right kind of flour. Most Chinese and Korean flours are heavily processed, so I have devised a way to create your own equivalent using a combination of organic all-purpose and pastry flours; see the recipe on page 386.

Flour, tapioca; *mùshǔfěn* 木薯粉 (tapioca flour) or *língfěn* 菱粉 (caltrop flour). Made from cassava roots, genuine tapioca flour is a fine, white, slightly sweet powder. Nowadays there is a lot of confusion in Chinese products as to what is truly tapioca flour, and the labeling is often incorrect. For that reason, purchase Western brands for these non-wheat flours whenever possible; most are available in health food stores.

Fungus, bamboo pith; *zhúshēng* 竹笙. This incredibly strange and beautiful mushroom grows in clumps of bamboo (see page 263). Purchase it at a Chinese herbal or dried-foods store; a busy Chinese grocery is a good second choice. The mushrooms usually come bundled in clear plastic bags. Look for places that offer them loosely packed so that you can see each piece. Bags that are stuffed tightly will often have all the nice mushrooms only on the outside. The absolute best fungi will be around 6 inches long, white, and a bit supple. Check for bug residue at the bottom of the bag, as well as crumbling. Store the mushrooms in a sealed container and try to use within a year.

Fungus, silver ear; *yíněr* 銀耳, *xuě'ěr* 雪耳 (snow ear), jelly fungus, and many other names in both Chinese and English. This very tender, bland, dried fungus grows on dead wood and is treasured by the Chinese for its slippery, gentle texture. It should be soaked for three days with multiple changes of water, which plumps it up and supplies a finer texture. The tough, darker parts are trimmed off and the fungus is separated into petals, which are then stewed in sweet or savory broth. Purchase from Chinese dried-foods stores, herbalists, and busy grocery stores. Look for large, unbroken heads that are not too white; whiteness means they were bleached. Store silver ears in a sealed plastic bag, where they will remain in good shape for a long time.

Fungus, wood ear; *mùěr* 木耳. This popular mushroom is used both fresh and dried throughout most of China. It is valued for its texture and health properties. Purchase fresh wood ears that are plump, completely dark on top, and a light brown underneath. There should be no signs of mildew. Store fresh wood ears in the refrigerator, preferably with something to absorb moisture, like a paper bag or paper towel, and cover them with a plastic bag. Dried wood ears come whole or sliced. Store dried mushrooms in a covered container and revive by soaking the wood ears in very hot water until plump. Black mushrooms (see entry) can sometimes be used as a substitute.

Gailan; *jièláncài* 芥藍菜. These beautiful flowering stalks of kale are at their tenderest when you do not see any opened flowers. Try to locate stems that are only about 6 inches long. Ideally, they will have just a couple of small leaves on their thin stems. If you're not too sure about your pick, do the fingernail test (see entry). To prepare them, trim off the ends and then rinse the stems under running water. Also known as Chinese flowering kale.

Garlic; *suàn* 蒜 or *dàsuàn* 大蒜. Garlic in this book always refers to fresh garlic. Purchase fat heads with no mildew, no dried cloves, and no green sprouts. If at all possible, buy American garlic, which has rootlets at the bottom (Chinese garlic bulbs are bleached and have the roots trimmed off), as fewer pesticides are generally used. It is also very easy to grow your own garlic from sprouted cloves—this allows you to enjoy the young plants called "green garlic" and the flowering shoots (see garlic stems) that come later in the season. These are delicious, yet often hard to find in the market.

Garlic stems; *suàntái* 蒜薹. The flowering stalk of garlic is tender and delicious when still young and completely green. See page 37 for directions on buying, storing, and preparing this vegetable. Also known as garlic scapes.

Ginger, fresh; *jiāng* 薑. One of the quintessential Chinese aromatics, mature ginger is used throughout China to season just about everything and is also an important herbal medicine. Purchase fresh organic rhizomes from Hawaii, rather than the ones from China, which are usually grown with pesticides. Chinese ginger tends to be thick and smooth, while Hawaiian ginger is more compact, with lots of branching. Refrigerate the ginger in a dry plastic bag. It can also be frozen for longer storage. Also known as mature ginger.

Ginger, young; *nènjiāng* 嫩薑. New growths on ginger plants are pale ivory with pink tips. Store in the refrigerator, covered in plastic, and use before they start to mildew or shrink. Buy fat rhizomes with pure ivory skins and no bruising. Baby ginger does not need to be peeled and is delicious when cut into the thinnest julienne as a garnish.

Ginger juice; *jiāngzhī* 薑汁. Ginger juice is easy to make: grate fresh ginger, use your fist to squeeze out the liquid over a sieve, and let it collect in a cup. Mature ginger gives you hotter juice, while baby ginger is very mild in flavor; mature ginger is preferred in most recipes calling for ginger juice. Make this juice a short time before cooking. If you want, let the juice settle and then use only the clear liquid that floats to the top of the white sediment. I use a special bamboo grater with large, sharp teeth (see page 467). A wheat grass juicer and a large-holed box grater are other options.

Ginkgo nuts; *báiguǒ* 白果. These starchy tree nuts are available fresh in markets during the fall. The smelly pulp that encases them will have already been removed. Ginkgo nuts can be purchased all year in vacuum-sealed bags in Chinese and Korean markets. Those nuts will have already been shelled and cooked. Avoid ones that are bright yellow, which means they have been dyed. To prepare them, all you need to do is simmer them in water for about 10 minutes. Store the sealed bags in the refrigerator, where they will remain usable for a long time. Also known in Chinese as "silver almonds" (*yínxìng* 銀杏).

Ginseng; *rénshēn* 人參 (also pronounced *rénsēn*). This is the most famous of all Chinese herbal medicines, and it can now be found fresh in some Chinese and Korean supermarkets. No special preparation is needed; just clean the roots and slice as directed. Dried ginseng is much more common, and the best-quality roots are found in busy herbalist shops. It should be washed carefully, soaked in hot water until slightly softened, and then sliced. Buy American ginseng—usually grown in Wisconsin nowadays—to avoid problems with pesticides and heavy metals. Use up fresh ginseng quickly. Dried ginseng stays tasty and viable for a while as long as it is stored in a closed container in a dark cupboard. Do not use extracts or candied ginseng as substitutes.

Gluten; *miànjīn* 麵筋. The proteins in wheat flour are made into three forms of vegetarian meat substitute: fried gluten, raised gluten, and gluten batons. Fried gluten is torn off into tiny balls that are deep-fried, while raised gluten is mixed with yeast and then steamed to form a fluffy breadlike cake, which can be torn into smaller pieces and deep-fried before braising (page 124). Large balls of fried gluten can be purchased in plastic bags in the refrigerated section. Raised gluten is also wrapped in plastic and sold near the fried gluten. Gluten batons are simply strips of raw gluten wrapped around chopsticks and boiled—these are sometimes called *miàncháng* 麵腸 (flour intestines) because of their long, lumpy appearance. Refrigerate or freeze all types of gluten and use them up quickly.

Glutinous rice; see Rice, sticky.

Hawthorn fruits, dried; *shānzhā* 山楂 (whole hawthorn fruits) and *shānzhāpiàn* 山楂片 (sliced hawthorn fruits). These look and taste a bit like tart crabapples, but they come from the Chinese hawthorn tree (*Crataegus pinnatifida*). They are presently available only in their dried form and are generally sold already sliced. They can be purchased at most Chinese grocery stores and herbal shops. Store them in a plastic bag in a dark cupboard and rinse before using.

Jamaica flowers, dried; *luòshénhuā* 洛神花. The dark red calyces of this hibiscus are mainly used to make a sour infusion. They can be found in many ethnic and health food stores; Latin American groceries often sell them in bulk. To prepare the infusion, simply pour boiling water over the blossoms. Store them in a closed bag in the pantry.

Jellyfish; *hǎizhétóu* 海蜇頭 ("jellyfish heads") and *hǎizhépí* 海蜇皮 ("jellyfish skin"). Jellyfish come salted, in plastic bags, and they can usually be found in the refrigerated section of Chinese markets near other dried but refrigerated seafood, like dried shrimp. Jellyfish are usually sold two ways: as the "head" or the "skin." These can be used interchangeably in most recipes; see page 253 for details. To prepare jellyfish, rinse it and then soak it in cool water for three days, keeping it in the refrigerator the whole time and changing the water twice a day. Store the bags unopened in the refrigerator, where they will stay fresh for quite a while.

Job's tears; *yìrén* 薏仁. These largish, round tropical seeds are sometimes used interchangeably with barley in Chinese cooking, and are occasionally even confused with it. Job's tears tend to have mahogany skins and are generally found split in half. Purchase in Chinese markets and store in a closed container. Soak before cooking.

Ketchup; see Catsup.

Lard; *zhūyóu* 豬油, *hùnyóu* 渾油, and *dàyóu* 大油. Rendered lard is pork fat that has been melted and strained. You can buy it already rendered from some butchers and ethnic grocery stores, but the best-tasting and whitest lard is generally made at home. Chop up pork fat into small cubes, add a bit of water to prevent the solids from burning before the fat melts, and bring everything to a slow boil in a saucepan over medium heat, regulating the heat as needed and swirling the pan now and then to stir the fat around. When almost all of the fat has been rendered, the solids will crisp up and become cracklings. Strain out the fat into a heatproof canning jar and cover; store it in the refrigerator. White shortening can often be used as a substitute for baking, while unsalted butter is better for other types of cooking.

Licorice root; *gāncǎo* 甘草. This is a common Chinese herb used for cooking and herbal medicine. Purchase the sliced tan roots from a Chinese herbalist. Store them in a closed container in the pantry.

Lily bulbs, fresh; *bǎihé* 百合. This delicate vegetable is beginning to appear with more frequency in some Chinese grocery stores. The bulbs are usually grown near Lanzhou, in Gansu Province, and they come packaged in small plastic bags, which are displayed in the refrigerated section. Lightly press the printed areas of the bag where the bulbs are hidden to determine whether they are firm, which is what you want. The prettiest bulbs will of course be in the front and visible through a clear window. These bulbs should be used within a week or two.

Just before using, dismantle the bulbs into separate petals, trim off any discolored or mushy areas, and rinse to dislodge the sawdust and dirt (see page 450). Shake them dry, and they're ready to use. Fresh lily bulbs are best if only barely heated through; their texture will soften and they'll turn starchy if they are overcooked. These bulbs can be planted if you find any rootlets at the bottom of them, and will produce tall stalks of orange blossoms that look like tiger lilies. Dried lily bulb petals are sold in Chinese grocery stores as well, but they are starchy and relatively flavorless. An acceptable substitute for fresh lily bulbs is thinly sliced fresh water chestnuts.

Long beans; *jiāngdòu* 豇豆. The entire pod of this strangely beautiful relative of the cow pea is enjoyed in China, either fresh or pickled. Almost always sold in bunches, these taste much like string beans but have a slightly rougher texture, and so for stir-fries, long beans are usually either diced or cut into short lengths, unless the seeds are very small and the pods are extremely tender. Select beans that are firm and slender with no shriveling at either the stem or blossom end. Wrap with a paper towel and refrigerate in a plastic bag for a day or two, at the most. Pickled long beans (*suān jiāngdòu* 酸豇豆) are sold in vacuum-packed plastic bags in the refrigerated section of many Chinese markets, but homemade ones are much more flavorful (see page 428). The fresh beans have a variety of English nicknames, including yard-long beans, snake beans, and so forth.

Longan fruits; *lóngyǎn* 龍眼. Eaten both fresh and dried, these are similar to lychees but have a deeper, heavier fragrance and less juice. Dried longans (*lóngyǎn gān* 龍眼乾) are usually sold already pitted and have a lovely perfume. They are available in Chinese herbal shops, dried-foods stores, and groceries. Purchase dried longans that feel slightly moist and have a mahogany color; dark brown ones tend to be older and harder. Rinse them in a colander and then soak them in boiling water to plump them up (the resulting liquid will be delicious). Store dried longans in a closed jar in the pantry.

Lotus leaves; *héyè* 荷葉. Only available in the States at present as dried leaves, these are packaged with grass ties and sold wrapped in plastic. Select leaves that have no signs of bug damage (holes in the leaves and black droppings in the bottom of the bag are sure signs). Soak the leaves in hot water until pliable and then wipe off carefully on both sides to remove any dust. Use whole or cut them into pie-shaped triangles. Store the dry leaves in a closed bag in the pantry.

Lotus roots; *lián'ǒu* 蓮藕. Fresh lotus roots are another item appearing with increased frequency in many local Chinese grocery stores. They are rhizomes rather than actual roots, and the lacy beauty of these vegetables is only revealed when they are sliced. Remove the thin skin with a potato peeler and trim off the hard ends, then rinse out the insides if any dirt can be seen. A chopstick is helpful for dislodging any mud you find (see page 451). The best rhizomes will be fat and heavy with absolutely no breakage, since cracks allow mud inside, as well as rot. They are best in autumn, when they've just been harvested. Select lotus roots that are connected to one another and are as pale as possible. If you can find local lotus roots, these will have fewer pesticides than the ones from China. Store refrigerated in a plastic bag and use within a week or so for best quality.

Lotus seeds; *liánzǐ* 蓮子. Starchy dried lotus seeds are available throughout the year but are best when purchased from a Chinese herbal or dried-foods store. The seeds need to be soaked in boiling or very hot water, and baking soda can be added to assist in the softening. (The ratio is around 1 cup dried lotus seeds to 1 teaspoon baking soda, with boiling water to cover.) Rinse the plumped-up seeds in a sieve, and then squeeze each one open to pluck out the bitter green shoot inside (see page 289). They will usually have a tiny vertical hole punched through them in an attempt to get rid of the sprouts, but this often misses the mark. The seeds should be boiled or steamed until tender. Store dried lotus seeds in a closed container.

If you are lucky enough to find fresh lotus seeds, remove them from the seed head and peel the seeds before using. As always, remove any green sprouts you find inside the seeds. Fresh lotus seeds should be eaten raw or cooked only very lightly to preserve their fragrance and texture.

Lovage root; *chuānxiōng* 川芎. Also known as Sichuan lovage, this member of the carrot family is widely used in traditional Chinese medicine. Buy in small amounts from a Chinese herbal store and keep in a closed container, out of the sun. An average thin slice is about the size of a quarter.

Lychees or litchis; *lìzhī* 荔枝. These tropical fruits are available canned and dried, but they are best when eaten fresh. A thin, leathery skin protects the juicy and fragrant interior, and at the core of each fruit sits a small brown pit. As cultivation of these fruits extends into Mexico and California, fresh lychees are becoming increasingly available in the States. Look for them in midsummer and select fruits that are firm and bright pink. They should smell very perfumey and feel heavy, as well. Refrigerate them in a plastic bag and wash before peeling. Canned lychees are often quite good, especially Taiwanese brands. Dried lychees are found in some Chinese grocery and dried-foods stores but are rarely used for anything other than snacks and for seasoning things like tea (page 240).

Maltose; *màiyátáng* 麥芽糖. This is a very thick liquid sugar made from sprouted grains such as barley. It is less sweet than corn syrup but much stickier and firmer. It is used widely in Chinese desserts and sweets. Purchase it in small (18-ounce or so) plastic tubs in Chinese grocery stores, where it will be in the sugar aisle. Maltose must be heated before it can be scooped into a measuring cup. This can be done in the microwave on low power in short bursts, or by placing the tub in a bowl of hot water until the syrup softens. I always spray my measuring cup with a light layer of oil beforehand so that the maltose slides out easily—that is the only trick I remember from my junior high home ec class. Store maltose in the pantry, where it will stay usable for a long time. Also known as maltose syrup.

Millet; *xiǎomǐ* 小米. The tiny round and yellow grains of millet create a fragrant mush when cooked. Get millet in bulk at a health food store. Before using, rinse it in a sieve. Store in a closed container.

Mingyou; *míngyóu* 明油. These seasoned oils are used to add a final sheen to many dishes while supplying a touch of fragrance. Aromatics are slowly fried in fresh oil and then strained out, leaving a scented and sometimes gently hued oil; see the recipes on pages 434 and 435. Any oil will do, as long as it does not have a strong aroma of its own, like toasted sesame oil. Store the oils in the refrigerator if you do not plan to use them immediately, as they can turn rancid.

Monosodium glutamate (MSG); *wèijīng* 味精. I do not use this Japanese invention myself, but it does appear in other cookbooks. Traditionally, Chinese chefs have relied on excellent chicken or pork stock to provide deep *xianwei* flavor. However, if you like MSG, use it. If not, I have found that more of that good stock, mushroom powder (see entry), or even white sugar are good substitutes wherever MSG is called for in other recipes. Do note that most commercial Chinese sauces (including soy sauce) and prepared foods already include MSG.

Mung bean powder; *lǜdòufěn* 綠豆粉. The best mung bean powder that I've found is sold in Korean grocery stores. It is labeled "green bean starch," "green bean powder," "mung bean powder," or something close to that. Most of the brands seem to be of comparable quality and price. Use this to make mung bean jelly (page 250). Store in a sealed container or bag in the pantry.

Mung bean sheets, dried; *fěnpí* 粉皮. These are available in just about any Chinese grocery store in the noodle aisle. The labels will feature different translations, such as "green beans starch sheet." Also, there will often be something on the package that says it's from the port city of Tianjin, which tells you you're on the right track. They stay fresh even after opened if kept in a plastic bag. Mung bean jelly (page 250) can be used in a pinch if cut into thin slices and treated with kid gloves so that it does not break apart— add it to the dish at the last minute.

Mushroom powder; *xiānggūfěn* 香菇粉. A flavoring agent much like dried bouillon, mushroom powder is a substitute for flavor boosters like MSG and "chicken essence" bouillon (*jījīng* 雞精). The best brands (my favorite is from Singapore) are made from nothing more than dried mushrooms, salt, and mushroom extract and can be found in many Chinese grocery stores. You can make a substitute by grinding (unwashed) dried black mushrooms into a powder and adding sea salt to taste.

Mushrooms, black, dried and fresh; *xiānggū* 香菇 (fragrant mushrooms) or *huāgū* 花菇 (flower mushrooms). A basic flavoring ingredient in almost every single Han Chinese cooking tradition, these large black fungi have a deep, meaty flavor, which intensifies during the drying process. Fresh black mushrooms are becoming increasingly available in Western metropolitan areas—most are imports from China, but others are grown locally. The dried ones are available whole or sliced, and while slices are convenient, the whole ones are much more flavorful.

Select thick, wide caps, preferably with decorative natural cracks along the top (these are flower mushrooms and have a better flavor). Avoid those with man-made cuts in the caps. Soak the mushrooms in cool water overnight; if you are in a hurry, the dried mushrooms can also be plumped up in hot water. Always remove the tough stems and reserve them for stocks; I dry mine and then pack them in jars for use in mushroom stock (page 381). Refrigerate fresh mushrooms covered, preferably in a paper bag or in a plastic bag with a dry paper towel. Dried mushrooms should be stored out of the sunlight in closed containers. Sometimes referred to by their Japanese name, shiitake.

Mushrooms, flower; see Mushrooms, black.

Mustard cabbage; *dàjiècài* 大芥菜. A variety of mustard that grows in rounded heads with thick, wide stems, these are prized for their texture and gentle bitterness. The leaves are floppy and long and can be used for something like salted Shanghainese greens; the stems can be prepared and enjoyed separately. Select heads that are fat and tight, with no flowering in the center. Refrigerate the unwashed mustard in a plastic bag and use within a couple of days. Also referred to by its Cantonese name, *gai choy*, and a number of English names, as there seems to be little unity in this family's nomenclature.

Oil, peanut or vegetable; *huāshēngyóu* 花生油 or *shālāyóu* 沙拉油. Like rice bran oil (see below), the oil that is expelled from unroasted peanuts has a high smoke point (437°F or 225°C) and offers a faint scent of peanuts that intensifies as it is heated. Vegetable oil is a good substitute. Canola, corn, and soybean oil can also be used when cooking Chinese dishes, but be sure to get non-GMO (genetically modified organism) and organic products. Keep all oils in a dark cupboard and discard if they smell stale; refrigerate for longer storage.

Oil, rice bran; *dàomǐyóu* 稻米油, *mǐkāngyóu* 米糠油, or *mǐpēiyóu* 米胚油. Made from the germ and inner husk of rice, this oil has a very high smoke point (450°F or 232°C) and a mild, nutty flavor. It's perfect for deep-frying, but also works for stir-frying.

Olives, preserved Chinese; *lǎnchǐ* 欖豉. The fruits of the Chinese olive (*gǎnlǎn* 橄欖) are much different from Mediterranean olives, but they have a similarly savory taste that is brought out through curing. The black fruits are cut in half, pitted, and squashed flat to form what the Chinese call "olive corners," or *lǎnjiǎo* 欖角. These can be found in groceries and dried-foods stores that cater to Cantonese customers. Simmer olive corners in some fresh oil and sugar to bring out their flavor and then refrigerate them in a covered jar; see page 181.

The preserved fruits of the *Canarium album* tree are also mashed and fermented with shredded mustard leaves to make a dark, savory paste called preserved olive vegetable (*lǎncài* 欖菜). It is available in small glass jars in many Chinese grocery stores.

Osmanthus blossom syrup; *guìhuājiàng* 桂花醬. Also known as "sweet olive" in English, these intensely fragrant little blossoms are an indispensable flavoring in many Chinese desserts. They come dried and can be mixed with tea leaves to make a scented beverage but are most often seen suspended in a sweet syrup. They should be stored in a dark pantry after opening. *Osmanthus fragrans* bushes can also be grown in the garden, where their sweet scent will welcome the first cool days of autumn. This syrup is sometimes translated as a "sauce" or "jam."

Honey plus a dash of salt can sometimes be substituted, but the flavor will not be the same.

Pepper; see Pepper, black, or Sichuan peppercorns.

Pepper, black; *hēihújiāo* 黑胡椒. Always buy whole peppers and grind them just before using. Tellicherry pepper from India is especially fragrant. Store in closed containers in a dark cupboard and use within a year. White pepper is merely black peppercorn with the outer layer removed. It is used in pale sauces and has a slightly milder flavor.

Pickled napa cabbage; *suāncài* 酸菜. The Chinese version of sauerkraut, this is a specialty of North China, from Shanxi in the west to Heilongjiang in the northeast. Buy sealed plastic bags of the pickled cabbage from the refrigerated section of a Chinese grocery store. Rinse off whatever amount you wish to use in cool tap water and gently squeeze it dry. Refrigerate any leftovers in a sealed plastic bag.

Plums, dried black; *wūméi* 烏梅. Very dry, very hard, and very sour, these dried fruits are sold almost exclusively in Chinese herbalist shops. They are so incredibly tart that they cannot be eaten as is; instead, dried black plums must be combined with other ingredients to balance out their flavors. There is an alternative variety of dried plum known as *suānméi* 酸梅 (sour plums), which have been tempered with sugar and salt and function wonderfully as a tea snack or in sauces (page 205). Store dried plums in a container away from the sunlight.

Pork, cured; see Charcuterie.

Pork belly; *wǔhuāròu* 五花肉. The Chinese call this "five-layer meat," which means that ideally there is an almost equal ratio of fat to meat in alternating ribbons of red and white. A thick flap of meat will often be attached to one end of the innermost layer: trim this off and use it for something else, because the lack of fat will render it tough even after a long

braise. The skin is usually sold attached to the pork.

Pork fluff; *ròusōng* 肉鬆. This is a common snack food and condiment from southern China. To make it, meat cubes are stewed with aromatics and then shredded. Constant tossing as the pork is fried turns the meat a golden brown. Plastic jars of this (as well as fish fluff and vegetarian fluff) can be found in Chinese supermarkets. "Fluff" is sometimes translated as "floss." Keep the jar closed to preserve the gentle crunchiness.

Preserved mustard greens; *méicài* 梅菜. A special variety of mustard green is salted and dried to produce this condiment. The Hakka variety (page 300) is called *Kèjiā méicài* 客家梅菜, and as it is a specialty of the Huizhou region of Guangdong, it's often labeled *Huìzhōu méicài* 惠州梅菜. This type of preserved vegetable is mainly found in small dried-foods stores in Chinatowns, although it may eventually be sold in grocery stores. Select long hanks of salt-flecked *meicai*, which are thick mustard heads that have been split down the middle before being dried. Rinse the leaves and stems very carefully to remove all of the grit and then chop them finely.

Hakka *meicai* is very different in flavor and texture from the *meicai* of Shaoxing in Zhejiang Province (*Shàoxīng méicài* 紹興梅菜), which is darker, finely chopped, and sold in small plastic bags in grocery stores (page 118). The two cannot be substituted for each other because their seasonings and textures are completely different. Store all *meicai* in sealed plastic bags in a cool place, where they will pretty much keep forever.

Radish, Chinese; *luóbó* 蘿蔔. Often mistranslated as "turnips," these are actually giant sweet radishes. They come with white, green, or red flesh. Younger radishes will not be woody or thick skinned; look for green, leafy tops with small diameters at the leaf base, as this signifies fast, juicy growth. The radishes should feel hard and have no "give" when you press them. Chinese radishes

are similar to Japanese daikon and can be used interchangeably with it. Korea's football-shaped turnips, another related vegetable, are especially good when fresh and are so mild and sweet they can be eaten raw, like apples. Refrigerate all of these and keep them dry to discourage rot and root growth. Small, Western-style radishes can sometimes be substituted, but they are much hotter than Chinese ones. All radish greens can be used to make salted Shanghainese greens (page 426).

Radishes, salted; *càipú* 菜脯. Chinese radishes are often alternately sun-dried and salted until they turn leathery. The resulting tan ingredient is always chopped before it is cooked. Popular in Southern Fujian, Chaozhou, Taiwan, Hakka, and Guangdong cuisines, as well as in Hong Kong and Macau, salted radish is lightly crunchy and full of *xianwei* depth. Rinse the salted radish until its saltiness is tamed and then use as directed. Store in a closed container, where it will generally stay fine for a long time. Often sold in plastic bags as "salted turnip" or something similar.

Red bean paste, sweetened; *hóngdòushā* 紅豆沙 or *hóngdòuní* 紅豆泥. Small red (adzuki) beans are soaked and then simmered until very soft before being mashed and cooked with sugar to form a sweet paste. This is easily made at home (page 442), but is also available canned, in both smooth and chunky form. Taiwanese, Korean, and Japanese brands tend to be good. Commercial sweetened bean paste always tastes better if it is first fried in a bit of toasted sesame oil until it bubbles. Be sure to stir it constantly to keep it from burning.

Rice, broken; *suìmǐ* 碎米. These are tiny shards of rice that were broken during the milling process. Broken jasmine rice is especially fragrant and tasty, and my go-to brand is the one from Thailand with three ladies on the label. Use this for Congee (page 226) and rice crumbs (page 383).

Rice, jasmine; *xiāngmǐ* 香米 (aromatic rice). This long-grain polished rice is used almost exclusively in the southern areas of China. As its name suggests, these grains have an almost floral perfume. The rice cooks up into separate grains with a slight chewiness. Basmati rice from India can be substituted, but it is not as fragrant or gently sticky.

Rice, regular; *niánmǐ* 粘米 (黏米) or *báimǐ* 白米. This name is used to refer to polished short- or long-grained rice. The grains remain separate when steamed or boiled, rather than stick together, as with sticky rice (see entry). Unless you eat large amounts, buy small bags or from bulk bins and store in a closed container. Be on the lookout for the harvest year, which is often printed along the top of sealed bags. Bulk rice should be smelled before it is purchased to determine its freshness. Also called white rice.

Rice, sticky; *nuòmǐ* 糯米 (creamy rice). Also known as "glutinous" or "sweet" rice, despite the fact that it contains no gluten and is no sweeter than any other rice, sticky rice encompasses a number of different types of grains, from the Thai purple long to Chinese white round. They all share one quality, though: the longer they cook, the creamier they become. This is what gives them the stickiness to hold together in such things as rice tamales (page 384) or be ground into rice cakes (see entry). Sticky rice is also the preferred main ingredient for fermented rice (page 415). It is almost always soaked until the grains can pass the fingernail test (see entry), and then is steamed, boiled, or ground into a paste. Purchase small bags of this rice unless you use it often, store it in a closed container, and toss out if bugs show up.

Rice cakes; *nián'gāo* 年糕. Chewy rice cakes are a specialty of Ningbo in Zhejiang Province, but their popularity has spread throughout the country and even into Korea. They are made by pounding steamed sticky rice into a paste, forming it into batons, and then slicing these batons into ovals. Purchase sliced rice cakes, whole thick batons, or finger-width rice cakes at either Chinese or Korean grocery stores; my favorites are the Korean brands. They are vacuum-sealed in plastic bags in the refrigerated section, and the rice cakes will stay fresh if kept cold and unopened. Use up any leftover rice cakes within a week before they mold. The unopened packages can also be frozen and then defrosted before use.

Rice crumbs; *zhēngfěn* 蒸粉. To make these crumbs, regular or sticky rice is dry-fried until dry and barely golden (often with a ground spice), and then crushed into smallish bits. Rice crumbs are used to coat meats and other ingredients before they're steamed, which turns the crumbs into a delicately sticky coating. Easy to make at home (page 383), these can also be purchased in tiny boxes at Chinese supermarkets. An excellent substitute is dry-fried broken jasmine rice (see entry). Keep in a closed container.

Rice flour, Indica; *niánmǐfěn* 粘米粉. Finely ground regular rice. The English translation on the package is usually not very helpful—something like "rice flour"—so be sure that you can find the Chinese characters on there. Both Taiwan and Thailand have good products; the Thai version usually has red print on its plastic bag. (The similar-looking green-printed bag is probably sticky rice flour, see entry.)

Rice flour, sticky; *nuòmǐfěn* 糯米粉. Finely ground sticky rice. This is also known as sweet rice flour or glutinous rice flour, and my go-to brand is Mochi-ko Sweet Rice Flour.

Rice vermicelli; *mǐfěn* 米粉. Made out of regular (non-sticky) rice, these noodles are popular all through southern China. Depending upon the area, they can be very fine or thick, but all are dried and need only to be boiled before serving. The best thin variety I have found is from the town of Xinzhu in Taiwan, and it comes (at least at present) in large, clear plastic bags marked "Hsin Chu Rice Stick." Store these in sealed plastic bags.

Rice wine, mild; *liàojiǔ* 料酒 or *Táiwān mǐjiǔ* 台灣米酒. Almost any mild, relatively colorless rice wine like Japanese sake can be used for cooking, but my favorite brand is Taiwan *mijiu*, which comes in dark green bottles. It's a slightly salty cooking wine, which sets it apart from the rice wine meant for drinking.

Cantonese clear rice wine (*Guǎngdōng mǐjiǔ* 廣東米酒) is so much stronger—around 60 proof—that it is considered a type of grain alcohol or a white liquor (see entry), and therefore cannot be used as a substitute for mild rice wine.

Rice wine, Shaoxing; *Shàoxīngjiǔ* 紹興酒. Shaoxing-style rice wine has an amber color, is around 30 proof, and blends aromas of sherry with dried mushrooms. Although it is a specialty of Zhejiang, the best-quality ones at present come from Taiwan. I prefer the "TTJ" brand with a red label and a clear, square glass bottle. This same brand also makes a better-flavored and more aged wine with a gold and red label that reads *Chénnián Shàoxīngjiǔ* 陳年紹興酒, as well as, in English, "Shaoxing V.O. (Rice Wine)." This is excellent in dishes where the wine's aroma is pronounced, as on pages 84 and 114.

Sometimes spelled Shao-hsing or Shaohsing, the superior-quality wine should be reserved for sipping, and tastes best when it is hot or warm. The cheapest ones are not very good and should be avoided, but good-quality wines for cooking can be found at present in the $3 to $5 range. Store any rice wine in a cool, dark place, where it will keep pretty much indefinitely if unopened.

Rice wine balls, Chinese; see Yeast balls.

Rose petal jam; *méiguījiàng* 玫瑰醬. Chinese recipes usually call for candied rose petals, but I have found that rose petal jams from places like Turkey are much more flavorful. Find these in Middle Eastern stores.

Salt, pink. This is the curing salt used in this book instead of the traditional potassium (*xiāo* 硝), which can lead to health issues. Also called Prague powder #1, pink salt is composed of 94 percent table salt and 6 percent sodium nitrate; it is tinted pink to differentiate it from regular salt. Pink salt lends an appetizing rosy color and a hamlike flavor to meats. Purchase small amounts (you won't need a whole lot unless you are a dedicated charcuterie maker) from specialty butcher shops and spice stores. Keep in the pantry in a closed, well-labeled container out of the reach of children.

Salt, sea; *hǎiyán* 海鹽. Salt in all its various guises is basically sodium chloride. However, I specify sea salt in most of this book's recipes because it measures differently from, say, kosher salt, which is flaked. The salt made from evaporated seawater has a purer flavor than iodized salt, which I find has a bitter, chemical edge. You, of course, can use whatever type of salt you like as long as you adjust the amount to suit your taste. In this book, sea salt refers to fine sea salt unless otherwise noted; coarse sea salt is sometimes preferred for its texture when salting vegetables and as a coating for meat or fish. It is available in just about every grocery store.

Salted Shanghainese greens; *xuělǐhóng* 雪裏紅 (or 雪裏蕻). This is one of the signature flavoring ingredients of the lower Yangtze River area, especially in Jiangsu, Zhejiang, and Shanghai. A special variety of long-leafed green mustard is used to make it, although similar greens such as other leafy mustards and even radish leaves can be used in a pinch. Salt is rubbed into the well-washed leaves, which lightly cures the greens, reduces the bitterness, and makes them crunchy and aromatic. You can get this in the refrigerated section of some Chinese groceries, but it is easily made at home (page 426).

Sand ginger; *shājiāng* 沙薑. This dried root is commonly used as a spice in southern Chinese dishes, as well as in traditional herbal medicine. The English name is a direct translation of the Chinese, although it has other appellations throughout Southeast and South Asia, such as kencur and

cutcherry; in Chinese, sand ginger is also sometimes referred to as *shānnài* 山奈. Locate the sliced dry roots in a busy herbal store, if you can; it is also stocked in most Chinese grocery stores. Instead of buying it already ground, always get sliced sand ginger, which has a much better flavor, and then pulverize it as needed in a spice grinder. Store this in a closed container in a dark cupboard.

Sauce, bean; *dòubànjiàng* 豆瓣醬. Completely different from sweet wheat paste, which is often mislabeled as a bean sauce, this is not sweet, but rather deeply savory and usually fairly smooth. It is made from cooked fava beans or soybeans that have been inoculated with mold and then fermented with various seasonings. Many parts of China have their own versions of this heavy, dark brown sauce full of rich *xianwei* flavors. Har Har brand is recommended.

Sauce, char siu; *chāshāojiàng* 叉燒醬. A reddish mixture of oyster, hoisin, and soy sauces, as well as sugar, rice wine, red fermented bean curd "cheese" (see entry), garlic, five-spice powder (see entry), and honey, this can be made at home (see Tip on page 206), although some grocery stores carry it already prepared in jars.

Sauce, hoisin; *hǎixiānjiàng* 海鮮醬. The name of this Cantonese seasoning literally means "seafood sauce"; it can be made at home (see Tip on page 206), but most commercial brands nowadays are simply thickened, sweet pastes mildly seasoned with garlic, chilies, salt, fat, red wine lees, and vinegar.

Sauce, oyster; *háoyóu* 蠔油. Made mainly from oysters fermented in brine, this thick, slightly sweetened sauce is used for the most part in southern-style cooking. It was invented in 1888 by the founder of the Hong Kong food manufacturer Lee Kum Kee, which is still the best. Vegetarian versions are also available. Store covered in a cool place.

Sauce, plum; *sūméijiàng* 蘇梅醬. This Chaozhou-style sauce is both tart and

sweet, thanks to the sour salted plums that provide fruity undertones and the sugar that balances them out. It is thickened with starch and comes in small glass jars; the Lee Kum Kee brand is good.

Sauce, satay; *shāchájiàng* 沙茶醬. Chinese satay sauce is a specialty of the Chaozhou region of Guangdong. It is completely different from peanutty Indonesian satay sauce, as this is a coarse brick-red mixture of dried chilies, crustaceans, and seasonings in oil. The Taiwanese brand Níutóupái 牛頭牌 (Ox Head Brand) is reliably tasty—this comes in traditional (clear plastic lid), vegetarian (green lid), and hot-and-numbing (red) varieties, so check the label carefully to get the right kind; I prefer the traditional recipe. This needs no special care once opened.

Sauce, Sichuan hot bean; *là dòubànjiàng* 辣豆瓣醬. Made from dried fava beans that are steamed and then inoculated with mold before they are allowed to ferment for a few months in a mixture of ground dried chilies and salt, this is a deeply savory and spicy paste. The most famous of the Sichuan hot bean sauces come from Pixian County 郫縣, but the popularity of this condiment has led to many copycats. I've used Taiwan's Har Har brand of Sichuan hot bean sauce and regular bean sauce for years.

Scallops, dried; *gānbèi* 乾貝. The best ones can be found at a Chinese herbalist's or a specialty dried-foods store, although some Chinese grocers will keep them behind the counter with other expensive goods like dried ginseng root. When using them to flavor stock, go for the cheaper small ones, which are just as tasty as the large, very expensive ones. The dried scallops should have a slight "give" to them when pressed and possess the fresh scent of the sea. Keep them in a jar in a cool, dark place. Also known by their Cantonese name, *conpoy*, or as *gānyáozhù* 乾瑤柱. Dried shrimp can sometimes be used as a substitute.

Sea moss; *táitiáo* 苔條. This is not a variety of seaweed, but rather green algae; see page 102. Like jellyfish, this is a nuisance in many areas, and yet it also happens to be quite tasty. Sea moss is dried in hanks and sold in sealed plastic bags in larger Chinese grocery stores, especially ones that cater to customers from East China. Store it in a sealed plastic bag in the pantry, where it will keep for a very long time. Seaweed cannot be substituted.

Seaweed; *hǎidài* 海带. Many varieties of kelp are used in China's dishes (see page 102), but the most widely preferred ones are the broad-leaved sea vegetable called *kūnbù* 昆布 (*kombu* in Japanese) and the laver seaweed called "purple vegetable," or *zǐcài* 紫菜 (nori). *Kunbu* has very long, wide, thick leaves that lend themselves nicely to braising; soak these in hot water before using to soften them and remove any grit. Laver seaweed is usually sold in thin sheets that are toasted and salted, and should be used up before the oil turns stale. Store both in sealed plastic bags.

Sesame oil, toasted; *máyóu* 麻油. Chinese sesame oil is always toasted, giving it a deep amber color and the strong aroma and flavor of the toasted seeds. The best toasted sesame oils are from Japan, and are most economically available in larger metal cans; always check the ingredient list to ensure that there are no extenders in there, like cottonseed oil, as you only want 100 percent sesame oil here. Untoasted sesame oil cannot be substituted.

Sesame paste, toasted; *májiàng* 麻醬. Toasted sesame seeds are ground into a nut butter to make sesame paste. There is usually nothing else in the paste except for a little toasted sesame oil; these pastes are never salted, although some have sugar added. Found in most Chinese grocery stores, it is easy to make at home (page 413). Refrigerate in a closed container unless you use it very often.

Sesame seeds; *zhīmá* 芝麻. Sesame seeds are used throughout China as a seasoning, as well as for their oil. Mainly white or unhulled seeds are turned into oil or paste; black sesame seeds are used more for decoration and in sweet fillings. The best sesame seeds can be found in busy health food stores where there is a good turnover; if purchased in bulk, you can taste them first to make sure they are fresh. If you purchase seeds from China, check them over for grit and foreign matter before using; Japanese brands tend to be much cleaner. Sesame seeds are generally toasted before use; see the recipe on page 413. Store raw and toasted sesame seeds in closed containers and use them within a month or two to ensure freshness.

Shark fin, vegetarian; *sùyúchì* 素魚翅. This can be found in the frozen section of some Chinese grocery stores and is usually sold in 1-pound bricks. Keep it frozen until needed and defrost it either by placing it in a cool area on the counter overnight or by soaking the unopened package in hot water. Open the package into a sieve in the sink and work the pieces apart under warm tap water. Drain thoroughly in a sieve (not a colander) before using. The labels tend to translate the main ingredient for this shark-fin alternative as gelatin, but my guess is that it is actually something like Japanese yam (*konnyaku*), since veggie shark fin can be simmered without melting. As with the real deal, it is flavorless and provides a fragile, gelatinous texture.

Shortening, white; *báiyóu* 白油. Lard is the preferred shortening for Chinese pastries, but I have found that organic white shortening, which can be found in health food stores, is an excellent substitute. Since it has a neutral flavor, the other aromas employed alongside it become more distinct. Look for shortening that is made from palm fruit oil and is nonhydrogenated, with zero trans fat.

Shrimp, dried; *kāiyáng* 開洋 or *xiāmǐ* 蝦米. Dried shrimp provide a signature flavor in dishes all over China but particularly in the coastal southern areas. They can be found in just about any Chinese grocery store, but the best are the plump specimens displayed in the refrigerated section or purchased at a dried-seafood shop, where they are sold by the ounce. Select shrimp that look whole rather than smashed up. I avoid shrimp that are too brightly colored, as this usually means they were dyed. Instead, I prefer ones that are a nice peach color, about the diameter of a penny, and pliable when gently squeezed. Rinse dried shrimp just before using and discard any detritus, shells, and blackish areas; then pour boiling hot water over them to plump them up before chopping or cooking. Refrigerate the dried shrimp in a closed container, where they should stay fresh for quite a while.

Shrimp, fresh; *xiānxiā* 鮮蝦. What to look for in shrimp: alive is best, but only if they are wild and from unpolluted waters. Second best are fresh or frozen wild shrimp from unpolluted waters, either with or without the head. Avoid farmed fish from countries where there are lax controls on aquaculture, as well as Thai producers, due to disturbing reports of slave labor there. Even if the shrimp are gorgeous and have orange roe in their heads, make sure you know where they were raised and how.

Shrimp roe, dried; *xiāzǐ* 蝦子. Dried shrimp roe is a lovely fillip, particularly in Jiangsu and Zhejiang dishes, as it lends a subtle taste of the sea along with a sandy texture and gentle red dots. The roe is usually lightly fried before it is slipped into a dish, as this releases its fragrance. This ingredient is not readily available at present but can occasionally be found in dried-seafood shops, where it is generally sold by the ounce. The roe will either be in a glass canister and the salesperson will weigh it out for you or in small plastic packages. Store the roe in a sealed freezer bag in the freezer, where it will stay tasty for a long time.

Shudi; *shúdì* 熟地. Also called *shúdìhuáng* 熟地黃, this root of the Chinese foxglove (*Rehmannia glutinosa*) is most often used in traditional herbal medicine, but it also lends itself nicely to soupy dishes that have a therapeutic nature. The curing process turns the naturally yellow root an inky black, and it is sold already sliced. The standard slice thickness is the width of a quarter. Purchase small amounts from a Chinese herbal store and keep in a closed container out of the light.

Sichuan peppercorns; *huājiāo* 花椒. This native Chinese spice has the scent of pines and gives a numbing sensation to the mouth, rather than the burning normally associated with peppers. Called "flower pepper" in Chinese because the reddish seed capsules seem to bloom and open when they are ripe, this is the signature flavor of Sichuan, though it is used in many areas of the country. Both the ripe red and immature green peppercorns are harvested, with the red ones more readily available. The red ones are usually either fried in oil or dry-fried and ground before use to release their fragrance. Purchase dried peppercorns from a busy Chinese grocery store and store them in a closed container. Sichuan peppercorn trees may also be grown in many temperate areas. No substitutes.

Sichuan pickled tubers; *zhàcài* 榨菜. This sour and salty pickle is made from the knobby, thickened stems of a variety of mustard plant. The stems are not tubers, but that seems to be the name they are stuck with. The mustard, *Brassica juncea*, is salted and partially dried and the juices squeezed out. It is then coated with chili powder and allowed to ferment.

The pickles can be purchased in most Chinese grocery stores, either in the refrigerated section, vacuum-packed in plastic, or canned. Select ones that are firm all over and have a nice coating of red chili powder. Refrigerate them—including canned ones after they have been opened—in plastic bags, where they will keep for a long time. Cut off whatever amount you wish to use, rinse, and then either julienne or chop as needed.

Soured napa cabbage; See Pickled napa cabbage.

Soy batons; *fǔzhú* 腐竹. When soy skins are rolled up and dried, they become soy batons, which must be soaked in warm water until pliable, then drained before using; also referred to as soy sticks or yuba sticks.

Soy custard; *dòuhuā* 豆花 (bean flower). Soymilk is coagulated with plaster, creating a silky, puddinglike ingredient that is naturally bland, and so sweet or savory sauces are usually added. It is very fragile and must be kept refrigerated. Use within a day or two for optimal flavor and quality.

Soy paste; *jiàngyóugāo* 醬油膏. Used mainly as a dipping or finishing sauce in southern Chinese cooking, this is basically soy sauce slightly sweetened and then thickened to give it a creamy texture.

Soy sauce; *jiàngyóu* 醬油 (in most of China). The main Chinese seasonings, bar none, are soy sauce and salt. However, not all soy sauces are alike, as each region has its own formulas and names. Taiwan has some good organic brands worth trying, and both Wan Ja Shan and Kim Lan have proved reliable over the years.

Basically, soy sauce is made by inoculating boiled soybeans and wheat with mold; the resulting mixture then ferments in brine, and the liquid that is produced is regular soy sauce. Light soy sauce (*dànjiàngyóu* 淡醬油 or *shēngchōu* 生抽) is paler in color, but slightly saltier; a good substitute is Bragg's Aminos, especially if you have wheat allergies. Dark soy sauce comes from the bottom of the liquid and is often mixed with things like molasses to deepen its color and flavor; this is called *lǎochōu* 老抽.

In the Guangdong area, soy sauce can also be referred to as *chǐyóu* 豉油, while in places like Fujian and Sichuan it may be called *dòuyóu* 豆油. The Yangtze area also has a variety seasoned with shrimp roe called *xiāzǐ jiàngyóu* 蝦子醬油.

The seasoning known as either *làjiàngyóu* 辣醬油 (spicy soy sauce) or *wūcù* 烏醋 (dark vinegar) is actually Worcestershire sauce. Sweet soy sauce (*tiánjiàngyóu* 甜醬油) has sugar and other seasonings added to the brew and is used mainly in South China; see the recipe for an excellent caramel version on page 439. Store the closed bottle away from heat.

Chinese-style soy sauce is not to be confused with tamari たまり, which is a Japanese product made from the liquid that forms when miso is fermented, although the latter can be used in Chinese cooking if you prefer the flavor. Japanese soy sauces have a lighter flavor than Chinese ones and are much saltier to my taste, so adjust the seasoning accordingly.

Soy sauce, sweet; see Soy sauce.

Soy skins; *dòufǔpí* 豆腐皮. This is the skin the forms on soymilk when it is boiled; it can be fresh, frozen, or dried. These generally are sold as large, thin, tan circles around 24 inches in diameter. When they are moistened, the skin turns light beige and becomes very fragile yet supple. Always keep fresh or frozen ones covered to prevent the skins from cracking. Sometimes referred to as tofu skins or by its Japanese name, *yuba*.

Soybean flour, toasted; *huángdòufěn* 黄豆粉. Soaked soybeans are either fried or baked until crisp and then ground to a fine powder (page 410); the flour is used either as a flavoring agent like ground toasted peanuts, or as a thickener. Cornstarch can be used as a substitute for thickening such sauces as the one in Mapo Doufu (page 268).

Soybeans, fresh; *máodòu* 茅豆 (or 毛豆). Mainly known in the West by their Japanese name, *edamame* 枝豆, these are widely used in various Chinese cuisines. They can be cooked without shelling to serve as appetizers (page 9). Shelled fresh soybeans are a beautiful jade green and can be added to stir-fries and braises. Both shelled and unshelled fresh soybeans are available frozen in many supermarkets, both Chinese and Western; look for non-GMO soybeans, preferably organic.

Sprouts, mung bean; *lǜdòuyá* 綠豆芽. Available in just about every Chinese grocery store, these sprouts are best when very fresh. Select solid sprouts with springy rootlets and no brown areas. Refrigerate them immersed in water and use within a few days for optimal quality. Some recipes suggest trimming the sprouts, which gives them a refined texture and appearance; to trim them, use your fingernail to nip off the dark heads and slender roots, leaving only the ivory-hued stem (see page 450). Cover trimmed sprouts with ice water to keep them crunchy. To sprout them yourself, see Sprouts, soybean.

Sprouts, soybean; *huángdòuyá* 黄豆芽. The best soy sprouts are usually found in Korean grocery stores, where they are almost always available. Select sprouts with white rootlets and the least amount of brown speckling on the heads, as that indicates the onset of rot. The yellow heads have a nutty crunchiness that sets them apart from mung bean sprouts (above). Smell the sprouts, as their aroma will tell you how fresh they are. Refrigerate soy sprouts covered with water; trim off rootlets for more refined presentations (see page 450).

If you want to grow your own, soak organic (non-GMO) soybeans overnight until they plump up. Place them in a large jar and cover the opening with wire mesh or cheesecloth to keep the insects out. Rinse the beans twice a day, place the jar in a warmish place out of the light (you want the sprouts to stay as white as possible), and when the beans have provided you with lots of long sprouts—but haven't formed leaves yet—transfer the sprouts to a container, cover them with water, and place them in the fridge for a couple of days.

Squid, dried; *yóuyúgān* 鱿鱼乾. Fresh squid are opened up along the bottom, cleaned out, and then flattened before they are dried in the sun. These come in a variety of sizes, but generally speaking, the larger the squid, the meatier it is. They can usually be found in loose piles in either dried-seafood or Chinese dried-foods stores. Select squid that are still pliable, for old ones cannot be bent without breaking. Refrigerate dried squid in closed plastic bags. To reconstitute, see the detailed directions on page 334.

Star anise; *bājiǎo* 八角 (eight corners) or *dàliào* 大料 (big spice). The licorice taste of this beautiful star-shaped brown spice is indispensable to many Chinese braises and seasoning mixtures. Always sold dried, it is available in Chinese grocery stores. Store in a closed container.

Starch, potato; *shēngfěn* 生粉. Like the name says, this is nothing more than the starch extracted from potatoes. Bob's Red Mill and other Western brands are reliable. Store in a covered container.

Starch, sweet potato; *fānshǔfěn* 蕃薯粉 or *dìguāfěn* 地瓜粉. This should be 100 percent starch from yams or sweet potatoes. The best comes from Taiwan, where it has a crumbly texture that lends a crunchiness and chewy texture to deep-fried foods and a sticky chewiness to steamed or panfried foods.

Starch, wheat; *chéngfěn* 澄粉. This is the stuff that is left over from making wheat gluten, dried into a fine white powder. It is available in most Chinese grocery stores next to the flour. The English on the packages will vary, so check the Chinese name to be certain.

Stock; *gāotāng* 高湯. This is the secret element to the best sauces. Good stock—be it the regular standby of chicken stock, or pork, mushroom, fish, or something else—gives the depth of flavor that the Chinese refer to as *xianwei* and the Japanese call umami. You can make your own (see the recipes on pages 380 and 381), or you can purchase it ready-made.

Sugar, brown slab; *piàntáng* 片糖. This is just sugar formed into thin sheets about ½ inch thick; the outside layers will be a darker brown than the center. It is widely available in Chinese supermarkets. Brown sugar or *piloncillo* sugar can be used as a substitute. Store in a sealed container.

Sugar, dark brown or black; *hēitáng* 黑糖. Chinese recipes often call for a particularly dark brown sugar, so dark it is almost

black. The best comes from Korea and is sold in plastic bags at most Korean supermarkets. Store in a container with a damp paper towel to keep it from hardening.

Sugar, rock; *bīngtáng* 冰糖. Crystallized into large chunks, rock sugar does not have the sour aftertaste that granulated sugar has. Yellow rock sugar is preferred because it has not been bleached. Most Chinese grocery stores carry it; store in a closed container. Use the large chunks for braises or smash them at will once they have soaked in liquid. The best way to measure the chunks is to place a tablespoon next to the sugar and compare them visually (in almost all cases, an approximation will do just fine), as these are difficult to crush. Use an approximate equivalent of white sugar as a substitute, though it can produce a sour aftertaste (see page 463).

Sweet bean paste, see Sweet wheat paste or Red bean paste, sweetened.

Sweet wheat paste; *tiánmiànjiàng* 甜麵醬 (sweet flour sauce). *Tianmianjiang* is mainly used in North China, and it is traditionally made out of steamed breads (plain *mantou*) that have been allowed to mold. These are then mixed with seasonings before the resulting mush ferments into a thick, rich sauce of the deepest, darkest brown. *Tianmianjiang* is often mistranslated as "black bean sauce" or "sweet bean sauce" or something on that order, but no beans were injured during the making of this sauce. To be sure that what you buy is what you want, check the ingredient list: it should mainly be wheat, water, caramel, and salt. If any beans or bean powder or soy sauce are mentioned, it should be as an afterthought. The best brands are, for my money, made in Korea. Store in the pantry, where it will stay fresh for quite a while. Bean paste (*doubanjiang*) may sometimes be substituted if only a small amount is called for.

Tamales, Chinese; *zòngzǐ* 粽子 (糉子). Sticky rice takes the place of cornmeal and bamboo leaves are used instead of corn husks, but otherwise they are similar to Mexican tamales. They can be sweet or savory, and different parts of China have their own specialties. See the recipes on pages 228 and 384.

Tangerine peel, aged; *chénpí* 陳皮. Guangdong's dried tangerine peel is deeply hued and has a wonderful perfume that homemade dried peels cannot match. The peels are usually sold in flat stacks bound with pretty red string, and the best come from dried-foods stores and herbal shops. Rinse before using. Store in a closed container out of the light and they will never go bad.

Tapioca pearls, Chinese; *Xīgòngmǐ* 西貢米 (Saigon rice). These tiny little balls shaped like pale BBs are made out of cassava root. Starchy and flavorless, they are beloved for their tensile texture. Chinese tapioca is almost always white when dry, but it turns translucent as it cooks. Store the uncooked tapioca in a covered container. Do not substitute Western tapioca, as this does not have the requisite round shape. Tapioca pearls are closely related to *boba* (see entry), and Southeast Asia also produces multicolored varieties. Sometimes labeled pearl sago.

Taro; *yùtóu* 芋頭. This tropical tuber is enjoyed mainly in the Coastal Southeast in both savory and sweet dishes. A mature taro can grow to the size of a football and will have a dry, mealy texture, as well as a sweeter flavor than a young taro. Immature taros are golf ball size, juicier, and their flesh has a grayer cast. Both need to be peeled before eating and must be fully cooked. If you are allergic to raw juices, wear gloves when peeling and cutting them. Select taros that are firm all over, with no bruises or gashes. Store like potatoes in the refrigerator.

Tendons, beef; *niújīn* 牛筋. In Chinese cuisine, the long tendons below a cow's shins are stripped clean of muscle and bone, leaving only slender white cords. These tendons are as tough as leather when raw but will turn tender and slightly gummy when slowly braised. Look for them in Korean and Chinese markets, usually in the frozen foods section. Rinse before using and don't bother trying to cut them before they are fully cooked; see the recipe on page 120 for directions.

Toon leaves; *xiāngchūnyè* 香椿葉. The young, tender leaves of the tree variously called *Toona sinensis* or *Cedrela sinensis* are mainly used in Anhui-style cuisine, as well as in other Yangtze-area dishes; you can sometimes find them in the frozen foods section or in jars. The older dried leaves are called for in some Hakka-style dishes, but I've rarely seen them outside of Taiwan. Your best bet is to grow them yourself or find someone who does. If you can locate a tree, see if you can dig up one of the suckers that it sends out and then plant it in a confined area where the rangy roots won't take over your yard.

Vinegar, black; *hēicù* 黑醋. China has a long tradition of making great vinegars out of grains such as rice and sorghum. They have a deep, rich flavor that is highlighted in many dishes. However, quality controls have not been able to keep up with the steep climb in demand, and as a result you should do your homework before buying any Chinese vinegars. I often use balsamic vinegar in my cooking instead of traditional black vinegar, and the taste is pretty comparable. For dipping, where the flavor of the balsamic can overwhelm at times, I use half cider or pale rice vinegar and half balsamic. Taiwan is beginning to offer some good-quality organic vinegars, and Japan has a honey vinegar that is my favorite for including in dipping sauces for *xiaolongbao* (page 132) and *jiaozi* (page 45).

Vinegar, pale rice; *mǐcù* 米醋. As with black vinegar, use common sense when selecting rice vinegar, for quality can be iffy at times. I like the better Taiwanese and Japanese brands, which have a lovely taste without chemical undertones.

Water chestnut flour; *bíqífěn* 荸薺粉. Made from water chestnuts that are first squeezed dry and then pulverized, this gently sweet flour is available in most Chinese markets. Just be sure and crush the flour in a food processor or blender, as it tends to have a crumbly texture right out of the box. Store in a closed container.

Water chestnuts; *bíqí* 荸薺 or *mǎtí* 馬蹄, not to be confused with either water caltrop (*língjiǎo* 菱角) or *Sagittaria safittifolia* (*cígū* 慈姑). These aquatic corms grow in mud, and inside their dark brown skins lies a sweet, crunchy flesh that is adored throughout southern China. Select water chestnuts that are firm all over, with no signs of bruises or mold. Refrigerate them covered with water in a closed container, where they will stay fresh for a surprisingly long time. To prepare water chestnuts, rinse them well to remove any mud, and then peel with a paring knife; remove both the hard root end and the sprouts on the top, and keep the peeled corm covered with water to prevent it from discoloring.

Frozen peeled water chestnuts from China are increasingly available, and they can be used in a pinch, but they are neither as sweet nor as crisp as fresh ones. Canned ones are not recommended, ever. Instead, use peeled jicama as a source of crunch and sweetness in most recipes that do not use water chestnuts as the main ingredient.

Water spinach; *kōngxīncài* 空心菜. A delicious aquatic vegetable popular throughout southern China, as well as Southeast Asia, water spinach is a member of the morning glory family and has the funnel-shaped blooms to prove it. However, the new growths that make it to the market are usually too young to have flowered.

The flavor of *kongxincai* is much different from that of spinach, though the latter can be used as a substitute if water spinach is not available. The stems are hollow like long straws, which is why the plant is called "hollow vegetable" in Chinese; the leaves are long and pointed.

There are two main varieties of water spinach: the regular dark green one and a paler variety that is both more tender and milder in flavor. They can be used interchangeably.

Select bunches that show absolutely no signs of rotting or damage, as they disintegrate fast and then require lots of time to clean. The stems should be firm and the leaves bouncy. Refrigerate water spinach in a plastic bag with a paper towel around the leaves, but use it within a day or two for maximum quality. Also called *wèngcài* 蕹菜 or *tōngcài* 通菜.

White liquor; *báijiǔ* 白酒 or *báigār* 白乾兒. This clear, high-alcohol liquor made from sorghum, rice, or other grains gets its flavor from the variety of grain used, as well as through additives that lend it a specific aroma, such as in the rose-scented *méiguīlù* 玫瑰露 ("rose dew"). Others, like *gāoliáng* 高粱 and *māotái* 茅台, taste strongly of sorghum; Taiwan's *gaoliang* from the island of Kinmen (Jīnmén 金門) is especially recommended for quality and flavor. Vodka or gin can be substituted in a pinch.

Winter melons; *dōngguā* 冬瓜. A word of caution when purchasing a winter melon: make sure that the slice you buy is really fresh. It should be completely white all over with no yellow or soft spots on the white flesh, which tell you quite insistently that it has been sitting around for a while. Smell it, as it should have just a faint squash smell and no sourness.

Press it gently through the plastic wrap to ensure that it is firm.

Wolfberries; *gǒuqǐ* 枸杞. I prefer to get my *gouqi* from either a good Chinese herbalist or from reputable health food stores. Organic wolfberries are becoming increasingly available, too. Select berries that are plump, the color of ripe persimmons, and as large as possible. Check for insect infestation by shaking the bag around and discard any that show holes or that have dark, round dust (insect poop) at the bottom. Store them in a freezer bag in the freezer if you are not using them within a month or two, as this will keep them fresh. Also sold under their Japanese name, *goji*, or as boxthorn.

Xianwei; *xiānwèi* 鮮味. This is the Chinese term for flavors that are deeply savory (see page 56), like tomatoes or black mushrooms. Also known by the equivalent Japanese term, *umami* うま味.

Yams, Chinese; *shānyào* 山藥. Chinese yams are unusual tubers that can grow to 3 feet or more, with beige skins covered with wiry little roots. They look much like a human leg. The flesh is white, sweet, and mucilaginous, which means that a jellylike goo seeps out once the yams are cut. Raw, they are sweetly delicious and taste a bit like a water chestnut. When cooked, this sugary character turns starchy and tastes more like a new potato.

These yams are also incredibly good for you and are seen as a sort of tonic in

Chinese herbal medicine. They are called *nagaimo* in Japanese, and nowadays they are becoming more available outside of Asian markets. The best place to buy them is at a busy market that caters to a Chinese and Japanese clientele. Chinese yams are usually packed in dry sawdust after they are harvested to help absorb the water that can lead to rot. Keep them dry and refrigerated, preferably in a plastic bag with a paper towel inside to wick up any moisture. Select yams that are firm and evenly beige all over, with no dark spots or bruises.

Yeast balls, Chinese wine; *jiǔbǐng* 酒餅. Used throughout China to make fermented sauces (including soy sauce and bean sauces), rice vinegar, and rice wine, these balls are little more than a variety of yeasts, molds, and bacteria mixed with finely ground rice and then dried. See the recipe for fermented rice on page 415 for instructions on how to use them. Freeze the yeast balls in a resealable plastic bag to prevent a bug infestation. In Japan, this mold is sold as the coated grains of rice known as *koji* 麴.

Yeast rice, red; *hóngqúmǐ* 紅麴米. Rice grains are given a deep scarlet coating of *Monascus purpureus* to make this ingredient. When these are brewed with fermented rice (page 415), the lees become the unique Northern Fujian seasoning called *hóngqú* 紅麴, while the liquid can be aged and used as a cooking wine. Purchase it in Chinese markets that cater to a non-southern clientele.

SUGGESTED MENUS

The serving sizes in this book are for Chinese-style meals built on multiple dishes. A recipe that says it serves four to six will most likely feed only two people if served on its own or with a starch like rice or bread. If you plan to eat in the Western way, adjust your amounts accordingly.

If you'd like to plan a full Chinese meal, though, I have provided some suggested combinations on the following pages. I have kept the foods organized around their respective regions, but you can, of course, mix and match as you please. Just aim for balance, such as one steamed dish, one fried, one stir-fried, and so on, so that you get as much contrast as possible. A simple plate of stir-fried green vegetables seasoned with garlic or ginger would also fit in perfectly with any of these menus instead of— or in addition to—one of the other dishes. Asterisks (*) denote the items that don't require detailed recipes, namely fried eggs and fresh fruit. Everything else can be found in this book.

The North & Manchurian Northeast

BREAKFAST OR MIDNIGHT SNACK FOR 4
Steamed bread (page 398 or 400)
Fried eggs*
Soymilk (page 64)

LUNCH OR LIGHT SUPPER FOR 4
Clear Beef Soup with Chinese Herbs and Radishes
    (page 18)
Fried Scallion and Flaky Flatbreads (page 54)
Fresh fruit*

FAMILY DINNER FOR 4
Spinach and Peanuts (page 10)
Beijing-Style Smoked Chicken (page 26)
Napa Cabbage with Dried Shrimp (page 36)
Steamed bread (page 398 or 400)
Laughing Doughnut Holes (page 61) or fresh fruit*

BANQUET FOR 6 TO 8
Soybean Pods (page 9)
    and/or Cold Garlic Chicken (page 13)
Stewed Peanuts (page 412)
Braised Prawns (page 25) with Fried Scallion and
    Flaky Flatbreads (page 54)
Rock Sugar Pork Shank (page 32)
    with Flower Rolls (page 397)
Stir-Fried Garlic Stems (page 37)
Wood Ears Braised with Green Onions (page 40)
Mock Shark Fin Soup (page 16)
Toffee Apples (page 62)
The Perfect Pot of Chinese Tea (page 150)
    and fresh fruit*

The Yangtze River & Its Environs

BREAKFAST OR MIDNIGHT SNACK FOR 4
Fried Green Onion Noodles (page 134)
Fried eggs*
Red Date Nectar (page 151)

LUNCH OR LIGHT SUPPER FOR 4
Suzhou "Smoked" Fish (page 85)
Oil-Braised Spring Bamboo Shoots (page 122)
Gold and Silver Fried Rice (page 138)
Fresh fruit*

FAMILY DINNER FOR 4
Raw Radish Threads with Green Onion Oil
    (page 78)
Fish Head Sandpot (page 94)
Bitter Melons in Golden Sand (page 123)
Crusty Vegetable Rice (page 131)
Sea Moss Sandies (page 145) or fresh fruit*

BANQUET FOR 6 TO 8
Crystalline Jellied Pork (page 90)
Sprouted Fava Beans (page 80) and/or Bean Curd
    with Pine Flower Preserved Eggs (page 81)
Shanghai Mustard Pickles (page 427)
Fried Fish in a Sea Moss Batter (page 102)
Dongpo Pork (page 114)
Slow-Braised Bok Choy (page 125)
Four Happiness Gluten and Vegetables (page 124)
Gold and Silver Fried Rice (page 138)
Sister-in-Law Song's Fish Chowder (page 93)
Crystal Lychees (page 146) and Sea Moss Sandies
    (page 145)
Chrysanthemum Tea (page 151) and fresh fruit*

The Coastal Southeast

BREAKFAST OR MIDNIGHT SNACK FOR 4
Congee of any kind (page 226)
Yuanyang Tea (page 241) or
    The Perfect Pot of Chinese Tea (page 150)

LUNCH OR LIGHT SUPPER FOR 4
Crusty Rice with Charcuterie (page 221)
Gailan with Oyster Sauce (page 211)
Fresh fruit*

FAMILY DINNER FOR 4
White-Cut Chicken (page 196)
Water Spinach with Bean Curd "Cheese"
    and Chilies (page 210)
Steamed rice (page 382)
Pork Rib and Dried Bok Choy Soup (page 173)
Baked Coconut Tapioca Custard (page 231)
    or fresh fruit*

BANQUET FOR 6 TO 8
Cold Bamboo Shoots with Mayonnaise (page 162)
    and/or Oyster Spring Rolls (page 168)
Shunde Raw Fish (page 164)
Pickled Lotus Root (page 425)
Whole Dry-Fried Flounder (page 182)
Pork Belly with Preserved Mustard Greens (page 207)
Crispy Silk Gourd Crêpes (page 213)
Steamed rice (page 382)
Flower Mushroom Soup (page 170)
Sun Cookies (page 234) or Water Chestnut Gelée
    (page 237)
The Perfect Pot of Chinese Tea (jasmine
    recommended, page 150) and fresh fruit*

The Central Highlands

BREAKFAST OR MIDNIGHT SNACK FOR 4
Pork and Preserved Mustard Green Baozi (page 300)
Peanut Milk (page 310)

LUNCH OR LIGHT SUPPER FOR 4
Guilin Rice Noodles (page 303)
Black Bean Asparagus (page 292)
Fresh fruit*

FAMILY DINNER FOR 4
Big, Thin Slices of a Pig's Head (page 256)
Crossing-the-Bridge Rice Noodles (page 302)
Raw Chinese Yam with Osmanthus Syrup
    (page 305) or fresh fruit*

BANQUET FOR 6 TO 8
Mouthwatering Chicken (page 255) and/or
    Spicy Mung Bean Jelly Shreds (page 250)
Sichuan-style pickles, traditional (page 428)
    or fast (page 431)
Cod with Crispy Bean Sauce (page 269)
Camphor Tea Duck (page 284) with Lotus Leaf Buns
    (page 408)
Twice-Cooked Pork (page 281)
Ginkgo Nuts, Chinese Celery, and Lily Bulbs
    (page 291)
Mustard Cabbage with Schmaltz and Ginger
    (page 294)
Steamed rice (page 382)
Bean Curd Quenelle Soup (page 258)
Water Chestnut Pastries with Red Date Filling
    (page 304)
Floral Tisanes (page 311) and fresh fruit*

The Arid Lands

BREAKFAST OR MIDNIGHT SNACK FOR 4
Crêpes and Chili Potatoes (page 366)
Fried eggs*
Butter Tea (page 374)

LUNCH OR LIGHT SUPPER FOR 4
Vegetable Confetti Salad (page 321)
Lanzhou Beef Noodle Soup (page 328)
Fresh fruit*

FAMILY DINNER FOR 4
Tossed Cilantro and Peanut Salad (page 323)
Xinjiang-Style Lamb Kebabs (page 346)
Golden-Edged Cabbage (page 349)
Grilled Sesame Breads with Green Onions (page 361)
Fried Cookies (page 370) or fresh fruit*

BANQUET FOR 6 TO 8
Sesame Lamb (page 325) and/or
    Lettuce with Three Shreds (page 320)
Sweet pickled garlic cloves (page 433)
Hot-and-Sour Pork (page 339)
Buddha's Hand Rolls (page 342)
Chicken with Walnuts and Lotus Root (page 337)
Lily Bulbs and Wolfberries (page 348)
Golden-Edged Cabbage (page 349)
Uyghur Pilaf (page 369) or Coiled Bread (page 360)
Ningxia Midwinter Soup (page 331)
Sweet Pear Soup with Silver Ears (page 372)
Eight Treasure Tea (page 375) and fresh fruit*

ABOUT THE AUTHOR

Carolyn Phillips is a food writer, scholar, artist, and the author of *The Dim Sum Field Guide: A Taxonomy of Dumplings, Buns, Meats, Sweets, and Other Specialties of the Chinese Teahouse*. Her work has appeared in numerous places, including *Best Food Writing 2015, Lucky Peach, Gastronomica*, BuzzFeed, *Alimentum*, Huffington Post, *Zester Daily*, Food52, and at the 2013 MAD Symposium in Copenhagen, as well as in her weekly blog, *Madame Huang's Kitchen* (MadameHuang.com). She can be found on Twitter as @madamehuang and on Instagram as @therealmadamehuang.

Carolyn's art has appeared everywhere from museums and galleries to various magazines and journals to Nickelodeon's *Supah Ninjas* series. She was a professional Mandarin interpreter in the federal and state courts for over a decade, and she and her husband recently acted as cultural consultants for the third *Ghostbusters* movie (2016). She lived in Taiwan for eight years, has translated countless books and articles, and married into a Chinese family more than thirty years ago.

ACKNOWLEDGMENTS

No book is ever created without the help of many generous and talented people, and that is especially true here.

To the people over at McSweeney's who made this book a reality, I want to say that there are no words to express how much this experience has meant to me. You allowed me to write and draw whatever I wanted, a genuine dream come true. Of all the kind people there, I owe my greatest thanks to Dan McKinley, the talented art director responsible for *All Under Heaven's* brilliant design—this book turned out more beautiful than I had ever imagined—and to my editors, Daniel Gumbiner and Jordan Bass, who somehow managed to wrest prose out of my scribbles and give this book style and coherence. Thanks to former McSweeney's publisher Laura Howard, executive editor Andi Winnette, and CFO Elizabeth Hanley for standing firmly behind both this book and me—I couldn't think of better people to have in my corner—and to intern extraordinaire Taylor Stephens for all the help, as well as to Ethan Nosowsky and Rachel Khong for a great beginning, Gabrielle Gantz for publicity, and Dave Eggers for creating such a welcoming place for authors.

My endless appreciation also goes to the wonderful people at Ten Speed Press who shepherded this book to its final publication in cooperation with McSweeney's, including editors Emily Timberlake and Kaitlin Ketchum, designers Ashley Lima and Mari Gill, publishing director Hannah Rahill, publisher Aaron Wehner, indexer Ken Della Penta, proofreaders Sharon Silva and Karen Levy, and Michele Crim, Kristen Casemore, and David Hawk in publicity and marketing.

Thank you, Ken Hom, for greeting this book with such unbridled enthusiasm, for writing the perfect foreword, and for extending a very generous helping hand whenever I asked. In addition to Ken, it has been my immense good fortune to have some of the best food writers around as my friends and mentors, including Florence Lin, Robyn Eckhardt, Deborah Madison, Mollie Katzen, Diane Kennedy, Madhur Jaffrey, Madeleine Kamman, Cecilia Chiang, Flo Braker, and Elissa Altman, all of whom were exceedingly gracious with their time and knowledge and contacts.

My lasting gratitude goes out to the many great teachers of China's cuisine, including Fu Pei Mei, Chen Kenmin, Ma Chun-ch'uan, Grace Zia Chu, Virginia Lee, Mary Sia, Chan Mung-yan and his talented family, and Barbara Tropp, all of whom provided wonderful templates for my initial forays in the kitchen—may your books never go out of print—and to the editors of the groundbreaking series Zhōngguó càipǔ 中國菜譜 ("The Recipes of China"), who back in 1979 gave me my first structured glimpse at the country's many cuisines. To scholar E. N. Anderson, wine expert Gerald Asher, and food science writer Harold McGee, thank you for your amazing depth of knowledge; a special expression of gratitude also goes out to the late Liu Zhenwei for his fabulous reminiscences of a bygone age (see page 364).

Lizbeth Hasse, Esq., of Creative Industry Law is my knight in shining armor, the one who repeatedly put everything back on track with amazing alacrity. I am grateful to Jane Dystel, Miriam Goderich, and Joe Regal for encouraging the mere germ of an idea of a plan for an outline of this book. And because everything needs a beginning, thanks especially to Wendy and Mom: I was set on an Asian trajectory by my oldest friend, Sumiko Wendy Ichikawa, and then my late mother gave me the money for a one-way plane ticket to the other side of the world in order to pursue my then very vague notion of someday, somehow mastering Chinese.

During my first year in Taipei, I lived with a lovely family, the Chens; it was the mother, Auntie Lee, who first taught me how to cook Taiwanese dishes and who introduced me to the absolute bliss that is a freshly baked coconut moon cake. Endless thanks to two of my favorite "spice girls"—Helen Chang and Chia Ying Fong—for sharing so many recipes and wonderful meals with me. My appreciation goes out to Corie Brown and Cecilia Wedgeworth at Zester Daily, as well as to the folks at Lucky Peach, the MAD Symposium, Gastronomica, Alimentum, Food52, and The Cleaver Quarterly, as well as Holly Hughes for including me in Best Food Writing 2015. I want to also express my sincere thanks to a very long list of people, including Jay Rayner, Mark Bittman, Edward Behr, Michael Ruhlman, Susie Heller, Michael Bauer and Jonathan Kauffman and Marlena Spieler at the San Francisco Chronicle, Martin Yan, Helen Luo, Raghavan Iyer, Dr. Li Yuanzhi, John and Margaret Fang, Ah Hong Lin Wu, Ken Fletcher, YenLu Wong, and Zhou Guiyuan, as well as his wonderful daughter, Ally Yang. And last but certainly not least, my deepest gratitude to my blog readers and the recipe testers: you are the unsung heroes here.

The graciousness of the Chinese people is legendary, and my life is incalculably richer as a result. I learned from complete strangers by watching them and asking them questions, and they invariably greeted me with good humor and kindness. Cooks in restaurants, ladies in street stalls, and gentlemen in wet markets showed me how to select and prepare food the right way, while close friends whispered cooking secrets their mothers had taught them and then gave me permission to tell the world. To the people of China—and especially in my second home, Taiwan—I can never thank you enough and hope that this book properly honors your knowledge and traditions.

I am in eternal debt to the Chinese friends who welcomed me into their lives and at their tables, and who nurtured a growing appreciation for the most wonderful things I have ever tasted. Many of them are mentioned throughout this book with affection, and I thank you from the bottom of my heart, especially the late Dr. Ho Hao-tien and my old colleagues at the National Museum of History, and both Prof. Wang Chen-ku and Teresa Wang Chang of the National Central Library. Over the years, countless others have shared their knowledge on how to cook the Chinese way and appreciate the country's ancient food culture. Some taught me in their kitchens, such as my late father-in-law, Col. Lung-chin Huang, while others, like my late mother-in-law, Chou Yueh-ming, reminisced about their childhood with such detail that these food memories sparked the initial ideas for this project.

Last but not least, anything I have achieved is due in no small part to my companion on this long, strange trip: J. H. Huang. You were the best thing to ever happen to me.

INDEX

MEASUREMENT CONVERSION CHARTS

VOLUME

U.S.	IMPERIAL	METRIC
1 tablespoon	½ fl oz	15 ml
2 tablespoons	1 fl oz	30 ml
¼ cup	2 fl oz	60 ml
⅓ cup	3 fl oz	90 ml
½ cup	4 fl oz	120 ml
⅔ cup	5 fl oz (¼ pint)	150 ml
¾ cup	6 fl oz	180 ml
1 cup	8 fl oz (⅓ pint)	240 ml
1¼ cups	10 fl oz (½ pint)	300 ml
2 cups (1 pint)	16 fl oz (⅔ pint)	480 ml
2½ cups	20 fl oz (1 pint)	600 ml
1 quart	32 fl oz (1⅔ pints)	1 l

TEMPERATURE

FAHRENHEIT	CELSIUS/GAS MARK
250°F	120°C/gas mark ½
275°F	135°C/gas mark 1
300°F	150°C/gas mark 2
325°F	160°C/gas mark 3
350°F	180 or 175°C/gas mark 4
375°F	190°C/gas mark 5
400°F	200°C/gas mark 6
425°F	220°C/gas mark 7
450°F	230°C/gas mark 8
475°F	245°C/gas mark 9
500°F	260°C

LENGTH

INCH	METRIC
¼ inch	6 mm
½ inch	1.25 cm
¾ inch	2 cm
1 inch	2.5 cm
6 inches (½ foot)	15 cm
12 inches (1 foot)	30 cm

WEIGHT

U.S./IMPERIAL	METRIC
½ oz	15 g
1 oz	30 g
2 oz	60 g
¼ lb	115 g
⅓ lb	150 g
½ lb	225 g
¾ lb	350 g
1 lb	450 g

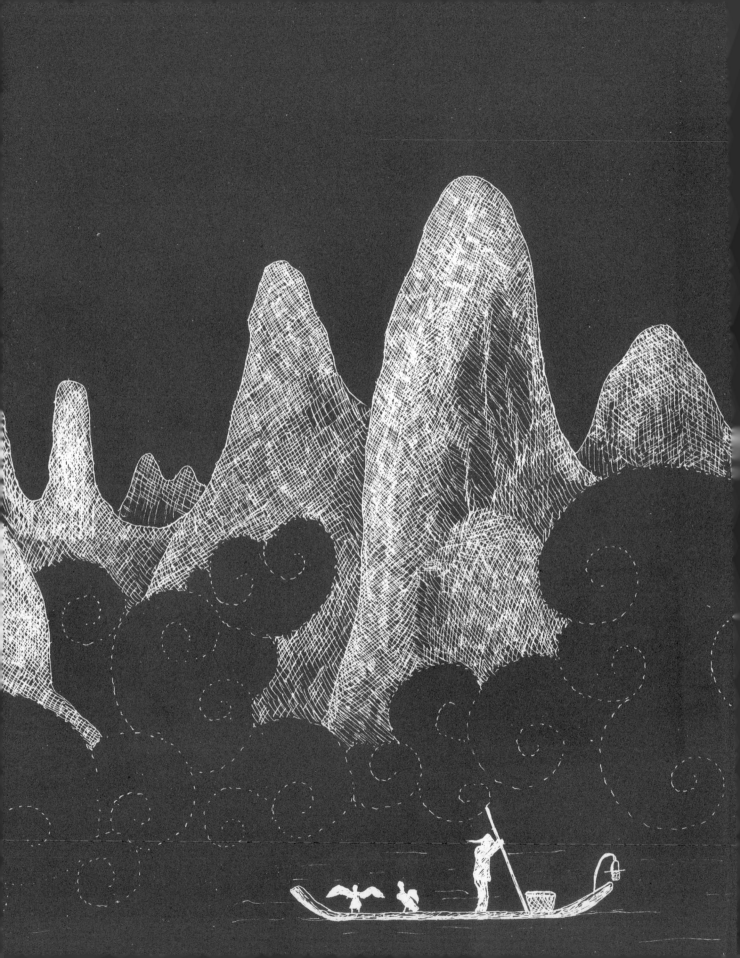